D1062846

SECOND EDITION

PEOPLE, WORK, AND ORGANIZATIONS

An Introduction to Industrial and Organizational Psychology

BERNARD M. BASS
State University of New York
Binghamton, New York

GERALD V. BARRETT
University of Akron
Akron, Ohio

ALLYN AND BACON, INC.
Boston   London   Sydney   Toronto

To our ever-patient and ever-loving wives,
Ruth and Pat

Library of Congress Cataloging in Publication Data

Bass, Bernard M
  People, work, and organizations.

  First published in 1972 under title: Man, work, and
organizations.
  Bibliography: p.
  Includes index.
  1. Psychology, Industrial. 2. Organizational
behavior. I. Barrett, Gerald V., joint author.
II. Title.
HF5548.8.B249 1981   158.7   79–23875
ISBN 0–205–06809–X

Printed in the United States of America.

CONTENTS

PREFACE

This edition differs from the original in a number of ways. It includes important research studies completed since the first one appeared, including several recent developmental projects carried out by both authors on designing jobs to make them more attractive, on applying open system analyses to management development, on transnational aspects of managerial behavior, on driving safety, and on enhancing attitudes toward affirmative action for women and black employees.

The five chapters in the first edition dealing with engineering and consumer psychology have been eliminated because of space considerations and because these two fields have split off from the mainstream of interests.

The most significant additions are three new chapters that expand upon issues mentioned in the earlier text. Chapter 9 discusses questions of values and research designs in validating selection programs. Organizational development is the theme of Chapter 14, where the various techniques to improve organization are explored. Chapter 15 deals with the theories and approaches to job design which have been used in research and to change organizational, and at times national, policy to improve the quality of working life.

Public policy questions posed in the last chapter lead to expanded discussions of such topics as the need to increase the human side of enterprise, what is a fair test, and how industrial/organizational psychology is involved in implementing affirmative action programs.

As in our first edition, we have attempted to provide references to source material that can guide students to additional research in an area. We have also attempted to present both sides of controversial issues in the field.

This has not precluded us from stating our position on certain issues that may be still debated within the field.

We would like to express our thanks to Mrs. Juanita Van Haren and Miss Deborah J. Thrash, who assisted in the various tasks involved in preparing and typing the final draft.

Bernard M. Bass
Binghamton, New York

Gerald V. Barrett
Akron, Ohio

Introduction to Industrial and Organizational Psychology

1 FIELDS OF INDUSTRIAL AND ORGANIZATIONAL PSYCHOLOGY

IN BRIEF   Although work is of central importance to individuals in our modern industrial society, the study of people at work has not been part of a liberal education.

Industrial and organizational psychology has drawn some of its methods and principles from general psychology and more particularly from social psychology. Nevertheless, most of its problems for investigation come from the world of work, and most of the understandings we develop emerge from study in the working environment itself or efforts to simulate it in the laboratory.

As jobs in organizations have changed over time, so have the major concerns of industrial psychologists. Industrial psychologists have branched out so much into nonindustrial organizations, such as hospitals, merchant ships, government agencies, and military services, that we now refer to the entire area as that of industrial and organizational psychology. Generally, when we mention *industrial* psychology we will be implying *industrial and organizational* psychology.

People spend as long as 20 years preparing to enter the world of work. During the middle 40 to 50 years of life they devote as much as half of each waking day to work. They spend an additional one or two hours daily commuting to and from work. Success in life, a sense of well-being and accomplishment, security, and prestige all may be tied to a person's work. Work usually determines one's standard of living and economic status

3

relative to others in the same community. A person's merit usually is no longer measured by his or her family connections but by his or her accomplishments on the job.

The central concern of life was different in many preindustrial societies. There, work was done only to provide for subsistence. Better yet, work was delegated to women or slaves. The Tibetans concentrated on their prayer wheel, the Talmudists on studying the Law, the Balinese on art, the Athenians on citizenship, and the Iroquois on military honors. Success, material welfare, security, and prestige depended not on one's job but on contemplative zeal, scholarship, artistic efforts, oratory, or bravery in battle.[3]

Despite the "work-intoxicated" nature of the world in which we live today, the study of people at work has been regarded as an applied subject —a practical extension of the study of the psychology of perception, learning, and motivation. Some aspects of general psychology, too, are applicable to the world of work. What is learned about the performance of rats in a maze, of children in a sandbox, or of college sophomores in a classroom may aid our understanding of the performance of people at work; however, the results of such investigations can only be suggestive. We must study people at or near work to develop reliable and valid understandings of their performance in work situations.

THE CASE OF THE SOCIAL SECURITY ADMINISTRATION

The Social Security Administration was confronted with new health and welfare legislation, which required it to expand its services rapidly. Its fifteen thousand interviewers (soon to double), accustomed mainly to handle retiring workers, survivors' insurance, and pension benefits, were now to deal with Medicare and welfare clients as well. Interviewer morale reportedly tumbled. Commonly shared beliefs in the efficiency of the administration were shaken.

Faced with this situation, what could a psychologist do to help?

Is There Really a Problem?

The psychologist could assist in detailing the existence, size, and scope of the perceived problem. More specific effects could be measured to see whether or not the negative impact had occurred as believed as well as how great the impact was. Thus, an industrial psychologist could attempt to measure changes in the quality of service by examining changes in client satisfaction, load handled per interviewer, errors, complaints, cost of service, reputation in the local community, and reputation with other agencies.

The interviewers themselves could provide indications about how well things were going and how satisfied or dissatisfied they themselves were. The psychologist could check grievance records, suggestions received, absenteeism, lateness, and rates of quitting.

What's Causing the Problem?

If some or all of these indicators pointed toward reduced efficiency, the industrial psychologist might then attempt to pinpoint what was specifically causing the negative outcomes. Environmental factors might be checked: for example, were there regional differences? Were things worse in the Midwest than elsewhere? Was there a rural–urban difference? Were the problems concentrated in the metropolitan inner cities? Did racial or ethnic or sex differences between interviewer and client make a difference?

Were there particular problems in the task requirements that were difficult to administer: for instance, ambiguities in the law leading to a great deal of interviewer–client conflict as each interpreted the meaning of the law differently?

What about the organization's policies and objectives as they affected interviewer performance? For example, did new policies impose a paperwork burden that reduced the interviewer's willingness to spend time in discussion with clients? How clear to the interviewers were the goals of their job? Were they to process as many clients as possible per day; were they to administer the law as fairly as possible; were they to satisfy clients as much as possible; or were they a compromise among these?

To what extent were relations among the interviewers and other staff a source of conflict? Were their interests and the organization's interests in conflict? To what extent did their supervisors help or hinder their work?

How skilled were the interviewers? Were their training and education adequate? Did they have the intelligence, aptitudes, and knowledge required for the work?

What about their motivation? How committed were interviewers to their work? What did they expect from their work? What outcomes did they value from their work?

What about the personalities of interviewers? To what extent were they authoritarian rather than democratic in ideology? Were many so ethnocentric ("our ethnic group is better than your ethnic group") that they couldn't deal fairly and adequately with clients from other ethnic groups? How strong was their interest in social service—the desire to help people for the people's sake? What were their attitudes about helping people on public welfare?

What Kind of Remedial Action Should Be Taken?

Depending on what causes for the problem seemed most salient, the psychologist might propose one or more of three kinds of remedial action: developmental, individual, and sociotechnical.

For example, the psychologist might have found that turnover is highest and dissatisfaction greatest among the newly hired interviewers. Improved development activities might be suggested for new recruits. A "joining up" workshop might be conducted, where new interviewers first discussed among themselves in small groups their expectations. Then these would be shared with a supervisory group, who in turn would note what it expected from new interviewers.

Many other developmental activities might be considered, depending on what the analysis of the problem revealed. These could include extended individual counseling and consultation with interviewers and supervisors, sensitivity training, periodic attitude surveys the group results of which are fed back to the interviewers, training in interviewer skill, training to promote better understanding of the client or the law.

Again, depending upon the problem analyses, the psychologist might focus attention on individual differences. It might turn out that only some interviewers have many problems completing their assignments. Only a subset of others are highly disgruntled. Improvement in recruiting, selecting, and placing interviewers by means of psychological tests and other assessment procedures might be recommended to improve the hiring and placing of more competent and satisfied employees.

Sociotechnical changes could be tried if relevant to the problem at hand. Some interviewers could be selected and trained as specialists in insurance, others in welfare. Physical rearrangement of the office where interviewer and client meet might be called for. The interviewer could be provided with performance aids such as a minicalculator to expedite his or her work. Centralized computing services might make the interviewer's job easier. Changes might be proposed in the traditional hierarchical command structure. Instead of reporting to a supervisor, the interviewers might see themselves as members of a small team.

It is one thing to propose remediation; it is another to implement it. It is still another to evaluate its effectiveness. All three efforts form part of the psychologist's work in the service organization as well as in the manufacturing establishment. So the industrial and organizational psychologist, after diagnosis of the problems at hand, designs remedial programs, works with those who will carry them out, and plans suitable evaluations of the efforts.

PSYCHOLOGISTS AND INDUSTRY

The industrial/organizational psychologist and other behavioral science personnel engaged in the human side of the enterprise are now commonplace in industry. Currently, AT&T employs 20 Ph.D.'s in the behavioral sciences, General Motors 150.[17] Most larger firms employ comparable numbers of behaviorally oriented professional personnel, who concentrate their efforts inside the firm on work in industrial/organizational psychology: selection, training, attitude surveys, job design, compensation programs, marketing, and so on.

Relations of Industrial Psychology to Other Disciplines

The methods and principles of social psychology are more directly relevant to industrial psychology than are the contributions of general psychology. In particular, interests in communications, attitudes, attitude change, group structure and process, interpersonal relations, social roles, and leadership are shared by industrial and social psychology.

Industrial psychology also shares with developmental and educational psychology a concern for the study of individual differences in talent and performance and methods of training and evaluation. In turn, the three fields of industrial, developmental, and educational psychology have been strongly affected by advances in applied mathematics, statistics, and computer technology.

Industrial psychology also has had in common with industrial engineering and industrial management interests in job design, job evaluation, and environmental influences.

Contributions to Industry

The understandings developed from psychological research in industry are playing an increasingly important role in the production and distribution of goods and services. Many managers have been satisfied to rely on their own experience and rules-of-thumb in dealing with "people problems" affecting their organizations' success. Now, however, many recognize the utility of systematic behavioral research when trying to answer questions about individual differences in employee performance, about social aspects of work, about the design of the workplace, or about consumer preferences for their goods. Through survey, field study, controlled experiment, or simulation, efforts are made to formulate and verify reliable generalizations. In particular, methods and principles are developed and tested for routine use as aids in increasing the accuracy of forecasting performance and in improving training, relations between people in the organization, and in bettering equipment, products, and services.

In a large-scale survey of over 300 diversified companies, 80 per cent reported an interest in the behavioral sciences. Of special significance was the fact that all the companies with more than 100,000 employees reported either "moderate" or "great" interest.

The companies were involved in a large variety of research and application projects. Among 241 firms, almost 3,000 behaviorally oriented projects were cited. These were in the areas of communication, performance appraisal, selection and placement, motivation, training and development, interpersonal and intergroup relationships, attitude measurement, compensation, career planning, and operator–machine relationships. The projects dealt with employees from all sections of the companies, but they tended to be concerned more with managers, scientists, and professionals than with other categories of employees.

Approximately three-quarters of all the companies surveyed reported that the behavioral sciences brought new and valuable insights to management. Furthermore, the companies reported that interest in behavioral sciences was increasing at all levels of management.[15]

In a national survey of over 300 personnel administrators, approximately three-quarters believed that an industrial psychologist could be useful in increasing productivity and satisfaction.[18] The survey was consistent with other surveys of executives over the past 20 years in showing that over half believed it would be desirable to have a professionally trained psychologist in their company. But despite the fact that over 50 per cent think it desirable to employ an industrial psychologist, only 11 per cent do so. This would seem to indicate an opportunity for qualified individuals.

Personal interviews, meetings, and questionnaires with a carefully selected sample of 75 top executives from large, medium, and small companies revealed the strong, sophisticated interest of a large majority in the new behavioral approaches to motivating employees, but they have done little to put new theories to work. They have heard about enriching jobs, integrating the goals of the employees and the organization, leading rather than driving employees, and participative management. Yet few know what really is involved in introducing the new approaches.

A majority saw the benefits to their firm of putting psychologists to work in their firm to deal with the following: motivation (84 per cent), human relations (81 per cent), attitude measurement (76 per cent), management development (77 per cent), job enrichment (76 per cent), communication (73 per cent), emotional problems (71 per cent), employee selection (71 per cent), resistance to change (71 per cent), supervisor selection (70 per cent), appraisal of managers (68 per cent), decision making (67 per cent), measurement of performance (67 per cent), aptitude testing (66 per cent), group behavior analysis (66 per cent), productivity improvement (66 per cent), counseling on how to manage (64 per cent), creativity (64 per cent), goal setting (64 per cent), boredom (62 per cent), and incentives (64 per cent). Many other issues on which psychologists may work, such as marketing research, training, accident reduction, fatigue, and occupational requirements, were given lower priorities.

More evidence for interest in industrial and organizational psychology can be seen in a survey of educational courses managers regard as most useful to them in their careers. Former Boston University business students who were in top or middle management were questioned. Among the several hundred top and middle managers who were asked, behavioral science courses were chosen as most useful for top management as well as for middle management.[12]

Industrial Psychology for Whom?

Despite its efforts toward scientific objectivity, industrial psychology has been charged, often with good reason, with being management-oriented and antilabor in its outlook. Often its work was circumscribed by what management, its sponsor, wanted done. The industrial psychologist was seen as a servant of management, rather than as an objective scientist trying to understand and improve the organization. Problems were assigned by the dominant management elite, and answers had to be found within the constraints imposed on the psychologist by these sponsors.[1]

Psychologists are human. Unfortunately, it is too easy for them to be victims of phenomena with which they are supposedly familiar. They, too, can see what they want to see and blind themselves in self-interest, particularly when data are complex, errorful, and ambiguous. Some psychologists may slip into parroting a line that management wants to hear.

While this charge of favoritism toward management contains a considerable degree of truth, it is certainly not the whole story, for it implies that management and labor must be engaged in a zero-sum game. It suggests that if you are for one side, you must be automatically against the other. (In a zero-sum game with two competing players, if one wins, the other must lose by the same amount.) The game is not this simple. Management and labor are largely engaged in a non-zero-sum game. Each side can profit from the cooperation of the other. In aiding either side, the psychologist is also likely to be helping the other.

Industrial psychology has often been seen by labor proponents as an ally of management because the sponsors of psychological research in industry have typically been big business or big government. Even the independent university researcher has had to have management's permission to conduct studies in industry. However, this management-oriented view of industrial psychology has been reinforced by a narrow conception of the goals of organizations. This conception, which sees profits and rates of return on investment as the only goals of consequence (and productive efficiency as the key to such profits and returns), is incomplete and misleading. The objectives of management have been found to be anything but one-dimensional, even though many in labor and management may believe otherwise.

Industrial Psychology and Management Goals

A total of 715 managers from 13 countries were given a year-end profit-and-loss statement as part of a training simulation, *Exercise Objectives*. Then they were asked to make five budgeting decisions and to note what goals they had in mind when they made the final decisions. These decisions were whether or not to allocate expenditures for the forthcoming year on safety equipment, wage increases, management counseling, product improvement, and alleviation of stream pollution. In distributing 100 points over six possible goals, their median weightings of goals were as follows: profit, 33.1; satisfactory operation, 20.3; employee welfare, 14.1; meeting competition, 12.1; growth, 11.1; public goodwill, 9.3.[5] About three-quarters of the distribution could thus be seen as directly concerned with economic success. Nevertheless, employee and public were also considered.

In a similar way, 145 chief executives or their deputies were asked in another study: "What are the aims of top management in your company?" Three-fourths of the managers mentioned more than one goal. One-sixth mentioned more than three goals. Consistent with our earlier comments about profits as a goal, only 36 per cent of these top executives mentioned as their first aim "to make money, profits, or a living," and only 52 per cent mentioned these financial goals at all.[7] Depending on the size of their firm, its past rate of growth, and whether the employees were unionized, the chief executives in the study tended to concern themselves about good products, public service, employee welfare, growth, organizational development, and meeting competition, as well as about profits as such.

Bass[2] suggested that the ultimate criterion of a firm's success should be measured by the extent to which the firm provides satisfactions for its various constituent members and clients, owners, managers, employees, customers, and the community at large. "Free market" economists such as Milton Friedman are the most outspoken critics of this position. Any business expenditure for social responsibility (apart from the goodwill it may earn) is a nonprofit-maximizing expenditure. And in a free market for products, corporate managements who pursue such social responsibility in a substantial way against the self-interests of their stockholders may risk losing out in the competitive market of stockholders.

But many scholars, beginning with Berle and Means'[6] seminal attack on big business, share our position, as do a majority of a sample of 3,453 subscribers to the *Harvard Business Review*. "Only a small minority feel that a corporation's duty is only to its owners, as described in nearly all classical business doctrine. More than 60% believe that the interests of owners must be served in competition with interests of three other groups —i.e., employees, customers, and the public" (p. 13).[9]

These findings are consistent with various studies of executive compensation. Their compensation only partly depends on the profitability of their firms. For instance, in 1972 the remuneration of top management of 823 corporations correlated only .56 with the reported profits and only .31 with the sales.[14] The size of the firm, as measured by its assets, correlated even less with the compensation of its top management. Prasad[14] concluded that only about 50 per cent of the variance in executives' remuneration could be accounted for by profits and sales.

The small stockholder may be concerned solely with current profitability or future profitability of a firm, but the managers who control the firm are also likely to be interested in their own tenure, in their power and prestige as well. Often the trust departments of the major banks are the principal stockholders of a firm because they gather together the wealth of many individuals. Management becomes increasingly autonomous as a firm's size increases over time.

Pickle and Friedlander[13] actually measured the extent to which a random selection of 97 small businesses in the state of Texas satisfied the interests of 7 constituents: owners; community; relevant federal, state, and local government agencies; customers; suppliers; creditors; and employees. *Owners* indicated their (1) financial satisfaction, including dollar amounts, return on investment, return on hours of work, profit relative to other organizations, previous financial record, and growth potential; and (2) nonmonetary satisfactions, including enjoyment of and pride in ownership. *Employees* completed detailed questionnaires covering their satisfaction with their jobs. *Customers* were surveyed by a questionnaire administered in an interview. They rated firms on 22 attributes such as quality of goods and services, speed of service, and dependability. *Supplier* satisfaction was measured in three categories: the supplier's cost of filling orders for the business organization, the organization's record of meeting its financial obligation to the supplier, and its record of stability in the continuity of relationship with the supplier. Levels of *creditor* satisfaction with each organization were obtained from statistical data gathered from Dun & Bradstreet and interviews with bankers, and members of retail merchant associations. *Community* satisfaction was measured in three categories: support of organizations in the community, support of charities and schools, and participation in political activities. *Relations with federal, state, and local governments* dealt with such items as (1) concerned communication with state and federal officials, (2) the support of lobbying groups, (3) questioning of income tax returns by Internal Revenue Service officials, (4) penalties paid on taxes, or (5) reprimands or censures by tax officials. In general, these items reflected the degree to which the organization carried out its explicit and implicit responsibilities with governmental agencies.

It was interesting to find for the 97 firms that if one constituent part was satisfied, others were likely to be satisfied also. For example, if owners were satisfied with a firm, so were the customers and employees. Satisfaction of the interests of one constituent part is not necessarily a detriment to others. The inside of a firm is not a competitive market. Owners and employees, for instance, are not necessarily in competition with each other. Rather, they can operate in a collaborative way to ensure that their mutual interests are satisfied.

Nevertheless, while we may espouse common interests and collaborative effort, we need realistically to be aware of how different interests in the firm can compete with each other. Supposedly, it is good for business to have satisfied customers and employees. It is good for public agencies to have satisfied clientele. Supposedly, high employee morale is good for employee productivity. But we know that the effects of morale on productivity may vary from negative to positive. At the same time, when profits are threatened, concerns for employee welfare are likely to diminish. Concern for good human relations may increase with profitability rather than vice versa. The pursuit of worker nonmaterial satisfactions seems to thrive and is tolerated by materialists mainly in prosperous times. In an economic recession, companies tighten their belts and employee-centered programs are abandoned. Yet, when slower economic growth occurs, and when firms and agencies have less material wealth to share, they still can try to provide the nonmaterial psychic benefits of satisfying jobs to offset declining productivity associated with employee insecurity.

The Impact of the Changing Economy on Goals

The slowing down in the rate of increase in real income and standard of living due to the increasing cost of nonrenewable resources such as oil and of pollution control can yield an unfavorable present in contrast with the past. A sense of relative deprivation may cast a pall. The outlook of the 13,000,000 unemployed during the Great Depression or the masses of underemployed in India today may give some insight into the potential for a psychological mass depression. Fewer jobs and overqualified job occupants with the threat of discharge hanging over their heads are real dehumanizing possibilities of slower economic growth.

But there is an alternative. Limits do not need to be maintained on the growth of psychic inputs of new information and psychic outputs of added nonmaterial satisfactions. We need to start getting more psychic "bang for the buck"—more psychic rewards from the same expenditures of energy and nonrenewable resources.[4] Industrial and organizational psychology can play an important role in this effort.

The firm is a complex system of people, money, materials, and information. From the investments in these are generated products, services, and profits, as well as stockholder, management, and employee satisfaction and maintenance. Managers are systems balancers who search for a mix of expenditures and investments that will yield satisfactory levels of products, services, profits, and satisfaction to all concerned. Industrial psychology supports this effort by providing managers with ways of testing and experimenting with changes in expenditures, particularly those involving human effort, and by providing ways of evaluating or forecasting the effects of such changes. For example, managers may see the need for a more flexible work force so that during different seasons workers can concentrate on different products. Industrial psychologists can recommend, develop, and test recruiting and screening practices and training programs to increase the flexibility of the work force. Also they can formulate objective employee transfer and promotion procedures based on systematic reviews of current employee performance. In this instance, the benefits that result accrue to the management of the firm, who are able to maintain a more varied production schedule with smaller required inventories to meet the seasonal markets, as well as to the employees, whose employment with the firm is stabilized. No layoffs occur because of seasonal demands for products. Society in general benefits, too. Fully employed workers have a higher standard of living than seasonal employees. They do not have to draw on unemployment insurance funds. They make a continuous contribution to the gross national product. Their families can plan and budget with confidence. Society benefits by receiving better goods and services with less expenditure and waste of its natural and human resources. What psychology contributes to improving the operations of the business firm is likely to benefit management, worker, and society.

Industrial Psychology and the Union Movement

Despite the handicaps of one-sided sponsorship, the industrial psychologist has maintained a creditable record in the union-management controversy of the past half-century. On some issues the work has been applauded by trade unionists; on others it has been deplored, sometimes with good reason and sometimes without. It is probably fortunate that so many of the outstanding industrial psychologists of the past had considerable training in engineering, statistics, and various other scientific disciplines that helped them to maintain professional objectivity in the face of controversial issues where self-interest might have dictated otherwise.

If we look at the three major areas of industrial psychology, we see that trade unionists have viewed relatively favorably what has been done in the psychology of the workplace and work methods, have had mixed feelings about vocational testing, and have been generally negative toward psychologists' efforts to better human relations in industry. The reasons for these attitudes are quite complicated.[10] Negative feelings of labor about vocational testing were partly due to historical coincidence. At the time when employers in the 1920s were sponsoring the development of vocational tests, they were also engaged in an open-shop campaign to destroy the unions that had become established during World War I. A second reason for trade unionists' negative feelings about testing has been the considerable predictive error in even the best of vocational tests. Although management's overall ability to discriminate the good from the poor prospect is improved with testing, the individuals for whom the test errs can organize and complain, particularly if the test is used for determining their advancement within the company after they are on the job.

On the other hand, the trade unionist endorses industrial psychology for having demonstrated that there may not be just "one best way" to do a job. Trade unionists are equally supportive of the behavioral scientist who argues that piece-rate systems fail to produce efficient worker behavior, as claimed. Rather, the piece-rate system may become (as noted by W. F. Whyte)[19] a game played daily, a psychological experiment used to produce neuroses.

Trade unionists also applaud similar demonstrations of the errors of omission of human factors in otherwise seemingly well-engineered job evaluation systems. These efforts by psychologists have resulted in more realistic job evaluation plans, to which unionists can subscribe.

Trade unionists argue that the rise of the "human relations movement" among managers coincided with the declaration by the Supreme Court of the constitutionality of the Wagner Labor Act. Management now *had* to bargain collectively with labor unions. Good human relations were seen as offering potential support for continued management control. Improve in formal human relations within the plant and the unions (assumed by management to survive only in the presence of continued management-labor warfare) would wither away. "The happily unorganized worker," voluntarily and spontaneously cooperating with management in a conflict-free organization of management and workers, was at variance with the trade unionist's ideals, for the trade unionist saw in conflict—and negotiation to resolve the conflict—the way to bring about social change and improvements in the worker's position in society.[10]

Current Issues

Psychological problems in industry are dealt with from three points of view: the responses to various stimuli present in industry, individual differences in response to the same stimulus situation, and social-psychological elements influencing such responses. But industrial psychology cannot be described fully in terms of what psychologists do in industry, nor can its future be charted by studying current practices of the staff psychologist, for much of the progress in the field has been made through contributions from the university, from the basic research laboratory, and from developments within the whole field of psychology, as well as from the psychologists working in industry. (In the same way, modern medicine has grown much more as a result of advances in biology and chemistry than from the discoveries of the practitioner of medicine.) The future of industrial psychology depends less on its own past practices than on the continuing development of research and theory on the psychology of work, its branches, and related disciplines. In industry itself, there has been a shift of psychological research toward basic issues and away from applied problems that are defined by management but have narrow applications. Nevertheless, industrial psychology is still in the midst of the transition from shallow issues, preoccupation with methods, and negative, simple, and static goals. Although we can discern the direction toward which we are moving, the transition is by no means complete. Much is left to be done.

A critic in 1954 argued that industrial psychology suffered from an absence of theory. The subject matter of industrial psychology was seen to be fragmented. It lacked integrative evaluation and systematization. There was no broad theory concerning the improvement of our use of human resources at work.[11] Matters have improved only somewhat since then. As we shall see, a number of limited theories about limited aspects of work have been developed, such as equity theory (which deals with a worker's response to his or her relative level of compensation). Wherever possible, we will attempt to connect concepts and principles from these limited but useful theories; we do so with the hope of linking organizational, personnel, and engineering psychology. Here a dilemma arises. If the discipline is to thrive, basic research must be fostered. But if the psychologist hopes to gain acceptance of recommendations from the research, the research must be conducted in terms readily understood by lay persons. Unfortunately, such research results are hard to generalize to make possible an advance in the science.

Industrial psychology suffers from methodological weaknesses. We are often unable to establish the generality of analyses across different organizations because we have failed to replicate investigations. At the same time, we seem to place more emphasis on statistical accuracy than on the practical significance of results. We escape through a flight into statistics to avoid difficulties involved in working on the real problems. Often we invent problems to fit existing research methods, rather than vice versa.[8]

We tend to rely too much on survey methods for reaching generalizations. Ordinarily, surveys at one point in time cannot predict effects from causes, but only tell us how two or more effects correlate. Such surveys cannot result in establishing functional relationships. We are unable to tell by questioning a group of millwrights or their supervisors how much we will alter their hourly and weekly productivity if we change from three shifts to two shifts. We need to make the change for some employees and not for others and then see what happens to the productivity of those who were changed in comparison to those who were not changed.

Whenever possible, the authors will call the reader's attention to those research studies that tend to corroborate or fail to corroborate generalizations that were drawn from other, independent studies. We shall point to the communalities among what at first might appear to be unrelated findings. Above all, we will avoid bogging ourselves or our readers down in statistics.

The utility of a test of statistical significance is often questionable. Given a large sample of workers, almost any result obtained is likely to be statistically significant, although it may be the result of a small effect. It may have even smaller practical importance. On the other hand, using a small sample of workers from one department of one organization, the likelihood is low that this sample is an unbiased replica of a larger population, for which our tests might have statistical significance. It is probably more useful to employ statistics as summary descriptions of what happened to a given sample and to what degree it happened. Seeing the same thing happen again elsewhere will increase our confidence in the result more than a statistically significant result in the one situation would. Conversely, even where a single study lacks statistical significance, if it can be replicated in separate studies, although no one study by itself attains statistical significance, the generality shown may be significant as well as relevant and meaningful.

CHANGES IN INDUSTRIAL AND ORGANIZATIONAL PSYCHOLOGY

Like most other behavioral sciences, industrial psychology has experienced rapid growth and change since the first industrial psychology text, by Hugo Munsterberg, appeared in 1913. At that early date there had already been investigations into the areas of employee selection, training, and consumer psychology. Even before that date, Scott in 1903 had written a book concerned with the application of psychology to advertising.[16]

In the 1920s, if one had asked what industrial psychology was all about, the answer would have been that industrial psychology deals with individual differences in aptitudes and proficiency for work and with the physical factors of the workplace. In the 1940s there would have been added concern for the social factors at the workplace. In the 1960s attention was also given to how differing individuals interact with differing kinds of work organizations. Not only are we interested in working associates and physical arrangements, but also in the peculiarities of the communication networks in which workers find themselves, as well as the effects of the historically and traditionally prescribed rules surrounding the workplace. By 1980 the interactions between employees and their industrial psychologist had become primary concerns of many. Industrial psychologists are now also likely to be at the forefront of ecological studies, looking at how persons at work systematically alter the total environment and how work and the workplace will have to be modified in order to maintain the health of the total environment.

Since the 1920s, industrial psychology has shifted its main attention from the manual worker and problems associated with repetitive work and physical deterrents like poor lighting, to the technician and administrator and to the social, organizational, and technological impediments present in the working environment. This shift, of course, parallels the changing nature of work in industrialized society — the reduction of the proportion of manual workers and the increase in the proportion of service, technical, and administrative workers in the total work force.

These changes in industrial psychology have been encouraged by social, scientific, and technological change, within and outside psychology. Thus, World War II focused attention on operating complex high-speed equipment, generating the vast growth of the engineering psychology branch of industrial psychology.

The depression of the 1930s resulted in concentrated research on counseling the unemployed. This research directly stimulated work on occupational information and aptitude testing. The growth of labor unions in the United States, as a consequence of industrialization and of New Deal legislation, aroused interest by some managements in better human relations in industry. Even more important in encouraging the application of psychology was an increase in our society in permissive child-raising, in social legislation, in democratic education, and in more liberal attitudes toward others in general. As a result, management began to sponsor psychological research and supervisory training on the subject of improving interpersonal relations.

The 1950s saw much greater regard for problems of creativity in scientists and engineers, because of the heavy increase in research and development in industry and pressures for their economic success. The trend was coupled with a reduction in interest in selecting workers for repetitive jobs—jobs that were fast disappearing as a consequence of automation. The vigilant behavior required for monitoring automated equipment became a far more significant issue for psychological study than the physical load-carrying behavior demanded of the unskilled manual laborer.

With increasing automation starting in the 1960s, a steady trend of workers away from direct production and into sales, clerical, and technical service was observed. In the United States, many more persons are now working in service-oriented occupations than in production. The microprocessors and minicomputers of the 1980s are accelerating the trend.

Organized labor will continue to press for a shorter work week and for more holidays. Thus, there could be increasing manpower costs proportional to net sales. There may also be less mobility of the individual member of an organization because of the benefits of seniority. Both these factors would place a further premium on accurate selection practices and improvements in training and upgrading procedures.

Shorter workdays, coupled with the increasing cost per worker of plant and equipment, will further increase the economic need for shift work and experiments with different plans. Larger numbers of women in the work force have made innovations such as the four-day work week and flexitime increasingly popular, although much study and analysis is still required before we fully appreciate the effects of these new schedules for work.

New Roles for Industrial and Organizational Psychology

The advent of automation has led to new roles for the industrial psychologist and new relations with other fields. Psychologists may find themselves members of operations analysis teams involved with operations research, linear programming, systems analysis, and computer applications. Their former concentration on methods has given way to serving on operations analysis teams as critics, problem solvers, researchers, and theoreticians, dealing with problems in terms of general psychological concepts.

Psychologists in industry have learned that if their research findings are to result in subsequent remedial actions, it is important to involve in the research, planning, and execution those managers who will be responsible for initiating and maintaining the remedial action. Moreover, managers are beginning to receive education and training on how to conduct routine research on human performance, and they are being encouraged to carry on such research as part of their job assignment. As a consequence, one may foresee that the psychologist in industry will assume more of a consulting role on research projects directed by staff or line managers.

As a staff advisor to top management and to organizational planners, the industrial psychologist may become more like the operations-research scientist in proposing systems modifications, then checking with laboratory simulations of the workplace to see if their forecasts about the effects of modifications indeed occur as expected.

With the current and future roles of industrial psychology in mind, the authors of this text hope to achieve what will prove to be a useful range of emphases by devoting somewhat more attention to organizational considerations than to matters of personnel selection and evaluation. These allocations will reflect the current and future distribution of interest and effort in psychology concerned with organizations. Furthermore, wherever possible, we will call the attention of the reader to some of the broader implications to organizations and to society of these industrial psychological endeavors.

If we look at where industrial psychologists work, and in what they say they are interested, we see that we can divide the subject matter of industrial and organizational psychology into three parts. The part with greatest emphasis is *organizational psychology,* the study of morale and attitudes toward work, organizational theory, organizational development, and interpersonal relations within the organization.

About as popular is *personnel psychology*—the study of individual differences in performance and of methods to assess such differences. Personnel psychology also includes concern with training, compensation, and employee development policies and practices.

The design of work and concern about human factors of design is less frequently of primary interest. Such efforts concentrate on describing, evaluating, and/or designing jobs and equipment. Focus on environmental factors affecting the quality of work and the quality of life in general is increasing in importance as concern by the public in ecological issues mounts.

PLAN OF THIS BOOK

After considering how we conduct research in industrial psychology, we see how it has been applied to further our understanding of why people work, how they are organized, and how management and supervision play a central role in the life of the organization.

Then we turn to the relationship between the formal organization's objectives and the objectives of the job occupant within the organization, looking particularly at how we appraise the extent to which the job occupant meets these objectives. This leads to a consideration of how we can forecast the likelihood that particular individuals will meet given job objectives. Techniques of psychological assessment and appraisal are covered, along with the technical and administrative problems involved.

Next, we look at how we can better train and educate individuals to meet personal, job, and organizational objectives. Then we consider how the job itself and the workplace can be designed or redesigned so that a job occupant can meet these objectives. The effects of environmental and psychological stress on the worker will also be considered. Finally, we consider industrial psychology in multinational settings, and the broader implications of applied behavioral science on public policy in our society.

SUMMARY

In the lives of most men, gainful employment has been essential. Increasingly, this is becoming true for women, yet the psychology of work has not been seen as part of a liberal education. However, we can be confident about understanding the world of work only if we devote special attention to studying it. Even here, the study itself must be replicated in a variety of ways for us to develop confidence in its conclusions.

The discipline of psychology can help by providing ways of defining problems at the workplace so that the methods of that field can be applied to dealing with those problems. Understanding drawn from similar situations can then be applied to coping with the problems. Such applications are now commonplace in the world of work.

The aims of industrial psychology tend to mirror those of managers who see themselves as stewards of firms and agencies entrusted with the responsibility for satisfying the various competing and collaborating constituencies of the firms and agencies.

In 80 years, industrial/organizational psychology has moved from crude studies of aptitudes, physical problems at the workplace, and advertising research to the application of some of its accepted principles to national policies. What we hope to show is the contemporary relevance of I/O psychology to why we work, how we are organized and supervised, and how we can increase satisfaction and productivity at the workplace. But to do this, we must begin with I/O's research strategies.

REFERENCES

1. Baritz, L. *The Servants of Power.* Middletown, Conn.: Wesleyan University Press, 1960.
2. Bass, B. M. "Ultimate Criteria of Organizational Worth," *Personnel Psychology,* 5 (1952): 157–173.

3. Bass, B. M. The Interface between Personnel and Organizational Psychology," *Journal of Applied Psychology*, 52 (1968): 81–88.
4. Bass, B. M. "Self-Managing Systems, Z.E.G. and Other Unthinkables." In H. Meltzer and F. Wickert (eds.) *Humanizing Organizational Behavior*. Springfield, Ill.: C C Thomas, 1976.
5. Bass, B. M., P. C. Burger, R. Dokter, and G. V. Barrett. *Assessment of Managers: An International Comparison*. New York: Free Press, 1979.
6. Berle, A. A., Jr., and G. C. Means. *The Modern Corporation and Private Property*. New York: Macmillan, 1932.
7. Dent, J. K. "Organizational Correlates of the Goals of Business Management," *Personnel Psychology*, 12 (1959): 365–396.
8. Dunnette, M. D. "Personnel Management," *Annual Review of Psychology*, 13 (1962): 285–314.
9. Ewing, D. W. "Who Wants Corporate Democracy?" *Harvard Business Review*, 49 (1971): 12–28, 146–149.
10. Gomberg, W. "The Use of Psychology in Industry: A Trade Union Point of View," *Management Science*, 3 (1957): 348–370.
11. Lanier, L. H. An evaluation of the *Annual Review of Psychology* (vols. 1–4), *Psychological Bulletin*, 51 (1954): 180–190.
12. Pearse, R. F. *Manager to manager*. New York: Amacom, 1974.
13. Pickle, H., and H. Friedlander. "Seven Societal Criteria of Organizational Success," *Personnel Psychology*, 20 (1967): 165–178.
14. Prasad, S. B. "Top Management Compensation and Corporate Performance," *Academy of Management Journal*, 7 (1974): 554–558.
15. Rush, H. M. F., and W. J. Wikstrom. "The Reception of Behavioral Science in Industry," *The Conference Board Record* (September 1969): 45–54.
16. Scott, W. D. *The Theory of Advertising*. Boston: Small, Maynard, 1903.
17. Singular, S. "Peering into the Corporate ID." MBA, March 25–30, 1975.
18. Thornton, G. C. "Image of Industrial Psychology among Personnel Administrators," *Journal of Applied Psychology*, 53 (1969): 436–438.
19. Whyte, W. F. *Money and Motivation*. New York: Harper, 1955.

2 RESEARCH: THE FOUNDATION OF INDUSTRIAL AND ORGANIZATIONAL PSYCHOLOGY

IN BRIEF Research findings form the basis of much of the substance of industrial and organizational psychology, as they do for psychology and science in general. These findings have been gathered in many diverse situations with a variety of methods. In the past, research efforts resulted primarily from desires to solve practical problems as they arose in industrial organizations. Increasingly, theoretical ideas from psychology and other behavioral sciences have become a second significant source of stimulation to research in industrial psychology.

There are five research techniques commonly employed in industrial psychology: the laboratory experiment, the simulation, the field experiment, the field study, and survey research. Each approach has its own advantages and disadvantages, and one investigation may use a combination of approaches.

The industrial psychologist has particular difficulties in conducting research in organizations. An organization may wish to obtain a certain finding or may take a short-term view of the research process. The problem is complicated by the fallacy of personal experience, which may lead some persons to deny the results of more objective investigations.

Approaches

There are a number of different ways of approaching any research question. We will attempt to classify some of the common techniques of conducting research and relate them to work that has been done in areas of personnel and organizational psychology. This approach will convey the flavor of the different research techniques. While there are many guidelines, formulations, and statistical procedures for research, creative research remains an art that often eludes precise formulations.

The real nemesis of workers in the behavioral and social sciences is the multitude of variables with which they must deal. Because of this perceived complexity, people often substitute "common sense," armchair philosophy, and intuition in behavioral analysis, rather than really using the data and variables scientifically. In the industrial situation, a good example is provided by the question of why people work. The data indicate that people work for many reasons, and that these differ from one person to the next. Nevertheless, the popular after-dinner speaker finds it more convenient to assume one master motive that will describe what motivates all people, such as money or the challenge provided by work.

The Scientific Ideal

In the sciences, the ideal is for research to begin with the formulation of one or more hypotheses—educated guesses about reality. The formulation is guided by a theory, a systematic generalized explanation of reality, or by a model, a simplified representation of reality rather than a broad explanation. A test is run to examine the truthfulness, the validity, of the hypotheses. Those hypotheses that fail to meet the test are modified, and new tests are run. The model or theory is then changed to conform to the modifications that were required to validate the hypotheses. While there is an increasing trend for theories and models to influence research in industrial and organizational psychology, it is still more usual to begin with a problem. Consideration of the problem leads to observations in the organization about the problem. Hypotheses are then formulated on the basis of previous work, models, theories, and intuition. The hypotheses are tested in an experiment or survey and revised until some relatively satisfactory way to deal with the problem is found.

For example, we may hypothesize that hospital nurses will be motivated to work harder under heavy patient loads than under light loads. This follows from Locke's theory of how goals affect behavior.[18] Or we may formulate the hypothesis from a model of how nurses' activity levels are associated with patient loads. We then would collect data over time from a sample of nurses to check the validity of the hypothesis.

More will be said later in the chapter about this process.

PARTICULAR DIFFICULTIES WITH THE SCIENTIFIC IDEAL   Especially in industrial psychology, we must be fully aware of the fact that the process of science is a very human one. Although scientific endeavor attempts to be logical, objective, and rational, there may be inconsistencies or biases that creep into investigations.

This is especially true when research is done by an industrial psychologist for an organization that may explicitly wish to obtain a certain finding. For example, an industrial organization may initiate a morale survey with the expectation that results will show the employees to be happy with management policies. It is extremely important for a psychologist in this situation to recognize the dangers involved and possible influences on and biases in the research.

Self-diagnoses. Another problem common in organizational research is like that of patients diagnosing their own ailments. For example, the first author was called into an organization as a consultant to reduce what management believed was excessively rapid turnover of sales personnel. An analysis of data collected by the consultant showed, however, that very few employees quit the company because they were dissatisfied. Rather, the sales personnel were asked to resign because of lack of sales ability after they had been with the organization for a period of time. The problem was not one of turnover, but one of matching abilities with job requirements.

Therefore, the consultant recommended a plan that might actually increase the rate of turnover by forecasting in advance who would be discharged six months later for lack of ability. The plan was based on the fact that an analysis of performance appraisal forms filled out by the employees' supervisors showed a high consistency in rated ability over time. This meant that if the supervisor rated a salesperson in the lowest 10 per cent in ability today, six months later the salesperson would be discharged for lack of ability. It would be better for both the company and the sales personnel if the latter were discharged early; the company could replace the employee with someone who had a greater probability of success, and the individual could find a position that would match his or her aptitudes.

For a longer-run solution, aptitude tests were introduced into the initial selection procedure to increase the ability level of sales personnel hired. More attention to training was also suggested.

Biased diagnoses. Industrial psychologists must be aware of not only organizational biases toward problems, but also of their own predilections. A behavioral scientist interested in communication might well see the problems of an organization in terms of failure to listen, inability to transmit, and motivated distortion of communications. Similarly, a training expert might see the organization's problem in terms of lack of adequate management development; and a systems analyst might attribute the organization's inefficiency to its failure to use its computer adequately.

The behavioral scientist must recognize biases in order to offset a tendency to see research problems from only one perspective.

The need for integration.   There is considerable evidence that the major advances in science result not from short, disconnected studies, but from long series of coordinated and integrated research projects. Unfortunately, long-term research is often discouraged in industry, for a variety of reasons. One of the most common is a shift in company management. A manager who wants some research accomplished in a certain area is transferred, and the new manager turns out not to be interested in the project. Also, as the organization changes, industrial psychological problems change. Last year's research project may be less relevant this year.

In the past, business and industry took a short-range view of psychological research efforts. The government and universities were left to carry out most of the long-term substantial research efforts. As a consequence, much of industrial psychology has been a product of university, institute, or government research. Increasingly, however, major corporations have instituted basic long-term research projects in the area of industrial psychology. Thus, for instance, companies may now sponsor projects involving five-, ten-, and fifteen- year follow-ups of managers as they rise in the organization.

Communication of Research Results

As in all science, the communication of results is extremely important. It is not enough to make a significant discovery through the execution of a creative study. It is also necessary for investigators to publish and disseminate the results of their investigations and thereby perhaps change behavior. For example, after discovering the manner in which blood circulates in the body, William Harvey eventually succeeded in having his new information recognized, although his theory contradicted the accepted folklore of his time. One may even argue that scientists have an obligation to present their findings with the objectivity, clarity, meaning, and relevance that will be persuasive to those who can make use of their conclusions. Discovery and verification are not enough. The personal actions and lack of tact of Ignaz Semmelweis, the discoverer of the causes of puerperal fever, the maternity scourge, contributed to the rejection of his principles during his lifetime.[8] Countless deaths in childbirth continued unnecessarily as a consequence.

The point is particularly relevant for industrial psychologists. They have not only to define the problem and design and execute the study, but they must also be proficient in summarizing the results and ensuring that they receive a fair hearing. For their research to have any effect, they must gain attention and acceptance for their research findings by the pertinent public. This is an especially difficult problem for all behavioral and social scientists, and for the industrial psychologist in particular. Many people think that a pure heart and a little common sense will let them understand complex social systems.[9] Sponsors of research often reply to the results of an investigation with "This doesn't jive with my experience," or "So what? I knew it all the time." Actually, their replies in either case might have been identical if the investigation produced opposite results.

The Fallacy of Personal Experience

One cannot underestimate the value of personal experience, but personal experience can be fallacious in meeting and solving behavioral problems. The plant manager may initiate a wage and salary program and therefore feel that the employees are extremely well satisfied with it. But a more objective evaluation by an industrial psychologist using an attitude questionnaire may reveal the reverse. It is clearly easier for the plant manager to question and deny the results of an attitude study than to question a report by the plant chemist. As the world becomes more complex and technical knowledge increases, the advances in areas such as theoretical physics and biochemistry outdistance the understanding of most individuals. But most people pride themselves on their ability to understand other people.

The misleading conclusions given by personal experience, as opposed to more objective scientific investigations, can be illustrated by what has been labeled the Barnum effect.

Even knowledgeable individuals can be misled. This was dramatically illustrated by a study performed with approximately 70 personnel managers, who were requested to take a personality test. Unknown to them, all were given identical results in the form of statements chosen to apply to almost all individuals — for example, "You have a need for people to like and admire you."

The managers examined their own "personal" analyses, then judged how accurately the test had described them individually. Approximately 50 per cent marked the description as "amazingly accurate," while 40 per cent said it was "rather good." Ten per cent said it was "about half and half." [22] This "Barnum effect" illustrates that a personal trial, which on the surface might seem to be a straightforward, logical way to check on the accuracy of personality tests for use in industrial organizations, is in reality meaningless. Test "results" that were considered accurate by the individual personnel managers gave the same answer for everyone.

If we will concede the point that unsystematic personal experience will not always give us insight into behavior, we may choose the alternative of scientific research.

SCIENTIFIC RESEARCH TECHNIQUES

There are five research techniques commonly employed in industrial psychology: the laboratory experiment, the simulation, the field experiment, the field study, and survey research.[16] Each has its own advantages and disadvantages. The five approaches overlap, and a single investigation may employ several. Variants also make it possible to conduct a survey with characteristics of an experiment, or a field study that also employs simulation. Following are some of the characteristics of each type and their advantages and disadvantages.

The Laboratory Experiment

In the laboratory experiment in industrial psychology, investigators are likely to manipulate systematically such *independent* variables as the time allotted to subjects to complete a task, the size of groups, the organizational level from which subjects are drawn, or the speed of a moving belt delivering goods to be assembled. Typically, the *dependent* variables they examine are presumed to be affected by, or be dependent on, the amount, strength, intensity, or degree of the *independent* variable. *Dependent* variables include such measures as costs of production, rated satisfaction with work and speed and accuracy of performance.

If in a laboratory study one were to study the influence of monetary reward on job satisfaction, one might systematically give different amounts of money to different subjects and then have them rate their satisfaction with performing the same task. If it were determined that as the money given to a particular subject increased, there was a concurrent rise in reported job satisfaction, one could then make the statement that the money (independent variable) caused a positive change in attitude (dependent variable).

It should also be understood that a variable can at one time be considered the independent variable and at another time or in another study be considered the dependent variable. For example, if we were to study the effect of attitude upon work performance, we might design a study where we would choose individuals with varying degrees of positive attitude toward work and then measure performance. In this case, attitude toward the work is considered the *independent* variable.

On the other hand, we might study how increasing the participation of nurses in the scheduling and sharing of their work loads affected their attitudes toward their work. In this case, attitude toward the work is the *dependent* variable.

Experiments require some independent control, usually easiest to introduce by means of a control group. The purpose of a control is to eliminate an alternate explanation of the results. If we had designed a study to test a new method of instruction and we took a sample of students and found that the instruction was indeed effective, we would not know if this was any better than the old technique. It would be necessary, therefore, to have a control group of similar students go through a training procedure using the old teaching technique. Then, if there were marked differences between the groups, with the new technique being the better, there would be some basis for saying that the new technique was superior. Claims about the efficacy of a particular training program are without merit if they fail to consider whether the effects obtained with training could have been obtained without training.

The laboratory experiment allows investigators the most control over what they are studying. It also can give researchers precise measurements of relevant variables. Its one major disadvantage is that it tends to be abstract and artificial, for ordinarily the laboratory experiment is conducted in an environment where the investigator tries to eliminate or control all but one variable, so that outcomes of the experiment can be attributed to that particular variable. Variables seldom operate with such lonely independence in nature or industry; they tend rather to interact with one another. As a consequence, the one-variable-at-a-time laboratory study often lacks generality to real-life situations, where many variables are operating at once.

The attitudes and motivation of the subject are often critical in a laboratory experiment. Experimental effects in a laboratory with college sophomores may be impossible to replicate with factory employees at their workbenches. The student and worker are likely to feel quite differently about the experimenter, the experiment, and the conditions surrounding it, and these differences are all apt to affect the results of the experiment.

The laboratory investigation in industrial psychology can be illustrated by experiments in vigilance factors that affect the efficiency of such work as inspection. In laboratory studies of vigilance, subjects are typically seated at a console where they monitor a display for either an infrequent signal or one of a low intensity, such as would be seen in real life by a radar operator or an inspector of small parts that pass by on an assembly line. Subjects respond whenever they think they have observed a signal. The experimenter precisely controls independent variables such as the frequency and intensity of the signal and the number of irrelevant signals, to see what effects they and individual subject differences have on the accuracy of the subject's response. But unfortunately, laboratory experimentation, particularly in the more social aspects of behavior, has limited validity when generalized to real life. We put into the controlled experiment a minimum number of stimuli abstracted from real life that' we expect will affect the behavior of consequence — the *dependent* variable such as accuracy of response. Then we manipulate the presence or absence of those stimuli — the *independent* variables such as the different signals in the display going on or off. But the total contextual situation in which the stimuli are embedded in real life is deliberately made sterile in the experiment. This is done to prevent us from finding ourselves in a situation where we wouldn't know which one of several *independent* variables was affecting the *dependent* variable.

For example, if we want to study how noise as such affects a worker's performance, we use a random mixture of "white" noise. But in real life most noise is not random, so we may learn much more about the effect of the noise with which we are really concerned by using in the laboratory a simulation (say by tape-recorded examples) of real-life factory noise. The problem for the industrial psychologist is that the pure variable, "white noise," has one effect, but real-life factory noise may have another.

How do we promote the generalization of our results to day-to-day applications? We do this by creating a more faithful replica of the real-life setting. This replica provides the context, the background, in which the stimuli of interest to us are manipulated. Performance is studied in the presence or absence of those particular stimuli. We still hold constant in the aggregate "all but one variable," but we provide a more realistic, more complex, noisy background, a background that is a complex replica of real life as the context in which the main stimulus of interest is varied. More will be said about controlled experiments and quasi-experiments and their problems later in this chapter.

Simulation

Because the results of single-variable experiments lack generality or applicability to many of the complex problems of organizational life, *behavioral* simulation has been used more and more often as a research technique. Here, the investigator creates a simplified replica of the system or situation being studied. Physical replicas can be constructed, such as a simulation of the automobile and the typical driving environment. (A detailed study of such a simulator will be described later.) Other ways of simulation are available. If we are interested in the flow of information and decisions in a firm, we can program a computer to reconstruct the flow in the past, then study the situation by systematically altering some of the programmed events to see what would have happened if these alterations had actually occurred. Or we can move the computerized replica forward to forecast what may be the flow of information and decisions at different points of time in the future. Such *mathematical* simulations seem particularly useful for manpower planning. We may know something about labor we shall later be able to recruit, the percentage of these who may pass various selection tests for different jobs in the organization, and the time it takes to train replacements. With this knowledge, we can simulate organizational manpower needs.

Why simulate? Because the complexity of variables makes it impossible for us to comprehend specifically how they will operate as a system. Only by manipulating the replica of the system can we see how it will look (assuming that we have correct estimates about the current system). Simulations can be equally useful in planning and designing complex systems, or assessing the likely costs and effects of different management development approaches.

The Field Experiment

The field experiment is performed in an organizational setting. Variables are manipulated by the experimenter as in a laboratory experiment, but since the researcher is operating in the real environment, there are often uncontrolled sources of variation that act on the design. This more natural setting increases the possibilities of generalizing to similar settings, although the potential for inconsistent results and errors is greater. Paradoxically, the abstract laboratory experiment may have implications for a diversity of natural situations. But with a field experiment, the research results are likely to be applicable to fewer situations. As an example, later in this chapter we will discuss a field experiment conducted to determine the effect of emotional disruption on productivity at General Electric.[22]

The field study is less precise and controlled than the field experiment, but again it is performed in a real organizational setting with real employees. Here there is no manipulation of variables. For this reason, of course, there is some lack of precision, and support for the statements of relationships are of necessity much weaker. Essentially, the investigator, like an anthropologist, observes a particular situation or situations, and then tries to organize meaningful generalizations about what has been observed. The consistency of observations at different points in time may be examined. Results depend greatly on the skill of the observers and their freedom from bias. Generalizations run the risk of being statements of what the investigator wanted to see rather than what actually happened. Sometimes we learn from the reports more about the observers than about what was observed.

Most business or organizational cases are based on field studies. They serve as familiarization exercises and are extremely popular in business and professional education. For research purposes, a collection of such cases can be compiled and generalization sought from among them. For instance, we can examine the extent to which nonprofit public service agencies tend to adopt more bureaucratic practices than profit-making firms when the costs and benefits of the former are difficult to measure objectively.

Survey Research

Survey research is conducted by questioning a sample of individuals. Questions and answers can be communicated by interview, mail questionnaires, panels, or telephone polls. This technique is less well controlled than the laboratory or field experiment, since there is no manipulation of variables by the investigator. Groups from which samples are drawn can be varied systematically. Different variables can be statistically associated, but cause and effect will often remain obscure. In a typical survey study, a questionnaire on leadership behavior was correlated with departmental turnover.[12] The turnover was found to be lower in departments with considerate supervisors. The question remained: do considerate supervisors produce low turnover, or can a supervisor of a low-turnover department afford to relax and be more considerate? We shall see in chapter 6 that the latter explanation may sometimes be as good or better than the former.

Cross-lagged correlations provide the solution to this problem of whether the chicken or the egg comes first. Here we measure the consideration of supervisors and turnover in their departments twice, say in January and in June. Then, if the correlation is higher between the supervisors' consideration in January and turnover in June than the correlation between the supervisors' consideration in June and turnover in January, we infer that the supervisors' consideration is affecting turnover and not vice versa. We will see examples of cross-lagged correlational analyses in the next chapter.

The opinions or attitudes expressed by the respondents may also fail to match subsequent behavior. For example, workers may express considerable dissatisfaction with work rules, but may go on strike for higher pay rather than altered rules.

TWO ILLUSTRATIONS

The comprehensive investigation is likely to involve several approaches, such as a field study followed by a simulation. The best way for a student to develop some appreciation for the research techniques used in industrial psychology is to examine in detail a few studies which illustrate some of the main points. The first investigation we will discuss combined a laboratory experiment with simulation to solve the problem of so-called motion sickness. The second is a field experiment on how the performance of assembly line workers can be affected by the way they are treated by management.

A Laboratory Experiment Using Simulation

The study to be described involved both a laboratory and simulation research technique. The main experimental apparatus used in the laboratory experiment was a simulation of the automobile driving task. The simulation was an actual physical reproduction of driving conditions.

Rudimentary simulation appeared in industrial psychology as early as 1908 when a streetcar motorman's mockup was used to test job applicants. Extensive use was made of simulation for pilot and gunnery training during World War II. But the use of simulation in experimentation can be traced to a time shortly after World War II, when complex computer-based simulators were developed. These simulators were designed to re-present, by means of a visual scene and appropriate controls, such tasks as automobile driving, gunnery training, avionic equipment, and the flying of helicopters. In the typical simulator, the vehicle's controls were operated and the results of the "operator's" actions were viewed upon a screen. The scene viewed by the subject gave the illusion of motion without actual motion.

The use of these complex devices for training and research has proved valuable, but the operation of these devices often resulted in symptoms of motion sickness. These included nausea, cold sweating, upset stomach, dizziness, and, in some cases, vomiting.[21] Since these simulators did not move, and motion is known to cause motion sickness, the phenomenon was hard to understand. We should pause here for a moment to consider one difficulty in behavioral research that is illustrated by this case. The phenomenon was termed motion sickness even though no motion had been present. Such premature labeling, based on physical symptoms, is often an impediment to efficient research progress. (The labeling problem is important to the area of industrial psychology. The lay person's use of imprecise terminology requires careful interpretation and refinement before experimental work can be carried out on problems as defined.)

The "motion sickness" problem was important economically as well as scientifically. In economic terms the cheapest simulator costs over $100,000. Much larger simulators are important research tools in a variety of scientific investigations to be discussed in Chapters 13 and 16. Simulators are also an important element in military and commercial aviation, driving, and space training programs. For example, much of the total training time in learning to fly a jumbo jet is spent in a simulator. It is simply too expensive, because of high costs of operation, to use a real airplane for training. Simulators also avoid any risk of accident.

As is true in many research investigations, there were a number of reasons that had been tentatively proposed to explain what we will now call the simulator sickness phenomenon:

1. Distortion of vertical objects in the visual scene
2. Rapid change in the brightness of the visual display over a period of time
3. Scene containing too much detail, leaving a feeling of disorientation like that sometimes encountered by individuals when they enter a large city for the first time
4. Poor resolution of the visual system
5. Control lag between the simulator controls and the corresponding shift in the visual display
6. High-frequency vibrations of the visual scene, disrupting accommodation of the eye
7. Distance between the visual display and the observer such that the accommodation of the eye is different from that experienced in the real world
8. Conflicting cues between the apparent motion seen on the visual display and the lack of any corresponding motion of the simulator

As in many research investigations, these hypotheses could be tested only when opportunity arose. It was after a study involving an evaluation of an automobile simulator that an opportunity presented itself to study the simulator sickness phenomenon. As with previous simulators, a certain number of the drivers experienced discomfort. Twenty-five subjects felt the experiences so unpleasant that they were unable to remain in the simulator longer than 10 minutes. An equal number of drivers managed to remain in the device for the full 45 minutes of the research program with varying degrees of discomfort.

Obviously, the fact that many individuals became ill in the device put severe restrictions on use of the research tool. On examining the possible reasons given above for sickness, it can be seen in general that there were two possible ways the simulator could be improved. First, the visual scene could be improved, giving the driver better resolution, a wider field of view, and so on. A second approach would be to add a motion system that would give the driver a degree of physical motion similar to that experienced by a driver in the real situation. Since both alternatives would have been very costly, it was necessary to determine which one would be most likely to solve the sickness problem. The investigators decided on the second approach for investigation, testing the hypothesis that sickness was caused by the conflict between the apparent motion of the visual display and a lack of any corresponding physical motion.

The analysis was carried one step further. One of the outstanding findings of all simulator sickness phenomena is that some people are affected by it to a greater extent than others, possibly because they experience greater difference between apparent and actual motion. Therefore, the hypothesis was refined to state that those who are most sensitive to body cues would be most aware of the difference between apparent and actual motion and would experience the greatest conflict. This, in turn, would result in greater severity of illness. The sensitivity to body cues was measured by the rod and frame apparatus developed by Witkin and his associates.[27]

The drivers were tested for body-cue sensitivity; the results are shown in Table 2–1. As can be seen, all those individuals who were extremely sensitive to body cues became sufficiently uncomfortable to demand to leave the simulation before the trial was completed. Those insensitive to body cues according to Witkin's test were less affected by whether or not apparent and real motion conflicted. Sensitive persons were more likely to report specific symptoms of motion sickness.

The results confirmed the fact that the simulator sickness was at least partially a function of the conflict generated between the visual presentation of apparent motion and lack of any corresponding body sensation of motion.[2] These results were later confirmed by another investigation, using a different driving simulator, supporting the generality of the phenomenon.[25]

As with many research programs, the results not only led to answers to the problem but also generated new ideas and concepts to be tested. The results of this research program suggested that the obvious way to alleviate the simulator sickness for all subjects, whether or not they were sensitive to body cues, was to introduce a certain degree of motion into the simulator. But instead of being on some kind of expensive moving, vibrating platform, the driver was put on an inexpensive air-filled seat that, by pressure on the body, would give the sensation of movement to the driver. Evidence so far suggests that this simple solution can give body cues to drivers.[3]

Table 2–1. Relationship between body sensitivity and simulator sickness (individual response)

Degrees of sickness	Those extremely sensitive to body cues	Those sensitive to body cues	Those not sensitive to body cues
Quit simulator	12	6	3
Remained in simulator	0	21	2

Adapted from Barrett and Thornton, "Relationship between Simulator Sickness and Perceptual Style," *Journal of Applied Psychology*, 52 (1968): 306.

A number of important points are revealed by this research study. First, the problem arose not from any basic psychological theory, but from a practical situation that demanded a solution. Second, a number of other hypotheses could have been tested by the investigator. Third, the solution to the problem was based on the knowledge of some basic psychological theory. It has often been said that good theory is the most practical thing in the world. In this case it can be seen to be true, since theory gave a focus for the investigation. Since the research was conducted in an industrial concern, its focus was on an extremely practical problem. Industrial situations also provide opportunities to test more basic theories that are not generated by a problem, but more often the specific theory testing by industrial psychologists is left to the university setting.

This study also illustrates a pattern frequently seen in our field: theory and method are used as tools to solve a narrowly defined problem, leading to findings that have potentially broader and broader implications. One of the joys of research is that one finding leads to another, so that there is a continuity in research work.

A Field Experiment

One of the main problems faced by many industrial organizations is the change in working procedures required by the introduction of designs, new models, or methods of manufacturing. The necessity for change is well understood in the modern industrial corporation, but the degree of smoothness of change is highly variable. In some cases the work group may accept a change quite well, and within a relatively short time they will again be operating efficiently. In contrast, other groups may take months to regain their former level of proficiency. A study was conducted at several plants to determine the effects of various psychological factors on the workers' productivity and ability to make a change in working procedures. The investigators refined their hypotheses to say that emotional factors will have an effect only on the production of those workers at the time of a change in working procedures.[21] When assembly-line workers are performing tasks in a routine manner, emotional states will not affect their productivity. When they have fully mastered operations, they will repeat the same task many times daily. It then becomes automatic, and it is only when the work operation is changed and a new work procedure is being learned that emotional factors can disrupt productivity.

To test this proposition, the investigators matched groups of assembly line workers. They selected groups who had equal experience on the job and who were performing identical work operations. Groups were either "favored" or "disfavored." Conditions were made as pleasant as possible for the favored groups. These groups were subject to praise and to flattery on the high quality of their work from supervisory personnel. The supervisors also attempted to be helpful and pleasant throughout the period, so that the favored groups had a relatively smooth and pleasant work environment. In contrast, the disfavored groups were systematically subjected to a series of common annoyances. They were emotionally upset by confrontation with annoying incidents every day during a two-week period. These incidents usually centered around a time study of the operators and attacks on the workers by quality control and supervisory personnel, usually complaining about the quality of work. The manipulation of these emotional states stopped as soon as the groups made a change in procedure.

During the course of the study, detailed production records were kept on all work groups. After the manipulation had continued for a period of time, a change in job procedure was introduced into both groups. In this manner the researchers could determine the effects of both emotional state on productivity of workers — first, when the work is routine and, second, when the work procedures are changing and the work requires very close attention.

The experiments were conducted in three manufacturing plants of General Electric. In all experiments the groups were assembly-line workers, with 5 to 11 workers per group. On each job the work was arranged so that a piece of material would pass from worker to worker, and each worker had a different job on the piece, which was repeated precisely for every piece that was worked. In all the groups, the work consisted of small manual movements, such as parts assembly or connecting wires.

The change for the workers in every group consisted of a change in some detail of the work or the manufacture of a slightly different product. It was accomplished by the established procedure of having the foreman and the trainer work for a few hours with the operators, showing them the new procedures, after which the operators were left pretty much on their own.

The results of the study confirmed the fact that when the work was routine and fully learned, the emotional state had virtually no effect on the productivity of the work force. In other words, making life very pleasant for the favored group and very unpleasant for the disfavored group had little effect on the quantity or quality of work. But after a change in work procedure, emotional factors did play a role. This was manifested by the fact that, after the change in work procedure, the favored group was consistently higher in quality of work (and also in quantity, if work was not on a paced conveyor belt). If work was on a paced assembly line (with no opportunity to increase productivity), the quantity of production would remain the same but the quality was lower for the disfavored group. It is clear that the result of the study supports the hypotheses advanced by the researchers.

This investigation sheds light on the realities of research and research design — how studies are actually conducted in an industrial situation. It will be useful to look a little deeper into the problems of a field experiment of this type. The authors of the report listed a number of factors existing during the time of study which have to be expected in this type of industrial research. For example, the experimenters had hoped to counterbalance the effects of day and night shift operations, to review operators repeatedly and perform other experimental controls during the course of study. The authors reported that the problems encountered in a major industrial organization forced them to abandon many of the niceties of the research design in order to have any experiment at all. This is an important fact of field experimentation that researchers must often face. They generally cannot have the same control over the variables that they have in laboratory studies. They must sacrifice some of their control to perform a meaningful study. Unexpected events often occur. For example, on the day of changeover of work procedures, a severe snowstorm occurred at the location of one of the plants. There was so much absenteeism that none of the experimental groups was working as a group. On subsequent days there was still a great deal of absenteeism, and some of the groups worked, while others did not. Therefore, data were discarded because so many individuals in the group were replaced by others who had not been given the full experimental manipulations. In another plant it was discovered that the favored group rotated their jobs, not only among themselves but also with individuals in other groups. Again, data had to be discarded because the members of the group were not receiving the same experimental treatment as members of the other groups. Other problems occur in field experiments. For an eleven-day period, at least one of four data collectors was at home, sick.

These factors have been mentioned to illustrate the difficulty involved in good industrial research. Despite difficulties, a field experiment of this sort probably offers the only means for testing hypotheses in a real-life situation.

After a finding has been obtained at a field setting, its generalizability can be confirmed in a laboratory investigation. In order to test the generality of the proposition that emotional arousal would disrupt performance of a newly learned task but not the performance of a well-learned task, a laboratory study was conducted. Subjects were given a simple repetitive task to do; it consisted of pressing switches in sequence. After the task was learned by both groups, an investigator gave two minutes of harassment, which consisted mostly of downplaying and ridiculing the subjects' responses to a questionnaire. The same investigator asked identical questions of a control group, but greeted the responses with mild approval instead of active disapproval. When both groups continued the well-learned task, no difference in performance was found between the two groups. There was a dramatic difference in performance when a new task was given to the subjects, with those subjected to emotional disruption performing significantly less well.[17] The laboratory study conducted under controlled conditions confirmed the field experiment.

It is apparent that the route to answering research questions is not always clear, and the astute investigator will build on what has been learned in one study to design a better research project. This approach is a feature of all scientific disciplines. As we mentioned at the beginning of this chapter, the inductive approach starts with multiple hypotheses, a finding is made, and then the procedure is repeated with the resultant new hypotheses. Studies are conducted to verify the results, and the cycle is repeated until answers are found.

METHODOLOGICAL ISSUES IN THE SCIENCE AND PRACTICE OF INDUSTRIAL AND ORGANIZATIONAL PSYCHOLOGY

Science and Practice

Industrial and organizational psychology is a science. But it also is a practice. In industry or the nonprofit agency, it can be employed in either way. One can be engaged in basic psychological research. However, one is more likely to engage in a variety of problem-finding and problem-solving activities in which available knowledge and intuition are used to handle day-to-day problems at work that do not call for or permit a scientific research project to seek out problems, determine a solution, and verify its correctness. Even if one has the opportunity to complete a relevant research project in order to discover and verify best solutions, ways must still be bound to arrive at solutions implemented through others, usually at higher organizational levels.

Problem Finding

Problem finding is critical for the would-be successful employment of psychology in the work setting.

> [One] may believe, for example, that the organization has correctly identified significant problems and is prepared to support research and any necessary changes in practice to solve them. In actuality, one of the reasons organizations experience persistent difficulties is their inability to determine the nature of the basic problem. This, combined with a lack of understanding of [psychologists'] possible contribution, makes it particularly risky . . . to accept as given

the problems posed by management. The temptation to accept management's diagnoses uncritically is greatest for neophytes. They want to produce for their new employer, and it is difficult for them to diagnose problems until they develop some familiarity with the organization.[24]

Policy Research

Industrial and organizational psychology is heavily involved in *policy research*. This is different from the purely scientific investigation, which is undertaken to search for or to test the truth of a proposition. Policy research is undertaken to help policy makers decide whether or not to take certain actions having long-term consequences to the organization. Here the independent variable is mandated by authority, the policy maker, and not usually under experimental control. For instance, the management of a company may wish to learn if a program to recruit college graduates for a firm is more effective over a five-year period as a consequence of a policy that allows prospective candidates to visit company headquarters in the summer of the last year in school. A *quasi-experiment* can be applied to studying the effects of the policy.

A quasi-experiment lacks the controls that would give us a high degree of confidence that it is indeed the summer program and not something else that is making recruiting more effective. Thus, we may institute a uniform policy: all prospective candidates pay a summer visit to headquarters. We measure the quality of recruits yearly after the new policy has gone into effect and compare it with the quality before the new policy was instituted. If quality improves we must depend on our judgment about whether or not it was the summer program that led to the increase.

What's Plausible?

Events other than the new policy can contaminate the results. Jobs may be harder to find because of a downturn in the business cycle. We may have better candidates to choose from as a consequence of conditions that have nothing to do with our new recruiting policy. Only if we can introduce a control group that does not hear about or benefit from our new recruiting policy can we be more confident that the new policy resulted in better recruits. We could institute the new program only east of the Mississippi and keep the old policy in force west of the Mississippi. If recruits improved in the East but not the West, the most *plausible hypothesis* would be that our new policy was effective. But we still could entertain less plausible alternative hypotheses. For instance, we might speculate that recruits improved in the East more than the West because the company increased its *institutional advertising* in the East, or because the company opened an attractive new office in the East, or because Easterners were more influenced by the new policy than Westerners would have been. But we could argue with some confidence that all of these alternative explanations were *less plausible* than the explanation that summer visits by prospective candidates to company headquaters attracted better recruits.

Most research in social science is like this. Most experiments are really quasi-experiments. There is almost always a string of plausible hypotheses that we can offer to account for the effects of a program. Highly controlled experimentation is usually costly and/or near impossible if we are engaged in a study of complex behavior of any consequence. We seldom are able to follow narrowly the simple traditional scientific model of controlling all but one independent variable and studying its pure effects on one dependent variable. Consider all the ways in which Eastern college graduates collectively differ slightly from Western college graduates that are of no practical importance. In the aggregate, the graduates are likely to differ beyond chance expectations in ethnic composition, height, weight, eye color, hair color, blood type, percentage of enrollment in private rather than public colleges, interest in ballet, and knowledge about agriculture. Yet, we would be hard pressed to argue that any of these differences would account for the fact that after we introduced our new program in the East but not the West, the quality of recruits improved in the East but not the West.

This is why industrial psychology is much more than just data gathering and "flights into statistical analyses," for it is theory and associated models that will guide our conceptions of a problem, and it is theory and models that will guide our thinking as to what empirical results make sense and what empirical results are just nonsense. It makes sense to expect that inviting college juniors to visit a company's headquarters will increase their enthusiasm about and understanding of the company. More seniors will want to join the company upon graduation. They will have more realistic reasons for their enthusiasm. The company will be able to choose from a large pool of interested applicants. So the East, with the summer program, ends up with better recruits than the West, without the summer program. On the other hand, suppose we find that more graduates in the East than the West are black-haired. Can this explain why the East graduates improved and the West did not? We are unlikely to include hair color in our model about what improves recruiting.

The Place of Theory

So, models and theory are needed. But often they are constructed prematurely before we have gathered enough evidence to justify the framework of variables. Often the framework constructed is just too elaborate, given what evidence we have gathered to support it. At an early stage in our knowledge about a problem, theories and models need to be kept simple. As we learn more about the problem we can profitably increase their complexity.[6] For example, we have little information about how the style of a communicator in an industrial organization affects his or her credibility. Therefore, we start with a simple model that lists the different styles of communicating and the different aspects of credibility. Then surveys are completed, identifying six dimensions along which styles of managers differ, such as carefulness in transmitting and listening, and three factors of credibility such as trustworthiness, informativeness, and dynamism. A more complex model can now be constructed, linking specific styles and aspects of credibility.[7] Theory generalizes to all cases; models cover a few specific situations. Models can be simple lists of possible factors of consequence or they can be complex arrangements specifying functional relationships between variables and constants.

Starr described three models.[23] The models increase from simple to complex.

A shopping list of purchases designed to increase a family's satisfaction is a simple model. It may include soap of an unspecified brand, size, and price, as well as coffee of a particular brand and amount.

Less simple is a model that specifies relationships: for example, satisfaction can be expected to depend on price, taste, and shopping convenience. It also says in advance that given outcomes will depend on given antecedent conditions. For example, the model can specify that the amount of coffee purchased will be a function of the amount remaining on the home shelf, the amount of coffee consumed each day, and the frequency with which the shopper visits the grocery store.

The most complex model has feedback that alters values of the variables of the model. Relationships can be changed on the basis of data gathered. For example, price rises may force family discussions about continuing to purchase the particular brand rather than turning to a less expensive one. At this point we probably are ready to start formal theorizing with some purpose.

The theory that might ultimately emerge from working with this complex model would concern family-based buying decisions. Sometimes we are at a stage in our data gathering and model building when more theory is needed before further understanding is possible. At other times, however, more theory may hinder rather than help. It used to be thought that to solve problems we conducted scientific investigations to generate and test fundamental broad generalizations. Once the generalizations had been proved, it was believed that solutions to particular problems (applications) would follow automatically. But, as Glaser noted:[14] "The sequence from basic research, to applied research, to development, to practice and

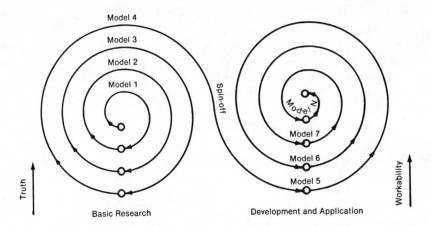

Figure 2–1. Ineffective relations between basic research and development. (Adapted from Bass, "The Substance and the Shadow," *American Psychologist*, 29 [1974]: 878.)

application on which most of us were weaned is no longer applicable if, in fact, it ever was" (p. 2).

The idea that basic research comes first and application comes last is illustrated by Figure 2.1. Basic research spins around its own axis, producing increasingly truthful models of the reality and problems under study. Then it spins off for application some portion, which is developed into more and more workable models of reality to solve the problem.

In industrial and organizational psychology, progress in a field of study is likely to be greatest if increasingly true *and* workable models to solve the problem are constructed, moving back and forth, as shown in Figure 2.2, between applications in the real world and the controlled experiments and simulations of basic research.

Information flow between those who conduct basic research and those who try to apply it is essential. They must disseminate to each other the results of their work. Figure 2.3 attempts to show how each proceeds and where the work can be linked.

Threats to Validity of Experimental Conclusions

In the typical controlled experiment, we first measure the experimental and the control groups. (It is hoped that there are no real extra-chance differences between the groups.) Then the experimental group is given the experimental treatment; the control group receives no treatment. Finally, we remeasure the two groups. If the experimental group now differs from the control group beyond what we might expect from chance,

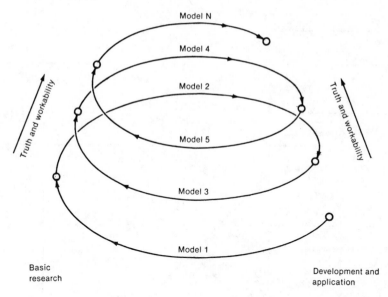

Figure 2–2. Effective relations between basic research and development and application. (Adapted from Bass, "The Substance and the Shadow," *American Psychologist,* 29 [1974]: 879.)

we infer that the treatment had an effect. But we may not be confident about the effect. The *internal validity* of the experiment will be suspect if we have strong doubts as to whether the effect was really due to the experimental treatment or to something else. The *external validity* will be suspect if we lack confidence that the treatment would work in other situations.[11]

A THREAT TO INTERNAL VALIDITY   We may suspect that the experimenter guided the experimental participants unconsciously by unintended non-verbal behavior toward them which caused the experiment to come out the way the experimenter wanted. This threat to the internal validity of the conclusions of an experiment is not unusual. In the psychological experiment, it appears to be difficult to avoid unintended covert communication between the experimenter and the subject. Without meaning to the experimenter influences subjects to respond in accordance with his or her expectations. Such unintended fulfillments of expectations have invalidated hundreds of experiments. Experimenters' hypotheses (expectations about how the treatment will affect the subject) serve as self-fulfilling prophecies — the Pygmalion effect.

The experimenter tends to act toward the subjects in such a way as to achieve a set of purposes that were defined in advance. The experimenter is hoping to win something, not lose, in the process. Negative feelings are

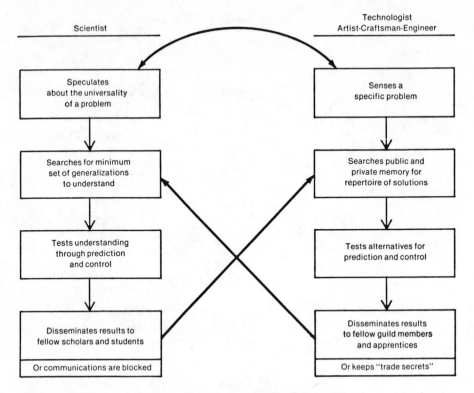

Figure 2–3. Informational links that need to be strengthened in the social sciences. (Adapted from Bass, "The Substance and the Shadow," *American Psychologist*, 29 [1974]: 880.)

to be suppressed. Above all, the experimenter is to remain rational rather than emotional. But a dilemma emerges as a consequence. These standards for the ideal experimenter result in subjects who either fight or flee (covertly, of course).[1] Or they may try to modify the experiment or raise the price for their participation. Such experimentation is unlikely to generate a mature and valid understanding of the total problem being investigated. Often it results in erroneous conclusions about the impact of the experimental variable on the subject or is limited in applicability to rather simple-minded people. Argyris proposes that experimenters reduce subjects' defensiveness by trying to be more open with the subjects about objectives in order to increase their internal commitment to the experiment. (Unfortunately, this may make the subjects, like the experimenter, push to fulfill their own expectations.)[1]

UNOBTRUSIVE MEASURES We try to reduce the experimenter's possible influence on the outcome of the experiment by using a tape-recorded voice, so that all subjects receive the same standard message. Or the experimenter is made blind to the treatment to be received by each subject; or *unobtrusive measures,* over which the experimenter has no influence, are employed.[26] We examine data that have accumulated without the contributors of the data necessarily being aware that it will be used for research. (If the data are not anonymous or if for some reason it was collected in confidence or should remain confidential, ethical considerations would require us to ask permission to use such data, of course.) However, many unobtrusive measures are quite anonymous. For instance, we can learn if people tend more often to turn left or right when they enter theaters by measuring the wear on carpets in the left and right aisles. (People tend to turn to the right.)

A favorite source of industrial psychological information is obtained from a firm or agency's personnel records. For example, we can determine how termination rates differ for different types of employee or from department to department. (Privacy-of-information legislation requires careful control of when and how many data are used.)

PROBLEMS WITH OBSERVATION   Simple observations of employees in their everyday activities may or may not be unobtrusive. An individual engineer clocking an assembly-line worker completing a cycle is clearly a very obtrusive observer. Employees call such observers "bird dogs." Workers may speed up to show off or slow down for fear that the rate at which they are paid to complete the cycle will be reduced if they complete cycles quickly. On the other hand, one may unobtrusively observe something like the interaction of assemblers and supply room workers when the assemblers come to the supply room for more parts.

OTHER VALIDITY THREATS TO THE PSYCHOLOGICAL EXPERIMENT AND WAYS TO COPE WITH THEM   Numerous factors could contaminate our experiment and reduce our confidence that the experimental treatment was the reason the experimental group differed afterward from the control group.[10] Suitable experimental designs have been developed to deal with each of these when we suspect they are present and must control them. For instance, we may suspect that the tests of our subjects before the subjects are treated in some special way will influence how they react to the treatment.

To eliminate this *reaction threat,* we use a second control group. This group is treated, then measured only afterward. Doing this eliminates the possibility that the measurement given before the treatment affected subjects during the treatment or their measurements after the treatment. Then, afterward, we compare our experimental group with the two control groups.

Or, suppose we suspect that our experimental group knows in advance that they will be treated and the control group knows in advance that they will not be. We can use a *"holdout"* design. All participants are treated, only we holdout and don't treat those who will be the controls until we have measured them at the same times as we have measured the experimental group. (This is an ethically attractive design, as everyone gets the opportunity to receive the treatment.)

In field experiments and studies that last for a period of time, we are likely to have participants dropping out. Dropouts are not the same as those who remain in the experimental and control groups. This *experimental mortality* has to be suitably accounted for. From the time when we begin collecting data to the time when we finish, events take place out of our control which may contaminate the effects of our treatments. In the middle of a study the company may announce a new promotion policy, which sharply raises the morale of those in our experiment or survey. We may lose some volunteers because of their being laid off from work. A new boss may force a change in the experimental program. All these *historical threats* to the validity of our conclusions need to be taken into account.

We may unconsciously load the dice in our favor by selecting for the experimental group participants who will differ from those in the control group in the ways they respond to the treatment, so that results will come out as we had expected. For example, suppose we want to evaluate the specific impact on male managers of PROFAIR, a half-day activity aimed at increasing awareness and understanding about the upgrading of women employees.[5] The validity of our conclusions is threatened if we choose for the experimental group, but not the control group, male managers who already are favorably disposed toward women.

We try to control this threat due to selection by randomly assigning participants to our experimental and control groups (or by various statistical control procedures, which cannot be discussed here because of space limitations).

A threat to validity occurs in a continuing training program where earlier treatments affect later treatments. The experimental group may be reminded now of an earlier occurrence (say, a film on women's rights) that makes it more receptive to PROFAIR than it would have been without the earlier treatment.

Notice that if we are not concerned about research, we may happily build all these biasing threats to validity into our program to increase the effects. We can deliberately promote the changing of people and organizations with these research contaminants. But, if we want to know just how good in operation PROFAIR will be by itself, then we need to keep our investigation clear of these threats to validity.

Threats occur in surveys and field studies as well as in controlled experiments. Thus, nonrespondents to a survey may or may not be the same as respondents in their attitudes. If anything, they are likely to be more opposed to the survey's objectives, so that conclusions we draw from the respondents are unlikely to apply accurately to the nonrespondents. Here we can test for the external threat to validity and discount it by trying a second time to get some of the nonrespondents to respond, to see what some nonrespondents were really like.

Most often, we'd be safer to assume that nonrespondents are unlike respondents. For example, survey questionnaires were given to 552 checkers in 14 food stores of a supermarket chain in Washington, D.C., along with a stamped return envelope. The questionnaire, to be completed anonymously, was designed to identify workers' attitudes about supervisory practices, the social climate, and personnel policies in the firm.

The 204 nonrespondents differed from the 348 respondents on five of seven characteristics analyzed. As shown in Table 2.2, nonresponding was associated with lower levels of education, single marital status, male status, being younger or older than the middle-aged group (between 30 and 49 years of age), and ranking in the bottom fifth of all employees as measured by supervisory ratings. These findings confirm previous re-

Table 2–2. Predictors of response rates among workers   N = 552

	Respondent (percentage)	Nonrespondent (percentage)
Education		
Under 11 years	57.4	42.6
11 and 12 years	26.9	37.1
13 and 14 years	64.6	35.4
15 years and over	80.3	19.7
Marital status		
Single	51.3	48.7
Married	64.7	35.3
Widowed, divorced, or separated	76.4	23.6
Age		
Under 20 years	57.7	42.3
20–24 years	66.9	33.1
25–29 years	51.1	48.9
30–49 years	69.4	30.6
50 years and above	52.4	47.6
Sex		
Male	56.8	43.2
Female	66.0	34.0
Supervisory ranking		
20th percentile and under	53.4	46.6
21st percentile and over	68.0	32.0

Adapted from Gannon, Nothern, and Carroll, "Characteristics of Nonrespondents among Workers," *Experimental Publication System,* 10 (1976): Ms. no. 378–12.

search, which showed that males, those with lower educational levels, and those with lower intelligence have lower response rates to surveys.[19] But, as shown in Table 2.2, the results of the analysis indicate that mail surveys of workers may be biased toward more stable, older, more effective employees. In addition, typical attitudes of female workers, to the extent that they differ from those of male workers, may be weighted too heavily by such surveys.[13]

SUMMARY

Research in industrial/organizational psychology is not for amateurs. We have seen how we cannot design the perfect experiment. Nevertheless, we have also seen how we can apply reason to the design of data gathering so that we can make some sense out of the outcomes. We are not engaged here in pure science. But we are far advanced from depending on personal experiences alone. Five research approaches work for us in I/O psychology: laboratory experiments, simulation, field experiments, field studies, and survey research. Usually several such approaches are combined in a line of investigation of a problem.

Policy research and quasi-experimentation is common in I/O psychology, usually leading us to ask what is most plausible, not what is absolutely true. We must learn to cope with the various threats to the validity of our conclusions.

REFERENCES

1. Argyris, C. "Dangers in Applying Results from Experimental Social Psychology," *American Psychologist*, 30 (1975): 469–485.
2. Barrett, G. V., and C. L. Thornton. "The Relationship between Simulator Sickness and Perceptual Style," *Journal of Applied Psychology*, 52 (1968): 304–308.
3. Barrett, G. V., P. A. Cabe, C. L. Thornton, and H. E. Kerber. "Evaluation of a Motion Simulator Not Requiring Cockpit Motion," *Human Factors*, 11 (1969): 239–244.
5. Bass, B. M. "The American Advisor Abroad," *Journal of Applied Behavioral Science*, 7 (1971): 285–308.
6. Bass, B. M. "The Substance and the Shadow," *American Psychologist*, 29 (1974): 870–886.
7. Bass, B. M., and R. Klauss. "Communication Styles, Credibility and Their Consequences," *Personnel Administrator*, 20, no. 6 (1975): 32–35.
8. Beveridge, W. I. B. *The Art of Scientific Investigation* (3rd ed.). New York: Vintage Books, 1957.
9. Boulding, K. E. "Dare We Take the Social Sciences Seriously?" *American Psychologist*, 22 (1967): 879–887.

10. Campbell, D. T., and J. C. Stanley. *Experimental and Quasi-Experimental Designs for Research.* Chicago: Rand McNally, 1963.
11. Cook, T. D., and D. T. Campbell. "Experiments in Field Settings." In M. D. Dunnette, ed., *Handbook of Industrial and Organizational Psychology.* Chicago: Rand McNally, 1976.
12. Fleishman, E. A. "The Description of Supervisory Behavior," *Journal of Applied Psychology,* 37 (1953): 153–158.
13. Gannon, M. J., J. C. Nothern, and S. J. Carroll. "Characteristics of Non-Respondents among Workers," *Experimental Publication System,* 10 (1976) Ms. no. 378-12.
14. Glaser, R. "Educational Psychology and Education." Presidential address to Division of Education Psychology, American Psychological Association, Honolulu, September 1972.
15. Haggard, H. W. *Devils, Drugs and Doctors.* New York: Harper, 1929.
16. Kerlinger, F. N. *Foundations of Behavioral Research.* New York: Holt, Rinehart & Winston, 1965.
17. Latane, B., and A. J. Arrowood. "Emotional Arousal and Task Performance," *Journal of Applied Psychology,* 47 (1963): 324–327.
18. Locke, E. A. "Toward a Theory of Task Motivation and Incentives," *Organizational Behavior and Human Performance,* 3 (1968): 157–189.
19. Macek, A. J., and G. H. Miles. "IQ Score and Mailed Questionnaire Response," *Journal of Applied Psychology,* 60 (1975): 258–259.
20. Miller, J. W., and J. E. Goodson. *A Note Concerning Motion Sickness in the 2–FH–2 Hover Trainer.* Report no. 1. Naval Aviation Medical Center, Pensacola, Florida, Project NM 17–01–11 Subtask, February 1958.
21. Schachter, S., B. Willerman, L. Festinger, and R. Hyman. "Emotional Disruption and Industrial Productivity," *Journal of Applied Psychology,* 45 (1961): 201–213.
22. Stagner, R. "The Gullibility of Personnel Managers," *Personnel Psychology,* 11 (1958): 347–352.
23. Starr, M. K. *Management: A Modern Approach.* New York: Harcourt-Brace-Jovanovich, 1971.
24. Task Force on the Practice of Psychology in Industry. "Effective Practice of Psychology in Industry," *American Psychologist,* 26 (1971): 974–991.
25. Testa, C. J. "The Prediction and Evaluation of Simulator Illness Symptomatology." Unpublished doctoral dissertation, University of California, Los Angeles, 1969.
26. Webb, E. J., D. T. Campbell, R. D. Schwartz, and L. Secrest. *Unobtrusive Measures: Nonreactive Research in the Social Sciences.* Chicago: Rand McNally, 1966.
27. Witkin, H. A., H. B. Lewis, M. Hertzman, K. Machover, P. B. Meissner, and S. Wapner. *Personality through Perception.* New York: Harper, 1954.

II Organizational Psychology

3   MOTIVATION TO WORK

IN BRIEF   The meaning of work and the motives that induce people to work have undergone considerable change over the centuries.

People work for outcomes they desire and expect from doing the work itself or from what is obtained from it. However, satisfaction with what one is doing does not automatically result in better performance, yet unmet expectations will result in dissatisfaction, absenteeism, or quitting.

Maslow's, Herzberg's, Homans's and Vroom's theories have stimulated continuing research and practical applications on how to increase motivation to work.

Behavioral theories about why people work, along with parallel changes in society, have resulted in greater attention in industry to employees' expectations. Challenging work and greater opportunities for personal growth are seen as being as important as equitable sharing of the costs and benefits yielded by the effort and performance.

Concern with how people feel about their jobs is of relatively recent origin. Before 1930, studies concentrated on the physical surroundings of the worker and how they could be improved. There was little consideration of a worker's attitudes about the job he/she performed. From the 1930s onward, interest increased in trying to learn about the thoughts, feelings, and attitudes of people that motivate them to work.

Reasons for Increasing Concern

Three reasons underlay this increased concern about job attitudes and the motivation to work. First, social critics were prodding society to pay more attention to individuals and their feelings. They were reacting against Taylor's "scientific management" and the treatment of workers as if they were machines. A sentiment developed that a person's work should have meaning. At an earlier time, social critics had been concerned mainly with the conditions and physical hardships imposed on workers by the industrial revolution. Then, as the physical conditions of jobs improved, they focused attention on the meaningfulness of an individual's job: a job which gave satisfaction.

The German sociologist Max Weber struck a responsive chord with his observation that people resent being under the control of an organization. An extreme example is the assembly line, where workers have no options about the timing or the kinds of tasks they perform. Charlie Chaplin's movie *Modern Times* reflected these feelings.

The assembly line was seen to contrast with the supposedly happy but bygone days of the skilled worker and apprentice, the ideal of which was the medieval craftsman. The craftsmanship of old was probably over-romanticized; no more than 10 per cent of the population in medieval times were in this skilled category, so the benefits could accrue to relatively few. In fact, in our modern society there are more people engaged in professions and skilled trades than ever before in the history of the world. Even in the automotive industry, fewer than 5 per cent of all workers are actually on assembly lines.[12]

The second reason for focusing on job attitudes was the increasing awareness of managers that jobs were changing and that greater discretion and responsibility would be needed from workers. As work became less repetitious and mechanical, so that more skilled individuals working at their own pace rather than machine pace were required, there was an increasing realization that workers' feelings about their jobs might well affect their job performance. Positive job attitudes could be measured in dollars and cents. In some cases, the improvement of employee attitudes was seen as a goal in itself; in others, it was assumed or hoped that improving employee attitudes would result in improved effort and performance.

A third reason for the attention to worker attitudes in the United States in the 1930s was the renewed vitality of labor unionism at that time. The rise of successful industrial unions, led by the C.I.O., and the legitimatization and legalization of collective bargaining began with the passage of the Wagner National Labor Relations Act in 1937. Up to that time, conspiracy and restraint-of-trade laws placed unions in a weak position in their dealings with management. Now legislation backed up their organizing efforts.

THE HAWTHORNE STUDIES

The first studies of motivation to work to gain prominence were conducted in the Hawthorne works of Western Electric between 1924 and 1932.[65] At the outset, the primary interest was in physical conditions such as temperature and humidity, and the incidence of monotony and fatigue among the workers. The first studies investigated the relationship between illumination and productivity. An improvement in lighting was expected to increase the employees' output. Contrary to expectations, the output bobbed up and down without any clear relationship to changes in illumination. To refine the experiment, a control group in another building worked under constant lighting while the experimental group worked under varying lighting. Both groups showed appreciable gains in production. In order for the researchers to convince themselves that the effects of lighting were "psychological," additional experiments were run. The illumination was decreased until it was equal to an ordinary moonlit night, and still the output remained constant. In the coil winding group, the experimenters increased the light day by day and solicited favorable responses from the women, who said that they liked the increased light. The experimenters then permitted the women to observe the electrician come and ostensibly change the light bulbs, though in reality he merely replaced the bulbs with others of the same wattage. Unaware that the amount of light remained unchanged, the women commented favorably about the increased illumination. It was now clear to the researchers that light was only a minor factor affecting employee output and that a better-controlled study would be necessary to identify the pertinent variables.

Relay Assembly Test Room

In order to maintain better control of the research, five women were isolated from their department in a separate location, the relay assembly test room. The women in this room assembled telephone relays composed of approximately 35 small parts. Each day's output was kept on tape and the significant events and interactions of the group were recorded by an observer who also acted as a supervisor. Over a two-year period, a 30 per cent increase in productivity was obtained.

The investigators concluded that social satisfaction derived from interaction with others at work was more important to productivity than either the physical aspects or the economic incentives of work.[78] Unfortunately, during the relay assembly investigation, many other changes were introduced, confounding understanding of what had contributed to the increased productivity. These included changes in the assembly task, shorter working hours, rest pauses, friendly supervision, and a preferred incentive plan. The women were accorded special privileges such as parties with ice cream and cake. In addition, the study did not continue for the entire two-year period with the same five workers. Two of the original five received continued reprimands for talking too much and were eventually replaced with two other women by the "friendly" supervisor. The two replacements were more willing to cooperate with the aims of the experimenters and lead the rest of the group to higher productivity.[14]

In addition to the above shortcomings in research design, the investigators did not have a *control* group. Indeed, results from five individuals could at best be considered suggestive in this quasi-experiment.

Significance

While the Hawthorne studies thus have very limited scientific worth, the "Hawthorne effect" has become a widely used term and concept. The term has become synonymous with "placebo effect" to describe a phenomenon where the results are due to suggestion rather than objective changes in relevant variables.[73] Nevertheless, even after fifty years, analyses of the Hawthorne studies continue. A reanalysis by Parsons led him to conclude that the studies illustrate how worker performance can be controlled by its consequences, combining information feedback and financial reward.[57] He noted that introducing rest pauses did increase output rate. Shorter hours also may have increased rate of output. But what made for the overall effect was that these changes in lighting, ventilation, and friendly supervision were combined with a change in the incentive plan. In the new arrangement, incentive earnings for a worker were based on the productivity of the worker and her 4 co-workers rather than the entire department of 100 employees. Franke and Kaul completed a statistical analysis of the effects of what had been regarded by the investigators as three minor threats to the validity of the conclusions.[25] But Franke and Kaul found that over 90 per cent of the improvement in performance of the employees could be accounted for by (1) improvements in the quality of raw materials to be processed by the workers, (2) tightening up of supervisory discipline, and (3) business declines, which brought anxiety about being laid off.

The Hawthorne studies illustrate the extent to which it is possible for invesigators to find what they are seeking, whether it is there or not. But most important, in their erroneous conclusions that performance was shaped primarily by improved human relations, the Hawthorne studies redirected attention from a strict economic and engineering view of the completely rational worker in a completely rationalized workplace to more socioemotional considerations. The Hawthorne studies gave birth to the human relations movement a half-century ago at a time when the pin factory idealized in Adam Smith's *Wealth of Nations* [71] was seen as the ultimate in perfection with complete job specialization, job simplification, and division of labor. In Chapter 15 we will explore more recent concepts of job design.

WHY PEOPLE WORK

Superficially, the reason why people work appears to be absurdly simple. They must work to put bread on the table. While this response certainly has been valid in the past, it has become less true today, with the spread of government welfare programs. But, despite the availability of welfare, it is essentially true that most people must be gainfully employed to meet their economic needs. The more subtle question is what factors associated with the work situation promote individual satisfaction and productivity over and above marginal subsistence and performance.

People work because they expect to be paid, but why else do they work? Men work because it's expected of all of them and women work because it is expected of many or most of them and to supplement the family income.

But why else do they work? Because they like the activity and the setting in comparison to other activities, such as housekeeping. Because it may give them power, particularly control over their own fates. Because it may help them to make friends. Because it gives them a sense of achievement. Because it gives them prestige, and so on.

Why is it useful to study what motivates people to work? Because working is usually the most important thing people do in their lives. Because work affects their sense of well-being and mental health. Also, because how they feel about working affects their absenteeism, rates of quitting, and productivity.

Motivation has become most important because of the way jobs have changed. Workers no longer supply the energy for industrial production. As technology advances, increasingly they become the regulators of an industrial process, the adjusters, the monitors, and diagnosticians dealing with unprogrammed, unpredictable fluctuations in the system. For effective performance in this kind of employment, they must be ready, willing, and able to react without necessary consultation with higher authority, and they must be adaptable and committed to their roles in the organization.

Changing Meaning of Work

The meaning of work and the motives that induce people to work have undergone considerable change over the centuries. With the exception of economically underdeveloped societies, where working may be motivated by nothing more than the need for basic physical survival, the motives and meaning of work have become extremely complex. These motives are especially important in our era, where people's options concerning the amount and type of work they do are the widest in history.

BEFORE THE INDUSTRIAL REVOLUTION   To the Greeks, work was a burdensome curse. They had a special distaste for manual work, probably because most manual work was performed by slaves.[79] Reports indicate that modern Greeks still have that distaste.[81] Cicero spoke for the Romans when he said that agriculture and big business were the only occupations worthy of a free man. Often the Hebrews found that manual labor was drudgery (Ecclesiastes 2:17): "Therefore I hated life; because the work that is wrought under the sun is grievous unto me." The early Christians regarded work as God's punishment for Adam's original sin. But work also had a postive value. By working one could earn enough to share with one's less fortunate brothers. Early Christians believed that in the Promised Kingdom they would be freed from toil and this belief, of course, engendered a lack of concern for the material world.

The downgrading of manual work still permeates modern society. The "guest workers" of the poorer Mediterranean nations, Asia, and Africa perform the manual labor in more advanced northern Europe. In the U.S., successive waves of immigrants supplied the manual labor force, and their children and grandchildren sought white-collar and professional careers.

A slow evolutionary process had to take place before work and the motivation to work became something more than an act of charity or a means to expiation. With the Renaissance and Reformation, new ideas were developed about the value of work. Luther taught that work was a means of serving God, and one of the best ways to serve Him was to work to the best of one's ability. Calvin fostered similar attitudes because he believed that work was the will of God and that by the sweat of man's brow the Kingdom of God could be established on earth. Success in one's work, or profession, was a sign that one's labor was pleasing to God. The rich man was now extolled because his profits attested to his success in serving God. Many thinkers claim the Calvinistic doctrine as the beginning of modern capitalism and the ideological foundation for the modern factory. This ideology, which exalts the person who survives in the competitive world of work and who also "knows the value of a dollar," evolved into what Max Weber has described as the Protestant ethic.[87]

Along with the new conceptions of work, the concept of managing work and workers began to receive attention.[11] There have been marked alterations in the goals of management through the years from the Industrial Revolution in England to the present.

SURVIVAL OF THE FITTEST   An early conception of management during the Industrial Revolution in England was labeled by John Stuart Mill as the "theory of dependence." The laboring classes were looked on as merely thoughtless children who required direction to perform tasks assigned by their superiors. If the workers performed their tasks well and were deserving, they would be provided for by the rich. As the pace of industrialization quickened, the view shifted from a feeling of responsibility toward the laboring poor to a feeling that the poor should attempt to better their lot by their own efforts. By the end of the nineteenth century, the managerial class embraced the doctrine of Social Darwinism, as expounded by Herbert Spencer. After the publication of Darwin's theory of evolution in 1859, it was assumed by industrialists that competition was the way of all life and that the industrialists' success was evidence of their fitness to manage the organizational complex. Conversely, the state of the laboring poor only confirmed the belief in their basic unfitness for survival.

A CHANGING PERSPECTIVE   In the early part of the twentieth century, still under the aegis of Social Darwinism, there arose the concept of "scientific management." Frederick Winslow Taylor is considered the popularizer of the application of scientific methods to industry, although, as we note in Chapter 5, he was preceded by many earlier innovators. One of the keystones of this approach was Adam Smith's simplistic notion that workers will put forth more effort the more they are paid for their work. Gradually, the methods of management have been forced through many revisions, as conceptions of people at work have changed. In the last fifty years, the occurrence of wars, the Great Depression, the rise of unions, and the advent of automation, as well as concern for energy, the environment and the quality of working life, have all served to broaden perspectives on worker motivation. Consequently, there is need for equally comprehensive views of managerial methods. Managers now talk not only of paychecks, but of pensions and fringe benefits, and of providing workers with meaningful work. No longer is any one motive seen to describe why people work, and numerous incentives are seen as potentially effective in increasing satisfaction and/or productivity at work.[6]

Even today, there remain strong cultural influences on whether a job is seen as meaningful and personally satisfying. "Dehumanizing work is in the eye of the beholder, which in turn is conditioned by societal norms."[9]

Redesigning jobs may be important, but it is equally important to value what one is doing in the organization, even if it is the most menial of tasks. Working as a farm laborer can be endowed with great value on an Israeli kibbutz or in a Chinese commune. "But just how can we endow the many holders of jobs in the U. S. which lack variety, skill demands, discretionary opportunities, prestige and so on with a sense that what they do for a living has purpose, meaning, honor and dignity when our culture in all its forms says just the opposite?" (page 145).[9] Mechanization and automation are answers (but they bring with them problems of displacing employees, technological unemployment, and a drain on our nonrenewable resources and environment). When automation of dull jobs is not possible, jobs can be modified sometimes to make them more attractive. Or job-holders can accept unattractive work (as do college students in the summer) if they see themselves in a temporary situation. Economists say that we should pay jobholders on unattractive work a competitive wage, a wage higher than they can obtain on any other job open to them. Or their hours should be shortened (as is done in garbage pickup work).

SATISFACTION AND PRODUCTIVITY

Satisfaction at work is an organizational objective. As noted in Chapter 1, most employers would rather have satisfied rather than unsatisfied employees. Employees themselves obviously prefer satisfying to unsatisfying jobs, unless they are masochists. But are satisfied employees more productive (as many employers argue to justify concern for job satisfaction)? Or are productive employees more satisfied? Is it possible that satisfaction and productivity are unrelated, or even negatively related? Does satisfaction correlate with productivity under some conditions but not others?

Satisfaction as a Predictor of Performance

It seems reasonable to expect that the more satisfied workers are on their job, the more effective they will be in performing their assigned task. If the happy worker is the more productive worker, productivity should be enhanced by eliminating negative job attitudes. As far back as 1932, studies were completed to see if this was so.[42] Surprisingly enough, however, after thirty years of repeated analyses, a thorough review by Brayfield and Crockett suggested that there was little reason to suppose that satisfied employees were more productive.[13] Subsequent reviewers agreed in general, but they felt there did seem to be a consistently low positive relationship between satisfaction and performance. For example, in reviewing some twenty studies, Vroom found a median correlation of 0.14.[82] Thus, it would seem that there is at best a tenuous relationship between performance on a job and attitudes.

There are many reasons to explain the lack of relationship. For example, if the work group itself sets a standard to restrict production to a certain fixed level, there will be a little variation in performance; and if performance is not varied, there can be no relationship to satisfaction. Also, there are wide individual differences in motivation among workers. Some workers would be satisfied with a job which specifically did *not* require them to produce at a high rate. Sometimes a more productive worker may actually be *less* satisfied with certain aspects of his/her work. For example, in one of two large departments of office workers, those most critical of the placement and rating systems were the most productive employees. These productive employees were also the most interested and informed members of the staff.[38]

The characteristics of a worker's occupational group also make the relationship between satisfaction and performance a complicated one. Navy enlisted men were compared with civilian scientists in Antarctica. Significant positive correlations between job satisfaction and job performance were obtained for the scientists, but no significant relationships were obtained for the enlisted men.[18]

Again, based on an average correlation of 0.32 between the need satisfactions of 148 managers and ratings by their superiors of how hard the managers worked and how well they performed on their jobs, Lawler[45] and Porter[58] suggested that the satisfaction-productivity linkage may be higher for managers than for employees as a whole, as reported by Vroom.

CONDITIONS THAT PROMOTE A POSITIVE ASSOCIATION OF SATISFACTION WITH PRODUCTIVITY   The performance of 103 physicians providing routine pediatric care in outpatient clinics was rated by other clinic staff members. These performance ratings were then correlated with measures of the physicians' satisfaction with their work. The correlations were much higher (0.55, 0.59) if the physicians had interned or completed residencies in community hospitals rather than in teaching hospitals (0.27, 0.31), if they earned little income (0.58) but a lot of recognition (0.71), rather than a lot of income (0.12) but little recognition (0.31) from working in the clinic. The satisfaction-productivity correlation was 0.26 if clinic work was important to their career goals but 0.84 if it was unimportant. In other words, *job satisfaction* was *linked with productivity primarily for those physicians who worked in the clinics because they were interested and trained in such community effort for its own sake.* The satisfaction-productivity correlation was much lower for those who worked in the clinical settings for the money or as a contribution to their career plans.[53]

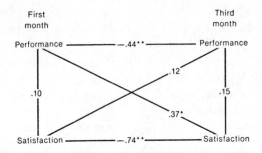

Figure 3–1. Intrinsic satisfaction with work itself and job performance (** p < .05; ** p < .01*). (After Wanous, "A Causal-Correlational Analysis of the Job Satisfaction and Performance Relationship," *Journal of Applied Psychology,* 59 [1974]: 142.)

WHICH IS CAUSE AND WHICH IS EFFECT? Wanous gathered job satisfaction and performance data from 80 newly hired female telephone operators after one months' work experience and again after three months.[86] Performance evaluations were based on supervisory ratings and company indexes of quality and quantity. Consistent with Vroom's summary review, as seen in Figures 3–1 and 3–2, the "static" correlations of satisfaction and performance at the same point in time were only 0.10 to 0.18. But performance at the end of one month resulted in greater intrinsic satisfaction (satisfaction with the work itself) in the third month (0.37) rather than vice versa (0.12). At the same time, extrinsic satisfaction (satisfaction

Figure 3–2. Extrinsic satisfaction with pay and workng conditions and job performance (** p < .05; ** p < .01*). (After Wanous, "A Causal-Correlational Analysis of the Job Satisfaction and Performance Relationship," *Journal of Applied Psychology,* 59 [1974]: 142.)

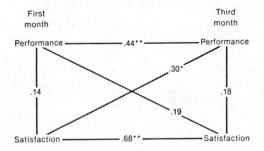

with pay and working conditions) at the end of one month contributed to better performance in the third month (0.30) rather than vice versa (0.19).

These results suggest that if we do well on the job, our subsequent satisfaction with the work itself is enhanced. If we are satisfied with pay and working conditions, our subsequent productivity on the job is enhanced.

RELATIVE STABILITY   Notice another interesting result in the two figures. While performance in the first month correlates only 0.44 with performance in the third month, the more subjective intrinsic satisfaction correlates 0.74 beween the first and third months. The comparable figure for the stability of extrinsic satisfaction is 0.68. That is, satisfaction, a "softer" piece of data bound up in emotion and feeling, is more stable than performance, which is a "harder" more objective piece of data.

One of the problems that most plagues the industrial psychologist is that of the relative lack of stability of some workers' productivity. Often productivity depends on factors outside the workers' control. The materials or equipment they use may vary from day to day or month to month. So, as we examine the linkage between satisfaction and productivity, we may find, as we did, that although satisfaction is a stable measure, productivity is not, and if it is not, we become faced with trying to predict the unpredictable. (The reliability of productivity measures will be addressed in more detail in Chapter 7.)

DISSATISFACTION AND WITHDRAWAL

Employees who are dissatisfied with their jobs reveal thoughts about quitting and intentions to do so. And if acceptable alternatives are available such workers will quit as a consequence of their dissatisfaction. If they do not quit, they may withdraw by frequent absences. Less consciously, they may withdraw by injuring themselves or through psychosomatic illnesses such as migraine headaches or ulcers.

Turnover and Job Dissatisfaction

In a review of 60 investigations, Porter and Steers found almost uniformly that job dissatisfaction correlated moderately with avoidable turnover — quitting that might have been prevented had the worker been more satisfied.[60] Dissatisfaction with pay, promotion opportunities, supervision, coworkers, and the job itself all tended to contribute to avoidable turnover. Working in larger rather than smaller groups also tended to result in more turnover.

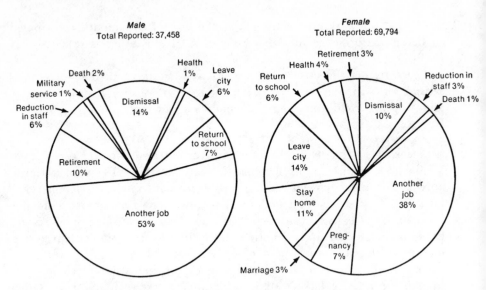

Figure 3-3. Reported reasons for turnover. (Adapted from *Administrative Management Society Report, 1973.* Survey conducted by the Administrative Management Society, Willow Grove, PA 19090.)

But actual turnover or quitting is often unavoidable. That is, an employee may need to quit because the family is moving to another town, because of pregnancy or health reasons, or because a clearly better job offer has been obtained. Therefore, actual quitting may be due to many reasons other than dissatisfaction with one's job. The stated reasons for 37,458 male and 69,794 female terminations in 1973 are displayed in Figure 3-3. Dissatisfaction is not shown in the figure, but obviously may play a strong part in the decision to accept another job, to retire, or even to behave in a way that results in dismissal. Nevertheless, one could be reasonably satisfied with one's job and still quit for any of the unavoidable reasons in Figure 3-3.

Avoidable quitting can often be an excuse or justification, or an emotional response (let's pick up our things and go west!). But, when it is a rational act, it comes as the completion of a process outlined in Figure 3-4. And so we can enter into the study of the withdrawal at a variety of steps in the process.

Unmet Expectations — The Connection Between Job Dissatisfaction and Avoidable Turnover

We can uncover the linkage between job dissatisfaction and quitting if we look at job dissatisfaction as a consequence of unmet expectations.

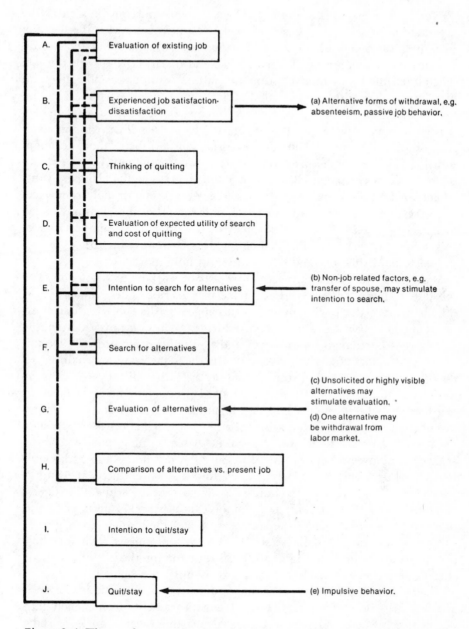

A. Evaluation of existing job

B. Experienced job satisfaction-dissatisfaction → (a) Alternative forms of withdrawal, e.g. absenteeism, passive job behavior.

C. Thinking of quitting

D. Evaluation of expected utility of search and cost of quitting

E. Intention to search for alternatives ← (b) Non-job related factors, e.g. transfer of spouse, may stimulate intention to search.

F. Search for alternatives

G. Evaluation of alternatives ← (c) Unsolicited or highly visible alternatives may stimulate evaluation. (d) One alternative may be withdrawal from labor market.

H. Comparison of alternatives vs. present job

I. Intention to quit/stay

J. Quit/stay ← (e) Impulsive behavior.

Figure 3-4. The employee turnover decision process. (From Mobley, "Intermediate Linkages in the Relationship between Job Satisfaction and Employee Turnover," *Journal of Applied Psychology*, 62 [1977]: 238.)

We see in Figure 3-4 that the final decision to quit can be seen as the culmination of a chain of events. Closely linked in time with the decision to quit is the intention to do so. Further back are thoughts about quitting. At the beginning of the chain is general dissatisfaction with the job. Therefore, intentions to remain on the job or to quit are more likely to correlate highly with current job satisfaction or dissatisfaction. Such intentions have been found, in turn, to forecast quite well subsequent tendencies to remain or to quit.[27] Studying 165 bank tellers, Gray found a correlation of 0.46 between their job dissatisfaction and their "thoughts about quitting."[33] The same correlation of 0.46 was found between their estimate of the career potential of the job and their thoughts about quitting. Closer to the final decision and, therefore, even more strongly connected, were the rated effort to find a new job and the following measures of job dissatisfaction: 0.53, lack of enjoyment of this job; 0.52 unimportance of this job; 0.51, lack of value in holding this current job; 0.51, effort required to hold this job; and 0.37, burden in holding this job.

Many employees quit during the first year of working at a new job. The job fails to meet the expectations of the new recruit. These unmet expectations may be dealt with by making changes in the job situation or by changing the expectations at the time of hiring.[60] Thus, turnover was reduced 18 per cent by changing promotion and pay policies for over 300 clerical workers in a manufacturing concern.[36] In the same way, a two-thirds reduction in turnover was accomplished in a textile mill by changing to more realistic production goals. A standard production norm of 60 units per hour had been established. The turnover rate of all current workers presumably fully skilled, who achieved a level of production above the standard of 60 units per hour was 13 per cent. After training, poorly performing new employees (who produced at 30 units per hour) also had a quit rate of 13 per cent. But newly trained hirees who produced at 45 units per hour had a even higher quit rate (60 per cent), while the highest turnover of all (96 per cent) was for those producing 55 units per hour, or only 10 per cent below the standard of 60. Thus, there were greater turnover rates for the "almost skilled" 55 unit producers than for those much farther behind the standard at 30 units or for those "fully skilled" current employees at above the standard 60 units per hour.

The explanation of these surprising findings appeared to lie in the operation of two opposing forces. First, the goal-gradient phenomenon may be involved, where individuals try harder as they near a goal—working a bit faster as they see the end of a production run. The second possible factor is the difficulty encountered by employees as their production increases. Starting from a low skill level, they may make rapid progress at first, but it becomes increasingly difficult to improve performance further. These two conflicting forces result in frustration and withdrawal for those very near the productivity standard—who don't quite make it. In contrast, those far away from the goal or those who have already reached it do not experience this intense conflict.

The textile company solved the problem by having the training program emphasize more intermediate and realistic subgoals instead of the 100 per cent standard of 60 units. These changes resulted in a two-thirds reduc-in the turnover rate for those in the critical "almost skilled" group.[48]

Changing initial expectations toward greater realism about the job has also been found to work to reduce turnover. Wanous demonstrated in a controlled field experiment with newly hired telephone operators that 43 who were shown a more realistic film containing both good and bad aspects of the work were more likely to remain on the job after three months than 31 who were shown a film with only the good points.[85] Those who saw the more realistic film had more realistic job expectations and fewer thoughts about quitting as well, in comparison to those who saw the film that emphasized only the good aspects of the telephone operator's work.

PERSONALITY AND TURNOVER   Another reason for early quitting is the hiring from the pool of "job hoppers," with their personal propensities to keep moving. Here, better screening of job applicants is required to forecast potential quitters.

Absenteeism and Job Satisfaction

Absenteeism—temporary withdrawal—may be the easiest and least painful way for employees to show their dissatisfaction. Indeed, the monetary loss to the individual may be insignificant, since many companies give employees full pay when they are "sick" and absent.

Furthermore, dissatisfaction may produce illness or injuries resulting in absences. Absences due to chiefly psychosomatic ailments (ulcers, migraine headaches, insomnia) may stem from job dissatisfaction. It has been suggested that even accidents resulting in injury and absences are sometimes a form of withdrawal.

In 29 investigations, Nicholson, Brown, and Chadwick-Jones found that dissatisfaction correlated with frequency of absences in 18, but was unrelated in 11 of the studies.[54] At best, the relationship is a weak one if one only attempts to complete gross statistical associations of job dissatisfaction of employees, on the one hand, and their absence records, on the other. But, when finer tuning is attempted, more clearcut results emerge. For instance, when extra effort is required to come to work, and there is no financial consideration one way or the other, to what extent is attendance at work connected with job satisfaction? Smith looked at what happened to 3,010 salaried employees on a single particular day in Sears,

Roebuck in Chicago and New York.[72] In New York, the weather had been good the day before. Chicago had suffered a crippling snowstorm. On the day analyzed, attendance in 13 New York departments averaged 96 per cent. Departmental attendance varied from 89 per cent to 100 per cent. In Chicago, the median attendance for 27 departments was only 70 per cent. Departmental attendance varied from 39 to 97 per cent. Table 3–1 shows the different results between job satisfaction levels and attendance records for the departments in Chicago and in New York. For Chicago, Table 3–1 reveals strong associations between department satisfaction levels and department attendance records for the day. In New York, since almost everyone came to work, it would have been difficult to find much relation between attendance and anything else. But the Chicago results are due to two things. First, there was enough variation among departments in attendance to make differences predictable. Second, individuals had to exert extra effort to show up for work on the day after the snowstorm.

REDUCING ABSENTEEISM   Again, a whole chapter on organizational development, Chapter 14, will address itself to improving those organizational conditions that promote job satisfaction and its consequences in better attendance. However, here we will consider briefly the direct attack on the problem of absenteeism as such. The infrequency of absences and the extent to which they may be due to the opening of the hunting season, to snowstorms and other factors outside the firm's or the workers' control suggest that it may be more useful to look at why workers absent themselves and then to attack those aspects that may be controllable by the firm or the employee.

Table 3–1. Correlations between job-satisfaction levels of departments and attendance levels on individual days for the Chicago and New York departments

Scale	Chicago [a] (n = 27)	New York [b] (n = 13)
Supervision	.54 **	.12
Amount of work	.36 *	.01
Kind of work	.37 *	.06
Financial Rewards	.46 **	.11
Career Future	.60 **	.14
Company Identification	.42 *	.02

* $p < .05$, one-tailed test
** $p < .01$, one-tailed test
a Group following storm, April 1975
b Group, April 1975
From Smith, "Work Attitudes as Predictors of Attendance on a Specific Day," *Journal of Applied Psychology,* 62 (1977): 18.

What motivates employees to stay away from work? Morgan and Herman checked the absences of 60 blue-collar employees in one department of a unionized automobile-parts foundry for 17 months before and 7 months after they questioned the employees about what motivated them to be absent, what deterred them from being absent and what the employees saw were the consequences of their absence.[51] Then, these authors correlated what the employees said with how often they were absent. Employees had higher past and future absenteeism records if they tended to give as reasons transportation problems, personal illness, the desire for a break from routine, and the desire to do other things, such as take care of their houses or engage in leisure activities. Less important were time with friends or family illness.

Those with high absenteeism rates said they would be most deterred from absenting themselves by loss of benefits, promotional opportunities, and disciplinary talks. Less important to them would be the loss of wages, a heavier work load on their return to work, a fear of losing their job, disciplinary probation, and so on.

Policies about absenteeism can make a difference. In investigating causes of absenteeism in a large assembly plant, the second author discovered that the union contract with the company was written so as actually to reward absenteeism. Employees could work on Saturday and Sunday and receive double time and then call in sick on Monday and receive their usual wage rate. There was no financial incentive to be a consistent worker.

ABSENTEEISM AS AN INDEX In many of the chapters that follow, we will be discussing absenteeism rates as an index (like turnover, lateness, and other forms of withdrawal) of job dissatisfaction and we will speculate on how it can be reduced. Sometimes absenteeism is the most important index. Thus, Volvo began its experiments in job redesign (Chapter 15) because it could no longer financially tolerate a 30 per cent rate of absence. In the late 1970s absenteeism along with underuse and oversupply of coal worked against the goal of expanding U. S. coal consumption. Some firms attack the problem directly through disciplinary measures without reference to employee job satisfaction. "One more absence, and you will be fired!" Other firms try direct incentives for good attendance without concerning themselves with improving job satisfaction as such. Unless the incentive plans are to be continued permanently, they work best in the long run if the reward for daily punctuality and attendance has some uncertainty built into it. For example, at an electronics plant, 120 employees became eligible for a monthly lottery drawing if they had perfect attendance for a month. There was an annual decrease of 28.8 per cent in sick-leave expenses and a 41 per cent reduction in absenteeism.[84]

To sum up, we are beginning to learn about the dynamics of the rela-

tions between job satisfaction and productivity and about job dissatisfaction and withdrawal from the job. Let's look at some of the theories
that have been constructed to explain the dynamics.

THEORIES ON THE BEHAVIOR OF PEOPLE AT WORK

Theories abound about why and for what people work. Just as the first
practical steam engine was designed by James Watt on the basis of the
soon-to-be-discredited phlogiston theory of heat, so we find that the most
pervasive practical applications of behavioral science to motivating people
at work have come from theories that, although they were interesting and
timely, often failed to be supported when tested by the many controlled
experiments they encouraged.

Abraham Maslow's theory stimulated concern for making work an opportunity for personal growth; Frederick Herzberg's theory stimulated
enriching the content of work itself; George Homans's theory led to fuller
appreciation of the relative meaning of fairness and equity; and Victor
Vroom's theory stimulated emphasis on worker expectations.

Maslow's Self-Actualization Theory

In contemporary culture the majority of the working population and
students who are about to enter the working force feel a deep concern
for the meaning of the jobs they are or will be performing.[63] We have
long been aware of the fact that laborer and factory worker have received
relatively little satisfaction from their work and definitely don't want their
children to perform that same work all their lives.[16] The concept of the children doing better than their parents is an ideal prominent in Western culture.
What is new is the dissatisfaction with work expressed by the middle class
worker in engineering, management, or the professions. This is vividly reflected in the trend for students such as those in the Peace Corps to seek personal fulfillment by choosing occupations considered to be more personally rewarding than business.

This need for self-actualization and personal fulfillment has been expressed recently in slightly different ways by several theories. Perhaps
Maslow's theory, which has had an enormous impact on modern concepts
of human development, best reflects the contemporary feeling.[49]

MASLOW'S HIERARCHY   Maslow postulated that all human needs can be
arranged in an ascending hierarchy, and that the lowest-level unsatisfied
needs are the main motivators of any individual. The lowest-level needs

are physiological — needs for food, water, and bodily survival. If these are satisfied, the next-higher-level needs become the motivating factors of the individual. As long as low-level needs are unsatisfied, one is dominated by them and cannot be concerned with needs of a higher order. The level above physiological needs contains the safety needs. Safety needs include, for example, security in one's work and various forms of insurance against the risks of life. The satisfaction of these needs leads to the next-higher need: for love and affection. For satisfaction of this love need, the individual seeks close relationships with his family and friends. If the love needs are met, esteem needs then demand attention. Most people have a desire for esteem from others as well as for self-respect for themselves. The top need identified in the hierarchy is the desire for self-actualization. This is the need of the individual to fulfill his or her potential. However, as a creative urge it applies only to those with the capacity for creation.

Maslow's theory asserts that each level of need in the hierarchy must be satisfied in part before higher-level needs become motivating. The hungry individual's behavior may be determined at any one time by several needs at different levels.

TESTS OF MASLOW'S THEORY   As with most theories that are any good, Maslow's theory was testable. And as with most good theories, the tests have led to modifications. For instance, Alderfer has shown with correlational analyses of workers' responses about their needs, that needs tend to cluster into three areas, rather than five: existence (safety and security), relatedness (love and affiliation), and growth (esteem and self-actualization).[4] Overall, attempts to establish evidence of Maslow's hierarchy have failed. Nor is there much to show that the stronger a need, the more likely we are to act to satisfy it.[83] Maslow's theory has been more interesting and more popular than true. Nevertheless, his theory and his efforts to apply his theory to life sparked the "human potential movement," which in turn influenced considerably what we will present in Chapter 14 on organizational development.

Herzberg's Theory of Motivation

Frederick Herzberg is the chief proponent of a specific theory of job motivation that has ideological similarities to Maslow's more general conceptualizations. The major support for this theory rests on a detailed study of 200 engineers and accountants. Respondents were asked to recall incidents when they may have felt extremely good or bad about their work. The interviewer then attempted to bring to light the factors that led to the respondents' reactions and to reveal the ultimate effects of these reactions.

An analysis of the results showed that although work itself, sense of responsibility, and opportunity for advancement produced the longest-lasting and most frequent positive attitudes toward the job, they did not play a significant role in producing poor job attitudes. These *intrinsic* elements were "motivators," since they fulfilled the individual's need for self-actualization and growth and were related only to the job itself. In contrast, *extrinsic* factors, such as working conditions, salary, interpersonal relations, and security, brought about dissatisfaction only when they fell below a certain point. Since the satisfaction of these factors led to neutral rather than to positive job attitudes, they were not "motivators" but simply "hygiene factors" surrounding the job, the presence of which prevented dissatisfaction. As was to be expected, most of those interviewed said they were more productive when they felt good about their jobs.[34]

FURTHER EVIDENCE   Similar results have been obtained with the same semistructured interviews[22] as well as with open-ended interviews[29] and questionnaires[28] in a variety of settings with many different occupational groups and in many countries.

Herzberg's original study was replicated at the Texas Instrument Corporation.[52] The sample included nearly 300 employees, drawn from all levels in the company. Most of the workers said that they derived their greatest satisfaction from achievement, responsibility, growth, and the work itself. These motivated workers showed a high tolerance for poor environmental factors, whereas another group, preoccupied with the hygiene factors, such as pay, working conditions, fellow employees, and security, showed little interest in the quality of their work. There were also differences among the five job levels studied. Scientists received their most positive and lasting good feelings from aspects of the work itself. Their bad feelings often stemmed from disappointments over responsibility. Engineers responded similarly to the scientists, with a little more positive emphasis on pay and the friendliness of supervision. In contrast, the manufacturing managers derived more positive satisfaction from advancement, growth, and responsibility, whereas the work itself was rarely mentioned. Hourly technicians were concerned about responsibility and advancement, while the work itself and the competence of the supervisor were dissatisfiers. Pay was an important source of both satisfaction and dissatisfaction. Fifty-two female assemblers felt that achievement and recognition were positive factors, while the opinion of their fellow workers acted only as a dissatisfier.

Thus, different motivation and hygiene factors were important to different classifications of employees. But some factors, such as pay for the hourly technicians, was a source of both satisfaction and dissatisfaction. Myers reported that Herzberg's concepts, motivation and hygiene factors, could be applied to an industrial setting with positive benefits to the employee by improving those aspects of the job situation that were most important to each classification of employee.

Just as there are differences among job levels regarding what factors give employees satisfaction, it appears there are similar differences according to employees' age levels. Two hypotheses derived from Herzberg's motivation-hygiene theory were confirmed by Saleh.[66] Pre-retirees looking backward to their middle age indicated that the motivators had been the factors that gave them the most satisfaction and the hygiene factors determined dissatisfaction. But when the pre-retirees looked toward the few remaining years before retirement, satisfaction was seen to come from hygiene factors.

CRITICISMS OF HERZBERG'S THEORY A variety of reasons lead numerous investigators to reject the main tenet of Herzberg's theory: that the separate factors that lead to satisfaction are different from the factors that result in dissatisfaction.[5] First of all, the theory flies in the face of what we know about good measurements of satisfaction. Some people are generally more or less satisfied, others neutral, still others are generally dissatisfied. They tend to distribute themselves on attitude scales along a single bipolar scale of satisfaction-dissatisfaction, not as demanded by Herzberg's two-factor theory.[32] Second, it is difficult to obtain Herzberg's results in any way other than by asking in interviews or questionnaires what workers like and dislike about their jobs, then scoring their answers according to Herzberg's conceptualization. Herzberg's findings are seen as illustrating defensive behavior[56] rather than a different attitude toward motivators and hygiene factors: that is, what's bad about my job is due to others, my boss or my organization; what's good about my job is what I bring to it.[20]

People rationalize their actions and feelings. It is easier for the individual to claim that success and positive feelings are the result of his or her own achievements (motivation factors) and that dissatisfaction does not arise from the person's own inadequacies but is caused by another person or by environmental conditions (hygiene factors).

There are many other criticisms of Herzberg's theory of work motivation. People are often not good judges of their own behavior. For example, nine out of ten drivers who have been objectively classified from their accident records as poor drivers feel they are good drivers.

Another, better explanation of Herzberg's findings is that his methodology does not afford respondents equal opportunity to respond positively and negatively to both job content factors (the work itself) and job context factors (the surroundings). If the investigator gives this opportunity, one finds that the intrinsic job content is more important to the respondents than is the extrinsic job context.[31]

Then there is a great deal of evidence, which we will discuss in detail in Chapter 4, which shows that individuals differ widely in what they find more or less satisfying about their work. For example, Wilkins found that among 300 young men, those of higher intelligence sought long-term incentives associated with the work itself, such as variety and prospects, while those of lower intelligence tended to value more extrinsic factors, such as pay and congenial work companions.[88]

Both Herzberg and Maslow assume that individuals enter the world of the formal organizations as mature, self-reliant, task-oriented, self-actualizing people and are constrained by the organization. So they become dependent, immature individuals. Classic enconomists or "scientific managers" would have us believe that employees enter organizations as individuals needing control and direction because they are immature and lack a desire to perform effectively on the job. Reality lies somewhere between the two positions. Individuals differ; while some may be at the Herzberg-Maslow extreme and others as described by scientific management, most are likely to be at different points along the continuum.

Needs also change over a period of time, and what motivates individuals at one period of life may be drastically different at another time. However, there is enough consistency in human behavior to make predictions possible based on employees' past performance. Overall, it is fair to say that when individuals enter the formal work organization, not only has their personality been determined but so, too, have many of their attitudes and much of their behavior. People enter the formal work structure with a multiplicity of needs; some are high and some are low in their need for achievement, affiliation, and power; some are mature individuals, and others are extremely dependent. From this aggregate, an enterprise must find the means by which it can motivate individuals to achieve and perform on the job. Money is the common device used to manipulate employee behavior. For some, this is an effective incentive. For others, socialization within the work group is more important. In some organizations, staffed by research scientists and other professionals, a great deal of freedom is given to the individual to perform effectively. These individuals are largely self-motivated and perform their tasks independently because of the nature of their work and by reason of their past graduate or professional training. Even here, there are a few individuals who abuse their privileges and fail to work effectively under their own volition. However, even realizing that most people are not always paradigms of energy, many organizations have tended to underutilize their employees.

Herzberg's theory, as we have already noted, despite its theoretical inadequacies, set in motion a widespread movement in industry to enrich jobs, to enhance the "motivators" as a way to increase job satisfaction. For example, American Telephone and Telegraph initiated such a program to add more meaning to the work itself with positive results.[23] The research and techniques of this job enrichment will be discussed in more detail in Chapter 15.

Homans: Distributive Justice and Equity Theories

Several theories have advanced the relatively simple and logical proposition that employees of an organization want an equitable return for the contributions they make. They want distributive justice. Homans expressed the belief that when people are in an exchange relationship with one another, they expect that the rewards of each person will be proportional to his or her costs.[35] Thus the locus of the employees' concerns is not just how well their needs are being satisfied but how well off they are in comparison with others at work.

For Adams,[1] distributive justice results when:

$$\left[\frac{\text{Person A's rewards minus A's costs}}{\text{A's investments}} \right] = \left[\frac{\text{Person B's rewards minus B's costs}}{\text{B's investments}} \right]$$

If either person felt that there was injustice, the individual who felt under rewarded would be angry. Conversely, the individual who felt over-rewarded would have a sense of guilt. It has been postulated that inequity creates a certain degree of tension, which is proportional to the magnitude of the inequity. The tension then creates a drive to reduce feelings of inequity. The greater the tension, the stronger the drive.

EVIDENCE   To test his theory, Adams designed several experiments.[2] He tested the hypothesis derived from the theory that workers overpaid on piecework would decrease their output and increase the quality of their work, since if they produced a substantial amount, their feelings of inequity would increase, and these impressions could be reduced only by low productivity. He also tested the proposition that individuals overpaid on an hourly basis would increase the quantity of their work to relieve their feelings of inequity. Students were hired for a proofreading task. The first group was informed that they were not qualified for the job, but that despite this fact they would be paid the usual rate for qualified workers: thirty cents per page. The second group was also led to believe that they were not qualified for the job, but they were paid the more equitable rate of twenty cents per page. The third group was told they were qualified for the task and were paid the full thirty cents per page. The hypothesis for overpaid piece-rate workers was upheld, since the group who felt they were overpaid proofread fewer pages in one hour but detected more errors in the pages than the two groups that had been led to believe that they were more fairly paid. As predicted, better-quality work (more errors detected) and lower productivity (fewer pages proofread per hour) resulted from a perception of being overpaid on piece rates. Equity was restored by reducing the number of pieces produced since pay per piece was seemingly too high. On the other hand, similar experiments revealed, as expected, that overpaid hourly workers would increase their output. For, seemingly overpaid workers, for the time they invested, could restore equity by being more productive during each hour for which they were paid.

In another more comprehensive experiment, 253 male college students were hired and worked for seven consecutive half-days. The pay system was deliberately changed halfway through the week's work to induce further perceptions of inequity. Again, subjects were led to believe they were being overpaid or underpaid. Subjects who thought they were overpaid, particularly as a consequence of the midweek change in the pay plan, did retard their productivity. Conversely, those who perceived underpay for performance tended to do the reverse. Effects on overall job satisfaction showed that employees in both the overpaid and the underpaid groups were less satisfied than employees made to feel equitably paid. Effects on job satisfaction were particularly strong under modified piece-rate payments, as opposed to flat hourly pay.[62]

EQUITY WITH REFERENT   A purely economic theory would have led to the erroneous prediction that more pay per piece would result in more productivity. Equity theory suggests that workers engage in some sort of calculation of costs and benefits relative to those with whom they compare themselves. The question then becomes: with whom do we compare ourselves? To answer this, interviewers asked 214 managers how they decided how much they were satisfied or dissatisfied with their pay. Interviewers did not suggest referents, but it was possible to categorize the referents into seven classes and to decide whether the comparison to the referent was seen as equitable or not. These seven classes of referents were as follows: (1) other-inside: (well, we managers got only a 5 per cent raise . . . but the unionized employees got 8 per cent and they have much less responsibility); (2) other-outside: (I get about the same as I would working in a similar job outside); (3) system-structure: (the present raise system permits graduations to reflect changes in cost of living as well as superior performance); (4) system-administration: (when I was promoted I got the 10 per cent raise to bring me up to the lower pay range of that job); (5) self–pay history: (I have received good raises in the past and expect the same in the future); (6) self-family: (I am able to provide for my family . . . we live well); (7) self-internal: (given my length of service and education, I feel I am paid well for what I do).

Table 3-2 shows that most managers used several referents. The most frequently mentioned are other persons inside the organization. But, as seen in the correlations with pay satisfaction in Table 3-2, a sense of equity with others outside was most important to such pay satisfaction; perceived

Table 3-2. Relationships between the perceived equity indices for the seven pay referents and the pay satisfaction criterion

Referent categories	Product moment correlations
Other-inside (N = 100)	.43 **
Other-inside (N = 93)	.68 **
System-structure (N = 43)	.59 **
System-administration (N = 65)	.49 **
Self-pay history (N = 67)	:27 **
Self-family (N = 86)	.62 **
Self-internal (N = 62)	.53 **

** $p < .01$

From Goodman, "An Examination of Referents Used in the Evaluation of Pay," *Organizational Behavior and Human Performance,*" 12 (1974): 183.

equity with one's own past history was least important. The more highly educated managers were more likely to compare themselves with referents outside the organization.[30]

One problem with focusing on perceived equity is that this equity may be largely outside the control of the organization or due to political, social, or economic conditions. U. S. workers asked by the Michigan Survey Research Center in 1972 and 1973 "How fair is what you earn on your job in comparison to the pay of others doing the same type of work you do?" were much more likely to feel they were getting less than they deserved in the fall of 1973 (43 per cent), than in the fall of 1972 (28 per cent). Strumpel attributed the change to the national inflation in 1973.[77] Similarly, compared to all workers, black workers felt a much greater sense of inequity in both 1972 (66 per cent) and 1973 (69 per cent). In the same way, Schuster and Atchison found that the better-performing, less well educated, higher paid, and older of 575 computer-science professionals generally felt a greater sense of fair pay.[67] Feelings of inequity were experienced by those individuals who gave relatively more weight to outside market considerations rather than to organizational factors.

Thus, distributive justice and its relation to job satisfaction is much more complex to determine than the simple equation with which we began this section. Laboratory research supports the basic prediction that equitable outcomes are more satisfying than inequitable ones.[41] Nevertheless, equity theory is plagued by a precision of *deduction* unmatched by the possibilities of precision of measurement in real life. This mismatch between what we can *deduce* from equity models and what we can *infer* in field studies is true also about expectancy models of motivation.

Vroom's Expectancy Model of Motivation

According to Vroom, people have two kinds of expectations. The first is that the more effort we exert, the better we will perform. Second, the better we perform, the more we are likely to attain a desired outcome. According to Vroom, our effort can be predicted by adding up all the pros and cons in the work situation and outside it, each literally multiplied by its expected probability of occurrence. Our performance can be predicted by adding up all the pros and cons of its consequences, again, each literally multiplied by its expected probability of occurrence.

EXPANSION. Elaborations on Vroom's expectancy theory came quickly. Among these was Porter and Lawler's formal model, which integrates the concepts of attitudes, motivation, effort, satisfaction, ability, performance, and the rewards of work.[59] Job satisfaction or good job attitudes are considered not just as a cause of high performance but as a complex function of the rewards of work. Their model includes the elements illustrated in Figure 3-5.

Figure 3–5. A performance-satisfaction model. (From Lyman Porter and Edward Lawler, III, *Managerial Attitudes and Performance.* [Homewood, Ill.: Richard D. Irwin, 1968], p. 165. © 1968 by Richard D. Irwin, Inc.)

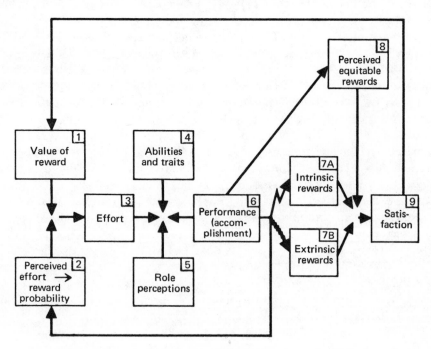

1. Value of reward.   There are a number of rewards that individuals can receive from any job situation. They include pay, promotion, achievement on a job, and the friendship of fellow workers. These rewards are differently perceived by individuals; some place more value on certain rewards than on others. The desirability of a given outcome is clearly a matter of "attitudes" as we have discussed them.

2. Perceived effort–reward probability.   This refers to the employees' expectation that their efforts will actually lead to desired rewards. For example, assume that promotion was a valued goal but the individuals know that all their efforts would not help because no opening is likely to be available. In this case the likelihood of effort, despite a highly valued goal, would be small.

3. Effort.   This is the central variable in the Porter and Lawler model; it is defined as the energy expended in attempting to perform a task. The emphasis here is on the attempt, which does not necessarily lead to effective or successful performance. Although there is a relationship between effort expended and success, we know that the relationship is far from perfect. We all know examples of individuals in the classroom and on the sports field who put in less time and energy than others but perform at a higher level. That effort is not the whole story is partly explained by variable 4.

4. Abilities and traits.   We know that there are great differences between people's abilities and traits, and that these differences are usually of a long-term nature, not easily changed. (Chapters 10 and 11 will be largely devoted to analyses of these differences.) Abilities and traits put an upper limit on the degree to which effective or successful performance will result from the application of effort.

5. Role perceptions.   These are the ways in which individuals define their job. Two people, both aiming for what they believe to be effective performance, may define the same job in different ways and thus spend their energies in different ways, achieving different levels of performance.

6. Performance.   This is the variable in which most organizations are interested. It is the degree of success achieved in accomplishing organizationally relevant tasks. It is the net effect of employees' efforts, modified by their abilities and traits and how they spend those efforts as a function of their perceived role requirements. (Chapter 7 and 8 will deal in depth with the problems of defining and measuring performance.)

7. *A and B rewards.*   Rewards are those desirable outcomes that individuals see as resulting from their own performance or the performance of others. Both the perception and the evaluation of these outcomes, of course, are matters involving attitudes, as discussed in this chapter. For example, if individuals receive from their performance something they don't want, it would clearly not be viewed as a reward, whether or not the organization defines it as one.

Intrinsic rewards (7A) are those that are administered by the individual himself or herself, derived from the work itself, the job content[21] These intrinsic rewards (for example, a feeling of accomplishment) satisfy higher needs of autonomy and self-actualization. They appear to produce attitudes that are significantly related to the individual's performance. The semiwavy line indicates that there can be a direct action between the performance of the worker and intrinsic rewards if the job design provides the necessary challenge to the worker. *Extrinsic rewards* (7B) are those that are given to the individual by the organization (for example, promotions or raises) or they are derived from the environment surrounding the work. The zigzag line in the diagram implies that these rewards may not always be tied to performance.

8. *Perceived equitable rewards.*   This is an expression by individuals of the reward they think is fair, taking into account their perception of their performance on organizational tasks. The dashed line from performance to perceived equitable rewards indicates that self-ratings of performance influence the way individuals feel about the level of reward they should receive.

9. *Satisfaction.*   Satisfaction is the extent to which the rewards received by individuals meet or exceed what they perceive to be an equitable level. If the actual rewards fall below perceived equitable rewards, the person will be dissatisfied. The feedback loop from satisfaction to value of reward indicates that once an individual has received some satisfaction from certain rewards, this satisfaction will have an effect on future value of rewards. For example, if an individual has just received a large raise and this reward is satisfying, the individual might feel that the value of additional money has been satisfied for the time being, so that some other reward might now be valued more highly (for example, recognition).

In order to test and refine the model presented above, Porter and Lawler conducted a large-scale investigation of over 400 managers.[59] Questionnaires and other techniques were designed to measure each of the variables. While the results of the investigation are too numerous to relate in detail, in general the predictions of the model were upheld for the sample. The model predicted that if an individual believes that significant rewards depend on job performance, the effort would be directed toward performing effectively. The evidence indicated that the managers who perceived their pay as being a function of their performance were rated as being the most effective and highly motivated workers.

SHORTCOMINGS OF EXPECTANCY MODELS   Taken as a whole, all the many studies of the past decade launched as a consequence of expectancy models and theories have unearthed only modest support for the theory that employees will perform better if they expect to obtain as a result of good performance outcomes they value. A review of 16 studies found the median correlation between expectations of valued outcomes at a given point in time and concurrent performance to be only 0.21.[39] However, Kopelman and Thompson suggest that expectancy models must take several conditions into account.[40] In a survey of 399 design and development engineers in three large, technology-based companies, they succeeded in raising the correlation from 0.24 to 0.45 between expected valued outcomes and the engineers' performance as rated by their supervisors. They measured performance a year after obtaining the engineers' expectations instead of measuring expectations and performance at the same time. Second, they improved the predictions from −0.15 and −0.04 to 0.48 and 0.28 respectively of the engineers' performance as gauged by the salary and organizational level they attained. A four-year lag was allowed between the time at which they assessed engineers' expectations and when they assessed the engineers' salaries and levels. Also, Kopelman and Thompson found that the initial salaries and levels of the engineers affected their expectations as well as their salaries and levels attained four years later. The expectation-performance predictions were improved further by holding constant the initial differences among the engineers.

There are other reasons why expectancy models have not done well in demonstrating relations among expectations, effort, and performance. First, expectations should affect effort and performance if it is clear to employees what outcomes they can expect if their performance is adequate: for example, piece-rate systems where for each piece or each batch of pieces there is a payoff. Even here, sometimes, unaccountably, subjects with low expectations of valued outcomes outperform those with high expectations.[61]

Expectancy models require workers to be hedonistic pleasure-pain calculators. As long as employees can make the appropriate cost-benefit calculation accurately, and they are unhappy, they should immediately switch to increase their happiness. The hedonist must prove that expected pleasure and the avoidance of pain are the sole basis for choosing what and how much to do.[47]

Another problem is that *intrinsic* and *extrinsic* valued outcomes are treated the same. Thus, Herzberg suggested that improving the job context, the *extrinsic* rewards of work such as pay, did not increase job satisfaction but only reduced job dissatisfaction. But the Porter-Lawler model simply combines the intrinsic and extrinsic rewards for work. Deci[17] proposed and was supported by evidence from a number of laboratory experiments that if people are *intrinsically* interested in what they are doing and enjoy their work for its content, if we add extrinsic rewards such as pay for good performance (piece-rate incentives), we actually *reduce* rather than increase their interest, effort and satisfaction with the work![55] And in real life it has been seen that providing more incentives to enlist or to reenlist in the navy does not necessarily increase intentions to enlist or reenlist in an additive fashion, as would have been predicted by expectancy models.[26,27] Instead of being able simply to pile one positive outcome on top of the other as a calculation for increasing its expected value, Deci shows that adding an extrinsic valued outcome (as would be required by expectancy models to make clear and contingent rewards for effort and good performance) sometimes can *decrease* rather than add to the total value of the combined outcome.[17] However, he suggests that receiving an equitable salary does not detract from one's being intrinsically satisfied with the work itself.

(We need to study in detail whether amateur tennis or golf players who enjoy the game for its own sake lose some of their enthusiasm for the game when they turn professional to compete for financial prizes.)

Another reason for the failure of expectancy models is the wide divergence of people in their experience, knowledge, intelligence, and thought processes in making projections of the outcomes of their actions and assessments of how much they value them.[47]

Another reason is that most people just don't ordinarily consider a wide variety of possible actions and their outcomes when they make decisions. Further, even if they do, they are often unlikely to let their final choice be based on an abstract mathematical analysis rather than a "gut feeling." A well-known behavioral scientist tells the story of the expectancy calculations he completed, adding up the different potential valued outcomes in pay, staff associates, teaching loads, students, programs, and so on, when offered jobs at several different institutions. After much analysis, he decided to go to Yale because of its prestige, not because it maximized his expectations of a valued outcome. In other words, expectancy models might work better if we were trying to account for the behavior of robots. (We get caught in circular reasoning if we argue that the decision to go to Yale actually maximized his expectations of valued outcome. The professor just didn't weigh prestige properly in his calculations.)

As Locke noted, what we need is to push ahead to discover how employees actually make choices among real alternatives.[47] We should begin with falling back on a simpler model that merely proposes that effort and performance are each influenced by a long list of variables. After we have found what variables are more or less important, then we can begin to construct a more workable model. Nevertheless, we are indebted to these expectancy models, for they have led us to start asking the right questions about what motivates us to work: for example, what are the employees' expected outcomes from their work; how much are these valued; how important are they in comparison with other outcomes; to what extent does pursuing such outcomes interfere with obtaining others; to what extent are employees dependent on others in order to obtain the outcomes; to what extent can others block their attempts; how much effort will be required; and are there short-cuts to obtaining the valued outcomes? [10]

Thus, Sims, Szilagyi, and McKenney found that among 1,161 medical employees, 11 variables contributed to a multiple prediction of 0.63 for the expectation that good performance would lead to valued outcomes.[70] The most important expectations were the extent to which the employees were rewarded directly by their supervisors; the extent to which they perceived that top management was receptive to their ideas; and the extent to which employees believed that events are the result of their own internal actions rather than external actions, luck or fate.

Much less predictable from these eleven variables was the expectation of the medical employees that their increased effort would result in better performance. Here, the expectation was most influenced by the employees' beliefs about the adequacy of communications in the organization and the lack of job pressure upon themselves.

Combining Motivation and Ability to Predict Performance

Expectancy theories of work motivation implicitly assume that if we know how to carry out the work, the amount of effort we make will depend on our motivation. Our performance will be the product of our ability and our motivation. Or,

$$\text{Performance} = f \ (\text{ability} \times \text{motivation})$$

This formula assumes that job performance is predicted better when motivation is a factor in the prediction. But why do we assume that ability should be multiplied by motivation? Can we find ratio scales (a 6 means three times as much as 2, not merely 4 units more than 2) for the measures of ability and motivation so that it is reasonable to multiply them? Perhaps ability and motivation should be added so that:

$$\text{Performance} = f \ (\text{ability} + \text{motivation})$$

In all the research to date that has attempted to combine ability and motivation factors, the results are surprisingly consistent — combining

Table 3–3. Comparison of ability, ability times motivation, and ability plus motivation in predicting sales performance

	Ability	Ability times motivation	Ability plus motivation
Sales volume	.28	.28	.30
Performance ratings	.38	.30	.31

Adapted from Barrett, Alexander, and Rush. *A Longitudinal Field Study Comparing a Multiplicative and an Additive Model of Motivation and Ability.* Technical Report 11, University of Akron, Department of Psychology, 1977.

ability with motivation does *not* predict performance better than does ability alone!

Typical results are shown in Table 3-3, where sales-force performance was predicted in three different ways for approximately 40 salespersons.[7]

It is evident that ability level, as measured by tests, is as good a predictor of both sales volume and performance (as rated by sales managers) as are ability and motivation. Neither multiplying by nor adding motivation factors improved the prediction of performance.

INCREASING MOTIVATION TO WORK

Zero Defects

Popular "fads, fancies, and folderol" [19] claim to increase motivation to work. Often, however, they only superficially fit with what we know about why people work and their effects may be superficial. For example, let's take a look at "Zero Defects," a widely used motivational program, which has produced a mixed bag of results.

The goal of any ZD program is to encourage employees to do the job right the first time, thereby reducing errors in the overall work. These programs seem to have a number of common features. A kickoff demonstration generally initiates the program, usually followed by the signing of cards pledging the individual employee to the goals of the program. A publicity campaign is also begun, featuring posters, slogans, badges, and news releases throughout the company and in local papers. The next stage of the program is an attempt to eliminate errors and the progressive charting of error reduction by each work group. On the basis of department progress charts, recognition is usually given to individuals and groups for superior performance.[24]

ZD's acceptance by employees turns out to depend a great deal on the degree to which employees who are involved have highly structured jobs.

Responses to open-ended items of a questionnaire completed by 94 male employees of a large manufacturer were analyzed for content. Although only 13 per cent of those in the production department (where meaningful performance measures were more easily obtainable) gave negative responses, in the other departments, where performance measurement was more difficult, from 44 to 64 per cent of responses were negative.[8]

In manufacturing operations, productivity and errors are often most easily measured by indices such as the number of parts produced and the number of scrapped pieces. But in engineering research and development work, for example, the criteria for effective performance and error-free work become much more complex. So it is not surprising that the ratings of effectiveness of the ZD program by the 94 employees followed fairly closely the degree to which their jobs were structured. Mean group ratings of favorability (on a scale of increasing favorability ranging from 0 to10) were as follows: research and development, 2.6; engineering, 4.6; sales, 4.8; administration, 5.6; and production, 6.4.

It is clear that certain features of the ZD program might apply more directly to certain employees' job functions than to others, and that, for example, more time must be spent determining relevant performance measures for engineering functions than for production work.

Any motivational program must be carefully assessed for its true value. Once a program has started and management time, effort, and money have been committed to it, there will be a great deal of pressure to show that it has been a success. This natural tendency often puts pressure on the employees so that management will hear and see what they want to.

Goal-Setting and Management-by-Objectives (MBO)

Goal-setting is a motivational technique that may be more consistent overall with expectancy, effort, and performance concepts of motivation. It has been found to work successfully in a variety of work groups. When attempted by an organization, it is management-by-objectives — a plan where supervisor and subordinate periodically meet to review past performance and set goals for the next period. MBO has been found useful in a wide variety of organizational settings, even in academia itself. For example, 109 faculty members at Utah State University completed a survey questionnaire after an MBO program had been in progress for the faculty for a year. Shetty and Carlisle concluded that the MBO program increased faculty awareness of organizational goals, improved planning, resulted in better understanding of job expectations, provided better data for performance appraisal, and improved performance and communication.[69] We will have more to say in Chapter 5 about management-by-objectives as a way of operating an organization. Here let us look at what we know about the practicalities of setting goals as a way of increasing productivity and improving the motivation to work.

NEED FOR GOAL CLARITY   Goal-setting is by no means new. It was practiced when Caesar harangued his troops before a battle in Gaul and when Vince Lombardi became famous for giving his football team rousing pep talks at half-time. This type of effort to arouse the motivation to perform probably still dominates meetings to open new sales campaigns by marketing divisions. They do arouse energy levels, but whether they necessarily improve long-term performance depends on the extent to which they help clarify expectations, identify goals, and provide understanding of what is to be accomplished. For example, in one laboratory experiment, subjects were asked to cut out as many paper forms as they could. Participants who where actually working by themselves were told that they were members of a trio. The two other persons in their trio whom they did not meet would build supposedly model paper houses with the forms. The subjects saw themselves as members of a team building model houses of paper. They were more satisfied and proficient than control subjects who cut out the same forms without being told their use, for the second group was quite unclear about why they were carrying out the work.[64]

The absence of clear goals for the control subjects is paralleled in an Air Force study of the survival (in training programs) of grounded air crews "behind enemy lines." Crews were much less able to survive if they were planless. But once a set of goals was formulated by the crew, their chances increased greatly for living off the land and eventually finding a way back home.[80] In the same way, Latham and Kinne demonstrated that productivity among loggers of pulpwood was higher if a supervisor set production goals for the men than if they worked without such targets.[44] Again, Ivancevich reported that 78 sales personnel with set goals had better sales records and were more satisfied than a control group without such set goals.[37]

What else can we say about goal clarity as a stimulator and definer of work?

Performance is likely to be better the more specific, explicit, and detailed the target, quota, or goal. Feedback of success or failure in attaining the goal clarifies what needs to be continued at work and what has to be modified. Goals provide the basis of establishing competitive efforts.

HARD VS. EASY GOALS   But all of this is fairly obvious and consistent with expectancy theory that we will exert effort if we believe it will lead to desired outcomes (the stated goals). Not so obvious and inconsistent with expectancy formulations is Locke's proposal that *the harder the goal set for us, the harder we will try to attain it, and the better will be our performance.*[46] This is like Parkinson's Law, that effort is adjusted to the difficulty of a task and the time available to complete the task. The hedonism or pleasure-pain calculations of expectancy theory would suggest that if the goal were very hard to attain, our confidence that we could reach it would be reduced and the perceived costs to obtain the goal would be increased. Therefore, a hard goal would become a less valued outcome for us. We would reduce our efforts to obtain it.

There are facts to support Locke. In the logging industry, drivers were loading trucks to about 60 per cent of what was legally permitted for travel on the roads. Then, in the manner of many "Caesar-Lombardi pep talks," log truck drivers were told about the problem and exhorted to "do their best." Nothing much changed in their performance during the next 3 months, as seen in Figure 3-6. Next, they were assigned the specific hard goal of loading their trucks with logs to 94 per cent of the maximum legal weight permitted. As can be seen in Figure 3-6, they increased the weights loaded each month until over the final 6 months of study after the intro-

Figure 3–6. Percentage of legal net weight of 36 logging trucks across months as a function of goals set. (From Lathan and Baldes, "The 'Practical Significance' of Locke's Theory of Goal Setting," *Journal of Applied Psychology,* 60 [1975]: 123.)

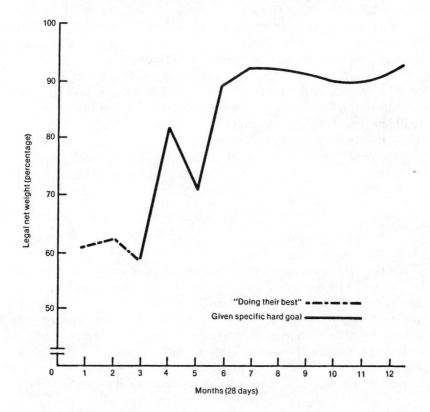

duction of the 94 per cent goal, trucks were loaded at an average exceeding 90 per cent. There were no incentives provided for the drivers for their better performance when assigned the hard goals.[43]

WHICH IS CORRECT?   Actually, it is possible to reconcile the different predictions of Locke from expectancy models. First, Shapira showed that if the task provides only extrinsic rewards for successful completion, college students choose the easiest tasks so they can make as much money as possible.[68] But if the task is inherently interesting and provides only intrinsic satisfaction and no external incentives, then they reject the easiest tasks as pointless and boring and choose to work on the difficult ones. Second, in reviewing the reported effects of management-by-objectives programs, Carroll and Tosi concluded that hard goals led to better performance only for employees who were confident and mature and therefore expected to succeed in attaining the goals.[15] Otherwise, the hard goals tended to produce expectations of failure and less adequate performance.

Third, expectations can be different depending on when and how goals are set. Stedry showed that if goals assigned to a group of subjects were higher than their own personal level of aspiration, the participants tended to reject the assigned harder goals as too difficult and failed to make a sincere effort to attain them.[74] If assignments were made before subjects could form their own personal goals, the subjects performed better. It may pay for supervisors to set standards, but then, when they believe they will set standards too low, ask for workers' opinions.[76]

Fourth, setting hard rather than easy goals, although resulting in unmet expectations according to expectancy theory, may also generate a search for the reasons for failing to attain the goals. In turn, this search may result in creative efforts to perform better, which would not occur if only easy goals were sought and obtained.[75]

Thus harder goals will be more motivating for confident people where the goals fit their aspirations and provide interesting challenges that easy goals fail to do.

SUMMARY

We have come a long way in the past 50 years in appreciating the importance of how we feel about our jobs. Work is seen now as much more than drudgery in exchange for pay. Challenging jobs are sought. Efforts are made by making orientation of new recruits more realistic or by making jobs more interesting, to avoid isolating employees' expectations.

Theories of why people work focus either on content (Maslow and Herzberg) or processes (Homans and Vroom). A key to increasing motivation is establishing and clarifying objectives. But people differ widely in what they want in life from their work and how satisfied they are with their jobs, as we will detail in the next chapter.

Attitudes play important roles in determining the degree to which both individuals and their organizations fulfill their goals. At least six of the nine variables in the Porter-Lawler model (1, 2, 5, 7, 8, and 9)[59] are "attitude" variables. The pervasive importance of attitudes leads us to devote particular attention in the next chapter to techniques currently used to measure attitudes in organizational settings.

As we shall see, the relationships among motivation to work, expectations, job satisfaction, and job performance are complex. They are modified by a large number of individual characteristics (age, sex, personality, job level, status, ability, for example) as well as characteristics of the organization (size, structure, management behavior, and so on) and of the environment (such as community size, wage rates, and union influences).

REFERENCES

1. Adams, J. S. "Inequity in Social Exchange." In L. Berkowitz (ed.), *Advances in Experimental Social Psychology*, vol. 2. New York: Academic Press, 1965.
2. Adams, J. S., and P. R. Jacobsen. "Effects of Wage Inequities on Work Quality," *Journal of Abnormal and Social Psychology*, 69 (1964): 19–25.
3. Adapted from *Administrative Management Society Report*, 1973.
4. Alderfer, C. P. "An Empirical Test of New Theory of Human Needs," *Organizational Behavior and Human Performance*, 4 (1969): 142–175.
5. Armstrong, T. B. "Job Content and Context Factors Related to Satisfaction for Differential Occupational Levels," *Journal of Applied Psychology*, 55 (1971): 57–65.
6. Barrett, G. V. *Motivation in Industry*. Cleveland: Allen, 1966.
7. Barrett, G. V., R. A. Alexander, and M. C. Rush. *A Longitudinal Field Study Comparing a Multiplicative and an Additive Model of Motivation and Ability*. (Technical Report No. 11). University of Akron, Department of Psychology, Contract N00014–75–C–0995, Office of Naval Research, 1977.
8. Barrett, G. V., and P. A. Cabe. "Zero Defects Programs: Their Effects at Different Job Levels," *Personnel*, 44, no. 6 (1977): 40–46.
9. Bass, B. M. "Self-managing systems, Z.E.G. and Other Unthinkables." In H. Meltzer and F. R. Wickert (eds.), *Humanizing Organizational Behavior*. Springfield, Ill.: C. C. Thomas, 1976.
10. Bass, B. M., and E. R. Ryterband. *Organizational Psychology* (2nd ed.). Boston: Allyn and Bacon, 1979.
11. Bendix, R. "Industrialization, Ideologies, and Social Structure," *American Sociological Review*, 24 (1959): 613–623.
12. Blauner, R. "Work Satisfaction and Industrial Trends in Modern Society." In W. H. Hill and D. Egan (eds.), *Readings in Organizational Theory: A Behavioral Approach*. Boston: Allyn and Bacon, 1966.
13. Brayfield, A., and W. Crockett. "Employee Attitudes and Employee Performance," *Psychological Bulletin*, 52 (1955): 396–424.

14. Carey, A. "The Hawthorne Studies: A Radical Criticism," *American Sociological Review*, 32 (1967): 403–416.

15. Carroll, S. J., and H. L. Tosi. *Management by Objectives: Applications and Research*. New York: Macmillan, 1973.

16. Chinoy, E. *Automobile Workers and the American Dream*. Garden City, New York: Doubleday, 1955.

17. Deci, E. L. *Intrinsic Motivation*. New York: Plenum Press, 1975.

18. Doll, R. E., and E. K. Gunderson. "Occupational Group as a Moderator of the Job Satisfaction–Job Performance Relationship," *Journal of Applied Psychology*, 53 (1969): 359–361.

19. Dunnette, M. D. "Fads, Fancies and Folderol in Psychology," *American Psychologist*, 21 (1966): 343–353.

20. Dunnette, M. D., J. P. Campbell, and M. D. Hakel. "Factors Contributing to Job Satisfaction in Six Occupational Groups," *Organizational Behavior and Human Performance*, 2 (1967): 143–174.

21. Dyer, L., and D. F. Parker. "Classifying Outcomes in Work Motivation Research: An Examination of the Intrinsic-Extrinsic Dichotomy," *Journal of Applied Psychology*, 60 (1975): 455–458.

22. Dysinger, D. W. *Motivation Factors Affecting Civilian Army Research and Development Personnel*. Report AIR–D–95–5/65–IR, American Institute for Research, Pittsburgh, Pa., 1965.

23. Ford, R. N. *Motivation through the Work Itself*. New York: American Management Association, 1969.

24. Fouch, G. E. "Motivation for Quality–Zero Defects Program," *Industrial Quality Control*, 22 (1965): 240–241.

25. Franke, R. H., and J. D. Kaul. "The Hawthorne Experiments: First Statistical Interpretation," *American Sociological Review*, 43 (1978) 623–643.

26. Frey, R. C., Jr., A. S. Glickman, A. K. Korman, B. E. Goodstadt, and A. P. Romanczuk. *A Study of Experimental Incentives as an Influence on Enlistment Intentions: More Is Not Better*. Report AIR–32201–6/74–TR-3. Washington, D.C.: American Institute of Research, 1974.

27. Frey, R. C., Jr., B. E. Goodstadt, A. K. Korman, A. P. Romanczuk, and A. S. Glickman. *Re-enlistment Incentives: More Is Not Better in the Fleet Either*. (Technical Report no. 4). Washington D.C.: American Institute of Research, 1974.

28. Friedlander, F. "Relationships between the Importance and the Satisfaction of Various Environmental Factors," *Journal of Applied Psychology*, 49 (1965): 160–164.

29. Friedlander, F., and E. Walton. "Positive and Negative Motivations toward Work," *Administrative Science Quarterly*, 9 (1964): 194–207.

30. Goodman, P. S. "An Examination of Referents Used in the Evaluation of Pay," *Organizational Behavior and Human Performance*, 12 (1974): 170–195.

31. Gordon, M. E., N. M. Pryor, and B. V. Harris. "An Examination of Scaling Bias in Herzberg's Theory of Job Satisfaction," *Organizational Behavior and Human Performance*, 11 (1974): 106–121.

32. Graen, G. "Addendum to 'An Empirical Test of the Herzberg Two-Factor Theory,'" *Journal of Applied Psychology*, 50 (1966): 563–566.

33. Gray, R. C. "The Problem of Turnover as It Relates to the Bank Teller." Unpublished report, 1975.

34. Herzberg, F., B. Mausner, and B. B. Snyderman. *The Motivation to Work.* New York: Wiley, 1959.

35. Homans, G. C. *Social Behavior: Its Elementary Forms.* New York: Harcourt, Brace and World, 1961.

36. Hulin, C. L., and M. R. Blood. "Job Enlargement, Individual Differences, and Worker Responses," *Psychological Bulletin,* 69 (1968): 41–55.

37. Ivancevich, J. M. "Effects of Goal Setting on Performance and Job Satisfaction," *Journal of Applied Psychology,* 61 (1976): 605–612.

38. Katz, D. "Survey Research Center: An Overview of the Human Relations Program." In H. Guetzkow (ed.), *Groups, Leadership and Men.* Pittsburgh: Carnegie Press, 1951.

39. Kopelman, R. E. "Expectancy Theory Predictions of Work Motivation and Job Performance: A Longitudinal Study of Engineers across Three Companies." Unpublished Ph.D. dissertation, Harvard Business School, 1974.

40. Kopelman, R. E., and P. H. Thompson. "Boundary Conditions for Expectancy Theory Predictions of Work Motivation and Job Performance," *Academy of Management Journal,* 19 (1976): 237–258.

41. Korman, A. K., J. H. Greenhaus, and I. J. Badin. "Personnel Attitudes and Motivation," *Annual Review of Psychology,* 28 (1977): 175–196.

42. Kornhauser, A. W., and A. A. Sharp. "Employee Attitudes. Suggestions from a Study in a Factory," *Personnel Journal,* 10 (1932): 393–404.

43. Latham, G. P., and J. J. Baldes. "The 'Practical Significance' of Locke's Theory of Goal Setting," *Journal of Applied Psychology,* 60 (1975): 122–124.

44. Latham, G. P., and S. B. Kinne III. "Improving Job Performance through Training in Goal Setting," *Journal of Applied Psychology,* 59 (1974): 187–191.

45. Lawler, E. E. "Ability as a Moderator of the Relationship between Job Attitudes and Job Performance," *Personnel Psychology,* 19 (1966): 153–164.

46. Locke, E. A. "Toward a Theory of Task Motivation and Incentives," *Organizational Behavior and Human Performance,* 3 (1968): 157–190.

47. Locke, E. A. "Personnel Attitudes and Motivation," *Annual Review of Psychology,* 26 (1975): 457–480.

48. Marrow, A. J., and G. David. "The Turnover Problem—Why Do They 'Really' Quit?" *Personnel Administration,* 14, no. 6 (1951): 1–6.

49. Maslow, A. H. "A Theory of Motivation," *Psychological Review,* 50 (1943): 370–396.

50. Mobley, W. H. "Intermediate Linkages in the Relationship between Job Satisfaction and Employee Turnover," *Journal of Applied Psychology,* 62 (1977): 237–240.

51. Morgan, L. G., and J. B. Herman. "Perceived Consequences of Absenteeism," *Journal of Applied Psychology,* 61 (1976): 738–742.

52. Myers, M. S. "Who Are Your Motivated Workers?" *Harvard Business Review,* 42, no. 1 (1964): 73–88.

53. Nathanson, C. A., and M. H. Becker. "Job Satisfaction and Job Performance: An Empirical Test of Some Theoretical Propositions," *Organizational Behavior and Human Performance,* 9 (1973): 267–279.

54. Nicholson, N., C. A. Brown, and J. K. Chadwick-Jones. "Absence from Work and Job Satisfaction," *Journal of Applied Psychology,* 61 (1976): 728–737.

55. Notz, W. W. "Work Motivation and the Negative Effects of Extrinsic Re-

wards: A Review with Implications for Theory and Practice," *American Psychologist*, 30 (1975): 884–891.

56. Ondrack, D. A. "Defense Mechanisms and the Herzberg Theory: An Alternate Test," *Academy of Management Journal*, 17 (1974): 79–89.

57. Parsons, H. M. "What Happened at Hawthorne?" *Science*, 183 (1974): 922–932.

58. Porter, L. W. "A Study of Perceived Need Satisfactions in Bottom and Middle Management Jobs," *Journal of Applied Psychology*, 45 (1961): 1–10.

59. Porter, L. W., and E. E. Lawler. *Managerial Attitudes and Performance.* Homewood, Ill.: Richard D. Irwin, 1968.

60. Porter, L. W., and R. M. Steers. "Organizational Work and Personal Factors in Employee Turnover and Absenteeism," *Psychological Bulletin*, 80 (1973): 151–176.

61. Pritchard, R. D., and P. J. DeLeo. "Experimental Test of the Valence-Instrumentality Relationship in Job Performance," *Journal of Applied Psychology*, 57 (1973): 264–270.

62. Pritchard, R. D., M. D. Dunnette, and D. O. Jorgenson. "Effects of Perceptions of Equity and Inequity on Worker Performance and Satisfaction," *Journal of Applied Psychology Monograph*, 56 (1972): 75–94.

63. Purcell, T. V. "Work Psychology and Business Values: A Triad Theory of Work Motivation," *Personnel Psychology*, 20 (1967): 231–257.

64. Raven, B. H., and J. Rietsema. "The Effects of Varied Clarity of Group Goal and Group Path upon the Individual and His Relation to His Group," *Human Relations*, 10 (1957): 29–45.

65. Roethlisberger, F. J., and W. J. Dickson. *Management and the Worker.* Cambridge, Mass.: Harvard University Press, 1939.

66. Saleh, S. D., and J. L. Otis. "Age and Level of Job Satisfaction," *Personnel Psychology*, 17 (1964): 425–430.

67. Schuster, J. R., and T. J. Atchison. "Examining Feelings of Pay Equity," *Business Perspectives*, 9, no. 3 (1973): 16–19.

68. Shapira, Z. "Expectancy Determinants of Intrinsically Motivated Behavior." Unpublished Ph.D. dissertation, University of Rochester, 1975.

69. Shetty, Y. K., and H. M. Carlisle. "Organizational Correlates of a Management by Objectives Program," *Academy of Management Journal*, 17 (1974): 155–160.

70. Sims, H. P., Jr., A. D. Szilagyi, and D. R. McKemy. "Antecedents of Work Related Expectancies," *Academy of Management Journal*, 19 (1976): 547–559.

71. Smith, A. *The Wealth of Nations.* New York: Modern Library, 1937 (London, 1776).

72. Smith, F. J. "Work Attitudes as Predictors of Attendance on a Specific Day," *Journal of Applied Psychology*, 62 (1977): 16–19.

73. Sommer, R. "Hawthorne Dogma," *Psychological Bulletin*, 70 (1968): 592–595.

74. Stedry, A. C. *Budget Control and Cost Behavior.* Englewood Cliffs, N.J.: Prentice-Hall, 1960.

75. Stedry, A. C., and E. Kay. "The Effect of Goal Difficulty on Performance: A Field Experiment," *Behavioral Science*, 11 (1966): 459–470.

76. Steers, R. M. "Task Goals, Individual Need Strengths, and Supervisory Per-

formance." Unpublished Ph.D. dissertation, Graduate School of Administration, University of California, Irvine, 1973.

77. Strumpel, B. *Inflation, Discontent and Distributive Justice*. Survey Research Center, University of Michigan, 1974.

78. Sykes, A. J. M. "Economic Interest and the Hawthorne Researches," *Human Relations*, 18 (1965): 253–263.

79. Tilgher, A. "Work through the Ages." In S. Nosow and W. Form (eds.), *Man, Work, and Society*. New York: Basic Books, 1962.

80. Torrance, E. P. "The Behavior of Small Groups under Stress Conditions of 'Survival,'" *American Sociological Review*, 19 (1954): 751–755.

81. Triandis, H. C. "Interpersonal Relations in International Organizations," *Organizational Behavior and Human Performance*, 51 (1967): 1–24.

82. Vroom, V. H. *Work and Motivation*. New York: Wiley, 1964.

83. Wahba, M. A., and L. G. Bridwell. "Maslow Reconsidered: A Review of Research on the Need Hierarchy Theory," *Organizational Behavior and Human Performance*, 15 (1976): 212–240.

84. Wallin, J. A., and R. D. Johnson. "The Use of Positive Reinforcement to Reduce the Costs Associated with Employee Absenteeism." Industrial Relations Research Association meeting, Dallas, Texas, December 28–30, 1975.

85. Wanous, J. P. "Effects of a Realistic Job Preview on Job Acceptance, Job Attitudes, and Job Survival," *Journal of Applied Psychology*, 58 (1973): 327–332.

86. Wanous, J. P. "A Causal-Correlational Analysis of the Job Satisfaction and Performance Relationship," *Journal of Applied Psychology*, 59 (1974): 139–144.

87. Weber, M. *The Protestant Ethic and the Spirit of Capitalism* (Parsons, T., trans.). New York: Scribner, 1930.

88. Wilkins, L. T. "Incentives and the Young Worker," *Occupational Psychology*, 23 (1949): 235–247.

4 PERSONNEL ATTITUDES AND MOTIVATION TO WORK

IN BRIEF People differ in what they find satisfying and motivating at work. These differences can be measured and scaled. Pay is among the important sources of satisfaction. It depends on whether it is by piece-rate incentives, by hour, or by straight salary. Group and organizational conditions in which the payment is received are also of consequence. Such conditions may result in restriction of output by workers. The way to counter this is by encouraging workers to participate in decisions of consequence to them as a way of increasing their motivation, commitment, and involvement.

People's satisfaction or dissatisfaction with a particular job can be correlated with their sex, race, age, job tenure, job and occupational level, job proficiency, self-esteem, job involvement, organization, life satisfaction, personality, and mental health.

Job opportunities differ widely in time and place. Job satisfaction will be greatest where an individual's needs, abilities, and objectives can be matched to a job that fulfills them. But this matching is fraught with difficulties. Many of us have to settle for compromises between what we think we want in a job and what we can get.

When they first begin their careers, few people have a good idea of their own abilities, needs, or goals. Even fewer have much knowledge of the organization they are joining. Moreover, organizations and their environments are seldom stable enough to allow employees to predict which of their goals and needs will be met or which of their abilities will be used. For example, a young woman might be looking for an opportunity to advance quickly in systems analysis, her field of specialization, while working on innovative projects. To pursue these goals, she might join an aerospace company. After she joins the corporation, cutbacks in government funding could result in the young analyst's finding herself in a stagnant or shrinking organization instead of an expanding one. Instead of holding an exciting job, she might find herself working on mundane projects. This, of course, could cause a great deal of unrest and job dissatisfaction for her.

Our attitudes toward our work and our satisfaction with it depend on many aspects. Who we are — our age, education, experience, abilities, and objectives — makes a difference in the type of work we will be satisfied with. The job we hold — its pay, advancement opportunities, supervision, our organization coworkers, the work to be done — likewise makes a difference. Particularly important to our satisfaction is the extent to which who we are matches what we do. So our study of personnel attitudes and motivation to work must concentrate on both — the job and the jobholder.

Mismatching and consequent dissatisfaction may be due to changes in the job or changes in the jobholder.

TECHNIQUES FOR ASSESSING JOB ATTITUDES

Thoughout history, attempts have been made to measure attitudes. The ancient Chinese mandarins content-analyzed the themes of village songs to gauge morale.[4] In more recent times, Karl Marx (in 1880) was one of the first to attempt to survey workers. An interesting aspect of his survey (for which he never was able to obtain respondents) was that all of his 101 questions concerned objective facts such as wages and sizes of plant and none asked about the feelings of workers.[8] The pendulum has swung so that it is now perceptions and feelings that are elicited in the typical survey of employee attitudes. And which particular approach we use will make a considerable difference in the conclusions we will draw.

Scaling

SOME SCALING METHODS We may try to assess an employee's attitude by asking a single question. For example, we might ask "Are you satisfied with your job? Yes, ?, No." We would then note the percentage of employees who responded "Yes" in contrast to the percentage who responded "?" or "No." But this result by itself is likely to contain a great deal of error. For instance, the way a single question is worded can change employees'

responses to it. "Are you happy at work?" is likely to yield different results from "Are you satisfied with your job?"

For this reason, we resort to asking a set of similar questions and scaling
the combined answers to them to obtain for the individual employee a
composite that is both a more reliable (consistent or stable) measure of
his or her attitude and more valid or relevant. That is, the composite score
accurately measures the attitude in question.

Among the many scaling procedures available, the method originated
by Rensis Likert remains the most popular prototype.[50] A large number
of favorable, neutral, and unfavorable statements concerning an issue are
collected and edited. Respondents in trial runs check whether they strongly
agree, agree, are undecided, disagree, or strongly disagree with each statement. The response to each item is then scored, according to categories
with preassigned values of 5, 4, 3, 2, and 1. About half the items are worded
so that "agree" denotes a favorable attitude, while half are worded so that it
indicates a negative attitude.

The final items for the scale are obtained by correlating each individual
item score with the total score. If an item correlates highly with the total
score, this indicates an internally consistent measure of attitude, and the
item is retained. An example of a Likert attitude scale toward supervision
is shown in Figure 4–1. The respondent is not shown the scale values.

The Likert technique's popularity may be due to the fact that it is
relatively less time consuming to construct, has slightly higher reliability,
and ordinarily is easier to administer than more complex alternatives.[81]

For a survey to be of much use to an organization, employee feelings
about a variety of issues are ordinarily measured. Multiple scales are used.
The different scales can be based on factor analyses of responses of large
numbers of employees to large numbers of questions. Factor analysis
makes it possible to determine the dimensions on which the responses
differ. In the physical world, all cardboard cartons, regardless of size and
shape, can be described by the dimensions of their length, height, and
width. Similarly, employees' attitudes can be described fully in terms of
15 to 20 dimensions. First, there is a general factor. That is, some employees are more satisfied than others across all areas. Then there are

Figure 4–1. Attitude toward supervisor scales (Likert technique)

My supervisor treats me fairly.

Strongly agree   Agree   Undecided   Disagree   Strongly disagree specific factors such as satisfaction with physical working conditions, management, co-workers, the work itself, and so on. Moreover, these dimensions remain the same with employee populations separated by as much as 10 years, according to surveys of 4,052 employees of the same firm in 1956 and of 4,882 employees in 1966.[62]

THE JDI.   A widely-used instrument, the Job Descriptive Index (JDI) taps five of the dimensions. Employees use a 3-point Likert procedure: "Yes, ?, No." The JDI is based on a number of factor analyses of the possible dimensions of job satisfaction. Five were chosen for the JDI: (1) satisfaction with work, (2) satisfaction with pay, (3) satisfaction with opportunities for promotion, (4) satisfaction with supervision, and (5) satisfaction with co-workers. These categories are measured by the words or phrases shown in Table 4–1.

Each of the five scales is presented on a separate page. The instructions for each scale ask the employee to put "Y" beside an item if the item describes a particular aspect of the job (work, pay, and so on), "N" if the item does not describe that aspect, or "?" if the employee cannot decide. The response shown beside each item is the one scored in the "satisfied" category for each scale.

Scoring involves assigning a value of 3 to a "Yes" if it is a positive item and 3 to a "No" if it is a negative item. A "?" on any item is scored as 1. Any other response is given zero weight. The higher the score, the greater the reported satisfaction.

THE EAS   The shortness and simplicity of the JDI makes it a favorite research tool, but if a more comprehensive survey is desired for organizational improvement (see Chapter 14), then a questionnaire like the Employee Attitudes Survey (EAS) is used.[77]

As shown in Figure 4–2, the questions (90 altogether) use the Likert format. Employees mail back their anonymously answered questionnaire to a computer center which provides a printed detailed profile of results for each department of the firm. Figure 4–3 shows a sample printout of the 15 scale averages for a quality-control department of 31 employees in a division of 221 wage-earning employees. Sixty-nine per cent of the department responded favorably to 10 questions on the survey about their job benefits. They agreed or strongly agreed with favorable statements about each benefit and disagreed or strongly disagreed with unfavorable statements. In this example, the norm of 76 per cent is provided by the corresponding percentages of the entire division who responded favorably. The department and the division were equally dissatisfied with pay. In both, only 18 per cent responded favorably to questions about pay. The differences between the department and the division were graphed. Each + or − repre-

Table 4-1. Job descriptive index (JDI).

Work	Pay	Promotions
Y Fascinating	Y Income adequate for	Y Good opportunity for
N Routine	normal expenses	advancement
Y Satisfying	Y Satisfactory profit	N Opportunity somewhat
N Boring	sharing	limited
Y Good	N Barely live on income	Y Promotion on ability
Y Creative	N Bad	N Dead-end job
Y Respected	Y Income provides	Y Good chance for
N Hot	luxuries	promotion
Y Pleasant	N Insecure	N Unfair promotion policy
Y Useful	N Less than I deserve	N Infrequent promotions
N Tiresome	Y Highly paid	Y Regular promotions
Y Healthful	N Underpaid	Y Fairly good chance for
Y Challenging		promotion
N On your feet		
N Frustrating		
N Simple		
N Endless		
Y Gives sense of		
accomplishment		

Supervision	Co-workers
Y Asks my advice	Y Stimulating
N Hard to please	N Boring
N Impolite	N Slow
Y Praises good work	Y Ambitious
Y Tactful	N Stupid
Y Influential	Y Responsible
Y Up-to-date	Y Fast
N Doesn't supervise enough	Y Intelligent
N Quick tempered	N Easy to make enemies
Y Tells me where I stand	N Talk too much
N Annoying	Y Smart
N Stubborn	N Lazy
Y Knows job well	N Unpleasant
N Bad	N No privacy
Y Intelligent	Y Active
Y Leaves me on my own	N Narrow interest
N Lazy	Y Loyal
Y Around when needed	N Hard to meet

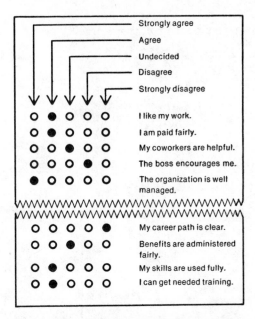

Figure 4–2. Excerpts from employee attitude questionnaire (courtesy of Transnational Programs Corporation, 1976)

sents a difference of one percentage point. It can be seen that satisfaction tended to be lower in the department than in the division, particularly in response to questions about benefits, identification with the organization, affirmative action, job training, and workload pressure. But the department was slightly more satisfied than the division with the effectiveness of management and the firm's evaluation and development procedures.

Computer analysis, of course, makes for exhaustive displays of the responses to each item. For example, the responses to the ten benefits provided by the firm are shown in Figure 4–4.

Weighting Responses According to Their Importance

The theories advanced in Chapter 3 would all suggest that if we wanted to determine more accurately employees' overall job satisfaction and their subsequent behavior as a consequence, we should give more weight to their satisfaction on those factors of importance to them and less weight to those factors of little importance. Once again, as we have pointed out before, behavioral science theories tend to outrun what works in measure-

GROUP = ALL QUALITY CONTROL EMPLOYEES . . . . (31)
NORM = ALL PRODUCTION EMPLOYEES . . . . (221)

PERCENT ABOVE (•) OR BELOW (-) NORM

CORE CATEGORIES	GROUP SCORE	NORM SCORE
1. PAY	18•	18
2. BENEFITS	69•	76
3. MANAGEMENT EFFECTIVENESS	32	28
4. ORGANIZATION IDENTIFICATION	56•	67
5. AFFIRMATIVE ACTION	19•	29
6. OVERALL COMMUNICATIONS	43	45
7. JOB TRAINING AND INFORMATION	48•	61
8. WORKING CONDITIONS	57	58
9. JOB SATISFACTION	54	54
10. WORK ORGANIZATION	38	43
11. WORKLOAD AND PRESSURE	47•	60
12. IMMEDIATE SUPERVISOR	50	52
13. WORK ASSOCIATES	54•	60
14. EVALUATION AND DEVELOPMENT	29•	24
15. REACTION TO THE SURVEY	38	44
16. OPTIONAL QUESTIONS	66	66
OV. ALL CORE ITEMS	47•	50

• = SIGNIFICANT DIFFERENCE BETWEEN GROUP AND NORM

Figure 4-3. Computerized display of attitude results on 15 dimensions for the quality control department in contrast to the entire production division

PERCENT ABOVE (•) OR BELOW (-) NORM

2. BENEFITS

	GROUP SCORE	NORM SCORE	10 20 30 40 50
10 PROBLEM RESOLUTION	61	56	
45 KEEPING CURRENT	39 •	63	
86 OVERALL RATING	74	87	
89A PROFIT SHARING	58	54	
89B MEDICAL INSURANCE	77 •	92	
89C LIFE INSURANCE	71 •	89	
89D VACATIONS	74	76	
89E HOLIDAYS	61	68	
89F PAID ABSENCES	77	85	
89G TUITION AID	94	87	

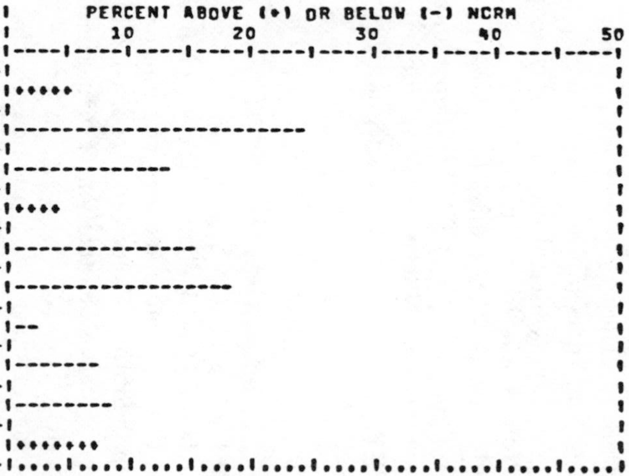

• = SIGNIFICANT DIFFERENCE BETWEEN GROUP AND NORM
GROUP = ALL QUALITY CONTROL EMPLOYEES . . . . . . (31)
NORM = ALL PRODUCTION EMPLOYEES. . . . . (221)

Figure 4–4. Computerized display of reactions to questions about benefits for the quality control department in contrast to the production division

ment. Quinn and Mangione collected data from a national probability sample of 1,533 U.S. workers. They compared many different ways of combining the importance employees attached to different facets of their work with their satisfaction. The combined results for each employee were used to predict his or her mental health, job-related tension, and the likelihood that he or she would quit. But rather than increasing the accuracy of predictions, Quinn and Mangione concluded that importance-weightings actually *reduced* their accuracy because of various statistical problems and unmet assumptions about how scales interact mathematically![62]

Open-ended Questionnaires

An open-ended question like "What can be done around here to improve management-employee relations?" will elicit a variety of free responses. After these are collected, their content is analyzed and categorized, and the percentage of responses in the various categories is reported. This technique is especially helpful in bringing to the attention of management problems of which they are not aware.

One reason for resorting to open-ended questions is that structured attitude questionnaires can only tap prejudged dimensions. Often very strong feelings are expressed in response to open-ended questions that would not otherwise be expressed. If undetermined "sore spots" are paramount, the write-in question is the best technique.

Figure 4–6 shows a typical response to the open-ended question at the end of the Employee Attitude Survey: "What do you dislike about your job?" Comments were obtained for this analysis on fifteen themes. The number in a large sample of employees who mention one of the particular themes is noted in Figure 4–5.

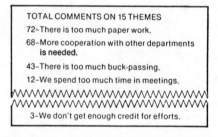

TOTAL COMMENTS ON 15 THEMES
72–There is too much paper work.
68–More cooperation with other departments is needed.
43–There is too much buck-passing.
12–We spend too much time in meetings.
3–We don't get enough credit for efforts.

Figure 4–5. Content analysis of frequency of responses to the question to sales personnel "What do you dislike about your job?" (Courtesy, Transnational Programs Corporation)

Figure 4–6. Response to
the open-ended question
"What do you dislike
about your job?"

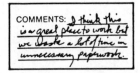

Interviews

In general, interviews have not been very successful in predicting employee performance (as we shall see in subsequent chapters), nor are they particularly effective in predicting what employees will report on structured attitude questionnaires about the job. For example, in one interview investigation, psychologists attempted to predict eighty-eight employees' attitudes toward various dimensions of their jobs. The psychologists' predictions of employees' attitudes were then correlated with employee attitude questionnaire responses. While there was a significant correlation in four out of six dimensions, the highest correlation was only 0.30.[3] Minimally, interviews do not necessarily measure the same content as questionnaires, assuming that one can obtain reliable interview results.

The interview is a necessary but not efficient technique. It is time consuming and expensive, and the attitudinal results obtained by the technique are not consistently related to the employees' own judgment in questionnaires, yet interviews with key people can give an in-depth picture of a situation that might be missed in questionnaires answered more perfunctorily. Generally, interviews serve useful purposes in pilot studies, for collecting speculations, and for formulating plausible hypotheses rather than verifying their validity.

THE EXIT INTERVIEW   Although it usually occurs too late to prevent an employee's quitting, the exit interview provides an opportunity to find out whether the separation could have been avoided or whether it was due to such unavoidable reasons as ill health, family relocation, desire to return to school, or a better job offer. (See Figure 3–3.)

If the reasons for termination are unavoidable, the important grievances resulting in quitting are likely to be mentioned, although departing employees may still feel reluctant to express their real feelings if they must depend on a good recommendation from their old employer. Where possible, the exit interview should be conducted by a person remote from the previous chain of command over departing employees to avoid recommendation fears or feelings of awkwardness that might prevent candid discussion of grievances.

Often inadequate pay is given as the reason for leaving. This is a neutral factor that may mask more personal feelings that departing employees prefer not to discuss.

The misleading nature of information gained from exit interviews was demonstrated in a study of eighty female sewing-machine operators. Six months after the women quit their jobs, a questionnaire was mailed to their homes. The reasons for quitting given in the exit interview could then be compared with the questionnaire responses.

Fifty-nine per cent of the women in the interview offered different reasons from those reported in the questionnaire. Most revealing was the finding that all the employees who stated in the exit interview they were leaving for "no specific reason" gave a specific reason in the subsequent questionnaire. About half the specific reasons concerned personal relations with peers or supervisors about which the employee "clammed up" during the exit interview.[48]

Several hundred IBM employees who had voluntarily resigned were routinely given exit interviews by a management representative. Later, a random sample of forty-eight were interviewed by an outside consultant. And all terminees were mailed an anonymous questionnaire to which 58 per cent replied. The consultant came up with much more negative information than had the exit interview. Furthermore, in comparing the results of the exit interviews with the results for the anonymous questionnaires:

> . . . in comparison with the questionnaire, the exit interview seemed to downgrade the importance of "freedom of action" and upgrade "nature of the work" and "personal reasons." . . . the organization would draw a different conclusion [from the exit interview] about how to deal with attrition than it would through the more structured questionnaire.[37]

Unavoidable terminations (due, for example, to pregnancy or "leaving town") appeared to be the only kind in which the exit interview gives accurate information.[48]

Management Estimation of Employee Attitudes

Perhaps the simplest, most widely used, but least accurate way to assess employee attitudes is to have managers give their "gut feelings" about the morale of their work group. Managers' subjective impressions suffer from all the defects of the interview, plus the fact that the information and impressions managers receive are often highly biased, both by the small number of people with whom they communicate and by the topics they discuss. For example, it is doubtful that many employees will directly express their dissatisfaction with their manager's supervisory style.

Anonymity

Many employees will be reluctant to contribute to any survey if their responses can be personally identified. It puts them at risk with managements they do not trust. Thus, the second author noted that some respondents in an industrial survey he conducted went to the trouble of photocopying their questionnaires because, due to a clerical error, their names remained, slightly indented, in the original paper questionnaires but disappeared in the photocopy. On the other hand, other employees will sign their names to attitude surveys if they are given the option to do so.

Results sometimes are not much different when anonymous surveys are compared with signed results. Obviously, how secure and trusting an employee feels makes the big difference. For example, Fuller contrasted the results of the Navy Personnel Survey completed anonymously by 2,469 officers and completed by another 3,147 officers with self-identification numbers attached. Identification raised the rate of return! With identification, the response rate was 51 per cent.[29] With instructions to maintain anonymity, the response rate was only 40 per cent. But more important, only slight differences in attitude responses between the two samples appeared. Results were similar for 11,000 enlisted men, but their rates of returning the questionnaire were the same whether or not they were asked to identify themselves. The higher return rates for signed officer questionnaires may have been due to officers' concern that their personnel files would show that they returned a questionnaire rather than that they had been remiss.

Indirect Methods

A number of techniques have been devised to measure employees' attitudes without directly asking people to state their feelings. These techniques have taken a variety of different forms.

An essay contest on "Why I Like My Job" was run by General Motors. The different theme employees used to write the essays formed the basis for comparing problems in G.M.'s divisions.[22]

Projective techniques have been tried. Here the employee is shown an ambiguous sketch, cartoon, or photograph. Employees are asked to describe what has happened, is happening, and will happen to those in the picture. Their answers are assumed to be projections of their own thoughts and feelings.

Sentence-completion techniques have also been used. For example, employees are asked to complete sentences such as: "*The trouble with this company is* . . ." Response themes are analyzed.

Another disguised technique, "error-choice," has also been utilized. This requires the respondent to make a choice between two equally erroneous response alternatives. The direction of error is taken as an indication of underlying attitude. For example, an employee might be asked if fringe benefits amounted to 10 per cent or 90 per cent of a typical employee's salary. Assuming that the true answer might be 50 per cent, the employee's choice of 10 per cent would be taken as an indication of a negative attitude; if 90 per cent were chosen, it would indicate a positive attitude.[34]

VALUE OF INDIRECT METHODS AND DISGUISED TECHNIQUES   Direct and indirect measures of job satisfaction were compared for over 500 insurance agents. The direct measures of job dissatisfaction correlated significantly with job turnover, but the indirect measures did not.[84] Since, as noted in Chapter 3, ordinarily we would expect job dissatisfaction to correlate with turnover, the indirect technique was considered an inappropriate measure of true job feeling.

There seems to be little reason for using indirect techniques for measuring employee attitudes except where (1) respondents cannot remain anonymous and we have reason to believe that they will consciously hide their true feelings, or (2) respondents are assumed to be unaware about how they really feel, and these subconscious feelings are of consequence to their behavior. But, as we have shown in Chapter 3, it is *conscious* expectations and satisfaction that are likely to be of importance in determining effort and performance in the work situation. And it is such conscious expectations that the organization is most likely to be able to deal with, rather than fantasies or wishes unknown or unclear to the employees themselves.

PAY AND JOB SATISFACTION

The subject of pay is extremely complex, and its exact influence is hard to determine. Some critics argue that it is the most important source of job satisfaction. But the pay individuals receive is only part of what motivates them to work, although additional pay may increase production. It determines one's possible standard of living. For some, pay is a symbol of success. For some, it may mean security in old age. To others, it may mean a new car or boat, a college education for their children, or a source of power and standing in their community. Considering the manifold uses of pay and the meaning it imparts to people, it is little wonder that precise statements of its incentive value are difficult.

Rated Importance

When workers are asked directly about the importance of pay to their overall job satisfaction, pay ranks relatively high compared with other factors. However, if workers are questioned more indirectly about the importance of pay, its significance drops substantially. The absolute amount of dollar earnings is of great importance to some workers, but there is also evidence that workers' perception of whether their pay is fair or not fair is often even more important to their morale than their actual absolute dollar earnings, as we have noted in discussing equity in Chapter 3.

In a more sophisticated approach to determining the importance of money, workers were asked to express their preferences for either increased pay or different type of fringe benefits. All the alternatives had equal monetary value. Over a thousand electrical workers indicated, on the average, that direct pay increases were not as important as fringe benefits, such as increased sick leave and extra vacation time.[58] In another study, nearly 200 industrial workers ranked a pay raise fifth in order of preference.[59] For the relatively affluent worker in America, simply earning more money often is less important than the opportunity to have more time for leisure activities. In addition, by 1980, sizable salary increments for middle-income workers could often result in relatively little increase in real disposable income because it moved them into higher income-tax brackets and because of the erosion of continuing inflation. Thus, in the late 1970s, many U.S. deep coal mines were experiencing operating difficulty because miners were refusing to work more than three days a week. Again, Ford Motor reported that thousands of its workers immediately began exercising a newly won option to refuse overtime work. Such action costs millions of dollars in potential sales and has an impact on other workers who want to put in additional time but can't because Ford needed to halt weekend production. About 35 per cent of the assemblers refused overtime beyond a fifty-hour week during the first months following the winning of the option to refuse such overtime. The director of industrial relations declared that Ford was "mystified by the experience."

Nevertheless, where income is low and psychological safety and security needs are unmet, pay is still considered to be of prime importance to the average worker.

The Meaning of Money

Money means the opportunity for conspicuous consumption, power and fate control for a few, the measure of success for many, and safety and security for most. Money literally means something completely different for a salesperson than for a service-oriented member of a religious order.

Wernimont and Fitzpatrick[85] asked 533 trainees, college students, and employees in various occupations to indicate what "money" meant to them by completing 40 semantic differential ratings of "money" like:

Good : —— : —— : —— : —— : —— : —— : Bad

Five interpretable factors emerged from an analysis of the responses. Respondents differed from each other in the extent that (1) money implied failure, embarrassment, and degradation; (2) money was a good thing; (3) money was unimportant; (4) money was a moral evil; and (5) money meant comfort and security. The 130 salespersons in the sample tended to view money more favorably than did the 44 nursing nuns. For the salespersons, money did not imply failure as it did for the nursing sisters. It was a good thing for the salespersons but not for the sisters. It was less of a moral evil to the salespersons than the nuns. Technical supervisors tended to see money in the same way as did the salespersons. College students and "hard-core unemployed" trainees were closer to the sisters. Managers, scientists, engineers, and secretaries were in between.

Incentive Plans, Hourly Rates, or Straight Salaries?

Regardless of what money means to them, the earnings of most gainfully employed people are of consequence to them. They are paid (1) according to incentive plans for each piece or batch they produce, (2) for the hours they work, or (3) with a straight salary from the firm or agency.

Expectancy theories suggest that piece-rate incentive systems should be most motivating. For instance, here it should be easiest to relate expectations, performance, and desired outcomes. But with a sample of 124 incentive-paid blue-collar employees, Schwab and Dyer found a correlation of only 0.13 between their *actual* productivity and their expectation that their effort determined how much they earned.[70] And there was only a correlation of 0.17 between their productivity and how important "making good money" was to them. Humanistic theories like Maslow's or Herzberg's suggest the reasons for this kind of result. For them, a straight salary should be most motivating. A salary should make it easier to attach meaning to the whole job and its implications for self-actualization. Salaried persons are more likely to see themselves as mature adults who can be treated with responsibility; workers on an incentive plan are more likely to see themselves treated as if they were dependent children.

There are no simple answers as to which is likely to be most motivating:

piece rate, hourly rate, or straight salary. Actually, they are often mixed. The piece-rate worker gets a base hourly pay, then extra incentive payments above production standards; the executive on salary gets a year-end bonus if profits have been good.

Incentive payments can increase productivity if workers are clear about how their performance results in quality output, if they understand how the incentive pay is calculated, if they trust management to keep the payment rates from being reduced, if the work group does not feel that it may "overproduce," with a potential loss of jobs, if workers feel that their earnings are equitable, and so on. Hourly wages or salaries can increase productivity where employees feel responsibility for what they are doing, see common interests between the firm and themselves, and see that merit raises and advancement will come from good performance by them. Let's now look in more detail at incentive plans, what makes them fail as motivators and what makes them succeed.

INCENTIVE PLANS Most incentive plans are based on a time study, and many of the problems of incentive plans are problems in time study. The usual objective of a time study is to obtain a standard time for any given task. Ordinarily, it is assumed that this standard time will represent the performance of the average employee working with normal effort. This assumption is often unrealistic. Two engineers timing the same operator simultaneously should get the same standard time. However, when Rodgers and Hammersley tested this proposition, they found a 9 per cent variation between similarly trained time-study engineers timing the same employee.[64] They also estimated that the typical experienced time-study engineer would be in error by 21 per cent.

There are many different systems of time study. Each has its own allowance for such items as personal needs and unavoidable delays. These allowances vary from 4 per cent to 50 per cent.

Another common problem occurs when time study is completed by estimation. Here, the time-study engineer does not time a so-called average employee but instead times an operator who is willing to cooperate or who is a superior worker. Then the time-study engineer compares the performance of the operator with what is considered to be normal. This estimation is likely to contain considerable error.

The time-study engineer often arouses mistrust and resentment. Whyte describes a factory where the engineers followed the common practice of trying to outsmart the time-study engineer.[87] The art of doing a job slowly but appearing to move fast while under the surveillance of the engineer was very much admired. The real heroes of the factory were the workers who could cause a machine to break down when the time-study engineer urged them on to greater speed.

There is little doubt that the time-study system is open to grave errors and that the system's inaccuracies can be a legitimate source of concern to workers. It often appears, too, that workers' ingenuity can beat the system to their advantage and the firm's disadvantage. Yet time study can be a useful basis for making budget proposals, bidding on contracts, or negotiating salespersons' commission rates. What is needed is a sophisticated point of view concerning the range of errors that can easily creep into the system.

OTHER PROBLEMS WITH INCENTIVE SYSTEMS   Most incentive-payment plans rest on two main assumptions. First, it is assumed that the work of each employee can be measured in a way that allows individual payment to be linked directly to individual performance. Second, it is assumed that the employees improve their performance in order to earn more money. Piecework can increase performance by 30 per cent over hourly wages if these assumptions are valid, but unfortunately more often than not, they are not. The validity of these assumptions was investigated by studying nearly 4,400 workers in 6 factories operating under incentive-payment plans. The only thing the employees knew about their system was that it started with a time study. Only a small percentage of them could explain how their bonuses were calculated. They could not tell the investigator how much bonus money they earned each day. Paradoxically, those who gave the best explanation of the bonus system were not the ones who were the best judges of their daily bonuses.[73] In a similar investigation of one factory with a group bonus and another with a group piece rate, most of the workers in both circumstances did not know the results of their efforts until they received their paychecks, and thus were not able to anticipate payment on the basis of performance.[12]

What type of incentive system is preferred by the workers is very difficult to determine, since most evidence suggests that workers tend to favor whatever system they are working under at the time of the interview or survey. Many factors have to be considered when asking workers about the type of incentive they prefer. There are, of course, individual preferences, but incentive plans are also dictated by the nature of the task. For example, 18 semiskilled machine workers who were given their choice of payment plans chose the one that gave them security and stable earnings rather than the opportunity to make a lot of money when things went well. This consideration also limited the differential among the earnings of each employee in the working group. The reason given for the choice was that the employees could not always control their rate of production, since machines often broke down.[36]

WHEN INCENTIVE PLANS WORK   Incentive plans can work well. The Lincoln Electric Company of Cleveland, Ohio, has one of the most successful and widely discussed wage-incentive plans.[51] This manufacturer of arc-welding equipment avoided the flaws of many plans by never cutting a piecework rate once it had been established. The system rewarded employees who displayed exceptional achievement in their jobs. Since the company shared its profit by means of a yearly bonus, the employees were strongly motivated to make suggestions that would increase the productivity of the corporation. High production became a norm for every worker. In a social situation such as this, those failing to do their best would be considered deviant members of the group. This situation put pressure on all members of the group to produce at their highest level.

(This can be a source of discontent. Many employees feel trapped by the pressure to maintain the high income that makes for a life style their families force them to continue.)

Management believes that it is establishing standards; in fact, often the work group fixes the standard, then all members produce up to this limit. Anyone who goes over this standard is a "rate buster." In a series of studies of machine operators, coil winders, chocolate dippers, and butter wrappers, Rothe and colleagues found that the groups lowered the standard for all their members when the economy was bad and raised the standard when it was good. [66,67] They actually were more consistent (worked up to the group's standard for everyone) under piecework than if paid by the hour. More will be said about the extent of the work group's control of output later. It is sufficient to note here that incentive plans over which the group can exert control, that pay for performance without threatening security, are most likely to generate increased quality and quantity of output. The Scanlon plan illustrates how this can be done.

Scanlon plan. The Scanlon plan has two parts. First, it shares any reductions in unit costs that are under the control of labor on a plantwide basis. Such reductions are determined against a normal labor cost for the factory. Usually, this cost is established by a joint labor-management agreement. Whenever labor costs fall below the norm, the workers receive anywhere from 50 to 100 per cent of the amount saved. This differs from profit sharing. Profits depend not only on what the workers can control but also market demand, investment decreases, and so on. With its emphasis on labor-cost savings, the Scanlon plan focuses on what workers can influence.

A second feature of the Scanlon plan is the unique implementation of a suggestion plan. In it, no one benefits individually from a suggestion; instead, the entire plant benefits through a reduction in the labor cost, thus eliminating any possible conflict among the originators of the suggestion. Reports indicate that as many as 80 per cent of the suggestions submitted in a Scanlon plan plant are accepted, while plants with individual suggestion plans commonly accept only 25 per cent of those submitted. Further, with the Scanlon plan there is no reason for the worker to withhold suggestions that will increase productivity for fear the rate of production will be correspondingly increased by the time study. If such suggestions do increase productivity, the only result is lowering of labor costs and consequently a bonus for the whole plant. Sharp increases in production are often reported after the introduction of the Scanlon plan.

A survey was made of nine firms with eleven plants that had introduced the Scanlon plan. They represented a wide variety of product lines. The workers' skills varied over a long range, from manual to highly technical labor. In the eleven plants surveyed, the gain in productivity varied from 11 per cent to 49 per cent, with an average gain of 23 per cent over a two-year period. Bonuses averaged 17 per cent of gross pay. In all the firms, the labor-cost savings were split 75 per cent to the workers and 25 per cent to the company. There seemed to be no consistent relationship between the skill of the employees, or the production process, and increases in productivity. Besides the direct benefits accruing from the increased production and higher profits, there seemed to be indirect benefits in the form of better service to the customer, higher-quality products, improvement in the firm's competitive position, and no decline in employment. The Scanlon plan has been adopted by several hundred firms here and abroad and its popularity remains undiminished.[61]

Pay as a Motivator

It seems obvious that whether pay, as such, actually motivates people to accept a job or to keep them happily working hard at the job will depend on whether or not they are satisfied with it. Therefore, the question of consequence is what determines such satisfaction. Using responses of 180 U.S. and 212 Canadian managers, Dyer and Theriault[20] tested Lawler's[47] model of what determines pay satisfaction. Lawler's model was built on equity and expectation theories. Dyer and Theriault built a modified model shown in Figure 4–7 which could account for 40 to 50 per cent of the variation in pay satisfaction of the 392 managers. It can be seen that pay satisfaction depended on the perceived adequacy of the pay system and the perceived equity of the amount of pay received. In turn, the system was evaluated in terms of its criteria, the way the managers' performance was assessed, and how well policies and contracts were adhered to. Equity depended on the discrepancy between actual pay received and amount of pay that should have been received. The latter amount, in turn, depended on a variety of standards and referents.

Minimally, we conclude that objectives of any well-thought-out pay policy of an organization plan include:

1. *Equity.* Differentially paid employees see themselves as making similarly differentiated contributions in their work.

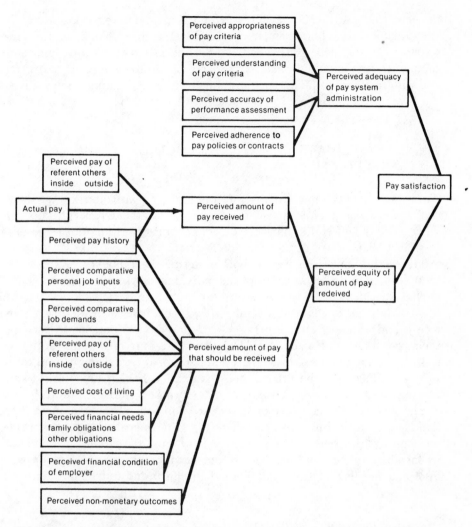

Figure 4-7. A modified model of the determinants of pay satisfaction. (From Dyer and Theriault, "The determinants of pay satisfaction," *Journal of Applied Psychology,* 61 [1976]: 596–604.)

2. *Motivation.* Effectiveness is rewarded with suitable salary increases.
3. *Security and comfort.* A "living wage" is paid.

Note that any payment plan will be in trouble if employees don't understand the plan or trust management. A plan that calls for group payments will have problems, if employees don't identify with the group. This is probably why performance improved in the relay-assembly room at Hawthorne when the bonus was based on the team of 5 rather than the department of 100. The bonus based on 100 could have worked as well if the 5 experimental women felt identification and shared mutual interests with the department of 100. Such sharing across divisions and companies does occur, as we have seen in the Lincoln Electric Company and with the Scanlon plans. Such building of trust and mutual interests is at the heart of organizational development (Chapter 14).

MOTIVATION AND THE SOCIAL SITUATION

Teamwork is not a modern invention. Loyalty to kith and kin predates civilization. The buddy system was practiced in the Greek phalanx by older soldiers befriending new recruits. The Arabs sweeping out of Arabia to spread Islam spoke of the spirit of the clan.

So it is not surprising to see how powerful the influence of the work group can be on the motivation of the individual worker to perform. Thus, during World War II, absenteeism and high turnover was prevalent in Plant X but not in Plant Y, a similar one. In Plant X, with the low absenteeism and turnover, the supervisor introduced new workers to each of their co-workers and made them feel they were part of a team. Workers' tasks and their relationship to the production of the total plant were carefully explained. On the other hand, Plant Y, with high absenteeism and turnover, did not attempt to integrate new workers into the groups.[38]

The group can be a source of satisfaction to its members. The more they find their membership satisfying, share the group's goals, identify as members, and "stick together" (are cohesive), the more the group can influence its members to increase their efforts and output. But the same group can also influence its members to *decrease* their efforts and restrict output.

Restriction of Output

As we have already seen in discussing incentive payment plans, workers often artificially restrict their output against their economic self-interest. This restriction is recognized as one of the frequent by-products of the informal group's influence, since the opinions, attitudes, and behavior of its members can be molded by the group.

Roy worked as a radial drill operator in a machine shop for eleven months. He soon learned that output was restricted in a very systematic fashion. His fellow workers let him know when he was not expected to earn the established standard. Roy classified restriction in two ways: If a "stinker" came in, a job on which the operators did not think it possible to make incentive pay, they would relax and hold production down well below the guaranteed day rate. This restrictive behavior was termed "goldbrick-ing." Conversely, if there were a "gravy job," one on which the operators felt it would be easy to make the incentive pay, they feared reclassification, so they would hold back production to a predetermined level, even though they might have been able to double their earnings. Roy's work record, which is typical of an experienced operator, indicated that he would make his quota and then spend the rest of the day loafing. By the end of the working period, Roy could make his quota and have two hours a day left to relax with his fellow workers.[87]

TOLERANCE FOR RESTRICTED QUANTITY OR QUALITY   Supervisors, themselves former members of the work group, may accept the group's standards. They may wish to avoid conflict with the group and bickering among group members for departing from group standards even where the stan-dards violate company policy. Workers accept the group only so long as production does not drop to a level that would jeopardize their standing with their superiors.[5]

A case in point was found in the aerospace industry. To assemble the wing section of a plane, a bolt is inserted through the wing plate to a recessed nut. Sometimes the alignment between the nut and plate open-ing becomes distorted. To insert the nut in such a case, the assemblers use a tap, an extremely hard tool that cuts new threads in the nut. The tap destroys the effectiveness of the stop nuts. Therefore it conceals a serious defect. Company policy is so strong on this point that an assembler can be fired just for having a tap in his possession. However, the supervisor knows that the taps are used and may even ask an assembler to tap a nut in order to meet production quotas. The supervisor is caught in the tradi-tional role of the man in the middle. On the one side is company policy and its demand for production. On the other is the unreconcilable inability of the workers to produce without breaking company regulations. The supervisor is thus forced to meet the conflicting demands of the manage-ment, assuming responsibility for the assemblers' deviations from man-agement policy.

PERSONAL REASONS FOR OUTPUT RESTRICTION   Three personal reasons may underlie restriction of output along with social motives. First, workers often feel that if they produce an exceptional quantity of one part, man-agement will cut the rate on the job. Frequently, the worker expects and fears that time-study engineers will retime the job and demand more for the same money if a quota is exceeded. (Management in certain companies at certain times has taken just such action.) A second fear is that employ-ment will be reduced if the worker produces too much at one time, leaving nothing for the next day. Obviously this fear is well grounded in certain industries.

To this must be added the workers' social concerns if one or several dare to exceed the group's production quota and outshine others. There is probably no quicker way for a worker to become an outcast. Again, at times there are built-in inequities. A worker with a good machine may produce 20 per cent more of the same product than a worker with a bad machine, irrespective of the operator. In such a case good social relationships may be maintained and friction avoided by a constant output from each worker with equal incentive pay.

The third personal factor stressed by the workers is the satisfaction derived from maintaining at least a minimum amount of control over their own behavior. They like the feeling that they can work at their own paces and not be forced to follow someone else's rules, subject to frequent layoffs of employees. Thus, restriction of output prevents competition among the group, which could disturb established interpersonal relationships. There will be conflict if the employees in the same department, doing the same job, find that an inexperienced worker is making more money than an older, more experienced worker. For this reason, the new workers on the job are told to produce a certain amount less than the experienced employees, even though they may be capable of producing much more. A major conflict can also develop between members of different departments doing different jobs. Often the jobs in one department have more status and prestige attached to them and correspondingly more pay than the jobs in another department. If the members in the department with the lower job status exceed an informal shop production quota and thus make more money than the members of the higher-prestige department, conflict will result. The destruction of established relationships causes a great deal of conflict throughout the shop.

DEVIANTS   There are employees who defy the group standard and produce more than the group deems advisable. These "rate-busters" are intensely disliked by the conforming members of the group. Thus, in a large machine shop, of eighty-four men on incentive pay, there were nine rate-busters who continually exceeded the group standard. These men differed in several important respects from the other workers. The rate-busters generally grew up either on farms or in urban lower-middle-class families, whereas the other workers came from typical working-class homes in large cities. The rate-busters were socially isolated in the shop and tended to avoid clubs or social activities in the community. Generally, the rate-busters were more acquisitive and were known to invest sizable sums in savings bonds.[87]

Zaleznik, Christensen, and Roethlisberger reported on the behavior of fifty workers who did or did not abide by group standards for production.[89] The group that restricted output, the regulars, was identified by its valuing generosity, which included a willingness to lend and spend money, and helpfulness, which took the form of giving aid to other members of the group in illnesses, or in a job too difficult to handle. To be loyal to the group was considered to be an important attribute, as was to be friendly and lead a happy, carefree life.

The deviant group was the reverse. Members were serious. They saved, and tried to get ahead. They did not indicate clearly that they always enjoyed the friendship of their fellow workers.

There seemed to be a fundamental difference in values between the regular group members and the high-producing deviant group members. The attitude of the regular group members was not to outproduce their fellow workers, but to be sure to produce just enough to avoid special attention by management.

The deviant members were oriented differently. They felt it their duty to work hard and produce as much as possible. Their point of view revealed their Protestant middle-class backgrounds. The regular group members, on the other hand, typically were Catholic, of immigrant parentage. The standard of the regular group members offered little attraction for the task-centered deviants.

Output and Cohesiveness of Work Groups

The impact of group norms depends greatly on the group's cohesiveness. This cohesiveness provides the means whereby the group can control the efforts of its members to raise or to restrict output. It is clear that work team members strongly attracted to a group by its usefulness, its spirit of friendship, or its prestige will conform more readily to their group standards than will members of groups lacking these qualities.[44]

In a review of the performance of teams, each composed of five employees and a plant supervisor, Danzig and Galanter showed that the greater the cohesiveness of the teams, the less time they took to assemble factory products.[17] Reporting on the performance of eighty-one eleven-man bomber crews, Berkowitz determined that crews with high cohesiveness and high regard for the worth of their jobs were superior in effectiveness as measured by supervisors and by percentage of missions flown.[7]

Cohesiveness can result in higher or lower production, depending on whether the group's norms conform to the interests of the company or are antagonistic toward them. Cohesive groups with high production standards will produce more than uncohesive groups. But cohesive groups with *low* production standards will produce substantially less than looser groups with similar standards.[6] In studying 228 work groups ranging in size from 5 to 50 members, Seashore clarified this relationship between cohesiveness and productivity. Cohesive work groups were more likely to deviate in either direction from plant averages.[72]

Assuming that workers' interests are connected with company goals, it pays to build cohesive groups. Thus, carpenters and bricklayers permitted to select their own work partners increased productivity by 5 per cent.[79] Selecting one's work partner is but one example among many of how worker *participation* in decisions enhanced the motivating possibilities of the social situation.

Group cohesion may be enhanced by severe initiation of new members. College fraternities, many military units, and some work groups such as certain railroad shops often operate in this manner. Initiation is an obstacle to be met and overcome, thus making achieved group membership more attractive to the individual. Initiation and membership thus foster cohesiveness and uniformity in response to the group goals.[1]

Participation and Motivation to Work

During World War II, meat was in unusually short supply in the United States. The shortage could be relieved if housewives made more use of less popular cuts, such as beef hearts, sweetbreads, and kidneys. To induce housewives to modify their cooking habits, one group of women was given a lecture that stressed the nutritional value of these less popular meats, while another group participated in a discussion. Both groups were asked to try one of the less traditional meats in the following weeks. Of those who participated in the group decision, 32 per cent tried the less popular meats, as compared with only 3 per cent of the women in the lecture group.[49]

SUPERVISOR TRAINING   Industrial applications followed quickly. In a large manufacturing plant the supervisors were making gross errors in merit rating their subordinates. In effect, the supervisors did not rate the performance of the worker on the job, as they should have, but rated the difficulty of the job. The ratings were important because they determined the worker's pay. (The difficulty encountered with these merit-rating plans will be discussed in Chapter 8.) The 29 supervisors responsible for rating the performance of 395 employees were divided at random into three groups. The first group received a lecture on the technique and theory of performance rating, were instructed on how to improve their ratings, and were shown past errors. The second group, under a discussion leader, were asked why they had rated the performance of workers in high-skill jobs as superior to the performance of workers in lower-skill jobs. The group discussed the question, and their own conclusion was that it was necessary to disregard the skill required for the job and concentrate on rating only the performance of the employee. A third group served as a control and received no instruction of any kind.

The lecture group made a small but insignificant shift in their post-training merit ratings, whereas the discussion group made a significant improvement, distributing their good and bad ratings among workers on all jobs regardless of skill required. There was no change in the control group's ratings. It was apparent that the group discussion had modified behavior, whereas the lecture had not.[49]

HARWOOD   The Harwood Manufacturing Company, which employs mostly women to sew pajamas, had an incentive plan. The nature of the business often required operators to learn new jobs. Marked resistance by operators to these changes was due to the learning period necessary for the new job, since old skills were no longer useful in the new job. To ease the transition, each operator was paid a bonus while learning the new job. Despite the efforts of management, many operators preferred to quit rather than learn a new job. The majority of those who did transfer took longer than new employees to learn new jobs.

Analysis of data revealed that the major determinant of the time employees needed to learn a new job was not their skill but their motivation. It was decided to test whether participation would increase motivation and willingness to put up with the frustration generated by a change in jobs.

Three comparable groups whose jobs were to be changed were selected for the experiment. The first group held a meeting for all operators whose jobs were to be changed. The reason for the change was explained. Management presented a plan to institute the required changes. The group accepted the plan and chose a small number of operators to be trained in the new methods. These, in turn, would train the remaining members of the larger group. The second group also had the need for the changes explained and the plan for the change presented to them. However, this time all members of the group were to participate in the design of the new job and to be trained in the new methods. The third group was a control group, which went through the usual factory routine, in which the change was explained and new methods and piece rates were presented.

After the transfer to the new job, the control group expressed hostility toward management. Seventeen per cent quit in the first forty days. Their output after thirty days was 10 per cent below standard. In contrast, the first experimental group was cooperative, and reached the production standard after fourteen days; none of the operators quit during the first forty days in this group. The second experimental group recovered their efficiency in the new jobs even faster, reaching the production standard in two days. They increased their production in subsequent days to a level about 14 per cent above the standard; no one quit during the relearning period in this group. It is clear that the degree of participation afforded to the group materially affected their acceptance and/or ability to change. To dramatize the effect of total participation, the remaining members of the control group were brought together some months later for a second experiment. They were then transferred to a new job, following the procedure used with the second group in the earlier experiment. As a result of their total participation, the group reached the standard in two days and within eight days exceeded the production standard by over 10 per cent.[16] More about the Harwood experience will be presented in Chapter 14.

A PROGRAM IN PLANT MODERNIZATION   Semiautomatic flow procedures were to be introduced in a plant and the sequence of operations was to be changed. Using participative techniques, management informed the workers of the anticipated changes in a series of group meetings. After the first meeting the workers were told that their wages would stay at the same rate as the average of the past six weeks until new rates were established. In the following weeks the changes were initiated on the production floor. There were many informal discussions among the engineers, supervisors, and workers to iron out the changes and make new suggestions. After the new system and procedures had been operating for a short time, the workers again met to discuss the revised wage rates. In this meeting the basis for the new rates was explained. At this time, the workers voiced numerous complaints, many of which had little to do with the modernization program. Management listened, investigated, and then offered remedies where feasible. As a whole, the workers' reaction to the system was favorable. A more direct measure of the success of the program was the slight increase in production by the company plus a 10 per cent saving in direct labor cost for each item. From management's point of view, the overall change that attempted to maximize the employees' participation resulted in a smooth transition from an established production method to a more modern system.[24]

CLOTHING STORE   Participation in solving a problem may not always be initiated by management.[2] Competitive selling in a clothing store where eighteen salespersons worked on commission resulted in "sales grabbing" and avoidance of such cooperative functions as arranging displays. The commission system, with its unequal pay, destroyed the morale of the employees. Management's efforts to solve the problem proved futile. Finally, the sales force decided informally among themselves that they would pool their sales and divide the total commissions equally. Management approved the scheme, and both morale and total sales increased for the group.

Participation is the reason why employee planning pays off, as will be discussed in the next chapter. Participation is a style of management particularly suited to "people" development and is at the heart of organizational development discussed in Chapter 14. Participation is central to the movement toward industrial democracy in Western Europe, Yugoslavia, and Israel. Nevertheless, it is no panacea. Often it depends strongly on who is going to participate.

When Participation Fails

Whyte reported a case where the technique was so successful that it failed.[87] The operation was the spray-painting of toys, hung from moving hooks before going through a drying oven. Eight women sat in a straight line in front of the moving hooks, each taking a toy from the tray beside her, painting it, and then hanging it on a hook as it passed by. The speed of the hooks had been calculated so that each woman would be able to hang a painted toy on each hook before it passed. All of the women were paid on a group bonus basis. Since the job was new, the women were given six months to learn the procedure. During these months they were to receive a learning bonus, which decreased monthly until it ended after six months, when it was assumed they would have mastered their jobs. During the second month the women appeared to learn more slowly than had been anticipated. They complained that the hooks moved by too quickly, and a few of them quit, ostensibly for this reason. A consultant advised the supervisor to meet with the women and discuss their complaints. One complaint was of too much heat in the room, and the women's solution was to install several large fans. Even though the supervisor thought that this would not solve the problem, he had the fans installed. The women were jubilant and very pleased with their supervisor. Another meeting followed, and the women still maintained that the speed of the hooks was too fast; they wanted to be able to adjust the speed themselves. Reluctantly the supervisor installed a speed control with fast, medium, and slow adjustments. The women worked out their own pattern and actually, on the average, ran the hooks faster than at the old constant speed. Within three weeks the women were operating 30 per cent to 50 per cent above what was expected for their training time, with the result that they were earning more than many skilled workers in the plant. The increased production of the paint room resulted in an excess of toys in the next process and a deficit of toys coming into the paint room. This caused so much dissension among the workers in other parts of the plant that the superintendent arbitrarily revoked the learning bonus and returned the hooks to the old time-studied, constant speed. Production dropped and within a short time, the supervisor and all but two women had quit. In this instance, participation was successful in terms of production and worker satisfaction, but failed because it disrupted established relationships prevailing throughout the plant. It ignored the fact that the work group was a system embedded in a larger one. What occured inside the group influenced and was influenced by what went on outside of it.

OTHER REASONS FOR FAILURE   Participation has been found to be less motivating for employees lacking in self-assurance,[14] in education,[74] and in need for achievement.[77] Again, participation has been found also to be less motivating, satisfying, and productive for employees weak in needs for independence and authoritarian rather than egalitarian in personality.[80]

Culture may also mar the profitability of participation. A Norwegian factory underwent seasonal changes in production. Twenty workers met with their foreman to participate in the changeover, while sixteen workers served as a control and were given less opportunity to participate in any decision-making process. In contrast to the Harwood program and results of other studies, there was no difference in productivity between the two groups. One explanation offered was that the areas of decision making were not relevant to production, and possibly the workers did not feel that participation in this case was legitimate. Another explanation was that the Norwegian factory workers, according to Norwegian character,[54] had a low need for independence, and were therefore people for whom participation was not motivating.[25] The importance of culture to work motivation will be discussed more thoroughly in Chapter 17.

JOB SATISFACTION RELATED TO PERSONAL CHARACTERISTICS

For the U.S. population of male workers aged 21 to 65 as a whole, sampled by Gallup, there was surprisingly little change over a ten-year period (1963–1973) in job satisfaction. A large majority continued to report themselves as satisfied.[30] Table 4–2 shows the percentages of a national sample who responded that they were satisfied with their jobs. The range between the years 1963 and 1973 was from 86 to 92 per cent who so reported themselves.

But just as the success of participation depends on personal differences

Table 4–2. Percentage of "satisfied" workers, 1963–1973 based on eight Gallup polls —men only, ages 21 through 65

July 16, 1963	89%
August 6, 1965	87%
September 6, 1966	92%
September 29, 1966	89%
March 25, 1969	92%
August 17, 1971	88%
December 7, 1971	86%
January 23, 1973	88%

Note: "Don't Know" answers were excluded from the percentage bases.
From Gallup, G. *Congressional Record* (April 30, 1973)

among employees, so motivation and satisfaction of employees generally may depend as much on their own personal histories, abilities, personalities, and individual preferences as on their job assignments. Let's look at some personal characteristics that make a difference.

Sex and Job Satisfaction

There is no simple relation for several reasons. First, women are statistically more likely to work at less skilled jobs and to receive lower pay for their work than are men. (This situation is being dramatically changed with the enforcement of federal regulations outlawing discrimination between male and female workers, as we will describe in Chapter 18.) Since workers of lower status, making less pay, are generally less satisfied, we would expect female workers, as a group, to be less satisfied with their work. Second, in the past, many female workers received more of their overall job satisfaction from different factors from those that satisfied male employees. The female employee tended to gain more satisfaction from social relationships in the workplace and less from the task itself than did male employees.[57] In more recent studies where males and females are equated for occupational level the importance of job attributes such as pay, security, and feelings of accomplishment have been found equivalent for the sexes.[11]

As life styles change, as sex discrimination is reduced, as sex role differences are blurred, as pay is equalized with men doing the same work, as more women seek and succeed in careers from which they have been excluded in the past, as more women become the single heads of households, we should find that sex differences would disappear in attraction to work and satisfaction with it. Already in the late 1970s, career orientation has become commonplace for the educated woman. Economic interests dictated the need for a majority of U.S. women to remain gainfully employed. By 1977, 58 per cent of working women were either fully self-supporting or married to men earning less than $7,000 a year and therefore working as a means to support their family.

RACE AND JOB SATISFACTION   Again, we are in the midst of societal change. The average level of jobs held by blacks (particularly black women) and other minorities is rising, aided by legislation and affirmative action programs. But so are black expectations and consequent frustration. The income gap, particularly between unskilled black and white men, remains high, although by 1977 a young black man with a college degree could expect to earn 9 per cent more than a young white man with a comparable education.[23] Annual unemployment rates for unskilled black youth (37 per cent) were still much higher than that of white counterparts (19 per cent) in the late 1970s, so that rising expectations were also producing rising frustrations and dissatisfactions as well. What about more specific preferences?

During one-hour interviews with 89 black and 756 white male workers, representing a national probability sample, the following was asked:

"Would you please look at this card and tell me which *one* thing on this list you would *most* prefer in a job?
1. High income
2. No danger of being fired
3. Working hours are short, lots of free time
4. Chances for promotion
5. Work important and gives a feeling of accomplishment."

Table 4–3 shows the responses in percentages for the black and for the white workers. It can be seen that while there were no differences in preferences for promotion and shorter hours, greater percentages of blacks chose security and income while greater percentages of whites chose meaningful work. Weaver concluded:

The black worker's differentially higher preference for income and lower preference for interest and meaning in a job may, at least partially, be the result of what has been learned from a history of considerable insecurity in jobs in the less desirable occupational categories. Knowing that having a job is at best tenuous, the black worker may focus on the tangible, immediate security of income and be less mindful of the intrinsic satisfactions in his work, which are, in fact, comparatively few in the types of jobs blacks have traditionally held.

These results further show that black workers with good jobs are very concerned about the danger of being fired. This insecurity may be related to the recent rapid inflation and falling employment, since . . . the level of black employment closely follows fluctuations in the labor market.[83]

Table 4–3. Preferences among job characteristics by black and white male workers

Job characteristic	% White (n = 756)	% Black (n = 89)
Income	16.01	39.33
Security	7.67	12.36
Short hours	5.29	5.62
Promotion	18.52	16.85
Work important	52.51	25.84

From Weaver, C. N., "Black-White Differences in Attitudes toward Job Characteristics. *Journal of Applied Psychology,* 60 (1975): 439. Reprinted by permission of the author.

Age and Job Satisfaction

Cross-sectional studies at a given point in time of the job satisfaction of employees who differ in age show that job satisfaction tends to increase in age. For instance, Figure 4–8 shows such results for a random sample of blue-collar workers in 1973 in a large manufacturing firm.

But evidence also indicates that when male managerial employees reach preretirement age, between 60 and 65, they experience a drop in overall job satisfaction.[69] This drop is best explained by the fact that in looking back over their careers, they perceive intrinsic aspects of the job to have been satisfying, but they now find satisfaction only in the more extrinsic factors of the job, such as social relationships. This conclusion appears logical, since the company is probably not willing to give the individual about to retire new opportunities to advance in the company nor to increase his or her skill or knowledge. This phenomenon may also be changing as the retirement age is extended and mandatory retirement requirements are eliminated for many jobs.

Changes also occur as a consequence of time for different age groups. Evidence of rather dramatic changes in youth from the late 1960s to the early 1970s comes from a survey by Yankelovich.[88] In 1973, 3,522 persons between 16 and 25 in age were interviewed. One-third were in college. Only 56 per cent would agree that hard work always pays off.

Figure 4–8. Increasing job satisfaction with increasing age. (Reprinted from Stagner, "Boredom on the assembly line: Age and personality variables," *Industrial Gerontology*, 2 (1975): 23–44. Published © The National Council on the Aging, Inc., Washington, D.C.)

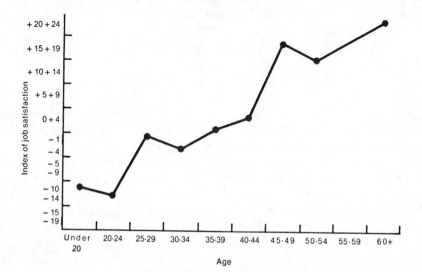

But 79 per cent had agreed in a 1969 survey. Conversely, 74 per cent would welcome less emphasis on money in 1973, compared to 54 per cent in 1969. Yankelovich saw these expressed values boding major changes in the workplace. The 1960s generation gap was between college youth and their parents. The 1970s gap was more likely to be between youth in general and their parents. "The new values off campus pose a new and different kind of challenge in the workplace. . . . [The young employees'] incentives and what they want as pay-offs have begun to change."

In the 1970s youth chiefly wanted jobs that provide self-expression and self-fulfillment. Wanted also were opportunities for special education to seek new aspirations. But only three out of ten were optimistic about finding such jobs. Nevertheless, young employees were less fearful of economic insecurity, less responsive to hierarchical discipline and fear of being fired.[88]

The economic cycle is likely to affect such results for youth entering the labor market for the first time. Continued high unemployment is likely to increase concern for safety and security needs; continued prosperity is likely to focus more attention on self-actualization.

One of the most pressing issues of concern to modern industrial organizations is the change in attitudes of college graduates. The older incentives of prestigious title and money are now being rivaled as sources of job satisfaction by personal recognition and more responsibility. In a survey of over 300 chief executives of the largest companies in the United States, 76 per cent said that they were reorganizing the company in some manner to allow younger executives to demonstrate their ability.[18]

Almost three-quarters of the chief executives also reported that younger executives are less patient and less willing to work their way up than were the older executives. This impatience is seen as causing resentment among older managers, who perceive younger managers making more money and moving into positions of responsibility sooner than they did.

Job Satisfaction and Job Tenure

Obviously, younger workers cannot have held any job for, say, 25 years. Only older workers could have put in such time on a job. And, if the older workers are more satisfied, so are those with longer job tenure. Thus, the age of workers and job tenure can account for the fact that it is possible to find a small set of 10 to 20 per cent of workers (i.e. older ones) who accept and even prefer assembly-line work, though the vast majority do not.[77] Assembly-line jobs generally are assigned to those under 30. In the automotive industry, fewer than 15 per cent on the line are likely to be over 45. When they get some seniority, most assembly-line workers show their dissatisfaction by arranging to be transferred off the line or else they quit the company. Those few older employees who remain on the line are likely to report they are satisfied with it (although they want their children to do better). And as we have already stated, it is the older workers who are likely to be satisfied with whatever they are doing.

Job Satisfaction and Job Level

The higher one's level in an organization, the greater is the status — the importance of the position in the organization. Job satisfaction tends to be greater with higher status level. This means that when supervisors are compared with workers, the supervisors have higher job satisfaction. Also, when managers are compared, research indicates that the higher the level of a manager, the greater his or her job satisfaction.

Situational variables can influence perceived status. Ratings of status from individuals in the same occupation but with half working on the day and half the night shift showed that the nonsupervisory night-shift workers perceived their jobs as having less status than did those on the day shift.[9]

This finding of increased satisfaction with each succeeding level in the organization is not surprising, since a number of other, satisfaction-related job factors are implied by higher levels, including responsibility, money, prestige, fate control, and more intrinsically rewarding work.

More than a thousand managers were questioned about how well five of their needs were being satisfied. Satisfaction was found to increase with each level of management for the esteem, autonomy, and self-actualization needs. But security and social-need satisfaction was high and relatively constant across all levels of management samples.[63] Moreover, at different levels in the organization, different needs are important to employees. At higher occupational levels, more intrinsic job factors (such as the work itself and the opportunity for self-expression) were more valued than at lower job levels, where extrinsic job characteristics (such as pay and security) assumed more importance for the employee.[15]

Occupational Level and Job Satisfaction

Occupations vary in average compensation, training required, or perceived status. In general, the higher the level of an occupation the higher the expressed satisfaction with it.[35] In addition, workers in different occupations look for different kinds of satisfaction. For example, in a comparison of over 1,000 white-collar workers with over 400 blue-collar workers, the social environment was found to be of greater importance to the blue-collar workers.[26]

Among others, Locke tested for Herzberg's job content as a satisfier and job context as a dissatisfier with white-collar and blue-collar workers.[52] He did not find job content potentially satisfying and job context potentially dissatisfying. Rather, he observed that white-collar workers were likely to be more satisfied by job content, especially achievement opportunities. Blue-collar workers were more likely to be more satisfied as a consequence of job context factors such as their pay. Lack of achievement was more dissatisfying to white-collar workers; lower pay was more dissatisfying to blue-collar workers.

Job Proficiency and Satisfaction

In the first year of study of 25 successful and 29 unsuccessful managers from the Bell System, no difference was found in satisfaction between the two groups. But after five years, the successful group significantly increased their satisfaction with achievement and esteem, while the unsuccessful managers experienced a marked drop in satisfaction.[10]

In the same way, a survey of 221 production employees working on batteries for heart pacemakers (which must be of extremely high quality), demonstrated that workers judged more accurate in their performance were generally more satisfied with the firm, particularly in their willingness to identify with it.[31] The evidence seems clear that the more successful employees become in an organization, the more satisfying their jobs become.[33]

Self-Esteem and Satisfaction

Esteem refers to the way a person's colleagues evaluate him or her; it is usually measured by sociometric methods — by asking others how they like or respect or accept or rely on the person being evaluated. It is a characteristic of informal organization and therefore different from formal status, which is usually regarded as the official rank or position of the person, as measured by his or her title or salary.

A number of studies have attempted to link esteem, as measured by reports from co-workers, with job satisfaction, but these studies show no consistent relationship. When self-esteem is measured by what the persons themselves believe their value to be, however, there does appear to be such a relationship.

A survey study of 151 employees in 18 repair crews concluded that self-esteem was more important to job satisfaction than esteem from fellow workers.[43] This illustrates the point that objective evidence is sometimes less important than what people believe to be true. But Lawler advanced the simple idea that there would be a positive relationship between job

Table 4-4. Correlations between job satisfaction and job performance, by ability–job requirement correspondence type and level

Match of abilities of worker with abilities required by job	Blue collar		White collar	
	r	N	r	N
High correspondence	.50 *	116	.34 *	111
Average correspondence	−.02	111	.12	113
Low correspondence	−.04	27	.09	28

* Statistically significant at .05 probability levels.
Adapted from Carlson, "Degree of Job Fit as a Moderator of the Relationship between Job Performance and Job Satisfaction," *Personnel Psychology,* 22 (1969): 167

performance and satisfaction only for those individuals with the necessary ability and experience to perform the job well.[46] For those with lower ability to do the job there would be a smaller or no relationship between satisfaction and performance. This proposition was confirmed by Carlson, who related job satisfaction with abilities to do the job for approximately 500 white- and blue-collar workers.[13] Psychological tests were given to all subjects, along with estimations of job requirements, job performance, and job satisfaction. Some of the results are shown in Table 4–4.

Those blue- and white-collar workers who had the ability for the job and could do it well were the most satisfied. But those with lower ability to do the job were neither likely to be more nor less satisfied with their work.

Job Involvement and Job Satisfaction

There seem to be at least three elements to what is meant by job involvement, according to a factor analysis of the response of 245 college students and 313 sales representatives by Saleh and Hosek.[70] The first factor concerns how much one actively participates on the job (I use the skills I have learned for my job); the second factor deals with how much one's job is central to one's life interests (The most important things I do are involved with my job); the third factor considers how much one's job performance is central to one's self-esteem (I feel badly if I don't perform well on my job).

Job satisfaction among blue-collar men and women clerks and bank employees, particularly with the work itself, seems to be much higher for those with a central life interest in work rather than with a central life interest in family, church, or community.[19] Thus, on a scale developed by Lodahl and Kejner assessing the extent to which work is a central life interest (The major satisfactions in my life come from my work) correlated with four of the five job satisfaction variables of the Job Descriptive Index. All the relationships were moderate (0.29 to 0.38).[53] It would appear that employees who are more involved in their job do gain more satisfaction from it. But how deeply involved they are in their work seems to depend more on the intrinsic satisfaction received from the work itself than the extrinsic satisfaction.[86] The composite picture of job-involved workers indicates that they tend to be older, show less consideration for others if they are leaders, score higher on tests of initiative and intelligence, and work with other people.[53] Also, according to a survey of 2,400 employees, they tend to be religious and moral and to see themselves as ambitious and capable.[70]

Being out of step with those with whom we compare ourselves in pay, as we have seen, can be a source of pay dissatisfaction. Being out of step with our peers in how fast or slowly we advance can be a source of stress and dissatisfaction. A study of 2,080 Navy enlisted men showed that those whose pay grade was relatively lower or relatively higher than ordinary for their job experience, their age, and their marital status tended to be less satisfied with their jobs and under more stress. Those whose pay grade was normal for their age, experience, and marital status were more satisfied and reported themselves under less stress.[21]

Incongruities and Dissatisfaction

Job dissatisfaction, as we have seen, can arise from unmet expectations. These expectations may be due to lack of realism about one's abilities, skills, and opportunities. Unwarranted aspirations may be a source of deep frustration, resentment, and dissatisfaction in a job setting that in itself is attractive to less ambitious employees. In the United States, as in many other countries, we are faced increasingly with frustrated workers who have much more formal education than is demanded by the jobs they are able to find. The reality here is recognizing that education, as such, is no longer a meal ticket but instead valuable for its own sake.

ENVIRONMENT AND JOB SATISFACTION

Employee job satisfaction is affected by where employees live and work. For example, Katzell, Barrett, and Parker found that employees' attitudes and behavior in 72 geographically dispersed warehouses were influenced by situational characteristics.[42] Using five situational variables — community size, number of employees in the division, union representation, average wage rate, and proportion of employees who were male — they found a small-town versus an urban cultural pattern. Employees in areas with the small-town cultural pattern were characterized by greater job satisfaction and productivity. While the correlations were modest, ranging from 0.21 to 0.32, they were consistent in showing the positive influence of the small-town cultural pattern.

Employees are influenced by their environmental frames of reference. For example, equally paid workers in communities where the cost of living is high are not as satisfied with their pay as are those in communities where the cost of living is lower.

Job attitudes are moderated both by the preferences people have for elements in their job situation and by the surrounding community environment. Women, for example, tend to prefer different job characteristics from men, and the standards people use for judging various aspects of their work environment are conditioned by the surrounding environment in the community.[39]

The Organization and Job Satisfaction

An employee's job satisfaction is likely to be strongly affected by his or her organization. For example, management policy is likely to affect worker satisfaction. Thus, workers are more satisfied with their jobs if they perceive policies that "get the organization moving" without managerial hindrance or busy work.[27] Again, we know that line managers (those directly supervising others in the chain of command) are likely to be more satisfied than staff managers.

More will be said about this in the next chapter.

PERSONALITY, MENTAL HEALTH, AND JOB SATISFACTION

Job and Life Satisfaction

There is fairly clear evidence that the job satisfaction expressed by employees is related to their satisfaction with life in general. Moreover, usually those who are less satisfied with their jobs are also those whose adjustment tends to be lower than normal. Dissatisfied workers have poorer personal relationships and more serious symptoms. They tend to be less outgoing and more discontented with their personal adjustment.[35] This, of course, is not to imply that all those who are dissatisfied with their jobs are emotionally maladjusted. In attempting to explain these findings, we can see how adults at work are products of their childhood experiences. Those who make a better adjustment to family life as children also make more satisfactory adjustment to work situations.[28]

JOB AS COMPENSATION? It is a popular but untrue conception that people who are unhappy with life in general compensate by seeking more satisfaction from their jobs. They "bury themselves in their work." The correlational data do not support this "compensatory" view of job and life satisfaction. On the contrary, the evidence supports a "spillover" of job to life satisfaction and vice versa.[45]

Clarification of what is cause and what is effect was sought by surveying two groups of supervisors. One group was in a good job setting; the other group was in a poor one. The supervisors in the good situation reported more satisfaction from all aspects of their job.

The most interesting aspect of the study was the relationship between the importance of job elements to the supervisors and their life satisfaction. The correlations are shown in Table 4–5.

Supervisors in a poor job situation, providing little job satisfaction, who believed facets of the job such as "work" were important to overall job satisfaction tended to have low life satisfaction. Conversely, supervisors in a good job situation who felt that the various facets of the job were important had greater life satisfaction. In a poor job situation it appears to be healthy to downgrade the importance of the job.[40]

Mental Health and Job Level

The myth persists that anxiety and stress are highest among executives and salespersons living in a world of overwhelming pressure and that it is lowest among those in blue-collar work. The facts are just the opposite, according to a thorough study of stress among different kinds of work groups.[32,41] Over 1,000 individuals in different kinds of work were asked to describe on a personality scale of how anxiety-ridden they were. Figure 4–9 displays the results. The hourly industrial laborers and the

Table 4–5. Correlation between importance of job elements and life satisfaction for two groups of supervisors

	Life Satisfaction	
Importance of	For supervisors in poor job situations	For supervisors in good job situations
Promotions	−0.53	0.18
Co-workers	−0.24	0.03
Supervision	−0.39	0.22
Pay	−0.11	0.17
Work	−0.52	0.59

From Iris and Barrett, "Some Relations between Job and Life Satisfaction—and Job Importance," *Journal of Applied Psychology*, 56 (1972): 302.

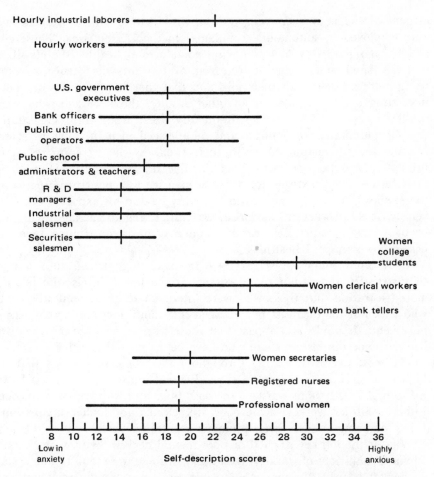

Figure 4–9. Middle 50 per cent of the distributions of selected job groups on self-decription of being anxiety-ridden. (Reprinted by permission of the publisher from *The Motivated Working Adult.* p. 78, by R. C. Hackman, © 1969, by the American Management Association, Inc. All rights reserved)

hourly wage-earning workers reported more anxiety; the salesmen and managers reported less. The pattern is the same for women. Clerical workers and bank tellers reported more anxiety; registered nurses and professional women reported less.

A Summary Survey: Mental Health and Job Satisfaction

Over 400 workers were interviewed by Kornhauser concerning the work they did and the satisfaction they gained from both their work and life in general.[45] The workers ranged from unskilled to skilled workers and were employed by automobile companies in the Detroit area. Those employees who were classified as having good mental health (the classification was based on an index derived from over 40 interview items) reported being more satisfied with their jobs and that they found their work both interesting and enjoyable. As in other studies, those workers who were satisfied with their jobs were less frequently absent from work. The sample was dichotomized into younger and middle-aged men in order to reveal possible age interactions. Men in their twenties who were interested in promotion had positive mental health. The reverse was true for men in their forties. It seemed that for a young man it was a positive virtue to try to get ahead, because there was some reality base to his expectations. Conversely, if the worker in his forties was still trying to get ahead, his was probably an unrealistic expectation and may have contributed to or reflected lower mental health.

As is often found in scales used in psychology to measure human characteristics, it was not those workers at the lowest levels who felt the most frustration, but those who were intermediate or in semiskilled jobs who felt most the inconsistency between their ambitions and actual accomplishments. It would also appear that those workers who are most realistic in their expectations are those who have better mental health.

The most pervasive finding throughout the whole survey was that the higher the occupational level of the individual (on the average), the better his mental health. This was true for both blue- and white-collar employees. Either healthier workers achieve or are selected for higher occupational levels, or being at such levels promotes mental well-being.

What is the job key to good or poor mental health? Security on the job? Physical conditions of work? Wages? None of these were found to be related to mental health. But one job attitude was very strongly related to the mental health of workers at all occupational levels: workers' perceptions that their abilities were not being used. For example, of the middle-aged workers in the lower-level jobs who said that the work did not use their abilities, 53 per cent had low mental health scores. In contrast, only 18 per cent in the same jobs who said that their abilities were being used had low mental health scores. In other words, mental health is associated with the belief that one's potential is being used. This idea relates to a number of theories concerning workers' desires to experience self-realization or self-actualization, which we have discussed.

While wages, as such, were relatively unimportant to mental health, the perception of being in an economic pinch did have a relationship with mental health for the middle-aged workers, but not for the younger workers. In the lower-skilled grades, income satisfaction was related to mental health, and those who were dissatisfied with their income had poorer mental health. In summary, the strongest job influence on mental health was whether employees had a chance to use their best abilities. When they felt they didn't, this feeling was related to poor mental health. Somewhat surprising was the finding that job monotony and repetition did not relate to poor mental health. Such working conditions played only a minor role in the poor mental health of the workers at lower occupational levels.

Social critics often paint a bleak picture about factory work. In fact, taken as a whole, workers are neither overjoyed about work nor bitter about their jobs. In the Kornhauser study, the 400 workers were asked how they felt about their jobs, and 58 per cent of the young men and 78 per cent of the middle-aged men said they were completely satisfied or well satisfied. Only 17 per cent of the young and 1 per cent of the middle-aged gave a clearly negative response, saying they were very dissatisfied. Of course, we have to remember that most of middle-aged factory workers usually have little expectation of ever having a job other than their current one. They realistically know that this is their position in life until they retire. So for them to say they are still dissatified with what they are doing would be in effect saying that they are failures in their life's work — an admission that would be painful for them.

There is also a selection factor operating. Those younger men who intensely dislike the work leave the factory, while those who are more satisfied stay on the job. But, nevertheless, those young and middle-aged workers who do admit to being dissatisfied with their work also reveal the poorest mental health.

On the whole, most people report being satisfied with their jobs, but the answers to another question give us a different perspective on the problem. Workers were asked whether, if they had a chance to start over again, they would choose the same type of work they are now in or a different type of work. Almost 80 per cent of the young and the middle-aged workers who were in the semiskilled category said they would choose a different type of work if they had a choice. Approximately 50 per cent of the skilled said they would choose a different type of work. While the majority of workers may now express satisfaction with their jobs, if they had a choice they would choose a different line of work. Coupled with responses from samples of professionals (most of whom report they would choose the same work again), we see that a more accurate inference is that most factory workers would rather be doing something else but, seeing no real opportunities to do so, report satisfaction with their lot.

SUMMARY

To get a true picture of how employees feel about their work requires asking them many questions in many different ways about many different facets of their work: pay, supervision, co-workers, job challenge and opportunities, company or agency policies, and so on. Concentration on effective salaries and payment plans is not enough. Social forces and personal characteristics also have important influences on job satisfaction and attitudes toward productivity.

REFERENCES

1. Aronson, E., and J. Mills. "The Effect of Severity of Initiation on Liking for a Group," *Journal of Abnormal and Social Psychology*, 59 (1959): 177–181.
2. Babchuk, N., and W. J. Goode. "Work Incentives in a Self-Determining Group," *American Sociological Review*, 16 (1951): 679–687.
3. Barrett, G. V., B. Svetlik, and E. P. Prien. "Validity of the Job-Concept Interview in an Industrial Setting," *Journal of Applied Psychology*, 51 (1967): 233–235.
4. Bass, B. M. "Social and Industrial Psychology: 2000 B.C.–400 B.C.," *American Psychologist*, 13 (1958): 78–79.
5. Bensman, J., and I. Gerver. "Crime and Punishment in the Factory: The Function of Deviancy in Maintaining the Social System," *American Sociological Review*, 28 (1963): 588–598.
6. Berkowitz, L. "Group Standards, Cohesiveness, and Productivity," *Human Relations*, 7 (1954): 509–519.
7. Berkowitz, L. "Group Norms among Bomber Crews: Patterns of Perceived Crew Attitudes, 'Actual' Crew Attitudes, and Crew Liking Related to Air Crew Effectiveness in Far Eastern Combat," *Sociometry*, 19 (1956): 141–153.
8. Blauner, R. "Work Satisfaction and Industrial Trends in Modern Society." In W. H. Hill and D. Egan (eds.), *Readings in Organizational Theory: A Behavioral Approach*. Boston: Allyn and Bacon, 1966.
9. Bohr, R. H., and A. B. Swertloff. "Work, Shift, Occupational Status, and the Perception of Job Prestige," *Journal of Applied Psychology*, 53 (1969): 227–229.
10. Bray, D. W., R. J. Campbell and D. C. Grant. *Formative Years in Business: A Long-term AT&T Study of Managerial Lives*. New York: John Wiley & Sons, 1974.
11. Brief, A. P., G. L. Rose, and R. J. Aldag. "Sex Differences in Preferences for Job Attributes Revisited," *Journal of Applied Psychology*, 62 (1977): 645–646.
12. Campbell, H. "Group Incentive Payment Schemes: The Effects of Lack of Understanding and of Group Size," *Occupational Psychology*, 26 (1952): 15–21.
13. Carlson, R. E. "Degree of Job Fit as a Moderator of the Relationship between Job Performance and Job Satisfaction," *Personnel Psychology*, 22 (1969): 159–170.
14. Carroll, S. J., and H. L. Tosi. "Goal Characteristics and Personality Factors in a Management by Objectives Program," *Administrative Science Quarterly*, 15 (1970): 295–305.
15. Centers, R., and D. E. Bugental. "Intrinsic and Extrinsic Job Motivations among Different Segments of the Working Population," *Journal of Applied Psychology*, 50 (1966): 193–197.
16. Coch, L., and J. R. P. French, Jr. "Overcoming Resistance to Change," *Human Relations*, 1 (1948): 512–532.

17. Danzig, E. R., and E. H. Galanter. "The Dynamics and Structure of Small Industrial Work Groups," Institute Report no. 7. Philadelphia: Institute of Research in Human Relations, 1955.
18. Diamond, R. S. "What Business Thinks," *Fortune* (December, 1969): 115–116.
19. Dubin, R., J. E. Champoux, and J. T. Stampfl. *Individual-Organizational Linkages*. Technical Report no. 17, ONR Contract N00014–69–A–0200–9001, University of California, Irvine, July, 1973.
20. Dyer, L., and R. Theriault. "The Determinants of Pay Satisfaction," *Journal of Applied Psychology*, 61 (1976): 596–604.
21. Erickson, J. M., W. M. Pugh, and E. K. E. Gunderson. "Status Congruency as a Predictor of Job Satisfaction and Life Stress," *Journal of Applied Psychology*, 56 (1972): 523–525.
22. Evans, C. E., and L. N. Laseau. "My Job Contest—An Experiment in New Employee Relations Methods," *Personnel Psychology*, 2 (1949): 1–16.
23. Freeman, R. B. *Carnegie Commission Report*, 1977.
24. French, J. R. P., Jr., I. C. Ross, S. Kirby, J. R. Nelson, and P. Smyth. "Employee Participation in a Program of Industrial Change," *Personnel*, 35 (1958): 16–29.
25. French, J. R. P., Jr., J. Israel, and D. Ås. "An Experiment on Participation in a Norwegian Factory: Interpersonal Dimensions of Decision-Making," *Human Relations*, 13 (1960): 3–19.
26. Friedlander, F. "Motivations to Work and Organizational Performance," *Journal of Applied Psychology*, 50 (1966): 143–152.
27. Friedlander, F., and N. Margulies. "Multiple Impacts of Organizational Climate and Individual Value Systems upon Job Satisfaction," *Personnel Psychology*, 22 (1969): 171–183.
28. Friend, J. G., and E. A. Haggard. "Work Adjustment in Relation to Family Background," *Applied Psychological Monograph*, 1948, p. 16.
29. Fuller, C. "Effect of Anonymity on Return Rate and Response Bias in a Mail Survey," *Journal of Applied Psychology*, 59 (1974): 292–296.
30. Gallup, G. *Congressional Record*, April 30, 1973.
31. Greatbatch, W. "Attitude as a function of craftsmanship." Unpublished report, University of Rochester, Rochester, New York, 1977.
32. Hackman, R. C. *The Motivated Working Adult*. New York: American Management Association, 1969.
33. Hall, D. T., and K. E. Nougaim. "An Examination of Maslow's Need Hierarchy in an Organizational Setting," *Organization, Behavior and Human Performance*, 3 (1968): 12–35.
34. Hammond, K. R. "Measuring Attitudes by Error-Choice: An Indirect Method," *Journal of Abnormal and Social Psychology*, 43 (1948): 38–48.
35. Herzberg, F., B. Mausner, R. Peterson, and D. F. Capwell. *Job Attitudes: Review of Research and Opinion*. Pittsburgh: Psychological Service of Pittsburgh, 1957.
36. Hickson, D. J. "Worker Choice of Payment System," *Occupational Psychology*, 37 (1963): 93–100.
37. Hinrichs, J. R. "Measurement of Reasons for Resignation of Professionals: Questionnaire versus Company and Consultant Exit Interviews," *Journal of Applied Psychology*, 60 (1975): 530–532.

38. Homans, G. C. "The Western Electric Researches." In S. D. Hoslett (ed.), *Human Factors in Management.* New York: Harper & Brothers, 1951, pp. 152–185.

39. Hulin, C. L. "Sources of Variation in Job and Life Satisfaction: The Role of Community and Job-Related Variables," *Journal of Applied Psychology,* 53 (1969): 279–291.

40. Iris, B., and G. V. Barrett. "Some Relations between Job and Life Satisfaction and Job Importance," *Journal of Applied Psychology,* 56 (1972): 301–304.

41. Kahn, R., D. M. Wolfe, R. P. Quinn, J. D. Snock, and R. A. Rosenthal. *Organizational Stress: Studies in Role Conflict and Ambiguity.* New York: John Wiley & Sons, 1964.

42. Katzell, R. A., R. S. Barrett, and T. C. Parker. "Job Satisfaction, Job Performance, and Situational Characteristics," *Journal of Applied Psychology,* 45 (1961): 65–72.

43. Kavanagh, M. J., and A. Lowin. "The Relationship between Status and Satisfaction in Industrial Work Groups," *Experimental Publications System,* 1 (1969): Ms. 012A.

44. Kelman, H. C. "Effects of Success and Failure on 'Suggestibility' in the Autokinetic Situation," *Journal of Abnormal and Social Psychology,* 45 (1950): 267–285.

45. Kornhauser, A. *Mental Health of the Industrial Worker.* New York: John Wiley & Sons, 1965.

46. Lawler, E. E. "Ability as a Moderator of the Relationship between Job Attitudes and Job Performance," *Personnel Psychology,* 19 (1966): 153–164.

47. Lawler, E. E., III. *Pay and Organizational Effectiveness: A Psychological View.* New York: McGraw-Hill, 1971.

48. Lefkowitz, J., and M. L. Katz. "Validity of Exit Interviews," *Personnel Psychology,* 22 (1969): 445–455.

49. Levine, J., and J. Butler. "Lecture versus Group Decision in Changing Behavior," *Journal of Applied Psychology,* 36 (1952): 29–33.

50. Likert, R. A. "A Technique for the Measure of Attitudes," *Archives of Psychology,* 140 (1932): 1–55.

51. Lincoln, J. F. *Lincoln's Incentive System.* New York: McGraw-Hill, 1946.

52. Locke, E. A. "Satisfiers and Dissatisfiers among White-Collar and Blue-Collar Employees," *Journal of Applied Psychology,* 58 (1973): 67–76.

53. Lodahl, T. M., and M. Kejner. "The Definition and Measurement of Job Involvement," *Journal of Applied Psychology,* 49 (1965): 24–33.

54. Milgrim, S. "Nationality and Conformity," *Scientific American,* 205, no. 6 (1961): 45–51.

55. Mukherjee, B. N. "Interrelationships among Measures of Job Satisfaction and Job Involvement," *Experimental Publication System,* 1 (1969): Ms. no. 036A.

56. Myers, M. S. "Who Are Your Motivated Workers?" *Harvard Business Review,* 42, no. 1 (1964): 73–88.

57. Nealey, S. "Pay and Benefit Preferences," *Industrial Relations,* 1 (1963): 17–28.

58. Nealey, S. M., and J. G. Goodale. "Worker Preferences among Time-Off Benefits and Pay," *Journal of Applied Psychology,* 51 (1967): 357–361.

59. Opsahl, A. L., and M. D. Dunnette. "The Role of Financial Compensation," *Psychological Bulletin,* 66 (1966): 94–118.

60. Porter, L. W. "Job Attitudes in Management: I. Perceived Deficiencies in Need Fulfillment as a Function of Job Level," *Journal of Applied Psychology*, 46 (1962): 375–384.

61. Puckett, E. S. "Productivity Achievements: A Measure of Success," In F. G. Lesieur (ed.), *The Scanlon Plan*. Cambridge: M.I.T. Press, 1958.

62. Quinn, R. P. and T. W. Mangione. Unpublished report, Survey Research Center, University of Michigan, 1973.

63. Roach, D. E., and R. R. Davis. "Stability of the Structure of Employee Attitudes: An Empirical Test of Factor Invariance," *Journal of Applied Psychology*, 58 (1973): 181–185.

64. Rodgers, W. and J. M. Hammersley. "The Consistency of Stop-Watch Time-Study Practitioners." *Occupational Psychology* 28 (1954): 61–76.

65. Ronan, W. W. "Industrial and Situational Variables Relating to Job Satisfaction." *Journal of Applied Psychology Monograph* 54, no. 1, part 2, 1970.

66. Rothe, H. F., and C. T. Nye. "Output Rates among Coil Winders," *Journal of Applied Psychology*, 42 (1958): 182–186.

67. Rothe, H. F., and C. T. Nye. "Output Rates among Machine Operators: II. Consistency Related to Methods of Pay," *Journal of Applied Psychology*, 43 (1959): 417–420.

68. Ruh, R. A., J. K. White, and R. R. Wood. "Job Involvement, Values, Personal Background, Participation in Decision Making, and Job Attitudes," *Academy of Management Journal*, 18 (1975): 300–312.

69. Saleh, S. D., and J. L. Otis. "Age and Level of Job Satisfaction," *Personnel Psychology*, 17 (1964): 425–430.

70. Saleh, S. D., and J. Hosek. "Job Involvement: Concepts and Measurements," *Academy of Management Journal*, 19 (1976): 213–224.

71. Schwab, D. P., and L. D. Dyer. "The Motivational Impact of a Compensation System on Employee Performance," *Organizational Behavior and Human Performance*, 9 (1973): 215–225.

72. Seashore, S. E. *Group Cohesiveness in the Industrial Work Group*. Ann Arbor: University of Michigan, 1954.

73. Shimmin, S. "Workers' Understanding of Incentive Payment Systems," *Occupational Psychology*, 32 (1958): 106–110.

74. Siegel, A. L., and R. A. Ruh. "Job Involvement, Participation in Decision Making, Personal Background and Job Behavior," *Organizational Behavior and Human Performance*, 9 (1973): 318–327.

75. Smith, P. C., L. M. Kendall, and C. L. Hulin. *The Measurement of Satisfaction in Work and Retirement*. Chicago: Rand-McNally, 1969.

76. Stagner, R., "Boredom on the Assembly Line: Age and Personality Variables." *Industrial Gerontology*, 2 (1975): 23–44.

77. Steers, R. M. "Task-Goal Attributes, in Achievement, and Supervisory Performance," *Organizational Behavior and Human Performance*, 13 (1975): 392–403.

78. Transnational Programs Corporation, Employee Attitude Survey, Scottsville, New York, 1976.

79. Van Zelst, R. H. "Sociometrically Selected Work Teams Increase Production," *Personnel Psychology*, 5 (1952): 175–185.

80. Vroom, V. H. *Some Personality Determinants of the Effects of Participation*. Englewood Cliffs, New Jersey: Prentice-Hall, 1960.

81. Weaver, C. N. "Black-White Differences in Attitudes toward Job Character-istics," *Journal of Applied Psychology*, 60 (1975): 438–441.

82. Webb, S. C. "Scaling of Attitudes by Method of Equal-Appearing Inter-vals: A Review," *Journal of Social Psychology*, 42 (1955): 215–239.

83. Weiss, D. J., R. D. Dawis, G. W. England, and L. H. Lofquist. *Minnesota Studies in Vocational Rehabilitation: 22nd Manual for the Minnesota Satis-faction Questionnaire*. Minneapolis: University of Minnesota, 1967.

84. Weissenberg, P., and L. W. Gruenfeld. "Relationship between Job Satisfac-tion and Job Involvement," *Journal of Applied Psychology*, 52 (1968): 469–473.

85. Weitz, J., and R. C. Nuckols. "The Validity of Direct and Indirect Questions in Measuring Job Satisfaction," *Personnel Psychology*, 6 (1953): 487–494.

86. Wernimont, P. F., and S. Fitzpatrick. "The Meaning of Money," *Journal of Applied Psychology*, 56 (1972): 218–226.

87. Whyte, W. F. *Money and Motivation*. New York: Harper, 1955.

88. Yankelovich, D. *The New Morality:A Profile of American Youth in the 70's*. New York: McGraw-Hill, 1974.

89. Zaleznik, A., C. R. Christensen, and F. J. Roethlisberger. *The Motivation, Productivity, and Satisfaction of Workers*. Cambridge: Harvard University Press, 1958.

5 ORGANIZATION OF WORK

IN BRIEF   More has been written with less evidence about organization than about perhaps any other field of human endeavor except theology. Five themes have come down through the centuries: how to organize work, how to deal with money, how to make management rational, how to deal with socioemotional humans, and how to study organization. Current theories emphasize objectives, systems, and the limits on rationality.

As people begin to work in groups, it becomes advantageous to divide the labor so that each specializes in only one part of the task. However, there are many potential costs as well, particularly when planning a job is separated from carrying it out.

If work is divided, coordination must be introduced among the workers. Predictability and accountability are increased by formal coordinating rules. The structure becomes more complex as a consequence of technological requirements and organizational climate, but we seem better able to describe organizational effects than to prescribe organizational arrangements.

We move now from examining the individual's attitudes and performance at work within an organization to a detailed review of theory and research about the formal organization itself — the functions it fulfills, the assumptions on which it is predicated, the reasons for formalizing relationships within the organization, and the consequences of formalization for the organization's climate.

141

FULFILLING THE NEED FOR PREDICTABILITY AND REDUCED UNCERTAINTY

When tasks are to be completed, services to be rendered, policies to be established, decisions to be made, or people and property to be protected, organization is necessary. Where the actions may involve the efforts of people using money, equipment, materials, information, access to markets and facilities, organization is equally necessary. Why? Because organization reduces the uncertainty about the needed performance of the people, money, and equipment. When two or more people work together to achieve some common purpose, the speed and accuracy of their joint performance depends considerably on how well each can predict what the other will do — how *certain* each is about the other's forthcoming performance. They are temporarily organized to some degree in their efforts if they can predict rather than guess what each will do. Two auto drivers approaching each other from opposite directions are temporarily organized in the sense that they can predict with considerable accuracy (and hope) that they will pass each other and remain on their own sides of the white center line of the road.

Some theorists focus on organizations that provide *certainty* by assuming that the decision-making members have complete and accurate knowledge of the consequences that will follow each alternative. (Because the other driver is trained, rational, obeys the rules, and wants to avoid accidents just as I do, I feel certain that the driver approaching me will pass me safely.) To be organized means to behave rationally with full knowledge of the rules required to do so.

Other theorists concentrate on *risk preference* by assuming accurate knowledge of the risks of alternatives. I know that 99.99 per cent of drivers will behave as I expect if I continue on as before. To be organized means that I make descisions based on my knowing my risks if I take particular actions. I am in a hurry. I may judge that the probabilities are very high that the driver in the car approaching me on a two-lane highway will maintain a steady speed. I'll take a bigger risk for a bigger payoff if I am a risk-taker by nature. I'll decide to pass with less tolerance the more I am in a hurry and the greater my preference for risk (or my lack of preference to avoid risk).

Still other theorists pursue a *doctrine of uncertainty*. My rationality must be limited. I cannot know fully what is in the mind of the other driver or whether one of the other car's front wheels might suddenly fall off. The other driver and I are dealing with each other as a temporary two-person organization. Although I can never be certain about the other driver, our temporary organization helps to reduce my uncertainty.

THE PRERATIONAL WORLD

How people worked together in the traditional, prerational world (and how they still do in many nonindustrialized societies) was strongly associated with ritualistic ways of relating to each other, where the outcome of work might not be as important as the specific way each person behaved. People did what was expected of them as a consequence of their relatives' status, their family connections, age, sex, or clan identification. Among the Incan peoples of Peru, work itself became what we would describe as a form of religious worship. Today, in Nigeria, it is still very difficult to introduce merit ratings, since this would require evaluating subordinates according to their actual performance, not their tribal identification.

The prerational approach to organized work emphasizes status deference and doing things in particular ways. Ignored are costs and accomplishments. There is little concern for planning, time requirements, and searching for better ways to attain objectives by improving the method of attainment. However, work is rewarding in its own right. Working relations between people have importance without reference to the contribution of the relations to costs or accomplishments.

BEGINNINGS OF RATIONAL INDUSTRIALIZATION

Medieval Europe already was the site of considerable rationality of industrial organization. An outstanding example was the arsenal at Venice for constructing and outfitting warships, which still stands. Double-entry bookkeeping emerged in early Renaissance Italy and was common practice in the world of business and commerce by 1800. About this time, James Watt (of steam-engine fame) introduced cost accounting into factory management. Thinking about how to organize has evolved slowly over the past 500 years in five parallel themes: work, money, scientific management, socioemotionality, and organizations as subjects of inquiry.

ON WORK   A thread of rational, deductive thinking and writing about work can be traced from Leonardo da Vinci's notebooks onward. In the 300 years between Leonardo da Vinci and Eli Whitney (who originated the mass production of equipment and the interchangeability of component parts in rifle manufacture), rational questions about work such as timing of operations, improving worker performance, production methods, costs and profits, and what a person could do in a day were subjects of letters, articles, and books.

ON MONEY   A second historical thread of ideas dealt with business and money. The commercial and industrial revolutions were seen by those who espoused a materialistic or economic determination of history to be built on money as the prime motivator and the accumulation of capital as the basis of how society develops. Arguments varied from almost pure propaganda to mathematical elegance of explanation. Economists and social philosophers as different in ideology as Adam Smith (free enterprise under conditions of perfect competition) and Karl Marx (business is the exploitation of the surplus created by labor) shared in common the assumption that business management was motivated primarily by the self-interested acquisition of material goods and the maximization of profits. Smith and Marx differed in that this assumed behavior was good for society according to Smith and evil according to Marx. These lines remain drawn today, but the free enterprisers and socialists continue to share in common a belief in economic determinism. Furthermore, they have moved closer to each other in ideology about the importance of profits to enterprise and of incentive payments to workers. Both share a deductive approach to understanding based on assumptions about people that are convenient but not necessarily valid. These include such empirically questionable axioms as the assertion that workers innately dislike work and are motivated mainly by money, material benefits, and the need for security. Money is the cement for building reliability and predictability in the continuing relations among people at work.

ON SCIENTIFIC MANAGEMENT   A third theme in the history of ideas about organization centered around scientific management. Adam Smith's discussion in *The Wealth of Nations* in 1776 of the division of labor in the pin factory was well known to early factory managers; they adopted what they regarded as highly rational procedures for organizing the work efforts under their control. Division of labor became widely practiced in the Soho foundry managed by James Watt in the 1790s. Careful consideration was given by Watt to plant layout, departmentalization, planning, and the control of material flow.[47]

Extensive production recording and rudimentary time study were used at the Soho foundry along with piece-rate incentive payments (which in 1791 were responsible for a strike). With reference to the rationalization of work, Frederick W. Taylor, like Newton, stood on the shoulders of many giants (Smith, Bentham, Watt, Babbage, and Jevons), only unlike Newton, he preferred not to acknowledge them.[23] Moreover, many of Taylor's reported studies have been found to be more fiction than fact. He seems to have made up much of his data as he went along.[62]

Nevertheless, from the late nineteenth century onward, out of the practice and observation of Taylor and others (including Henry Fayol, L. F. Urwick, J. D. Mooney, and R. C. Davis), came a series of propositions based on a mixture of wisdom, experience, and what passed for logical deduction about how to rationalize the workplace and the working environment. To the assumptions held by the economic determinists about people's inherent dislike for work and the prime importance of money as a motivator were added assumptions that workers have to be coerced into attaining what they are capable of doing, that they lack initiative or willingness to accept responsibility, that they are unable and unwilling to plan ahead, and that they are likely to make errors they would not be able to correct. Like the economic determinists, these proponents of scientific management provided *normative prescriptions* — the one best way — usually about how to maximize productivity. Their advice on how to organize to maximize operational efficiency has evolved into a variety of exhortations about the effective planning, direction, and control of work of others. Axiomatic for them are such propositions as the following:

1. *Scalar principle.* Persons should know who reports to them and to whom they report. Authority and responsibility should flow in a clear unbroken line from the top to the bottom of the hierarchy. Authority to make decisions should be commensurate with responsibility for those decisions. Moreover, authority should be delegated so that decisions take place as close as possible to the point of action.
2. *Unity of command.* No one should receive orders from more than one superior. Responsibility for specific areas should not be duplicated or overlapping.
3. *Exception principle.* Recurring decisions should be programmed, routinized, and delegated downward to subordinates. Only non-recurring issues should be referred to superiors.
4. *Span of control.* There is some maximum number of subordinates who can be supervised (classicists debate whether it is three to five or five to seven at higher levels in the organization, whether one can be available for discussion with many more subordinates, etc.).
5. *Specialization.* Labor should be divided so that common activities are meaningfully clustered into one job or one department; unrelated activities should be grouped elsewhere. No one position should have too numerous or complex duties.
6. *Clarity of responsibilities.* Responsibilities should be written clearly and understood by job occupants.

We are beginning to see empirical research on the validity of these principles. For example, several surveys show that violation of the principle of unity of command generally leads to role conflict, employee dissatisfaction, and ineffective performance, particularly in a bureaucratic organization. Thus, 123 managers in a government bureaucracy who reported to two or more superiors were more likely to find difficulties with their organization than 181 managers who reported to a single superior Those who reported to two or more superiors were more likely to say that employee selection is not based on ability in their organization, that role conflict and pressure are high, and that there is need for more coordination and delegation.[21]

ON SOCIOEMOTIONALITY   A fourth stream of ideas about how to operate organizations effectively dealt with socioemotional elements in people. Two opposing tendencies could be discerned. On the one hand, as in Machiavelli's advice to the Prince, emphasis was laid on political approaches to directing and controlling an organization by maintaining social distance, withholding information, diversionary tactics, bluffing, and the like. People are inherently evil and need the strong imposition of rules and order to do good. Mutual predictability and organizational reliability require manipulation, "managing the news," promises of payoff for reliability, persuasion with extrinsic rewards, and veiled threats to unleash punishment.[3]

Dale Carnegie's *How to Win Friends and Influence People* was in this tradition.[11] First, Carnegie advocated giving support and approval to the target of one's persuasive attempts, then asking the person to change to avoid losing one's support and warmth. While such a manipulative approach is practiced, in fact, by many managers,[40] surveys of middle managers and students here and abroad suggest relatively low espousal of such political, manipulative methods as effective management styles.[4]

The opposite view was advanced by Ralph Waldo Emerson, John Dewey, Thomas Jefferson, and Robert Owen, as well as by the nineteenth-century anarchists. They saw people as inherently good and believed that if people were freed from the constraints of arbitrary maladaptive rules and orders and allowed to participate in matters affecting themselves through consultation, group discussion, open communication, and shared decision making, they would be highly motivated to do their best, would be most stimulated into creative accomplishment, and would be willing and able to accept responsibility for directing and controlling their own actions.[4] With these positive assumptions about people, it follows that mutual predictability and organizational reliability accrue from the participation, involvement, and understanding by its members of an organization's methods and objectives. Successful operation requires authentic communication between members, striving for consensus and commitment.

The "human relations movement," the modern proponents of this viewpoint, began with the observations by Elton Mayo and his associates of the effects on productivity of supervisors' interest in workers' morale, personal needs, and attitudes. This was in comparison with the effects of improving lighting, opportunities for rest, or work methods. We have already discussed the lengthy studies of Mayo and others at the Hawthorne Works of the Western Electric Company in the mid-1920s. The worker's primary group, the informal organization, was seen as most significant for understanding employee performance. The contribution of Kurt Lewin and his students was in this tradition, starting with emphasis on the greater efficacy of democratic over authoritarian and laissez-faire leadership in a controlled experiment with boys' clubs.[31] Along with Leland Bradford and Kenneth Benne, they began to evolve techniques and principles of process via observations of small-group interactions, feedback, and sensitivity training, which in one form or another has become a common approach to management and organizational development — particularly as it has been modified for widespread industrial use.[7] (We will discuss these approaches in Chapter 14.) Most prominent in recent years, Douglas McGregor pushed for the participative type of management, based on a "theory Y" that says that workers are self-starting, responsible, and self-controlling, rather than the "theory X" that workers are lazy, irresponsible, and in need of authoritarian direction and control.[43] Summarizing much survey research, Rensis Likert argued for overlapping groups of organizational members at different succeeding levels so that each manager is a linking pin member of two groups — one with his/her boss and his/her peers, the other with his/her subordinates and himself/herself.[32] Chris Argyris emphasized the need for the organization to become more integrated with the needs of its individual members.[1] Warren Bennis saw the need for organizations of temporary functional teams in lieu of highly structured bureaucracies.[6]

Closely associated with this "people" approach are theorists like Whyte and Homans, who focused on the interconnecting roles people play in organizations, how these roles are learned, how expectations, attitudes, feelings, norms, and perceptions are built up about them that result in conflict or coordination.[24,59]

ON ORGANIZATIONS AS SUBJECTS OF INQUIRY   A fifth line of thought about organizations is sociological and philosophical. As March pointed out, ". . . there is scarcely a major philosopher, historian or biographer who has overlooked the management and perversities of organizations."[38]

On the basis of observations of labor unions and political movements, Michels, a sociologist, formulated an "iron law" of oligarchy, which said that because of the desire by the "incompetent" members for strong leadership in any organization, a continuing proliferation of departments, branches, and roles would occur.[45] In describing the Prussian bureaucracy, Weber in the same sociological framework, emphasized the functionality and utility of the high degree of structuring found in such an organizational form.[58] Such bureaucratic and oligarchic structures were seen by him to provide a reduction in potential uncertainty and an increase in predictability in relations between people who must work together. Building on this rationale, Merton saw this demand for reliability in formal organizations as stemming from the sponsors of the work effort, the owners of a business or the directors of a public agency.[44] This emphasis on relia-bility makes each individual strive to follow the rules laid down for him/her. Personal relations are minimized, and individuals avoid responsibility for their own actions (they are fully programmed; they are only following orders). There is increased use of categorization as a decision-making pro-cedure (once you can locate the category in which a problem can be placed, the rule to be applied is automatically given). Maintaining and understanding the organization of formal roles, prescriptions, categories, and rules become more important than accomplishing task objectives. The rigidity of behavior produces conflicts with the external world of suppliers, customers, and clients, but insiders rush to one another's defense, building in-group status symbols to coerce or persuade each other about the adequacy of their approach, thus minimizing uncertainty inside the organization.[39]

Continuing in this vein today are analysts who look at the structure of each of many organizations in a search for underlying dimensions to describe how such organizations differ from one another. They examine the effects of such formal aspects as size, shape, span of control, degree of hierarchy, spatial dispersion, and other aspects of organization likely to be related. Many present-day structuralists measure such differences among organizations, then factor-analyze the results to determine the minimum number of dimensions required to describe variations among organiza-tions as entities. For example, Pugh, Hickson, et al. completed such an analysis of fifty-two work organizations in Great Britain and uncovered fac-tors such as the amount of the organizations' formalized activities, the extent to which authority was concentrated, line versus staff, personal versus impersonal control of flow, and the extent to which support services were available.[49]

Shortcomings of Preceding Approaches

Considerable criticism has been leveled at each of the five approaches because of their simplistic assumptions about people, the marketplace, or the consequences of the work to be done. The limited static views of the *economic* and *scientific management* theorists about people and organi-zations were built on assumptions about human behavior that often were no more than legalistic or ethical hopes. For example, they assumed that once employment was accepted, people could and would fully complete all the terms of their contractual obligations if the organization's goals and job responsibilities were clear.[30] This assumption was based on the premise that people are completely rational. Furthermore, they assumed that organization dynamics linking machines in a coordinated effort could as well be applied to link people and machines. Thus, the simpler the job assignment for a worker, the more stable would be the output and the easier the task. They saw coordination and direction from on high through formal authority structures built on assumptions that people were irresponsible, lazy, and lacking in initiative.[42] Detailed guidance was required for cooperation and coordination. People worked primarily in exchange for money. Maximizing production or minimizing its cost was assumed to be the organization's only goal. Efficiency related to a mechanical process and the economic utilization of resources, without consideration of human factors. The important considerations in management were only those which involved individuals and groups of individuals heading logically toward their goals. Unless clear limits to jobs were defined and enforced, workers would tend to be confused and to trespass on the domains of others. The theorists further assumed that human beings prefer the security of a definite task and do not value the freedom of determining their own approaches to problems, that they prefer to be directed and will not cooperate unless a pattern is planned formally for them. The activities of a group should be viewed on an objective and impersonal basis without regard to personal problems and characteristics. Finally, in complete opposition to what we will detail in the next chapter, engineering and economic theorists assumed that managerial functions in varied types of activities have universal characteristics and can be performed in a given manner, regardless of the environment and qualities of the personnel involved.[41]

Another shortcoming of the economic and engineering theorists was their failure to generate verifiable propositions that could be tested experimentally. Most often, their propositions were collections of wisdom based on intuition, personal experiences, and methods varying in value; they often contained contradictory elements. For instance, workers were supposed to cooperate with each other, but such cooperation was a consequence of being ordered to do so by higher authority — an approach almost guaranteed to minimize rather than maximize cooperation. (Worse still, given powerful enough authority, surface cooperation can be forced, but the underlying hostility and resentment militating against full cooperation may be that much greater.)

The *sociological* approach could be criticized for its emphasis on organization survival as a main criterion of organizational success. Often analyses comparing organizations dealt with them as a series of black boxes, undifferentiated entities whose insides were unimportant compared with how they differed from one another on the outside. Another shortcoming lies in the data-gathering method of observing and recording organizations *in vivo* by participant observers or outside observers. Although sociologists were far more controlled and systematic than the "wisdom researchers" who generated the mass of economic and engineering propositions, premises, and proposals, still the biases of the sociological observer often strongly influenced the published accounts of organizational behavior.

The *socioemotional* theories of organization — what Leavitt calls "people" approaches — have their shortcomings also.[30] They often oversimplify the environment in which the organization must operate. The political manipulators have to avoid being caught in the act. Their credibility is directly dependent on their ability to simulate sincerity. Their opposites, the human relationists, have tended to ignore the external environment and the way in which it impinges on the behavior of those inside the system. The president of a manufacturing firm truly does have to meet a payroll and has overriding needs to be responsive to customers, clients, and stockholders. If the chief executive concentrates mainly on satisfying the needs of those inside the system — workers and managers — the firm may easily become sluggish in its response to the demands of the marketplace. The paint-spraying example discussed in Chapter 3 provides an excellent example of how an effort to apply understanding of human motivation in one department, a subunit of a larger system, failed because of factors outside the department that should have been taken into account.[59]

Leavitt sums up the shortcomings of "people" approaches, which emphasize the "human side of enterprise," shared decision making, collaboration of superiors, peers, and subordinates, openness and leveling, mutual goal setting, and participative management.[30] This approach tends to be pushed as universally applicable when in fact it may fail to be useful, as we will note in the next chapter, in situations where tasks are highly programmed, environments are constrained, and speed, quantity, and stability of output are at a premium. In addition, when different units in a system (say, management and workers) truly do not share aspirations and aims, when increased wages for workers mean reduced profits for management, then understanding of the situation is advanced by seeing it as a negotiation exercise, where the relative power and authority of the two parties will go far to explain what happens. If management accedes readily to worker demands for pay increases, a human relationist might see management as forward looking and trying to increase worker satisfaction with management. An analyst with more appreciation for political-manipulative approaches would suggest that management was acting weakly in the face of worker power and creating dangerous precedents for future bargaining. Both analysts might be partially correct in their interpretations, but neither would be likely to accept the other's analysis.

SOME CURRENT THEORIES OF ORGANIZATION

Today, efforts to understand the organization build on much of the work that has gone on in each of the earlier approaches just enumerated, despite the shortcomings we have noted. Indeed, current progress in the field has depended on our understanding of the strengths and weaknesses of earlier approaches. Thus, current thinking represents a shift of focus rather than a fundamentally new beginning.

For example, each of the earlier approaches yields one best way — a prescription for doing things — whereas current approaches tend to emphasize careful descriptions of the mix of people, money, and materials. Then understanding of how people actually behave in organizations flows from the careful descriptions. If the descriptions can be cast in terms of behavioral, mathematical, or economic concepts which are generally applicable, then descriptions of what happens in samples of organizations, units, or people can be summarized and used to see whether what is normative in the sample also occurs in the particular group under study, and, if not, what conditions of the organization, unit, or people under study are different from the sample.

Some of these newer approaches include emphasis on (1) management by objectives, (2) limited rationality, and (3) open systems analysis. Open systems analysis leads naturally into contingent approaches to hierarchical relations, which will be discussed more fully in the next chapter.

Management by Objectives

The formulation of Peter Drucker minimizes concepts and theory and is more prescriptive than other newer approaches to be discussed.[15] According to Drucker, managers live in a world of multiple objectives and their problem is how to make adequate judgments about these objectives, how to set them, and how to measure progress toward attaining the objectives sought. Rules are unimportant; it is performance in reaching stated goals that counts. Management by objectives involves (1) setting specific objectives for performance, (2) establishing ways of assessing managerial performance and development, and (3) challenging and stimulating employees to work toward the desired ends. Consistent with this approach, organizations are structured around the concept of profit centers (originated by GM's Alfred P. Sloan, Jr.). Each center within the larger organization is accountable for its own profits and losses. Attention of managers is focused directly on performance and results, permitting a much closer concern for and examination of costs and waste within units of the organization. The approach makes possible greater spans of control and more decentralization, since higher-level management can allow lower management more latitude as long as costs are in line and gains in attainments of objectives are met or surpassed. Lower-level managers have more opportunity to develop, as they are given greater opportunity within the constraints of stated objectives and profit expectations.[41]

SHORT- VS. LONG-TERM PROFIT PLANNING   A danger is that excessive short-run profits will be sought by the manager responsible for a profit center. The decision may be made to show a higher profit this year by cutting expenses for training. Then, next year when unit performance falls in quantity or quality, subsequently reducing long-term profitability, the manager hopes to have been promoted to a new unit. This danger can be avoided only by conceiving profits in the long term and taking into account the importance of other objectives including service, product quality, employee and management satisfaction, and so on. Methods for measuring each of these tangible and intangible aspects of performance have been suggested (human cost accounting) and it becomes quite possible to combine profit center notions with this broader concept of profit.[33] Furthermore, the need to provide for lag effects in assessing the contribution to profits of management policies and actions is beginning to be realized. There may be a lag of several years between the time some *causal* variable, some management decision, is made, and its subsequent effect on intervening changes in motivation and attitudes and on *end-result* variables such as productivity, costs, scrap, growth, market share, and earnings.

The lag is longer in larger organizations. It is longer in repetitive, highly engineered assembly operations than in sales and service industries. It is longer in more complex organizations when effects have to cross many layers and boundaries.[34]

Illustrative of the lag were results obtained in a continuous-process plant employing over 500 persons. No statistically significant relations were found among concurrent data from 40 departments on managerial performance, motivation of employees, and departmental productive efficiency. However, *current* managerial performance did correlate for the 40 departments between 0.48 and 0.58 with various measures of departmental productive efficiency *obtained one year later*. Again, while managerial performance showed *no immediate* relation with such intervening variables as worker motivation, communications, and coordination, correlations as high as 0.68 were obtained for the 40 departments between *current* managerial performance and departmental motivation, communications, and coordination *one year later*.

PERVASIVE USE   Management-by-objectives is now a widely accepted practice. Goal setting is effective in a variety of organizations and over extended periods of time.[27] Effects will depend on the complexity of the job, the interdependence among jobs and support by top management.[25]

And as we already noted in Chapter 3, MBO's effects will depend on whether the goals set are clear and challenging.

Behavioral Theory of the Firm: Rationality Is Limited

Dissatisfied with the economic theory of the firm that assumes that the firm is a single decision maker that maximizes profits under environmental constraints, Cyert and March propounded a behavioral theory that assumes that within the firm are many fallible decision makers.[13] Being human, they are subject to perceptual biases, unconscious motivations, forgetting, and lack of perfect knowledge about the marketplace, all of which lead to flows of decisions within the firm that need to be carefully observed, described, and explained. One cannot sit back and deduce the flow from pure logic without taking the humans into account, together with the situations in which they find themselves as they proceed to make their particular decisions in the total decision flow. While managers might like to be completely rational, they cannot be so because they lack the requisite complete information.[39] Therefore, their behavior can be described as limited in rationality. The behavioral theory of the firm pursues a description of the chain of events, *actual* and *probable*, that take place in organizations — not those prescribed by economists as the events that *should* take place. Information and decision chains are the keys for understanding organizational behavior.

Study of the decision-making processes at each point in the chain of events makes it possible to develop generalizations about the total patterns and hence to predict what will happen in similar circumstances elsewhere. It becomes possible to develop simulations of total organizations of decision makers. Thus, by studying how department-store buyers looking at the market respond to earlier decisions of merchandising managers in their own stores, and so on, it becomes possible to forecast and simulate the decisions buyers will make under specified conditions.[13] Or it becomes possible to understand the decision to innovate a new program in a firm by examining (a) the costs of innovating versus allowing the prevailing conditions to continue, (b) the tendencies and norms for novelty and search for new ways among the management, and (c) the current state of dissatisfaction with things as they are. Such analyses can yield predictions about whether or not an innovation will be considered. Then the decision on whether or not to adopt the innovation involves identification and selection of alternatives, which in turn depend on the cost and time required for search for and development of alternatives. Finally, the difficulty or ease with which the innovation is adopted depends on the complexity of the organization, its environment, its climate, and the attitudes of its members toward change, as well as the ways in which the innovation is introduced.[39] At each decision point of "go" or "no go" one can study the factors involved, the probabilities of various outcomes from effects. From the total chains of events examined with their respective probabilities of occurrence, one can forecast with some accuracy whether or not a particular innovation will be selected, adopted, and introduced successfully.

PRINCIPLES The behavioral theory of the firm advances four key principles about organizations:

1. *Organizations strive to avoid uncertainty.* Wherever possible, short-range decisions are preferred over long-range decisions. Members tend to be kept busy "putting out fires" rather than planning long-term policies.
2. *Organizations engage in searching for solutions to problems, not understanding processes.* They behave like cooks baking a cake, rather than chemists trying to understand the underlying chemistry of cake baking.
3. *Organizations learn.* They adjust aspirations, adapt to what can be done and what can't be done. They develop rules from experience.
4. *Organizations resolve conflicts of interests through compromise.* Not the best solution, but one that will satisfy the interests in conflict is sought.[14]

Organizations as Open Systems

Building from a dynamic engineering approach, the system theorist views the organization as an *open social system.*[26] The system is open to the outside environment but is searching for ways to maintain control over how it imports, processes, and exports energy and information.[57] In viewing the organization as an open system, we can apply what seems to be true about all living systems in general to the study of organizations. Living systems such as cells, tissues, and organisms are open systems, as are organizations, and tend to follow similar patterns of growth, energy processing, and decline.

DESCRIPTION As an open system, a formal organization to produce goods or services is continually or periodically receiving inputs from the outside world of energy, money, people, materials, and information. Likewise, although physically designed to provide an output of goods or services, it also is created to generate profits for its sponsors, owners, or shareholders, salaries and other benefits for its managers and employees, in addition to job satisfaction. The organization may both benefit and cost the community and environment in which it is located. It may yield desired goods and services, taxes, and job opportunities; it may generate costly pollution of air and water, and misuse of land, people, and natural resources. At the highest decision levels of the organization, a net gain of benefits over costs is sought. In turn, as one moves down in the organization, at each lower level, the kinds of operations required to convert the inputs into outputs need to be managed so that the benefits to the system outweigh the costs.

The formal organization is designed to reduce uncertainty or to increase predictability. The open system, with its inputs and outputs to the environment, strives for closure, for the greater certainties of a closed system like a thermostat connected with a furnace where all actions are fully programmed and automated.

Two flows occur within the organization. One is a flow of information; the other, a flow of energy. All systems of coordinated effort have these two flows. They are open systems in that the energy and information enter from outside the system and eventually lead to outputs of energy and information.

Typically, organizations, unless extremely temporary, tend to complete a cycle of events beginning with imports, continuing with various transformations of what is imported, and concluding with exports that form the reason, source, or stimulation for a new wave of imports. Unlike a closed, physical system, like a bar of soap in a bathtub of water, an open system does not dissolve into a uniform distribution as would soap and water in a closed vessel. The coordinated work force can continue to import energy (materials, electric power, worker nourishment) and to export finished products. Meanwhile, the system of coordinated workers continues to grow and become more intricate in its means of transforming information and energy. The organization as an open system seeks a steady state of imports, transformations, and exports, but to avoid dissolution or stoppage of its function due to import fluctuations, builds up reserves inside the system. More generally, it grows and expands to incorporate and anticipate new changes in the environment. The meat packing firm may grow in size and diversity, so that eventually it gets everything but the squeal out of the pigs it processes.

WHAT'S THE DIFFERENCE? This emphasis on organizations as open systems contrasts with the earlier approaches of the economists, engineers, and behaviorists in a number of ways.

1. More attention is now paid to the environmental forces that interact with the organization and modify in a continuing way what is going on inside of it.
2. Open systems do not require the endowing of organizations with mysterious, built-in vital forces driving their growth and expansion.

3. The organization maintains staff and expands as a consequence of feedback about how it is functioning in its environment. A dynamic balance is achieved by this means. New states of development are reached when feedback is received that some dysfunction is occurring. For example, a firm marketing computers in the United States receives information about the unmet demand for computers in Canada and increases its production and distribution facilities to a new level until it can satisfy the Canadian demand.

Open systems are governed by the *principle of equifinality*. For example, the computer manufacturer can reach this new state of heightened productivity and distribution from different initial stimulation and through different ways of developing. The signal for growth could have been given by changes in the domestic United States market or some new technological breakthrough. Or growth could have come from licensing a Canadian counterpart as well as from internal expansion of the original manufacturing facilities.

COMMON PRINCIPLES   We can use the same reasoning to look at a unit, say a finance department in a larger organization. We can do the same with much smaller subsystems in the same firm: for example, the finance director and his or her subordinates. Whatever the system or subsystem examined, similar principles are likely to apply: input, transformation, and output of energy and information through permeable system boundaries, cycles of events, growth and development toward new steady states under equifinality, arriving at these new steady states of operating as an organization by one of many different possible pathways.[26]

SYSTEMS MANAGEMENT   The management of any organization or any subunit of it can be understood as an effort to coordinate the system through influence processes that select and identify common objectives, and as an important agency for information transformation and transmission about programs and task interdependency.

IMPLICATIONS FOR LEADERSHIP   Possibly of the greatest immediate practical import is what this system's approach means to effective leadership. As we will see in the next chapter, there is no one best way to lead. Rather, where uncertainty is high and the system lacks order and regulation, the effective leader is one who can initiate and direct, who can provide the needed structure for the system to improve its performance. On the other hand, if uncertainty is low, if objectives are clear, if rules and regulations provide order and structure, then the effective leader is one who is less directive, less initiating, less concerned about giving orders and more ready to give more freedom of choice to subordinates.[46]

REDUCING UNCERTAINTY If organizations are open systems searching for closure (for more certainty about the future), then this fact helps account for several important aspects of organizational behavior. According to Thompson, there are several generally uncertain issues for organizations such as business firms, which lack certain knowledge about how, what, when, and why things happen in their external environment.[57] Business firms lack perfect knowledge of all the cause-effect relations in the markets in which they deal. And even if they fully understand all the forces of the marketplace, they cannot predict with complete accuracy what is going to happen because of unstable demands and lack of complete control over such demands. *Buffering* is undertaken to cope with these fluctuating demands. A firm maintains an inventory, which will expand and contract with varying demands for the business's finished products. This allows the business to produce such goods at a steady rate. Or the firm will deal with the vagaries of the marketplace by bargaining or cooperating with other firms, suppliers, government regulators, and customers to smooth out supply and demand, the inputs and outputs of the firm. When it cannot regulate its environment, the firm invests in forecasting and builds its plans on its forecasts. At the same time, it may be moved to expand itself to incorporate some of the uncertain elements in its environment. An automobile manufacturer may buy control of a headlight manufacturer on which it depends. There is an increase in coordination costs as a consequence, but if the need for stable inflow of those headlights is critical, the company may find it useful to do so despite the additional overhead and coordination costs.

Another source of uncertainty is internal — how the interdependent components of the organization coordinate with each other. For this, as we shall see, structures are created, formal ones usually specifying the grouping and patterns of relations between positions in the firm regardless of who occupies them — the patterns of formal relations between people built up out of position-based mutual expectations, attitudes, and experiences, because informal personal patterns lack the certainty desired.[57]

Other strategies organizations employ to reduce uncertainty are as follows:

1. If they face a variety of different outside environments, they establish different units to deal with each. Internal flexibility is maintained. Control and authority are pushed out toward the boundaries of the organization. For example, a national foods distributor may see its markets as industrial firms and retail grocery chains. It will create an industrial sales force and a completely separate retail-chain sales force. The units may be subdivided further to deal with particular local changes. The industrial division will have different policies, training programs, ways of dealing with customers from

those of the retail division. Decisions made in one will not affect the other.

2. The organization facing a stable environment will generate uniform rules and precedents to dictate how its departments and members will operate. It will centralize controls. A federal agency insuring savings-and-loan banks may view itself in a stable environment where more similarities rather than differences exist among the banks it serves. Effects on the banks due to changes in the economic cycle are buffered by conservative rules for loans. Uniform rules and approaches can be followed in all of its regional offices with controls highly centralized in Washington.[56]

ORGANIZING FOR ENVIRONMENTAL UNCERTAINTY   Burns and Stalker studied twenty British industrial firms and found that if a firm's environment was stable it was likely to have a *mechanistic* system.[10] If a firm's environment was turbulent, it was likely to have an *organismic* system. The mechanistic organization and its members were highly specialized in knowledge, task, and function. The chain of command was rigid. Superiors directed; subordinates obeyed. Communications flowed vertically. Only top management was concerned about the organization as a whole.

On the other hand, the organismic system generated continuous adjustment of tasks and functions. Members had generalized knowledge and responsibility and were committed to the organization as a whole. Superiors consulted and advised subordinates. Much communication flowed horizontally. According to Burns and Stalker, organizations performed better in stable environments if they were mechanistic; they performed better in turbulent environments if they were organismic.

Similarly, Lawrence and Lorsch showed that firms from three different industries — plastics, packaged foods, and standardized containers — had to be organized properly to match the stable or turbulent environments they confronted.[28] Plastics firms were in a turbulent market; container manufacturers, in a stable one; and packaged food companies were in between. In the turbulent environment of the plastics industry, the most effective organization successfully differentiated its subparts. That is, it permitted or even fostered different goals, expectations, norms, standards, and orientations in its different departments. But it also successfully managed to coordinate and integrate these differences. At the same time, the most effective container firm in a stable environment was the one that exhibited the least differentiation among its departments.

WHY DO ORGANIZATIONS GROW?   Conceiving organizations as open systems makes it easier for us to link the many elements that cause an organization to form and grow. As a living system, the growing organization can be seen as a combination of reactions to its internal needs and capabilities and the external sources of energy and information with which it is supplied. For example, the organization expands to exploit fully the technologies it has developed; it expands to meet customers' demands for complete service.

Adventurous managerial entrepreneurs who enjoy risk for big payoffs will push out toward newer activities; bored bureaucrats may take on expanded roles to give their work more variety. Running a bigger operation should provide more prestige and power. Most studies show that salaries of executives depend mainly on the size of the organizations they lead rather than the profitability. Nevertheless, expansion often is dictated by the expectation that the larger organization will have lower unit costs and greater earnings. Within the constraints imposed by antimonopolistic government regulation, larger firms have more power and influence over their markets. In the same way, to some extent, the larger labor union is more powerful than the smaller labor union. Larger organizations can maintain more stable operations. They can stabilize the volume of orders they process by suitable use of buffer inventories even if the demand in their market ebbs and flows. Finally, although the larger organization may not be any more efficient or profitable than the small one and innovations may be harder to introduce, it has the surplus resources to survive a disaster that could destroy the smaller organization. Thus, we see many forces underlying the growth of organizations.[52]

ORGANIZATIONAL STRUCTURE

Several fundamental attributes of an organization affect member satisfaction and performance. It is important to know how complex the division of labor is within the organization. It is equally important to know the ways in which the organization, as a consequence, achieves coordination by informal and formal structuring of relations among its members.

Division of Labor

A task may be too large for one person to handle. It may involve more knowledge than any one person can possibly have. Whenever people are banded together to carry out such tasks, it becomes necessary for them to differentiate what each will do. This division of labor is a basic attribute of organization. The total amount of work to be done can be divided up in at least seven ways.

1. Those portions requiring different tools, equipment, and procedures can be located separately or assigned to different workers.

2. Those portions requiring less skill can be assigned to lower-paid, less skilled workers; those requiring more skill, to higher-paid operators.

3. Different shifts during the day and night can concentrate on different segments of work, and on different time segments of work.

4. Work can be divided according to the nature of the output of goods or services. A manufacturer of radios and clocks may divide into two divisions, one for each.

5. Work can be divided according to the type of client served. A government agency may divide itself into a division for serving other government agencies and a division to serve the public at large.

6. Work may be divided by location. The marketing department may divide itself into northern, southern, eastern, and western divisions.

7. Work may be divided by functional areas. Business firms typically form divisions of marketing, finance, manufacturing, and so on.

The *complexity* of an organization describes how much it divides up its work, how many separate parts it forms and then needs to coordinate. It can be gauged directly or indirectly from the following facts about an organization:

1. The number of its distinct goals or major activities

2. The number of its major divisions or the average number of subdivisions per major department

3. The number of hierarchial levels in the deepest division or the average number of levels per major division

4. The degree to which physical facilities and/or personnel are spatially dispersed.[22]

ADVANTAGES   Many benefits accrue from the division of labor. As pointed out by Adam Smith and Charles Babbage, the division of labor permits one to produce products of more uniform quality, although the actual level of the quality may deteriorate, since the responsibility for the final product no longer resides in a single skilled worker who has produced all the parts as well as assembled the product by himself.[2,51]

Another advantage of dividing up the work is that production can be speeded up to complete a product composed of many parts where the various parts are produced by different people concurrently. Workers can become more skilled in the production of their specialized parts. Simpler parts can be produced by lower-paid workers with fewer skills, thus freeing the more skilled workers (whose wages are higher) from tasks that yield products of less worth than the cost of their labor.

These same arguments apply to groups and divisions of workers. A specialized division can be more attentive to its particular needs and products than an amorphous organization in which this specialized effort is buried. Again, different levels of investment can be justified for different divisions of the organization. More support for growth can be given to the more profitable and less to the less profitable.

DISADVANTAGES   Along with the benefits are technical and sociotechnical requirements and the costs of dividing up the work. The output of different subassemblies must be balanced if they are produced at different rates and are used in different amounts in the final product. Controlling the rates and amounts in order to limit the oversupply of some parts or speed up the output of others requires an overhead of planners and supervisors, as well as programs and schedules developed for the producers. Individual worker output is constrained by the needs of the larger system.

As the division of labor is refined, each worker becomes a specialist. Being absent from work as a link in a chain of interdependent producers of parts for the final composite product can become more costly. One missing part can stop the whole assembly. On the other hand, this same division of labor can lead to much greater simplification of individual jobs so that training a replacement is easier than training a replacement for a skilled worker who could complete all the parts and the final product.

Since a group of specialists must be kept supplied with their particular portions of the work to be done, the flow of inputs to them must be stabilized. Again, if the supply to one of the parts producers fails, the entire assembly must stop until the production of the missing part is brought back up to normal, or else an oversupply of the other parts will ensue.[35]

Standardization of parts becomes necessary. If six workers each produce A parts, and six produce B parts, which are assembled as ABs, usually any A part should be able to be assembled with any B part.

Specialized workers must be ready to change their method of work or their entire job. Only small portions of a skilled worker's job change as the product is modified to meet changes in the marketplace. But a change may entirely eliminate a specialist's part. This situation may plague the scientific or engineering experts who work on a five-year project to design and build highly specialized equipment. When the project ends, the former scientists and engineers have become obsolete, since they failed to keep up with their overall field of endeavor and have concentrated on only a small area during the five-year period.

There are sociopsychological costs of division of labor which often offset many of the technical benefits of the division. First, job and unit specialization may become so extensive that work lacks sufficient challenge and loses its intrinsic interest. The drill-press operator who punches holes of a particular size all day may find little in the work itself that is satisfying; the manager of a shoe sales department in a large store may feel similarly limited. In both instances it is a matter of with whom the employees are comparing themselves. The drill-press operator may regard his brother-in-law's work as an auto mechanic as far more challenging; the shoe department manager may remember her mother's small business for which her mother had total responsibility. At the same time some persons may benefit. They may prefer simple, routine work about which they do not have to think much as they carry out their assignments, permitting them to daydream as they work.

Again, comparisons with what associates are doing on other parts of the total task may be sources of conflict. Some more complex jobs may be seen as more desirable because they yield higher status than the simple specialized work does. But there are many more subtle costs, particularly where the division of labor is by staff and line so that, for instance, planning (a staff function) is separated from the line function of carrying out the plans, a common industrial practice that is seemingly efficient for the reasons cited earlier. An illustration of the advantages and disadvantages of dividing up the work is seen in the case of whether planning should be separated from the execution of the plans.

Who Shall Plan?

As much as we might want to encourage self-planning so as to maximize commitment to what is planned, the utility of the division of labor dictates separating planners from doers for several reasons. First, if planning is a full-time, continuing task for a person or unit, and self-planning were practiced, no time would be left to execute the plans. Second, planning may require special skills, education, and experience. By dividing up labor so that some persons or units specialize in planning, we obtain more effective plans than if planning were done equally by every employee in the organization. Third, some people are uninterested in planning and prefer to concentrate on carrying out plans. So the division of labor makes it possible to place persons differentially in work according to interest preferences. Fourth, plans can be standardized as blueprints automated by computerized programs. Labor can be divided up between people and machines, so that people are freed from some aspects of planning and can devote more of their efforts to carrying out the plans.[5]

But with the gains of separating planning from doing come costs. The costs of this separation were demonstrated by engaging 600 managers in a training exercise where they carried out plans under two conditions: (1) where they had developed the plans themselves and (2) where the plans had been developed for them by colleagues.

In all, working in teams of 3, the 600 managers did almost 19 per cent better operating their own plans than carrying out plans assigned to them by other trios. Productivity averaged 77.0 units when operating self-

Table 5–1. Productivity of managers of different nationalities operating their own plans and plans assigned to them by others

| | | (percentage) | |
| | | Productivity when operating | |
Number and location of managers		Own plan (self-developed)	Other plan (assigned)
Scandinavian	78	71.7	62.2
Dutch	108	86.7	62.5
Belgian	78	68.9	49.1
British	132	94.9	79.2
American	162	80.9	69.9
Indian	42	63.0	41.1
Total	600	77.0	64.8

Reproduced by special permission from *The Journal of Applied Behavioral Science,* Table 1 from "When Planning for Others" by Bernard M. Bass, 6:2 (1970) 155, NTL Institute for Applied Behavioral Science.

developed plans and 64.8 when operating assigned plans. Half the managers operated the plan they devised themselves first, and then the other plan. The other half did the reverse to counterbalance the effects of practice.

Table 5-1 shows the productivity of the 600 managers working in 200 trios in Scandinavia, the Netherlands, Belgium, Great Britain, the United States, and India. Results were similar for managers in all the nations. Trios assembled more units when they operated their own plan rather than the plan assigned to them by other trios.

Subjective results were the same. For the 600 managers, 63.0 per cent were more satisfied with their jobs when working on their own plans, only 20.2 per cent preferred working on the other plan, and 16.8 per cent did not care one way or the other.

Dividing up work into the staff function of planning and the line function of carrying out the plans tends to produce operations that are less productive and less satisfying for a variety of reasons: (1) the sense of accomplishment is less when executing someone else's plan; (2) there is less tendency to try to confirm the validity of another's plan by executing it successfully — less confidence that it can be done; (3) there is less flexibility, less room for modification and initiative to make improvements in an assigned plan; (4) understanding of the plan is less; (5) there are more communication problems and consequent errors and distortions in pursuing instructions; and (6) there are competitive feelings aroused between planners and doers; if the former "win," the latter "lose."

There is still another cost associated with dividing organizations into line producers and staff supporter operations. Among 155 managers and professionals in a large industrial manufacturing firm, those in operating line units saw their units as esteemed, and powerful when compared to other units. They felt better about their own units than did those in staff support services who saw their staff service as lower in esteem and power.[9]

Given these results, two alternatives are available. Wherever possible, doers should plan for themselves. Fisch would formalize this by abolishing the staff function of planning in favor of organizing temporary project teams responsible for planning and execution of the plans.[19] The alternative is to counteract these sociopsychological costs of dividing into planners and doers.

COUNTERACTING THE SOCIOPSYCHOLOGICAL COSTS OF THE DIVISION OF LABOR
The preceding analysis of the psychological costs of division of work into planners and doers suggests its own remedies to help reduce such costs. Thus, for example, to foster a sense of accomplishment, the means for providing more frequent feedback of success or failure must be built into plans for others.

To promote confirmatory behavior, the planners can try to make the doers aware of provisions for various contingencies. The confidence of the planners in the adequacy of their plans can be communicated. Reservations of the doers need to be brought into the open and discussed with the planners. If the doers believe that the plans are unrealistic, even if the plans are actually sound, the doers may behave in such a way as to confirm their own beliefs. Planners need to share with the doers the reasons for their optimistic expectations.

Promoting commitment likewise hinges on communication and consultation. Those involved in only a portion of the total task can be consulted at various stages in the planning process. Wherever possible, their ideas can be incorporated into the plans for the total effort, or when such ideas are unusable, the reasons can be discussed with them. They can be involved in preliminary trials of the operations, with emphasis given to their own evaluations of the trials. Plans can provide for some discretion on the part of the subassembly operators to modify noncritical elements of the operations, increasing the feeling that they have some control over the fate of the total operation and hence responsibility for the successful execution of the total plan.

Flexibility is obtained by making provision for it in the design of the systems to be operated. Groups of 40 technicians each were assigned to operate a simulated air defense system. Plans had been carefully engineered to maximize the load that could be handled safely by the operators and their equipment. However, built into the plan was permission for the operators to modify their relations with each other in dealing with the load as they saw the need to do so. Following a period of trial and error, organizational innovations occurred, not foreseen by the planners, which resulted in the ability of the groups to handle much heavier loads than the planners had thought possible.[12]

A task should be explained in terms simple enough to be understood by the least sophisticated operators. If they can understand the total operation, all can do so. Attention to reading or speaking level and interest is important, as is appreciating what should and should not be assumed about what operators know and do not know about the total task. Each situation will call for different means for promoting understanding. In one production situation, understanding may be promoted best by pretests and modifications of presentations, demonstrations, and instructions. In another, it may best be aided by testing for individual differences in understanding and then working further with those who fail to understand. What is necessary is concern for understanding and suitable attention to it.

Maximizing the effective use of people is a matter of making the most of what is available by whatever means the situation allows. One case may call for self-assessments of the differential capacities of the operators, so that people and jobs are similarly matched. Still another scheme may permit the rotation of assignments until optimum arrangements are found, or rotation may be continued in order to reduce boredom.

Communications can be improved by seeing that all parts of the total system use the same code or language. If procedures are simple to understand, one-way communications (for example, from the planners to the doers) are likely to be fast, effective, and satisfying to both parties. But if the planners are using different concepts, "speaking a different language," and presenting what seems to the doers a complex set of instructions, then it becomes important for communication to flow in two directions: from planners to doers and from doers to planners. The doers must have (and must feel that they have) plenty of opportunity to question the planners for clarification of the plans.

The planners need to attend to whether or not they are overestimating the comprehension of those who are receiving the plans. The planners need to judge whether they are transmitting too much or too little, too fast or too slowly, with too great or too little enthusiasm, with too much or too little confidence. The planner-senders have to be alert to the extent to which their messages are being filtered by the receiver-doers, who may "hear" only what they want to or what fits their past understandings.

Minimizing competition involves avoiding a situation in which one subgroup of operators (or one operator) sees itself in a zero-sum game with another subgroup. If one subgroup (or one operator) succeeds, it must do so without the other losing status, prestige, power, or material benefits. Conditions must be established in which the subgroups share the same superordinate goals. The division of labor should be seen to benefit all subgroups. Maintaining a non-zero-sum game where all subgroups win through cooperation with each other and lose if they compete with each other is essential.

Coordination

Once work has been divided among several workers, coordination among them is required. When interdependent departments are created to handle only parts of the total output of an organization, coordination is again required. Such coordination of workers or departments can be fully programmed by establishing a formal organization. Each worker who is to contribute a part to the whole can receive specific instructions and training to notify an associate when the worker's contribution is ready to be fitted together with the components provided by others. Departments can receive specific schedules of deliveries to each other of subassemblies and can be advised of what routines to follow to maintain balanced efforts so that one department does not overproduce while another underproduces. As long as inputs and outputs of each interdependent worker or each independent department remain stable, coordination can be maintained by program. But when perturbations occur — customers change their requests to some department, a worker is absent, a delivery is held up by traffic, a machine breaks down — then information must flow from and to the interdependent units to achieve the coordination of required changes in the program. Here, then, communication, influence, and control become keys to coordinated effort. One can provide this by authority, rules, orders, and direction from above, emphasizing the formal relations between jobs and levels in their system, or one can emphasize understanding of the purposes and needs for coordination and purposeful collaboration to achieve a coordinated effort. In either case, the managers, their superiors, peers, and subordinates, and their respective attitudes, preferences, and interrelationships are keys to understanding what happens. These are all reflected in the *control hierarchy*. To be constructed, organization members are asked to indicate how much influence different components of their organization do exert and should exert on particular outcomes.[53]

For example, when 275 managers and professionals of 16 Brazilian banks were asked how much influence on decisions to grant loans should be exerted by the different levels, as seen in Figure 5–1, top management called for control to be higher at successively higher levels in the organization. Managers and professionals at lower levels proposed that there should be more equality of control at the different organizational levels.

Nevertheless, rather than managerial level making a difference in control effects, more specialization of control was seen in the more effective organizations. The effectiveness of the banks was greater if department heads had the most control over determining methods, if technical personnel had the most control over evaluating grant applications, and if top management had the most control over the final approval of loans.[17]

Figure 5–1 Amount of control reported by 275 managers and professionals of 16 Brazilian banks. (Adapted from Farris and Butterfield, "Control Theory in Brazilian Organizations," *Administrative Science Quarterly*, 17 [1974]: 574–585.)

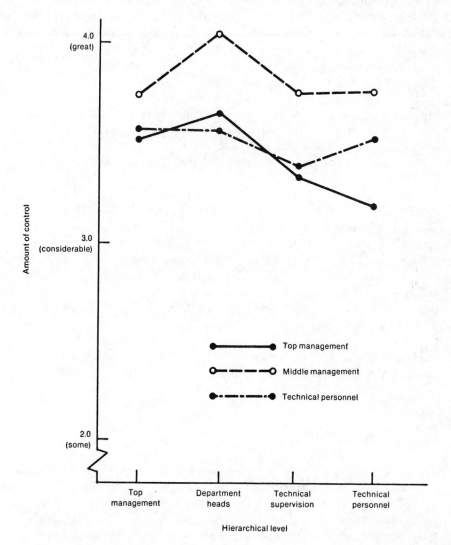

INFORMAL COORDINATION   This is accomplished by relations between people regardless of their positions. One person may be able to exert more influence over other persons when coordination between units is required. Or mutual influence may result in satisfactory coordination. What is implied here is a process. First, one or more persons in a system perceive the need to coordinate completion schedules, work flows, use of resources, etc. Second, one or more persons attempt to influence the others to modify their current behavior, to speed up or slow down, shift efforts, and the like. One person can succeed in influencing others because others see the person as more valued or more esteemed. What the person says is seen to have more merit. And it may actually have more merit. Mutual esteem between parties may be established, with the result that issues of coordination are settled between them primarily on the basis of the perceived merit of the suggestions rather than on the source of the suggestion.

This informal approach to coordination will be facilitated if *task interdependency* exists between parties. Thus, two or more persons will coordinate without much need for specific leadership on the part of one or the other as a consequence of task interdependence. If the task of two people is to carry a heavy table from one room to the other, they will keep pace with each other. When one stops for a rest, so will the other. The interdependency of the two parties is such that the efforts must remain highly coordinated.

In the same way, informal relations are sufficient when goals of the parties who must work together are clear and compatible. People can be directed or direct themselves toward objectives. Once directed, they will coordinate activities if that is seen to be instrumental in their own goal attainment. Thus, two or more persons motivated to attain a common objective will coordinate their activities in a manner that enables each to attain what is wanted. If two persons wish to see how often they can pitch a ball to each other and catch it without error, each in turn will get into and remain in the receiving position while the other goes through the throwing activity. We will discuss many aspects of informal teamwork in Chapter 6. Now we are more interested in looking at the importance of *formal* relations in coordinating work where division of labor exists.

Formalization

Two or more units of a system can develop or be given plans of action, assigned duties, standard operating procedures, and decision rules that if obeyed to the letter will produce the requisite coordination between the units. Such programming can be effective to the extent that required unit activities are simple and routine. This *structuring* or *formalization* of relationships can be seen in the extent to which jobs are codified and tolerances established for whatever deviation will be permitted. Formalization is seen in "statements of procedures, rules, roles, and operation of procedures which deal with decision seeking (applications for capital, employment, and so on), conveying of decisions and instructions (plans, minutes, requisitions, and so on), and conveying of information including feedback." [49] Indicators of formalization include: (1) concretely defined positions; (2) written job descriptions; (3) a clearly defined hierarchy of authority; (4) a written description of the hierarchy; (5) emphasis on written communications; (6) emphasis on following established channels of communication; (7) large numbers of written rules and policies; (8) clearly stated penalties for violating rules; (9) a written code of penalties for violations; (10) formalized orientation programs for new members; and (11) formalized in-service training programs for new members.[22]

TALL VERSUS FLAT HIERARCHIES   Ordinarily, as organizations enlarge, levels of authority are established following the scalar principle. Each job incumbent knows which jobholders at the level below are supposed to report to him and to which jobholder at the level above her/him she/he is supposed to report. The hierarchy may tend to be tall or flat. Thus, fifteen employees may be organized in a tall hierarchy of four levels or in a flat one of two levels, as in Figure 5–2. For the same total number of organization members, tall hierarchies are made up of more levels than flat hierarchies. A major corporation with a tall hierarchy may have fifteen to twenty levels between the first-line supervisor and the president. On the other hand, some large firms such as Sears Roebuck maintain a relatively flat hierarchy with as few as five levels from lower to top management. There is an obvious direct relation with the span of control. To deal with the same size organization, in a *flat* hierarchy, all managers must have a relatively large number of subordinates reporting to them. In our fifteen-person example, fourteen subordinates report to one superior. At lower levels in flat hierarchies, it

Figure 5–2. A tall hierarchy compared to a flat hierarchy

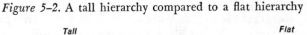
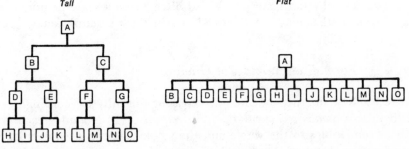

is not uncommon to see twenty to thirty subordinates reporting to one supervisor. For the same number of employees in a *tall* hierarchy, a single manager will be responsible for many fewer employees. In our example, only two subordinates report to a superior. Tall hierarchies may require only two or three subordinates to report to a single superior.

BEHAVIORAL EFFECTS   Some behavioral effects are apparent. In the flat hierarchy, the superior with a large span of control is forced to practice *management by exception*. That is, managers cannot hope to pay continuous attention to what all their subordinates are doing, so they concentrate on dealing with exceptions and variances to the general procedures that all their subordinates are expected to follow. For this system to work well, superiors must have continuing access to good data about how all their subordinates are faring. Objective records of the subordinates' performance must be readily available so that the managers can be apprised of problems and exceptions.

The flat organization requires that the superior delegate authority to subordinates so that they can be free to carry on without continued intervention by their superior. But in the flat hierarchy, there are fewer opportunities for advancement, since the competition is greater for each movement up the shorter ladder than in the tall hierarchy. Nevertheless, as Machiavelli pointed out, the single individual in a flat hierarchy can be rapidly pulled up from the bottom to the top of the organization by the central authority. Since one superior is responsible for so many subordinates in the flat hierarchy, the supervisor can also be a complete communications clog. Subordinates wait in line to schedule an appointment. The superior can use this as a device to veto or slow down changes.

SATISFACTION AND HIERARCHICAL LEVEL   As we have already noted in Chapter 4, a strong behavioral effect of hierarchy is that persons at the upper levels are more satisfied with their jobs than are those at lower levels. This has been demonstrated in both capitalist and socialist societies and in countries as diverse as the United States, Italy, Austria, Israel, and Yugoslavia.[54] It can be demonstrated in the classroom by asking students to carry out an exercise as members of different levels in a hierarchy. The pervasive effect is one reason why top managers fail so often to appreciate or understand the discontent that may lie at lower levels in their organization.

Formalization and Coordination

Three levels of interdependence, of increasing difficulty to coordinate, may be required: *pooled, sequential,* and *reciprocal.* In *pooling*, each component contributes to the whole and the whole supports each component. Coordination requires standard routines and expectations that all components will generally follow the routines. It is relatively easy to accomplish. An example would involve the cooperating efforts of several snow-removal plows. Each would plow a different section of a main thoroughfare, but when each had done its own section, the entire route would be clear and all plows would be removed to another assignment.

When they are *sequentially interdependent*, one component's activities must follow another's. In addition to each component's following standard routines, planning, and scheduling, additional communications are required among components. It is more difficult than mere pooled interdependence. As an airplane leaves one traffic space, ground control of the plane is transferred to another station in charge of the space the aircraft is now entering. Ground controllers are sequentially interdependent here.

Still more difficult to coordinate is *reciprocal interdependence.* Mutual adjustments must be maintained in addition to standard routines, planning, scheduling, and communicating. A five-man basketball team is obviously in almost continuous reciprocal interdependence.[57]

The amount of uncertainty faced in the external environment will be met, as we discussed before, by efforts of the firm to reduce it. Here it means that the formal structure of those departments like marketing, which deal with the outside world, will be broken into as many subdivisions as necessary to maintain surveillance over the different special markets which develop. For example, a food products manufacturer will divide the sales force into those dealing with industrial buyers and those dealing with retail store buyers. If large government contracts become significant, a third division might be created to deal with government institutional buyers. *Pooled interdependence* is involved among the three divisions, for the most part. Coordination remains relatively easy and new divisions can be created without significant increase in coordination costs unless their markets begin to overlap for some reason.

Suppose manufacturing and marketing are in pooled interdependence. Manufacturing schedules are coordinated only generally with marketing orders. Then an overall centralized manufacturing division and an overall centralized marketing division can be created. On the other hand, suppose they are reciprocally interdependent. Suppose a sales engineer must design the customer's purchase to provide the details of the order to manufacturing. Suppose marketing is involved with checks and modifications before the product is released from manufacturing for delivery to the customer. Then a decentralized, self-sufficient cluster of manufacturing-marketing units will evolve.[57]

Effects of Size

Most organization theorists have assumed that large organizations are more complex and formal than small ones. In actual fact, the differences in complexity and formality between large and small organizations are not so great as has been assumed, according to a survey of seventy-five trade, industry, government, and voluntary educational organizations.[22] Nevertheless, size may still be an important variable in the study of organization, although it seems to have little relation to the complexity or the formality of relations in the organization. Usually a negative relationship has been shown between employee morale and organization size. For Sears Roebuck employees morale was lower in larger Sears divisions and higher in smaller ones.[61]

The individual in a large organization may feel "lost" in the great number of people. Organizational size also is an important variable in interorganizational relations, since size and organizational power are probably positively related. Similarly, larger organizations probably have more financial resources. Thus, organizational size should not be dismissed as a variable but should rather be utilized where it is likely to have more predictive significance than it has for complexity and formalization.[22]

A review of the many studies of the effects of group size and organization on interaction processes, satisfaction, and productivity yielded two main conclusions:

1. As organizations enlarge, the capacity of individuals to form relations with all others becomes exhausted. Subgroups must develop within the larger organization. There is pressure toward subgroup cohesion and adoption of subgroup norms, sometimes at the risk of producing larger organizational conflicts. In short, the stage is set for subgroup-group conflict, as well as for conflict among subgroups.

2. The satisfaction of individual workers tends to decrease as their work organization enlarges. Their opportunities to participate in decisions affecting themselves decrease along with their identification with the goals of the larger organization and their sense of achievement from attaining such objectives.[20]

INERTIA We have already suggested that inertial effects are likely to be greater in larger organizations. There are longer time lags between the introduction of a new management approach and its subsequent effect on motivation and productivity.[34]

FLEXIBILITY Mahoney, Frost, et al. studied 386 organizational units of different sizes from 19 firms.[37] The firms also differed in size. They were engaged in finance, insurance, electronics, heavy manufacturing, agricultural processing, and pharmaceuticals. Both unit size and the firm's size made a difference in three ways: larger units and the larger firms revealed: (1) more flexibility in personnel assignments and the development of employees for promotion within the firms; (2) more delegation of work responsibility by supervisors; and (3) more emphasis on results, outputs, and performance rather than procedures. Thus, it would seem that with more employees, more varied tasks, and greater opportunities, larger entities can provide more flexibility in assignments. But more delegation and more attention to results may be needed in larger entities where there may be greater difficulty in closely monitoring and coordinating the larger number of employees who are likely to be engaged in a greater variety of tasks.

Effects of Technology

No simple conclusion seems to explain the extent to which technology shapes the way an organization will be structured.[55] Woodward inferred from empirical studies that as its operating technology becomes more advanced, a firm is likely to become more flexible and informal, with more individual worker freedom and satisfaction.[60] On the other hand, Dubin saw advanced technology producing more rigidity, centralization, less freedom, greater complexity, and specialization.[16] It all depends on which workers we are looking at and where they are in the system. When a computer is installed in a large office, the department heads and staff may be freed of much drudgery and find themselves with enlarged jobs involving greater responsibility, but the clerks — now keypunch operators — may find their jobs much more restricted in scope. In the same way, automation in the factory increases the skill demands among maintenance employees but often not among those in production.[18]

In south Essex, England, interviews were held in 100 firms ranging in size from 100 to 8,000 or more employees. The firms were classified into three categories according to their technology: small batches and unit production, large batches and mass production, and process production. Small batches and unit production were in companies producing for special orders from customers for specific kinds and types of products: men's suits, special turbines, and so on. Mass production and large batches were on assembly-line products such as appliances. Process production was exemplified by petroleum refining.

Process production featured smaller spans of control with taller hierarchies of four to eight levels.

Unit production had the flattest structures, with two to four levels and much wider spans of control. The proportion of administrative and clerical employees was greatest in process industries and least in unit production. Duties and responsibilities were most formally specified in mass production. Unit production firms favored straight-line organizations with each supervisor serving as his/her own staff. Few specialists were available. Mass-production industry favored line and staff arrangements where line was responsible for supervision but staff was responsible for planning, scheduling, and quality control.[60]

TECHNOLOGY AND ATTITUDES Such technological differences between firms — small-batch, mass, and process — were found to affect systematically the attitudes of 1,023 professional, technical, and managerial employees in 18 Norwegian firms. Satisfaction with extrinsic benefits such as pay and working conditions was highest with small-batch operations and lowest in mass-production ones. As might be expected, satisfaction with advancement, recognition, and sense of accomplishment — intrinsic satisfaction — was lowest in mass-production firms. Organization was seen as most "organic" — living, responsive, flexible, and dynamic in small-batch production — and most "mechanical" — static, inflexible, fixed — in mass production. In the same way, supervision was most general in small-batch production and closest in mass production.[48]

TECHNOLOGY AND EFFECTIVENESS When we ask what makes for an effective organization, we must consider the organization's technology. The managers of 386 organizational units from 17 firms engaged in manufacturing, insurance, wholesale trade, electronics, and finance described their units' work processes and function and provided judgments of the units' effectiveness. The units were classified according to their technology, as proposed by Thompson.[56]

Long-linked technology described those with serially interdependent tasks such as for mass-production assembly lines. Mediating technology operated in standard ways to sort inputs. For example, technology is mediating where it is used to decide how clients are to be treated when they first indicate their problems. (All patients waiting in a physician's office may have their temperatures taken.) Intensive technology is involved in custom applications and specialized treatments. (The X-ray machine is adjusted specifically for each new patient who is to be scanned.) Good planning was most important for effective long-linked operations, but flexibility was seen as contributing the most to the effectiveness of mediating technologies, and cooperation was particularly important to the effectiveness of intense technology.[36]

TECHNOLOGY AND CONTROLS Technology also affects the controls in an organization. The controls, in turn, often help to explain how and why an organization behaves as it does. The controls may be unitary or fragmented. That is, there may be a uniform standard for approval or disapproval, success or failure, applied all over the organization, or different standards in the different units of the organization. Also, the controls may be personal (one person over another) or impersonal (automatic as in the case of a profit center or an automated production process). Table

5–2 shows how their technology affected what kinds of controls were used by 100 British firms. It can be seen that in continuous production controls are almost always impersonal and unitary, in mass production most diverse, and in small-batch production most often personal and unitary.[50]

ORGANIZATIONAL CLIMATE, COMPLEXITY, AND FORMALIZATION

The term *organizational climate* is used loosely and in a variety of ways by different psychologists. Forehand and Gilmer see the organizational climate as those stimuli, constraints on freedom, and rewards and punishments that affect worker attitudes and performance.[20] For many it is anything in the working environment that affects worker satisfaction and/or productivity.

The concept of organizational climate, however, becomes more useful when, as defined by Likert and his colleagues, it is more limited to *conditions inside the organization but outside the immediate face-to-face working group.*[33]

In this sense *organizational climate* involves such matters as extent of upward receptivity, lateral communications, and interdepartmental decision making, control, and coordination. Judgments are obtained from managers, employees, and observers on such questions as the following:

Table 5–2. Controls associated with different technologies.

	(percentage)			
	Type of control			
	Personal		Impersonal	
Technology	Unitary	Fragmented	Fragmented	Unitary
Unit and small-batch production	75	25	—	—
Large-batch and mass production	15	35	40	10
Continuous-process production	—	—	5	95
Total number of firms	28	21	18	33

Adapted from Reeves and Woodward, "The Study of Managerial Control." In J. Woodward (ed.), *Industrial Organization: Behavior and Control* (Oxford: Oxford University Press, 1970) p. 54.

How receptive are those above you to your ideas and suggestions?

How adequate for your needs is the amount of information you get about what is going on in other departments?

To what extent are there things about working here (people, policies, conditions) that encourage you to work hard?

How are objectives set in this company?

To what extent are decisions made at those levels where the most adequate and accurate information is available?

When decisions are being made, to what extent are the persons affected asked for their ideas?

To what extent is information widely shared in this company so that those who make the decisions have access to all available know-how?

To what extent are the persons who make decisions aware of problems at lower levels in the company?

In general, how much say or influence does each of the following groups of people have on what goes on in your department (foremen, top managers, department heads, etc.) ?

Between departments, how frequently is work time lost because of failure to do proper planning or coordinating with relevant people?

In working with other departments, problems are bound to arise from time to time. When these problems do occur, to what extent are they handled well? [8]

As we will discuss more fully in Chapter 6, proponents of the participative approach to management argue that satisfaction and productivity will be greater with less structure, complexity, and formalization. There is more freedom to contribute to objectives and methods and to have a personal influence on what happens than where jobs and relations between jobs are highly structured. Thus, (with reference to the preceding questions about communications, decision making, control, and coordination) satisfaction and productivity would be expected to be greater if upward and lateral communications flow more easily, where policies are stimulating, where decisions are shared, where people have control over their own fates, and where coordination between people is smooth. Nevertheless, experimental results, particularly for the hypothesized relation between less structure and more productivity, are mixed and may apply only to some jobs in some parts of the organization.[29] As we have noted earlier, proponents argue and offer evidence that generally there will be a payoff from reducing structure but that effects may lag. It may take several years before productivity and reduced absences, quitting, and accidents reflect a change in the extent to which a company has shifted from a highly structured, complex, formalized operation to one where individuals feel much freer to communicate upward and outward, to suggest changes, to participate in goal setting, to have greater discretion about their own work, and to be under less close supervision.[34]

SUMMARY

Organizational structures arise out of the need for predictability and reduced uncertainty, so that people will work with each other rather than against each other toward common goals. In the past, the ways we organized have been influenced by ideas about work, about money, about scientific management, about socioemotionality, and about the utility of comparative studies of different organizations. The operation of modern organizations has been further influenced by the practice of management by objectives, by the concept of limited rationality, and by an open systems point of view. A firm or agency's technology, size, and organizational climate influence and are affected by its planning processes and its hierarchical structure.

As with the imprecise meanings given to organizational climate, an unfortunate lack of clarity exists also concerning what is meant by organizational structure and how much of it is necessary for a given set of tasks and objectives. And, as we will note in the next chapter, the amount of organizational structure that is optimal for maximizing satisfaction and performance depends on characteristics of the task, the people involved and other circumstances surrounding the situation. This fact will be seen more clearly as we examine in greater detail the roles the manager plays in the organization's structure.

REFERENCES

1. Argyris, C. *Integrating the Individual and the Organization.* New York: Wiley, 1964.
2. Babbage, C. *On the Economy of Machinery and Manufacturers.* London: Charles Knight, 1832.
3. Bass, B. M. "The Interface between Personnel and Organizational Psychology," *Journal of Applied Psychology,* 52 (1968): 81–88.
4. Bass, B. M. *A Preliminary Report on Manifest Preferences in Six Cultures for Participative Management.* (Technical Report No. 21). Management Research Center, Contract NONR N00014–67(A). Rochester, N. Y.: University of Rochester, 1968.
5. Bass, B. M. "When Planning for Others," *Journal of Applied Behavioral Sciences,* 6 (1970): 151–171.
6. Bennis, W. G. *Changing Organization.* New York: McGraw-Hill, 1966.
7. Blake, R. R., and J. S. Mouton. *The Managerial Grid.* Houston: Gulf Publishing, 1964.

8. Bowers, D. G. *Work Organizations as Dynamic Systems*. Technical Report, Office of Naval Research, September 30, 1969.
9. Browne, P. J., and R. T. Golembiewski. "The Line-Staff Concept Revisited: An Empirical Study of Organizational Images," *Academy of Management Journal*, 17 (1974): 406–417.
10. Burns, T., and G. M. Stalker. *The Management of Innovation*. London: Tavistock, 1961.
11. Carnegie, D. *How to Win Friends and Influence People*. New York: Simon and Schuster, 1936.
12. Chapman, R. L., J. L. Kennedy, A. Newall, and W. C. Biel. "The Systems Research Laboratory's Air Defense Experiments." In H. Guetzkow (ed.), *Simulation in Social Science: Readings*. Englewood Cliffs, N.J.: Prentice-Hall, 1962.
13. Cyert, R. M., and J. G. March. *A Behavioral Theory of the Firm*. Englewood Cliffs, N.J.: Prentice-Hall, 1963.
14. Cyert, R. M., and J. G. March. "The Behavioral Theory of the Firm: A Behavioral Science–Economics Amalgam." In W. W. Cooper, H. J. Leavitt, and M. W. Shelly (eds.), *New Perspectives in Organization Research*. New York: Wiley, 1964.
15. Drucker, P. F. *The Practice of Management*. New York: Harper, 1954.
16. Dubin, R. "Supervision and Productivity: Empirical Findings and Theoretical Considerations." In R. Dubin, G. C. Homans, F. C. Mann, and D. C. Miller (eds.), *Leadership and Productivity*. San Francisco: Chandler, 1965.
17. Farris, G. F., and D. A. Butterfield. "Control Theory in Brazilian Organizations," *Administrative Science Quarterly*, 17 (1974): 574–585.
18. Faunce, W. A. "Automation in the Automobile Industry: Some Consequences for In-Plant Social Structure," *American Sociological Review*, 23 (1958): 401–407.
19. Fisch, G. G. "Line-Staff Is Obsolete," *Harvard Business Review*, 39, no. 5 (1961): 67–69.
20. Forehand, G. A., and B. von H. Gilmer. "Environmental Variation in Studies of Organizational Behavior," *Psychological Bulletin*, 67 (1964): 361–382.
21. Gannon, M. J., and F. T. Paine. "Unity of Command and Job Attitudes of Managers in a Bureaucratic Organization," *Journal of Applied Psychology*, 59 (1974): 392–394.
22. Hall. R. H., E. J. Haas, and W. J. Johnson. "Organizational Size, Complexity and Formalization," *American Sociological Review*, 32 (1967): 903–912.
23. Hoagland, J. H. "Historical Antecedents of Organization Research." In W. Cooper, H. J. Leavitt, and W. Shelly (eds.), *New Perspectives in Organization Research*. New York: Wiley, 1964.
24. Homans, G. C. *The Human Group*. New York: Harcourt, Brace, 1950.
25. Ivancevich, J. M. "Changes in Performance in a Management by Objectives Program," *Administrative Science Quarterly*, 19 (1974): 563–574.
26. Katz, D., and R. L. Kahn. *The Social Psychology of Organizations*, 2nd ed. New York: Wiley, 1978.
27. Korman, A. K., J. H. Greenhaus, and I. J. Badin. "Personnel Attitudes and Motivation," *Annual Review of Psychology*, 28 (1977): 175–196.

28. Lawrence, P. R., and J. W. Lorsch. *Organization and Environment.* Cambridge: Harvard University Press, 1967.
29. Leavitt, H. J. "Unhuman Organization," *Harvard Business Review,* 40, no. 4 (1962): 90–98.
30. Leavitt, H. J. "Applied Organizational Change in Industry: Structural, Technological, and Humanistic Approaches." In J. G. March (ed.), *Handbook of Organizations.* New York: Rand-McNally, 1965.
31. Lewin, K., R. Lippitt, and R. K. White. "Patterns of Aggressive Behavior in Experimentally Created Social Climates,' *Journal of Social Psychology,* 10 (1939): 271–301.
32. Likert, R. *New Patterns of Management.* New York: McGraw-Hill, 1961.
33. Likert, R. *The Human Organization: Its Management and Value.* New York: McGraw-Hill, 1967.
34. Likert, R., and D. G. Bowers. "Organizational Theory and Human Resource Accounting," *American Psychologist,* 24 (1969): 585–592.
35. Litterer, J. A. *The Analyses of Organizations.* New York: Wiley, 1965.
36. Mahoney, T. A., and P. J. Frost. "The Role of Technology in Models of Organizational Effectiveness," *Organizational Behavior and Human Performance,* 11 (1974): 122–138.
37. Mahoney, T. A., P. Frost, N. F. Crandall, and W. Weitzel. "The Conditioning Influence of Organization Size upon Managerial Practice," *Organizational Behavior and Human Performance,* 8 (1972): 230–241.
38. March, J. G. "Introduction." In J. G. March (ed.), *Handbook of Organizations.* New York: Rand-McNally, 1965.
39. March, J. G., and H. A. Simon. *Organizations.* New York: Wiley, 1958.
40. Martin, N. H., and J. H. Sims. "Thinking Ahead: Power Tactics," *Harvard Business Review,* 34, no. 6 (1956): 25–36.
41. Massie, J. L. "Management Theory." In J. G. March (ed.), *Handbook of Organizations.* New York: Rand-McNally, 1965.
42. McGregor, D. *The Human Side of Enterprise.* New York: McGraw-Hill, 1960.
43. McGregor, D. *The Professional Manager.* New York: McGraw-Hill, 1967.
44. Merton, R. K. "Bureaucratic Structure and Personality," *Social Forces,* 18 (1940): 560–568.
45. Michels, R. *Political Parties.* New York: Dover, 1915.
46. Miller, J. A. *Structuring/Destructuring: Leadership in Open Systems.* Technical Report no. 64, Management Research Center. Rochester, N. Y.: University of Rochester, 1973.
47. Morris, W. T. *Management Science in Action.* Homewood, Illinois: Irwin, 1963.
48. Peterson, R. B. "The Interaction of Technological Process and Perceived Organizational Climate in Norwegian Firms," *Academy of Management Journal,* 18 (1975): 288–299.
49. Pugh, D. S., D. J. Hickson, C. R. Minings, and C. Turner. "Dimensions of Organization Structure," *Administrative Science Quarterly,* 13 (1968): 66–105.
50. Reeves, T. K., and J. Woodward. "The Study of Managerial Control." In J. Woodward (ed.), *Industrial Organization: Behavior and Control.* London: Oxford University Press, 1970.

51. Smith, A. *The Wealth of Nations.* New York: Modern Library, 1937 (London, 1776).
52. Starbuck, W. H. *Organizational Growth and Development.* Institute for Quantitative Research in Economics and Management, Paper no. 67. Lafayette, Ind.: Purdue University, 1964.
53. Tannenbaum, A. *Control in Organizations.* New York: McGraw-Hill, 1968.
54. Tannenbaum, A. S., B. Kavačič, M. Rosner, M. Vianello, and G. Wieser. *Hierarchy in Organizations: An International Comparison.* San Francisco: Jossey-Bass, 1974.
55. Taylor, J. C. *The Conditioning Effects of Technology on Organizational Behavior in Planned Social Change.* Technical Report, Institute for Social Research. Ann Arbor: University of Michigan, 1969.
56. Thompson, J. *Organizations in Action.* New York: McGraw-Hill, 1967.
57. Thompson, J. D. "Organizations in Action: Social Science Bases of Administrative Theory." Paper presented at the 77th Annual Convention of the American Psychological Association, Division 14, Systems Theory and Organization Theory, Washington, D.C., 1969.
58. Weber, M. *Gesammelte Aufsätze zur Sozial- und Wirtschaftgeschichte.* Tübingen: Mohr, 1924.
59. Whyte, W. F. *Money and Motivation.* New York: Harper, 1955.
60. Woodward, J. *Industrial Organizations: Theory and Practice.* Oxford: Oxford University Press, 1965.
61. Worthy, J. C. "Organizational Structure and Employee Morale," *American Social Review,* 15 (1950): 169–179.
62. Wrege, C. D., and A. G. Perroni. "Taylor's Pig-Iron Experiments," *Academy of Management Journal,* 17 (1974): 6–27.

6 MANAGEMENT, SUPERVISION, AND LEADERSHIP

IN BRIEF The working supervisor and the company president share in common the need to get work done through subordinates.

As long as business and government are organized in hierarchies, some will supervise and others will be supervised. Possibly every fifth member of the work force will have a substantial supervisory role at some time in his or her working life. Although the first-line supervisor and the company president both supervise others, the natures of their supervisory roles are quite different. The supervisory process changes as we rise in the hierarchy, but we also see two contrasting approaches at all levels: directive and participative. Neither approach is uniformly practiced, nor is one better than the other. Some managers do one or the other. Others do both. Still others do neither. What managers actually do, what they think they should do, and what approach actually is more effective depends on their own personalities, backgrounds, and objectives, as well as on those of their subordinates. Also important are the cultural and economic environment outside the firm, the organizational climate outside the work group but inside the firm, and the requirements of the task being supervised.

In Chapter 4 we briefly noted the extent to which supervisors and management affect worker satisfaction and performance. In Chapter 5 we observed that division of labor and the resulting need for coordination are fundamental to organization. Here we will explore in detail the role of managers in the division of labor, and then consider the different ways managers may play the role and the consequences to themselves and others.

It is not uncommon for 10 per cent or more of the work force of a modern business firm or governmental agency to be members of management. Thus, in covering managerial behavior in supervising, we will be discussing one of the most common occupations in the world of work as well as the most important single occupation in the industrial firm or non-profit agency.

THE MANAGER'S ROLE

Many observers have written about their own experiences as managers, or what they have seen about the behavior of other managers. As president of New Jersey Bell Telephone, Chester Barnard saw management as an art rather than a science, involving feeling, proportion, balance, appropriateness, and the ability to make decisions under conditions of risk (risk is the known probability of success or failure) and uncertainty (uncertainty is the lack of knowledge about one's risks).[5] For him, managers were concerned with three areas: (1) formulating purposes and objectives, (2) maintaining organizational communication, and (3) securing necessary services from others.

Roles at Different Levels in the Hierarchy

Like most other commentators, Barnard emphasized that the manager's level in the hierarchy was most important in determining what was expected of him or her. Top management is concerned with broad policies, objectives, and plans. These purposes and objectives become more specific as they filter down to lower levels, where the work is actually done.

Top management is both teacher and judge of subordinates in an ultimate sense and must be sensitive to the interactions among subordinates and to the material resources with which they work. "Top management must have the ability to detach itself from the internal imperatives of coordination and to reflect on the general purposes and objectives of the company in its industry. . . ."[83] Conformity is the rule at lower levels in the organizational hierarchy. Here, the primary problem is to perceive one's task accurately and conform to it.[103] Technology and controls are most influential. Higher in the hierarchy, job objectives and interpersonal factors become more important in influencing the jobholder's effectiveness.[2] However, for the broad objectives and policies set at the top to be made operational and successfully carried out, managers at lower levels must exhibit considerable initiative.[28]

Other differences are seen between managers at various levels in the organization. For instance, consider the difference between first-level supervision and middle managers. The supervisors are often in direct personal contact with subordinates, whereas middle managers see their subordinates less often. Supervisors are more likely to be expert in the technical aspects of the job. Middle managers spend more time with their own superiors than do supervisors. Middle managers use formal communications in their work to a greater extent than do supervisors.[72]

TIME PERSPECTIVE   Other aspects of the manager's role that change as one rises in the organizational hierarchy are the use of resources, and particularly time perspective.

Table 6–1 displays the time perspective of the decisions made by a sample of British managers at four levels, from foreman at the bottom to general manager or works manager at the top of the same factory. It can be seen that almost all decisions of a shift foreman at the bottom of the hierarchy are about matters that occur within a two-week period. On the other hand, only 3.3 per cent of the decisions of the works manager involve questions of such short duration. Fifty per cent of the decisions of the works manager involve policies with one year or longer time perspectives. No one at lower levels gets involved in decisions involving such periods of time.[60]

The time perspective required of managers at higher levels means that they must live with more uncertainty and risk. They must consider longer-range goals and be able to remain for long periods without evaluation of the effects of their decisions.

CONCERNS   In Chapter 1, we noted that the manager of a firm or agency must balance a system of conflicting interests. The manager must be satisfied with attaining "a workable balance which constitutes the best solution

Table 6–1. Time perspectives of decision situations at four levels of management (in percentages)

Time	Works manager	Division superintendent	Department foreman	Shift foreman
Short (0–2 weeks)	3.3	54.2	68.0	97.7
Moderate (2 weeks–1 year)	46.1	41.4	30.4	2.1
Distant (1 year and beyond)	50.0	4.3	1.5	0.0
Total	.99.4	99.9	99.9	99.8

From Martin, "Differential Decisions in the Management of an Industrial Plant," *Journal of Business,* 1956, p. 251. Copyright 1956 by The University of Chicago Press.

available within the constraints of time, resources, and vision that limit his or her ability to adapt at any given point in time." [45] But at each level, the manager's constituents and their interests are different. At the top, the manager is concerned with sponsors, clients, and community as well as his or her own subordinates. At the bottom, the first-level supervisors are concerned with the interests of their superiors, their peers, and their subordinates as well as others such as union stewards or outside inspectors.

FUNCTIONS   Most managerial jobs seem to require some minimal degree of the function of planning, although the planning may involve employees, finances, materials, purchases, sales, methods, facilities, or equipment. Eight functions are recognized: planning, investigating, coordinating, evaluating, supervising, staffing, negotiating, and representing. These eight functions can be used to differentiate among managerial jobs reliably and validly. For example, 76 per cent of the reports by 452 managers on time spent performing these functions varied no more than 5 per cent over a three-week period. A questionnaire survey of these managers from thirteen companies in a variety of industries, varying in size from 100 to over 4,000 employees, provided the data of Table 6–2. The five functions of planning, investigating, coordinating, evaluating, and supervising account for almost 90 per cent of all the time spent at work by the sample of managers. More time was directed to supervision than any other function (28.4 per cent), but to equate all of management with supervision or leadership is clearly a serious error.

Since most of the 452 managers tended to concentrate on a single func-

Table 6–2. Percentage of work day spent by managers on various performance functions and areas of competence (N = 452).

Performance Function		Area of Competence (Subject Matter)	
Planning	19.5	Employees	27
Investigating	12.6	Money and finances	9
Coordinating	15.0	Materials and goods	15
Evaluating	12.7	Purchases and sales	10
Supervising	28.4	Methods and procedures	26
Staffing	4.1	Facilities and equipment	11
Negotiating	6.0		
Representing	1.8		
Totals *	100.1		98

* Totals do not add to 100 per cent because of rounding.

From Mahoney, Jerdee, and Carroll, "The Job(s) of Management," *Industrial Relations,* 4 (1965): 103.

tion, it was possible to classify them according to this function. Figure 6-1 shows the proportions that fell into various job types based on their single most time-consuming function according to whether they were in lower, middle, or upper management levels. Here we see that being a supervisor predominates as a main job of 51 per cent of lower-level managers, 36 per cent of middle managers, and 22 per cent of those nearer the top of their organization. On the other hand, planners increase in percentage as we rise in the hierarchy. At upper levels, planners are the single largest group. At this top level, generalists are a distinct minority of 20 per cent — not the large majority that is assumed for this level by many commentators.[56]

Management and Leadership

Management entails much more than face-to-face leadership. Nevertheless, skill as a leader and in relating to others is a most important requirement at all levels of management. Interviews with seventy-one corporate executives noted that at the top of the corporation, the group of consequence is relatively small. Its members have highly personal relationships. They interact with each other as in a small firm. A high proportion of group involvement is usual. Informal procedures supplant formal ones.[35]

When queried about what kind of continuing education was most needed by middle managers, eighty-seven business-school deans, fifty-eight business executives, and forty executives in trade associations gave top priority to improving human relations skills. Improving quantitative and technical skills was seen to be of secondary importance. And, as already noted, the single most important function of first-line supervisors surveyed by Mahoney, Jerdee, and Carroll was that of supervising others.[56]

INITIATION (DIRECTION) AND CONSIDERATION (PARTICIPATION)

The traditional view of the manager is of one who gets work done through others by planning, directing, and controlling their work. But evidence has accumulated (as we have noted in previous chapters) that self-planning is more fruitful, that participative approaches often are more effective than directive leadership, and that self-regulated control is often more successful. Hence, many modern managers now see themselves as planning collectively and sharing the decision process through consultation with subordinates. They substitute clear objectives, group norms, and feedback mechanisms for control through threat of punishment or promise of reward.

But we must emphasize that there is no one best way. As we shall see, effective management may call for planning *with* others in some situations and planning *for* others in other situations; being directive at times, and participative at other times; imposing arbitrary controls in some circumstances and emphasizing self-regulation in others. What seems least effective is for managers to do nothing, to abdicate leadership responsibilities, to play laissez-faire roles, shuffling papers behind closed doors and remaining unavailable for consultation.

Considerable evidence is available to suggest that the way in which man-

Figure 6–1. Distribution of assignments among job types at each organizational level (totals do not add up to 100 per cent because of rounding). (From Mahoney, Jerdee, and Carroll, The Job(s) of Management, *"Industrial Relations,* 4 [1965]: 109)

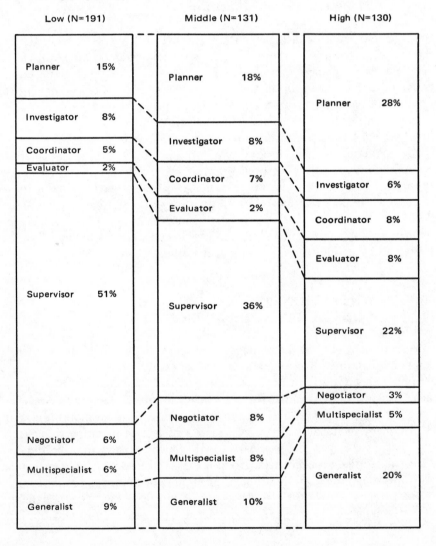

agers carry out their supervisory roles strongly affects the attitudes and performance of their subordinates. A pool of 1,790 items was assembled to describe all possible supervisory behavior. Then eleven field surveys of subordinate ratings of their superiors in industry, business, the military, and in educational organizations were completed.[90] Several factor analyses eventually reduced the pool of items and important clusters of them to two factors: *consideration* and *initiation*.

A review of 72 studies using these two factors suggests when managers are asked whether they should be *considerate* or behave in ways to *initiate structure,* they do see these two as completely independent issues. How much managers *think* they ought to be considerate is unrelated to how much they *think* they ought to initiate. Nevertheless, most often there tends to be a positive correlation between the actual amounts of consideration and initiation of a manager according to their subordinates.[99]

There are numerous unresolved problems with these two widely used instruments (LOQ and LBDQ).[46] Yet there is little question that some supervisors are more active, displaying both consideration and initiation, than others. And, it is usually the more active managers, concerned both about involving their subordinates and about providing direction for them, who are judged as more effective by their subordinates.[14] But, as found in a survey of 54 semiprofessionals working for a national black social-services agency, a leader who is *inconsiderate* and yet high in initiation of structure is detrimental to subordinate productivity.

As with initiation or consideration, and direction or participation, Blake and Mouton describe a manager as concerned about people and/or about production. Each concern can be measured on scales of 1 to 9.[15] Managers may have concern both for production and for people, "9, 9," or they may be "9, 1" (high in concern for production but low in concern for people), or "1, 9" (the reverse), and so on. That is, some managers can be considerate or not without reference to how much they will initiate structure. They can be concerned about people or lack concern about them without reference to their concern for task accomplishment. Managers tend to see themselves as "9, 9," although subordinates are less likely to accord their superiors such doubly positive ratings. More will be said about this in later chapters.

The Considerate or Participative Approach

Considerate supervisors tend to emphasize concern for their subordinates' opinions on matters of importance. Although the supervisors have been endowed with authority over their subordinates, they are willing to equalize with their subordinates their power to decide appropriate courses of action. They seek involvement and commitment from their subordinates. They stress the importance of people and their satisfaction at work, strengthen the self-esteem of their subordinates by treating them as equals, make them feel at ease in discussions, are easy to approach, put subordinates' suggestions into operation, and gain their approval before going ahead.

At the other extreme are inconsiderate supervisors. They frequently demand more than can be done, criticize subordinates in front of others, treat subordinates without considering their feelings, act without consulting subordinates, and refuse to accept suggestions or to explain their actions.[29]

EMPHASIS ON PARTICIPATION   Other characteristics of considerate managers may include their tendencies to make use of participative approaches, such as regular group meetings with subordinates. These managers are likely to try to be open in discourse with subordinates, in an effort to achieve reciprocal openness, so that they communicate what the managers ought to hear, not what subordinates think they want to hear.[9] Consideration and participation are not identical but are correlated. Thus, for example, consideration among fifty-five company presidents, described by their staff, correlated 0.45 with conciliating conflicting demands, 0.49 with representing their interests, and 0.41 with tolerating freedom of action among subordinates.[90]

Consideration takes several forms. Among managers studied so far in the United States, Britain, Spain, and India, subordinates report that, compared to other forms of joint effort, their managers most frequently *consult* with them. That is, their managers most frequently make the final decisions only after obtaining their subordinates' ideas on the subject. The behaviors described as *"consultation,"* according to 46 judges, are completely distinct conceptually from true participative decision making. In true participation, the final decisions are a shared consensus of the managers and their subordinates. However, according to a survey analysis of 75 managers by more than 300 of their subordinates, the same managers who are reported to be consultative also tend to be participative as well, but to a lesser extent. The correlation is 0.84.

Participative managers are also more likely to be reported by their subordinates as delegating decisions to them. The correlation is 0.68. While leaving matters completely in the hands of one's subordinates is quite different conceptually from hammering out a decision in discussion with them, the same managers who reveal one type of behavior also show the other.[14]

Participative, considerate managers are also likely to provide support for their subordinates and to facilitate interaction among their subordinates.[16] Such managers maintain the group through attention to the human relationships involved.

The Initiating or Directive Approach

Myers has described the relationship between participative supervisors and operators doing electronic assembly work.[66] The operators plan their work and have considerable control over what happens as well as over carrying out the task at hand. This situation is in contrast to the relations seen when supervisors are directive. When supervisors are directive, all planning and control remain with them. The operators are rewarded for submissiveness, loyalty, and effort exerted. Highly initiating, directive supervisors insist on maintaining standards, see that subordinates work to full capacity, offer new approaches to problems, emphasize the meeting of deadlines, make their attitudes clear, and decide in detail what should be done and how it should be done. This is what Blake and Mouton refer to as concern for production.[15] Concern for production or production emphasis is not identical with initiation of structure but tends to correlate fairly strongly with it. For example, among fifty-five corporation presidents described by a member of their staff, a correlation of 0.64 was found between emphasizing production and initiating structure.[91]

Directive leadership (initiation) can be coercive. Supervisors can coerce subordinates by threatening them with punishment or promising them rewards. But experiments suggest that supervisors who coerce must maintain continual watch over the situation. Further, their subordinates are likely to remain overly dependent on them.[76] Coercion also is likely to generate dissatisfaction and hostility on the part of subordinates unless they see it as a legitimate part of the supervisor's role.[34]

Directive supervision can be persuasive, or "tell and sell." Supervisors exert influence in one of several ways. Their subordinates may acknowledge the supervisors as experts, they may see the supervisors as referents or models to be imitated; or they may be influenced by virtue of legitimacy — the superior status of the position the supervisors occupy. That is, those in lower positions will accept the influence of anyone who occupies the particular higher position. When directive leadership is exerted through what Raven calls expert, referent, or legitimate power, experiments demonstrate that the influence is more lasting and does not require continued close monitoring by supervisors.[76]

Manipulation is less frequently reported than true direction. Subordinates feel they are being manipulated when they think managers know in advance what they will decide and what they want the subordinates to do. The manager strikes bargains and plays favorites. Such manipulative behavior tends to be exhibited by more directive managers but not by managers who tend to be participative.[14]

Direction or Participation? Initiation or Consideration?

These are the central questions for managers in their role as supervisors. Should they initiate activities, give direction, threaten or promise, emphasize getting the work done and how to do it, or should they share with subordinates the need for solving problems or handling situations, and involve them in working out what and how to do what needs to be done?

For convenience, we will dicuss as two extremes *direction* and *participation*. But, in fact, at least five levels of direction and participation can be categorized. At one extreme, the supervisor gives directions and orders with no explanation to subordinates. The supervisor expects unquestioning obedience. Participation by subordinates is minimal. At the next level, the supervisor accompanies directions with detailed explanations. The supervisor expects to persuade the subordinates or to bargain with them. At the third level (in between direction and participation) is the supervisor who consults with subordinates before deciding what is to be done. Full participation of both superior and subordinate occurs at the fourth level, when they join in deciding what is to be done. Finally, at the fifth level, the superior delegates to the subordinate the task and instructions on how to handle it. The superior's own participation becomes minimal. Whatever the subordinate decides is acceptable to the supervisor.[41]

CONSIDERATION, INITIATION, AND JOB SATISFACTION When subordinates see that they have considerate superiors, the departments of those superiors tend to be departments with fewer grievances.[31] Figure 6-2 shows the grievance rates of 57 production supervisors, each described by three of their subordinates with the leader Behavior Description Questionnaire. It

Figure 6-2. Relation between consideration and grievance rates. (From Fleishman and Harris, "Patterns of Leadership Behavior Related to Employee Grievances and Turnover," *Personnel Psychology,* 15 [1962]: 47.)

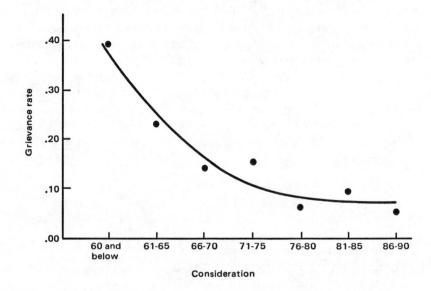

can be seen that considerate supervisors (as described by subordinates) coincide with lower grievance rates.

Initiation works in reverse. Grievance rates are higher where bosses are described as exhibiting more initiation. Corresponding results were obtained for turnover (Figure 6–3). Turnover is high with inconsiderate, directive superiors; turnover is low with considerate superiors who exhibit less initiation.[31]

Since grievances and turnover are expressions of dissatisfaction, we can say that considerate supervision goes with increased satisfaction with work. This is a conclusion reached in numerous studies of the effects of participative management. But there are related questions that need to be answered before we can agree that participation pays off in higher productivity as well. If participation promotes satisfaction, does it also promote productivity? Under what conditions does it promote productivity, if it does so at all? Under what conditions is directiveness more likely to contribute to productivity? And finally, to what extent does supervisor consideration itself *result from* higher productivity and/or worker satisfaction?

INITIATION, CONSIDERATION, AND PRODUCTIVITY   Numerous surveys have demonstrated a postive relationship between departmental productivity and a supervisor's consideration and emphasis on participation. Thus, personnel at 27 delivery stations were more likely to meet their quotas when their

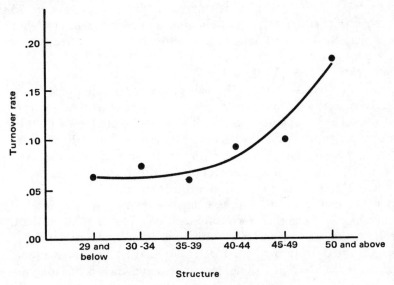

Figure 6–3. Relation between initiation of structure and turnover rates. (From Fleishman and Harris, "Patterns of Leadership Behavior Related to Employee Grievances and Turnover," *Personnel Psychology,* 15 [1962]: 51.)

supervisors were participative.[96] *But laboratory experiments fail to consistently demonstrate the same thing,*[80] so while high productivity in the work situation may coincide with considerate, participative management, laboratory experiments fail to prove that being a considerate, participative supervisor results in more productive subordinates.

In fact, as noted below, we find that directive leadership and initiation of structure are just as predictive of productivity as considerate or participative leadership, when we look at results from many organizations and many independent investigations.[89] Subordinates do become more committed and feel more influential with participative supervisors. But participation may lead to the buildup of expectations that evaluation and rewards depend upon subordinates' participation in goal setting. Further, rewards for goal attainment have to be commensurate with feelings of "ownership" of the goals.[47]

What marketing subordinates under a participative supervisor might say to themselves is: "We contributed to the decision to launch the new media campaign. It was a success. We should receive special acknowledgement, bonuses, or pay raises because it was our idea and it worked. If the rewards are not forthcoming, our expectations will be violated."

The coincidence in industry of participative leadership and productivity may often be due to the fact that supervisors of productive, competent employees can as a consequence afford to be considerate, consultative, and participative. The supervisors can also afford to give less direction and structure to their subordinates if the subordinates already are highly productive. When things go poorly, and workers are incompetent, it is probable that the supervisors are more prone to be directive and inconsiderate. Evidence supporting this possibility is beginning to appear.[25] In a simulated study involving 200 management students, supervisors were more likely to be described as encouraging participation if the supervisors had been told earlier that their subordinates were performing well rather than poorly.

WHICH COMES FIRST? Additional evidence is available dealing with what is cause and what is effect. A "human relations" training program to raise supervisors' consideration scores was conducted. Eighteen months afterward the supervisors' job performance was rated more highly than before.[40] Again, as an experiment, teachers deliberately increased their initiation of structure. Student work productivity improved as a consequence. And when the teachers increased their consideration deliberately, student work group productivity again was increased as a consequence.[21]

First-line managers in insurance, finance, marketing and research, and engineering described their own consideration and initiation on the Leadership Behavior Description Questionnaire. Two subordinates of each of 103 managers rated their own work satisfaction. Peers of these subordinates rated their productivity. The measures were picked up on successive occasions one month apart. Cross-lagged comparisons of "X" at time 1 correlated with "Y" at time 2, in contrast to "Y" at time 1 correlated with "X" at time 2 (shown below), strongly suggests that (1) considerate, participative management *results* in subsequent increased subordinate satisfaction; (2) subordinates' productivity *results subsequently* in their managers' increased consideration for them; and (3) subordinates' productivity *results subsequently* in a reduction in the managers' initiation and directiveness.[36]

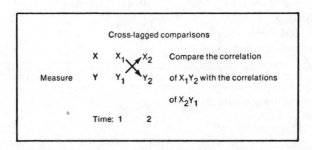

SEEING WHAT YOU EXPECT TO SEE   The issue of what is cause and what is effect is further complicated by the possibility that the correlations reflect the *implicit leadership theories* of the supervisors and/or the subordinates. For example, if subordinates believe that considerate supervision results in more satisfied subordinates and if they are satisfied with their supervision, they will judge the supervisor to be considerate. If subordinates believe that directive supervision results in greater productivity and if they are more productive, they will see their supervisor as directive.[78] Thus, knowledge that a group performed well caused increases in the rated consideration and initiating structure of that group's supervisor, whereas knowledge that a group performed poorly caused large decreases in rated consideration and initiating structure.[64] This happened even when the supervisors behaved identically.[54]

CONTINGENCIES OF SUPERVISION AND LEADERSHIP

The proponents of participative management assume that, in most work situations, (1) everyone wants to share in the more important decision processes; (2) everyone can contribute usefully to the decision process; (3) generally, there is underutilization of this available talent. In turn the proponents react against the other extreme, which argues for supervisory direction under all normal working conditions and for supervisors who plan, initiate, and control subordinates.[41,62]

Table 6–3. Number of positive, negative, and zero findings on the relationships of participative and directive leadership to measures of group performance.

Variables related	Direction of relationship		
	Positive	*Zero*	*Negative*
Productivity			
and participative	10	5	3
and directive	10	4	1
Satisfaction			
and participative	8	3	1
and directive	2	2	2

Adapted from Stogdill, *Handbook of Leadership.* New York: Free Press, 1974. Copyright © 1974 by The Free Press, A Division of Macmillan Publishing Co., Inc.

Nevertheless, when one looks at the many studies on the subject, one finds that results are mixed. For example, as is seen in Table 6–3, in 33 studies 10 investigators reported positive relations between participative supervision and productivity and 10 reported positive relations between directive supervision and productivity. On the other hand, satisfaction was more frequently connected with participative leadership.[89]

Support for the exclusive use of the two extremes — participation versus direction — is giving way to evidence and argument that suggest that we need first to know something about the supervisor in a given situation, about his or her subordinates, about the external environment of the organization in which the supervisor works, about the climate within the organization, and about the task to be performed by the group supervised. With this knowledge, one can both prescribe what might be the more effective approach of the manager — directive or participative — and predict the approach the manager is more inclined to use.

Tables 6–4, 6–5, 6–6, 6–7, and 6–9 list those significant aspects in a supervisor-subordinate situation that influence whether the supervisor will try to pursue a directive or a participative approach with subordinates. These include attributes of the supervisor, of subordinates, of the environment outside the organization, of the organizational climate, and of the task to be accomplished. We shall discuss effects, one at a time, although we recognize that *in vivo* many of these effects are likely to be interacting at the same time, obscuring what is happening. Thus, each effect will be discussed as if all others were being controlled or held constant. Wherever possible we shall comment on the likely supervisory effectiveness of what occurs.

Table 6–4. Tendency of supervisors to be directive or participative, related to their own attributes.

Attributes of supervisors	They will tend to be	
	Directive if:	Participative if:
1. *Interpersonal esteem:*		
Valued and liked, identified with, acknowledged as expert, rewarding figure	Very much or very little esteemed	Moderately esteemed
2. *Personality and attitudes:*		
a. Social ideology: authoritarian or egalitarian; theory X or theory Y	Authoritarian, theory X	Egalitarian, theory Y
b. Attitudes toward own capabilities	Confident, but insecure	Confident and secure, or not confident
c. Attitudes toward subordinates' capabilities		
(1) Capabilities	Does not value	Values highly
(2) Ideas	Uninterested	Interested
d. Specific beliefs about effects of management style		
(1) Participation promotes morale	No	Yes
(2) Participation promotes productivity	No	Yes
(3) Supervisors are rewarded for directiveness	Yes	No
(4) Legitimacy of directiveness	Legitimate	Illegitimate
e. Personality traits		
(1) Locus of control	External	External
(2) Assertive	More	Less
(3) Fair-minded	Less	More
f. Age	Younger	Older
g. Education	Less	More
3. *Culture*	North European, Greek, Indian	U.S., U.K., Latin
4. *Training*	Pattern A Untrained	Pattern B Trained to be trusting, open, experimenting

Table 6–4. Continued

Attributes of supervisors	They will tend to be:	
	Directive if:	Participative if:
5. *Status and power:*		
a. Importance of position, legitimacy of position, position of control and power	Very much or very little status, power	Moderate or high power, status
b. Centrality of information	Central	Peripheral
c. Span of control	Large	Small
6. *Personal objectives:*		
a. Time perspective	Short-term	Long-term
b. Esteem sought	To be valued	To be liked
c. Desired source of esteem	Superiors	Subordinates
7. *Job objectives*	Output quantity (avoidance of risk and uncertainty); orderliness; lower costs, more sales	Creativity; morale; flexibility; understanding of subordinates; development of subordinates; personnel development

Attributes of the Supervisor

Seven clusters of attributes of supervisors in the situation have been identified as making a difference as to whether they will tend to be directive or participative. As noted in Table 6–4, these attributes are interpersonal, personal, cultural, and educational. Others relate to the supervisor's status, to personal goals, and to goals as a supervisor.

1. INTERPERSONAL ESTEEM   What supervisors can do will be affected by how subordinates evaluate them. In early studies, a good deal of experimental evidence had been gathered that suggested that supervisors could be directive if they were esteemed and valued by subordinates, if they were liked, if they could be identified with easily, if they were acknowledged as expert, and if they were seen by subordinates to control rewards that they could allocate among the subordinates if they desired to.[76]

Patchen qualified this.[70] He found that close, directive supervision resulted in high group output only if the group was not only cohesive but also directed by a supervisor who was seen to be a rewarding figure. Furthermore, the matter is complicated by the fact that for many subordinates with strong needs for independence, supervisors will be likely to lose much of their esteem if they are too directive of their subordinates.

Fiedler further qualified the proposition.[27] On the basis of his many studies with survey teams, infantry squads, steel-mill work groups, and many other task groups, Fiedler formulated a contingency theory of leadership, which says that such groups are likely to be most productive under directive supervisors if the supervisors are either very highly esteemed or very little esteemed by the group. On the other hand, these same groups are likely to be most productive under participative supervisors of moderate esteem. Presumably supervisors who are very highly esteemed have too much power to share it readily in a participative approach. Paradoxically, if they have too little power, the supervisors cannot set the boundaries within which it is possible for participation to take place. Under such circumstances, if the supervisors try to be participative but have no power, their subordinates tend to engage in a free-for-all struggle for power.[6]

2. PERSONALITY AND ATTITUDES   Four types of personal characteristics on the part of the supervisor need to be looked at here. A supervisor's implicit theories about effective management are important. As might be expected, a supervisor who subscribes to an authoritarian ideology is more likely to be directive, while one who is more egalitarian in ideology (as measured by the F scale, for instance) is more likely to engage in participative management. In the same way, a manager will be more directive who subscribes to what McGregor called theory X — the theory that workers cannot be trusted.[61] Such workers are seen as immature, lazy, irresponsible, and in need of firm guidance. Managers will tend to be participative if they believe in theory Y — that workers in general are responsible, mature, and capable of taking initiative when necessary. All other things being equal (which they seldom are), pursuing a management approach that is consistent with one's own personal beliefs probably works best. Naturally, if we could select supervisors all of whom were egalitarian and who endorsed theory Y, or if we could provide the educational and therapeutic experiences to make authoritarian managers and subordinates more comfortable with participative approaches, more flexibility of approach would be suggested. However, it is likely that the extreme "theory X" authoritarians who attempt to be participative are likely to be seen by subordinates as insincere if they try power-equalization approaches without really believing in them.

Supervisors who regard themselves as completely competent to deal with a particular task situation are more likely to pursue a directive approach. Where they are unsure about what to do or how to do it, it would be more profitable for them to be participative. Unfortunately, the reverse often happens. Unsure executives try to bluff their way through by being extremely directive. They cover up their feelings of inadequacy by closing the doors on discussion with their subordinates about the issues at hand. At the same time, supervisors who are truly expert in a given situation may feel obligated to spend considerable time in a participative power-sharing stance with their subordinates, when the subordinates in fact would appreciate much more direct orders on the matter, since they see their supervisors as clearly more knowledgeable than they are about what to do.

Supervisors who lack confidence in their subordinates' capabilities will tend to prefer to direct them; if their attitudes are realistic about the subordinates' competence, the supervisors will indeed be more effective if they are directive. If they are uninterested in the ideas the subordinates may have, they may do better to avoid asking the subordinates' ideas if they have no intention of giving the ideas serious consideration. Conversely, if the supervisors value their subordinates highly and are interested in what they have to offer, the supervisors will tend toward a participative approach.[51] Thus, 200 management students examined a work procedure in groups of four. Twenty supervisors of groups were each led to believe their group was highly productive; in 20 more, the supervisors were told that their groups were unproductive. The remaining 10 groups served as controls. In comparison to supervisors of control groups and groups reported to be poor performers, supervisors of the supposedly high performing groups were more likely to encourage speaking out and to listen with respect (according to their subordinates' evaluations of them). The supervisors were also seen to be more open to influence from their subordinates.[25] A manager's specific beliefs about what style is appropriate, legitimate, and effective will dictate whether he or she is directive or participative. If, through reading, experience, and education, the managers come to the conclusion that participation promotes morale, they will more likely be participative. If they come to the belief that participation promotes productivity, they will also be more likely to be participative. On the other hand, if they believe that their success in their organization or the rewards they will achieve from their superiors will depend on their adoption of a directive approach to management, they will be more likely to pursue a directive approach.

If supervisors believe that it is most legitimate for supervisors to direct, control, and plan for subordinates, they will most likely do so. And managers whose behavior is consistent with their specific beliefs about management are more likely to be effective than managers whose behavior is inconsistent with their beliefs — managers who, for instance, "practice Jeffersonian democracy with their subordinates but really believe in the Divine Right of Kings." Such inconsistency was common among managers from traditional cultures surveyed by Haire, Ghiselli, and Porter.[38]

Personality traits as measured by managers' completion of personality inventories tend to account considerably for the managers' leadership behavior as recorded by their subordinates. Thus, 45 managers of a Midwestern textile and plastics firm were seen by their subordinates as higher on initiation of structure if the managers believed that what happened to them was externally controlled, that is, due to forces outside their own control rather than to their own actions.[23] In another study, 77 managers in light industry and nonprofit agencies were more likely to be seen by their subordinates as highly directive if the managers scored high in *assertiveness* and *social boldness* on a personality assessment. However, the managers' *assertiveness* was unrelated to whether or not they were highly participative. Managers who characterized themselves on personality inventories as unwilling to believe that people were *fair-minded* were more likely to be directive. Those who felt people were *fair-minded* tended to be participative. This is consistent with the expectation that "theory X" managers will be directive, since they believe that people cannot be trusted.[26]

Age and education also appear to affect managers' leadership behavior. *Younger* managers tend to be more directive, while *older* managers tend to be more participative, according to a study of 200 managers by Pinder, Pinto, and England.[73] And Bass, Valenzi, and Farrow found among 76 managers a correlation of -0.37 between their educational level and their tendency, according to their 277 subordinates, to be directive.[13] But education was unrelated to their tendency to be participative. However, contrary to popular beliefs and contrary to some laboratory experiments, *sex* seems to have no consistent effect on style of leadership in real-life settings. For example, data on first-line supervisors in two residences for the mentally retarded show that the supervisors' amount of consideration and initiation, according to their subordinates, was unrelated to whether the supervisor was a man or a woman.[68]

3. CULTURE   While some authorities subscribe to a universal style that is equally applicable in all cultures, the evidence from cross-cultural studies shows a consistent pattern for preferences for directive rather than participative approaches in some countries and preferences for participative rather than directive approaches among managers from other countries.[66] For example, managers from the United States, the United Kingdom, and from the Latin countries are more likely to favor participative approaches. On the other hand, managers from Greece and India are more likely to favor directive approaches.[79] (The effects of culture on management will be discussed in more detail in Chapter 7.)

4. TRAINING   Although many supervisory training programs remain unevaluated, at least some have been shown to bring about specific changes in the supervisory style of the trainees.[40] Argyris calls Pattern A behavior that of people who have not been involved in a successful sensitivity training program, which would shift them to what Argyris calls Pattern B behavior.[3] Pattern A behavior occurs in groups where conformity is the norm in dealing with both ideas and feelings. Members are unable to trust one another. This climate prevents experimenting with new ways of relating to others, of being open and owning up to one's feelings and ideas as well as helping others to do the same. As a consequence of sensitivity training, according to Argyris, it is possible to move people to become trusting, open, and able to experiment with their own ideas and feelings, and to own up to them. Moreover, such people can help others to become more trusting and open.

There is evidence that supervisors without sensitivity training are likely to be more comfortable with directive approaches. On the other hand, supervisors who have been through sensitivity training are more likely to be interested in participative approaches with their subordinates. They will probably be more comfortable with such approaches and more effective in sharing their power with their subordinates.[19] More will be said about this in Chapters 13 and 14.

5. STATUS AND POWER   For a decade, much was made of the different kinds of power of consequence to leaders. *Referent* power was ability to set an example to subordinates. *Expert* power was using knowledge to exert influence. *Legitimate* power was due to the leader's position. *Coercive* power was power to punish subordinates. *Reward* power was ability to reward subordinates.[76] It turns out that these powers tend to be highly intercorrelated, so that it is not unreasonable to look at more and less generally powerful people in the organization.[22] If experimentally we suddenly increase the power of leaders in an experiment, we increase the amount by which they can be directive and, in fact, leaders given more power do tend to increase their directiveness.[88] Nevertheless, more powerful executives — that is, those at higher levels — *if secure*, don't necessarily use their power in this way. Paradoxically, it also takes power to be participative.[7] Consistent with what we have already noted in finding that older, more secure managers tend to be participative, Heller and Yukl reported in a study of 203 British managers in all levels in 16 organizations that senior managers, particularly those who had been in their positions for a considerable amount of time, were more likely to share in decision making with their subordinates.[42]

The *status* of managers is the importance of their position in the hierarchy, the position's legitimacy in the eyes of the organization — the amount of power that is associated with the position regardless of who occupies it. Numerous investigations have shown that such status relates to the success and style of the managers in their relations with their subordinates.[76] As with esteem (the value of individuals regardless of their positions), status tends to be an important determiner of success as a leader in a group. If managers have a great deal of esteem and status in the eyes of their subordinates, and *if they choose to be directive*, they will be quite successful in influencing their subordinates. On the other hand, Fiedler suggests that the managers' best tactic in an unstructured task, if they have very little esteem and status, may be to be directive.[27] For this to be so, we assume that in an amorphous situation, if group supervisors have little more esteem or status than their subordinates, the subordinates will conduct a struggle among themselves and with the supervisors unless the supervisors provide firm direction.

A particularly important aspect of one's status is the amount of information one is given. Communication studies strongly support the contention that if group leaders are in the center of a network, so that they are in two-way contact with all the people at the periphery, their group will be more effective if they are directive. On the other hand, if the leaders occupy peripheral positions, their groups will be most effective if the managers are more participative.[86]

6. PERSONAL OBJECTIVES   The supervisors' own goals play an important role in their choosing to be directive or participative. If their time perspective is short, supervisors may find it most effective to be directive. If they have some immediate objectives to be obtained, or if they have little need to concern themselves with involving their subordinates in a long-range commitment to the effort, directive approaches are likely to be most efficient. On the other hand, if the long-term efficiency of their groups is an important objective of the managers, particularly their groups' morale, then participation is more likely to pay off.[37]

If supervisors are seeking to be known for their intelligence, creativity, skill, and general ability and to be valued for such capabilities, they are more likely to pursue directive approaches. They are more likely to suggest what needs to be done, more likely to demonstrate initiative, and in general are more likely to be directive. On the other hand, if they are seeking to be personally liked by those with whom they work, to be popular with their associates, they will try to be good listeners. They will encourage participation and equalization of power with those with whom they work. The evidence lies in how the subordinates evaluate their supervisors. Subordinates tend to report more favorable attitudes toward those supervisors who are considerate and participative. Subordinates are less apt to like directive supervisors. For example, in a wholesale pharmaceutical company that operates 80 decentralized warehouses throughout the United States, 1,760 employees described their supervisors; the attitudes of subordinates were much more favorable when their supervisors in turn felt that consideration and participation were more important.[69] The correlation between how well supervisors were liked by their subordinates and how much the supervisors felt they should be considerate was 0.51. On the other hand, the supervisors' popularity correlated only 0.22 with the extent to which they felt the need to initiate and be directive. But it matters whose esteem you are seeking. If supervisors are more interested in gaining esteem in the eyes of their superiors, they will be more directive. On the other hand, if their main aim is to please their subordinates, they are more likely to show consideration for their subordinates and to emphasize subordinate participation in planning and decision making.[39,102]

7. JOB OBJECTIVES   How supervisors define the purposes of their jobs will affect whether they will be directive or participative. Consider how they choose to communicate with their subordinates. Supervisors can tell their subordinates some specific information. This one-way communication is directive. The communication is two-way if the subordinates can talk back

and question the supervisors. In numerous studies and demonstrations comparing one-way and two-way communication, Leavitt showed that one-way communication tends to be faster; two-way is more satisfying and more likely to be accurate.[50] From these results and from discussions with those who engaged in this experiment, Leavitt further inferred that supervisors are more likely to be comfortable with one-way communication if they are seeking orderliness and minimum "noise" in the system, from their point of view. If their job objective is to minimize risk and uncertainty, they are more likely to avoid opening up prolonged discussion with their subordinates about what is to be done. However, if they are searching for more creative solutions, if their job objectives are to promote commitment, satisfaction, and morale, if they are seeking to develop their subordinates and improve their subordinates' understanding of what is happening, they are more likely to pursue participation.

From the supervisors' standpoint, participation will be worthwhile if they are concerned about their subordinates' growth, understanding, and satisfaction.[51]

Since job objectives depend on one's function in the organization, function makes a difference in leadership style also. Consistent with the managers' relative concern for money and products rather than people, Heller and Yukl found that British managers in sales, production, and finance were less willing than those in personnel to share in decision making with their subordinates.[42] At the same time, Bass, Valenzi, and Farrow reported more direction and negotiation in production, finance, and accounting than among personnel executives.[13]

To sum up, we see that whether managers are more directive or more participative depends on their interpersonal situation, on their personalities, ideologies, culture, and training, on their current positions in the organization and, most important, their objectives as leaders. Whether they reach their objectives depends on whether or not the style of leadership they choose meets the needs of their subordinates to attain their goals and clarifies for them the paths to their goals.[43]

Attributes of Subordinates

As with supervisors, a variety of subordinates' characteristics in a given situation will determine whether or not directive or participative supervision is likely to be attempted and more effective. These subordinate attributes, shown in Table 6–5, include the state of relations among them, their abilities and beliefs, their culture and training, the importance of their positions, and their objectives.

1. INTRAGROUP RELATIONS   How subordinates relate to one another affects what the supervisor can do with them. One of the most important elements

Table 6–5. Tendency of supervisors to be directive or participative as related to attributes of their subordinates

Attributes of subordinates	They will tend to be:	
	Directive if:	Participative if:
1. *Intragroup relations:* Shared norms, purposes, interests; cohesion, absence of conflict, homogeneity of attitudes	Very high or very low cohesion	Moderate cohesion
2. *Personal and interpersonal attributes:*		
a. Level of skill and knowledge; esteem	Low	High
b. Authoritarian vs. egalitarian	Authoritarian	Egalitarian
c. Acceptance of participation as legitimate for subordinate	No	Yes
d. Differential motivations	Requires nurturing; responsive to reward and punishment; prefers order, principle	Need to belong; need for information; need for understanding
e. Independence needs	Weak	Strong
f. Externally oriented	More	Less
3. *Culture, tradition*	Greek	Dutch-Flemish
4. *Training*	Pattern A	Pattern B
5. *Job attributes:*		
a. Importance of position	Low status	High status
b. Centrality to information	Peripheral	Central
6. *Personal objectives:*		
a. Time perspective	Short-run	Long-run
b. Esteem sought	To be liked	To be valued
c. Desired source of esteem	Superior	Peers
7. *Task objectives*	Low risk and uncertainty; low involvement; uninterested	Creativity; personal growth; satisfaction; involvement; interested

determining whether or not supervisors can be directive or participative is the extent to which their subordinates are cohesive, are free of conflict, and share norms, attitudes, beliefs, purposes, goals, and interests. Where members of a group are very cohesive or homogeneous in beliefs and purposes, it is relatively easy to direct them toward their goals, since, to a considerable degree, they are already moving toward them. At the same time, groups in severe conflict, suffering divisive lack of cohesion, usually see the utility of turning to an arbitrary authority, a directive leader, to settle matters that divide the group. Some level of agreement about procedures, interest, and norms is necessary before effective participation can take place.[41] We thus conclude that moderate cohesiveness among subordinates is likely to give rise to effective, participative supervision of them.

2. PERSONAL AND INTERPERSONAL ATTRIBUTES   Skill, esteem, belief, and motives of subordinates all condition whether their supervisor will tend to be directive or participative with them. If subordinates are uncertain because the situation is ambiguous, because the problem is unclear, or because contact time is brief, they prefer direction. On the other hand, when the subordinates think they know what to do, they prefer general orders and the opportunity to participate in the decision. Thus, supervisors of *unskilled* employees in a manufacturing plant were able to be more directive than supervisors of *skilled* employees in the same plant. They were the same, however, in their consideration.[44] Elsewhere, subordinates in a textile and plastics firm who felt that their success or failure was in the hands of forces outside their own control tended to see their supervisors as initiating more structure, but they also felt that their supervisors were less considerate.[23] Using students who thought themselves to be on part-time jobs, Lowin showed that when subordinates perceive that they lack competence for the tasks to be done, they are more appreciative of close, directive supervision than when they consider themselves competent.[55] A survey study of eighty-three British managers was consistent with these findings. Whenever the managers reported seeing a big skill differential between themselves and their subordinates, they were more likely to use autocratic decision methods. Attributes of particular importance were technical ability, decisiveness, and intelligence.[41] On the other hand, when subordinates are esteemed or valued for their expertise and personal qualities, they are more likely to be invited to share in the decision process with their supervisors.

In a survey of 108 supervisors, Vroom showed that satisfaction on the job was increased by participation, but only for subordinates with egalitarian rather than authoritarian attitudes.[95] Closely related to these results are experimental findings in a Norwegian replication of a field experiment carried out in a factory. An earlier, classic study by Coch and French found a marked increase in productivity on the part of work groups that were permitted to participate in goal-setting decisions affecting them.[20] These results were in contrast to findings with control groups not permitted to participate in the same manner. The experiment failed with Norwegian factory workers partly because the decisions permitted them were of a minor order of importance, and partly because Norwegian workers did not see participation by themselves as legitimate, as did American workers.[33] In addition, Norwegian workers are likely to be less independent, as discussed in Chapter 3.

Individual differences among subordinates in a variety of motives also affect the extent to which participation or directive supervision would be more effective. For example, in the preceding survey of 108 supervisors, Vroom showed that individuals with relatively weak needs for independence were less likely to find satisfaction in participating in decision making that affected themselves, in comparison to individuals with strong needs for independence.[95] Similar results would be expected if we contrasted subordinates who required much nurturing, were more immediately responsive to direct promises of reward or threats of punishment, who perfer order and structure (as do authoritarians) rather than remaining in a state of uncertainty with lack of closure, and who tend to be highly materialistic bargainers for whom interpersonal relationships are matters of contractual obligation. According to Clare Graves, these subordinates are more likely to be effectively led by directive rather than participative management.[1] On the other hand, for subordinates with strong needs to belong, to develop cohesive relations with their fellow workers, and to have understanding and information about matters that affect themselves, Graves suggests that participative approaches are more likely to be effective.

3. CULTURE   Managers from six different countries engaged in a decision-making exercise where each experienced authoritarian-directive supervision in two instances and participative supervision in a third role-playing session. Following the three experiences, they indicated which one had been most satisfactory. On a chance basis, participation would have been selected 33 per cent of the time. But among 40 Dutch and Flemish managers, 62.5 per cent were most satisfied in decision-making meetings with participative supervisors. Of 50 Latin managers, 50 per cent were most satisfied with participation; and 46 per cent of 72 British and American managers were most satisfied with participation. The participative mode was preferred over the directive by 42 per cent of Indian managers, 36 per cent of Scandinavian managers, and only 22 per cent of Greek managers.[9] These results are consistent with survey research completed by Haire, Ghiselli, and Porter in 18 countries varying in cultural background.[38] The preference by subordinates for participation in decisions varies as a consequence of the cultural background of the subordinates.

4. TRAINING   As in the case of supervisors, subordinates who have been through some type of sensitivity training — who are what Argyris refers to as Pattern B people — are more likely to appreciate the opportunity to participate in open discussion, to experiment with new ideas, to discuss feelings, and to feel free to own up to how they feel about issues and matters

at meetings with their supervisors.[3] On the other hand, Pattern A subordinates are less likely to be comfortable with the open participation and more likely to accept, at least publicly, direction by the supervisors.

5. JOB ATTRIBUTES As the obverse of what we said earlier about the status of supervisors and how it affects the extent to which they will be directive or participative, it follows that subordinates of relatively low status, peripherally located in information networks, are more likely to operate effectively under conditions of directive supervision. On the other hand, subordinates of high status, who are more central in a communication network, will operate more effectively under conditions of participative management. Thus, participation becomes more common at upper management levels, where all the subordinate managers are of high status.

6. PERSONAL OBJECTIVES What subordinates need and want makes a difference. It seems obvious that where subordinates have a short-run time frame, they will be more likely to put up with authoritarian direction on the part of their supervisor. On the other hand, if the subordinates' time span is of longer duration — for example, if they see their own personal growth tied up with the development of solutions of what is to be done, if they see that their satisfaction over a long period of time is involved — they are more likely to want to participate in decisions of consequence to themselves.

Many subordinates are of a mind to tell their superiors what they believe the superiors want to hear rather than what they should hear; many subordinates wish to ingratiate themselves with their superiors; many subordinates strive above all for being liked by their supervisors. A supervisor will tend to be directive with such subordinates. On the other hand, if subordinates have strong needs to be valued, they must be in a position to demonstrate this value. Often this is only possible if the subordinates can participate in some manner in the decision process. Thus, if subordinates mainly want to be liked, directive supervision is more likely to occur. If subordinates want to be valued by their superior, participation will be more commonly acceptable. Similarly, if it is most important for subordinates to gain esteem in the eyes of their peers, opportunities to do this will be sought and a supervisor will be preferred primarily if he/she permits such peer group participation. But, if ingratiation with their superior is most important to subordinates, directive supervision is going to be more workable.

7. TASK OBJECTIVES OF THE SUBORDINATE What subordinates seek in their jobs affects what their supervisor can and will do. If the subordinates prefer to avoid risk and uncertainty, if they do not wish to get deeply involved in the task at hand, if they are uninterested in the task and their interest is of no great importance in the overall situation, then directive approaches seem in order.[57] On the other hand, if subordinates are seeking personal

growth, if subordinates are seeking to be more creative, if subordinates are seeking involvement and satisfaction, if subordinates are strongly interested in the objective of the task at hand, participative approaches seem more appropriate. Thus, among the British managers surveyed by Heller, when a decision was seen as important to subordinates but not to the company, a high degree of power-sharing was used.[41] Conversely, when a decision was a matter of concern to the company but not to subordinates, power central-ization was preferred.

Attributes of the Outside Environment

Managers differ in what aspects of the outside environment they regard as most important to their work, and they behave differently inside the organ-ization as a consequence. Seventy-six managers described the importance of economic, political, social, and legal influences on the work of their imme-diate subordinates. Their 277 subordinates, in turn, described the fre-quency with which the managers displayed direction, negotiation, con-sultation, participation, and delegation. Highly directive or negotiative managers tended to see economic events such as inflation and taxes as having stronger effects on their work situation. Highly consultative or participative managers tended to see political, social, or legal issues playing a stronger role.[13]

As Table 6–6 shows, the tendency of the supervisor to be directive or participative also will be affected by whether the market or clientele that the organization serves is stable or turbulent, whether the economy as a whole is prosperous, and by the culture of the supervisor and the subordi-nates.

STABLE OR TURBULENT MARKETPLACE   Emery and Trist called attention to the fact that firms that must operate in turbulent fields are more likely to share power of decision making inside their organizations.[24] Faced with

Table 6–6. Tendency of a supervisor to be directive or participative related to the environment outside the organization, market place, community, clients

Attributes of outside environment	They will tend to be:	
	Directive if:	Participative if:
Stable or changing marketplace	Stable	Turbulent
Current economic situation	Recession	Prosperity
Culture; client attitudes, expectations	Traditional	Postindustrial

economic and political uncertainties in British industry, the way out is seen if social-technical conflicts can be solved at the lowest possible levels in an organization. Consistent with this are the observations of Burns and Stalker, who contrasted the relatively stable environment of a rayon mill with the more unstable conditions faced by firms in the electronics industry.[17] For the mill, in its stable environment, a mechanistic, hierarchical system of relationships calling for directive supervision seemed most appropriate. On the other hand, in the electronics field, with its rapidly changing environment, a more consultative, participative, organic system seemed most effective. Similar conclusions were reached by Lawrence and Lorsch, who compared decision making they observed in the relatively stable container industry with decision making in a more turbulent plastics industry.[49] Again, in the stable environment, the decision-making processes within the container firm were likely to be directive; in the more turbulent environment of the plastics firm, decision processes were more likely to be participative.

CURRENT ECONOMIC SITUATION   Our reasoning here is as follows: When the economy is in a recession, money is tight and profit margins are likely to be slim. Management tends to "tense up," to be less willing to risk the consequences of loss of control over decision making. Management anxiety is high and tolerance of uncertainty is low. Also important, the labor supply is more abundant during a business recession, and management becomes less concerned about labor turnover. In fact, often at this time it may look for ways to increase quitting to reduce overhead. On the other hand, during periods of prosperity, there is increased effort to hold on to workers at all costs, to spend what it takes to keep workers happy, and to feel more indulgent about permitting consultation and participation. Human relations training programs are fully funded during conditions of prosperity when the pursestrings are loosened. The glow of prosperity takes pressure off management and increases the likelihood of an easy acceptance of participation and consultation from their subordinates.

CULTURE, CLIENT ATTITUDES AND EXPECTATIONS   Here we suggest that members inside the firm tend to try to be consistent with what they see is expected of them by those outside the firm. Particularly if these inside relationships (in a service agency or business office, for instance) can be observed by outsiders, the organizational climate will tend to reflect outside culture, norms, and expectations. For example, suppose a firm is engaged in producing and marketing educational materials to a clientele with a progressive egalitarian ideology. Some effort will probably be made to encourage participative practices inside the firm.

Attributes of the Organizational Climate
(Elements outside the immediate work group)

As noted in Chapter 5, organizational climate involves elements inside the organization but outside the immediate work group.[94] These elements, listed in Table 6–7, include the organization's current economic health, top management's policies and attitudes, and the organizational structure in which the work group is embedded.

1. CURRENT ECONOMIC HEALTH OF THE FIRM   Various surveys have searched for positive correlation between participative management and profitability, between good social relations and good business, and between employee and community satisfaction and productivity. The results have been mixed and the explanations unconvincing.

When positive associations have been found, indirect inferences have been drawn that the profitability was a consequence of efforts to maintain participative relations, although as we shall see, it may be the reverse: profitable firms may be more willing and interested in promoting satisfactory human relations through participative approaches. But those firms facing economic hardship may be more likely to do the opposite. As some consultants and directors of employee relations have discovered to their chagrin, their efforts to promote good interpersonal and social relations have been scrapped in the name of economy. During economic boom periods, they have been able to expend funds generously on management training, employee morale surveys, and social betterment activities. One might suggest that it is mainly the successfully established firms with a continued history of profitable growth that are most likely to favor participation and consideration along with elegant human and social relations programs.

An experiment was run to test indirectly the proposition that when a firm is making money, its managers become more open to participative approaches.[11] In a simulated budgeting situation, whether or not their company had just finished a profitable year strongly influenced the concern of decision makers for employee satisfaction and well-being and willingness to accept more participative, employee-centered, considerate solutions to problems in safety, labor relations, and management development.

The simulation was "Exercise Objectives," which provides management trainees with the background facts about a hypothetical company and permits each trainee to make a series of decisions including whether to spend $225,000 on safety equipment or let matters ride, knowing that without the equipment a fifty-fifty chance exists for a serious accident or death, whether to negotiate a wage settlement at $750,000 or take a prolonged strike. Afterward, each trainee is asked to rank the goals he had in mind when he made his decisions.

Table 6–7. Tendency of a supervisor to be directive or participative related to the organizational climate outside immediate work group

Attributes of the organizational climate	They will tend to be:	
	Directive if:	Participative if:
1. Current economic health	Unprofitable (profit squeeze): tight money; losing money; intolerable costs; contracting business	Profitable: surplus money; highly profitable enterprise; tolerable costs; expanding business
2. Top management and its policies		
a. Directive or participative	Directive	Participative
b. Time perspective	Short	Long
c. Objectives	Order, stability	Flexibility, creativity
d. Clarity of objectives; ease of measurement of progress	Unclear	Clear
e. Job prescriptions	Simplification	Enlargement
f. Secrecy required or demanded	Yes	No
g. Desired public image	Conservative	Liberal
h. Religious identification of top management	Catholic, homogeneous	Jewish, heterogeneous
3. Structure in which work group is embedded		
a. Departmental function	Production, accounting, finance	Research, personnel, general management, service
b. Line or staff	Line	Staff
c. Level in the organization	Lower	Higher
d. Production system	Mass, batch	Process
e. Centralization	High	Low
f. Negotiating requirements	Flexibility	Support
g. Immediate boss of supervisor	Directive	Participative
h. Number of hierarchical levels trained in participation	Few	Many
i. Person-to-person or overlapping groups	Person-to-person	Groups

Of 72 graduate business students shown a firm's year-end profit-and-loss statement, 24 saw figures that an $86,000 net loss had occurred, while 52 were given a profit-and-loss statement indicating that moderate or large profits had been earned. Both groups learned that over a 10-year period, the company returned approximately 6 per cent on investments.

While 73 per cent of the business students in the profitable circumstances decided to recommend buying the safety equipment, only 50 per cent in the unprofitable situation so decided. Similarly, 40 per cent of those in the profitable enterprise and only 25 per cent of those in the firm losing money last year were willing to spend the required funds to settle a strike quickly.

In comparison with those showing an unprofitable record, students in the profitable situation more often saw as goals in their decisions employee welfare, goodwill, and satisfactory operations. Students in the firm that had experienced a loss were more concerned about meeting competition and profits.

2. TOP MANAGEMENT AND ITS POLICIES   It is easy to envisage the variety of top management attitudes and policies that are likely to affect management styles throughout the organization. If top management has a short time perspective and pushes for production at all costs, demands immediate payoffs, and maintains a close check on how well its policies are being carried out, its supervisors throughout the system are likely to be more directive than participative. On the other hand, if top management is concerned about long-range growth, about employee satisfaction with prospects and opportunities, about maintaining and building a dedicated work force, then greater attention to participative approaches is likely throughout the system. In the same way, if order and stability are repeatedly demanded by top management, directive supervision is more likely to pay off. But if top management is searching for creative activity and for flexible response from its organization, then participation is likely to be promoted.

Conditioning the above effects is the extent to which objectives of operations are clear and easy to measure. For example, if dollar values can be attached readily to the outcomes of performance, or if units of productivity can be assigned, or if quotas and standards to be met can be put into effect, participation is more likely to be acceptable as a management style. Top management can feel at ease about allowing for considerable discretion among subordinates of different levels as long as they are able from time to time to have clear checks on accomplishment. If no such checks are possible, top management is less likely to countenance as much discretion and will be more likely to try to reduce uncertainty by requiring more directive action on the part of its supervisors.

It would also seem apparent that if top management is interested in providing challenging work for subordinates throughout the organization, and keeps looking for ways of enlarging subordinates' jobs, participative management styles will be promoted throughout the system. On the other hand, if top management is imbued with the need and desirability of simplifying jobs within the organization as much as possible, then correspondingly more directive management approaches are likely to be maintained.

An obvious condition which affects whether or not managers can be participative with their subordinates is the extent to which secrecy concerning products, techniques, and business strategies is required of employees by top management. If there is a clear emphasis on people in the organization knowing only "what they need to know," participation becomes much more difficult to maintain than more directive supervision. Employees cannot be asked to participate in or be consulted about decisions where much of the information required to discuss and consider such decisions cannot be revealed to them.[93]

While no concrete evidence supports the contention, it seems reasonable to assume that if top management wishes to promote itself in its institutional advertising and in its recruiting efforts as a liberal, progressive, forward-looking organization, it will tend to emphasize the extent to which its employees contribute to the organization's success through participation. This would be particularly true in those cultures that put a premium on the individual and on democratic ideals. At the same time, if an organization wished to stress as its public image its reliability, solidity, steadfastness, orderliness, discipline, and the like, what would come through in its communications to the outside world would be strong central leadership and quick acceptance within the system of the necessary directions to carry through projects quickly and expeditiously. Again, the culture in which the organization was found would make a difference. Discipline, for example, would be a more important selling point in a traditional society. What top management was trying to convey to the outside world would filter down to lower levels of the organization.

It is obvious that top management that prides itself on its hard-headed, pragmatic, tough-minded, directive approach to work will be less tolerant of participative supervision than a top management that sees itself as more considerate and democratic. Less obvious and less well known is the extent to which personal attributes of top management and the composition of the top-manager group affect supervisory-subordinate relations throughout the system. Most relevant is a large-scale survey by Ward of top managements in the United States, which suggested strongly that the religious affiliation represented by top management in a firm affected to a considerable degree the personnel policies promoted within the firm.[98] Personnel practices were more likely to be liberal and participative where top management was not restricted to members of one religious group. Where managers were all of one religion, policies were more likely to be liberal if top management were exclusively Jewish than if it were exclusively Protestant. Managements that were exclusively Catholic were the most conservative.

3. STRUCTURE IN WHICH THE WORK GROUP IS EMBEDDED   Despite the fact that much more attention has been paid by behavioral scientists to the dynamics within the work group itself — within the primary informal organization of people in face-to-face relationships — there is a growing body of evidence and speculation about the critical importance of the larger structure in which the work group is embedded. That is, much of what goes on inside a work group can be understood only by looking at the relations of the group with components outside the group but within the organization. As with any system or subsystem, external factors play an important part in determining internal dynamics.

We can discern nine attributes of the organization immediately surrounding the work group that are likely to influence the style of supervision seen inside the work group. These nine include departmental function, whether the type is line or staff, the level of the group in the organization, the production system of the organization, centralization of the organization, the supervisor's negotiating requirements, the management style of the immediate boss of the supervisor, the number of hierarchical levels in the organization trained in participation, and the extent to which links are between people or between overlapping groups.

Departmental function has a distinct effect on the department head's supervisory style. Heller's survey of British managers noted that those in personnel and general management functions typically used less centralized decision procedures than colleagues in finance and production.[41] Managers who led groups in purchasing, stores, and sales tended to be in between. This is consistent with earlier work by Fleishman, Harris, and Burtt, who noted that foremen in manufacturing departments or other departments working under time constraints were likely to receive higher merit ratings if they tended to be directive, while the reverse was true for foremen in service departments.[32] In addition, in the nonmanufacturing service departments, considerate supervisors were seen as more proficient. More direction and initiation contributed to greater absenteeism and more grievances mainly in manufacturing departments, and to greater turnover in service departments. Table 6–8 shows a summary of these International Harvester results.

Although manufacturing often demands routinization and coordination, they may be contraindicated in a service function. Child and Ellis found in a study of 787 managers that managers in service organizations, indeed, saw their roles as less formal, less well defined, and less routine than the roles of manufacturing managers.[19] Service implies a "people orientation" in contrast with the "concern for things" of manufacturing. Supervisors,

Table 6–8. Comparison of manufacturing and service departments.

	Proficiency	Absenteeism	Accidents	Grievances	Turnover
Consideration					
Manufacturing	−0.31 **	−0.49 **	−0.06	−0.07	0.13
Service	0.28	−0.38	−0.42 *	0.15	0.04
Initiating Structure					
Manufacturing	0.47 **	0.27 *	0.15	0.45 **	0.06
Service	−0.19	0.06	0.18	0.23	0.51 *

* $p < .05$.
** $p < .01$.

Adapted from Fleishman, Edwin A.; Harris, Edwin F.; and Burtt, Harold E. *Leadership and Supervision in Industry.* Columbus, Ohio: Ohio State University, Bureau of Educational Research, (1955): 85

say in a welfare agency, who remain highly directive set for their case workers an example of how to relate to clients that is likely to reduce client satisfaction and the effectiveness of consultation with the clients.[81]

In their examination of the impact of a firm's market on internal dynamics within the firm, Lawrence and Lorsch also noted that within the firm itself, different departments require different modes of decision making.[49] For example, marketing is usually under shorter time constraints than is research. Within working units in marketing, directive styles may more often than not be appropriate, whereas in research they are likely to be less appropriate.

Line and staff distinctions make a difference, consistent with what was learned about management style in production, where time constraints are often involved. Line executives frequently complain about their lack of time to do creative long-range thinking, while staff executives are often hired just for this purpose. So it was not surprising that line executives in Heller's survey reported using more centralized directive decision styles than did executives in staff positions.[41]

The level in the organization of superior and subordinates is a particularly salient factor affecting the superior's style.[84] At higher levels, managers are concerned with longer-range problems and policies, norms, and values. They are dealing with more creative, educated, higher-status subordinates, who expect more opportunity to participate. They show more interest in long-term commitments from subordinates as well as in the development of subordinates. At lower levels, managers are dealing with more routine types of work, more clearly defined objectives, and with subordinates of lower status and fewer expectations about participating in the decision process.

The production system makes a big difference. Woodward's study of the impact of technology on decision processes in 100 British firms concluded that in those companies involved in mass or batch production, decision making was more likely to be centralized and directive and often not precedent-setting.[101] On the other hand, in continuous-process industries, such as petroleum refining, decisions were more likely to be made by committees with considerable participation, and the decisions were more likely to have long-term implications.

Centralization leads to more directive supervision. If supervisors find themselves and their immediate subordinates embedded in a highly centralized structure, the supervisors need to be more immediately responsive to demands from higher authority and are likely themselves to need to be directive in relations with their subordinates. On the other hand, if the organization as a whole is highly decentralized, supervisors are more on their own and freer to choose participative approaches. This does not necessarily mean that supervisors will choose participative styles. In fact, decentralization makes it possible for supervisors to be extremely dictatorial with their subordinates if the supervisor so chooses.

Negotiating requirements are of consequence. Simulated collective bargaining experiments demonstrated that negotiators who were committed to their own group's strategies were likely to be less flexible and effective in negotiations.[8] Thus, we infer that supervisors who must often negotiate with other department heads about schedules, budgets, working relations between departments, and personnel transfers are likely to want to remain relatively independent of the strong influence of those within their departments, if they wish to maximize their flexibility in negotiating outside their own department. They want a free hand so that they can be as flexible as possible in negotiations. They do not want to be locked into positions by consensus decisions that have been reached beforehand within their groups. Such consensus decisions would arise from participative discussions about issues to be negotiated by the supervisors when they meet with other department heads. These decisions would tend to bind the supervisors when they entered managers' meetings. If they saw themselves representing their work group, pushing the point of view that had strongly been supported inside their work groups, their flexibility in the negotiations would be much more limited than if such participative efforts had not been made. But if supervisors need to present a united front as part of their negotiating argument, if they are concerned that whatever they are able to negotiate outside the department is strongly endorsed by their subordinates, then the participative mode makes more sense. For example, if supervisors are seeking among their own subordinates commitment, understanding, and acceptance of schedules to be negotiated with other departments, then obviously the supervisors need to consider the utility of being more participative before negotiations begin. If the supervisors permit discussion of negotiations only after they have occurred and matters are completed, then they obviously are preventing much participation and are likely to have less acceptance by their subordinates of whatever decisions were reached in negotiations.

The immediate boss of the supervisor is an important element to be considered. Fleishman followed up International Harvester foremen who had been in two weeks of human relations training.[80] At the end of training, the foremen as a whole had shifted in the direction of favoring more considerate, participative supervisory behavior. Whether these new attitudes were still maintained and revealed in practice six months later depended on the behavior and attitudes of the foremen's immediate bosses. Some foremen returned to a department where their own boss was strong in initiation of structure and less concerned about consideration and participation on the part of his subordinate foremen. Such foremen were more likely to drift back to an earlier position of less considerate and more directive behavior and attitudes, according to descriptions by themselves and their subordinates. To sum up, supervisors are more likely to be initiating and directive if their bosses behave in the same way; they are more likely to be considerate and participative if their bosses are so inclined. Furthermore, they tend to share the same attitudes about these approaches.[75] Training to change this behavior can be effective only if the goals of the training are also accepted by the immediate supervisors of the supervisors being trained.

The number of hierarchical levels trained in participation obviously increases the tendencies to be participative throughout the system. Further, a necessary key to shifting an entire organization in the direction of more participation and consideration of subordinates lies in full acceptance of the ideology by the sponsors of the organization and its top management.[58]

Lowin hypothesized that the effectiveness of participative decision making would increase with the number of administrative levels in the organization that would pursue this approach.[55] He argued that experiments introducing the participative approach and moving away from the more traditional, directive style of management at lower levels would be arbitrarily terminated prematurely if upper-level executives were opposed to the approach. Moreover, great lateral and cross-functional conflict would occur if participative approaches were practiced in one section of the organization but not in another.

The story is often told by management educators and change agents in large organizations of the temporary success they achieved, within the units they were working in, in shifting management toward more consideration and participation. But eventually they failed because of rejection of the approach and program by higher authority or because of conflicts with other units, which were not changing.

Person-to-person overlapping groups are a double way of organizing the web of supervisor-subordinate relations in an organization. Traditionally, managers tend to establish person-to-person relationships with their immediate subordinates. Discussions are held with each subordinate individually. The supervisors' power outweighs the subordinates' and influence is likely to flow one way: downward. But where superiors see themselves as members of a group including all their subordinates, power equalization is more likely. This change from person-to-person to group approaches was proposed by Likert and subsequently tested out in a variety of situations.[52,65,58]

Satisfaction and morale tend to be positively enhanced over time in organizations of overlapping groups. Productivity may or may not be so positively stimulated, although here Likert argued that there is a time lag of as much as two years between the time of shifting toward an overlapping group organization and the time at which increases in productivity begin to appear.[53]

The "overlapping" group design, shown by crosshatching in Figure 6–4, is superimposed on the traditional hierarchical design represented by the vertical lines of authority also seen in the same figure. Instead of individual person-to-person relationships between superiors and their subordinates at each level of the chain of command from bottom to top of the hierarchy, Likert envisages an organization of overlapping groups. Each group contains a superior and a number of subordinates, so that (except at the very top and bottom of the organization) each manager is a member of two groups. The first group contains peers and the superior; the second group contains subordinates and the manager. Given such overlapping groups, participation at all levels becomes the more appropriate style of management. The assumed payoffs to management with this conversion are greater organizational flexibility and adaptability.

In the traditional organization, with its single vertical communication

Figure 6–4. The overlapping-group form of organization. (From *New Patterns of Management,* p. 107, by R. Likert. Copyright 1962 by McGraw-Hill, Inc. Used with permission of McGraw-Hill Book Company.)

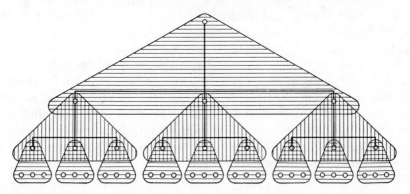

lines upward and downward, diagonal and horizontal flow of information is often more difficult to effect. Overlapping groups reduce the obstacles to this required flow of information among peers.

The organization increases its adaptability and flexibility because the overlapping groups permit and encourage their members to respond quickly and intelligently when they detect problems. The detection and rapid communication to the decision makers of unforeseen changes inside or outside the organization give the decision makers opportunities to learn, to experiment, to profit from mistakes, and to modify the organization to increase its effectiveness in dealing with new conditions. (In many companies, it is the salespersons, who meet the public, who must be sensitive to customer reactions of consequences to the company and who must feel free and willing to communicate their opinions back to the management. In other companies, it is the first-line supervisors and workers who must be ready, willing, and able to detect and transmit upward perceived production problems.)

Task Requirements

For convenience, we compartmentalize the discussion here into three aspects of what is required for task accomplishment and how each affects supervisory style: (1) problem and decision requirements of the task, (2) potential outcomes from completing the task, and (3) motives and constraints imposed by the task.

1. CHARACTERISTICS OF PROBLEMS AND DECISION REQUIREMENTS   As noted in Table 6–9, eight elements of the problem at hand influence the extent to which the supervisor will tend to be directive or participative in working with subordinates in completing the task. The eight elements include the nature of the solution, quality requirements, whether or not rapid decisions are required, the amount of structure of the task, whether the task is routine or varied, whether or not there is machine pacing, whether the goal is practical or theoretical, and whether the problem is intellectual or manual and manipulative.

It matters whether the task requires *convergence* or *divergence,* according to a laboratory study by Shaw and Blum of groups of five men each who performed three tasks with different types of solutions to be sought.[87] Directive supervision was more effective when the problem called for a single final decision or involved the convergence of judgments into some final unification. On the other hand, when the problem required multiple alternatives for a final answer, if the problem ended in divergency, then participative approaches were more effective.

Where *decision quality* is demanded and varied types of input are re-

Table 6–9. Tendency of a supervisor to be directive or participative related to task requirement

Task Requirements	If the task requirements are as below, a supervisor should be:	
	Directive	Participative
1. Characteristics of problem and decision requirements		
a. Solution to problem	Unitary, convergent	Multiple, divergent
b. High quality required	No	Yes
c. Emergency action; rapid decisions	Yes	No
d. Routine or varied	Routine	Varied
e. Machine-paced	Yes	No
f. Practical or theoretical	Practical	Theoretical
g. Intellectual problem-solving versus manual, manipulative	Manual	Intellectual
2. Consequences of task completion		
a. Conflicts of interest for subordinates (e.g., salary increases)	Yes	No
b. Outcome of consequence to	Organization	Subordinates
3. Motives and constraints		
a. Stressful, pressure, strain	Very high; very low	Moderate
b. Can be delegated; subordinates have control or skills	No	Yes
c. Interaction potential, group size, worker connectivity, worker proximity	Low	High
d. Cost of participation	Expensive	Cheap

quired to achieve quality, participative approaches tend to be in order, contrary to traditional thinking on the subject.

There is voluminous evidence that groups achieve better solutions to problems than their average member does working alone — although the group solution may not be as good as the best single solution achieved by one of the members working by himself.

The primary reason for managers in 15 firms to use participation, they reported, was to improve the technical quality of decisions. Other supposed advantages of participative management were increased satisfaction, improved communications, subordinate development, and overcoming resistance to change, But these were seen as secondary in importance to promoting decision quality.[41] In fact, participation becomes mandatory in highly technically oriented organizations, where the technical expertise available does not reside in the heads of the supervisors but is distributed in varying amounts among their immediate subordinates.

Emergency action obviously limits or prevents lengthy discussions. Where rapid decisions are called for, executives are likely to become more directive than participative.[55] Consistent with this, the more an organization wishes to be prepared for emergency action, the more likely it is to stress a high degree of structure, attention to orders, and authoritarian direction. The military, particularly at lower levels in the organization, stresses rapidity of response to orders from high authority, despite the fact that it may actually operate under battlefield conditions a relatively small amount of the time.

Routine tasks call for directive supervision. In their detailed study of the worker on the assembly line, Walker and Guest emphasized the extent to which supervision was likely to be more directive when tasks to be performed were extremely routine. In the same way, we would guess that where pacing is established by machines over which subordinates and supervisors have little or no control, directive supervision is in order, consistent with higher authority that does control the pacing. Contrariwise, participation is more characteristic of situations where tasks are varied and not machine-paced.

Practical outcomes favor directive supervision. Korten observed that if the final product of a task were practical, more directive supervision was in order.[48] On the other hand, if the outcome were theoretical, then participation was of more utility. In this same vein, McGregor argued that where the task calls for intellectual problem solving, participative approaches are more effective, whereas for manual, manipulative types of activities, directive approaches are favored.[62]

2. CONSEQUENCES OF TASK COMPLETION   Several potential consequences affect the extent to which supervisors can be directive or participative. For example, where they suspect the existence of conflicts of interest between subordinates and organization, say in recommending salary increases for subordinates, supervisors must take a directive stance. On the other hand, where solving the problem is in the common interest of all subordinates, participation is more likely to be effective. More generally, where the outcome is of primary consequence to the organization alone, supervisors may have to be directive, but where subordinate interest is paramount, participation seems to be the obvious approach of choice.[41]

3. MOTIVES AND CONSTRAINTS   Several motives and constraints associated with the task and its completion are likely to modify the manager's style of supervision. If the task generates great stress and strain, if employees must work under great pressure and tension in order to achieve success on the task, then the most effective leadership is from a directive leader, who, given the ability and power to do so, can help to provide authority in coping with the situation.[77] Thus, among 54 semiprofessionals in a national black

social-service agency, under conditions of high stress, supervisory considera-tion of 19 department heads was *negatively* associated with performance of their subordinates, but under conditions of low stress, considerate super-vision was *positively* associated with subordinate performance.[82] Never-theless, we guess that the directive approach may also be more effective if the task were so relaxing and leisurely that some prodding on the part of supervision is required to keep work flowing along. Thus, again an in-between state of affairs seeems most conducive to participation on the part of employees, where they are stressed neither too much nor too little by the nature of the task.

The obvious characteristic of the task that affects the extent to which supervisors can be participative is whether the task is easy enough for subor-dinates to handle without the supervisor's intervention.[41] We have already noted that if they believe that their subordinates have the requisite skill, supervisors are more likely to be participative. It seems equally true that if in fact the subordinates do have the skills, supervisors will be more effective if they permit subordinate participation in the decision process. On the other hand, if the task constraints prevent delegation to subordinates, then direction may be required from the supervisors.

Interaction potential between individuals refers to how much they can contact each other. Such contact becomes difficult if they belong to a large group; if they are physically distant from each other; if they are unfamiliar with each other, as telephones are not available; and so on. Where the task must be accomplished by a large group, by "disconnected," unfamiliar workers operating at a distance, interaction potential is low. Directive leadership is required. On the other hand, under conditions where workers can operate in small, intimate, face-to-face groups, interaction potential is higher and participation works better. In one study, 489 employees of a large manufacturing company working in 42 groups described the initia-tion and consideration of their supervisors. In the smaller groups only, the greater the supervisor's initiation (or direction), the less effective were those groups.[4]

Another element in deciding whether a supervisor should be directive or participative is the *cost of participation*. It seems obvious that directive rather than participative leadership is desirable if the cost of the time re-quired of subordinates is more expensive than the value of the outcome of their participation.[93]

Direction, Participation, Supervision, and Power

Some of the key elements in what we have said so far can be joined rationally to prescribe what is most likely to succeed: direction or participation. Vroom and Yetton pose ten questions that leaders should ask themselves in deciding whether to be directive or participative in decision making with their subordinates.[97] Essentially, they argue that supervisors ought to be directive if they are confident that they know what needs to be done and their subordinates do not have this knowledge. Furthermore, Vroom and Yetton suggest that in this situation the decision will be accepted by subordinates if supervisors make it by themselves. On the other hand, if the subordinates have more of the information than the supervisors, if their acceptance and commitment are of a paramount importance, and subordinates can be trusted to concern themselves with the organization's interests, the supervisors should be participative.

This is consistent with what Bass and Valenzi theorized and Shapira confirmed, that where supervisors have more power and information than their subordinates, they can be directive.[12,85] If they have more power, but their subordinates have the information, they can and should be more consultative. Where subordinates are relatively more powerful but supervisors know what needs to be done, supervisors can mainly negotiate with the subordinates. Finally, if subordinates are both more powerful and better informed than supervisors, supervisors might as well delegate the decisions to subordinates.

Supervision, Organization, and Motivation to Work

In completing this section on organizational psychology with an examination of management and supervision, we need to emphasize that to understand what makes for effective organizations, good supervision must be buttressed by a healthy organizational climate and by job assignments for subordinates that meet their needs for meaningful work, worthwhile outcomes, and feedback about accomplishments.[74] The supervisor plays an important role in bringing about these conditions for motivation to work. When the organization's goals are unclear, and there is disorderliness, threat, and uncertainty, the effective leader initiates needed actions and takes a strong directive stance. On the other hand, when arrangements are predictable, when the organization functions with clear objectives in an orderly fashion, when what needs to be done and how to do it is clear, the effective supervisor is still active, but he or she now consults with subordinates or shares the decision making with them. As we have already noted, such participation and consultation are more likely to pay off, particularly at higher levels in the organization, if subordinates have knowledge and control in service operations and where high priority is placed on obtaining the enthusiastic commitment of the subordinates to the organization's objectives.

Regardless of the organizational circumstances, ineffective supervisors are those who take a laissez-faire position. They display neither directive nor participative leadership. They bury themselves in paperwork. They are uncommunicative, unavailable for consultation, seemingly unconcerned with either the productivity or the satisfactions of their subordinates. When pressed to influence their subordinates, they tend to try to cajole or manipulate them by promises of rewards or threats of punishment. They bargain for favors and play off one subordinate against another.[12] Under such leadership, each individual's goals or aims take precedence over organizational objectives.[92] The organization is likely to be plundered. Thus, when such laissez-faire leadership occurred in research and development labs, overall laboratory output of the scientists and engineers suffered.[71]

SUMMARY

After describing what managers do and the organizational purposes they serve, we see that whether they are directive or participative, whether they initiate structure or are considerate in their supervisory behavior depends on a variety of personal, interpersonal, and organizational conditions as well as the nature of the task in which they are engaged with their subordinates. Whether they should be directive depends on how much more they know than their subordinates about what needs to be done; whether they should be participative depends on how much they want the fully committed contribution of their subordinates to what needs to be done.

In moving next into personnel psychology, we will see that organizational issues will continue to be involved. In fact, we will conclude our examination of personnel psychology that follows by showing how we can increase understanding and prediction of individuals' abilities and performance by taking into account what's going on around them on and off the job.

REFERENCES

1. Albrook, R. C. "Participative Management: Time for a Second Look," *Fortune* (May 1967): 166–170, 197–200.
2. Argyris, C. *Integrating the Individual and the Organization.* New York: Wiley, 1964.
3. Argyris, C. "The Incompleteness of Social-Psychological Theory: Examples from Small Group, Cognitive Consistency, and Attribution Research," *American Psychologist,* 24 (1969): 893–908.
4. Badin, I. J. "Some Moderator Influences on Relationships between Consideration, Initiating Structure, and Organizational Criteria," *Journal of Applied Psychology,* 59 (1974): 380–382.
5. Barnard, C. I. *The Functions of the Executive.* Cambridge: Harvard University Press, 1950.
6. Bass, B. M. *Leadership, Psychology and Organizational Behavior.* New York: Harper and Row, 1960.
7. Bass, B. M. *Organizational Psychology.* Boston: Allyn and Bacon, 1965.

8. Bass, B. M. "Effects on the Subsequent Performance of Negotiators of Studying Issues or Planning Strategies Alone or in Groups," *Psychological Monographs,* 80 (1966): 1–31.

9. Bass, B. M. *A Preliminary Report on Manifest Preferences in Six Cultures for Participative Management.* Technical Report 21, Contract NONR N00014–67 (A), Management Research Center, Rochester: University of Rochester, 1968.

10. Bass, B. M. "A Systems Survey Research Feedback for Management and Organizational Development," *Journal of Applied Behavioral Science,* 12 (1976): 215–229.

11. Bass, B. M., J. M. Binder, and W. Breed. "Profitability and Good Relations: Which Is Cause and Which Is Effect?" *Management Research Center Brief* 4. Pittsburgh: University of Pittsburgh, 1967.

12. Bass, B. M. and E. Valenzi. "Contingent Aspects of Effective Management Styles." In J. G. Hunt and L. L. Larson (eds.), *Contingency Approaches to Leadership.* Carbondale: Southern Illinois University Press, 1974.

13. Bass, B. M., E. R. Valenzi, and D. L. Farrow. *External Environment Related to Managerial Style.* Technical Report No. 77–2. U. S. Army Research Institute for the Behavioral and Social Sciences, Grant No. DAHC19–76–G–0008. Rochester: University of Rochester, 1977.

14. Bass, B. M., E. R. Valenzi, D. L. Farrow, and R. J. Solomon. "Management Styles Associated with Organizational, Task, Personal, and Interpersonal Contingencies," *Journal of Applied Psychology,* 60 (1975): 720–729.

15. Blake, R. R., and J. S. Mouton. *The Managerial Grid.* Houston: Gulf Publishing, 1964.

16. Bowers, D. G., and S. E. Seashore. "Predicting Organizational Effectiveness with a Four-Factor Theory of Leadership," *Administrative Science Quarterly,* 11 (1966): 238–263.

17. Burns, T., and G. M. Stalker. *The Management of Innovation.* London: Tavistock Publications, 1961.

18. Campbell, J. P., and M. D. Dunnette. "Effectiveness of T-Group Experiences in Managerial Training and Development," *Psychological Bulletin,* 70 (1968): 73–104.

19. Child, J., and T. Ellis. "Predictors of Variation in Managerial Roles," *Human Relations,* 26 (1973): 227–250.

20 Coch, L., and J. R. P. French, Jr. "Overcoming Resistance to Change," *Human Relations,* 1 (1948): 512–532.

21. Dawson, J. A., L. A. Messe, and J. L. Phillips. "Effects of Instructor-Leader Behavior on Student Performance," *Journal of Applied Psychology,* 56 (1972): 369–376.

22. Dieterly, D. L., and B. Schneider. "The Effect of Organizational Environment on Perceived Power and Climate: A Laboratory Study," *Organizational Behavior and Human Performance,* 11 (1974): 316–337.

23. Durand, D. E., and W. R. Nord. "Perceived Leader Behavior as a Function of Personality Characteristics of Supervisors and Subordinates," *Academy of Management Journal,* 19 (1976): 427–438.

24. Emery, F. E., and E. L. Trist. "The Causal Texture of Organizational Environments," *Human Relations,* 18 (1965): 21–32.

25. Farris, G. F., and F. G. Lim, Jr. "Effects of Performance on Leadership, Cohesiveness, Influence, Satisfaction, and Subsequent Performance," *Journal of Applied Psychology*, 53 (1969): 490–497.

26. Farrow, D. L. and B. M. Bass. *A Phoenix Emerges: The Importance of Management and Subordinate Personality in Contingency Leadership Analyses.* Technical Report No. 77–1, U. S. Army Research Institute for the Behavioral and Social Sciences, Grant No. DAHC19–76–G–0008. Rochester: University of Rochester, 1977.

27. Fiedler, F. E. *A Theory of Leadership Effectiveness.* New York: McGraw-Hill, 1967.

28. Fiedler, F. E., and S. M. Nealey. *Second-Level Management.* Washington, D. C.: U. S. Civil Service Commission, 1966.

29. Fleishman, E. A. "The Description of Supervisory Behavior," *Journal of Applied Psychology*, 37 (1953): 1–6.

30. Fleishman, E. A. "The Measurement of Leadership Attitudes in Industry," *Journal of Applied Psychology*, 37 (1953): 153–158.

31. Fleishman, E. A., and E. F. Harris. "Patterns of Leadership Behavior Related to Employee Grievances and Turnover," *Personnel Psychology*, 15 (1962): 43–56.

32. Fleishman, E. A., E. F. Harris and H. E. Burtt. "Leadership and Supervision in Industry," *Business Education Research* (1955).

33. French, J. R. P., Jr., J. Israel, and D. As. "An Experiment on Participation in a Norwegian Factory: Interpersonal Dimensions of Decision-Making," *Human Relations*, 13 (1960): 3–19.

34. French, J. R. P., Jr., H. W. Morrison, and G. Levinger. "Coercive Power and Forces Affecting Conformity," *Journal of Abnormal and Social Psychology*, 61 (1960): 93–101.

35. Glickman, A. S. and Hahn, "Top Management Development and Succession: An Exploratory Study" New York: MacMillan, 1969.

36. Greene, C. N. "The Reciprocal Nature of Influence between Leader and Subordinate," *Journal of Applied Psychology*, 60 (1975): 187–193.

37. Hahn, C. P., and T. G. Trittipoe. *"Situational Problems for Leadership Training: III. Review for Petty Officers of Leadership Research.* Naval Contract Report, Washington, D. C.: Insitute for Research, 1961.

38. Haire, M., E. E. Ghiselli, L. W. Porter. *Managerial Thinking: An International Study.* New York: Wiley, 1966.

39. Halpin, A. W. "The Leader Behavior and Effectiveness of Aircraft Commanders." In R. W. Stogdill and A. E. Coons (eds.), *Leader Behavior: Its Description and Measurement.* Bureau of Business Research Monograph 88. Columbus: Ohio State University, 1957, pp. 65–68.

40. Hand, H., and J. Slocum. "A Longitudinal Study of the Effect of a Human Relations Training Program on Managerial Effectiveness," *Journal of Applied Psychology*, 56 (1972): 412–418.

41. Heller, F. A. *Managerial Decision Making.* London: Human Resources Center, Tavistock Institute of Human Relations, 1969.

42. Heller, F. A., and G. Yukl. "Participation, Managerial Decision-Making, and Situational Variables," *Organizational Behavior and Human Performance*, 4 (1969): 227–241.

43. House, R. J., and T. R. Mitchell. "Path-Goal Theory of Leadership," *Journal of Contemporary Business*, 3, No. 4 (1974): 81–97.

44. Hsu, C. C., and R. R. Newton. "Relation between Foremen's Leadership Attitudes and the Skill Level of Their Work Groups," *Journal of Applied Psychology*, 59 (1974): 771–772.

45. Jacobs, T. O. *Leadership and Exchange in Formal Organizations*. Ft. Benning, Georgia: Human Resources Research Organization, 1970.

46. Kerr, S. and C. Schriesheim. "Consideration, Initiating Structure and Organizational Criteria — An Update of Korman's 1966 Review," *Personnel Psychology*, 27 (1974): 555–568.

47. Kim, J. S., and R. S. Schuler. "Contingencies of the Effectiveness of Participation in Decision Making and Goal Setting," *Proceedings of the Eastern Academy of Management* (May 13–15, 1976).

48. Korten, D. "Situational Determinants of Leadership Structure." In D. Cartright and A. Zander (eds.), *Group Dynamics: Research and Theory*, New York: Harper and Row, 1968.

49. Lawrence, P. R., and J. W. Lorsch. *Organization and Environment*. Cambridge: Harvard University Press, 1967.

50. Leavitt, H. "Some Effects of Certain Communication Patterns on Group Performance," *Journal of Abnormal and Social Psychology*, 46 (1951): 38–50.

51. Likert, R. "Motivational Approach to Management Development," *Harvard Business Review*, 37, No. 4 (1959): 75–82.

52. Likert, R. *New Patterns of Management*. New York: McGraw-Hill, 1961.

53. Likert, R. *The Human Organization: Its Management and Value*. New York: McGraw-Hill, 1967.

54. Lord, R. G., J. Binning, M. C. Rush, and J. C. Thomas. "The Effect of Performance Cues and Actual Behavior on Questionnaire Based Measures of Leadership Behavior," *Organizational Behavior and Human Performance*. 21 (1978): 27–39.

55. Lowin, A, "Participative Decision Making: A Model, Literature Critique and Prescriptions for Research," *Organizational Behavior and Human Performance*, 3 (1968): 68–106.

56. Mahoney, R. A., T. H. Jerdee, and S. J. Carroll. "The Job(s) of Management," *Industrial Relations*, 4 (1965): 97–110.

57. Maier, N. R. F. *Psychology in Industry*, Boston: Houghton Mifflin, 1965.

58. Marrow, A. J., S. E. Seashore, and D. G. Bowers. *Management by Participation*. New York: Harper and Row, 1967.

59. Martin, N. H. Differential Decisions in the Management of an Industrial Plant," *Journal of Business*, 29 (1956): 249–260.

60. Martin, N. H., and J. H. Sims. "Thinking Ahead: Power Tactics," *Harvard Business Review*, 34, No. 6 (1956): 25–36.

61. McGregor, D. *The Human Side of Enterprise*. New York: McGraw-Hill, 1960.

62. McGregor, D. *The Professional Manager*. New York: McGraw-Hill, 1967.

63. Miller, J. A. "Leadership in Open Systems." Unpublished doctoral dissertation, University of Rochester, Rochester, New York, 1974.

64. Mitchell, T. R., J. R. Larson, and S. G. Green. "Leader Behavior, Situational Moderators and Group Performance: An Attributional Analysis," *Organizational Behavior and Human Performance*, 18 (1977): 254–268.

65. Morse, M., and E. Reimer. "The Experimental Change of a Major Organization Variable," *Journal of Abnormal and Social Psychology*, 52 (1956): 120–129.

66. Mouton, J, S., and R. S. Blake. "Issue in Transnational Organization Development." In B. M. Bass, R. Cooper, and J. A. Haas (eds.), *Managing for Accomplishment*. Lexington, Mass.: D. C. Heath, 1970.

67. Myers, M. S. "Every Employee a Manager," *California Management Review*, 10, No. 3 (1968): 9–20.

68. Osborn, R. N., and W. M. Vicars. "Sex Stereotype: An Artifact in Leader Behavior and Subordinate Satisfaction Analysis?" *Academy of Management Journal*, 19, No. 3 (1976): 439–449.

69. Parker, T. C. "Relationships among Measures of Supervisory Behavior, Group Behavior, and Situational Characteristics," *Personnel Psychology*, 16 (1963): 319–333.

70. Patchen, M. "Supervisory Methods and Group Performance Norms," *Administrative Science Quarterly*, 7 (1962): 275–294.

71. Pelz, D. C., and F. M. Andrews. "Detecting Causal Priorities in Panel Study Data," *American Sociological Review*, 29 (1964): 836–848.

72. Pfiffner, J. M., and F. P, Sherwood. *Administrative Organization*. Englewood Cliffs, N. J.: Prentice-Hall, 1960.

73. Pinder, C., P. R. Pinto, and G. W. England. *Behavioral Style and Personal Characteristics of Managers*. Technical report, Center for the Study of Organizational Performance and Human Effectiveness. Minneapolis: University of Minnesota, 1973.

74. Porter, L. W., E. C. Lawler, and R. C. Hackman. *Behavior in Organizations*. New York: McGraw-Hill, 1975.

75. Rambo, W. W. "The Construction and Analysis of a Leadership Behavior Rating Form," *Journal of Applied Psychology*, 42 (1958): 409–415.

76. Raven, B. H. "Social Influence and Power." In I. D. Steiner and H. Fishbein (eds.), *Readings in Contemporary Social Psychology*. New York: Holt, Rinehart and Winston, 1965.

77. Rosenbaum, L. L., and W. B. Rosenbaum. "Morale and Productivity Consequences of Group Leadership Style, Stress, and Type of Task," *Journal of Applied Psychology*, 55 (1971): 343–348.

78. Rush, M. C., J. C. Thomas, and R. G. Lord. "Implicit Leadership Theory: A Potential Threat to the Internal Validity of Leader Behavior Questionnaires," *Organizational Behavior and Human Performance*, 20 (1977): 93–110.

79. Ryterband, E. C., and G. V. Barrett. "Managers' Values and Their Relationship to the Management of Tasks: A Cross-Culture Comparsion." In B. M. Bass, R. C. Cooper, and J. A. Haas (eds.), *Managing for Accomplishment*. Lexington, Mass.: D. C. Heath, 1970.

80. Sales, S. "Supervisory Style and Productivity: A Review," *Personnel Psychology*, 19 (1966): 275–286.

81. Schneider, B. "The Perception of Organizational Climate: The Customer's View," *Journal of Applied Psychology*, 57 (1973): 248–256.

82. Schriesheim, C. A., and C. J. Murphy. "Relationships between Leader Behavior and Subordinate Satisfaction and Performance: A Test of Some Situational Modifiers," *Journal of Applied Psychology*, 61 (1976): 634–641.

83. Scott, W. A. *Organization Theory: A Behavioral Analysis for Management.* Homewood, Ill.: Irwin, 1967.
84. Selznick, P. *Leadership in Administration.* Evanston, Ill.: Row, Peterson, 1957.
85. Shapira, Z. "A Facet Analysis of Leadership Styles," *Journal of Applied Psychology,* 61 (1976): 136–139.
86. Shaw, M. E. "Some Effects of Problem Complexity upon Problem Solving Efficiency in Different Communication Nets," *Journal of Experimental Psychology,* 48 (1954): 211–217.
87. Shaw, M. E., and J. M. Blum. "Effects of Leadership Style upon Group Performance as a Function of Task Structure," *Journal of Personality and Social Psychology,* 3 (1966): 238–241.
88. Shiflett, S. S. "The Effects of Changing Leader Power: A Test of Situational Engineering," *Organizational Behavior and Human Performance,* 7 (1972): 371–382.
89. Stogdill, R. *Handbook of Leadership.* New York: Free Press, 1974.
90. Stogdill, R., and A. E. Coons. *Leader Behavior: Its Description and Measurement.* Bureau of Business Research Monograph 88, Columbus: Ohio State University, 1957.
91. Stogdill, R. M., O. S. Goode, and D. R. Day. "The Leader Behavior of Corporation Presidents," *Personnel Psychology,* 16 (1963): 127–132.
92. Tannenbaum, A. S. *Control in Organizations.* New York: McGraw-Hill, 1968.
93. Tannenbaum, R., and F. Massarik. "Participation by Subordinates in the Managerial Decision-Making Process," *Canadian Journal of Economics and Political Science,* 16 (1950): 408–418.
94. Taylor, J. C. *The Conditioning Effects of Technology on Organizational Behavior in Planned Social Change.* Technical Report, Institute for Social Research, Ann Arbor: University of Michigan, 1969.
95. Vroom, V. H. "Some Personality Determinants of the Effects of Participation," *Journal of Abnormal and Social Psychology,* 59 (1959): 322–327.
96. Vroom, V. H. "Ego Involvement, Job Satisfaction and Job Performance," *Personnel Psychology,* 15 (1962): 159–177.
97. Vroom, V. H., and P. Yetton. *Leadership and Decision-Making.* New York: Wiley, 1974.
98. Ward, L. B. "The Ethnics of Executive Selection," *Harvard Business Review,* 43, No. 2 (1965): 6–28.
99. Weissenberg, P., and M. J. Kavanagh. "The Independence of Initiating Structure and Consideration: A Review of the Evidence," *Personnel Psychology,* 25 (1972): 119–130.
100. Whyte, W. H. *The Organization Man.* New York: Simon and Schuster, 1956.
101. Woodward, J. *Industrial Organization: Theory and Practice.* London: Oxford University Press, 1965.
102. Zentner, H. "Morale: Certain Theoretical Implications of Data in the American Soldier," *American Sociological Review,* 16 (1951): 297–307.

III Personnel Psychology

7 PERSONNEL PSYCHOLOGY

IN BRIEF Organizational objectives are translated into desired and required performances through the process of *job analysis*. The job analyst spells out the work to be done, the skills needed, and the training required by the jobholder. The documents that result from this analysis — job descriptions and job requirements, which specify the elements of the work to be done and the skills and training needed — are used in almost every aspect of personnel research and administration.

Once requirements for each job have been specified, the relative value of each job to the organization must be determined. Five standard approaches to *job evaluation* are used: ranking, classification, factor comparison, point system, and questionnaire.

Both job analysis and job evaluation are conducted without reference to the specific individual who will do the job; job descriptions represent ideal, or standard, performances for the job — *criteria* against which the jobholder's *actual performance* is measured. In the last analysis, the contribution the jobholder makes to the overall objective of the organization becomes the ultimate criterion of effective performance, toward which the improvement of selection and training efforts are directed. More often than not, however, this ultimate criterion cannot be meaningfully measured, so performance evaluation must rely on more immediate measures of contribution.

Personnel psychology begins where organizational psychology leaves off. Concern for the individual's performance in a firm must be viewed in terms of the firm's objectives. For instance, Henry Smith sells more merchandise faster than Mary Jones does, but Henry's customers complain more about their purchases. Henry brings in more new, nonrepeat business, but Mary has more steady, satisfied customers. Who is the better salesperson? The answer depends on the firm's goals, on what it values most. Henry is the better salesperson if the firm is concerned most about its current share of the market. Mary is the better salesperson if the firm is concerned about its long-term standing in the market.

If a firm had but a single goal — say, to maximize immediate sales — then the individual worth of the firm's sales personnel, or the *criterion* of effective job performance, would be the amount of goods sold by each individual salesperson. Personnel psychology could contribute to the firm by providing means to identify individuals more likely to sell above-average amounts of goods.

A firm or agency is likely to have many objectives. As noted in Chapter 5, it is a system of inputs and outputs of people, money, and materials. The overall strategy is to achieve high levels of output coupled with low levels of input and waste, levels that are satisfactory to all those involved with the organization. Thus, the firm's objectives are likely to include high levels of such outputs as sales, service to the public, and satisfaction to management, workers, and stockholders. At the same time, the firm strives for low levels of input; the less material, energy, time, and financing required, the better. Similarly, minimum waste is desired, since it diminishes the output/input ratio. Scrap, accidents, excess inventory, idle capital, excessive interest charges, and inadequate use of human resources are misuses of people, money, and materials. In business firms, the degree to which these objectives are achieved is usually measured by some number which summarizes the output/input ratio — for example, profits, earnings per share, growth rates, productivity, or dividends.

Criteria of effective job performance by the individual employee are selected to measure how well the employee's performance meets one or more of these organizational objectives.

Developing and Evaluating Criteria

A most significant problem for the personnel psychologist is to establish the *relevance* to the firm's success of these criteria of individual effectiveness: that is, whether or not a specific individual performance actually contributes to organizational performance.

The answers to these and related questions can be determined only with respect to the goals of the organization. This determination begins with the study of how the organization divides its tasks into individual jobs. We need to describe the ways in which one job differs from another in terms of all the demands to be made on the jobholder. This description is the task of *job analysis*.

The second step in the determination of the worth of an individual job-holder involves making judgments about the dollars-and-cents values (usually expressed in ranges) to be attached to the various jobs that need to be done. This is the task of *job evaluation*.

Both the description and the evaluation of jobs are independent of the particular individuals who currently happen to be assigned to them. In theory, at least, the jobs stay the same even though different people may be assigned to them. It is only in the third step that the focus turns to an evaluation of individual performance — how well jobholders actually do what their job requires of them. The last section of this chapter will discuss the problem of the *criteria* to use in deciding whether one employee is better than another, and Chapter 8 will be devoted to a presentation of the most widely used techniques for evaluating employee performance.

JOB ANALYSIS

In the broadest sense, job analysis is a personnel function, devoted to the gathering and analysis of any kind of job-related information for use in a wide variety of ways. The job analyst is concerned with providing clear and accurate descriptions of the activities that ought to be performed by a typical or standard holder of a given job. The job analyst is interested in specifying the unique characteristics or combinations of characteristics that differentiate one job from another, as well as the required knowledge, skills, and training that a typical jobholder would need to perform a given job. Two approaches are possible, one using systems analysis; the other focusing on jobs as they now are carried out.

Systems Analysis

This is a deductive procedure. It begins with a specification of the overall task of the organization, and proceeds by step-by-step logical subdivision until the total task has been broken down into pieces small enough to be handled by individual workers. While systems analysis is logically appealing, it would represent an enormous waste of effort, for it "reinvents the wheel" for the large majority of relatively standardized jobs already being performed in industry. A more detailed discussion of this approach will be reserved until Chapter 16.

The Inductive Approach

Here, the job analyst begins by noting the characteristics of jobs as they are actually being done. By careful examination of these activities, the analyst is able to produce summary statements in the form of job descriptions (what the typical worker in a given job actually does), which are then normally refined or broadened into statements of job specifications (what the worker in a given job ought to do), and job requirements (the personal characteristics, abilities, skills, knowledge, and training required to perform the specified tasks). This approach represents the process of job analysis as it is usually practiced.

Differences among Jobs

Important aspects of each job differ from each other with respect to their demands on the employee. So, to perform a job analysis, many kinds of information about the job must be collected, including: (1) an exact description of the work performed and of supervision given and received; (2) the degree of responsibility for the work of others, for material, equipment, safety, and public relations; (3) the specific knowledge, experience, and training required for the job; (4) the amount of initiative necessary to anticipate and meet new situations; (5) the amounts of mental alertness, judgment, skill, dexterity, and adaptability required for success on the job; (6) the standards of production for the job and how they were devised; (7) the equipment and material used; (8) working conditions and the physical demands of the job; (9) evaluations of worker characteristics required for success on individual parts and on all of the job; and (10) the number employed on the job.

The analyst may also be expected to judge how: (1) the job is related to other jobs; (2) one gets promoted or transferred in and out of this job; (3) the job could be combined with another, or broken into two or more jobs for workers with less training; (4) workers ordinarily are recruited for the job; (5) screening procedures are used in deciding whether to place the applicant on the job.

Uses of Job Analysis

Job analysis constitutes the first phase in the establishment of a formal performance appraisal system. It provides the basis for job evaluation in a program of wage and salary administration. In addition, job analysis has other important uses.

The descriptions of work performed and how it is supervised may be used by organizational designers to suggest realignments of chains of authority or of the flow of work. The traditional personnel functions of employee selection, training, promotion, and transfer can all be based on the information contained in an analysis of the jobs in an organization.

Statements of the specific knowledge required can be used by the training department in establishing suitable curricula. Information about equipment and material used, work done, and transfer patterns helps in the formulation of job families, or logical groupings of jobs. These set career patterns can readily be used in counseling employees concerning opportunities for promotion or transfer. Information about human resource requirements and selection procedures is used by the employment department to establish the priorities with which they will recruit, hire, and place applicants and the hiring standards they will employ. Finally, the judgments of the worker characteristics required for effective performance aid the personnel psychologist in deciding (1) how to construct criteria or yardsticks of success on the job, and (2) what traits sort out the potentially good from the poor performers. Such traits ought to be considered when formulating the trial battery of psychological tests and other screening devices for forecasting success on the job.

Unfortunately, in practice, job analyses are usually completed without considering all their potential uses. A review of 307 publications about job analyses of technical positions noted that unless a specific future purpose is kept in mind in formulating what will be collected, job analyses are likely to be performed without realizing the full uses possible.[23]

Techniques of Job Analysis

Employing the approach that begins with an analysis of jobs actually being performed, the job analyst will use a combination of techniques to gather, verify, and integrate information.

INTERVIEWS   The interview is probably the most common technique used to obtain job information. The job analyst usually follows a specially prepared form, which systematically covers the information to be obtained. The success of this technique depends partially on the interviewing skills of the job analyst. The cooperation of the employee must be gained and an atmosphere provided where free discussion about job duties and responsibilities occurs. If conducted properly, interviewing can obtain much of the necessary information.

There are, of course, drawbacks to this approach, especially if it is known that the job analysis will culminate in a job evaluation that could affect wages. Under these circumstances employees may "puff up" their jobs by attaching special importance to duties and responsibilities that are rarely or never performed. It often takes time and subtle questioning to obtain a valid picture of some employees' actual duties and responsibilities. There is also the factor of honest misunderstandings as to what the responsibilities of an employee actually are. For example, two supervisors may believe that they are both primarily responsible for the supervision of the same employee. The clarification of such ambiguities in an organization may be a valuable by-product of the job analysis procedure.

Besides interviewing the employees, the job analyst should also interview the immediate supervisor of the employees. In this way the analyst obtains a more complete picture of the job. While for some simpler jobs, interviewing only the workers and their supervisor might suffice for job analysis, it is still prudent to observe also the job being performed. Observation is a natural complement to interviewing.

OBSERVATION   For jobs requiring a great deal of manual standardized activity, much of the needed job information can be obtained by the analyst's observing the worker. Of course, the possibility exists that during the observation period critical duties might not be performed. What is even more important, this technique can be used mainly only with blue-collar jobs. Obviously, this technique is not applicable for most administrative and many clerical jobs, since observation would indicate only that the incumbent was seated at a desk manipulating papers. An exception might be a job that involves much meeting with others, so that interaction patterns could be noted.

JOB PERFORMANCE   On occasion the job analyst will actually perform the job in question to get a "feel" for the actual duties and responsibilities entailed. Again, this technique is applicable only for the simpler types of jobs, and would usually not be adequate for obtaining all the desired information.

QUESTIONNAIRES   On the surface, the questionnaire would appear to be an easy way to obtain a great deal of information in a standardized form.

One such widely researched questionnaire is the Position Analysis Questionnaire.[27] It can be scored both in terms of the job content and the attributes required for satisfactory performance. The questionnaire may be filled out by job incumbents or by a job analyst.

As with any questionnaire, questions may be misinterpreted and ambiguities remain unresolved that can be corrected in an interview. The questions about the job are couched in terms that are readily translated into behavioral dimensions. The questionnaire deals with the information that is received by the job incumbent, mental processes required on the job, the work output of the job, relations of the jobholder with other persons in the company, and various other attributes of the job, such as whether it requires a regular or irregular work schedule.

The Position Analysis Questionnaire is decribed as "worker-oriented" since the questions concern performance acts such as "operates keyboard." [35]

Unfortunately, the Position Analysis Questionnaire is written at the reading level of a college graduate. This means that a majority of incumbents and supervisors would have difficulty in using the instrument.[4]

Another problem with the Position Analysis Questionnaire when it is used by trained individuals is that females appear to give consistently lower ratings than males to the same job.[2]

TRAINING MATERIALS Occasionally it is possible to examine the process by which an employee is trained for the job. From this, we can develop an understanding of what is required for success in learning how to do the work. Training manuals and standard operating procedures are often good sources of information in this respect.

A content analysis of these manuals can provide a comprehensive review of what must be learned in order to succeed on the job, what worker traits are thought to be important, and what the attributes of effective performance are. In the same way, the analyst may find it useful to study records of trainees, reasons for failure, reasons for terminating training, success or failure of transferees into the job, and the educational and occupational backgrounds of successful and unsuccessful trainees.

OTHER SOURCES Within the firm's files there may also be other descriptive materials of considerable use. Daily reports from sales personnel might be analyzed. One rich storehouse of information was found in ten years of back issues of the newspaper of a large national manufacturer of food products, which had featured in each issue anecdotes of unusual success experiences. Each report was an experience that resulted in a sale or an increase in sales. When content-analyzed, these provided a reasonably thorough statement of the behavior required of sales personnel in this particular firm if they were to demonstrate outstanding performance. An illustrative anecdote was as follows:

> I worked out a plan last week that helped me get a couple of large advertising mats run by grocers who usually want only the smallest I have. I checked their current advertising and picked those of our mats which would look best in the ads. Then, instead of displaying my entire assortment, I pulled out only the biggest mat that would fit their ads to best advantage. In a number of cases they went for that larger mat without even asking to see anything smaller.

THE DICTIONARY OF OCCUPATIONAL TITLES The *Dictionary of Occupational Titles* is a standardized and comprehensive body of information of approximately 20,000 jobs compiled by the United States Employment and Training Administration. The *Dictionary of Occupational Titles* is based upon 75,000 on-site job analyses. The job analyst can turn to the *Dictionary of*

Occupational Titles to get a concise definition of almost any job in American industry.

The first item for each job is a nine-digit occupational code. The first three digits identify particular occupational groups. The next three digits are ratings of functions performed in the occupation. This code is based upon the concept that every job requires a worker to relate in some way to data, people, and things. For example, under the "people" function the lowest level is taking instructions, while a higher level is supervising. The last three digits indicate the alphabetical order of the titles.[46]

Dimensions on Which Jobs Differ

Observations, content analyses, ratings, estimates, and checklist descriptions yield hundreds of specific items differentiating one job from another. It becomes useful to try to condense these into a smaller set of general headings, or "job families," accounting for these hundreds of differences.

Factor analysis is a powerful statistical technique used to determine a minimum set of factors, or underlying dimensions, which can account for the elements common to a large number of intercorrelated items. Using factor analysis, researchers have been able to extract a number of general common dimensions along which virtually all jobs can be described, no matter how dissimilar these jobs appear to be on the surface.

Job analyses by the United States Training and Employment Service estimated how much workers on each of 4,000 jobs needed each of forty-four traits. Seven dimensions were found to be sufficient to describe how these jobs differed.

The first dimension on which jobs differed was in how much educational and mental ability was required. A metallurgist required a lot; a warehouse laborer, very little. Second, some jobs (like that of wheel alignment mechanic) required much more adaptability to precision operations than did other jobs (like that of county agricultural agent). Third, some jobs (like that of plumber) demanded more body agility than others (like gas station attendant). Fourth, jobs differed in degree of artistic ability and aesthetic appreciation required. A commercial photographer needed much, while a teamster required little of this. Fifth, manual art ability was a fundamental job separator, differentiating the precision lens grinder from the airways observer, for example. Personal contact ability was a sixth dimension, differentiating jobs like that of a front-office cashier from that of a rag sorter. Seventh, jobs seemed to differ basically in whether heavy manual labor was a requirement (as by a wharf laborer) or whether nonmanual work was involved (as by a file clerk).[28]

THE POSITION ANALYSIS QUESTIONNAIRE GOES INTO FAR MORE DETAIL ABOUT JOBS The PAQ yields forty-five psychologically-oriented factors. For example, in the visual-perceptual or information input aspects of the job

alone, five factors emerged according to a factor analysis of over 8,000 jobs
in 125 different organizations. The five dimensions were: (1) perceptual
interpretation (for example, recognizing sound patterns) ; (2) evaluating
sensory inputs (for example, estimating the speed of processes); (3) visual
input from devices or materials (for example, inspecting); (4) input
from representational sources (such as written materials); and (5) environmental awareness (for example, detecting man-made features of the
environment). Using these five dimensions, jobs can be differentiated in
terms of the amount of input of information.[26] Although limited to use
by professionals and college graduates, the PAQ provides a sophisticated
research and analytical tool constructed to match readily with psychological
assessment procedures.

If the work of the job analyst results in clear descriptions of the actual
and required behaviors of jobholders, such as is possible with the PAQ,
multiple purposes can be served. Out of such analyses of worker behaviors
are distilled estimates of what is and what is not important for performance
of the job. They provide suggestions as to what criteria to establish for
evaluating how well the employee is performing on the job, bases for deciding which employees are doing well and which ones are doing poorly.
They provide guides to the recruiter on what to look for in prospective
employees. They indicate to the personnel research investigator who is
trying to develop a screening battery what kinds of tests and measurements
should be tried out to see whether they will be valid in forecasting which
applicants will be successful on the job and which ones will not. They focus
the attention of instructors on what behaviors should be emphasized in
training new employees. These estimates provide clues to ways in which
we can evaluate the job in its worth to the company, as we shall see in the
next section.

JOB EVALUATION

Jobs differ in value within the firm in many ways. In establishing compensation schedules, it becomes important to judge these ways. It is the
task of those responsible for the job evaluation program to make decisions about the relative importance of different job behaviors to the
goals of the organization.

Worth to the company is not the only basis for deciding what makes
the job more valuable. Also to be considered is the need for equity in compensating employees for the time, effort, and energy they expend in performing a job. A fair exchange must take place so that employees with
relatively unimportant but dirty, dangerous, or distasteful jobs receive a
"just" or "fair" return for their inputs to the firm's operations. Furthermore, a job is more valuable if its incumbents must exert much time and
effort to achieve the necessary skill level to perform the job.

Job Evaluation Methods

There are five methods used for evaluating jobs: ranking, classification, factor comparsion, a point system, and questionnaires. Each will be discussed separately.

RANKING   The ranking method requires a responsible committee, say, composed of employee representatives and management representatives from production, personnel, and finance to review the job descriptions provided from job analyses. The committee then ranks the jobs in a given department in terms of their overall worth according to an agreed-on set of criteria. For instance, they may agree to rank highest those jobs entailing the greatest responsibility, mental ability, and effort. Then, management members may scale the departments so that the job with an average rank in a more important department receives more credit than a job with an average rank in a less valued department. Following this, the committee groups the jobs with similar scores into classes and assigns different pay rates for the different classes. While this procedure is simple to set up, easy to explain, and better than no plan at all, it suffers from lack of reliability. (If the committee were to repeat the ranking of the jobs, there would be considerable fluctuations when jobs were ranked the second time.) Moreover, the task becomes difficult or impossible if a large number of jobs must be evaluated together.[32] Also, afterward there is a lack of substantial data to justify the relative positions of certain jobs.[33]

CLASSIFICATION METHOD   The committee reads the job descriptions. Then it sets up a classification of grades. Finally, it assigns the jobs to appropriate grades. This method is favored by many offices, particularly the U.S. Civil Service agencies. The system is simple to establish and does provide a general yardstick against which to evaluate all the jobs in a firm, but it contains a number of inadequacies. Often it is difficult to establish grades. Jobs, we have seen, differ along different dimensions, and while Job 1 may be higher on one dimension than Job 2, they may reverse positions on another dimension. The classification method forces jobs to be evaluated on a single but complex scale.[32] Judges' biases can easily lead to upgrading certain positions erroneously, for example, if they are jobs that ordinarily are hard to fill.[33]

FACTOR COMPARISON METHOD*   This method is most difficult to understand, although it is easy to develop. Because it depends on certain key jobs remaining stable both in operations and pay rates, it is less popular

---

* The word factor is used here in its general meaning of attribute or characteristic, not as that which is extracted in a factor analysis.

as a quantitative job evaluation procedure than is the point method, to be discussed later.

First, a number of factors differentiating the worth of jobs to the company and to the employee are arbitrarily identified, such as skill level, mental demands, physical demands, responsibility, and discomfort of working conditions.

Next, every job is rated on every factor. Ten to twenty-five key jobs are then isolated. A key job is one that the committee (of management and employee representatives) agrees is properly compensated. A key job is also a common one in the area and has an established pay rate in the community. The key jobs cover the range of requirements on all five factors. They are ranked by the committee on each of the five. For example, ten key jobs might be ordered on the first factor of mental requirements as follows: pattern maker, substation operator, machinist, pipefitter, painter, drill press operator, carpenter's helper, and laborer.

Next, the total pay for each key job is broken down, and an appropriate portion assigned according to the key job's ranking in each factor. For instance, suppose the pattern maker is paid $10 per hour. Of this, $3.00 or 30 per cent may be apportioned for the first factor, mental requirements, $2 or 20 per cent for skill, $1 for physical demands, $1 for working conditions, and the remaining 30 per cent of $3.00 for responsibility. Thus, monetary amounts are established for each key job. Then all other jobs are compared with the key job. All other jobs with the mental requirements comparable to that of pattern maker are given $3.00 as part of the total pay to be assigned to them. The other parts depend on how they match up with the various key jobs on the other four factors.[33]

The advantages of the key-job or factor-comparison method are that jobs are directly compared with one another, factor by factor, and the scale of value is in monetary terms so that no one need argue about the financial value of a grade or a point as in other methods. On the other hand, the system must be custom-made for each business establishment; the system is strongly dependent on the accuracy and fairness with which the key jobs have been selected and evaluated. If community wage rates change for some of the key jobs but not others, the scales must be revised.[32]

POINT SYSTEM   The point system is the method most widely used. For instance, a point plan developed by the National Electrical Manufacturers Association was put into operation in from 1,200 to 1,500 plants, and that of the National Metal Trades Association was adopted in 500 establishments. Of 72 companies surveyed, 81 per cent were found using a point plan, 13 per cent a factor-comparison method, and 6 per cent other procedures. The percentages were fairly similar for plans for blue-collar, white-collar, and management employees.[43]

In using the point system, a set of from three to 40 factors (most com-

242   PERSONNEL PSYCHOLOGY

monly 10 to 15) is selected. It is assumed that these factors are required to some degree by all jobs to be evaluated. A set of factors might be those such as the 17 selected for evaluating nonexempt clerical employees of Fieldcrest Mills:

1. Education
2. Experience in related jobs
3. Experience with this job
4. Complexity
5. Supervision received
6. Supervision given
7. Number supervised
8. Dexterity
9. Accuracy
10. Responsibilty for confidential matters
11. Responsibility for contacts
12. Responsibility for money
13. Monotony
14. Pressure of time limits
15. Attention
16. Distracting interruptions
17. Job conditions

The degrees that may be required on each of these factors are then described. Figure 7–1 shows an example of factor 9, accuracy required. Then, points are assigned to the degrees for each factor. Figure 7–2 shows how points have been assigned, according to a hypothetical scheme, to the five degrees defined for six factors of a standard plan. Note that the job evaluation committee has decided to weight the factors differently.* Experience,

Figure 7–1. Description of the five degrees of estimated accuracy required on nonexempt clerical jobs at Fieldcrest Mills. (Adapted from *Job Evaluation Manual for Evaluation of Nonexempt Clerical Jobs,* Fieldcrest Mills, Spray, N.C., 1953).[22]

Degree

1. Possibility of error is very slight or error is of little consequence even if not detected.
2. Considerable possibility for error but error would be detected in the operation itself and could be corrected in less than an hour. Mistakes are normally detected upon completion of work cycle. Operation itself may provide a check against errors.
3. Considerable possibility for error. Error would be detected in succeeding operations (within department). Up to three hours may be required to correct error.
4. Errors difficult to detect or require considerable time to correct. Error might affect other departments or relationships with public or employees. Considerable dependence placed on employee.
5. Where cost of detection or correction would be great. Or where error would have considerable effect on other departments or upon relationships with employees or public. Great reliance placed on employee for accuracy.

* The committee may weight these factors one way, but statistics may weight them quite differently as a consequence of how the jobs are seen to vary on each of the factors. For example, if all the jobs were seen to require the same degree of physical exertion and were all given 40 points as a result, then physical demands would actually have no weight at all in differentiating jobs. Every job would have a constant of 40 added to it, keeping it in the identical position vis-à-vis the other jobs likewise raised by 40 points.

Factor	1	2	Degrees 3	4	5
1. Education	10	20	30	40	50
2. Experience	30	60	90	120	150
3. Physical demand	20	40	60	80	100
4. Responsibility	10	20	30	40	50
5. Supervision	10	20	30	40	50
6. Working conditions	5	10	15	20	25

Figure 7–2. A hypothetical point plan.

in any degree, is given three times more weight than education in the example shown in Figure 7–2.

Then, a simple arithmetic progression has been applied, so that for each of the five degrees of education, as an illustration, there is an addition of 10 more points. Some plans use a geometric progression. For instance, education might be scaled for the five degrees at 10, 20, 40, 80, and 160 instead of 10, 20, 30, 40, and 50.

All jobs are then evaluated in terms of the estimated degree to which they require each of the factors, and points are assigned accordingly and cumulated for each job. Thus, a sweeper may receive 10 points for education, 30 for experience, 60 for physical demands, 20 for various responsibilities, 10 for supervision, and 15 for working conditions — a total of 145 points. A welder might obtain 20 for education, 90 for experience, and so on, for a total of perhaps 220 points.

A wage survey of the community or the industry is then completed to determine the going rates for the jobs being evaluated. Then a chart, as in Figure 7–3, is prepared relating current average wages to total points assigned each job. A fitted trend line* is likely to curve upward as in Figure 7–3 if arithmetic scales have been used for the factors. A first job with double the points of a second job may provide four times the earnings. For this reason, geometric scales for the factors like 10, 20, 40, 80, and 160 are

---

It follows that the weight of a factor depends on how differently the jobs are seen to require the factor, as well as what multiplier is used by the committee.

Another way of viewing the same thing is to note that raters differ in how reliably they can rate the different factors. Thus, they agree much less with each other in evaluating the physical demands of the job. They correlate most highly in evaluating responsibility for safety. Each rater is likely to cancel the other rater's high or low scores assigned for physical demands, for if one is high the other is likely to be low.[13] Therefore, the jobs will vary less in combined points received for physical demands, and physical demands will have less weight in the total system than responsibility for safety, all other things being equal.

* This line of best fit (the fewest-squares solution) is that line from which the square of the distances to all plotted points approaches a sum of zero.

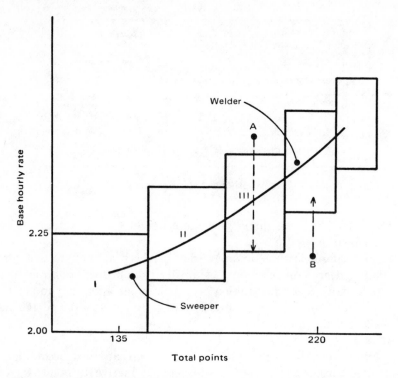

Figure 7–3. A wage-point chart.

sometimes used. Total points based on such scales then are likely to fit in a straight line with current wages, since both points awarded and wages are increased together in geometric rather than arithmetic fashion.

A classification of grades can now be established for successive steps of points, as shown in Figure 7–3. Starting wages are given by the bottom line of each step; the highest wages that can be earned in that grade as a consequence of seniority and merit are given by the top line of the step. For step 1, minimum and maximum wages are $4.00 and $6.00 respectively. A job like that of A, whose actual rate is too high for the points assigned, is left unchanged. However, when new incumbents are placed in job A, they will start at the considerably lower rate, at the bottom of Grade III. On the other hand, the wages of the occupants of job B are adjusted upward as soon as possible.

The point system has certain inherent qualitative advantages. The point system makes use of readily understood and widely used rating scale techniques. It yields results that are most reliable: that is, in comparison to the other methods, jobs evaluated in the point system will shift around less if the evaluation is repeated.

The point system is independent of economic trends or changing wage rates. There is a ready conversion of points to dollars and cents, and a single job can be changed in content and evaluation without upsetting the rest of the system, for each job's evaluation is supposedly independent of the points assigned any other.[32]

On the other hand, the point system must rest on many arbitrary restrictions. The number of factors to describe a job is fixed, as is the number of degrees. The system may be more complex than it needs to be. For instance, while each factor is supposed to be independent, in fact, factor ratings are highly intercorrelated. Ratings are actually needed on only two or three factors (for example, skill demands and job hazards) to arrange industrial jobs in their value in an almost identical order such as would be obtained from summing up of ratings of the jobs on a dozen or more factors.[15] In the same way, two factors, supervisory responsibility and skill demands, were found sufficient to order in value 800 clerical and professional positions, serving the same function as 8 originally used to arrange the jobs.[3]

QUESTIONNAIRE   The Position Analysis Questionnaire has also been used for job evaluation purposes. This is because certain job dimensions obtained from the questionnaire are highly related to compensation. In the case of a utility with 131 jobs, the correlation between the dimensions "making decisions" and the job evaluation score from using a point system was 0.82.[36] The questionnaire approach has the advantage of saving time over the other systems. The Position Analysis Questionnaire has even been applied to homemakers. The predicted salary was approximately $1,000 per month.[1]

Equity and the Need for Job Evaluation

Wage and salary administration represents an activity in which both economic and psychological issues are critical for success. Employees' pay needs to be adequate to provide them with a satisfactory standard of living. At the same time, they need to feel that the pay they receive is fair for what they do relative to the pay received on other jobs and what those jobs require. Compensation must be perceived as equitable.

There are many temporary economic situations, historical accidents, and traditional conditions that result in inequity. Thus, certain jobs may be accorded out-of-the-ordinary wages because of a labor scarcity. Supply and demand may operate to give brick masons, for instance, a 20 per cent premium over and above compensation for their actual contribution or worth to the firm. At the same time, the current wages of particular jobs may be high relative to what they contribute to the company simply because of historical accident. If there was a scarcity of personnel to fill this job at the same time when it was created or when occupants were replaced, premiums may have been paid that remain in effect subsequently.

Union activity may bring about higher wages for some jobs favored by the union leadership, or, conversely, may lead to management attempts to restrict unfairly the wages of some classes of jobs. Regional and industrial traditions may also lead to systematic inequities. The relative pay of electricians to carpenters may vary from one locality to another for no reason other than history and tradition. Despite legislative and judicial attempts at correction, a job done mainly by black workers or by women may be underpaid for no reason except that the job is held by incumbents who traditionally have been paid less or are in a weaker bargaining position with management. Dealing with such inequities remains one of the centrally important tasks of personnel psychologists — and, indeed, of all persons concerned with the problems of industrial organizations. Today it is illegal to maintain inequities for reasons of race or sex.

It is precisely in dealing with such inequities that the benefits of a systematic job evaluation program such as the point plan become clear. An internally consistent ordering of the worth of jobs to the organization, without respect to the characteristics of the jobholders, provides the basis for establishing equitable compensation to all employees. At this point we must also make it clear that for higher-level positions (executives) the individual will make the job. Individuals must take on increased responsibility, increasing their worth to the organization.

The establishment of a job evaluation system provides other related benefits. It furnishes a general framework for management-union collective bargaining. (Negotiations can be about the structure as a whole rather than job-by-job.) Pay rates for newly established jobs can be determined easily. Employees can discern readily the structure within which they can progress in earnings, how much they can hope to earn in their current job, and what kind of job they must be promoted to in order to move into a higher grade level with new maxima and minima. Grievances about pay can be reduced considerably once a generally acceptable framework has been established.[45]

With the determination of job worth, expressed in ranges irrespective of the quality of the jobholder's performance, we are now ready to turn to the question of the value of an individual's contribution to the organization.

DIFFERENCES IN EMPLOYEE PERFORMANCE

So far, we have examined how jobs differ regardless of who performs them. Now, let us consider how a group of employees working at the same job differ from each other in effectiveness, in their service-ability or worth to the firm, and in their contribution to the organization. On what basis can we decide that one employee is better than another?

Before comparisons can be made, employees need to be grouped according to the work they do. If only a few people work on any single job in the firm, to obtain sufficient samples of employees to compare with a set of standard performance measurements we may need to group together employees working on clusters of similar jobs. Once a decision is reached about what the appropriate comparison group should be, we need to consider what specific elements to measure. This problem — the problem of *performance criteria* — is one of the most enduring and most critical topics in the field of personnel psychology.

Job performance criteria are those specific elements chosen to measure the degree to which jobholders are meeting requirements as detailed in job descriptions and/or job specifications. If the value of an employee's performance in contributing to the objectives of the firm rests solely in, say, the quantity of pieces produced per day, the criterion problem is trivial: we simply count pieces produced per day. The problem is rarely that simple, however. Our workers' job descriptions may require that they produce a large number with minimum errors, and that they be able to switch to the production of other pieces from time to time. Thus, we may decide that speed, accuracy, and versatility are the appropriate elements identifying the value to the firm of an employee's performance. But then we may find that the employees vary very little in accuracy, or that errors occur only rarely. In other words, we may attempt to use a criterion that is *not sensitive* enough to discriminate between employees; in such a case, our efforts devoted to measuring it are wasted. We may find error measurements *unreliable:* that is, employees who are relatively accurate in one time period may be inaccurate the next. Or errors may depend primarily on the material the employee works on. With easy material, some employees make relatively fewer errors than others do with hard material. Sometimes, although not usually, speed and accuracy may be *highly correlated* so that all that is needed is a measure of one or the other.

But if speed, accuracy, and versatility are all sensitive, highly reliable (as for proofreaders), relatively uncorrelated, and relevant criteria (to the extent that all three are truly necessary to the success of the firm), then we face the problem of deciding how much weight to attach to each. For example, we can ask judges to rate the extent to which each of the three criteria is important to the firm or to the department. We can convert measures of each criterion into standard scores so that scores on all three criteria are on the same scale, with the same variance, and can be combined, giving equal weight to scores regardless of the scale from which they come.

Another preference or value judgment may be involved. Management and/or employees' representatives may find any or all of these three measurements (speed, accuracy, and versatility) unacceptable. For instance, if the criteria are to be used to provide the basis for merit raises, employees may argue that versatility is of no consequence. On the other hand, management may find versatility more important than either speed or accuracy for the long-term contribution it makes to the firm.

Immediate, Intermediate, or Ultimate Criteria

Establishing a true worth of an employee to an organization is a long-term affair. What we need to know ultimately is the employee's value to the firm or agency over an extended period of time. For example, the *ultimate criterion* of salespersons' performance may be total sales over their entire careers. But neither the sales personnel nor the firm could wait for the final reckoning to decide on salary, raises, promotions, training needs, evaluating tests, and other personnel actions. Thus, in lieu of an ultimate criterion, an organization develops more readily available intermediate or immediate criteria, such as weekly sales, grades in training courses, or supervisors' ratings of performance over, say, the past six months.

An *immediate* criterion of success in the organization might be some measure of performance in a training program such as grades obtained in a school. An *intermediate* criterion of success would be a supervisor's rating of performance after some time on the job, say two years.

Usually, the correlation between an immediate criterion such as training grades and later job performance, as exemplified by supervisors' ratings, is low or moderate. This only modest relationship occurs for a number of reasons. First, the training program is usually designed to impart specific knowledge or skill to the employee, and typically the job knowledge or skill is considered to be a necessary, but not sufficient, condition for job performance. For example, an organization may have a sales training course that is designed to give the sales personnel explicit knowledge about the product. The course may not be designed to impart or improve interpersonal skills. Therefore, it is not surprising that the trainee's scores have only a modest relationship with subsequent success in selling in the field where much more than just job knowledge is required.

Composite or Multiple Criteria

THE COMPOSITE CRITERION   This is a general measurement of the overall success of an individual employee. Composite criteria are required for salary decisions, promotions, transfers, dismissals, layoffs, and test evaluations. Someone in the organization must make overall evaluations of employees and reach one decision about each of them. Various dimensions of job performance are combined to determine each individual's overall worth to the organization. Thus, suppose we need to evaluate two employees, one who is fast and wastes a lot of material; another who is slow but wastes little material. The value of speed and accuracy can be combined to provide a single index of performance for each employee.

MULTIPLE CRITERIA   If you combine different job dimensions into a single composite, you have an index the meaning of which cannot be readily interpreted if the correlations among the different criteria are low, as they often are.

Consider the job performance of proofreaders observed in one analysis. Here, each of three printing company objectives was involved: high quality and high quantity of output (both at minimum cost), and the flexible use of personnel. Consequently, three measures, or criteria, of the performance of the individual proofreader were employed: rate of productivity, number of errors per hour, and versatility as gauged by the foreman's ratings of the variety of work the employee could proof. Each of these three measures was highly stable: correlations between a first measurement and a repetition of it for a later period ranged from 0.95 to 0.99. Yet each of the three measures was almost completely independent of the others, intercorrelating close to zero on the average. That is, the fast proofreader was not necessarily accurate or versatile, nor was the inaccurate proofreader necessarily slow or lacking in versatility.[25]

Similar results were obtained in one study of approximately 1,000 delivery service drivers. Five criteria of drivers' effectiveness were intercorrelated: actual time needed to deliver parcels; supervisory ratings; accidents; unexcused absences; and an objective measure of errors. The accident and absence data were not related to the other criteria or each other.[42]

BOTH KINDS OF CRITERIA ARE USEFUL   The composite criterion is necessary for personnel decision making, but since it often lumps together "pears and apples" in the same count, we only can learn about "fruit" as a consequence. Therefore, if we want to understand something about productivity, job satisfaction, and interpersonal success, each independently of the other, we must employ multiple criteria. Since we usually are interested in both adequate personnel administration and in psychological theory (to promote better selection, training, and development), we should first develop multiple criteria and later combine the separate criteria into a composite criterion to aid the organization to reach a variety of decisions requiring a unitary criterion.[41]

Specific or Summary Criteria?

SPECIFIC CRITERIA   Five kinds of specific performance criteria are widely employed: examination scores, specific behavior checklists, standardized work sample scores, ratings of specific work results, and objective output measures.

An achievement or proficiency *examination* can be used to measure the knowledge and understanding achieved by employees. For example, after apprentice electricians have completed training, we measure how much each has learned about various phases of the electrician's work. This achievement examination taken by the apprentices upon completion of training serves as a specific criterion of success as an electrician. We assume, of course, that apprentices who do well on the exam will be more serviceable to any organization in which they work than those who do poorly. That is, if they know more at graduation, they can and will operate more effectively after graduation.

We may develop *checklists* or rating forms for competent observers to assess, fairly objectively, various phases of behavior of the trained electricians. Observers may watch the electricians at work and check to see whether they handle their tools properly, whether with a minimum expenditure of time and energy they find the electrical troubles for which they search, and whether they make proper use of their helpers. The completed checklist serves as a criterion.

Standardized work samples may be set up, and performance of the trained electricians noted. For example, ten standard defective electrical systems are rigged and the electricians are given a specified amount of time in which to troubleshoot each of them. The number of systems they correct serves as an estimate of their serviceability or worth to the organization which employs them.

Qualitative ratings may be made of the work the electricians complete. The quality of the splices they make, the firmness and neatness of the soldered connections, and the placement of the various electrical equipment in the system are rated. If the employees are in training, some of their grades for various phases depend on these latter two techniques and in turn may serve as specific criteria.

Objective output criteria may be appropriate for some jobs, such as routine piecework production, or certain standard clerical or sales jobs. For example, we can measure the number of units per hour the electricians finish, or the number of defective units they turn out, or the amount of material wasted, in comparison with other electricians with the same experience and type of work. Such measures of "objective results" are frequently proposed as being the best yardsticks to use in appraising employee effectiveness, and indeed they often provide the basis for evaluation and compensation in piece-rate production and sales commission systems.

But objective results may provide faulty criteria of job success. Results frequently bear little consistent relation to how well individuals actually perform on their job. Objective results often suffer from lack of consistency. That is, the high-scoring worker one day may be the low-scoring the next day. This may occur, for instance, when no financial incentive is associated with daily output.[38] When a financial incentive is connected with production, week-to-week output has been found to be relatively constant. A very short period of time, several days or one week, will not show consistent work performance, however.[37]

The proposition that job performance improves over time is certainly true for a large number of occupations. Perhaps the most extensive data have been provided from a study of keypunch operators. In one study involving over one billion key strokes, the operators' proficiency was shown to improve over time, reaching a plateau usually in the second year.[24]

Many factors affecting workers' output are largely beyond their control. The methods they use may be inadequate; the equipment they are given may be old or obsolete. Supplies may be slow or erratic in arriving. They may receive information or feedback about the quality of their work inadequate to tell them how and when to make corrections.

Employees' supervision may be poor. Studies in life insurance selling show, for instance, that aptitude will make a difference in salespersons' income only in territories supervised by good management.[17] They may be asked to work too many hours or at too fast a pace. They may have been given too little training or inadequate training. Often, departmental or territorial effort is paramount in governing the success or failure of individual employees. Many of the differences in effectiveness among employees may depend on the particular location to which they happen to be assigned. Whether or not employees sell much or little auto insurance, for example, may depend mainly on the number of autos registered in the territory or how well sales personnel are utilized.[16]

Thus, basing an evaluation of an employee's contribution to the organization on measures of objective results, especially over the short term, requires a careful determination of the nature of potential external factors, and an attempt to insure that the employees' performance is being judged, rather than the influence of conditions beyond their control.

SUMMARY CRITERIA   To avoid unwarranted effects of possible short-term external influences on employee evaluations, organizations often resort to summary criteria instead of, or in addition to, the specific measures described above. Such summary criteria are often based on these specific criteria, in the form of longer-term totals or averages. For example, if we have confidence in the relative stability of employees' work, we may use the quantity (objectively counted) and quality (provided, say, by ratings) of output for the electricians over a six-month period. But even with readily observed summary output measurements, many conditions like those that influence specific objective measurements can systematically distort one's reading of an employee's contribution to the firm.

The average grade that the electricians earn while in training is another example of a summary criterion that is often used. Many of the higher-level or professional aptitude tests have been validated against an evaluation of this sort.

Administrative actions represent a type of summary criterion. As an estimate of the worth of the electricians, we follow up their subsequent work history to determine how quickly they receive promotions, what job status they finally obtain, how well they are paid, whether or not they are discharged, whether or not they receive special commendations or awards, and whether or not they are assigned to special tasks requiring superior proficiency. These administrative actions are frequently employed for lack of a better criterion, but it must be pointed out that they can also be seriously affected by extraneous factors having nothing to do with the employee's value to the company. The ups and downs of our economy may be a more important determiner of the electricians' wages than their worth to the organization is. Favoritism rather than merit may determine promotions.

By far the most frequenty used summary criteria are various kinds of supervisors' ratings. The widespread use — and abuse — of performance rating systems requires that we devote considerable attention to a description of the various types possible and to an intensive analysis of their advantages and disadvantages. This we will do in Chapter 8.

The Dynamic Character of Criteria

Over time, we may see change in the relative standing of an employee on a particular criterion of job performance. We may make measurements early in training that do not reflect the employee's standing at the end of training. We may collect criterion measurements early in employee careers that may not reflect standings later on. Why?

One reason is that job requirements may change for employees as they gain more experience. The skills required by experienced employees may be different than those required by novices. For instance, technical proficiency may be most closely associated with criterion success as a staff accountant during the first two years of employment. After that, when staff members have gained two years' experience and are all technically competent, interpersonal competence may now be most important in determining continuing success on the criterion. Again, the skills and abilities required to be successful in learning a job may not be the same ones that are important in doing a job well after it has been fully learned. Therefore, some individuals who are very successful in doing well on the job initially through what was learned in a training course may be less successful once everyone has learned the job skills. Early success in a sales position might be based upon knowledge of the product, but later success is based upon a good relationship with purchasing agents. Those individuals who had the most product knowledge and were successful for this reason early in their careers may not be the ones who are also most skilled in building an effective relationship with purchasing agents.

A second reason is that the organizational environment may change. The interpersonal type, most likely to succeed in a growing organization, may be most likely to fail in a stable or declining organization. The same thing can occur for a salesperson operating in a territory with little competition, which over time changes when a highly competitive product is introduced.

A third reason is that people (or their lives) change. They may suffer illness, loss of interest in their work, divorce, and other life stresses, which result in top performers' dropping over time in performance.

Fourth, some criterion measures are inherently unreliable, as for example where the number of parts a machinist produces is highly dependent upon the quality of materials received, and quality of materials received is a random phenomenon across a group of machinists. So one week, a machinist may have very good material to work with, and the next week poor material, and therefore the resulting productivity index is unreliable.

Fifth, over time, evaluations of employees may be made by different supervisors with differing views about what is important and how to rate employees.

Illustrative of the steady change of a criterion over time is the example, Figure 7–4, showing the correlation between rated merit of several hundred sales personnel over a 42-month period dropping with the increasing length of time between ratings.[6] Similarly, correlations of only 0.26 to 0.41 were found in days to reach standard in learning different portions of Morse Code.[19] On the other hand, there is also plenty of evidence about the stability of some criteria of performance over time.

EXAMPLES OF STABILITY OF CRITERIA   In a training program for welders, the rate at which the trainees learned 14 separate tasks was quite consistent from the beginning to the end of training. The correlation between time to learn the various tasks of the course and total time to completion ranged up to 0.87. This indicated that training speed in the first few tasks could accurately predict the time it would take to complete the total program.[21] In a large aerospace firm, salary over a 20-year period was relatively constant for aerospace engineers.[8] Again, median correlations ranging between 0.48 to 0.78 for the same criterion measures over different periods of time were found for skilled factory workers.[38,39,40] Over an 18-week period, taxi drivers' sales correlated 0.96 from week to week.[10]

Thus, we are forced to conclude that criteria of success may or may not be stable over time. Fortunately, behavior is reasonably predictable. Early performance on a task is likely to correlate with later performance, to the degree that conditions and requirements to complete the task remain the

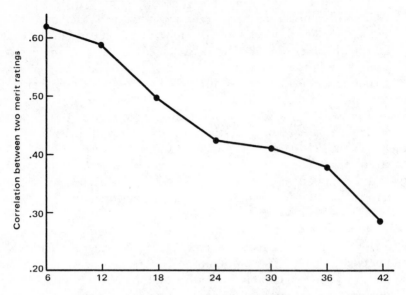

Figure 7–4. Correlation between two merit ratings on the same salesmen as a function of the time between merit ratings. (From Bass, "Further Evidence on the Dynamic Character of Criteria," *Personnel Psychology,* 15 [1962]: 95.)

same, and the employee does not change. The longer the intervening time period between our first and second collections of criterion data, the less likely we are to maintain these elements necessary for stability; the more change we will observe!

Biasing Factors in Criteria

The various biasing factors in criteria can be classified in a number of ways. First, the criterion may be deficient. *Criterion deficiency* is the failure to include important elements of the job in the criterion for success. For example, in measuring the effectiveness of a typist, we might count only the number of words typed per hour. This would be clearly a deficient measurement because we are not taking into account the number of errors made. A useful measure, of course, would be one that would take into account the errors and might be expressed as the number of usable manuscript pages per hour produced by the typist.

Second, the criterion may be contaminated. *Criterion contamination* involves the introduction into the performance appraisal process of elements that are not a reflection of individual performance. For example, we might be comparing two typists, using as the criterion the number of usable pages typed per hour and fail to note that one typist's performance was aided by the use of a superior typewriter with a mechanism for quickly correcting mistakes, while the other typist did not have this advantage.

The third biasing factor is *scale unit bias*. This occurs when there is a distortion of the scale units for a criterion. As an illustration, let's assume that we have developed a rating form that measures both *quantity* and *quality* of performance. Further assume that the raters assign a wide range of scores on the dimension of *quantity* of performance but rate everyone high on the *quality* dimension. This may not reflect the true quality performance but rather the fact that the scale does not adequately reveal the true underlying differences in the quality of the individual performance on the job. And so individuals who did high-quality work would not have this taken into account when the scales of quantity and quality were combined into a composite measure of individual performance. Conversely, those with low-quality performance would have a higher composite score than they deserved since no adequate distinction was made between poor- and high-quality performers.

Fourth, the criterion may be distorted. In *criterion distortion* the bias arises when the separate criteria are combined into an overall measure of organizational worth. The decision could be made to weight the quantity dimension twice as heavily as the quality dimension. A more careful analysis of the situation might indicate that this is a mistake, since in this situation a low-quality product is very costly to the organization. Sometimes criterion distortion can be eliminated. Thus, in keypunching, the correction of an error was found to take the same time as punching a total of 14 cards. Therefore, the overall measure of job proficiency involved subtracting 14 cards for each error from the total number of cards the keypunch operator produced.[31]

Fifth, there is often *opportunity bias,* especially when objective criteria are used. For example, for the police officer the number of arrests may be highly dependent on the assigned district. For the salesperson, total sales may depend on the number of accounts in the assigned territory.[11,14]

SUMMARY

Job analysis is a process that is basic for a number of personnel functions. The technique of job analysis includes interviews, observation, performing the job, questionnaires, and review of sources such as training materials and *The Dictionary of Occupational Titles.* Job analysis procedures are used to gather information for job evaluation, or for determining the worth of a job to an organization. Five common job evaluation methods are ranking, classification, factor comparison, the point system, and questionnaires. Employees differ in performance. The criterion chosen to establish an individual's worth to an organization must consider a number of factors including the concept of immediate, intermediate, and ultimate criteria. There are many potential biasing factors in criteria, including criterion deficiency, contamination, scale unit bias, criterion distortion, and opportunity bias. These will all be germane considerations when in the next chapter we discuss appraising performance by merit ratings.

REFERENCES

1. Arvey, R. D., and M. E. Begalla. "Analyzing the Homemaker Job Using the Position Analysis Questionnaire (PAQ)," *Journal of Applied Psychology*, 60 (1975): 513–517.
2. Arvey, R. D., E. M. Passino, and J. W. Lounsbury. "Job Analysis Results as Influenced by Sex of Incumbent and Sex of Analyst," *Journal of Applied Psychology*, 62 (1977): 411– 416.
3. Ash, P. "A Statistical Analysis of the Navy's Method of Position Evaluation," *Public Personnel Review*, 11 (1950): 130–138.
4. Ash, R. A., and S. L. Edgell, "A Note on the Readability of the Position Analysis Questionnaire (PAQ), *Journal of Applied Psychology*, 60 (1975): 765–766.
5. Atchison, T., and W. French. "Pay Systems for Scientists and Engineers," *Industrial Relations*, 7 (1967): 44–56.
6. Bass, B. M. "Further Evidence on the Dynamic Character and Criteria," *Personnel Psychology*, 15 (1962): 93–97.
7. Bass, B. M. *Organizational Psychology*. Boston: Allyn and Bacon, 1965.
8. Brenner, M. H., and H. C. Lockwood. "Salary as a Predictor of Salary: A 20-Year Study," *Journal of Applied Psychology*, 49 (1965): 295–298.
9. Brogden, A. E., and E. K. Taylor. "The Theory and Classification of Criterion Bias," *Educational Psychology Measurement*, 10 (1950): 159–186.
10. Brown, C. W., and E. E. Ghiselli. "The Prediction of Proficiency of Taxicab Drivers," *Journal of Applied Psychology*, 37 (1953): 437–439.
11. Cascio, W. F., and E. R. Valenzi. "Relations among Criteria of Police Performance," *Journal of Applied Psychology*, 63 (1978): 22–28.
12. Chesler, D. J. "Reliability and Comparability of Different Job Evaluation Systems," *Journal of Applied Psychology*, 32 (1948): 465–475.
13. Cohen, L. "More Reliable Job Evaluation," *Personnel Psychology*, 1 (1948): 457–464.
14. Cravens, D. W., and R. B. Woodruff. "An Approach for Determining Criteria of Sales Performance," *Journal of Applied Psychology*, 57 (1973): 242–247.
15. Davis, M. K., and F. Tiffin. "Cross Validation of an Abbreviated Point Job Evaluation System," *Journal of Applied Psychology*, 24 (1950): 225–228.
16. Dugan, R. D. "Evaluating Territorial Sales Efforts," *Journal of Applied Psychology*, 44 (1960): 107–110.
17. Ferguson, L. W. "Management Quality and Its Effects on Selection Test Validity," *Personnel Psychology*, 4 (1951): 141–150.

18. Fleishman, E. A. "Predicting Code Proficiency of Radiotelegraphers by Means of Aural Tests," *Journal of Applied Psychology*, 39 (1955): 150–155.
19. Fleishman, E. A., and B. Fruchter, "Factor Structure and Predictability of Successive Stages of Learning Morse Code," *Journal of Applied Psychology*, 44 (1960): 97–101.
20. Ghiselli, E. E., and M. Haire. "The Validation of Selection Tests in the Light of the Dynamic Character of Criteria," *Personnel Psychology*, 13 (1960): 225–231.
21. Gordon, M. E., and S. L. Cohen. "Training Behavior as a Predictor of Trainability," *Personnel Psychology*, 26 (1973): 261–272.
22. *Job Evaluation Manual for Evaluation of Nonexempt Clerical Jobs*. Fieldcrest Mills, Spray, N. C., 1953.
23. Jones, M. H., S. F. Hulbert, and R. H. Haase. "A Survey of the Literature on Job Analysis of Technical Positions," *Personnel Psychology*, 6 (1953): 173–194.
24. Klemmer, E. T., and G. R. Lockhead. "Productivity and Errors in Two Keying Tasks: A Field Study," *Journal of Applied Psychology*, 46 (1962): 401–408.
25. Lawshe, C. H., and A. D. McGinley. "Job Performance Criteria Studies: I. The Job Performance of Proofreaders," *Journal of Applied Psychology*, 35 (1951): 316–320.
26. Marquardt, L. D., and E. J. McCormick. *The Job Dimensions Underlying the Job Elements of the Position Analysis Questionnaire (PAQ) (Form B)*. Report 4, Office of Naval Research, Contract N00014–67–A–0016, NR 151–331, Purdue University, 1974.
27. McCormick, E. J. *The Application of Structured Job Analysis Information Based on the Positions Analysis Questionnaire*. Final Report, Office of Naval Research, Contract N00014–67–A–0016, NR 151–331, Purdue University, 1974.
28. McCormick, E. J., R. H. Finn, and C. D. Scheips. "Patterns of Job Requirements, *Journal of Applied Psychology*, 41 (1957): 358–364.
29. McGhee, W. "Cutting Training Waste," *Personnel Psychology*, 1 (1948): 331–340.
30. Nagle, B. F. "Criterion Development," *Personnel Psychology*, 6 (1953): 271–289.
31. Otis, J. L. "The Criterion." In W. H. Stead, C. Shartle, and associates (eds.), *Occupational Counseling Techniques*. New York: American Book Company, 1940.
32. Otis, J., and R. H. Leukart. *Job Evaluation: A Basis for Sound Wage Administration*. Englewood Cliffs, N. J.: Prentice-Hall, 1959.
33. Pigage, L. C., and J. L. Tucker. "Job Evaluation," *I.L.I.R. Publications, Bulletin Series*, 5 (1952): No. 3.
34. Prien, E. P., G. V. Barrett, and B. Svetlik. Use of Questionnaires in Job Evaluation," *Journal of Industrial Psychology*, 3 (1965): 91–94.
35. Prien, E. P., and W. W. Ronan. "Job Analysis: A Review of Research Findings," *Personnel Psychology*, 24 (1971): 371–396.
36. Robinson, D. D., O. W. Wahlstrom, and R. C. Mecham. "Comparison of Job Evaluation Methods: A 'Policy-Capturing' Approach Using the Position Analysis Questionnaire," *Journal of Applied Psychology*, 59 (1974): 633–637.
37. Rothe, H. F. "Output Rates among Industrial Employees," *Journal of Applied Psychology*, 63 (1978): 40–46.

38. Rothe, H. F., and C. T. Nye. "Output Rates among Coil Winders," *Journal of Applied Psychology*, 42 (1958): 182–186.

39. Rothe, H. F., and C. T. Nye. "Output Rates among Machine Operators: II. Consistency Related to Methods of Pay," *Journal of Applied Psychology*, 43 (1959): 417–420.

40. Rothe, H. F., and C. T. Nye. "Output Rates among Machine Operators: III. A Nonincentive Situation in Two Levels of Business Activity," *Journal of Applied Psychology*, 45 (1961): 50–54.

41. Schmidt, F. L., and L. B. Kaplan. "Composite vs. Multiple Criteria: A Review and Resolution of the Controversy," *Personnel Psychology*, 24 (1971): 419–434.

42. Seashore, S. E., B. P. Indik, and B. S. Georgopoulos. "Relationships among Criteria of Job Performance," *Journal of Applied Psychology*, 44 (1960): 195–202.

43. Smith, R. C. "Job Evaluation Plans," *Factory Management Maintenance*, 110, No. 1 (1952): 118–121.

44. Taylor, D. W. "The Learning of Radiotelegraphic Code," *The American Journal of Psychology*, 56 (1943): 319–353.

45. Tiffin, J. *Industrial Psychology* (3rd ed.). Englewood Cliffs, N. J.: Prentice-Hall, 1952.

46. U. S. Department of Labor. *Dictionary of Occupational Titles* (4th ed.). Washington, D.C.: U.S. Government Printing Office, 1977.

8 APPRAISING EMPLOYEE PERFORMANCE BY MERIT RATINGS

IN BRIEF   Decisions to promote, demote, train, or transfer employees are based more often than not on formal subjective ratings of them by their supervisors. Each of the many available rating methods has its advantages and disadvantages. Whatever method is used, it is important to insure that it is as reliable and as relevant as research, development, and resources can make it, free of the systematic biases and distortions that tend to emerge if raters are uncooperative or untrained, or if rating forms are poorly designed.

Ratings are sometimes used also as motivating techniques in employee counseling. Effective use of ratings is often made when appraisal interviews take the form of mutual goal-setting sessions.

We have looked at the ways in which work itself is analyzed, described, and evaluated. We have seen ways in which criteria of job success can be measured. Now we turn to merit rating, one specific method for appraising success on a job. Merit rating is the single most common method of formally appraising job performance. All organizations have some implicit or explicit means of appraising employee performance. A formal appraisal program serves many purposes.

Purposes Served

Merit rating may be used to help make decisions to promote, demote, transfer, determine salary, or train employees. The merit rating also may provide a rationale for discharge. From merit ratings, top management can learn how its supervision sees its subordinates. It may help top management to judge such supervisors as work evaluators. Employees can be assigned work according to abilities as described by merit ratings. Supervisors become more aware of differences among their subordinates if they must rate them periodically. Also, the changes in performance of a given employee may be assessed by periodic ratings. Snap judgments can be offset. Exceptional talent may be brought to the attention of higher authority.

Approximately 75 percent of companies also use merit ratings as the basis for counseling and guidance of employees and as means for providing feedback to employees about their performance, yet this use of merit ratings raises a number of serious questions.[88] We will return to a consideration of employee counseling and guidance using appraisal and goal-setting interviews at the end of this chapter.

Attitudes toward Merit Rating

The evidence on employee attitude toward merit rating is mixed. Naturally, those who make the ratings see them more favorably than those who receive them. Over 90 per cent of the top personnel administrators in key industrial firms were satisfied with their present performance appraisal systems.[88]

About 47 per cent of 2,487 Aramco supervisory employees responded to a questionnaire about merit ratings. Of these, 84 per cent felt that the company should continue its policy of requiring a performance review at least once a year. Twelve per cent were opposed, particularly if the ratings were to be made of low-level employees. Nevertheless, 88 per cent felt the report should be discussed with the ratee, while 60 per cent said that they observed improvements in subordinates as a consequence of such discussions. Sixty-one per cent of the respondents felt that such reports should be used for pay increases.[48]

On the other hand, in a survey of 340 employees from 14 firms, the typical respondent expressed only limited confidence in merit rating. Fifty-two per cent stated: "No weight should be given to merit rating in deciding who is to be promoted." Fully three-fourths stated that merit ratings are of little use in guidance and correction of workers. Merit ratings benefit the company, according to seven out of every ten of these respondents, while only one out of ten conceded some personal benefit from merit ratings. The remaining 20 per cent felt that merit ratings help neither the company nor the employee. Particularly negative in import is the finding that over half of these respondents said they were made to feel insecure by the merit rating programs to which they are subject.[84] Attitudes toward the merit ratings may depend on employee satisfaction with the postappraisal interview. Employees are more likely to favor a merit rating system that includes appraisal interviews, if they feel that the postappraisal interviews are handled well by their supervisors and they are monthly rather than semiannual.[87]

Inadequacies of Objective Appraisal

For some jobs it is possible to obtain completely objective measures of performance, which in turn can serve as appraisals of employee success. For instance, sales personnel often are appraised according to the number of shop calls they make per day, the number of new account calls they complete per day, the number of spot orders they obtain, the amount of new business they bring in, and/or the number of merchandising demonstrations they conduct. In the same way, the number of units assembled per hour by an assembly-line employee and the number of items rejected at inspection provide objective measures of performance. But, as we noted in Chapter 7, while these measures seem completely fair and objective, they often prove invalid. Instead of reflecting employee merit, they may depend primarily on conditions outside the employee's control. For instance, the extent to which a salesperson completes merchandising demonstrations will depend on factors in the territory, including the number of stores, the distances between stores, the nature of the competition, and the firm's advertising compared with the advertising of competitors. The quality and price of merchandise are also important factors that may be completely out of the salesperson's control. In the same way, the quality and quantity of output by the assembly-line worker may depend mainly on the speed of the assembly-line belt and the quality of parts coming down the line. Consequently, while the most common approach to appraisal — merit ratings — may seem to be more subjective than necessary, in the last analysis merit ratings may be fairer and more appropriate way to gauge the performance of employees than the seemingly more objective measures of performance.

RELIABILITY AND RELEVANCE IN MERIT RATINGS

A commonly used merit rating program requires supervisors to judge periodically whether or not each of their subordinates is doing superior, good, fair, or poor work on several of the dimensions of the job discussed in the last chapter. Any such rating program must meet two basic requirements before it can be used successfully in an organization. First, it must be acceptable to both the raters and the ratees in an organization. It is a truism that programs must have the support of those who use them or human ingenuity will be used to thwart them. One of the best ways to gain acceptance for a program is through the participation in its development of those concerned, both the rater and the ratee. The advantages of participation as a motivating technique were discussed in Chapters 3, 5, and 6.

A basic question is the effect of participation on the psychometric properties of rating scales. Thus, for example, rater participation in scale construction led to better psychometric properties in a study of college instructors.[34] It is a fair summary statement to say that participation does appear to have positive effects upon the rating process. Presumably, the many reasons we advanced in Chapter 5 for the utility of self planning are at work here also. Raters who participate in the design of the rating program have better understanding, more sense of accomplishment, and so on. Another possibility is that there is not only the increased understanding of the job and the dimensions which are being rated, but also the expectations one now has about the usefulness of the scale.

Finally, in order to be accepted, a new rating plan must be relevant to the jobs being rated. This means that it must cover areas important to job success and exclude those that are or seem irrelevant. But to be relevant, merit ratings must also be reliable.

Reliability of Merit Ratings

The reliability of merit ratings can be assessed in two general ways. First, a reliability coefficient can be obtained by correlating the merit rating obtained at one point in time with the rating obtained at a second point in time. As was illustrated in Chapter 7, in merit rating of sales personnel, a considerable drop in the reliability of their ratings occurred over time. The problem with this *rate-rerate* reliability is that for various reasons individuals do shift in performance. Merit ratings may fail in rate-rerate reliability because of actual changes in performance. Nevertheless, if rate-rerate reliability is extremely low, we will suspect that there is some deficiency in our merit rating scheme.

Interrater reliability is a second method of obtaining a measure of reliability. Two separate individuals rate the same group of employees. Ideally, we would hope to have a very high correlation between judgments of an employee's performance by two different observers. Even under ideal conditions, with all raters observing the same standard job performance on videotape, there is still considerable disagreement between raters.[20] This reflects the inability of one supervisor to observe relevant behavior, or a different perspective taken by supervisors at different levels in the organization when judging the same group of employees. However, training the raters can result in substantial improvement in interrater reliability.

We should note here that society in general and sporting contests in particular do not recognize the problem of low interrater reliability even when a million or more dollars may be at stake. In a world heavyweight title match, the boxing judges had only moderate agreement, about 0.60 correlation.[76]

Relevance of Merit Ratings

There are two general ways to establish the relevance of merit ratings. The first method involves judgments by employees, supervisors, and upper-level organization executives of the relevance of the dimensions being measured by the merit rating plan. They judge the extent to which the dimensions reflect the worth of the individual employee to the organization. As litigation concerning fair employment practices increases, this approach has become more common.

A second technique of determining relevance of merit ratings is to correlate the merit scores with other measures of employee performance that are seen as measures of the worth of the employee to the organization. If the merit ratings are relevant to the organization, it is a reasonable assumption that there should be at least some correlation between merit ratings and other conceptually similar measures of employee performance. The important point here is that the dimensions should be conceptually similar. A merit rating of quality of workmanship may never be related to accident involvement, for instance. This should not be taken to indicate that the merit ratings are not relevant for that position. In a typical study, substantial positive correlations were found between rankings of 294 Exxon service station dealers and their objective sales records.[81] Subjective ranking of performance by marketing personnel correlated 0.40 with gasoline sales by the dealers; 0.48 with their motor oil sales volume; 0.47 with their sales of tires; and 0.50 with their sales of batteries. One of the highest correlations was between rated motivation and new business orders earned.

SYSTEMATIC METHODS
OF SUBJECTIVE APPRAISAL

It is possible to ask supervisors to describe in their own words the performance of their various subordinates. As we shall see, some newer techniques have returned to this simplest unstructured form of appraisal. But where one is interested in comparing a relatively large number of such appraisals of many employees, it becomes important to bring some system and order to the ratings. The simple descriptions need to be categorized and ordered. Among the many methods for doing this are simple ranking, paired comparisons, forced distributions, graphic ratings, behavior check-lists, and critical-incidents reports. Each of these techniques may be subject to a greater or lesser amount of distortion.

Common Distortions in Ratings

The accuracy of ratings, primacy effect, leniency, error of central tendency, and halo effect are general tendencies that systematically distort ratings. They tend to occur regardless of the rater, the ratee, or the performance to be rated.

DIFFERENTIAL ACCURACY   Accuracy can be defined as the correspondence between a standard of measurement and the actual measurement. For physical measurements the accepted standard is typically maintained by the Bureau of Weights and Standards in Washington, D.C. For behavior the accepted standard would be actual recorded behavior.

Several studies illustrate that supervisors are differentially accurate in matching their ratings with standards of actual recorded behavior. That is, they tend to focus more on the effective compared to the ineffective aspects of the performance of their subordinates.[36] To study the differential accuracy of ratings, 118 managers rated specific dimensions of the observed behavior of an insurance agent who was calling a prospect on the telephone. All of the insurance agent's performance was videotaped, so that all managers saw exactly the same behavior. In this study, the accepted standard of accuracy was the actual videotaped behavior. This standard could then be compared to the ratings by the managers. The managers were 88 per cent accurate on behavior that was actually performed correctly (for example, repeating the time of the appointment before hanging up), but only 74 per cent accurate on behavior that was actually performed incorrectly (for example, failing to address the prospect by his correct name).

In a similar investigation, when objective production records were compared with supervisors' judgments of employee performance, the judgments paid most attention to the best work done by the employees.[35] Again, rating 200 computer systems analysts and programmers, raters made more errors when judging those with the poorest performance.[2]

PRIMACY EFFECT   Common sense suggests that an individual who starts off poorly and then improves in performance is more capable than one who starts off well and then goes downhill. Nevertheless, the reverse seems to happen to judgments about such individuals. Thus, individuals initially successful in performing a problem-solving task who then declined in success were judged to be more intelligent and to have greater potential than those individuals who either improved or fluctuated randomly.[41] This has been labeled a *primacy effect* where the raters recall the initial performance of of an individual. This memory of early performance dominates the total ratings of overall potential. But the effect is not always found.[69] The phenomenon may be situation-specific.

LENIENCY   More often than not most raters consistently rate almost everyone highly. Rating someone merely "good" damns the person with "faint praise." To call someone "average" is to downgrade the individual substantially. The grade inflation in colleges in the 1960s and 1970s was illustrative of the leniency effect. (Later in this chapter, we will discuss the motivation to be lenient.) If a supervisor has the chance to criticize the employee to be rated, he or she will be even more lenient.[75] Raters also will be more lenient in rating others when they know either that the ratings they make will be used for purposes of evaluation or they will have to be justified to the ratee. When the ratings are going to be used for research purposes only, then the raters are much more likely to show significantly less leniency in the ratings.[70]

SEVERITY   The reverse of leniency is severity. Some raters consistently assign low ratings to almost all ratees. Other raters apply more demanding standards to those they rate. Students are familiar with hard grading professors despite the grade inflation.

ERROR OF CENTRAL TENDENCY   Some raters consistently give everyone an average rating. No employee is judged as either superior or inferior. Consequently, the ratings have little value for any purpose, since no discrimination is made among employees.

THE HALO EFFECT   Raters develop a global or overall good or bad evaluation, which colors any judgments of other attributes of the ratee. If, for example, we believe an individual is a warm and friendly person, we often give favorable evaluations to other aspects of the individual about which we have little or no information. The halo effect seems to be even stronger than one might at first suspect. These is now evidence that halo effect can distort even judgments about an employee on dimensions for which there is contrary objective data. The rater develops an implicit belief in the goodness of a ratee. When presented with hard contrary data, the rater may reject or deny the validity of the data in order to maintain the belief. Raters are seldom aware of the pervasive influence the halo effect has upon their judgments. Over sixty years ago, Thorndike reviewed data from industrial organizations, the military, and the teaching profession to show that raters have a tendency to think of employees in rather general good or bad terms.[80] Raters seem to find it difficult to distinguish among individuals on the separate dimensions that they may be required to rate. For example, supervisors' ratings of a teacher's voice quality were found to correlate 0.63 with ratings of intellectual ability and 0.50 with ratings of interest in community affairs. Rated intellectual ability was found to correlate with rated discipline at about 0.80, while an objective measure of intellectual ability correlated close to 0.30 with rated ability to discipline students.

It is clear that raters have their judgments biased by an overall good or bad "halo" around the individual being rated. What is not clear for any position is the factor that is the most important in inducing the halo. Physical appearance, likability, and perhaps intellectual ability are chief among the factors that color our perceptions concerning an individual.

We have to be careful not to confuse actual positive relations among traits with halo.[16] Thus, the true correlation is not zero among intellectual, physical and interpersonal skills. Contrary to stereotyping brighter people actually are generally in better physical condition and better health than duller people. Nevertheless, to demonstrate the powerful effect that halo can have on judgment, an instructor was videotaped under two conditions. In one condition, he was presented as a very cold individual and the other as being very warm. Two groups of comparable students were then asked to rate the instructor on a variety of factors, including his physical appearance and mannerisms. In the "cold" condition, as would be expected, his physical appearance and mannerisms were seen to be quite shoddy as compared to the "warm" condition. Without the audio portion of the TV, a third group could not distinguish between the two videotapes as to his physical appearance or mannerisms. This result showed that the students in the first two conditions were evaluating objective factors such as physical appearance and speech mannerisms on the basis of their overall judgments of the individual as a warm or cold teacher.[57]

These results are somewhat similar to those of studies that have looked at the physical attraction of an individual and its effect upon judged performance. For example, in one study, judges of an essay upgraded their evaluation when it was written by an attractive woman, and downgraded their judgment when they believed the essay to be written by a plain woman.[46]

Many of these effects and errors are more prevalent with the graphic method of rating performance, while some errors such as central tendency are precluded by some methods such as ranking. We now turn to a consideration of various methods for rating the merit of employees beginning with one of the simplest — ranking.

Ranking

The ordering by rank of all employees to be compared is relatively simple and widely used. Except in those unusual circumstances where a single manager supervises a large number of subordinates, say more than 35, it is possible for the manager to rank the worth of the subordinates to the company according to the adequacy of performance on one or a composite of particular dimensions.

An alternation ranking procedure is usually suggested. Supervisors first identify their single best subordinate. Then they identify their poorest subordinate. The supervisors continue to fill in persons in this manner until all employees under them have been placed in rank order. If no tie ranks are permitted, the ranking method forces the supervisors to grade all their employees differently and prevents them from lumping all subordinates together at some point on a rating scale, thus avoiding the central-tendency error. For instance, they cannot report that all of the employees are identical or average. They must discriminate maximally.

At the same time, just because a rater is forced to discriminate does not mean that the discriminations are necessarily relevant or accurate. As a matter of fact, it is likely that the discriminations among employees in the central portion of the ranking distributions have little validity. That is, chance will determine that one employee is ranked slightly above the mean, while another employee who really is just as good is ranked a bit below the mean. For this reason it appears that flat rank distribution, which locates one case at each point on the scale and which assumes an equal distance between each case so ranked from highest to lowest, is not at all the best possible way of portraying the entire distribution of subordinates. It is suggested that the ranks be converted instead to standard scores, so that those with high and low ranks will be given highly differentiated standard scores, but those in between will obtain scores that are more nearly alike. This conversion assumes that in reality the employees are distributed as a normal frequency distribution rather than in the flat distribution created by ranking them in order.* It becomes mandatory to convert ranks to standard scores (or some other relative form such as percentiles) when we want to compare employees who have been ranked in different departments of different size. For example, it is obvious that the first employee out of 15 is seen as a better worker, all other things being equal, than an employee ranked first out of 5. After conversion to standard scores, the employee first out of 15 would have a standard score much farther from the mean of his distribution than the employee who was first out of 5.

However, problems in ranking may considerably decrease the accuracy of evaluation. These include (1) the likelihood that the rater will not be able to make the necessary discrimination between ratees without additional guides; (2) the tendency of the technique to penalize all the individuals of a superior group and to reward all those of an inferior group; (3) an increase in the difficulty of the task with an increase in the number of em-

---

* The conversion is simple to do since the standard deviation of any set of ranks is equal to $\sqrt{N^2-1}$ where N is the number of employees to be ranked.

ployees to be ranked by one supervisor; and (4) the likelihood that one supervisor may be judging employees on one dimension, with another supervisor using a completely different dimension, so that the ranks of employees in different departments may not be comparable.

Paired Comparisons

In this system, the supervisors are presented with a random pairing of their subordinates. In all, every subordinate is compared with every other, so that if the supervisor has 10 subordinates, 45 pairs are judged, choosing the better in each pair.* Although decisions about the quality of the performance of each subordinate are simplified considerably by the paired comparison method, these seems to be no appreciable difference in the validity, relevance, reliability, or discriminability possible when paired comparisons are used instead of the ranking procedure. It is probable that the typical rater has a rank order in mind when making paired comparisons. Moreover, when many more than 10 subordinates need to be rated, the number of pairs becomes extremely large; there seems to be little advantage to the paired comparison technique over ranking procedures and much disadvantage when the number of subordinates to be rated is large.[38] There are procedures that allow the rater to judge only half the possible pairs without lowering the validity.[60]

Forced Distribution

Forced distribution usually assumes that the ratees are normally distributed along a scale of effectiveness. The rater is forced to assign a certain percentage to each of the defined categories. Students are familiar with the forced distribution as "grading on the curve," in which their instructor assigns 10 per cent of them A's, 20 per cent of them B's, 40 per cent C's, 20 per cent D's, and 10 per cent F's. As with the ranking and paired comparison methods, the rater cannot pile up cases at the lenient end of the distribution nor assign a similar category to most or all of the subordinates to be rated. The supervisor must spread out and discriminate among subordinates as if they conformed in their performance to the forced distribution.

Again, the disadvantage lies in forcing raters to distribute their evaluations in a pre-set arrangement. Even if all ratees are generally good, only 10 per cent will receive A's. As students know, one effect of such forcing is to

---

* Number of pairs $= \dfrac{N(N-1)}{2} = \dfrac{10(10-1)}{2} = 45$

increase rivalry and competitiveness among ratees, reducing the possibility of profitable cooperation in learning and performance.

Nomination

The nomination technique is essentially a three-point rating scale with a forced distribution. First, raters eliminate all persons they do not know well enough to rate. Then, the raters are asked to choose a specified number of the remaining persons for a particular purpose: say, as persons they would most prefer to work with. Raters also may be asked to reject an equal number. In complying, each rater actually classifies all persons on the original list into three categories: those accepted, those neither accepted nor rejected, and those rejected. The greater the number of acceptances assigned a ratee compared with his or her rejections, the higher the ratee's score. The advantages of the nomination technique are that it requires only a rough judgment by the rater, and yet any ratee's final merit score is fairly precise and usually highly reliable, since it is a mean score based on a large number of raters. On the other hand, there is a likelihood that ratings based on the nomination technique will be biased by the popularity of the ratee. Thus, associates were nominated from among 203 salespersons. Nomination as individuals with whom raters would like to work correlated 0.60, 0.49, and 0.50 with nominations for value, ability, and influence.[7]

Graphic Rating Methods

Figure 8-1 shows graphic scales describing various aspects of performance. The figure shows nine different ways in which the quality of work can be rated on graphic scales. As can be seen, the scales vary in how many steps on them are defined verbally or numerically or not at all. Thus, in scale *a*, raters can check anywhere they like on a continuum between the cue locations, and the physical distance of their checkmark from the nearest cue is taken into account. The extra opinion obtained may not be worth the added cost of data analysis. The steps provide *anchors* for the rater in making the judgments. Care is needed in writing, selecting, and placing the definitions of the steps. To provide the most reliable structuring for the rater, step descriptions should be short, simple, and unambiguous. They should be consistent with the trait being rated and its definition. Each description should apply to a point or a very short range on the continuum. Its quantitative meaning ought to be relevant to its position and relation to the other graphic statements.

As much as possible the cues for each trait should be unique to that trait. General statements should be avoided: for example, when scaling

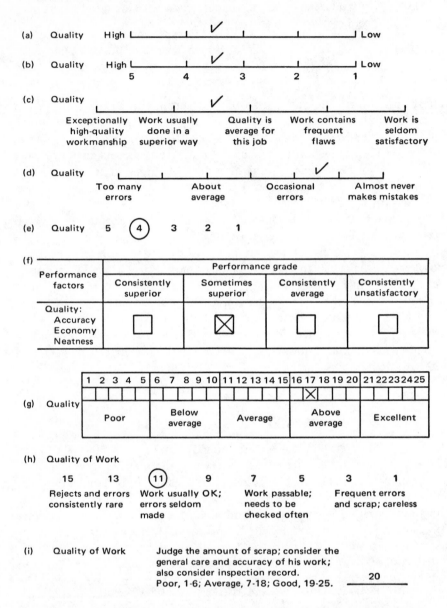

Figure 8-1. Variations on a graphic rating scale; each line represents one way in which a judgment of the quality of a person's work may be given. (From Guion, *Personnel Testing*, p. 98. Copyright © 1965, McGraw-Hill Book Company. Used with permission of McGraw-Hill Book Company.)

quality, it is preferable to talk about errors and mistakes, as in scale *d* in Figure 8–1, rather than high and low quality, as defined in scales *a* and *b*.

Many studies have been made linking the significance of the *number* of steps used in graphic scales with the reliability of the ratings that can be obtained. The evidence is mixed. Generally, reliability does not increase beyond five anchors.[52,40] Nevertheless, it is probable that an odd number of steps makes it possible to pile up more cases at the center of the scale, in the middlemost step, if the rater is so inclined. This cannot be done if an even number of steps is used, so that there is no exact middlemost category. To some extent, because the cooperation of the rater is all-important, it may be more necessary to satisfy the raters than to consider relatively slight effects on the ratings of number of steps when deciding on the number of rating steps to use.[55] Some raters may prefer a scale such as *g* in Figure 8–1, which permits as many as twenty-five different categories of rating. Others may prefer scale *f*, where only four categories are possible, yet scale *f* and scale *g* may be equally reliable, equally relevant, and equally discriminating. A survey of over 100 merit rating plans showed that the median number of steps was five.[12] Other evidence indicates that five to nine steps are preferable. If you use fewer than five you are probably not discriminating as well as you can and if you use more than nine the rater probably will find it difficult to make such fine distinctions.

The *man-to-man scale* is a graphic scale in which actual ratees are used to anchor particular points on the scale. Thus, supervisors might be asked to name an electrician with high quality of production, one with mediocre quality, and one with poor quality. After this, the supervisors rate the other electricians they supervise against those three "standard" ratees. The man-to-man scale is cumbersome compared with the paired-comparison and graphic rating scales, and has other disadvantages, such as administrative difficulty, extreme dependence on proper choice of "standard" individuals, and no means for equating scales of different raters. Because of these problems this scale is seldom used.[6]

Checklists

Checklists of various types have been developed to provide raters with more specific descriptive material to cover as they rate subordinates. The Likert method of summated responses described in Chapter 4 for attitude scaling can be the basis for scoring of a checklist. For example, raters can indicate whether they strongly agree, agree, are uncertain, disagree, or strongly disagree that an employee wastes a lot of material.

The same kinds of statements about an employee's performance can be scaled using the method of equal-appearing intervals. Judges assign values from 1 to 11 to each item. If an item were checked as applicable to a ratee, the ratee is credited with the mean value assigned for that item by the judges. A ratee's total merit score is the grand mean of all the item values checked as descriptive of him or her. Fortunately, it is not usually necessary to develop one's own items and judgments about the worth of these items, since work has been completed for 724 such items. It does not matter whether judges are supervisors, college professors, college students, or technically trained personnel.[59] As can be seen in the excerpts from Uhrbrock's standardized list shown in Figure 8–2, the main values assigned by the five samples of judges used by Uhrbrock did not differ very much from each other, although there was occasionally considerable difference in the variance within the five samples.[82] Nevertheless, personnel workers interested in constructing an equal-appearing interval scale can turn now to Uhrbrock's available list,[83] selecting items to try for their own purposes, then refining and scoring them according to the plan described above.

CRITERION-REFERENCED CHECKLIST Most performance appraisal techniques are "norm-referenced": the performance of the individual is either implicitly or explicitly compared to that of others performing the same job. This approach can be contrasted to "criterion-referenced" measures, which tie the job performance directly to acceptable or desirable performance of the individuals in the organization without reference to how others perform. Such an absolute scaling measure of job performance was constructed for aviation electronics technicians.

The objectives of the organization were obtained, and for each objective, supervisors were asked to determine on the checklist scales going from the

Figure 8–2. Excerpts from Uhrbrock's standardization of 724 rating-scale statements, using the method of equal-appearing intervals. (*Personnel Psychology*, 2 [1950]: 285, 316.)

Item Number		Mean Value Assigned Samples of Judges*				
		1	2	3	4	5
8	Usually does things wrong	1.4	1.9	1.8	1.6	1.5
98	Wants to be told what to do next	3.0	3.9	3.7	3.7	3.8
254	Is a good routine worker	6.0	6.2	6.8	6.1	6.0
414	Makes many useful suggestions	8.2	8.7	8.0	8.3	8.8
540	Merits the very highest recommendation	10.7	11.0	10.4	10.9	10.6

* Samples
  1. 20 foremen
  2. 10 technical assistants
  3. 24 U. Nebraska students
  4. 10 U. Nebraska faculty
  5. 25 U. Miami faculty

most to least proficient behaviors, the minimum point of acceptable performance and the minimum point of desirable performance.

A job-sample test of the knowledge and skills required in aviation electronics was then constructed and related to the checklist. The correlation was 0.40 between the two measures of job proficiency.[71]

This approach thus makes explicit, without reference to the job performance of anyone else, the minimum acceptable behavior of an individual performing a job.

Binary Scoring

A binary scoring procedure has been developed to correct for leniency errors. A sample five-point scale is shown in Figure 8–3. Those categories that clearly separate the inferior from the superior ratee as determined in a trial run are assigned weights of +1. All other categories are assigned weights of 0. It does not matter where on the continuum the categories discriminate. Thus, the technique is especially useful in correcting for the leniency error. Where the leniency effect is strong, the discrimination occurs at the positive end of the continuum, as shown in Figure 8–3. While superior sales personnel were described as "always" following through on sales, inferior personnel were most usually described as "often" following through on sales. The discrimination of consequence is between "always" and "often." Binary scoring makes it possible to discriminate among the personnel all along a continuum, yet the rater is able to assign relatively lenient ratings to all of

Figure 8–3. Excerpts from Binary Discriminant Scoring of Checklists to Reduce the Leniency Effect. (From Bass, "Reducing leniency in merit ratings," *Personnel Psychology,* 9 [1956]: 363.)

"He follows through on his sales"				
	Always	Often	Occasionally	Seldom	Never
Superior men, %	66	34	0	0	0
Inferior men, %	10	56	24	7	3
Weight given	1	0	0	0	0

"He knows how to handle all types of customers"				
	Very well	Fairly well	To some degree	A little	Not at all
Superior men, %	54	46	0	0	0
Inferior men, %	3	24	66	7	0
Weight given	1	1	0	0	0

"He keeps his products competitively priced"				
	Always	Often	Occasionally	Seldom	Never
Superior men, %	42	58	0	0	0
Inferior men, %	0	56	39	0	3
Weight given	1	0	0	0	0

the rated. The really good subordinate is described as always or almost always so; the inferior subordinate is "damned with faint praise." [6] Reliability of scores is as high as with other more traditional checklists.

The Mixed Standard Scale

Also designed to reduce leniency as well as halo is the Mixed Standard Scale. The rater is presented with three different degrees of the trait or attribute to be rated. The three degrees are a large amount of the trait or attribute, a moderate degree, and finally a statement that the trait or attribute is absent or very low.[17] An example of the three statements might be as follows:

"Extremely proficient in numerical operations";
"Satisfactory speed and accuracy in numerical operations";
"Very slow in performing numerical operations."

A large number of these descriptions are randomly presented to the rater. The rater's job for each description is to indicate whether the ratee is better or worse than the description, or if the ratee exactly fits the description.

The technique has the additional advantage of being able to identify systematically those ratings that are inconsistent or do not follow a logical pattern. It is somewhat less reliable than behaviorally anchored scales.[64]

Forced-Choice Methods

The forced-choice rating was developed to remove from the raters' control their opportunity to be either lenient to the ratee or to "damn a ratee unfairly." In the first form of forced choice, raters were presented with pairs of statements, both of which were favorable to the ratee. For instance, the rater was asked to indicate whether a ratee was intelligent or ambitious. The two items "intelligent" and "ambitious" were selected because preceding research had indicated that to be called "intelligent" was indicative of (correlated positively with) good performance, while to be described as "ambitious" was not a sign of good work in the particular situation for which the ratings were being made.

In the same way, two unfavorable statements — such as "dull" and "lazy" — could be paired on the basis of preliminary research. When raters objected to having to make such discriminations between two negative opinions about a ratee, the two pairs of ratings were combined on a rating form into a group of four choices containing two favorable statements and two unfavorable statements. Now the rater had to indicate which of the four statements was most true about the ratee and which was least true. Subsequently, it was found that putting together four favorable statements, two of which were discriminating, would work best.

Comparisons among Forced-Choice Techniques. Naval training instructors were rated using six different forced-choice formats, as follows:

Form A: Two statements per item, both favorable or both unfavorable; rater selects more (less) descriptive statement.

Form B: Three statements per item, all favorable or all unfavorable; rater selects the most and least descriptive.

Form C: Four statements, all favorable; rater selects two most descriptive.

Form D: Four statements, all favorable; rater selects the most and least descriptive.

Form E: Four statements, two favorable and two unfavorable; rater selects the most and least descriptive.

Form F: Five statements, two favorable, two unfavorable, one neutral; rater selects most and least descriptive.

While Forms *E* and *F* yielded the highest reliability coefficients (interrater agreement), Forms *C* and *D* tended to give the highest measures of the performance of the instructors being rated. Forms *C* and *D* produced the least tendency to leniency and halo effects. At the same time, Forms *A* and *C* were liked best by the raters and Forms *B* and *D* were least liked. As a consequence, Form *C*, in which four favorable statements are presented to raters and where the rater is asked to indicate which two are most descriptive, was identified as the format that was best to use in operation. As a consequence of this study, the general approach shown by Form *C* has been adopted most widely where the forced-choice merit-rating procedures are used in industry.[13]

Figure 8–4 shows an even more sophisticated version of a forced-choice merit rating procedure developed at Exxon. The rater is asked to indicate

Figure 8–4. Excerpts from a forced-choice appraisal form with qualification. (Reprinted with permission from *Social Science Research Reports*, vol. III, *Performance Review and Evaluation.* © 1962 by Standard Oil Company [New Jersey], all rights reserved.)

	Fits Poorly								Fits Well	
	0	1	2	3	4	5	6	7	8	9
1. A Keeps talks on discussion level and above argument level.	□	□	□	□	□	□	□	□	□	□
B Performs assignments efficiently and speedily.	□	□	□	□	□	□	□	□	□	□
C Performs duties with a minimum of supervision.	□	□	□	□	□	□	□	□	□	□
D Assumes his share of blame when things go wrong.	□	□	□	□	□	□	□	□	□	□
	0	1	2	3	4	5	6	7	8	9
2. A Follows work schedule closely.	□	□	□	□	□	□	□	□	□	□
B Has good work habits.	□	□	□	□	□	□	□	□	□	□
C Is a credit to his department.	□	□	□	□	□	□	□	□	□	□
D Makes decisions promptly.	□	□	□	□	□	□	□	□	□	□

which of the favorable statements best fits the ratee. Then the rater is forced to indicate which is next best, and finally which least fits the ratee. The rater can assign only one item to any given position on the scale, so that he or she is forced to discriminate among the four items or to order them to the extent to which they fit the performance of the ratee. Some raters may decide that all four items fit the ratee fairly well and will assign them 9, 8, 7, 6 on the scale. Other raters may choose to describe the ratee at 4, 3, 2, and 1 on the scale. Nevertheless, the same forcing occurs, and since only two of the items really have validity, while two of the items do not actually discriminate between good and poor employees, the same final scoring of performance can be effected.[74]

The main advantage seen for the forced-choice checklists is that the rater has difficulty in distorting the results in a desired direction. Nevertheless, uncooperative raters (if they know this trick) can distort results by checking the list as if to rate the best or worst ratee they ever knew rather than attempting to describe a specific ratee. In practice there is little evidence that raters attempt such a deliberate falsification of results. Rather, most studies tend to corroborate the finding that while graphic ratings tend to suffer from a leniency effect, the leniency disappears when the same ratees are rated by the same raters using forced-choice methods.[79]

Critical-Incident Technique

A rather different approach to appraisal is offered by the critical-incident technique developed by Flanagan.[31] First, interviews are held with supervisors to identify situations in which they have seen a subordinate do something effective or ineffective. The incidents are then content-analyzed and categorized. For example, 2,500 such incidents were collected from supervisors of ten Delco-Remy plants, yielding categorizations of critical incidents dealing with physical and mental qualifications, work habits, and so on.[32]

These categorizations and their subcategories form the basis of a performance record to be used by the supervisor. Such a performance record for the first category is shown in Figure 8–5. The supervisor simply enters any incidents observed during the given period that indicate good or poor performance by the employee in question. For instance, suppose at the end of each day the supervisor takes time to indicate personally observed incidents of both good and poor performance by various subordinates. The supervisor then keeps a running record such as is shown in Figure 8–5. At the end of some larger block of time, the information shown in the performance record can be used for employee counseling, research, and administration.

The more frequently the supervisor attends to the performance report, the better. Delco-Remy supervisors who recorded their incidents only once at the end of a two-week period reported less than one-fifth as many in-

PERFORMANCE RECORD

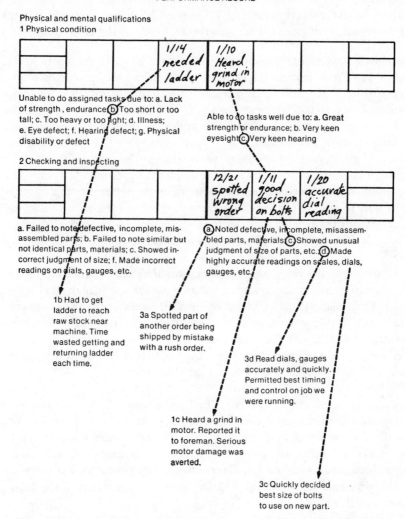

Physical and mental qualifications
1 Physical condition

1/14 needed ladder

1/10 Heard grind in motor

Unable to do assigned tasks due to: a. Lack of strength , endurance b. Too short or too tall; c. Too heavy or too light; d. Illness; e. Eye defect; f. Hearing defect; g. Physical disability or defect

Able to do tasks well due to: a. Great strength or endurance; b. Very keen eyesight c. Very keen hearing

2 Checking and inspecting

12/21 spotted wrong order

1/11 good decision on bolts

1/20 accurate dial reading

a. Failed to note defective, incomplete, mis-assembled parts; b. Failed to note similar but not identical parts, materials; c. Showed incorrect judgment of size; f. Made incorrect readings on dials, gauges, etc.

a Noted defective, incomplete, misassem-bled parts, materials c Showed unusual judgment of size of parts, etc. d Made highly accurate readings on scales, dials, gauges, etc.

1b Had to get ladder to reach raw stock near machine. Time wasted getting and returning ladder each time.

3a Spotted part of another order being shipped by mistake with a rush order.

3d Read dials, gauges accurately and quickly. Permitted best timing and control on job we were running.

1c Heard a grind in motor. Reported it to foreman. Serious motor damage was averted.

3c Quickly decided best size of bolts to use on new part.

Figure 8–5. An illustrative section of the performance record as kept on an hourly-wage employee in one of the divisions of the General Motors Corporation. (Reprinted by permission from "The Employee Performance Record: A New Appraisal and Development Tool," by John C. Flanagan and Robert K. Burns (September–October 1955). Copyright © 1955 by the President and Fellows of Harvard College; all rights reserved.)

cidents on the record as those who recorded incidents at the end of each day. All but one of 100 supervisors who were asked their preference indicated that they would prefer to make daily records of their observations of employee performance.

Of the incidents reported by the Delco-Remy supervisors, 98,556 were about effective performance and 7,670 were about ineffective performance. No incidents were reported for about one-fourth of the employees.

ADMINISTRATIVE AND RESEARCH USES   The data bank of incidents provides a rich store of information about job and organizational problems in general. The incidents are sufficiently specific to contribute considerably to job information and to specifying matters of consequence to personnel operation.[32]

To try to ascertain the reliability and relevance of the critical-incident technique, over 1,800 critical incidents were recorded concerning the behavior of grocery store managers.[1] Compared to the questionnaire approach, approximately twice as many critical incidents were derived from the interview. But the categories were the same for both techniques of collecting the critical incidents. There were variations in interviewer performance; the best interviewer obtained nearly twice as many incidents as the typical interviewer. Reliability was high with incidents being placed in the appropriate categories.

To ascertain the relevance of the critical incidents, the materials used by the organization for the internal training of the store managers were analyzed. The 1,800 critical incidents covered all issues in the training materials. The major problem with the critical-incident technique is the time required to collect and categorize information.

A variant of the critical-incident approach is the *behaviorally anchored scale,* originally developed by Smith and Kendall.[73]

BEHAVIORALLY ANCHORED SCALES   The first step usually involves collecting a large number of critical incidents of effective or ineffective performance by the employees performing the job. Ideally, we collect a large number of representative incidents from employees performing the job and their supervisors. Involving everybody creates more psychological commitment to the performance appraisal and feedback process when it is finally used operationally.

The second step involves sorting the separate job incidents into a number of dimensions of job performance such as speed, accuracy, cooperativeness, and initiative. The numbers will vary for each job, but are seldom over 10. This sorting procedure of the dimensions can be accomplished either by the employees, the supervisors, or the investigator.

The third step involves another group of judges. They are given the definition for each dimension and then asked to allocate each incident to the dimension that it best fits. This is called a *retranslation* procedure. Ideally, the job incidents should all fall under the same dimension as in the first analysis. The higher the percentage of the group assigning an incident to the same dimension, the less ambiguous is the job dimension. Different investigators use different standards, but at least the majority of the group must agree that an incident belongs to a particular dimension before it will be retained in the final scale.

The fourth step is for this group of judges to rate each incident on its effectiveness or lack of effectiveness for job performance on the appropriate dimension. Again, ideally, the group should be consistent in assigning numerical values to the range of job incidents. Those job incidents are retained that have the highest consistency (that is, they are consistently assigned a value indicating very effective performance).

As the final step in the process, usually five to eight job incidents are arranged on a vertical scale ranging from "very effective" to "very ineffective" performance, based upon the previous rating procedure. The task of the rater then is merely to indicate the *expected* behavior of the employee being rated, that is, whether or not the employee would be expected by the superior to exhibit each of the scaled incidents. Such expectations, of course, should be based on the fact that the same or similar incidents involving the employee have already been observed by the rater.

Figure 8–6 shows a behaviorally anchored scale developed to measure the dimension of personal relations of a salesperson with a client.

If two parallel forms of a behavioral expectancy scale result in similar ratings, one can have some degree of confidence that the scaling procedure is performing as expected. Evidence indicates that parallel but equivalent forms of behavioral expectancy scales can be contructed.[89]

Criticisms   A number of advantages have been claimed for this approach, but they have not always been fully supported by the research evidence. First, there is the belief that behaviorally anchored scales generate job performance dimensions that are relatively independent of each other.

Figure 8–6. Example of behaviorally anchored scales for sales representatives.

Personal Relations With Client

1. Could be expected to have a cordial, first-name relationship with all members of the client firm and the office staff on most accounts. □

2. Could be expected to be known by all people in most accounts, but on a formal basis. □

3. Could be expected to be known basically by one person in an account on a more formal basis. □

4. Could be expected that sales representative is recognized as such, but not by name. □

5. Could be expected that sales representative would be a near stranger in many active account calls. □

When the behaviorally anchored rating scales have been compared to other rating techniques, the results have been mixed. At best, it can be said that in certain specified situations, the behaviorally anchored rating scales do result in somewhat less halo effect than other rating approaches do. In other situations, the results have been equivocal.[68]

Second, it has been assumed that there would be less leniency exhibited by raters on this scale, since the anchors refer to concrete behavior. Again, the results are mixed, with some studies showing more, some showing less, leniency with the rater's using the behaviorally anchored scaling approach. When the effects of education and job experience of raters and ratees upon the behaviorally anchored rating scales were examined, it was found that neither of these characteristics affected the ratings. Both halo effects and leniency were found in the ratings.[25]

Third, there is at least some evidence that, as expected, participation by supervisors in formulating the rating approach will motivate them to be more conscientious and effective when they actually evaluate their subordinates. In addition, since the terminology used is taken from the actual job, there is less ambiguity concerning the meaning of any of these scale positions. Nevertheless, since people are promoted or transferred or quit, after several years, users no longer are the ones who participated in the development of the scales.

Fourth, it is very difficult to obtain behavioral examples that illustrate the average performance of an employee. It is much easier to obtain examples of very good or very poor performance.

Fifth, it is important to remember that one implicit assumption of the behavioral-expectancy scaling approach is that the ratees are going to be evaluated on *expected* behavior that they may have never carried out. This means that the rater has to recall observed behavior of the employees in a variety of situations and then make an inference concerning expected behavior of the employee that probably never has been observed. So, in some sense, "behaviorally anchored rating scales" are misnamed. At times, they call for superhuman performance as a result of extreme behavioral incidents that are cited for effective performance on the job.

Sixth, there is a real question whether behavioral-expectation scales are significantly *better* than simpler formats for rating the performance of employees. For example, it was found in two large hospitals that the behavioral-expectation-scale format was not significantly more effective on any of the rated dimensions than a simpler format.[21] Indeed, simple formats have been preferred over behaviorally anchored scales.[27]

Seventh, certain behavioral anchors may become dated. In contrast to many other formats, behavioral expectancy scales require periodic updating. Also, if behavioral-expectancy anchor points are quite specific to one organization, comparison across different units of the organization is difficult.

Eighth, research with nurses indicates that peers, supervisors, and incumbents rate employee performance from different perspectives. For example, it has been suggested that head nurses may be less able to discriminate items related to confidence from those that relate to job effort; but nurses who rate themselves and their peers can make the distinction between confidence and effort.[45]

Ninth, raters differ in their cognitive complexity or ability to deal with the many dimensions and behavioral anchors. The less cognitively complex rater prefers a simpler format.[67]

Tenth, developing behaviorally anchored scales is a time-consuming and costly process. As the present evidence indicates, all of this extra work and time may not produce better results than using one of the more common graphic rating scale approaches would.

Other uses   Yet the extra effort may be worthwhile if the data are used for other purposes. Data obtained from the behavioral-expectancy procedure can supplement or substitute for a job analysis, since they specify the concrete behavior that is expected of individuals on the job. The behavioral expectancy data can also be used as an aid in developing training programs since the behavioral anchor is specific in indicating the exact behavior expected of the employee. A behavioral-expectation procedure also provides information concerning how much agreement there is in organization policy and how well that policy is communicated to all employees. Since supervisors are asked to judge what effective and ineffectual behavior is, if there is a wide disagreement concerning certain behavior as to whether it can be considered effective or ineffectual, then there is clearly a problem in terms of organizational policy and how it is communicated.[18] There is limited evidence from a small group of computer programmers that both construction of a behaviorally anchored scale and feedback to the ratee increased rated performance.[11]

SOURCES OF VARIANCE AND ERROR IN MERIT RATINGS

No matter which rating procedure is used — rank, paired comparisons, graphic, forced distribution, behavior checklist, forced-choice, or critical-incidents technique — errors associated with the appraiser will creep into the rating, particularly if rater training and cooperation are lacking.

Various experiences with ratings tend to show that the most effective method for improving ratings in many ways is to train raters carefully. The rater who knows about the existence of the different kinds of errors can be on the lookout for them and can take steps to counteract them.[38]

Other errors will be associated with the ratee. Particular combinations of raters, ratees, rating methods, and the situations in which the ratings are made and used will influence the degree of error occurring in the ratings.

In addition to the above influences on the amount of unreliability, irrelevance, and bias is included in merit ratings, other factors also play an important part: the format, who rates whom, and peculiar errors that occur with particular combinations of ratees, raters, and formats.

The Format

Ratings that happen to be close on a rating form are more likely to correlate than those more distant from one another. It has been found that adjacent ratings correlate more highly than those further apart.[77] The same *proximity effects* occur when the locations of the traits are rearranged.

There is a current trend in performance appraisal systems to move away from ratings of personal traits of the employee, such as dependability and leadership. The trend is to rate actual job behavior. Yet, in reviewing the evidence, Kavanagh concludes that personal traits can be as reliable, relevant, and desirable to use as more job-oriented measurements.[43]

WORDING   According to research and experience, rating errors are likely to be smaller if:

1. Each trait covers a single activity rather than a composite of activities. Only one thought should be expressed and it should be readily intelligible to the rater.
2. There is objective evidence of the accomplishment that is being rated; more accurate ratings will be obtained if the rater can observe the behavior in question.
3. Abstract terms like *loyalty, honesty,* and *integrity* are avoided. Terms like these describe behavior and attitudes that are likely to vary in the typical ratee depending on specific circumstances and may mean different things to different raters.
4. General terms like *average* are avoided when describing a particular location on a scale, for the same general term will be interpreted differently by different raters.
5. Rating statements are kept short and clear. The statements should avoid double negatives and inconsistencies, which will confuse the rater.[4,28,77,38]

A trait to be rated is usually defined. Cues are also provided to distinguish different degrees of the trait. The cues have two purposes. They supplement the definition of the scale continuum and provide anchor points for the rater.

Cues should be short, unambiguous, and as specific to the trait possible. (That is, if the rating is about motivation, a good cue would be "eager," but not "excellent.") Cues should cover single points on the continuum and not overlap with other cues. For instance, "average" and "mediocre" are likely to overlap.

Although the reliability and validity may not be seriously altered by the number of cues used, it may be helpful to establish empirically the optimum number and type of cues. Different formats can be tried experimentally and compared. If the final formats are to be used operationally for evaluating hundreds or thousands of employees periodically, then the research effort involved may be well worth the cost.

EMPIRICAL RATIO SCALING OF CUES   One hundred seventy-five graduate, undergraduate, and high school students were asked to assign a number, any number, to what they conceived "sometimes" to mean. Then, given whatever number they had assigned to "sometimes," they were asked to assign a corresponding number to "always." For example, a student who said that "sometimes" meant 3 might then say that "always" meant 30, yielding a ratio of 1 to 10. Numbers were assigned in this way to 39 other adverbs. The mean choice for "sometimes" was 19.42. When this was set equal to 1.00, six of the adverbs scaled in ratio to "sometimes" were as follows: "always," 2.98; "very often," 2.18; "fairly often," 1.68; "sometimes," 1.00; "seldom, if ever," 0.19; and "never," 0.004.

Six expressions of frequency — *always, very often, fairly often, sometimes, seldom,* and *never* — roughly bear ratios to one another of 5:4:3:2:1:0. Rationally, "never" is a good zero point for the scale. We finish with a choice of six cues because there seem to be six that have a consistent relation to each other.

In the same way, the 175 students scaled 44 expressions of amount. In ratio to "some," assigned the mean amount of 18.63, nouns scaled as follows, for example: "all," 3.54; "an extreme amount," 2.59; "quite a bit," 1.83; "some," 1.00; "none," .008. The ratios were the same for an expression regardless of the educational level of the judges or whether the topic to be rated was important or unimportant.[10]

DIFFERENTIAL WEIGHTING   The fact that some characteristics that are rated are judged more important than others leads personnel departments to develop weighting procedures. For instance, *quality* of output may be judged twice as important a contribution to organizational success as *quantity* of output. Rated quality then may be assigned twice as much weight as rated quantity and a composite score calculated on the basis of both. However, in doing this it is necessary to take into account how much the ratings differ in assessing quality and quantity. Thus, if employee ratings differ very little or not at all about quality, regardless of the weight assigned to it, differences among ratees in composite score will depend primarily on the less important rating of *quantity*. In the same way, since the variance of ratings will be greater if their consistency or reliability is greater, the composite score will depend greatly on the reliability of the ratings of quality and quantity. In forming composites, it will be necessary to correct each subscore by dividing it by its own standard deviation or by using other available statistical techniques.

Nevertheless, if more than five ratings are to be combined, it has been shown algebraically that the correlation is practically 1.00 between a composite based on any particular differential weights for each rating and a composite where every rating is given the same unitary weight.[39] Thus, for checklist formats combining ratings on many activities, there is no utility in assigning different weights to the individual items.

The Ratee

Characteristics of the ratee may be a source of systematic error, that is, a source of systematic divergence between the distribution of merit ratings and the true or theoretical distribution of merit.

JOB TENURE   A study of 9,000 employee ratings in a steel mill showed that the ratings improved as the workers increased in age from 20 to 30 or 35 and, thereafter, declined with age. The longer workers had been on their *present* job, the lower was their rating. Some of this shift was meaningful. That is, it is likely that over time, learning occurred; then the more meritorious workers were promoted and the less meritorious remained in the same jobs, so that the mean first improved and then declined with age and service. Also, there may have been a distorted negative appraisal of very young and of older employees.

A comparative study of the same problem, completed for two steel mills and three laundries, concluded that other factors determined whether older, more tenured workers would be overevaluated or underrated.[63] For instance, if supervisors play favorites and make their ratings on the basis of familiarity, or if they are uninterested in establishing merit scores close to the truth, higher merit scores will be assigned to the older, longer-tenured employees. But, if older employees with long tenure on a given job are already at the top of their pay bracket, and only shorter-tenured workers can obtain raises if their merit scores are high, supervisors will give the shorter-tenured employees the higher merit ratings.

The Rater

DIMENSIONS PERCEIVED   Raters tend to generalize some particular feelings they have when they rate other persons. These general tendencies vary along at least four independent dimensions of consequence, according to a factor analysis of 100 subjects rating 225 photos on 15 personality traits. First, a clear halo effect is seen. Some pictured persons are judged by a rater as good, honest, thoughtful, relaxed; others are judged by the same rater as bad, dishonest, self-centered, and tense. A second dimension concerns harmfulness — good, safe, and kind versus bad, dangerous, and cruel. A third dimension deals with dependability: that is, honesty, reliability, and stability. A fourth dimension concerns affability: that is, generosity, happy disposition, relaxation.[50] Keep in mind that there is no relevance in the ratings at all. All the variance is bias, for the correlation is zero between judgments of personality on the basis of photos and true personality.

RESPONSE SET When confronted with the same choices, *regardless of what behavior or trait is being rated*, some persons generally tend to be more agreeable, favorable, and acquiescent than others. These generalized differences in response sets are likely to influence merit ratings completed by "yea-sayers" and "nay-sayers." [6]

COMPETENCE OF THE RATER Supervisors who themselves received lower merit ratings from their bosses tended to agree less with fellow supervisors in rating subordinates.[54] We infer that less meritorious supervisors' ratings of subordinates were less reliable and possibly less relevant. Differences among raters tend to reflect their own activities, achievements, and confidence. The raters higher in aptitude and achievement at Army Command and General Staff School tended to turn in more relevant or valid merit ratings of others.[66] The effect was particularly pronounced when graphic rating scales rather than forced-choice formats were used. In a more detailed analysis, 17 supervisors judged as effective by their bosses were compared with 11 judged as less effective. The merit ratings assigned subordinates were severe when completed by the 17 effective supervisors. They were more discriminating between good and poor subordinates. The more effective supervisors tended to concentrate on task matters: initiative, persistance, constructive action, anticipated planning. This is consistent with what we will discover when discussing predictors of good supervisory behavior: that is, that good supervisors are task-oriented. The less effective supervisors tended to be interaction-oriented. They overweighted the traits of following orders, cooperation, teamwork, and loyalty to company.

The effective managers saw more differences between their good and poor subordinates and were less lenient than the ineffective managers in assigning merit ratings.[51]

A review of research concluded that intelligence, knowledge of the appropriate norms, and standards of judgment increase one's ability to judge others.[78] For instance, a correlation of 0.33 was reported between the IQ and the consistency or reliability of given raters.[77] Furthermore, raters lower in IQ tended to be more susceptible to the influence of the popularity of the ratee when assigning ratings to him.

ACCURACY AND SIMILARITY   Supervisors overestimate their similarity to workers they rate highly and underestimate their similarity to workers given poor ratings.[85] This is because our own self-image tends to influence the accuracy with which we can rate others. If we esteem ourselves (as we usually do) and we also value another person, we will tend to ascribe to him many characteristics we think are desirable and admire in ourselves.[53] If other people are actually endowed with these characteristics, our ratings of them will be accurate. If they actually are not endowed with them, our ratings will be inaccurate. Contrast errors will occur if we regard other people as of little value. Then we will ascribe to them characteristics opposite to those we see in ourselves.[85] Our accuracy will depend on what they are really like.

DIFFERENTIAL ACCURACY   How accurate are raters in evaluating individuals across different types of jobs? Using videotapes with known "true" performance, the accuracy of raters could be assessed. Differential accuracy, the ability to rank the performance of individuals, was found to be moderately consistent.[19] Those raters who were accurate in judging the job performance of recruiters (on videotape) were moderately accurate (0.46) in judging the performance of managers.

RATER MOTIVATION   Raters are often motivated to be lenient rather than to downgrade unmeritorious subordinates. Many reasons underlie this tendency. The supervisors may:

1. feel that anyone under their jurisdiction who is rated unfavorably will reflect poorly on their own worthiness;
2. feel that anyone who could have been rated unfavorably had already been discharged from the organization;
3. feel that a derogatory rating will be revealed to the ratee to the detriment of relations between rater and ratee;
4. rate leniently in order to win promotions for their subordinates and therefore earn a reputation as a superior with "influence upstairs";
5. be projecting;
6. feel it necessary always to approve of others in order to gain approval for themselves;
7. be operating on the basis: "I am meritorious; therefore, whoever associates with me is meritorious";
8. rate leniently because there exists in the culture a response set to approve rather than disapprove.[6]

Rater cooperation and interest are of prime importance in avoiding the leniency effect and other errors and in securing accurate, reliable, and relevant ratings. Again, the amount of support and concern shown by top management when a merit rating system is introduced makes a considerable difference. If supervisors feel that their own reputations are involved, they will do a more conscientious job of rating subordinates.

In some situations, a lenient distribution may be accurate. It may be a more relevant representation of the situation than the psychologist's ideal of a normal distribution. For example, if a large proportion of poorer job applicants has been weeded out by a valid selection program, a "lenient" distribution may portray accurately the distribution of performance among a group of workers.

Interaction of Rater and Ratee

The location in the organization of the rater in reference to the ratee can make considerable differences in the ratings received by the ratee. One study found that supervisors' ratings of Air Force aircraft maintenance mechanics were more likely to correlate with actual tested job knowledge than did ratings given the same mechanics by their peers.[42] Moreover, in comparison with peers, supervisors tended to be less influenced by the length of time they knew the ratee, the age of the ratee, and the ratee's marital status. Employees may sense these greater biases among peers, for among 340 employees in 14 firms surveyed, 33 per cent favored being rated alone by their supervisor while only 23 per cent were willing to be rated only by their peers, and 44 per cent preferred having both done.[84]

There is some indication that the propinquity or physical distance that separates the supervisor and the employee may have some bearing upon the forming of friendships and thereby to some degree bias the performance ratings.

How long raters have known a ratee affects their rating substantially, although 80 per cent of the workers surveyed in 14 companies did not feel that the closeness of an acquaintanceship would influence a merit rater.[84] In an analysis of acquaintanceship and merit ratings by 104 traveling field representatives of 1,597 assistant life-insurance sales managers, it was shown that the rate-rerate reliability of the ratings increased systematically from 0.74 to 0.85 with the degree to which the representatives said they were acquainted with the ratee.[30]

Degree of acquaintanceship had the same effect on the extent to which representatives' ratings agreed with those of the manager's immediate superiors, increasing from 0.51 to 0.66 as acquaintanceship rose. Rated merit also rose with acquaintanceship. On the average, acquaintanceship correlated 0.24 with the merit rating assigned. Thus, acquaintanceship seemed to contribute to a leniency effect while it was increasing the reliability and relevance of the ratings (where relevance was estimated by the amount of agreement of the ratings assigned by the representatives with the ratings assigned by the ratee's superiors). A much greater leniency effect was noted in another study, where a correlation of 0.65 was obtained between merit rating received by 485 superiors and the length of time they had been known by the department head who rated them.[77]

To some extent, the tendency to be more lenient with acquaintances may be due to our proneness to identify with those with whom we are more familiar. Comparing the ratings assigned to a hypothetical subordinate, those who actually had had to play the role of the subordinate gave the most favorable ratings to the subordinate. Those who played the superior were least favorable, while those who only observed the role-play were in between in leniency.[62]

An important factor in elevating some ratings is the proportion of employees perceived by the supervisor of a group to have "basic weaknesses." The supervisor who has a relatively high proportion of inept subordinates will give the competent employees relatively high ratings and salary increases. The supervisor with few inept subordinates will give the other employees relatively smaller raises. Your co-workers can have an influence on how your job performance is rated.[37] This *contrast effect* can also influence interview selection decisions, as we will see in Chapter 11.

POTENTIAL BIASING FACTORS OF RATER'S AND RATEE'S SEX, RACE, AND AGE   A potentially serious problem is the extent to which the employee's sex, race, or age may influence the rating of performance by the worker's supervisor.

In a controlled study, eight ratees were filmed performing the identical task of stacking large cans on a grocery shelf. White and black men and women served as the employees performing the stacking either well or poorly. Sixty white men rated all eight conditions.

The results indicated that low-performing men and women were rated in a similar fashion, but, contrary to some previous research, high-performing women were rated significantly better as grocery clerks than the high-performing men. In terms of potential race bias, the raters tended to give higher ratings to blacks than to whites when performance was low, but gave equivalent ratings to high-performing blacks and whites.[15]

Evidence about the effects of race on ratings is mixed. Thus, one study of over 400 hospital medical technicians allowed groupings that resulted in interactions between white and black supervisors who were rating white and black employees. General results showed that black technicians when rated by black supervisors received higher ratings than blacks who were rated by white supervisors.[33]

Some effects of race were revealed in a study of over 400 bank tellers. The differences between the black and white tellers on both objective measures of criteria and supervisory ratings were small and mostly insignificant. The correlations between supervisory ratings and measures of objective criteria were mostly low except for a relationship between the supervisors' ratings for quality of work and the number of shortages and overages — objective measures of work quality. It is not surprising that supervisors' ratings of the tellers on dimensions such as relations with customers did not relate to the more objective measures of work quality.

But, in comparing separately the objective measures and the supervisors' overall ratings for the black and white tellers it was found that the white supervisors consistently rated the black tellers more in accord with the objective performance measures than they did the white tellers. It appears that the white supervisors were basing their judgments of performance more for the black tellers than for the white tellers on the objective measures. This may have been an attempt by the supervisors to be fair to the black employees.[5]

Some military research has suggested that peer raters tended to favor individuals of their own race by giving them higher ratings. Yet with 80 first-line supervisors during a training workshop, no significant correlations were found between race and judged potential. In other words, whites tended to rate blacks and whites equally, as did blacks tend to rate blacks and whites. It would appear, at least in some industrial situations and in some integrated situations, that race may not be much of a factor in the judgment of performance.[65]

Although generalizations are difficult to make, it also needs to be kept in mind that some rated differences between groups may reflect true differences rather than bias. For example, women with generally smaller hands, may perform certain small assembly tasks better than men.

There is a paucity of evidence about rating bias against the older worker. But there is a pervasive age stereotype. On performance capacity and potential for development, ratings of the average 30-year-old employee are significantly better than for the average 60-year-old employee.[61]

If this stereotype is translated into organizational personnel practices, then age discrimination may result, largely unsupported by the available evidence about the lack of relation between age as such and job performance.[22]

IMPROVING RATER PERFORMANCE

Training guides for raters may suggest that (1) raters should know in advance that they must make particular performance appraisals; (2) the rater should be in a position to observe firsthand the performance to be rated; (3) the firsthand observations should include many aspects of performance rather than a few; (4) appraisals should always be based on specific, actual performance; raters should avoid using anticipated or hoped-for performance, which may not occur; (5) raters should be careful not to be overly influenced by a major strong or weak point of employees' performance; (6)

raters should avoid making appraisals when in an unusual frame of mind, mood, or temporary attitude toward either the individual or the work situation; and (7) raters should set aside a definite time to make appraisals. They should obtain a quiet place and an uninterrupted period of time. If notes have been kept, they should be reviewed objectively.

Training Raters

Several studies have demonstrated that even short training periods will decrease leniency error and halo effect,[14,23] particularly if the training is participative.[49]

The U.S. Department of Agriculture teaches appropriate standards to supervisors. Supervisors rate the described performance of a hypothetical employee. A "correct" rating has been predetermined by staff specialists. The supervisor is then given feedback indicating deviations from the "correct" evaluation. This type of training increases the probability that all supervisors will be evaluating individuals against similar standards.[58]

APPRAISAL AND GOAL-SETTING INTERVIEW

Often merit ratings form an important part of an appraisal interview. Let us look at the advantages and disadvantages and some of the problems involved. To improve their performance, subordinates must know what is expected of them and know how well they are doing. Yet to disclose or not to disclose ratings to subordinates seems a major question for management, even though, as noted earlier, most supervisors are in favor of informing their subordinates about what ratings they have assigned them.

In the absence of solid support and mutual trust, it may be more profitable for merit ratings to remain confidential and for use only for administration and research, not for the guidance of subordinates. As long as the merit ratings are used only for administration and research, raters are not under pressure to confront their subordinates with the particular ratings they had assigned to them. Raters are less likely to be subject to the leniency effect.[77] Moreover, evidence has accumulated that a counseling discussion with a subordinate, particularly one whose performance has been less than adequate, which begins with the superior handing the subordinate a statement of the subordinate's shortcomings, is not conducive to employee development. Rather, the employee is likely to become defensive, (correctly) believing him- or herself to be under attack. The supervisor is likely to be downgraded by subordinates high in self-esteem who receive ratings of poor performance.[72] Nevertheless, if handled tactfully, performance appraisal interviews in which supervisors discuss the merit ratings they assign their subordinates may be useful. Thus, subordinates were likely to report that they had taken constructive action as a consequence of their performance appraisal interview.[56]

The critical incidents approach is particularly suited to providing material for easy opening of counseling discussions with subordinates. The supervisor can begin the interview by referring to an effective incident, such as when the employee called attention to the loosening of a guard on an overhead conveyor and suggested a different style of guard that would be more effective and durable. The concrete feedback is likely to make the employee feel appreciated. It also will tend to stimulate further suggestions in the future. Similarly, the supervisor can discuss specifically and objectively the criticism that when a pan of parts was accidentally spilled and an assembly line had to be shut down until more parts could be obtained, the interviewee was the only one who sat down and waited until the parts were available and made no effort to help pick up and sort the spilled parts. A frank discussion of this situation is likely to promote better insight on the part of the employee and improve the understanding between the employee and the supervisor.

Importance of Feedback

The importance of providing subordinates with feedback is demonstrated by the fact that there seems to be in many situations little agreement between the subordinates' self-ratings of their performance and the ratings of the subordinates by their supervisors. For example, in one study involving over 200 employees in a state agency, the highest correlations between self-ratings and supervisors' ratings were around 0.20.[3]

Costs of Feedback

In approximately 90 per cent of the organizations that have performance appraisal, results are discussed with employees.

An interesting question is "What is the effect of providing feedback when it is optional on the supervisor's part?" In one investigation of almost 2,000 employees of a state government, analysis of the personnel files showed that overall, the supervisor tended to discuss the performance rating results with subordinates who had been given low evaluations. In further analysis, other subordinate characteristics, such as sex, race, and age, were investigated. Perhaps the most significant finding was that for white employees there tended to be discussions when the evaluation was lower, but for black employees discussions were more frequent when they had higher performance ratings.[29] The supervisors in the study were all white, and this may have affected their willingness to provide negative feedback to black employees. It appears that from the supervisor's point of view, the psychological costs of giving negative feedback to black employees were perceived to be too high.

FIELD COMPARISONS   For 140 employees, an opportunity for a natural field comparison occurred when there was a switch from an old appraisal system to a new system that had distinctly different features. In the new appraisal system, salary recommendations were made by the first-level supervisor and were communicated directly to the employee along with the evaluation of the employee's performance. In addition, under the new system, each department developed its own appraisal forms. Under the old system, feedback to the employee was inconsistent, salary recommendations were made by the department heads instead of the first-level supervisor, employees were not told their salary recommendations, and the forms were standardized and established by the personnel department. About half the employees used the new appraisal system, while half remained under the old system.

During a one-year period, the group using the new appraisal system evaluated it favorably and believed it was clearer than the old system. Shifting the power of the department head to the first-level supervisor, presenting feedback to the subordinates, and involving subordinates in constructing the performance appraisal system appeared to be main ingredients in forming a successful performance appraisal program.[26]

A field study involving engineers and scientists compared participative setting of work goals during performance appraisals with control conditions. Only the participative goal setting resulted in higher performance after six months. Supervisors asking their subordinates to "do your best" did not result in improved performance.[47]

The biggest loss in most systems seems to be in the failure of supervisors to provide feedback to white employees (usually the vast majority of employees) who are doing a good job for it is most important that employees who are doing a good job receive periodic feedback and recognition for doing so. A mutual goal-setting program may provide the solution to the problem.

Mutual Goal-Setting as an Alternative

Considering the biases and errors likely to be contained in any particular merit rating and the defensiveness likely to appear in subordinates, particularly those of high self-esteem, who are informed that they have received a rating lower than they expected, the use of annual or semiannual appraisal interviews based on merit ratings for purposes of employee development and guidance presents inevitable difficulties.

One technique designed to overcome problems inherent in the traditional appraisal interview is the mutual goal-setting interview, often part of a management-by-objectives program (Chapter 5). In such a counseling session, independent of the merit rating program, superior and subordinate sit down together periodically to review the progress of the subordinate during the time preceding the meeting and to formulate joint plans for the period following the meeting. Major emphasis can be placed on comparing the subordinate's own present with his or her own past performance rather than with that of others, to avoid evoking defensiveness. Discussion about shortcomings can be in terms of failures to reach goals that had been agreed to by the subordinate in a previous mutual goal-setting interview.

COMPARISONS   Many firms, including Johnson's Wax, General Mills, and McKesson & Robbins, have concentrated on these "How Am I Doing" programs to provide feedback information. At the same time, the subordinates can provide appropriate feedback to their superiors. But this aspect of the interview may not be as important as the goal setting. Rather, it is the focus on plans for the future, rather than on past success or failure, that seems to make the difference, according to a study that contrasted the psychological effects of appraisal interviews and improvement-planning discussions between managers and their subordinates.[44] In an aircraft engine department of a General Electric plant, 84 manager-subordinate pairs were observed in performance-appraisal and goal-planning discussions. The subordinates were interviewed before and after these discussions. A follow-up check was made 12 to 14 weeks after the performance appraisal and goal-planning discussions to determine how much performance had improved.

Marked dissatisfaction with the regular appraisals was common. Most subordinates felt they deserved more favorable appraisals and greater salary increases than they actually received. As expected, criticisms of performance typically resulted in defensiveness on the part of subordinates. The more criticisms or "improvement needs" the manager cited in appraisal discussions, the more likely the subordinate was to be defensive. Such defensiveness was indicative of the lack of effectiveness of appraisal interviews, for the more criticism and defensiveness observed in the appraisal discussion, the less performance had improved 12 to 14 weeks later. On the other hand, the use of praise had no measurable effect on employee reactions to criticism or on subsequent job performance.

But the story was quite different for the interviews primarily devoted to joint planning for improvement. Performance improved when specific goals were established with deadlines set and result measures agreed on in advance.

In comparison, no matter how much emphasis the manager gave to an improvement need in the appraisal discussion, if this did not get translated into a specific goal, very little performance improvement was achieved.

Equality of participation by subordinate and superior in planning was more satisfying but did not seem to increase the likelihood of fulfilling plans. Subordinate participation in goal planning resulted in improved subordinate attitudes in subordinate-supervisor relations, but little difference in the degree to which goals were achieved. Actually, favorable attitudes and improved performance occurred most often if the interview was consistent with the "usual level" of participation subordinates experienced in day-to-day work-planning activities with their managers. The investigators concluded that there is more payoff in goal-planning interviews than in interviews that are intended to feed back appraisals. Such feedback for salary-administration purposes should be divorced from the efforts aimed at improving employee performance through goal planning.

The usefulness of shared participation in the process is illustrated in a laboratory study in which college students played the role of subordinates. A tell-and-sell appraisal interview, a tell-and-listen meeting, and a problem-solving session were compared. In the tell-and-sell method, the subordinates participated the least; the supervisor informed subordinates of their strengths and weaknesses and gave suggestions for improvement in job performance. In the tell-and-listen method, subordinates were again told their strengths and weaknesses, but were allowed time to express their feelings about the evaluation process. The problem-solving technique allowed subordinates the most participation. The supervisor had feelings or ideas concerning solutions to job-related problems. In the final part of the process, the goals and plans were formulated. The overall results indicated that both subordinate satisfaction and motivation were enhanced the most by the problem-solving method.[36]

TIMING   Some firms see goal-planning interviews as a procedure to be taken up whenever they are needed, daily if necessary. Six months or a year is usually much too long an interval for discussions between a subordinate and his superior about mutual objectives. Supervisors tend to save up improvements to discuss with subordinates instead of talking about them at the time their need is seen.[44]

SUBORDINATE PERSONALITY   Sometimes, the personality of the subordinates may make performance-appraisal interviews worthwhile. Some evidence suggests that interviewees who are self-oriented (primarily concerned about recognition and reward for performance) tend to be more satisfied with appraisal interviews than mutual goal setting, while others who are task oriented are more likely to feel satisfied as a consequence of a job well done and are more likely to favor mutual goal setting.[8] But examples can be cited where other personality traits made no difference. Authoritarianism and the need for independence had no effect on whether problem solving or goal setting was more motivating than more traditional performance-appraisal interviews.[36]

In sum, feedback about performance, to be effective, must include the opportunity for the subordinate to take an active role in the interview. In particular, employees should have a chance to express their feelings and fully participate in the interchange. A positive attitude on the supervisor's part is also found to be characteristic of a most successful interview. A negative and critical attitude is seldom helpful. This is especially true for those subordinates who have high self-esteem. They may become defensive and react negatively to the comments made to them. A timely appraisal interview can be an opportunity to try to solve any problems that might be hurting the employees' job performance. As we have seen, specific goal setting is a key to making feedback sessions an effective activity.[24]

ONE BEST WAY?

At this point, the reader may ask if there is one simple solution to all the manifold issues raised in this chapter. The answer is no. No final or simple solution has been found. This does not mean that the problems should be ignored.

In short, current industrial practice usually "solves" the many problems found in this chapter by ignoring them. It is hoped that practice will become more sophisticated as the importance of the problems is considered when designing appraisal systems. We may have come a long way since the military appraisals in the files of the Department of the Army for 1813 (shown in Figure 8–7) but we still have a long way to go in the development of appraisal systems that are relevant, reliable, and free from bias.

SUMMARY

The problem of obtaining merit ratings that are reliable and relevant is of major concern to organizations. There are a number of common distortions in ratings, including differential accuracy, primacy effect, leniency, severity, error of central tendency, and halo effect. Systematic methods have been devised to reduce distortions in ratings. Potential biasing factors such as sex, race, and age must be considered and eliminated if present. Participative goal setting appears to be an effective technique of improving employee performance. In the next chapter we will discuss how the appraisal of employee performance is an important element in validating selection procedures.

```
                                              Lower  Senaca  Town
                                              August 15, 1813

Sir:

        I forward a list of the officers of the 27th Regt. of Infty. arranged agreeably to
rank. Annexed thereto you will find all the observations I deem necessary to make them.

                                    Respectfully,
                                    I am, Sir,
                                    Yo. Cot. Servt.

                                        Lewis Cass
                                        Brig. Gen.


                         27th Infantry Regiment

Alex Denniston—Lieut. Col., Comdg.      —a good natured man.

Clarkson Crolins—First Major            —a good man, but no officer.

Captain Shotwell                        —a man of whom all unite in speaking ill, a
                                         knave despised by all.

   "    Allen Reynolds                  —an officer of capacity, but imprudent and a
                                         man of most violent passions.

First Lieut. Wm Perrin      )           —low vulgar men, with exception of Perrin,
  "      "    Danl. Scott   )            Irish and from the meanest walks of life—
  "      "    Jas. I. Ryan  )            possessing nothing of the character of offi-
  "      "    Robt. McElwrath )          cers or gentlemen.

  "      "    Robt. P. Ross             —willing enough—has much to learn—with
                                         small capacity.

2nd Lieut. Nicholas G. Carner           —a good officer but drinks hard and disgraces
                                         himself and the services.
```

Figure 8–7. Extracts from *The First Recorded Efficiency Report in the Files of the War Department, August 15, 1813.*

REFERENCES

1. Anderson, B., and S. Nilsson. "Studies in the Reliability and Validity of the Critical Incident Technique," *Journal of Applied Psychology*, 48 (1964): 398–403.
2. Arvey, R. D., and J. C. Hoyle. "A Guttman Approach to the Development of Behaviorally Based Rating Scales for Systems Analysts and Programmer/Analysts," *Journal of Applied Psychology*, 59 (1974): 61–68.
3. Baird, L. S. "Self and Superior Ratings of Performance as Related to Self-Esteem and Satisfaction with Supervision," *Academy of Management Journal*, 20 (1977): 291–300.
4. Barrett, R. S. *Performance Rating.* Chicago: Science Research Associates, 1966, pp. 80–84.
5. Bass, A. R., and J. N. Turner. "Ethnic Group Differences in Relationships among Criteria of Job Performance," *Journal of Applied Psychology*, 57 (1973): 101–109.
6. Bass, B M. "Reducing Leniency in Merit Ratings," *Personnel Psychology*, 9 (1956): 359–369.

7. Bass, B. M. *Leadership, Psychology and Organizational Behavior.* New York: Harper & Row, 1960.

8. Bass, B. M. "Business Gaming for Organizational Research," *Management Science*, 10 (1964): 545–556.

9. Bass, B. M. *Third Annual Report.* Contract NONR 6241141, University of Pittsburgh, 1965.

10. Bass, B. M., W. F. Cascio, and E. J. O'Connor. "Magnitude Estimations of Expressions of Frequency and Amount," *Journal of Applied Psychology*, 59 (1974): 313–320.

11. Beatty, R. W., C. E. Schneier, and J. R. Beatty. "An Empirical Investigation of Perceptions of Ratee Behavior Frequency and Ratee Behavior Change Using Behavioral Expectation Scales (BES)," *Personnel Psychology*, 30 (1977): 647–657.

12. Benjamin, R., Jr. "A Survey of 130 Merit-Rating Plans," *Personnel*, 29 (1952): 289–294.

13. Berkshire, J. R., and R. W. Highland. "Forced-Choice Performance Rating: A Methodological Study," *Personnel Psychology*, 6 (1953): 355–378.

14. Bernardin, H. J., and C. S. Walter. "Effects of Rater Training and Diary-Keeping on Psychometric Error in Ratings," *Journal of Applied Psychology*, 62 (1977): 64–69.

15. Bigoness, W. J. "Effect of Applicants' Sex, Race, and Performance on Employers' Performance Ratings: Some Additional Findings," *Journal of Applied Psychology*, 61 (1976): 80–84.

16. Bingham, W. V. "Halo, Invalid and Valid," *Journal of Applied Psychology*, 23 (1939): 221–228.

17. Blanz, F., and E. E. Ghiselli. "The Mixed Standard Scale: A New Rating System," *Personnel Psychology*, 25 (1972): 185–199.

18. Blood, M. R. "Spin-Offs from Behavioral Expectation Scale Procedures," *Journal of Applied Psychology*, 59 (1974): 513–515.

19. Borman, W. C. "Consistency of Rating Accuracy and Rating Errors in the Judgment of Human Performance," *Organizational Behavior and Human Performance*, 20 (1977): 238–252.

20. Borman, W. C. "Exploring Upper Limits of Reliability and Validity in Job Performance Ratings," *Journal of Applied Psychology*, 63 (1978): 136–144.

21. Borman, W. C., and W. R. Vallon. "A View of What Can Happen When Behavioral Expectation Scales Are Developed in One Setting and Used in Another," *Journal of Applied Psychology*, 59 (1974): 197–201.

22. Bowers, W. H. "An Appraisal of Worker Characteristics as Related to Age," *Journal of Applied Psychology*, 36 (1952): 296–300.

23. Brown, E. M. "Influence of Training, Method, and Relationship on the Halo Effect," *Journal of Applied Psychology*, 52 (1965): 195–199.

24. Burke, R. J., and D. S. Wilcox. "Characteristics of Effective Employee Performance Review and Development Interviews," *Personnel Psychology*, 22 (1969): 291–305.

25. Cascio, W. F., and E. R. Valenzi. "Behaviorally Anchored Rating Scales: Effects of Education and Job Experience of Raters and Ratees," *Journal of Applied Psychology*, 62 (1977): 278–282.

26. Cummings, L. L. "A Field Experimental Study of the Effects of Two Performance Appraisal Systems," *Personnel Psychology*, 26 (1973): 489–502.

27. DeCotiis, T. A. "An Analysis of the External Validity and Applied Relevance of Three Rating Formats," *Organizational Behavior and Human Performance,* 19 (1977): 247–266.

28. Edwards, A. L. *Techniques of Attitude Scale Construction.* New York: Appleton-Century-Crofts, 1957.

29. Field, H. S., and W. H. Holley. "Research Notes: Subordinates, Characteristics, Supervisors' Ratings and Decisions to Discuss Appraisal Results," *Academy of Management Journal,* 20 (1977): 315–321.

30. Ferguson, L. W. "The Value of Acquaintance Ratings in Criterion Research," *Personnel Psychology,* 2 (1949): 93–102.

31. Flanagan, J. C. "Critical Requirements: A New Approach to Employee Evaluation," *Personnel Psychology,* 2 (1949): 419–425.

32. Flanagan, J. C., and R. K. Burns. "The Employee Performance Record: A New Appraisal and Development Tool," *Harvard Business Review,* 33 (1955): 95–102.

33. Flaugher, R. L., J. T. Campbell, and L. W. Pike. *Ethnic Group Membership as A Moderator of Supervisors' Ratings.* ETS Bulletin PR–69–5. Princeton, N. J.: Education Testing Service, 1969.

34. Friedman, B. A., and E. T. Cornelius III. "Effect of Rater Participation in Scale Construction on the Psychometric Characteristics of Two Rating Scale Formats," *Journal of Applied Psychology,* 61, no. 2, (1976): 210–216.

35. Gaylord, R. H., E. Russell, C. Johnson, and D. Servin. "The Relation of Ratings to Production Records: An Empirical Study," *Personnel Psychology,* 4 (1951): 363–371.

36. Gordon, M. E. "The Effect of the Correctness of the Behavior Observed on the Accuracy of Ratings," *Organizational Behavior and Human Performance,* 5 (1970): 366–377.

37. Grey, R. J., and D. Kipnis. "Untangling the Performance Appraisal Dilemma: The Influence of Perceived Organizational Context on Evaluative Processes," *Journal of Applied Psychology,* 61 (1976): 329–335.

38. Guilford, J. P. *Psychometric Methods,* New York: McGraw-Hill, 1954.

39. Gulliksen, H. *Theory of Mental Tests.* New York: Wiley, 1950.

40. Jenkins, G. D., Jr., and T. D. Taber. "A Monte Carlo Study of Factors Affecting Three Indices of Composite Scale Reliability," *Journal of Applied Psychology,* 62 (1977): 392–398.

41. Jones, E. E., L. Rock, K. G. Shaver, G. R. Goethals, and L. M. Ward. "Pattern of Performance and Ability Attribution: An Unexpected Primacy Effect," *Journal of Personality and Social Psychology,* 10 (1968): 317–340.

42. Judy, C. J. *"A Comparison of Peer and Supervisory Rankings as Criteria of Aircraft Maintenance Proficiency.* AFPTRC Research Bulletin No. 53–43, San Antonio, Texas, 1953.

43. Kavanagh, M. J., A. C. Mackinney, and L. Wolins. "Issues in Managerial Performance: Multitrait-Multimethod Analyses of Ratings," *Psychological Bulletin,* 75(1971): 34–49.

44. Kay, E., J. R. P. French, and H. H. Meyer. "A Study of the Performance Appraisal Interview," *Behavioral Research Science,* General Electric, New York, 1962.

45. Klimoski, R. J., and M. London. "Role of the Rater in Performance Appraisal," *Journal of Applied Psychology,* 58 (1974): 445–451.

46. Landy, D., and H. Sigall. "Beauty Is Talent: Task Evaluation as a Function of the Performer's Physical Attractiveness," *Journal of Personality and Social Psychology*, 29 (1974): 299–304.

47. Latham, G. P., T. R. Mitchell, and D. L. Dossett. "Importance of Participative Goal Setting and Anticipated Rewards on Goal Difficulty and Job Performance," *Journal of Applied Psychology*, 63 (1978): 163–171.

48. Laurent, H. "Job Performance Review Survey," *Social Science Research Reports* (vol. III, *Performance Review Evaluation*.) Exxon, New York, 1962.

49. Levine, J., and J. Butler. "Lecture vs. Group Decision in Changing Behavior," *Journal of Applied Psychology*, 36 (1952): 29–33.

50. Levy, L. H., and R. D. Dugan. "A Constant Error Approach to the Study of Dimensions of Social Perception," *Journal of Abnormal and Social Psychology*, 61 (1960): 21–24.

51. Levy, S., and D. M. Stone. "Process and Content of Managerial Ratings of Subordinates." Paper presented at meeting of Eastern Psychological Association, New York City, April 1963.

52. Lissitz, R. W., and S. B. Green. "Effect of the Number of Scale Points on Reliability: A Monte Carlo Approach," *Journal of Applied Psychology*, 60 (1975): 10–13.

53. Lundy, R. M. "Self Perceptions Regarding Masculinity-Feminity and Description of Same and Opposite Sex Sociometric Choices," *Sociometry*, 21 (1958): 238–246.

54. Mandell, M. M. "Supervisory Characteristics and Ratings," *Personnel*, 32 (1956): 435–440.

55. Matell, M. S., and J. Jacoby. "Is There an Optimal Number of Alternatives for Likert Scale Items? Study I: Reliability and Validity," *Educational and Psychological Measurement*, 31 (1971): 637–674.

56. Meyer, H. H., and W. B. Walker. "A Study of Factors Relating to the Effectiveness of a Performance Appraisal Program," *Personnel Psychology*, 14 (1961): 291–298.

57. Nisbett, R. E., and T. D. Wilson. "The Halo Effect: Evidence for Unconscious Alteration of Judgments," *Journal of Personality and Social Psychology*, 35 (1977): 250–256.

58. Prather, R. "Training: Key to Realistic Performance Appraisals," *Training and Development Journal* (December 1970): 4–7.

59. Prien, E. P., and J. T. Campbell. "Stability of Rating Scale Statements," *Personnel Psychology*, 10 (1957): 305–309.

60. Rambo, W. W. "The Effects of Partial Pairing on Scale Values Derived from the Method of Pairing Comparisons," *Journal of Applied Psychology*, 43 (1959): 379–381.

61. Rosen, B., and H. J. Thomas. "The Nature of Job-Related Age Stereotypes," *Journal of Applied Psychology*, 61 (1976): 180–183.

62. Rothaus, P., R. B. Morton, and P. G. Hanson. "Performance Appraisal and Psychological Distance," *Journal of Applied Psychology*, 49 (1965): 48–54.

63. Rothe, H. F. "The Relation of Merit Ratings to Length of Service," *Personnel Psychology*, 2 (1949): 237–242.

64. Saal, F. E., and F. J. Landy. "The Mixed Standard Rating Scale: An Evaluation," *Organizational Behavior and Human Performance*, 18 (1977): 19–35.

65. Schmidt, F. L., and R. H. Johnson. "Effect of Race on Peer Ratings in an Industrial Situation," *Journal of Applied Psychology,* 57 (1973): 237–241.
66. Schneider, D. E., and A. G. Bayroff. "The Relationship between Rater Characteristics and Validity of Ratings," *Journal of Applied Psychology,* 31 (1953): 278–280.
67. Schneier, C. E. "Operational Utility and Psychometric Characteristics of Behavioral Expectation Scales: A Cognitive Reinterpretation," *Journal of Applied Psychology,* 62 (1977): 541–548.
68. Schwab, D. P., H. G. Heneman III, and T. DeCotiis. "Behaviorally Anchored Rating Scales: A Review of the Literature," *Personnel Psychology,* 28 (1975): 549–562.
69. Scott, W. E., Jr., and W. C. Hamner. "The Influence of Variations in Performance Profiles on the Performance Evaluation Process: An Examination of the Validity of the Criterion," *Organizational Behavior and Human Performance,* 14 (1975): 360–370.
70. Sharon, A. T., and C. J. Bartlett. "Effect of Instructional Conditions in Producing Leniency on Two Types of Rating Scales," *Personnel Psychology,* 22 (1969): 251–263.
71. Siegel, A. I., D. G. Schultz, M. A. Fischal, and R. S. Lanterman. "Absolute Scaling of Job Performance," *Journal of Applied Psychology,* 52 (1968): 313–318.
72. Sigall, H., and R. Gould. "The Effects of Self-Esteem and Evaluator Demandingness on Effort Expenditure," *Journal of Personality and Social Psychology,* 35 (1977): 12–20.
73. Smith, P. C., and L. M. Kendall. "Retranslation of Expectations: An Approach to the Construction of Unambiguous Anchors for Rating Scales," *Journal of Applied Psychology,* 47 (1963): 149–155.
74. Social Science Research Division, Exxon. *Performance Review and Evaluation* (vol. III, Supplement.) New York 1962.
75. Spector, A. J. "Influences on Merit Ratings," *Journal of Applied Psychology,* 38 (1954): 393–396.
76. Stallings, W. M., and G. M. Gillmore. "Estimating the Interjudge Reliability of the Ali-Frazier Fight," *Journal of Applied Psychology,* 56 (1972): 435–436.
77. Stockford, L., and H. W. Bissel. "Factors Involved in Establishing a Merit-Rating Scale," *Personnel,* 26, no. 2 (1949): 94–116.
78. Taft, R. "The Ability to Judge People," *Psychological Bulletin,* 52 (1955): 1–23.
79. Taylor, E. K., and R. J. Wherry. "A Study of Leniency in Two Rating Systems," *Personnel Psychology,* 4 (1951): 39–47.
80. Thorndike, E. L. "A Constant Error in Psychological Ratings," *Journal of Applied Psychology,* 4 (1920): 25–29.
81. Trawick, M., and A. M. Munger. "Objective Criteria of Service Station Dealer Success: Social Science Research Reports (vol. III)," *Personnel Review and Evaluation.* Exxon, New York 1962.
82. Uhrbrock, R. S. "Standardization of 724 Rating Scale Statements," *Personnel Psychology,* 2 (1950): 285–316.
83. Uhrbrock, R. S. "2000 Scaled Items," *Personnel Psychology,* 14 (1961): 375–420.
84. Van Zelst, R. H., and W. A. Kerr. "Workers' Attitudes toward Merit Rating," *Personnel Psychology,* 6 (1953): 159–172.

85. Vroom, V. H. "Projection, Negation and Self-Concept," *Human Relations,* 12 (1959): 335–344.

86. Wexley, K. N., J. P. Singh, and G. A. Yukl. "Subordinate Personality as a Moderator of the Effects of Participation in Three Types of Appraisal Interviews," *Journal of Applied Psychology,* 58 (1973): 54–59.

87. Zander, A. F., and J. Gyer. "Changing Attitudes toward a Merit-Rating System," *Personnel Psychology,* 8 (1955): 429–448.

88. Zawacki, R. A., and R. L. Taylor. "A View of Performance Appraisal from Organizations Using It," *Personnel Journal,* 29 (1976): 290–292.

89. Zedeck, S., R. Jacobs, and D. Kafry. "Behavioral Expectations: Development of Parallel Forms and Analysis of Scale Assumptions," *Journal of Applied Psychology,* 61 (1976): 112–115.

9 VALIDATION CONCEPTS AND DESIGNS

IN BRIEF   This chapter presents the important concepts involved in selection research, research on how to select and place job applicants who will be most likely to succeed on the job. Five possible models of personnel selection are discussed: probationary model, random selection, quota system, probability of success based on empirical consideration, and probability of success based on intrinsic attributes. Each personnel selection model makes different assumptions and rests on different values. The probationary model involves hiring all individuals applying for an actual job and rejecting those who then fail to perform well. The random selection model assigns individuals to jobs by chance. A quota system classifies and selects personnel according to such factors as age, sex, race, or religion. If it works, use it; selection model is based solely on whatever is found to be useful in predicting success on the job. Any identifiable characteristic related to job success serves as the basis for selection. In the last model, selection is based on intrinsic attributes that predict success.

Validation designs are concerned with inferences about job performance. Criterion-related designs establish an empirical relationship between the test score and some measure of job performance (called the criterion). There are a number of threats to validation designs. These include mortality, history, testing, criterion contamination, current-use validity curtailment, statistical power, fishing, and criterion reliability.

302

> In contrast to the criterion-related validity techniques, a content valid test is a representative sample of the knowledge, skills, or behaviors required on the job. Issues such as cross-validation and validity generalization are explored.

Our discussion of the individual's contribution to an organization began in Chapter 7 with the determination of the nature of the work to be performed and the characteristics required of the potential jobholder. We examined problems associated with the choice of reliable and relevant criteria of job success, and, in Chapter 8, we surveyed techniques used to measure the degree to which jobholders differ in meeting those performance criteria.

Chapters 7 and 8 contain some implicit assumptions that we will try to make explicit in our discussion. Good professional practice requires that adequate proof be provided that the selection procedures do result in the hiring of people with the most potential for success. Concern for making validation concepts define explicitly what is accomplished during personnel selection became more acute with the enactment of the Civil Rights Act of 1964 and similar legislation that barred discrimination in employment because of race, sex, religion, or national origin. The Equal Employment Opportunity Commission, established to enforce those regulations, has issued guidelines designed to ensure equal and fair treatment to all individuals seeking employment in organizations. We will discuss the issues of discrimination in greater depth in Chapter 19. For now, we will examine five models that have been used to select individuals for jobs in our society.[2]

Possible Models of Personnel Selection

We will discuss five possible models of personnel selection. Students will see that it would be possible to use a combination of two or more of the models to select individuals for organizations. The selection model chosen by any one organization invariably contains some implicit value orientations, which we will attempt to make explicit in our discussion.

PROBATIONARY MODEL   The probationary model involves hiring all the individuals who apply for a position in an organization. After a specified period of time, or period of probation, all individuals are evaluated on their actual job performance. The organization then retains only those individuals necessary to fill the number of available positions. This model is analogous to the one used by many state universities with open admission policies. All state residents with a high school diploma are allowed to enter the state university system. The retention of the freshmen in college is then based upon their coursework performance. The probationary model assumes that everyone should have an equal opportunity to attempt any job, without regard to prior qualifications. This model is appealing to many individuals and appears to be fair. Unfortunately, there are a number of practical disadvantages. For many positions in our society, the cost of training and evaluating all the potential applicants makes the model prohibitively expensive. Beyond that, in many types of positions individuals without the requisite qualifications could make a mistake resulting in injury to others or themselves. While the concept of self-selection of an occupation and trying it a while is appealing, the economic cost associated with that approach is so high that it is doubtful if it will receive widespread adoption in the foreseeable future.

RANDOM SELECTION The random selection model involves choosing by chance as many applicants for a position as there are openings. Drawing jurors by lot illustrates this approach. On the surface, it also seems to be a fair method of selecting individuals for positions; it again appears to be based upon the assumption that prior qualifications should not give any individual an edge in obtaining a position. The model assumes that everyone in our society can perform all jobs with equal proficiency. However, the evidence that we have reviewed in prior chapters certainly refutes that contention. The main difficulty with this model is the fact that many positions in our society require specific qualifications and abilities, which have been found to be related to successful performance. If we randomly chose applicants for such positions, we would in effect hire individuals whose overall performance would be quite a bit worse than that of qualified individuals. Of course, it is posible to argue that society should bear this cost in order to make entry into occupations as fair as possible. In that case, of course, the definition of fairness is based upon random selection.

QUOTA SYSTEM This selection model classifies applicants according to demographic categories based on sex, race, age, and national origin. Then a predetermined proportion from each designated category is hired, for example, 50 per cent men and 50 per cent women. While this model may appear fair to some, there are a number of inherent difficulties involved in its implementation. First, the decision must be reached about the appropriate categories for each position. Should the categories be based on sex, age, religion, ethnic group, or any of a number of other demographic and personal characteristics? Second, once the categories have been established, the decision must be made as to the number of individuals to be selected from each category. Should it depend on the number of individuals in that category who applied for the position, or on some broader population base? This decision can drastically affect the proportion of individuals hired in each category. (For example, we could reasonably expect that proportionately fewer women would apply for the position of lumberjack than their actual percentage in the population. If only 10 per cent of the applicants are female, should they all be hired? Or should more applicants be sought so that the proportion of women hired can rise to 50 per cent, which more nearly equals their representation in the population at large?) Third, after the decisions about establishing quota category proportions are made, then the method of actual selection from each category must be determined. The probationary, random selection, or some other model may be chosen.

PROBABILITY OF SUCCESS BASED ON EMPIRICAL CONSIDERATIONS   This model bases the selection of individuals for a job on *any* identifiable characteristic that has proved in the past to be related to success on that job. A rationale or theory for selection is not required. The only question asked is "Does it work?" For example, if an investigation has shown that single, blue-eyed females whose parents came from Albania and who lived no more than five miles from the plant were the most successful workers, then an organization would attempt to hire individuals with those characteristics. This model has obvious potential to discriminate against individuals because of sex, race, or age — exactly the factors that legislation has deemed illegal.

Let's take a more concrete example of how some organizations have used the empirical model. A warehouse job might require the manual lifting and stacking of heavy boxes during the workday. Initially, both male and female workers are assigned to the job. After six months, records of the number of boxes stacked are analyzed, and it is determined that males (who are generally stronger) performed better than females. Using this model, the organization would from then on hire only males for the warehouse job. We believe this to be a discriminatory selection practice. In our judgment, a better approach is illustrated by the next model.

PROBABILITY OF SUCCESS BASED ON INTRINSIC ATTRIBUTES   The fifth model involves a selection procedure based strictly upon intrinsic attributes that predict job success. It assumes that there are individual attributes that can be measured prior to employment and that these attributes predict subsequent performance on the job. This model, of course, assumes that selection of individuals for positions in our society should be based solely upon the probability of their success; it specifically rules out the use of coincidental predictors, such as age, race, sex, residence, occupation of parents, and other similar variables that are not intrinsic to the individual.

For example, in the case of the job stacking heavy boxes in a warehouse, sex would be a coincidental predictor and would not be used for selection. That is, men are stronger than women *on the average*. But there are *some* women who are stronger than *some* men. Instead, this method would involve developing an appropriate test to measure the strength required to stack the boxes. Strength would be the intrinsic attribute of the individual to be measured. Of course, we would expect that fewer females than males would reach the required level of strength, although some females would qualify. The important point is that if a female were rejected for the job, the reason would not be her sex (a coincidental predictor), but her relative lack of strength (an intrinsic attribute).

Another example, using age as a coincidental predictor, might help clarify this important concept. We might find that certain abilities or physical characteristics are distributed differently in the population as a function of age. Visual acuity, for instance, might be related to job success for a certain occupation; and yet we might find that visual acuity is, in general, diminished in older individuals. The intrinsic attributes model calls for measuring visual acuity as the means of selection for the occupation and not choosing according to age, despite the fact that we know a higher proportion of younger people would be qualified for the position than older people. The selection process is based strictly upon each individual's visual acuity, not on the coincidental predictor of age. Since some older people have visual acuity fully as good as younger individuals, older people should not be penalized because of the fact that, as a group, their vision is poorer than younger people's.

This is a subtle but important point. We want to emphasize it because it makes a great deal of difference in terms of how a personnel selection program is conducted.

Throughout the remainder of the book, our intention will be to advocate this fifth model, which involves selection of individuals for jobs based upon intrinsic attributes related to successful performance in that position. We recognize the fact that other models may be appropriate for certain situations. For example, the probationary model may have merit when a job is fairly complex and when there are no available measures to predict success in the occupation. In cases where an occupation is perceived as a burden or duty, a random selection model might be most appropriate, as has been used by the military services.

VALIDATION DESIGNS

The next question is how do we provide evidence that the "intrinsic" attributes of an individual are related to job performance? The inferences that a personnel psychologist makes are usually based upon a study or a series of studies using one of five validation designs. In validation, we are concerned with inferences about job performance that can be made from test scores or from other information about the individual tested. If we can demonstrate that a selection system is related to job performance, then we can infer that, in future uses of the selection system, individuals receiving superior test scores will be superior in job performance. In other words, the selection system is valid.

A number of experimental designs have been developed to help the personnel psychologist make such inferences. Each of these validation designs has advantages and shortcomings in terms of the inferences one can draw from the results of an investigation. The first three designs are *criterion-related*. That is, in each an effort is made to relate the test score to some measure (such as units produced per hour) of the individual's performance on the job — the criterion of job success. These three designs — *predictive, concurrent,* and *postdictive* validity — all involve the use of some external criterion.

Predictive Validity

Figure 9–1A presents schematically the design for an ideal predictive validity study. As the figure shows, we administer our selected test battery to all prospective employees. The tested individuals are all assigned to the actual job for some period of time, varying according to the nature of the job from one month to several years. At the end of that period, we collect our measures of job performance for each of the individuals originally tested. This gives us two sets of measures, the test scores collected initially and the criterion scores, or measures of job performance, collected subsequently. We then correlate the *test* scores with the *criterion* measures of job performance to obtain a *validity coefficient* — the test-criterion correlation coefficient. The more accurately the test predicts the subsequent criterion measure, the higher is the predictive validity coefficient.

This ideal design can seldom be applied, as such, in real life settings. What typically happens when individuals apply for a position is that some screening takes place. Some applicants may be "talked out" of joining the firm; others may be rejected for legitimate or not so legitimate reasons. Therefore, the individuals who actually start work are a special group based on the initial screening. For many jobs, there is another screening due to a training period required before individuals can start work. Again, the organization or the trainees may decide they are unwilling or unable to learn the job. Even after some exposure to the work, they may quit before there is a chance to collect criterion measures on them.

A more realistic perspective is given by Figure 9–1B. There is attrition of some of the sample even before testing. The attrition continues so that we can gather criterion data for only a part of the sample. Such *mortality* is a threat to the predictive validity of the test for the generality of prediction for *all* applicants.[4]

In Chapter 2, we noted how the validity of influence (the truth) about

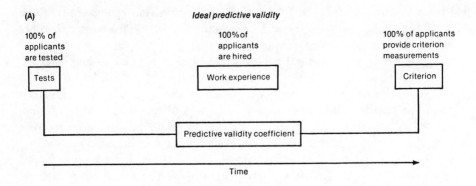

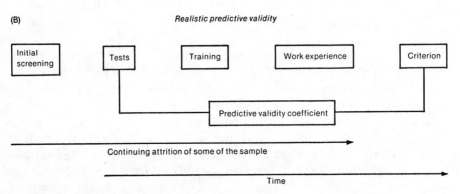

Figure 9–1. Predictive validity designs: (A) There is no attrition of the sample over time; (B) There is continuing attrition from before testing onward.

any experiment could be threatened in a variety of ways. Attrition is one such threat to the predictive validity design. Let's look now at other such threats. They include history, testing, criterion contamination, current-use validity curtailment, statistical power, fishing, and criterion reliability.

HISTORY The obtained relationship between the test and criterion may be due to a historical event, such as a business recession. A recession might result in a *lower* relationship because the more insecure individuals either worked harder in order to retain their jobs or slowed up to make the work last. Our test might plausibly measure feelings of insecurity caused by the business recession rather than true job performance under less stressful conditions.

TESTING Some individuals in the study may have had previous experience with the tests being used and therefore produce artificially inflated scores.

This would result in a *lower* relationship and thereby obscure the importance of the individual attribute being measured for job success.

CRITERION CONTAMINATION   The criterion errors discussed in the last chapter can lead to test-criterion correlations that are inflated or deflated from the true test-criterion relationship. The true relation between intelligence test scores and criteria of success as a police officer, for example, may be positive, yet fail to appear so because "politics" leads to errorful ratings of performance on the job. In the same way, criterion contamination can result in obtaining higher than true correlations between the test and job performance. This could occur, for instance, if supervisors rating their subordinates' job performance also knew their prior test scores. The supervisors might be influenced by those scores and base the ratings on this knowledge rather than on actual job performance.

CURRENT-USE VALIDITY CURTAILMENT   Here, the test results are used to screen out applicants so that the final test versus criterion correlation contains only examinees who scored higher in the test. There is a restriction in range, reducing the size of the relationship from the true one. For example, life insurance agents were selected using the Aptitude Index. Then the subsequent success was measured of the top scoring group. Here, 31 per cent were successful. Yet, when the test was not used for selection and all sales agents were hired regardless of their Aptitude Index score, 54 per cent of the top scoring group were successful.[13] In effect, only the individuals with the best probability of success were hired when the test was used for selection. This made it difficult to show how effective the test was in eliminating those with a lower probability of success.

STATISTICAL POWER   In much of the previous research, the number of individuals required to perform a selection study was seriously underestimated. The rule of thumb was that a sample size of 30 to 60 was adequate for validation research. In confirming the personnel psychologist's rule of thumb, the median sample size over 406 validity studies was 68.[13]

However, using this sample size of 68, and other realistic assumptions, recent studies have documented that a test will be reported valid only in 54 per cent of the studies and invalid 46 per cent of the time, when the true validity is 0.45.[16] The failure to have an adequate sample size will usually result in an underestimation of the true validity. *Power analysis* can be employed to determine the appropriate sample size for each situation.[4] Given the problem of current-use validity curtailment, it is not surprising to learn that research in the life insurance industry suggests that 2,000 to 3,000 agents are required to determine the validity of a test if it is currently in use for selection. The value of small sample size validation studies will be discussed in more detail later in the validity generalization section.

FISHING AND THE ERROR RATE PROBLEM   In most selection research, more than one test is used, and the more tests are used, the higher the probability that one or more will be significant by chance alone. "Fishing" for the valid test increases the probability of error. Therefore, this threat tends to result in inflated estimates of the true validity. (Techniques of cross-validation and "shrinkage" formulas to control for this problem will be discussed later on in this chapter.)

CRITERION RELIABILITY   As we discussed in Chapter 7, the lower criterion reliability, the more error variance and subsequently the lower the estimate of the true relationships between the test and job performance. The reliability of the criterion can be taken into account to adjust statistically (raise) the obtained validity coefficient to give a better estimate of the true validity.[16]

Concurrent Validity

The main difference between predictive and concurrent validation designs is that with concurrent validation both test and criterion data are collected at the same time from presently employed members of an organization. This is illustrated in Figure 9–2. Figure 9–2A shows the ideal concurrent design. It assumes that every individual who applies is hired and obtains subsequent work experience in the firm or agency. At some point in time, the experienced employees are tested and at approximately the same time, criterion information is obtained. A more realistic design is shown in Figure 9–2B, where there is a preliminary screening process. Only a portion of those applying are hired. This design also assumes that there will be some attrition due to the effect of the training and work experience.

In addition to the threats discussed concerning predictive validity designs the concurrent validity design reveals two additional threats to its validity. One of these is maturation, and the other is test-taking motivation.

MATURATION   Employees change over time. They grow older or change as a result of training and the work experience itself. These changes may affect the relationship between the test and the criterion. For example, test scores given after a work experience may reflect mainly differences in what the employees learned on the job; there may be no relationship to what their test scores would have been if they had not had the work experience. Evidence is mixed about the importance of the maturation threat.

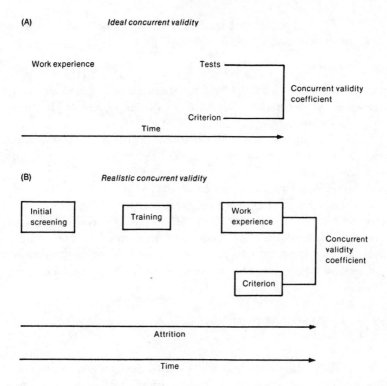

Figure 9–2. Concurrent validity designs: (A) Assumption that all individuals who apply are hired; (B) Assumption that only some proportion of those applying are hired.

Dvorak concluded from civil service test research that employees improve their test scores by the same amounts as a consequence of their work experience. That is, the differences among employees stay the same as they mature.[6] She therefore inferred that the validity coefficient was not biased by work experience. On the other hand, Alvares and Hulin found that students who went through pilot training had higher aptitude test scores after training than before, compared to students who did not have the benefit of flight school.[1]

Suppose cognitive ability is required during the first six months in learning a task, and suppose during the second six months finger dexterity becomes important for learning it, then, the validity of the tests for both the predictive and concurrent designs will depend on the point in time the criterion data are obtained. For example, if performance data are collected at the end of the first six months on the job, then a cognitive ability test will correlate with performance but not a finger dexterity test. But if performance data are collected at the end of the second six months on the job, the finger dexterity test will show a higher validity than the cognitive ability test. Thus, the effects of maturation tend to be specific to tests, tasks, and time of measurement.

TEST-TAKING MOTIVATION   Currently employed individuals taking tests for a concurrent research analysis may not be as motivated to do well as job applicants in the predictive design.[9] If all the employees are less motivated, a restriction in range of scores is likely. Or they may "fool around" or yield less reliable or true test scores. If some employees are less motivated than others, we are in danger of obaining test results about motivation rather than about the abilities that are important to job success. In each instance, the concurrent validity will be threatened.

To avoid this threat, employee cooperation must be sought in concurrent designs. Offers of personal feedback of results and counseling may help. But ethical problems will be generated if employees are stimulated to behave like job applicants by being made to believe that the test results will be used to make personnel decisions about them personally.

Comparisons of Predictive and Concurrent Validity Designs

The most salient difference between the two designs is the time of testing. In the predictive design, all testing is accomplished before the individuals begin their work experience. The criterion data are then collected some time after the individuals have had work experience. By contrast, in a concurrent validity design the test data and criterion data are collected at approximately the same point in time from present employees.

It could be argued that the predictive validity design is preferable to the concurrent design because the practical inferences that one wishes to draw are most analogous to the predictive design (i.e., individuals are tested before employment). If the test scores of employees after their work experience in the concurrent design are comparable to what their test scores would have been before employment, then the inference for future use of the concurrent validity tests may be as strong as inferences from a predictive validity design. Each validity design, whether predictive or concurrent, must be considered individually for threats to its validity. In some situations, the predictive validity design will allow more accurate inferences, while for other studies, a concurrent validity design will be superior. For example, a concurrent validity design is more practical in that it can be completed in a shorter time. With the predictive validity design, newly hired employees have to gain enough work experience that reliable measures of performance can be obtained. This may involve a year or more, depending on the specific job. Predictive validity may be mandatory if we determine that work experience enhances test performance differentially so that some individuals do better on the test and some do worse as a consequence of their work experience. Concurrent validation will suffer. On the other hand, concurrent validity will be required, say, where we cannot wait to collect the criterion data because we suffer continuously high turnover or transfers, or, the criterion may become contaminated with seniority effects. Merit may be confused with survival on the job.

Both predictive and concurrent designs are subject to the validity threat of *mortality* — the loss of people due to transfers, promotion, firing, quitting, retirement, or death. For both designs, the relationship between the test and the criterion can only be established for the group of employees who are present when the criterion data are collected.

A combination of concurrent and predictive validity designs, as illustrated in Figure 9–3, has some practical advantages. First, the investigator determines if the tests chosen do relate to the performance of current employees. If the concurrent results are positive, then the tests can be put into operation for hiring new employees. The newly hired employees can then be part of a longer-term predictive validity study. (This, of course, is not an *ideal* predictive validity study, since some persons are rejected because of test results.)

The last criterion-referenced design we present is the postdictive validity design.

Postdictive Validity Design

In the postdictive validity design, as shown in Figure 9–4, the investigator attempts to correlate a currently administered test with past behavior. This

Figure 9–3. Combination of concurrent and predictive validity designs.

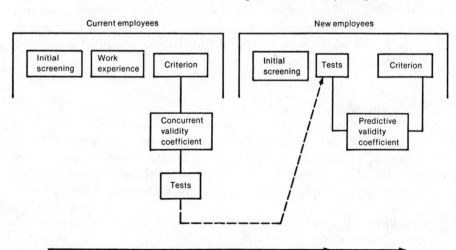

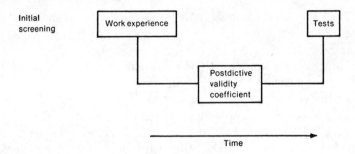

Figure 9-4. Postdictive validity design.

design is common in accident research. Five or more years of past accident records are required for a reliable criterion. For example, organizational records may be reviewed for the past five years. The sum of accidents for each employee during the five-year period is the criterion. An appropriate test battery would then be administered to the employees, and current test scores correlated with past behavior to yield a postdictive validity coefficient.

This design, even more than the concurrent design, is dependent upon the assumption or evidence that the attributes measured by the tests are consistent over the time period during which the criterion information was collected. It is subject to all the threats to validity already enumerated.

VALIDATION DESIGNS BASED ON CONTENT AND JUDGMENT

Two validition designs depend more on judgment, standards, and deduction, than on empirical, inductive inference. These are content validity and construct validity. They are based on comparisons with external standards and on deduction. Here, judgment is made of what the test measures in comparison with what is known about the job requirements, the population of examinees, and the other tests.

Content Validity Designs

If the content of a test situation actually samples the knowledge, skills, or behaviors that a test is supposed to measure, the test is said to have content validity. The adequacy of a content-valid test is determined by the care that is taken in constructing it. Such care requires the following steps:

1. A thorough job analysis is conducted. Details of each job duty or task are documented.

2. For each job duty, the associated knowledge and skills required to perform the task are also documented.

3. The amount of time that an incumbent would spend performing each job duty is determined.

4. Each job duty's importance is assessed. It is conceivable, for example, that some very unimportant job duties will take a major part of the incumbent's time

5. For each job duty, a determination is made of the knowledge and skills that the content-valid test should measure. (It is conceivable that certain knowledge or skills would *not* be measured by the test, since a training program might teach them before the individual begins the job duties.) In making this determination, an important consideration is whether increased knowledge or skill will result in improved job performance, or whether only a certain level of knowledge or skill is required to perform adequately.

6. A determination is then made of the proportion of the content-valid test to be allocated to each task and its associated knowledge and skill. This involves judging both the frequency and importance of the task, and the depth of knowledge or degree of skill required.

SELF-REPORTING A cautionary note should be mentioned here. If self-reported data are used to ascertain the amount of time an employee spends performing an activity, the accuracy is apt to be quite low in comparison to independent observations by others. Self-reporting of activity time has been found to be somewhat inaccurate. We tend to report that we spend more time on important than trivial tasks.[8]

FORMAT We need to consider the format of the test. Should it be oral or written? Should it be somewhat similar to the actual job duties? We need to consider whether or not the test should be timed, and how much individual speed in performing the test should affect the score obtained. The decision here is likely to rest upon whether or not the job duties will require an individual to use the knowledge or skills under time pressure.

Once the test has been constructed, it is reviewed by subject-matter experts to see if the test items are accurate, fair, and relevant to the job.

WORK-SAMPLE TESTS A work sample is one type of content-valid test. The job of a typist for instance, obviously requires skills in typing. A work sample could be constructed involving material representative of what a typist might encounter on the job. In this case, the assessment is based upon the performance of the major part of the job duties.

CONSENSUAL VALIDITY A variant of content validity is found in those tests based on *consensual* validity: for example, the visual acuity tests given to individuals for their driver's license. A consensus has been reached among experts that, first, visual acuity is important for driving, and, second, a minimal level of visual acuity, often 20/40, is required for safe operation of a motor vehicle. But the visual acuity test does *not* assume that individuals with superior visual acuity will be safer drivers. In fact, the evidence indicates otherwise. Visual acuity is not related to accident involvement.[2] The rationale behind the acuity test only assumes that individuals with deficient visual acuity will be unable to operate vehicles safely.

This distinction is extremely important, particularly for content-valid tests. Many content-valid tests assume that good performance on the test, up to a certain specified point, is an indication of a "necessary but not sufficient condition for satisfactory performance in the job." The driving case is a particularly good example, since research has indicated that once an individual has minimum visual acuity, then other information-processing abilities, unrelated to visual acuity as such, become important for the safe operation of a vehicle. This will be discussed in more detail in Chapter 16.

FACE VALIDITY   The visual acuity test may appear to be a test that simply looks valid, or has *face validity*. Although the test looks as if it should forecast whether or not an individual will be a safe driver, it does not. The mere appearance, or face validity, is no guarantee that a test will actually measure the aptitude it is purported to measure or will be related to subsequent job success. Nevertheless, in many sensitive selection programs, it is essential that the tests used have face validity. For instance, a finger-tapping test would not appear to Civil Service examinees to be valid for forecasting success as a clerk, whereas a test requiring the use of a pencil to check the accuracy of names and addresses would appear valid to them. Both tests might actually forecast job success, but personnel administrators would face criticism from examinees if the finger-tapping test were used. While face validity may be necessary in some testing situations, it is certainly not sufficient.

J-COEFFICIENT   A most sophisticated variant of content validation is used by the U. S. Civil Service to prepare job element examinations.[11] Although this detailed and complex procedure cannot be fully described here, we should note that it does depend upon the identification of specific elements for each job. This test involves the use of the J-Coefficient, which provides the estimated validity of a test for a specific job. The J-Coefficient is computed from the weights of the elements in the test and the importance of each element for the given job. It is a form of *synthetic validation*.[10]

SYNTHETIC VALIDITY   Here the most important specific components of each job are identified through job analysis. While no two *total* jobs are alike, several jobs may share the same basic skill or aptitude components. For example, the jobs of bookkeeper, salesperson, and telephone switchboard operator are different, but salesperson and telephone operator probably share a basic requirement for verbal fluency. Bookkeeper and telephone operator differ in total skills but share the need for perceptual accuracy. Thus, instead of developing different tests valid for each *total* job, we develop valid tests for each of the *basic* job aptitudes required. By combining the appropriate tests, we then "synthesize" a valid battery of tests for each job. For the job of telephone switchboard operator, for example, we put together and suitably weight differentially a verbal fluency and perceptual accuracy test battery.

It should be noted that both the J-Coefficient approach and the synthetic validity approach depend initially on the use of criterion-related validity designs. But to this, they add the subjective professional judgment of standards in deciding the nature of the job elements and the appropriate task to use. Thus, these approaches combine aspects of content validity with criterion-related validity.

Construct Validity

A construct is a theoretical dimension on which employees are thought to differ in test scores or in criterion performance. For example, "intelligence" is a psychological construct. The understanding of this construct is derived from a logical network of interrelationships. For instance, there is the relationship with maturation. As we grow from infant to adult, we become more competent with tests involving the manipulation of words, forms and shapes, and numbers. A genetic linkage is inferred because the competence is highly correlated among identical twins even when they are reared apart. It is also inferred from the substantial association of the competence of grandparents, parents and children. Yet some of this competence can be linked to our socioeconomic class and educational opportunities. The competence reveals itself in better performance in school and in skilled and professional work. Trauma, malnutrition, drugs and disease may cause physiological decrements as well as deterioration in performance at school and on the job as well as on tests involving working with words, judging forms and shapes and completing numerical problems. The underlying construct of intelligence connects competence revealed on particular tests with performance in school and on the job and helps deal with related social and biological effects.

The web of relations can be supported by concurrent and predictive validity studies as well as other ways of matching observed facts about this kind of competence with words, forms and numbers with logical expectations about its contributions to job performance.

OTHER VALIDITY ISSUES

In practice, inferences must be drawn and applied from our validity studies. To do this usually requires cross-validation and validity generalization.

Cross-Validation

Sampling errors, systematic effects of other variables on test performance, and extraneous conditions affecting test scores make it mandatory to determine after an initial validation analysis how valid a test remains with new samples of examinees. Furthermore, we may need to consider how the validity of the test is affected if the new samples are drawn from different populations of examinees. Depending on the purpose of the analysis, two somewhat different procedures are typically used in assessing the usefulness of a test battery which seems to be valid with a certain sample: replication and cross-validation.

Replication simply involves administering the same test to a new sample from the same population. For example, if our original validation study was done using young male adults, replication would require a second sample with the same characteristics. If the validity for the test obtained on the replication was about the same as on the original administration, we would have some grounds for assuming that the test could continue to be used validly with new samples of young male adults.

Cross-validation uses the weights for the separate tests developed in the first administration to predict criterion behavior for a second sample from the same population. Or we may complete an item analysis on a sample of young male adults, eliminating those items from the test which failed to correlate with a criterion of job success, such as supervisors' ratings of those young male adults. Our very next step will be to apply the test, with the invalid items removed, to a parallel sample of young male adults for whom the same kind of criterion success data are available. If scores on the test actually predict the criterion measures for the second sample — e.g., if high test scores tend to mean high supervisors' ratings — we have further evidence of validity.

Cross-validation is costly. We must split our available cases. If we have 200 test scores and matched them with 200 criterion scores, in order to cross-validate, we must set aside 100 of the cases to refine the test, then apply the valid test portions to the set aside cases. Since there are accurate ways of estimating how the test-criterion correlation will "shrink" as we apply it to provide predictions in the second sample, we can substitute such shrinkage estimations (based on the number of different tests in the battery and the sample size) for cross-validation.[17]

Validity Generalization

The basic issue of validity generalization concerns the degree to which we can generalize obtained validity coefficients between a test and job performance to a new situation. If we find in one department that a test accurately predicts the performance of welders, are we justified in believing that the test will do the same in a second department?

There has been a widespread belief in personnel psychology that validities obtained in one situation are highly situation-specific. This conclusion may have been based on some faulty assumptions and on the failure of many validity studies to use a sample of adequate size. That, in turn, is due to the fact that each investigator analyzes results as if no previous research had ever been done. (The tradition stems from classical statistical analysis of Pearson and Fisher.) For each new investigator, the question is always the same. Are the correlations obtained with the test and criterion data of this investigation due to chance, or not? Essentially, with each new investigation we begin as if we had no previous information to build upon.

If we adopt a Bayesian approach, however, we begin with whatever better-than-chance knowledge we have and continue to build upon it. Recently, Schmidt and Hunter have taken this Bayesian* approach to the issue of validity generalization.[15] Here, relevant information concerning the same or similar tests for the same or similar jobs is used to derive an estimate of validity. That estimate is based not only upon the present study and its data but also upon all of the past information available about the test's validity coefficients. Sample sizes, restriction in range, and criterion reliability are also taken into account.

The new approach was applied to the validity of an intelligence-type test for predicting success as a clerk. Results indicated that there was a 97.5 per cent probability that the true validity coefficient, using an intelligence test, was 0.40 for this general class of clerical jobs.

This represents a rational way to generalize results of validity studies without performing a specific new validity study in each organization. The approach makes possible the accumulation of sufficiently large sample sizes to establish adequate validity coefficients for different tests and jobs.

STEPS IN VALIDATION PROCESS

At this point we will specify the steps in the validation process before considering the various types of tests used as predictors. The typical validation study involves the following steps:

1. *Job analysis.* We have discussed in Chapter 7 the process that provides essential information for both criterion development and test selection.
2. *Choice of the personnel selection model.* At the beginning of this

* This type of analysis is based on Bayes' theorem. Using prior knowledge about a relationship, Bayesian analysis estimates for the investigator the probabilities of the occurrence of the relationship in the current investigation.

chapter, we enumerated five possible models of personnel selection. The model chosen will determine whether the next steps in the process will be taken.

3. *Choice of the validation design.* The types of validiation designs were previously discussed. If a criterion-related design is chosen, then this leads to the next step.

4. *Criterion development.* With the job analysis and the considerations discussed in Chapter 7 and 8 as a basis, the dimensions and necessities of job performance are specified and developed, if required (for example, developing a behaviorally anchored rating scale).

5. *Test selection and development.* Constructs are hypothesized to relate to the criteria. Tests are then either selected or developed to measure the constructs. The next two chapters will discuss various tests.

6. *Data Collection.* Test and criterion data are collected according to the dictates of the validation design.

7. *Data analysis.* The tests are combined if there are more than one, and the degree of association is established between the selection procedures and job performance.

8. *Determination of the utility of the selection procedure.* The utility or value of the selection procedure for the organization is determined (to be discussed in Chapter 12). This will include an analysis of any adverse impact on minorities.

9. *Recommendations for operational use.* Exact procedures for the use of the selection procedure are specified, including how to administer, score, and establish the passing points for the tests.

SUMMARY

This chapter has reviewed the conceptual basis for validation research. Five possible models of personnel selection may be used by an organization. The various validation designs have been reviewed, comparing and explaining threats to internal and external validity. Predictive, concurrent, and postdictive designs are termed criterion-related, since an empirical relationship is established between the test and job performance. Tests measuring aptitudes and abilities are used in criterion-related validation studies.

REFERENCES

1. Alvares, K. M., and C. L. Hulin. "An Experimental Evaluation of a Temporal Design in the Prediction of Performance," *Organizational Behavior and Human Performance*, 9 (1973): 169–185.

2. Barrett, G. V., R. A. Alexander, and J. B. Forbes. "Values and Professional Judgment in Validating and Litigating Tests for Civil Service Positions," *Professional Psychology*, 9 (1978): 137–144.

3. Brown, C. W., and Ghiselli, E. E. "The Relationship between the Predictive Power of Apptitude Tests for Trainability and Job Proficiency," *Journal of Applied Psychology*, 36 (1952): 372.

4. Cohen, J. *Statistical Power Analysis for the Behavioral Sciences*. New York: Academic Press, 1977.

5. Cook, T. D., and D. T. Campbell. "The Design and Conduct of Quasi-Experiments and True Experiments in Field Settings." In M. D. Dunnette (ed.), *Handbook of Industrial and Organizational Psychology*. Chicago: Rand McNally College Publishing Company, 1976.

6. Dvorak, B. J. *Differential Occupational Ability Patterns*. Bulletin, Employment Stabilization Research Institute. Minneapolis: University of Minnesota, 1935.

7. Ghiselli, E. E. *The Validity of Occupational Aptitude Tests*. New York: Wiley, 1966.

8. Hartley, C., M. Brecht, P. Pagerey, G. Weeke, A. Chapanis, and D. Hoecker. "Subjective Time Estimates of Work Tasks by Office Workers," *Journal of Occupational Psychology*, 50 (1977): 23–26.

9. Jennings, E. E. "The Motivation Factor in Testing Supervisors," *The Journal of Applied Psychology*, 37 (1953): 168–169.

10. Lawshe, C. H. "Employee Selection," *Personnel Psychology*, 5 (1952): 31–34.

11. Lent, R. H., H. A. Aurbach, and L. S. Levin. "Predictors, Criteria, and Significant Results," *Personnel Psychology*, 24 (1971): 519–533.

12. Mosvier, C. I. "Symposium: The Need and Means of Cross-Validation," *Educational and Psychological Measurement*, 11 (1951): 5–11.

13. Peterson, D. A., and S. R. Wallace. "Validation and Revision of a Test in Use," *Journal of Applied Psychology*, 50 (1966): 13–17.

14. Primoff, E. J. *How to Prepare and Conduct Job-Element Examinations*. Personnel Research and Development Center, U. S. Civil Service Commission, Washington, D. C., November 1973.

15. Schmidt, F. L., and J. E. Hunter. "Development of a General Solution to the Problem of Validity Generalization," *Journal of Applied Psychology*, 62 (1977): 529–540.

16. Schmidt, F. L., J. E. Hunter, and V. Urry. "Statistical Power in Criterion Related Validation Studies," *Journal of Applied Psychology*, 61 (1976): 473–485.

17. Schmidt, N., B. W. Coyle, and J. Rauschenberger. "A Monte Carlo Evaluation of Three Formula Estimates of Cross-Validated Multiple Correlation," *Psychology Bulletin*, 84 (1977): 751–758.

10 ASSESSMENT OF APTITUDE AND ABILITY

IN BRIEF   Since employees differ in what they can contribute to their organizations, it becomes useful to forecast such differences with tests and other means. But the tests need to be reliable and valid. Such reliable and valid tests are available to assess verbal, numerical, and spatial aptitude, and the complex of aptitudes — intelligence. Reliable and valid tests of perceptual speed, finger dexterity, and manual dexterity are also available for assessing potential performance in the clerical and mechanical occupations. Job sample tests and nonverbal tests have certain advantages for predicting job success: Many applicants may perceive these tests to be fairer.

The personnel psychologist is concerned with collecting and analyzing whatever information may be available about a job applicant that might reliably and validly be used to predict the potential jobholder's ability to perform. We will examine the development and utilization of predictive measures derived from a wide variety of information sources. Chapter 10 focuses on information provided by tests of aptitudes and abilities. The widespread use of such tests, many of which are available in relatively standardized forms, requires careful examination of the issues involved in both the construction of these tests and the evaluation of the information provided by them.

But aptitude test data represent only one kind of prior information that can be obtained for predictive purposes. Chapter 11 deals with data provided by tests of interests and personality, as well as with data from nontest sources such as application forms and interviews. In Chapter 12, we examine the processes used to combine and integrate predictive information from all sources, in order to make decisions about selecting and classifying job applicants.

TEST DEVELOPMENT AND APPLICATION

In Chapter 7, we looked at job analysis and concentrated on the determination of the relevant criteria of job success. These constitute two of the important steps in the development and refinement of a psychological test. But, before constructing a trial version of the test, we also need to hypothesize what *attributes of behavior* on which workers differ are likely to be testable in advance. The same rationale holds if we are going to select an already-prepared test. In short, we must decide on what attributes of behavior we should try to assess with the tests to be selected or developed.

What Attributes of Behavior Should We Try to Forecast?

Job information and information about currently available tests give us the basis for making educated decisions about the following questions which need to be answered.[19]

1. *How important is each attribute for job success?* The job analysis may disclose that while trainees with a high degree of finger dexterity have an easier time getting started, all workers seem to have enough dexterity to do the job well once they have been through a standard training program. We could decide not to bother trying to assess finger dexterity.

    We need to avoid snap judgments about what is and what is not important to job success. It seemed obvious that a high degree of visual acuity should forecast success of the performance of power sewing machine operators. Yet analysis showed that women could sew sheets well with their eyes closed.[22]

2. *Are criteria available to check the validity of what we might construct for assessing job applicants?* We might feel that "ability to handle emergencies" was an important trait. However, such emergencies might or might not occur on the job in sufficient frequency to make it possible to appraise whether or not individual workers actually respond differentially in emergencies.

3. *Is the trait important on all jobs?* The ability to get along with workers is likely to show up as important on a good percentage of jobs. If we are constructing a test to help transfer current employees to a job for which they are best suited, even if we could assess ability to get along with co-workers, we might decide to skip attempting to make this measurement.
4. *Are nontest methods available?* For adults, in particular, who often have a fairly good fix on their own interests, it may be sufficient to ask them if they think or expect they will be satisfied with a particular job which is described to them rather than having to select or develop an interest inventory to assess their interests in an effort to forecast their likely satisfaction with a given job assignment. Rank in one's high school class may provide an adequate predictor of job success in lieu of an academic achievement test.
5. *What are the prospects that we can develop a test to forecast a particular attribute deemed important?* Analyses of the job of airplane pilot shortly after the United States became involved in World War II suggested that two clusters of attributes were important: psychomotor coordination and motivation to fly. It was decided to place major effort in constructing psychomotor coordination tests to forecast success in training, as it was felt that the prospects were much poorer that equally valid tests of motivation could be constructed. Subsequently, generally unprofitable attempts to do the latter showed the correctness of this judgment.

Test Characteristics

Once we have in mind what content we wish to sample with the tests to be developed or selected for use, we must decide on what kind of methods we will use. Here the choice will depend on administrative issues, as well as expectation that the method of testing will forecast job success.

Job Sample versus Aptitude Tests

Should we construct a test that is a complex sample of real-life behavior? Such a test would involve several aptitudes and is likely to be highly predictive of success in the one situation for which the sample has been constructed. Or should we devise a test that intensively measures one aptitude and that may partially be predictive of success in many situations?

For example, to assess applicants for a job as a production machine operator, an apparatus was constructed to simulate the flow of bottles, crates, and packages with blocks, cans, conveyor belts, indexers, and guides, as on a real assembly line. This complex job sample assessed applicant skill in handling five adjustment tasks and using tools to correct five jams. There were 30 job applicants, who could attain a mean test score of only 43.4; while 40 experienced machine operators earned a mean score of 68.8, more than a full standard deviation higher (an experienced operator with a mean score was like the upper 10 per cent of the applicants).[20]

The investigator in this case could have used a battery of single aptitude tests, one dealing with facility in handling tools, another in mechanical knowledge, another purporting to measure perceptual speed, still another trying to test eye-hand coordination. Each of those single aptitude tests would have uses in forecasting success in other kinds of work. For example, an applicant with a high score on the mechanical knowledge test might be equally ready for a job in the sales service department. A different pattern of optimal weightings of the scores in these tests could be developed, so that after an applicant had completed the battery, one could calculate a variety of composite scores, each valid for forecasting success in a different kind of work. The same battery, with scores weighted differently, might be used to identify potential prospects for the machine shop.

Job sample tests seem to be favored by applicants over aptitude tests, at least among blue collar workers. Thus, in comparing a content-valid job sample test of metal trade skills with a content-valid written achievement test, both nonminority and minority group metal trade apprentices preferred the job sample.[15]

ADVANTAGES AND DISADVANTAGES One advantage of the job sample test is that it is likely to be a more valid predictor of success on the specific job for which it was designed than any battery of single-aptitude tests. Second, it looks valid — it has *face* validity, which helps make the test "politically acceptable." Applicants for Civil Service positions, as well as applicants from disadvantaged minority groups, are likely to view such tests as more fair to them than single-aptitude tests. The latter are more abstract and seem unconnected to the job in question, look more like school tests, seem more culture-bound, and are likely to contain some reading requirements.

Furthermore, examinees in general are more likely to be motivated and interested in a complex simulation of the job than by single-aptitude tests. Nevertheless, although the latter are individually and in combination less valid, and look less valid in forecasting success on most jobs, a battery of single-aptitude tests, each independently measuring a different aptitude, will provide a far more efficient test battery for properly placing applicants on a large number of widely diverse jobs (i.e., within a large organization). The various permutations and combinations of single-aptitude tests can be validated against many different complex criteria.

Which combination of tests will be the best predictor of a criterion will depend on which aptitudes are required for predicting the criterion.

There are other potential disadvantages to the job sample approach. For example, Campion arranged a job sample for mechanics.[4] To be fair, he made the assumption that each applicant had had an equal chance to install pulleys and belts, disassemble and repair a gear box, and install and repair a motor. Yet there was no reason to believe that even knowledgeable mechanics are equally expert in performing each of these separate tasks. Indeed, even experienced mechanics would have been unlikely to have had equal experience with these tasks. This is indicated by the low intercorrelations in success in performing these separate tasks ranging from 0.01 to 0.27. Thus, successful performance on these tasks was quite specific; proficiency was found to be highly dependent upon prior experience in performing the task. One of the problems of minority groups is that they often do not have the same prior work experience as others. The job sample task *may* put them at a comparative disadvantage despite the fact that job sample tests are seen as fairer to the disadvantaged for superficial reasons.

Speed Tests versus Power Tests

In *time limit* tests, the *speed* with which examinees answer is important. Such tests are designed so that no examinee will have time to finish all the items. In *work limit* tests, examinees are given sufficient time to complete all items they can handle to demonstrate their *power*. In fact, most tests fall somewhere between these extremes; it is impossible to set a clear distinction between them.[10]

In practice, speed factors are often built into aptitude tests. In doing so, test makers appear to assume that speed and power are opposite sides of the same coin — that an examinee can make up for slowness by high ability, or vice versa. Substantial research evidence, however, questions this assumption.[10] Speed and power appear to be independent, so that scores obtained on aptitude tests that also emphasize speed may provide quite distorted (unreliable) pictures of individual abilities, depending on the level of difficulty of the test items.

Speed factors are probably incorporated into aptitude tests for both practical and theoretical reasons. On the practical side, there are clear administrative and cost advantages to group testing, as opposed to examining applicants individually. Efficient group testing requires time limits. The existence of time limits *per se* does not make for a speeded test, but in practice, timed tests do represent speed pressures for at least some examinees. On a deeper level, there appears to be a theoretical reason, either overt or tacit, for incorporating speed factors into tests primarily

designed for power purposes. It is quite likely that most real-life performance situations, either in industry or in the classroom (where most
of the research on testing has been done), emphasize speed to some extent,
as well as power. As a result, performance on tests including speed elements
may tend to predict real-life performance better than would power-
oriented tests alone; i.e., they may show higher predictive *validity*, even
though scores on speeded tests may be less *reliable*. The exact effects of
speed factors on abilities tests have not been completely determined. There
is some evidence that moderately tight time limits do not distort results
so seriously as to outweigh the practical administrative advantages. (See
Nunnally for a detailed discussion of the issue of speed versus power.[14])

Whatever the effects of including speed elements in aptitude tests,
special care must be taken in interpreting test results based on restrictive
speed factors. Research results suggest that speed of work reflects personality or motivational factors rather than ability, so that if speed of work
is important to measure, it may be more efficient to do so with tests
specifically designed for that purpose, rather than penalizing slower examinees on power-oriented tests. Given our current technology, almost
any individual aptitude or proficiency test (i.e., a power test) can be converted into group form (i.e., where time pressures are involved), should
cost advantages require it, by making some appropriate allowances for
slower examinees. For example, extra unscored items can be included at
the end of each timed section to provide busywork for faster workers, while
the slower ones complete the items which are actually to be scored.[10]

APTITUDES AND APTITUDE TESTS

Aptitude versus Proficiency

A valid *aptitude* test is a simulation of a wide range of related real-life
problems. As problems for testing, it usually abstracts from the real situations those elements shared in common by the various real-life problems.
For instance, a test for measuring the aptitude of *spatial visualization* is
likely to contain a series of items that involve the ability to visualize the
effects of putting parts of objects together, manipulating objects in space,
and judging spaces, sizes, and shapes. Its *construct validity* is established
by its correlations with other tests and with measures that previously
have been identified as partially measuring spatial visualization; its *predictive* validity is demonstrated if it forecasts proficiency in training and/or
on a job with such visual requirements.

A valid *proficiency* test is a simulation of a more limited range of related real-life problems. It usually abstracts from real life a much more
specific set of elements as problems for testing. Because one must have had

specialized training or experience before taking a proficiency test, whereas one could handle an aptitude test without such previous specialized effort, we are prone to ignore the proficiency test as a predictive tool. Yet if we are interested in forecasting the success on the job of individuals already trained to some degree to do that job, a simple proficiency test may be much more predictive of success than any combination of aptitude tests. Thus, it was found that a 15-minute oral trade test had a validity of 0.53 for forecasting rated performance on the job as a first-class machinist in a naval shipyard.[18]

The Basic Aptitudes

Standardized tests have been developed to measure each of various different aptitudes. An effort has been made to keep the number of aptitudes to some minimum that would satisfactorily account for success in most types of vocational training and job performance. We have searched for a basic set of aptitudes, each of which is independent of the other and each of which will help to account for success in a wide variety of vocational activities. Factor analysis, a statistical technique used to determine "basic factors" or "underlying dimensions" of test scores, has aided this search.

How many factors there are depends somewhat on the varieties of abilities and occupational skills we include in our investigations. The Educational Testing Service identified 23 such basic factors.[12] If our tests sample the wide array of cognitive skills required in such a complex job as a space shuttle pilot we may emerge with as many as 120.[11] We can, however, concentrate on five more broadly framed aptitudes, which are most important for success among a large proportion of manual and knowledge workers. We will describe which behavior each of these aptitudes underlies and how more complex aptitudes may emerge from a combination of these basic ones. We will give examples of tests that in part or whole measure each of these aptitudes, and examples of the types of occupations that require these aptitudes for success both in training and in performance on the job.

The five general aptitudes are verbal aptitude, numerical aptitude, spatial relations ability, perceptual aptitude, and psychomotor aptitude (including manual and finger dexterity). *We must repeat that this list is by no means exhaustive,* nor are we entirely sure that the five enumerated are really all unique and independent of one another. In fact, most tests of mental abilities correlate to some extent with each other, but the differences are sufficiently great and sufficiently stable to permit descriptions of separate ability categories. We feel that these five will provide the opportunity for understanding behavior in a wide variety of vocational training and performance situations.

After describing the five basic general aptitudes, we will consider three constellations of aptitudes — intelligence, clerical aptitude, and mechanical comprehension — which, prior to developments in factor theory, were considered as single rather than complex factors.

Verbal Aptitude

We often speak of "verbal intelligence"; in fact, verbal fluency and intelligence go hand-in-hand. Essentially, this aptitude concerns successfully dealing with the meaning of words and verbal concepts, "juggling" or manipulating them, reasoning with them, and communicating ideas through them. Verbal fluency is one of the most important of the aptitudes necessary for success in school or in most training programs, since language is one of the basic tools of the student. Moreover, verbal aptitude is of considerable importance to most professional people, because of their need to communicate effectively with each other and with the public by means of reports, interviews, books, conferences, and public lectures.

Verbal tests may range from an easy five-minute vocabulary test like the *PTI Verbal* (Psychological Corporation) aimed at industrial applicants and apprentices to the *Miller Analogies Test* (Psychological Corporation) of about an hour's duration, valid for screening applicants to graduate schools and for assessing correspondingly well-educated applicants for professional and managerial jobs requiring at least a bachelor's degree. Readers are probably familiar with other test forms involving sentence completion, word fluency, speed of associations, and reading comprehension.

In particular, tests of reading comprehension have become increasingly important for predicting training and job performance in diverse jobs, such as cook, repairman, factory worker, and police officer.[1,18,16] For example, a content-valid reading comprehension test successfully predicted both training and job performance for police patrol officers, as shown in Table 10–1. Content-valid reading comprehension tests have the additional advantage of being *face* valid, since the material in the test is based on training-course information that is required eventually to perform the job.

It was popular for a period in the past to downplay the importance of reading ability, and nonverbal measures were advocated. But nonverbal measures have been remarkably unsuccessful in predicting either training or job performance for occupations that involve reading. This is true not only of professions such as the law, where it is evident that reading comprehension is important, but of other occupations, such as maintenance, where the need is not as obvious. Yet, accurately reading technical manuals and the monthly changes in them are mandatory for success as a copy machine service mechanic.

Table 10–1. Reading test correlation with police academy training and job performance.

Criteria of success	Reading test
In training	
Tests of achievement	.77
First aid test	.75
On the job performance	
Rated job knowledge	.32
Rated report writing	.48
Rated investigation performance	.57

Adapted from Barrett, Alexander, Burns, and Byers "Predictive Validity of a Content Valid Reading Test." Unpublished manuscript, 1978.

Note that scores on some predictive tests, such as word analogies, may combine the factors of heredity, cultural background, experience, and formal education. Such tests may be relatively insensitive to remedial instruction. But reading proficiency can be improved through remedial effort. For example, the U.S. Navy embarked in 1977 on a remedial program to bring all its recruits up to the sixth-grade level, since so many navy jobs require reading training and trouble-shooting manuals.

Numerical Aptitude

Numerical aptitude involves successfully performing arithmetical operations quickly and accurately. It is concerned with behavior requiring the judging of the effects of manipulating numbers. We have to reason with, combine, or separate numbers according to a set of formal rules. Problems in simple addition, subtraction, multiplication, and division would be one way to assess this aptitude; arithmetic reasoning would be another.

A numerical aptitude score is likely to contribute to the forecasting accuracy of most test batteries designed to predict success in technical training. A high level of numerical aptitude required for success in accounting, engineering, and other technically oriented professions, while a moderately high degree is of importance in recording and computing, in general clerical work, and in industrial designing. A moderate level of this aptitude is necessary for training and on-the-job success in machine shop and all-round mechanical repairing occupations, and for business machine operations.[19]

Spatial Relations Ability

Spatial relations ability concerns judging the relations among objects in space, — their shapes, shades, and sizes, — as well as forecasting the effect of manipulating objects in a certain way and visualizing the effects of putting objects together or turning them over or around. This factor, or parts of it, may be known by other names, such as form perception and spatial visualization.

Spatial relations ability has been related to a wide variety of industrial and clerical occupations and to the trades and crafts. It is of importance in engineering occupations, especially in the designing phases. To a lesser extent, it is important in technical and mechanical work like metal machining and mechanical repairing, and in such occupations as advertising layout and commercial design. On the average, spatial relations has correlated 0.44 with success in training machine workers and 0.28 with their success on the job.[9]

For many years, the *Revised Minnesota Paper Form Board* (Psychological Corporation) has been the test most widely used to assess this aptitude. Each item of the paper-and-pencil test consists of a geometric figure whose parts have been disarranged. The examinees must choose the one of five alternatives that best represents what the geometric figure would look like if all of its parts were properly reassembled. Although this test attempts to measure the spatial factor only, an examinee's score seems to be affected by a reasoning and a perceptual speed and accuracy factor.

The Revised Minnesota Paper Form Board has been found valid for predicting success in training in shop work, mechanics, printing press work, engineering, dentistry, and art. It has predicted success on the job for aircraft inspectors, aircraft mechanics, merchandise packers, and power sewing machine operators.[19]

Various other kinds of spatial tests have been used. A most common is block-counting. Examinees are presented with a picture of an orderly pile of blocks; they must try to determine the exact number in the pile by taking into account all the blocks that are obscured by those in the foreground.

Perceptual Aptitude

The ability to discriminate sensory inputs depends on perceptual speed and accuracy. Theoretically, perceptual aptitude deals with the ability to recognize and identify certain stimuli whether or not the meanings of those stimuli are recognized. For example, the ability to differentiate quickly and accurately between the letter patterns STAB, BATS, and TABS has theoretically nothing to do with the verbal aptitude of being aware of the semantic meanings of these patterns, nor does differentiating between 52381 and 58321 require numerical aptitude of knowing that one is smaller than the other.

In practice, however, it is extremely difficult to construct tests of perceptual speed and accuracy that do not also tap certain cognitive or intellectual abilities. Attempts to do so have resulted in tests of color sensitivity, pitch and loudness discrimination in hearing tests, and tests of size or length discriminations among symbolic stimuli. Spatial visualization factors are probably also involved in most perceptual aptitude tests, but tests are able to differentiate between these abilities by appropriately combining item difficulty levels with speed elements: spatial visualization tests normally include items with high difficulty levels and liberal time limits; perceptual ability tests stress rather easy problems (most items would be answered correctly by most examinees, given enough time), but impose tight time limits. An example is the *Minnesota Clerical Test* (Psychological Corporation). Examinees are required to indicate whether lists of paired numbers, such as 146712 — 147616, are the same or different. Pairs of names are also checked. Both speed and accuracy are scored. The *Short Employment Tests:* Verbal, Numerical, Clerical Aptitude (Psychological Corporation) require the applicant to check names against credit ratings. This test differentiates the better from the poorer workers for clerical tasks involving perceptual speed and accuracy.[3] Other tasks that require perceptual speed and accuracy are visual monitoring and vigilance, performed by radar operators and assembly-line inspectors.

Psychomotor Aptitude

The aptitudes underlying the motor skills have been factored into many independent dexterities. We will concentrate primarily on those skills of consequence to common occupations, since many motor skills are performed rarely. The complex coordination, timing, and strength of the acrobat or boxer probably involve many unique aptitudes rarely necessary for other types of work. Walking a tightrope might involve certain aptitudes of eye-torso coordination not found in any other motor activities.

Some common psychomotor aptitudes are manual dexterity, finger dexterity, tweezer dexterity, hand-and-arm dexterity, eye-hand coordination, eye-hand-arm coordination, and finger-wrist dexterity. Cutting across these aptitudes along with different dimensions are such concepts as motor speed, motor coordination, aiming, and kinesthetic sensitivity — the ability to sense accurately and quickly the movements of the muscles, tendons, and joints of the body.

Fleishman's program of studies of over 200 different tasks administered to thousands of airmen[7] yielded patterns of correlations accounting for performance on this wide range of tasks in terms of a relatively small number of factors. Moreover, Fleishman concluded "that there is no such thing as general physical proficiency or general psychomotor skill or general manual dexterity. Rather, each of these areas breaks up into a limited number of unitary abilities" (p. 461), such as wrist-finger speed, finger dexterity, speed-of-arm movement, aiming, and gross manual dexterity. He also noted that "skill in fine manipulation tasks is quite independent of skill in gross physical proficiency or skill in coordination tasks" (p. 462).

While all of these factors are important in forecasting success in highly complex psychomotor tasks, like piloting a plane, for industrial jobs in general it is the manual and finger dexterities that are likely to contribute to forecasting success. Many bench and assembly jobs require such dexterities.

MANUAL DEXTERITY   Workers possessing manual dexterity can move their hands easily, accurately, and quickly. Manual dexterity usually involves coordinations with arm and eye and more gross movements than those involved in finger dexterity. A fair degree of manual dexterity is likely to be required for repairing mechanical equipment, for carpentry, plumbing, grinding, industrial inspection, machine tending, and packing or wrapping.

The most widely used test of gross arm-hand manipulation is the *Minnesota Rate of Manipulation Test* (American Guidance Service). The form board has four rows of identical holes, 15 holes in each row. Sixty disks, somewhat larger than checkers, have to be placed in their respective holes by the examinee as quickly as possible. The flat sides of the disks are in different colors. The disks are thicker than the depth of the holes, so that in a second part of the test, the disks can be grasped easily by the examinee and turned over rapidly. The examinee's "placing" score is the time needed to place the 60 disks. The placing and turning scores correlate about 0.60.

These scores have been found valid to some degree for forecasting success in industrial jobs like seasonal department store wrappers and packers, pharmaceutical inspector-packers, can packers, and converting machine operators who remove and assemble tissue sheets. "Arm-and-hand dexterity as measured by the Minnesota test is important in packing, wrapping and inspection jobs and in gross-manual assembly and machine-operation jobs; however, the predictive value of the test depends somewhat upon the specific factors contained in each job." [19]

FINGER DEXTERITY   Finger dexterity is the aptitude for performing operations requiring the use of fingers, or of wrist and fingers, simply and quickly, avoiding fumbles, faulty performance, and superfluous movements — and manipulating small objects quickly and accurately. Average or better-than-average finger dexterity is likely to be required in such occupations as typist, check-writing machine operator, stenographer, key puncher, and Linotype operator. Fair finger dexterity is likely to be of importance to machinists, radio repairmen, business machine operators, plumbers, and sewing machine operators.

The *Purdue Pegboard* (Science Research Associates), is a widely used method for assessing the ability to manipulate one's fingers skillfully. The holes down the middle of the 12 × 18 inch board are $\frac{1}{8}$ inch in diameter. Fifty metal pins fit easily into the holes. Examinees' scores are based on how many pins they can insert in 30 seconds with their right hand, how many they can insert with their left hand in another 30 seconds, and how many they can insert with both hands in another run. In a fourth part of the test, the examinees assemble for each hole one pin, a washer, a collar, and then another washer. Their score is the number of assemblies they make in 60 seconds. The short time allowances produce test-retest reliabilties between 0.66 and 0.79, reliabilities too low for individual placement. Minimally, one should probably repeat the same test at least once with applicants and calculate mean scores for the repeated administrations. Or, one could use a board with more holes, pins, collars, and washers.[2]

Purdue Pegboard scores have been found to forecast piece rate earnings of small samples of workers learning to operate light machines ($r = 0.21$ to 0.56). Also predicted with some success were earnings after learning (0.07 to 0.52), productivity in textile mills (0.15), and simple small parts assembling (0.76).

Tweezer dexterity is closely associated with finger dexterity. As with the Purdue Pegboard in the O'Connor Tweezer Dexterity test (C. H. Stoetling & Co.) the object is to pick up a pin with a tweezer from the center tray of the board and rapidly insert it in a hole in a particular order. Scores depend on the time required to complete the task requirements.

The tweezer dexterity score correlated 0.32 with instructors' grades for mechanics trainees learning aircraft instruments, but generally failed to relate with success in training in other mechanical specialties. However, four separate studies have found validities ranging from 0.10 to 0.35 in forecasting success in dental training. The higher validities were obtained when the investigators attempted to predict specific dental laboratory success rather than overall grades.[6]

OTHER DEXTERITY TESTS   While the Minnesota and Purdue tests are most commonly employed, other dexterity tests may be found useful for particular selection purposes where other dexterity factors may be involved.

The *Flanagan Aptitude Classification Tests* (Science Research Associates) contain several dexterity assessments. The coordination test correlated 0.66 with the rate of salary increase of 45 construction workers. The precision test correlated 0.51 with the rate of salary increase of 33 electricians.[21] Both tests illustrate the possibilities of assessing dexterities with paper-and-pencil tests instead of individually administered apparatus such as pegboards or form boards.

Common Combinations of Basic Aptitudes

Our confidence in the nature of the basic aptitudes described above has been supported greatly by developments in factor theory and techniques of factor analysis, but efforts to assess individual differences in abilities long antedate such developments. In their attempts to design and use reliable tests that could validly predict performance in the most common industrial job categories, personnel psychologists have focused on *mechanical* and *clerical* aptitudes. In doing so, the assumption was made — either overtly or tacitly — that each of these aptitudes was a separate and distinct unitary power. The working assumption resulted in the construction and use of single tests of mechanical aptitude or clerical aptitude, which, when later subjected to factor analysis, proved to incorporate a variety of more basic aptitudes. More recent testing programs have taken advantage of factor analytic results in assembling batteries of tests known to tap more basic aptitudes required in specific job categories.

Tests for assessing *intelligence* — probably the most complex human "ability" — share a similar history. From an early history of attention to a limited number of unitary mental abilities, investigators have come to recognize the complexity of human mental abilities: Guilford lists 120 separate factors involved in human intelligence.[11] A detailed analysis of the nature and structure of human intelligence goes beyond the scope of our present discussion, but the widespread employment of intelligence tests in organizational selection and classification programs requires our attention. The personnel psychologist shares an intense interest in intelligence testing with educational and developmental psychologists, primarily because intelligence tests have proved to be particularly reliable and valid predictors of performance in certain job categories.

Examples of tests for some of these complex aptitudes follow.

MECHANICAL APTITUDE   The term mechanical aptitude has been used quite loosely by test constructors. One widely used mechanical aptitude test, the *MacQuarrie Test for Mechanical Ability* (California Test Bureau — McGraw-Hill), appears primarily to assess dexterity, perceptual speed, and spatial visualization. At the same time, the *Bennett Mechanical Comprehension Test* (Psychological Corporation) (Figure 10–1) and the *FACT-Mechanics Test* (Science Research Associates) seem to be primarily

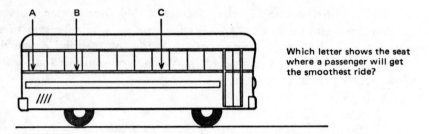

Figure 10–1. From Bennett Mechanical Comprehension Tests, by The Psychological Corporation, New York, N. Y. Copyright 1940, renewed 1967, 1968.

tests of knowledge of applied physics. Still other mechanical aptitude tests, like the *O'Rourke Mechanical Aptitude Test* (Psychology Institute) and the *Purdue Mechanical Adaptability Test* (Purdue University), concentrate on information about tools and materials in mechanical, electrical, plumbing, and carpentry occupations. Although those tests correlate with each other (from 0.40 to 0.70), probably because they share visualization and perceptual factors in common, each contains unique components.

Few occupations require all components of mechanical aptitude. While it was first thought that all work that involved working with machines, their products, or processes had a common set of highly interrelated requirements, mechanical work actually involves combinations of aptitudes and information that vary in kind and amount from occupation to occupation.

Each of the five mechanical aptitude tests mentioned earlier has been found valid for forecasting success in a variety of different mechanical jobs. Correlations ranging between 0.17 and 0.73 have been found between the Bennett Mechanical Comprehension Test and rated success on the job of 60 machine tool operator trainees, 587 ordnance factory employees, 85 instructors of auto body workers, 105 instructor-mechanics, 90 turbine floor assembly workers, 49 inspectors, 45 engine testers, 81 machine operators, 25 job setters, and so on.

Fewer validity studies have been completed with the O'Rourke or the Purdue mechanical tests. These tests focus more on knowledge of tools and materials than on understanding of mechanical principles, as do the Bennett or FACT-Mechanics. However, the validity data available on small samples of ice company mechanics and steel mill apprentices suggest that assessed knowledge of tools and materials may be a useful predictor of performance on mechanical jobs. Nevertheless, the utility of the Bennett or FACT concentration on principles has been more than adequately demonstrated already.[19]

CLERICAL APTITUDE Perceptual speed and accuracy appear to be the factors of prime importance in predicting success in clerical work, because central to most such work is the task of accurate and quick checking. However, complete tests aimed at forecasting success in a variety of clerical jobs are likely to be expanded to include assessments of other factors. For instance, the *speed* and *number* booklet of the *General Clerical Test* (Psychological Corporation) contains sections on checking, alphabetizing, and error location that are primarily assessments of perceptual aptitude. It also adds items on arithmetic computation and arithmetic reasoning. A verbal booklet examines spelling, reading comprehension, vocabulary, and grammar. In the same way, the *Thurstone Examination in Clerical Work* (Psychological Corporation) covers computation, spelling, coding, cancellation, and classification. The *SRA Clerical Aptitudes* concentrates on the assessment of checking, vocabulary, and arithmetic; the *Short Tests of Clerical Ability* (Science Research Associates) provide separate subtests in checking, filing, arithmetic, business vocabulary, language, and following directions.

Clerical employees who operate machines such as calculators and typewriters will require at least a fair degree of finger dexterity. Receptionists, telephone operators, and those in other "meet the public" clerical occupations will require a high degree of sociability. Stenographers must be proficient in grammar and spelling. Hence at one extreme, clerical aptitude may be identified as perceptual speed and accuracy. At the other extreme, however, it may be thought of as a complex of aptitudes and proficiencies including perceptual, numerical, and verbal aptitude, finger and manual dexterity, social intelligence, and proficiency in grammar, spelling, word usage, and other language skills.

The diversity of predictors has been shown in a review of validity studies for clerical occupations. The importance of intelligence and perceptual accuracy is reflected in the average validity coefficients shown in Table 10–2.

These results with clerical tests also illustrate the general finding that success in training is easier to predict than success on the job.

INTELLIGENCE TESTS Historically, techniques were developed for measuring the various aptitudes that combine to form intelligence. Intelligence has meant many things to many people. Most psychologists would agree that persons are more intelligent (1) the more difficult the problems they can solve; (2) the more complex the problems they can solve; (3) the more abstract the problems they can solve; (4) the more they can find solutions to problems with a minimum expenditure of time and energy; and (5) the more they can find original solutions to problems, when necessary. In modern society, the above problem solving requires that an individual minimally be able to manipulate, remember, substitute, and

Table 10-2. Validity coefficients of tests predicting success in various clerical occupations.

Test	Criterion	
	Achievement in training	On the job proficiency
Intellectual abilities	.47f	.27f
Intelligence	.48f	.30f
Immediate memory	.32d	.30d
Substitution	.24d	.24e
Arithmetic	.50f	.26f
Spatial and mechanical abilities	.33f	.20e
Spatial relations	.36f	.19d
Location	.27c	.17d
Mechanical principles	.30f	.25d
Perceptual accuracy	.40e	.27f
Number comparison	.34c	.27e
Name comparison	.35c	.31d
Cancellation	.49b	.21d
Pursuit	.21b	.12b
Perceptual speed	.42e	.42c
Motor abilities	.15d	.15e
Tracing	.15b	.19b
Tapping	.21c	.15d
Dotting	.18b	.12d
Finger dexterity	.09c	.24d
Hand dexterity	.30a	.11b
Arm dexterity	.09a	.11b
Personality traits	.17d	.23d
Personality		.24d
Interest	.17d	.12b

a.	Less than 100 cases	d.	1,000 to 4,999 cases
b.	100 to 499 cases	e.	5,000 to 9,999 cases
c.	500 to 999 cases	f.	10,000 or more cases

Adapted from, *The Validity of Occupational Aptitude Tests* by Edwin E. Ghiselli. Copyright © 1966 by John Wiley and Sons. Reprinted by permission of John Wiley and Sons, Inc.

otherwise work with *spatial, numerical,* and *verbal* content. These three kinds of content are covered in most tests of general intelligence. For example, the *Army General Classification Test* (Science Research Associates) consists of three parts, one devoted to each of these three aptitudes.

Most psychologists feel, however, that the variation among individuals on intelligence tests and on tasks or jobs requiring intelligence cannot be accounted for completely by spatial, numerical, and verbal aptitude.

Sometimes a reasoning factor independent of the other three is added to the complex. Or, two factors — induction and deduction — are added instead of reasoning. Or reasoning is reclassified into the categories of general reasoning, analogous reasoning, sequential reasoning, and judgment. Apart from the reasoning complex, there is often added a memory factor, which also may be single or complex. Memory span, paired associates memory, visual memory, and picture-word memory may be included in the memory constellation.

The *Otis Self-Administering Tests of Mental Ability* (Psychological Corporation) of 75 items and its 50-item shorter version, the *Wonderlic Personnel Test* (Wonderlic & Associates), represent two of the most popular short intelligence tests used in industry. The verbal, numerical, and spatial items involve vocabulary, sentence meaning, proverbs, analogies, number trends, and so forth. Indeed, the very popularity of these tests may make them a problem to test administrators, for a job candidate may have taken the test several times before in applying elsewhere for jobs: some practice effect is likely.

The *Thurstone Test of Mental Alertness* (Science Research Associates) is a 20-minute test yielding quantitative and linguistic assessments of intelligence. A 15-minute test of trainability for industrial jobs is the *Adaptability Test* (Science Research Associates) for literates. Its counterpart for illiterates, the *Purdue Non-Language Test* (Science Research Associates), consists of 48 geometric forms. The examinee crosses out the one different drawing in each series. Another such test for illiterates is the *SRA Non-Verbal Form,* a test of 60 pictorial reasoning items. The examinee indicates the one drawing of a person, object, or form that is different in each set.

Reviewing numerous studies completed between 1919 and 1964, Ghiselli showed that intelligence tests tended to forecast success in training in diverse skilled types of work.[8] The median correlation between intelligence test scores and trainability was 0.40 for mechanical repairmen; 0.50 for electrical workers; 0.29 for structural workers; 0.45 for process workers; 0.34 for machine operators; 0.36 for machining workers; 0.52 for computing clerks; 0.46 for general clerks; and 0.48 for recording clerks. Each of these coefficients was usually based on at least 10,000 cases. Nonintellectual tests of dexterity had little or no validity in predicting the same training criteria for such skilled workers.

On the other hand, for manipulative and observational occupations like machine tenders, bench assembly workers, inspectors, packers, wrappers, and gross manual workers, intelligence tests had little or no validity for predicting trainability, while dexterity tests or perceptual tests did.

In sum, intelligence tests are likely to prove valid for predicting trainability when training for a job calls for verbal, numerical, or spatial aptitude. Intelligence tests are likely to correlate with job success when such aptitude also is required on the job itself.

Nonverbal Tests

Most of the tests we have reviewed require some verbal skills, including a fair degree of reading ability. It has been thought that aptitude tests requiring verbal ability do not fairly estimate the aptitudes of individuals with deficient reading skills or those lacking a middle-class educational and cultural background. This problem was recognized during World War I, when the Army Beta Test was developed for illiterate or disadvantaged personnel.

The main problem in the past with nonverbal tests has been their failure to predict either training or job performance. In addition, nonverbal tests have usually had a low correlation with more traditional verbal tests of intellectual ability. However, the Air Force has developed and validated a battery of nonverbal tests that have apparently overcome many of these problems. The Air Force's Non-Verbal Aptitude Battery consists of eight tests, such as Dial Reading (a measure of numerical ability requiring quick and accurate reading of a dial), Wheels (a measure of mechanical reasoning requiring determination of the turning direction of a wheel), and Figure Analogies (a measure of abstract reasoning using figures).

The Non-Verbal Aptitude Test Battery was validated with over 13,000 personnel.[23] Three important results were found. First, grades in certain technical schools, such as mechanics, could be consistently predicted. Second, the nonverbal tests increased the accuracy of prediction of technical school grades, beyond that of the verbal tests. Third, the nonverbal tests could predict performance of both low- and higher-aptitude personnel.

Although the Air Force has been successful in predicting technical school performance, no data are yet available concerning actual job performance.

New Concepts in Measuring Abilities

The studies we have reviewed have a long history and can be considered traditional approaches to measuring abilities. Two newer approaches involving psychophysiology and information processing should be briefly noted.

By means of electroencephalographic (EEG) recordings, it has been demonstrated that if the left hemisphere of the brain is used to solve language and analytic tasks; the right hemisphere predominates in the solving of spatial and intuitive tasks. Diverse professions emphasize different cognitive styles. Such differences have been observed between high-level executives, who are thought to be more intuitive in their problem solving style, and with operations researchers, who have to construct complex mathematical models to solve difficult problems. Whatever the type of task, the executives used primarily the right hemisphere. In contrast, the operations researchers used the left hemisphere for analytical tasks and the right hemisphere for intuitive tasks.[5] It has been suggested that the difficulty in communication between the occupations may be partially explained by differing cognitive styles.

The second newer approach to measuring abilities attempts to understand the way individuals process information. The tests developed using this approach, often computer-based, are quite different from the usual paper and pencil tests of ability.[17]

The psychophysiological and the information processing approaches are limited to basic research at this time. But, we expect that understanding and measures will eventually evolve that will have practical utility.

SUMMARY

In this chapter, we have examined the nature of one kind of information used for predicting job performance: namely, that provided by tests of aptitudes and abilities. The advantages and disadvantages of the job sample approach were discussed. Descriptions were given of basic aptitude tests measuring verbal, numerical, spatial, perceptual, and psychomotor abilities. The usefulness of mechanical, clerical, and intelligence tests in predicting performance was explored. The promise of certain nonverbal tests has been confirmed. In Chapter 11, we turn to other sources of information — interests and personality.

REFERENCES

1. Barrett, G. V., R. A. Alexander, W. Burns, and D. Byer. "Predictive Validity of a Content Valid Reading Test." Unpublished manuscript, 1978.
2. Bass, B. M., and R. E. Stucki. "A Note on a Modified Purdue Pegboard," *Journal of Applied Psychology*, 35 (1951): 312–313.
3. Bennett, G. K., and M. Gelink. "Manual for the Short Employment Tests," *The Psychological Corporation*, 1956.
4. Campion, J. E. "Work Sampling for Personnel Selection," *Journal of Applied Psychology*, 56 (1972): 40–44.
5. Doktor, R., and D. M. Bloom. "Selective Lateralization of Cognitive Style

Related to Occupation as Determined by EEG Alpha Asymmetry," *Psychophysiology*, 14, no. 4 (1977): 385–387.

6. Douglas, H. R., and C. M. McCulloch. *Prediction of Success in the School of Dentistry*, vol 2, pp. 61–74. University of Minnesota: Studies Proceeding Scholastic Achievement, 1942.
7. Fleishman, E. A. "Psychomotor Selection Tests: Research and Application in the United States Air Force," *Personnel Psychology*, 9 (1956): 449–467.
8. Ghiselli, E. E. *The Validity of Occupational Aptitude Tests*. New York: Wiley, 1966.
9. Ghiselli, E. E. "The Validity of Aptitude Tests in Personnel Selection," *Personnel Psychology*, 26 (1973): 461–477.
10. Guilford, J. P. *Psychometric Methods*. New York: McGraw-Hill, 1954.
11. Guilford, J. P. *The Nature of Human Intelligence*. New York: McGraw-Hill, 1967.
12. Harman, H. H. *Final Report of Research on Assessing Human Abilities. Report ETS PR–75–20 ED 113–388*. Princeton, N. J.: Educational Testing Service, 1975.
13. McCormick, E. J., and N. B. A. Winstanley. "A Fifteen-Minute Oral Trade Test," *Personnel*, 27, no. 2 (1950): 144–146.
14. Nunnally, J. C. *Psychometric Theory*. New York: McGraw-Hill, 1978.
15. Schmidt, F. L., A. L. Greenthal, J. E. Hunter, J. G. Berner, and F. W. Seaton. "Job Sample vs. Paper-and-Pencil Trades and Technical Tests: Adverse Impact and Examinee Attitudes," *Personnel Psychology*, 30 (1977): 187–197.
16. Schoenfeldt, L. F., B. B. Schoenfeldt, S. R. Acker, and M. R. Perlson. "Content Validity Revisited: The Development of a Content-Oriented Test of Industrial Reading," *Journal of Applied Psychology*, 61 (1976): 581–588.
17. Sternberg, R. J. *Intelligence, Information Processing, and Analogical Reasoning: The Componential Analysis of Human Abilities*. Hillsdale, New Jersey: Lawrence Erlbaum Associates, 1977.
18. Sticht, T. G. *Reading for Working*. Alexandria, Virginia: Human Resources Research Organization, 1975.
19. Super, D. E., and J. O. Crites. *Appraising Vocational Fitness*. New York: Harper, 1962.
20. Uhlmann, F. W. "A Selection Test for Production Machine Operators," *Personnel Psychology*, 15 (1962): 287–293.
21. Volkin, L. "A Validation Study of Selected Test Batteries Applied to Fields of Work." Unpublished Ph.D. dissertation, University of Pittsburg, 1951.
22. Walker, W. B. "Vision and Production of Sewing Machine Operators," *Personnel Psychology*, 6 (1953): 291–295.
23. Wilbourn, J. M., N. Guinn, and S. A. Leisey. *Validation of Non-verbal Measures for Selection and Classification of Enlisted Personnel*. Personnel Research Division, Lackland Air Force Base, San Antonio, Texas, December 1976.

11 ASSESSMENT OF INTERESTS AND PERSONALITY

IN BRIEF Tests of interests, values, and personality, in addition to tests of aptitudes and abilities, are frequently used to provide information about job applicants, although opportunities for distortions and biases of various kinds may make such tests less reliable and less valid than other information sources. The importance of personal rather than ability factors for certain job categories is sufficiently great to require special care in the selection or construction of measures in this area.

Information sources other than tests are also used for assessment. They include recommendations, application blanks, peer ratings, and interviews. As with all sources of forecasting data, their utility depends on their reliability and validity. Yet certain traditional employment practices, such as interviews, continue to be used despite evidence of their lack of validity or despite the availability of less expensive, more valid techniques.

Individual differences in employee interests, values, and personal traits have relevance in understanding both the differential worth of the individual to the organization and the worth of the organization to individual employees. Again, we are faced with how many factors are of consequence. The Educational Testing Service has identified twenty-eight temperament factors, based upon individual self-reports.[35] Yet, some investigators, such as Hans Eysenck, concentrate on just two factors: introversion-extroversion and neuroticism. Others use four, six, or ten factors. It all depends on the

343

breadth of the behavioral content examined. In this chapter we will limit our concern to just those personality and interest factors most predictive of job success.

Importance of Personal Factors

The importance of personal factors (other than ability) in job success is shown by the large proportion of critical behaviors (incidents reported as examples of effective and ineffective job performance) that can be attributed to personality and interpersonal relations. The incidents have been reported for such diverse jobs as air route traffic controllers, research personnel, hourly wage earners, and dentists.[110]

When cross-validation is used, a study of architects found that interest and personality measures could reliably differentiate the creative from the more ordinary individuals. The personility traits of flexibility and self-acceptance are characteristic of creative architects, Their interests are least like those of a banker and president of a manufacturing firm.[34]

Personality traits such as conscientiousness can be added to intellectual ability measures to increase our prediction of school achievement.[105]

Interest, attitude, and personality assessment are more likely to add to the ability to forecast occupational success as the jobs under study become more complex and the job occupants have more discretion. It is also likely that the greater is the time interval between when the employees were tested and when their job performance was appraised, the more important are personality and interest factors compared with ability. At least this seems so in predicting the sales success and survival of life insurance agents.[25] Ability is significant in determining early success, but interests and personality play a more important role later on. The same is true for accountants. Personality factors increase in importance as the jobs in question involve working more with others. Thus, after two years as a staff accountant with one of the "Big 8" accounting firms, interpersonal skills with colleagues and clients become essential for continued success.

Conversely, many jobs are likely to be more satisfying to those lacking in gregarious tendencies and skills, again suggesting the importance of personality and interests but of a different kind. Here are some examples from a Bayer Process alumina plant.[84] Night shift maintenance workers are often the only representatives of their craft on duty in the whole plant; they may work alone for entire shifts. The samplers for the control laboratory make continuous rounds of the various stages of the "in line" chemical process by which alumina is produced, gathering samples for return to the laboratory' to be analyzed. It is quite possible for them to work an entire shift without having an opportunity to talk with other workers. Presumably, the interaction-oriented employee with strong needs to affiliate with others, as measured by the *Orientation Inventory* (Consulting Psychologists Press), would be dissatisfied in such isolated work.[10]

Interest in establishing, maintaining, or restoring personal relations has several dimensions. Factor analyses suggest that two fairly distinct subdivisions are required if we wish to understand what underlies an interest in working with others. Hard-sell salespersons associate with others in order to influence them. The social worker wishes to nurture interpersonal relationships to be of service to others.[94] The hard-sell salesperson wants to influence clients for the salesperson's sake; the social worker wants to influence clients for the clients' sake.

OCCUPATIONAL ADJUSTMENT   Six supervisors rated 80 unskilled workers doing individual piece work on their degree of job adjustment. Those workers who were described as poorly adjusted to their work were likely to reveal in tests many worries and annoyances. Self-disclosed irritability manifests itself in poor job adjustment.[37]

More extreme results were found in a ten-year follow-up study of disturbed war veterans. Nearly half of the sample with a service history of psychosis were unemployed at the time of the follow-up, whereas only 7 per cent of a normal control sample were out of work. Diagnosed neurotics did not fare so badly, although in comparison to a normal control sample, those with service histories of a neurosis tended to concentrate in lower-level occupations ten years afterward. They were more likely to be working in unskilled jobs and less likely to be supervisors.[71]

IDENTIFYING THE INEFFECTIVE   Complicating matters in identifying the ineffective is our need to look at the applicant's patterns of abilities and interests to determine whether they are consistent with each other. For example, job applicants of below average intelligence who want to be engineers have interests and aspirations that are out of line with their aptitudes. Despite the fact that they may have developed to a high degree the aptitudes and skills necessary for becoming carpenters, they may neither perform well nor be content as carpenters. Their personal discontent and their continuing vocational problems may also make it difficult for them to work well with others, to retain responsibility, and to withstand on-the-job stress.

Most personality inventories provide either global assessments of a cluster of neurotic items or subscales of anxiety, lack of emotional well-being, irritability, poor job adjustment, many worries, many annoyances, inability to concentrate, feelings of being disturbed, hostility, defensiveness, compulsiveness, obsessiveness, and so on. Efforts to diagnose symptoms and underlying patterns usually lead to the use of more detailed inventories, such as the *Minnesota Multiphasic Personality Inventory (MMPI)* (Psychological Corporation), more specifically designed to discriminate among different clinical populations seeking help from a counselor. A review of

346 PERSONNEL PSYCHOLOGY

the use of MMPI in industry found only a limited number of validity studies and very few relationships between test scores and job performance.[36] In addition, inclusion in it of many overly personal or offensive items about sex and religion limits its usefulness for industrial selection purposes.

It seems obvious that to account fully for the performance of employees we need to know their motivation to work at their jobs as well as their ability to do them. We need to know how much and in what ways they will be rewarded for their performance. We need also to determine what they want from their job, what they value in their work, what interests them, and what they would rather be doing. Often their success may depend at least partially on their reputation among their associates, their cooperativeness, tact, understanding, amiability, initiative, flexibility, energy level, or emotional stability.

FORECASTING OVERALL JOB SUCCESS. In a review of 113 studies in the United States, the validity of personality inventories in the selection of employees was obtained. Table 11–1 shows the results. The review summarized the correlations between relevant trait assessments and job success on those jobs for which the trait might be relevant (for example, sociability versus success as a salesperson). The average correlation between personality assessment and supervisory success was only 0.14. The average correlation was higher (but not much higher) for crafts and trades (0.29) and sales clerks (0.25) and at the low moderate level of 0.36 for salespersons.

Subsequent to this early review, a factor analysis by the Psychological Services of Pittsburgh revealed more promising results. Five motivation dimensions that could be related to successful job performance were found. The five factors were labeled as follows: *drive, achievement, status, anxiety,* and *aggression.* Data were gathered on eight samples of workers in different

Table 11–1. Weighted mean validity coefficients of personality inventories for various occupational groups.

Mean r	Total no. of cases	Total no. of r's	Occupation
.14	518	8	General supervisors
.18	6433	44	First-level supervisors
.25	1069	22	Clerks
.36	1120	8	Sales clerks
.36	927	12	Sales personnel
.24	536	5	Protective workers
.16	385	6	Service workers
.29	511	8	Trades and crafts

Adapted from Ghiselli and Barthol, "The Validity of Personality Inventories in the Selection of Employees," *Journal of Applied Psychology,* 37 (1953): 18.

occupations. Technical managers and sales personnel were highest in self-reported drive. For example, the mean drive score of the technical managers was considerably higher than the drive of hourly production workers. Each sample was separated into high- and low-criterion groups — those more and less successful. For technical managers and sales personnel, significant relationships were found between drive and the criterion.

As noted in Chapter 4, production workers had *anxiety* scores that were quite a bit above those of the salaried groups. Anxiety showed a negative relationship with job proficiency; those higher on the anxiety factor were generally less successful. (Bank officers were an exception.) Quite dramatic differences were reported in *aggression* for the criterion groups. Production workers showed a great deal of aggression compared to the other groups, and also a significant relationship with performance on the job.

The most important finding was that certain aspects of motivation are important for success in some jobs and unimportant or even maladaptive for other occupational groups. *Drive,* as a whole, appeared to be important for success in almost all occupational groups. It was somewhat more characteristic of men than women, especially in the upper end of the occupational hierarchy. In contrast, *anxiety* seemed to detract from job success and was more characteristic of those at the lower end of the occupational hierarchy. The motivational factor of *status* and *achievement* were predictive of success for some occupations, while for others they were not related to success. Middle and top managers have also been differentiated as to personality variables. Top managers have been found to be higher on measured general activity, sociability, and emotional stability.[32]

USEFULNESS OF PERSONAL ASSESSMENT   Personality, interests, and values, then, do affect behavior on the job. But we need to understand what particular aspects of job performance are accounted for by specific personal factors. Personality and interest assessments provide ways of evaluating what may be important dimensions in understanding given job behaviors. This understanding, if developed, may help us to design better individual and supervisory training, devise better systems of management, do a better job of counseling employees, assembling teams, suggesting transfer of individuals to more compatible kinds of work, and so on. Significant personal variables in work behavior are persistence, energy, flexibility, orderliness, originality, initiative, and task orientation. Dimensions for understanding relations with others are equally important for the organization, and these include sociability, status attitudes, conformist tendencies, consideration for others, and aggressive needs.

SITUATIONAL EFFECTS   A more complete understanding of personal factors involved in job performance requires a situational or contextual analysis. So far, we have concentrated on consistent individual differences, that is, on the fact that individuals, as such, make a difference, regardless of the situation. Some persons tend to be task-oriented in no matter what situation they find themselves — doing their daily chores, playing poker, or planning a reading assignment; others tend to avoid working hard whenever they can. Nevertheless, situations make a difference regardless of individuals. Almost anyone will show persistence on a dull task for a million dollar gain and a high probability of success. And in the absence of extrinsic rewards or punishments, a high probability of failure on a dull task will stop almost anyone from working hard.

It is more useful in the long run to search for the *construct validity* of personality tests, finding out the complex of observable behaviors of which the test is a sample, among what cultural and social groups the test tends to discriminate, and what other measurements and individual differences correlate with it. For instance, we become satisfied that task orientation as assessed by the *Orientation Inventory* [11] does measure persistence if we find that those who volunteer for work score higher on the task orientation scale and persist longer voluntarily on uncompleted assignments, that mountain climbers and design engineers score higher than the general public, or that college students tend to increase in scores with increasing amounts of age and education. In many instances, ultimate understanding would be demonstrated when we are able to induce changes in behavior in the dimension in question resulting in corresponding changes in test scores. Such, for example, seems to have been done by McClelland and Winter with a projective test of need for achievement.[61] They instituted a training program resulting in greater efforts by trainees to achieve, as well as increased need achievement scores on their test (see Chapter 18).

PERSONAL ASSESSMENT

Approaches

We can assess the applicants' or employees' personal tendencies, interests, and values in one of several ways. We can ask them for descriptions in their own words or from using a checklist of terms. Alternatively, we can ask other people who are acquainted with the examinees of interest to do the same, using specially prepared recommendation blanks or telephone interviews. We can observe the actions of the examinees in standard social and work situations and make judgments based on what we observe. We can ask examinees to describe their work history, education history, avocational experiences, and personal background either in an oral interview or on a specially prepared biographical information blank. We can use psychological tests and inventories that, as far as the examinee is concerned, may be either structured or unstructured, direct or indirect, as shown in Figure 11-1.

	Direct	Indirect
Structured	Inventories of questions, statements, or choices (examinee selects appropriate response from set provided)	Error choice or information tests (examinee estimates some statistic or value; direction and amount of error of the estimate is used as assessment)
Unstructured	Incomplete sentences (examinee completes sentence of which only the first few words are given, such as "I like people who . . .")	Thematic Apperception Test (examinee makes up story in response to ambiguous sketch) Rorschach Ink Blot

Figure 11–1. Kinds of psychological tests. From Kuder Preference Record, Vocational. Copyright 1942, by G. Frederic Kuder. Reprinted by permission of the publisher, Science Research Associates, Inc.

The advantages and disadvantages of these different approaches will be discussed as we proceed through this chapter.

The Fakability Problem

Unfortunately, it is one thing to observe on the job that personality, interest, and motivation factors are important in understanding differences in the adequacy of employee performance; it is another to assess successfully in advance such differences as they may affect an industrial setting, particularly when the examinees are applicants answering the tests in a way that they figure will land them the job. The more educated they are, the more likely they will be to try to influence test scores and to succeed.[39] Or if the examinees are employees being tested for a supervisory position or a transfer, they are again likely to try to look as good as possible. The ability of job applicants to influence test scores was empirically tested with 400 male applicants for the job of bus conductor.[38] A questionnaire was designed, using items from personality and clinical questionnaires. As part of the selection procedure, the questionnaire was administered to 200 men *before* they were told they had been selected for the position, while another 200 men were tested *after* they obtained the job. There was a definite difference in responses under the two conditions. For example, more emotional maladjustment was reported by respondents if tested after rather than before they obtained the job. Using the questionnaire's standard of 10 or more, 12 per cent of the research sample was "probably maladjusted." In contrast, only 1.5 per cent of the job applicants could be classified as "probably maladjusted." It was clear that job applicants do put their best foot forward and are unlikely to admit personality defects.

Even projective tests can be distorted. When test results were part of an appraisal of them by a consulting firm, 60 engineers and accountants gave significantly less self-punishing responses on the *Rozensweig Picture-Frustration Test* (a collection of cartoons, the verbal parts of which are to be completed by examinees) than did 154 similar examinees who took the test for a research survey.[57] Minimally, applicants can complete this test by trying to imitate someone they knew who was successful or had obtained a promotion. They may be wrong, but still their responses will reflect something other than a self-description. The procedure might have some validity as a projective device if every applicant completed the blank with the same effect in mind.

Less intention to distort the results may be present when examinees are tested for what they see as of value to themselves. For example, they will respond more honestly if the test results are used for their own counseling, for determining consistent tendencies about themselves, for promoting self-understanding so they can do a better or more satisfying job, identifying others with whom they would be more compatible, or for identifying problem areas for management (i.e., a department with a poor safety record might have a concentration of high risk-takers).

ATTEMPTS TO REDUCE FAKING   Psychologists have searched for less fakable assessment methods. Forced-choice personality inventories have been tried with some success. They are based on the same construction technique as the forced-choice rating described in Chapter 8, except that the raters rate themselves. Projective tests like sentence completion ones are more difficult to fake. But even empirically keyed biographical information blanks are susceptible to faking, however factual in nature the items may be.

Faking is lowered when the instructions indicate there is a lie-detection scale.[86] Various situational tests also can lower faking because candidates are placed in actual problem situations that they have to solve. But it would appear that the only tests reasonably free from the possibility of systematic distortion by examinees are those which look like aptitude or achievement measurements but actually assess personality factors. For instance, Kipnis developed a *Hand Skills Test* that seemed to examinees to be just that but actually was a test to measure persistence on tiring tasks.[47] Scores among men with low aptitude correlate between 0.26 and 0.47 with various appraisals of their merit and willingness to work and get along with fellow workers.

TEST METHODS FOR ASSESSING PERSONALITY FACTORS

There are over 300 published personality tests in print. So here we can only hope to call attention to a few of the most widely used, or to those most representative of a class of similar tests.

Direct, Structured Tests

As noted in Figure 11-1, direct tests are highly structured for the examinee. They confront examinees with direct questions about their personal tendencies. The typical personality inventory may ask the examinee to respond "yes," "?," or "no" to each of a set of statements such as: "I take life very seriously" or "I often feel grouchy" or "I like to entertain guests." The typical interest inventory would ask, "Would you like to be an actor?" "Do you like to garden?" The typical inventory of values would ask a direct question about how important a particular need, motive, goal, or value is to the examinee, such as, "How important is it to you to contribute to charity?"

Scoring is completely structured for the examiner. Responding one way rather than another adds to an examinee's score for a total cluster of highly correlated items. The clustering is based on previous factor analyses or item analyses. Thus, saying, "yes" to "I like to entertain guests" adds a point to an examinee's overall sociability score.

Sometimes each test item is keyed to discriminate among previously identified successful, contrasted with unsuccessful, employees. Saying "yes" might add to one's likelihood of matching the pattern of responses of successful rather than unsuccessful employees. Or keys may be developed to discriminate between, say, successful accountants and the general public.

An example of a widely researched factored personality inventory is the *16 PF Questionnaire* (IPAT), a list of 187 items that can be answered in less than 50 minutes. The 16 primary factors are assessments of such traits as outgoingness, emotional stability, assertiveness, enthusiasm, ventursomeness, and self-sufficiency. Norms on the 16 PF are available for a variety of occupations: accountants, administrators, advertising personnel, aircraft engineering apprentices, business executives, chemists, clerks, cooks, and kitchen help.

THE PERSONALITY RESEARCH FORM   This is one of the most carefully developed personality inventories.[42] Specific constructs that describe the normal person were the starting point for construction of the test. Twenty scales measure constructs such as achievement, affiliation, aggression, and endurance. The scales have been found to differentiate successful from unsuccessful trainees. The successful trainees expressed a higher achievement orientation before training. There are also occupational differences, based on personality characteristics: for example, successful radio operators in remote locations report a stronger desire for autonomy than clerical workers. Successful clerical workers expressed a need to give assistance to people before training.[89]

FORCED-CHOICE FORMAT   Because responses by job applicants can be distorted so easily, many of the newer widely used personality questionnaires now require the examinee to choose among equally desirable alternative descriptions of himself/herself. Forced-choice formats are employed, similar to those used in forced-choice merit ratings described in Chapter 8.

Forced-choice assessments include the *Edwards Personal Profile* (Psychological Corporation), the *Gordon Personal Profile* (Psychological Corporation), and the *Gordon Survey of Interpersonal Values* (Science Research Associates). Unfortunately, the problem of distortion has not been completely solved by forced-choice formats. Examinees can always take a chance and try to describe an ideal candidate rather than themselves. Thus, sales applicants tend to describe themselves more favorably on the *Gordon Personal Profile*[9] and on the *Edwards Personal Preference Schedule*[48] both forced-choice instruments, than do already employed salespersons in the same company.

MEASURES BASED ON STYLE OF RESPONSE   Another approach depends on assessing the consistent response tendencies of the examinee, regardless of the contents of the questions directed to him. For example, a *social acquiescence* scale has been developed, which scores the extent to which the examinee agrees with 56 proverbs, many of which have mutually incompatible content. Acquiescers tend to be "outward-oriented, insensitive, non-intellectual, and socially uncritical according to correlations between the social acquiescence scale and other tests."[8] Similarly, one can calculate the extent to which an examinee checks as true highly improbable but socially desirable statements about himself, such as "I never deliberately try to hurt people's feelings."[20]

Unstructured Tests

Personality tests can be made less structured for the examinee although remaining almost as structured for the examiner. Instead of limiting responses to "yes," "?," or "no," the examinee may be asked to complete the following sentences expressing his true feelings: "I take life . . ."; "I often feel . . ."; "I like to . . ." The responses can be reliably scored by following a manual of scoring instructions to yield an overall score on personal adjustment. Distortion of results seems less of a problem. Again, custom keys can be developed.

MINER SENTENCE COMPLETION SCALE   For instance, standardized scoring procedures make it possible for examiner variations to be reduced. Such a procedure was developed for the Miner Sentence Completion Scale.[70] With it, it is now possible to codify responses reliably for such constructs as desire to compete and attitudes toward authority.

The Miner Sentence Completion Scale has predicted managerial performance in a number of organizations. Both managers and sales applicants have considerably more motivation to manage than students in general. For sales personnel, motivation to manage is developed before entering a firm and is not usually modified by experience in the organization.[5] Research over the years with the instrument supports Miner's contention that managerial motivation is decreasing in the United States.[69] Presentday management students have been found to be more negative toward authority, less assertive, less competitive, and less responsible than students in former years. Miner believes that this shift will eventually result in a crisis, due to the estimated 35 per cent drop in the motivation to manage. Organizations in the 1980s won't have enough management talent (as Miner defines it).

A new source of individuals with the motivation to manage may be found in women and minority group members.[68] The evidence indicates that for both men and women, motivational patterns relate to success as a manager.

FUTURE AUTOBIOGRAPHY   A variant of the sentence completion test involves asking the applicants to write about their goals in life. The *future autobiography* is a relatively new technique, where respondents are asked to write about what they will be doing five years from now. They are requested to include "vocations, avocations, goals, jobs, interest, and concerns." These autobiographies are then scored to measure the degree to which respondents can shape their future in detail and take personal responsibility for outcomes. A predictive validity study showed that scores on *agency*, the feeling of personal control of the future, were related to sales managers' judgment of performance of sales personnel.[100]

THEMATIC APPERCEPTION TEST   Less structured for examinees and the examiner alike and less direct is the *Thematic Apperception Test (TAT)* (Harvard University Press). The TAT comprises a set of sketches into which examinees must project themselves, by telling a story about what happened before a sketch was made, what is now happening, and what will happen. It is assumed that in telling these stories in the Thematic Apperception Test, the examinees reveal consistent themes in their strivings and fantasies — and therefore their needs. The themes can be scored reliably after suitable training of the scorers, yielding assessments of the needs of examinees for *achievement, affiliation, power,* and so forth, with less likelihood of conscious distortion by the typical examinee.

A popular idea is that women have a *fear of success*.[96] Horner developed the concept based on analysis of TAT type stories.[47] Fear of success refers to the ambivalent feelings about the consequences of being a successful woman. Although Horner believed that many women were motivated to avoid success, more recent research has not supported this concept possibly because women are changing.[53, 112]

Both projective tests and more objective personality measures show little difference between male and female executives.[73]

RORSCHACH   The most widely used projective instrument is the *Rorschach*.[33] Unfortunately, results from the ink blot test when applied to the industrial situation have been uniformly negative. Even variations of the test which make it more standardized, such as the multiple choice Rorschach, have failed to obtain positive results. This is not surprising, since the *Rorschach* was developed as a clinical instrument and was not designed to differentiate among essentially normal adults.

PICTURE ARRANGEMENT TEST   One of the more successful projectives for industrial use is the *Tompkins-Horn Picture Arrangement Test (PAT)* (Springer Publishing). The test was designed with more than half of each set of three pictures depicting interpersonal relations in a work setting. The subject is requested to show the order of each set of three pictures so "they make sense" and write a sentence for each picture to tell a story. Consistently positive results have been obtained in the selection of both sales personnel and tabulating equipment operators. Miner found correlations ranging from 0.58 to 0.82, using supervisor ratings as the criteria.[65, 66, 67] He believed that highly significant results with tabulating operators might be due to the routine, repetitive nature of the job, where personality factors largely determined success after minimal levels of manual dexterity and intelligence had been met.

While one can be somewhat discouraged about the use of projective techniques and disguised personality tests, there is also a basis for optimism. First, there has seldom been adequate specification of job requirements in terms of personality required for success.[46] It is clear that different occupations require different personality patterns, and the pattern for success as a librarian is not the same as that required of a door-to-door salesperson. Second, the personality pattern for some occupations (like welding) may account for very little in terms of successful performance and it may count a great deal in others (like selling). Third, the organizational climate in which one works may detemine whether a particular personality will help or hinder one's success in that organization. Fourth, there is consistent evidence that certain projective tests do have validity, namely the PAT and TAT scored for such measures as *need for achievement* and *need for power*. Last, while hundreds of validation studies have been conducted with other types of tests, relatively few have been reported with projective tests. Further refining and development can be expected.

Illustrative of this is the line of investigation dealing with the *need for achievement*. At least 22 direct and indirect methods have been employed to measure the construct, but projectives have played a major role. And while outcomes depend on which method of measurement is used,[26] a body of evidence has been amassed indicating that *need for achievement* is an important construct for understanding work performance.

Need for Achievement

The *need for achievement* is a fairly consistent trait from early childhood to adult life. Mothers' attitudes seem particularly important in the development of the child's need for achievement. Mothers of children with a compelling need for achievement set high standards for them, expecting them to become self-reliant and to master at an early age such tasks as making friends, doing well in competition, and, in general, working hard. On the other hand, mothers of children possessing a low need for achievement tend to restrict their children's activities and discourage their decision making.[59]

High need for achievement in adults results in a variety of behaviors of consequence to their success or failure at different kinds of tasks. In general, such individuals prefer to work on tasks of moderate difficulty. They prefer not to take big risks, while their opposites tend to take no risk or to play the long shots. In comparisons of managers with staff specialists at General Electric, the managers scored higher in need for achievement, and in preference for intermediate over high or low odds in risk-taking situations.[64] Those with higher need for achievement tend to be more realistic in their expectations and rely more on their past performance to estimate chances of success. They are more *self-confident* because they have learned that they can control situations by their own efforts.

Individuals with high achievement motivation work longer and harder than others, but only at tasks that will give them some feeling of accomplishment. If the task is too easy, or routine, they will do no better than those with a low need for achievement. Persons with high achievement needs will work just as hard for group goals as for individual ones. Public recognition is not as important as the satisfaction of having initiated the action. Those high in need for achievement will strive to accomplish the job, and are far less concerned with socializing. They will choose an expert rather than friends to help them with a task, whereas those whose primary need is for *affiliation* will turn first to friends for help. High "need achievers" are interested in knowing how well they are doing the job. These individuals value money not so much for its own sake as for its value as a measure of achievement; it serves as an index by which they can compare themselves with others. For such people the introduction of money as an incentive will make them work no harder, whereas for those with lower achievement needs it acts as a spur to performance.

The need for achievement affects occupational choice. College sophomores were tested in need for achievement, and 11 years later these scores were compared with their occupational choice. Among those who were classified as being in business-entrepreneurial occupations, 83 percent had been high in need for achievement, while only 21 percent of those in the business-non-entrepreneurial classification had been previously judged high in need achievement.[60]

In American Telephone and Telegraph, a significant contribution was made to the prediction of managerial success from need for *achievement* as measured by the TAT.[31] But, more successful executives, also have been found to be higher in both need for *power* and need for *achievement*.[21] The most successful entrepreneurs, who have started and managed the fastest growing technical companies, are charaterized as having a high need for achievement and a moderate need for power.[104] Successful managers in general usually have at least a moderate need for power along with the high need for achievement.[6]

SITUATIONAL EFFECTS   Two firms were chosen by a knowledgeable industrial psychologist. One firm was achievement-oriented and successful in its ventures. The second firm was oriented toward power relationships and was more conservative and less successful in the marketplace. It was hypothesized that the executive group in any firm would have high scores on those motives that characterized the orientation of the firm as a whole. Studies of executives of the two firms confirmed the fact that the top executives of the achievement-oriented firm were higher in need for achievement and lower in need for power than those in the power-oriented firm. There was positive correlation between executives' need for achievement and their advancement in the achievement-oriented firm, but a negative correlation between need for achievement and advancement in the power-oriented firm. This meant that individuals with high need for achievement would advance in the achievement-oriented firm but would find their personality a drawback for advancement in the power-oriented firm. Conversely, the individuals with high power needs were promoted in the power-oriented firm but not in the achievement-oriented business.[2]

ASSESSMENT OF VOCATIONAL INTERESTS

Measures of Interest

The *Strong-Campbell Interest Inventory*, formerly the Strong Vocational Interest Blank (Stanford University Press), is the most widely researched interest inventory.[15] For over fifty years it has been the source of much information about the development and stability of interests.

The Strong-Cambell Inventory requires examinees to indicate whether they like, are indifferent to, or dislike certain school subjects, amusement, activities, peculiarities of people, vocational activities, well-known persons, clubs, and self-estimates. The examinee's response pattern is then compared with the patterns of successful persons in each of 46 different professional and skilled occupations. Factor scoring now is possible also. Scoring has been simplified so that examinees may determine from computer printouts in which occupational interest areas they most likely lie. These are biological science, physical science, technical, social welfare, business detail (C. P. A.), business contact (salesperson), and linguistic (lawyer). Many other item clusterings have been used to generate a variety of additional scores. Some border on personality assessments. For instance, the Strong-Campbell inventory can now distinguish among respondents who seek adventure and those who don't. The computer printouts also note books and experts with whom to consult depending on one's interest profile.

A forerunner of forced-choice inventories was the *Kuder Preference Record* (Science Research Associates), another popular interest assessment. Examinees are presented with triads of activities such as those shown as examples in Figure 11–2. They must choose the activity they would like most and the activity they would like least. Kuder scales were constructed originally by internal consistency item analysis — clustering together those responses which correlated highly with each other and a particular scale total. Preferences for activities in each of ten areas are calculated: outdoors, mechanical, computational, scientific, persuasive, artistic, literary, musical, social service, and clerical.

Stability of Interests

Interest patterns for adults tend to be remarkably stable over long periods of time. For instance, employees in 48 Minnesota banks were administered the *Strong Vocational Interest Bank* (SVIB) in 1934. Their average age

Figure 11–2. Example triads from the Kuder Preference Record. (Adapted from Kuder, *Kuder Preference Record: Personal.* Chicago, Illinois: Science Research Associates, 1959).

	Check Most and Least Liked Activity	
	Most	Least
Visit an art gallery	——	——
Browse in a library	——	——
Visit a museum	——	——
Collect autographs	——	——
Collect coins	——	——
Collect butterflies	——	——

was 38. They were reexamined 30 years later in 1964, when they were 68 years old on the average. Their overall patterns of interests — matching those of larger samples of bankers, real estate sales personnel, office managers, and accountants—were strikingly stable despite the 30-year interval.[16]

In the same way, the preferences as a whole of 103 bankers, in 1964, differed little from those of a comparable sample of 103 who had been tested in 1934, despite the changes that had occurred meanwhile in banking practices. Similarly, a median correlation of 0.80 was found for two administrations of the SVIB taken 10 years apart by 109 men for the various scales of the instrument.[82]

Interests Predict Job Choice

Although interests play some role in job success, they play a more important one in choosing a job and in satisfaction on the job. For example, while college achievement was forecast more accurately by high school grades and achievement tests, interest inventories more accurately forecast whether students chose to concentrate in medicine, business, education, or journalism.[12] On 16 specific occupational scales of the Strong Vocational Interest Blank, for an examinee with an "A" score (a close match with the stated preferences of a large sample of men in a designated occupation), the odds were 3.5 to 1 that he or she would be employed in that occupation 18 years after completing the SVIB. Conversely, for an examinee with a "C" score (a poor match), the odds were 5 to 1 that he or she would *not* be employed in that vocation.[50]

For 117 men 7 to 9 years after taking the *Kuder Preference Record,* men who now worked in a particular interest area of the nine areas assessed by the Kuder were more likely to have registered a high degree of interest in that particular area when tested earlier. For instance, men who as high school boys expressed a high degree of mechanical interest 7 to 9 years afterward were more likely to be working in mechanical occupations.[52]

Many more follow-up analyses of SVIB scores and future careers all point to the same conclusions. College graduates are much more likely to be pursuing a career for many years after graduation consistent with their SVIB scores obtained when they were freshmen. They are less likely to transfer out of a career field consistent with their SVIB scores. They are less likely to be in a field in which, as freshmen, they had indicated little interest on the SVIB.[93] Comparable scales have been developed and validated for women.

Interests and Abilities

Individuals often possess the aptitudes for many different types of work. Their choice of an occupation, then, will rest mainly on their interest and on

Table 11-2. Relation between interests and abilities.

Correlation	Kuder interest	Appropriate test of ability
.44	Mechanical	Survey of Mechanical Insight
.24	Computational	Stanford Arithmetic Test
.33	Scientific	Science Content Test
.29	Artistic	Meier Art Judgment Test
.47	Literary	English and Literature Achievement Test
.21	Musical	Seashore Musical Talent Test
.07	Clerical	Minnesota Clerical Test

Adapted from Wesley, Corey, and Stewart, "The Intra-Individual Relationship Between Interest and Ability," *Journal of Applied Psychology,* 34 (1950): 193–197.

opportunities for employment in what they choose to do. But interests are not independent of aptitudes. It is not unreasonable to expect that strong interests in a given area increase attention and learning of skills for work in that area. At the same time, it seems likely that aptitude for learning how to cope successfully with such work promotes interest in it.

Investigators correlated the Kuder Perference Record scores and appropriate tests of ability of 115 to 132 college students.[109] Correlations are shown in Table 11–2, generally supporting the positive association between interests and abilities.

NONTEST METHODS FOR ASSESSING PERSONAL FACTORS

Various nontest methods of assessment are available. As we will see, some offer freedom from distortion; several offer greater validity than psychological tests of nonability factors. They include reference checks, application blanks, and interviews.

Recommendations and Reference Checks

Checking work references, school references, and personal references of job applicants is a common practice. Probably 90 per cent of all organizations use some form of reference checking.[51] Both telephone and written letters of reference are used in the employment process. Privacy legislation may alter the practice and result in less candid references (discussed in Chapter 18).

LIKELY DISTORTION   To a considerable degree, recommenders face a conflict of interests that may distort the opinions they submit. On the one hand, they may feel happy to see a former colleague or subordinate leave their current firm or agency; furthermore, they may feel guilt as a consequence and want to assist in the rapid employment of the recommendee in a new job. They may emphasize favorable points about the applicant, omitting the unfavorable. Conversely, there is pressure to be fully honest if their own reputations as recommenders will suffer should they provide an unwarranted favorable portrait of the recommendee. They may also see themselves dependent in the future in their own personal operations on the recommendations of those to whom they are now giving information. At the same time, *examiners* also may err in failing to check on certain matters, or overweigh others, as well as vary greatly in what they listen to or look for each time they run a check on an applicant.

STANDARDIZATION To promote examiner and reference reliability or consistency, as well as to provide comparable items for all applicants that can be tested for predictive validity, it becomes useful to develop standardized methods of gathering information from references who have known the applicant elsewhere. Typical questions in a standardized recommendation checklist in the form of letters or standardized telephone interview forms include reasons for leaving, willingness to rehire, attendance, and work habits. Each of these forms can provide data for developing valid keys for forecasting success in designated jobs. Unfortunately, little research has been reported. We do know that the mental agility, vigor, cooperation, and dependability can be derived from the adjectives used to describe the applicant in letters of reference.[80] Also, we have learned from research that when a person is disliked the letter of reference tends to be shorter.[111]

EXAMPLE Mosel and Goheen had only modest success when they attempted to validate a mailed, standardized recommendation blank, the Employee Recommendation Questionnaire.[74] Only 56 per cent were usable; 23 per cent were returned incomplete; 18 per cent failed to return the blanks; and 3 per cent returned them unopened. Nevertheless, for 1,193 Civil Service employees in skilled operations, validities ranging from 0.21 to 0.29 were obtained between mean recommendation scores of employees and their rated performance on the job.

Acquaintances of recommendees in professional and skilled occupations were seen to give the most favorable evaluations when they used the Employee Recommendation Questionnaire. Former subordinates gave the next most favorable recommendations. Still less favorable were those from former co-workers, while the least favorable came from former employers.[74,75]

Application Blanks and Biographical Information Blanks

Almost every prospective employer from an organization of any size asks applicants to complete a standard application form. Usually, applicants are asked to answer some questions about their educational background, previous work history, and personal affairs.

For over half a century, successful assessment procedures have been obtained from treating many of the responses to an application blank as test responses.[30, 18] They can be correlated with subsequent job performance. Responses that discriminate between those applicants who are and who are not successful after they are employed can be the basis of scoring keys to be used with future applicants. The scoring keys can be cross-validated with new samples of applicants.

EXAMPLE   The application blank responses of 60 women office employees who had subsequently quit within one year of employment were compared with those who had remained two years or more. The responses of the shorter- and longer-tenure employees differed. Older women who lived within the city with older children were more likely to remain.[27] A scoring key was constructed and applied to the responses of a new sample of 85 clerks. A correlation of 0.57 was obtained between application blank scores and subsequent tendency to quit or remain on the job. Seventy-eight per cent of the short-termers could have been eliminated, at the expense of losing only 32 percent of the long-termers, had the application blanks been used to screen clerks in advance.

The biographical information blank (BIB) is a more extensive autobiographical self-report than the usual application blank. In essence, it is an interview with the applicant where all questions are asked in the same way of every examinee and the examinees respond by choosing among multiple alternatives. The predictive validity of the different alternatives can be discovered and the responses are free from the usual biases of human interviewers' interpretations.

A catalog of Life History Items lists possible items that can be tried covering various areas of the applicant's life.[78] The catalog makes it possible for BIB researchers to use the same standard forms of questions to provide the pooling of experience with the validity and utility of the different items. A typical BIB item from the catalog of Life History Items is shown in Figure 11-3.

ADVANTAGES   Numerous other advantages can be cited for the application blank and/or the biographical information blank as an assessment device:

Figure 11-3. Typical biographical item.

Which of the following is most likely to make you feel most uncomfortable or unhappy?
1. Having a friend not speak to you.
2. Making a mistake in your work.
3. Being laughed at when some circumstances make you look silly.
4. Having to introduce yourself to someone you don't know.

1. Applicants are relatively unlikely to falsify factual items and BIB responses, in contrast to what they have been found to do on interest and personality inventories. For example, Cascio found very accurate responses on 17 BIB items completed by police officers. A check of the weekly wages of 385 currently unemployed U. S. Employment Service clients against what their former employers said they had earned found correlations of 0.90 to 0.93 between the reports of the applicants and those of their former employers.[44] A correlation of 0.98 was found for how long they said they had worked and what their employer reported. There was 94 to 96 per cent agreement about the applicants' job duties.

2. The BIB is an inexpensive exploratory device. If an item reveals that previous shop work in school is predictive of the success of an industrial salesperson, then it may suggest trying out a mechanical interest and/or a mechanical ability test in the selection procedure.

3. The BIB has what is probably the best overall record for predictive validity of any nonintellectual assessment technique. Thus, Exxon studies obtained an impressive array of validity predictors from empirically constructed BIB keys. A median validity above 0.40 was obtained in 9 applications of BIB for predicting criteria of success as skilled craftspersons. Future success as manager was forecast by BIB keys with a median validity of 0.37 in 15 studies. The validities ranged from 0.14 to 0.64. Validities ranging from 0.30 to 0.60 have been found when BIB keys have been constructed to predict research creativity and competence.[90,14] In all, generally useful outcomes have been revealed in 60 reports of the use of BIB for selecting sales personnel, forecasting turnover, and predicting success as a supervisor or manager.[78] In comparison with other predictors, BIB items have superior validity.[4]

4. The BIB had validity stemming from the well-substantiated evidence that "what persons will do in the future is best predicted from what they have done in the past".[78] Life history items are good predictors of future criteria because they often contain all the elements of consequence to the criterion.[22] For example, rank in a high school class is one of the best predictors of grades in college. The intelligence, motivation, and study habits required to achieve high grades in college are equally present in high school, so high school performance is a good predictor of college performance. The correlation is usually near 0.50.

WHAT IS ASSESSED BY APPLICATION AND BIB ITEMS   Many studies of the predictive value of answers to application blank questions have focused on discrimination among employees who would quit versus those who would remain on the job.[98,72,27] These studies have shown that employees who are older, married, and have dependents at the time of employment are more likely to remain for longer periods of time. Average tenure on jobs also is often predictive of tenure on a current job.[18,71]

Other items found associated with subsequent tenure on a job include distance from home to work, differential between expected salary and salary received, unavoidable reasons for leaving last job, and source of reference to the company.[27,71,92,108] The successful performance of shop employees, of sales personnel, and of assistant district sales supervisors has been forecast by such application blank items as marital status, area of residence, organizational memberships, and special education.[45,88]

WHICH ITEMS FORECAST SUCCESS   In reviewing the published results, England was able to list 86 personal history items that had been found predictive of subsequent job success.[24] He was also able to note the extent to which items predicted success in one or more of the following fields of work: salespersons, production employees, clerical employees, sales clerks, and plantwide employee groups such as maintenance mechanics. Thus, club memberships predict sales success, while character of residence related to success as a production employee.

As seen in Table 11-3, age was a predictive item in all five occupational areas. Marital status and education were almost as widely valid.

DYNAMIC APPROACHES   The way applicants view the application process, or what seeking the job means for them, may provide clues to their future performance. For instance, unpublished research shown in Table 11-4 suggests that those applicants who become better sales personnel say it is all right to contact their current employer for references. Those applicants

Table 11-3. Generality of item predictions across occupational areas.

Items that proved predictive in—	Items
All five occupational areas	Age
Four occupational areas	Marital status
Three occupational areas	Education, previous occupations
Two occupational areas	Number of dependents, location of residence, occupation of father, previous selling experience, tenure on previous jobs, club memberships
One occupational area	Time lost from previous jobs, domicile, birthplace, major field of study — high school, college grades, previous salary earned, possession of specific skills, amount of life insurance carried, hobbies, relatives or acquaintances working for company and manner of filling out application blank.

Adapted from England, *Development and Use of Weighted Application Blanks*. Dubuque, Iowa: Wm. C. Brown Company, Publishers, 1961, p. 48.

Table 11–4. Response to the dynamic application item, "Is it all right to contact your employer?"

| Response on application | Subsequent performance record | | | |
| | Grocery products sales personnel | | Industrial products sales personnel | |
	Above 50th percentile in merit	Below 50th percentile or discharged	Above 50th percentile in merit	Below 50th percentile or discharged
Unqualified yes	48%	7%	73%	21%
Qualified yes; yes, but . . .; no	52%	93%	27%	79%

From unpublished research by B. M. Bass with Wesson Oil sales personnel.

who make poorer sales personnel according to subsequent merit ratings are reluctant to have their current boss contacted. In the same way, better prospects say they cannot begin work for two weeks; poorer prospects are available immediately.

POTENTIAL UNFAIRNESS OF BIOGRAPHICAL INFORMATION   As we discussed in Chapter 9, one model of personnel selection was probability of success based on *any* characteristic that was related to job success. As you recall the research on biographical information in this chapter, you will note that many of the successful predictions were "hard" verifiable items such as age, marital status and occupation of father. Recently, Owens has stated that since only items are used that have an empirical relationship to job success, "there can be no justified complaints of willful discrimination against minority groups." [77] It is our contention that many of these "hard" items do discriminate against various groups and need to be avoided.

Age, for example, is a convenient measure only for some psychological construct that is age-related. Therefore, in our judgment, considering current law, most "hard" biographical items should be avoided for selection purposes.[5,79]

For example, in a study of over 20,000 sales personnel, the biographical information provided by teen-age respondents formed the basis for predictions of sales success. Those items that indicated a middle-class background, such as "own a bicycle," "have a telephone," and "receive a newspaper," predicted sales success.[3] Yet such biographical items, while valid, would discriminate against those from lower socioeconomic backgrounds and against some minority groups.

Only one study using biographical information has specifically shown so far that it can be valid for predicting turnover for both minority and nonminority clerical personnel.[17]

Caution is indicated.

THE INTERVIEW

Almost all organizations use some type of employment interview. While many interviews are formal, structured affairs with standardized questions, most are informal, varying in content, time, and procedure. Who does the interviewing and how it is done differs from day to day, despite the fact that a half century of research has shown that the informal, unstandardized interview often has little or no reliability or validity. When the objectives of the interview are vague and no systematic pattern of questions is followed, reliability of assessment is likely to be low. Such an interview may have value for the applicants who learn what will be expected of them on the job, and it may give the interviewer a feeling of security to see the applicants before deciding to hire one, but the predictive value of the interview will be nil.

Problems with Interviewing

In less structured interviews, when, what, and how questions are asked varies from one interview to the next, and from one interviewer to the next. Different assessments of the applicants often are due more to the interview and the interviewer than to the applicant. For example, in those interviews where the interviewer does a lot more of the talking, and there is less silence, the applicant is more likely to be accepted for the job.[1]

THE ILLUSION OF VALIDITY   The unwarranted confidence that interviewers have in their predictions has been labeled the *illusion of validity*.[101]

It occurs because a good fit is perceived between a predicted outcome (she will be a good salesperson) and the input information (she is sociable). In this case, the interviewer's stereotype of a good salesperson (being sociable) matches the perceived personality of the interviewee (sociable). The interviewer's confidence in the interviewee's superior job performance is based on the congruence between the interviewer's stereotype of a good salesperson and the interviewer's judgment that the interviewee has the stereotype attribute. Thus, from a series of studies of such decisions by Canadian Army personnel interviewers, Webster concluded that interviewers tend to develop their own stereotypes of a good applicant, and then accept those applicants who subsequently match their stereotype.[106] It is interesting to note that the more information the interviewer obtains reinforcing the impression that the interviewee is sociable, the more confident the interviewer becomes that the prediction of success for the interviewee in sales is warranted.

The actual predictive validity of the interview is based on two questions. First, is the stereotype of the successful salesperson (being sociable) accurate, or is another attribute, such as being aggressive, the important trait. Second, if the stereotype is accurate, can the interviewer accurately assess the trait? If the stereotype is accurate and the interviewer can assess the relevant trait, then predictions will be valid.

SIMILARITY AND CONTRAST   When interviewing an applicant for a job, people can make a number of other errors that bias overall judgments. One of these potential effects is a *similar-to-me* effect. This occurs when interviewers judge applicants more favorably if they are similar to the interviewers on a variety of factors, such as attitude toward current events, social issues, marriage, and children, or if the applicants have a similar background in education, place of birth, and so on. Interviewers' predictions about an applicant are biased by what interviewers think of themselves, assumptions they make about their similarity to the applicant, as well as actual similarity to the applicant in the characteristics about which the interviewer is trying to make predictions.[95]

Another common error is that of *halo* (previously discussed in Chapter 7) where the interviewer has an overall good or bad impression of the applicant.

Then there is the *contrast effect,* which occurs when the rater interviews a highly qualified applicant for a position and then interviews an average applicant. When this occurs, the contrast is so strong that the average applicant is usually given a relatively low rating. Conversely, if the interviewer evaluates an applicant with very low qualifications and then an applicant with average qualifications, the applicant with the average qualifications may be rated higher than normal.

Another common error is overweighting the importance of *first impressions.* A judgment may be made too quickly. The initial impressions outweigh the information obtained from the rest of the interview. Biases may form early during the interview. Interviewers may be prepared to make their decisions after only four minutes of interaction.[91] As interviewers commit themselves to accept or reject the applicant, they become more likely to react suddenly and radically to a new piece of information that upsets their position. Unfavorable information about the applicant will affect interviewers to a greater extent than favorable information.[13]

PUFFERY   The information received in an interview may not always be accurate. For example, in one interview study of the physically handicapped, stated education level was in error 21 per cent of the time.[107] Puffery is more likely where applicants feel that their answers cannot or will not be subjected to verification.

EFFECTS OF TONE   The socio-emotional tone of the interview is predictive of what decision the interviewer will make about the applicant. When Bales' interaction process analyses were applied to interviews conducted by Canadian Army personnel officers, decisions to accept candidates occurred when there was much agreeing, giving of suggestions and opinions, and tension release. Decisions to reject applicants were more likely when much disagreement occurred, when tension and antagonism were shown, and when there was a great deal of asking for information, opinions, and suggestions.[95]

EFFECTS OF PROCESS   As for the process itself, the length of the interview seems to depend much more on the talkativeness of the interviewer than that of the applicant, according to an analysis of 60 interviews in eight companies.[24]   How much the interviewer talked correlated 0.90 with the total length of the interview time, while how much the applicant talked correlated only 0.55 with total time of the interview. The interviewer directly influences the length of time the interviewee will take to answer a question. Matarazzo and his associates [58,59] have found that during nondirective employment interviews, there is a direct relationship between the *time* the interviewer takes to ask an open-ended question and the time the interviewee takes to respond; if the interviewer's question takes 10 seconds, the interviewee's response will take 50 seconds. The content of the question (i.e., education, occupation, family history) does not influence this ratio.

A similar ratio has been found in the time for questions and the time for answers by astronauts and ground communications. The ratio is similar also for reporters' questions and the President's replies at news conferences.[83] In one study, it was found that fully one-fourth of the interview was about data already on record, 15 per cent dealt with information about the job and company, 12 per cent was in the form of advice and suggestions, while 12 percent was irrelevant. This left 36 per cent of the questions and answers which might produce data for predictive assessment.

NONVERBAL CUES   Interviews involve not only oral communication but a wide variety of nonverbal behavior. The *immediacy* conveyed by applicants has been found to be an important dimension in determining their acceptability. Immediacy is communicated by a pattern of behaviors that include eye contact, smiling, and attentive posture. A laboratory study showed that these nonverbal communication patterns accounted for 43 per cent of the variance in rating of an applicant. In reinforcing the folk wisdom that "It's not what you say, but how you say it," 86 per cent of the applicants who conveyed immediacy were recommended for the position, but only 19 per cent who didn't convey immediacy. The verbal interaction was identical for both groups.[41]

Usefulness of the Interview

Despite the almost universal employment of the face-to-face interview for selection screening, little strong evidence of its usefulness for predicting job success is available — but not for lack of trying. Mayfield [58] reviewed almost 80 studies and concluded, as Wagner [103] had done 15 years earlier in a similar review, that it was mainly intelligence that could be predicted satisfactorily. (And this, of course, can be done much more cheaply with a simple paper-and-pencil test.)

Widely varying results have been reported concerning validity of the interview assessment. Given specific objectives, patterned interviews, and foremen's ratings as criteria, McMurray reported a high correlation of 0.68 between interviewers' ratings and job success for 578 applicants.[62] On the other hand, a correlation close to 0 was found between 14 psychiatrists' ratings of applicants for psychiatric training and subsequent performance.[40] Wagner [103] did find that interviews were valid for predicting specific traits such as intelligence (0.45 to 0.94), academic achievement (0.66 to 0.73), sociability (0.37), social adjustment (0.22), and family and socioeconomic status (0.20). Looking at a somewhat different collection of studies, Ulrich and Trumbo [102] concluded differently that the interview had potential for assessing motivation and interpersonal competence if the interview was focused solely on such matters. But again it is doubtful whether the highly expensive interview is as valid as much more easily administered objective written tests for these assessment purposes. Also complicating matters is that in many validity studies of interviews, the interviewers base their judgments on application blanks and other information as well as on the interview itself. How much the validity of their judgment is a consequence of noninterview data is debatable. If current interviewing practice is to be evaluated, then we usually must ask what the interview *adds* to the total assessment on which a decision to hire is made, for interviewers are seldom asked to make these judgments without reference to available test or application blank information.

A series of studies from Psychological Research Services of Case Western Reserve University make a case that something is added to psychometric data by interviewers.[76] More definitely, SAS found that interviewers with test knowledge about applicants for co-pilot training exceeded the accuracy of statistical predictions.[99] While the gain was small, for critical jobs such as a pilot, the interview would seem to be worth the cost. More will be said in the next chapter about combining data and interviewer judgments. But first, the interview itself needs to be focused more sharply.

Making the Interview More Useful

FOCUSING THE INTERVIEW   When interviewers were restricted from access to any records about the applicant and confined to focusing on their own interaction with the applicant, a correlation of 0.37 was obtained for 1,359 interviewees between interviewer and peer ratings.[85] Restricting the interviewer to focusing just on "motivation to work," or just on "interpersonal competence" and standardizing questioning makes the process more of a psychological assessment, independent of other psychometric data about the applicant. This, in turn, increases the unique contribution the interview can make to augmenting the validity of prediction of a combination of assessments. If the interviewer is strongly affected, for example, by the intelligence of the applicant, which has already been assessed by a test, then the interview adds nothing when combined with the test to predict job performance. On the other hand, suppose the job requires both intelligence and interpersonal competence. If the interview is free of the effects of the applicant's intelligence and is a valid assessment of interpersonal competence, then the combination of the interview and the test will have a higher validity for predicting job success than the test alone. Indeed, focusing the interview, giving it specific behavioral objectives, may be more important to the utility of the interview than following too rigidly a standard review (like that shown in Figure 10–4) of what is usually covered in an application blank or BIB anyway.

DYNAMIC INTERVIEW   Yonge [113] developed a plan of somewhat freer social interaction between interviewer and applicant, concentrating discussion on more limited and well-defined traits, like self-esteem, which might better be assessed from social interaction than from a written test. The interviewer was mainly to evaluate the strength of applicant motivation from the dynamic interplay between the applicant and himself. The interview is made into a two-person situational test like those to be described in the next section for groups.

Forty-six young pharmaceutical employees doing routine manual work were subjected to the dynamic interview. Correlations ranging from 0.45 to 0.99 were obtained between interviewer ratings and supervisory ratings of the employees' productivity and job relations.

THE "KNOCK OUT" USE OF THE INTERVIEW   Often, by asking key questions, the interviewer can provide information that serves to "knock out" the applicant for further serious consideration for the position. For example, applicants have been interviewed for fire-fighting positions who did not want to climb ladders; for police officer positions who would never shoot their firearm; for traveling sales positions who didn't want to be away from their families overnight (where the accounts were widely dispersed, requiring overnight stays four days a week); for management positions who didn't want to leave their hometown when the job opening was in a different city; and for professorial positions who had no interest in research when the job required research productivity.

The basic point is that many jobs require certain critical behaviors. If the applicant is unwilling to perform those functions, the interview may reveal this and the applicant will be rejected. On a logical basis this can be considered a "valid" assessment approach, but because the applicant is never hired there is no way of proving the "knock out" factor was valid in an experimental design. For this reason, the value of the interview may be understated.

Interviewer Training

Videotaped training and workshops are useful in reducing interview errors. In one investigation the interviewers were evaluated six months after the workshop and videotaped training and errors were still low in occurrence.[49]

Interviews must be standardized, presenting the same conditions for each applicant, to make possible consistent assessments of those applicants. In an experimental study, 18 experienced job interviewers were assigned to interview applicants in either a structured, semistructured, or unstructured interview format. There was a high degree of reliability among interviewers' ranking of the same five job applicants in the structured interview situation, moderate agreement for the semistructured situation, and no significant agreement among the interviewers using an unstructured interview.[87]

Interviewers' consistency can be improved with training. They can be coached to reduce their own biases and idiosyncracies. Moreover feeding back to interviewers knowledge of their predictive success and failures can raise their rate of success.[97]

SITUATIONAL TESTS

In the early history of industrial psychology, it was common to construct a miniature replica of the real-life job, then see how well applicants for the job did in handling themselves in the simulation of the job. For instance, to predict success as streetcar motor operator, a mock-up of the motor operator's controls was constructed and applicants were tested on the working model. Such miniature tests are still used where many applicants are being tested for a single job, for they often provide greater predictive accuracy than any combination of abstract or single factor tests.

Similar simulated environments have been created for testing managerial and professional personnel. Two of these simulations tend to show considerable validity. One is the in-basket test; the other, the leaderless group discussion.

In-Basket Tests

An in-basket test is constructed by first analyzing the managerial or administrative job for which candidates are applying. Problems are created to

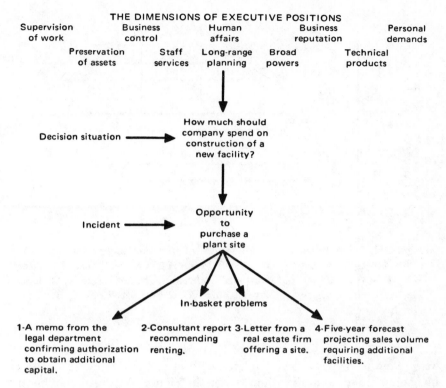

Figure 11-4. Analyzing a job for in-basket construction. (Reprinted by permission of the publisher from *Evaluating Executive Decision Making,* AMA Research Study # 75, F. M. Lopez, Jr. © 1966 by the American Management Association, Inc., page 33. All rights reserved.)

simulate issues to be faced by candidates if they are accepted for the job. As seen in Figure 11-4, an executive position has been analyzed into nine functions, each of which would be the locus of decision situations and incidents to be handled by the occupant of the position. A long-range planning decision concerns how much to spend on a new facility. The specific event that triggers the in-basket problem is an opportunity to purchase a plant site. The fictitious problems are created for the candidates by their in-baskets being filled with a legal memo, confirming authorization to obtain additional capital, a consultant's recommendation to rent, a real estate firm's offer of a site, and a five-year sales forecast.

Details are given about the company, its organizational structure, and the time available to review and react to the in-basket of memos, letters, statements, and reports. The candidates respond by preparing memos for their "secretary," dictating letters, requesting a committee meeting, and so on.

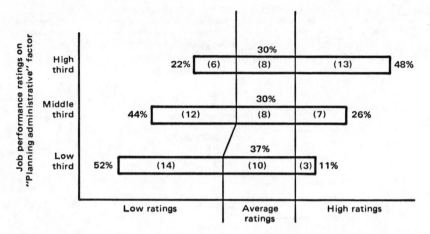

Figure 11–5. Validation of overall ratings of in-basket test performance for eighty-one General Electric managers. (From H. H. Meyer, "The In-Basket as a Measure of Managerial Aptitude," *Behavioral Research Service,* General Electric, 1961. Courtesy Robert F. Burnaska, Personnel Research, General Electric.)

VALIDITY   The in-basket profiles of 81 unit managers of General Electric were found to be positively correlated with rated performance as managers in planning and administration as seen in Figure 11–5.[63] Similar findings have been obtained in the Bell Telephone assessment program and in studies by Sears Roebuck, which we will discuss in more detail in Chapter 12.

Leaderless Group Discussions

It is interesting to note that the two situational tests on which we have elected to concentrate, the in-basket test and the leaderless group discussion (LGD), tend to correlate (about 0.25) with each other,[54] although each has substantially higher correlations with criteria of supervisory or managerial performance. The two might be profitably added to a supervisory selection program. And, in fact, they are both commonly employed routinely in the Assessment Center that will be described in Chapter 12.

DESCRIPTION   In its usual form, candidates are asked to discuss as a group some topic for some specific length of time, 30 minutes or one hour, for instance. Examiners act solely as observers once the discussion begins. Topics for discussion can be almost any subject about which the candidates have sufficient knowledge to discuss, but face validity is enhanced by using a job-related topic. Observers' ratings tend to cluster into three factors: *Ascendence* (confidence, initiative, boldness, striving for recognition); *task facilitation* (efficiency, cooperation, adaptability, pointed toward group solution); and *sociability*.[19] It is not difficult to train observers to make assessments that correlate highly (above 0.80). Test-retest reliability of performance in the LGD is high also.

Since the participants' own ratings of each other in the LGD correlate close to 0.90 or higher with observers' assessments,[43] it is possible to administer the LGD to a large mass of applicants by dividing them into small groups and having the participants rate each other. Such was done with military trainees. Validity and reliability held up as well under these circumstances as where independent observers were used.[29]

VALIDITY   A median correlation of 0.38 was found between LGD assessment and meritorious performance as a student leader, administrative trainee, shipyard foreman, foreign service administrator, civil service administrator, and oil refinery supervisor.[7] Finally, it has been demonstrated that LGD assessment added to the validity of predictions of supervisory success above and beyond what was possible with paper-and-pencil tests of basic abilities and supervisory practices.[28] A note of caution should be added. There is evidence that a 15-minute briefing about the purpose of the LGD can improve an individual's score.[81]

USE   Again, one may ask why a demonstrably useful assessment such as the LGD is actually applied less routinely than the demonstrably invalid routine interview. The LGD does tend to be an important portion of the activity in assessment centers, which we discuss in the next chapter. Convenience may be involved. It is often difficult and awkward to assemble groups of candidates for the same job. Ignorance of personnel psychology's findings may be a second reason. And habit and the need to feel in complete control of the selection process may prompt continued heavy emphasis on the individual interview rather than some other more valid procedure. Few employers (including the writers) are ready to fill important jobs with unseen candidates or candidates who have talked to each other but not the employer. Finally, candidates expect and desire to be interviewed, and find the nterview useful for learning about the job and their future employer. Since the interview occurs, it becomes natural to employ it as a source of data for assessing candidates.

SUMMARY

In this chapter, we have reviewed the various ways we can assess individual applicants' personality and interests with test and nontest procedures. Such assessments are generally more likely to be valid indicators of job choice and job satisfaction than job performance although they become increasingly important in higher level positions.

We now turn to an examination of how the various aptitude and non-ability tests and measures can be combined to maximize the utility of their applications to forecast occupational success.

REFERENCES

1. Anderson, C. W. "The Relation between Speaking Times and Decisions in the Employment Interview," *Journal of Applied Psychology*, 44 (1960): 267–268.
2. Andrews, J. D. W. "The Achievement Motive and Advancement in Two Types of Organizations," *Journal of Personality and Social Psychology*, 6 (1967): 163–168.
3. Appel, V., and M. R. Feinberg. "Recruiting Door-to-Door Salesmen by Mail," *Journal of Applied Psychology*, 53 (1969): 362–366.
4. Asher, J. J. "The Biographical Item: Can It Be Improved?" *Personnel Psychology*, 25 (1972): 251–269.
5. Barrett, G. V., R. A. Alexander, and K. Marshall. The Comparison of Female and Male Sales Applicants and the Prediction of Sales Force Performance by Use of the Miner Sentence Completion Scale. University of Akron, 1978.
6. Barrett, G. V., and R. H. Franke. *"Need for Achievement: A Reappraisal."* Unpublished manuscript. Management Research Center, University of Rochester, 1971.
7. Bass, B. M. "The Leaderless Group Discussion," *Psychological Bulletin*, 51 (1954): 465–492.
8. Bass, B. M. "Development and Evaluation of a Scale for Measuring Social Acquiescence," *Journal of Abnormal and Social Psychology*, 53 (1956): 296–299.
9. Bass, B. M. "Faking by Sales Applicants of a Forced Choice Personality Inventory," *Journal of Applied Psychology*, 41 (1957): 403–404.
10. Bass, B. M. "Further Evidence on the Dynamic Character of Criteria," *Personnel Psychology*, 15 (1962): 93–97.
11. Bass, B. M. "Social Behavior and the Orientation Inventory: A Review," *Psychological Bulletin*, 68 (1967): 260–292.
12. Berdie, R. F. "Aptitude, Achievement, Interest, and Personality Tests: A Longitudinal Comparison," *Journal of Applied Psychology*, 39 (1955): 103–114.
13. Bolster, B. I., and B. M. Springbett. "The Reaction of Interviewers to Favorable and Unfavorable Information," *Journal of Applied Psychology*, 45 (1961): 97–103.
14. Buel, W. E. "Biographical Data and the Identification of Creative Research Personnel," *Journal of Applied Psychology*, 49 (1965): 318–321.
15. Campbell, D. P. *Manual for the SVIB-SCII* (2nd ed.). California: Stanford University Press, 1977.
16. Campbell, J. P. "Stability of Interests within an Occupation over 30 Years," *Journal of Applied Psychology*, 50 (1966): 51–56.

17. Cascio, W. F. "Turnover, Biographical Data, and Fair Employment Practice," *Journal of Applied Psychology*, 61 (1976): 576–580.
18. Cawl, F. R. *A Method for Predicting Length of Service.* Philadelphia: Hill Memorial Library, 1926 (Doctoral Dissertation).
19. Couch, A., and L. F. Carter. "A Factorial Study of the Rated Behavior of Group Members," *American Psychologists*, 8 (1953).
20. Crowne, D., and D. P. Marlow. "Social Desirability and Response to Perceived Situational Demands," *Journal of Consulting Psychology*, 25 (1961): 109–115.
21. Cummin, P. C. "TAT Correlates of Executive Performance," *Journal of Applied Psychology*, 51 (1967): 78–81.
22. Dailey, C. A. "The Life History Approach to Assessment," *Personnel Guidance Journal*, 36, no. 7 (1958): 456–460.
23. Daniels, H. W., and J. L. Otis. "A Method for Analyzing Employment Interviews," *Personnel Psychology*, 3 (1950): 425–444.
24. England, G. W. *Development and Use of Weighted Application Blanks.* Dubuque, Iowa: W. C. Brown, 1961.
25. Ferguson, L. W. "Ability, Interest and Aptitude," *Journal of Applied Psychology*, 44 (1960): 126–131.
26. Fineman, S. "The Achievement Motive Construct and Its Measurement: Where Are We Now?" *British Journal of Psychology*, 68 (1977): 1–22.
27. Fleishman, E. A., and J. Berniger. "One Way to Reduce Office Turnover," *Personnel*, 37, no. 3 (1960): 63–69.
28. Glaser, R., P. A. Schwarz, and J. C. Flanagan. "The Contribution of Interview and Situational Performance Procedures to the Selection of Supervisory Personnel," *Journal of Applied Psychology*, 42 (1958): 69–73.
29. Gleason, W. J. "Predicting Army Leadership Ability by Modified Leaderless Group Discussion," *Journal of Applied Psychology*, 41 (1957): 231–235.
30. Goldsmith, D. "The Use of the Personal History Blank as a Salesmanship Test," *Journal of Applied Psychology*, 6 (1922): 194–195.
31. Grant, D. L., W. Katkovsky, and D. W. Bray. "Contributions of Projective Techniques to Assessment of Management Potential," *Journal of Applied Psychology*, 51 (1967): 226–232.
32. Grimsley, G., and H. F. Jarrett. "The Relation of Past Managerial Achievement to Test Measures Obtained in the Employment Situation: Methodology and Results," *Personnel Psychology*, 26 (1973): 31–48.
33. Grune & Stratton.
34. Hall, W. B., and D. W. MacKinnon. "Personality Inventory Correlates of Creativity among Architects," *Journal of Applied Psychology*, 53 (1969): 322–326.
35. Harman, H. H. *Final Report of Research on Assessing Human Abilities.* Report ETS PR-75-70. Ed 113–388. Princeton, N.J.: Educational Testing Service, 1975.
36. Hedlund, D. E. "A Review of the MMPI in Industry," *Psychological Reports*, 17 (1965): 875–889.
37. Heron, A. "A Psychological Study of Occupational Adjustment," *Journal of Applied Psychology*, 36 (1952): 385–387.

38. Heron, A. "The Effects of Real-Life Motivation on Questionnaire Response," *Journal of Applied Psychology*, 40 (1956): 65–68.
39. Herzberg, F. "Temperament Measures in Industrial Selection," *Journal of Applied Psychology*, 38 (1954): 81–84.
40. Holt, R. R., and L. Luborsky. "Research in the Selection of Psychiatrists: A Second Interim Report," *Bulletin of the Menninger Clinic*, 16 (1952): 125–135.
41. Imada, A. S., and M. D. Hakel. "Influence of Nonverbal Communication and Rater Proximity on Impressions and Decisions in Simulated Employment Interviews," *Journal of Applied Psychology*, 62 (1977): 295–300.
42. Jackson, D. N. *Personality Research Form Manual*. Goshen, New York: Research Psychologists Press, 1967.
43. Kaess, W. A., S. L. Witryol, and R. E. Nolan. "Reliability, Sex Differences, and the Validity in the Leadership Group Discussion Technique," *Journal of Applied Psychology*, 45 (1961): 345–350.
44. Keating, E., D. G. Paterson, and C. H. Stone. "Validity of Work Histories Obtained by Interview," *Journal of Applied Psychology*, 34 (1950): 6–11.
45. Kerr, W. A., and H. L. Martin. "Prediction of Job Success from the Application Blank," *Journal of Applied Psychology*, 33 (1949): 442–444.
46. Kinslinger, H. J. "Application of Projective Techniques in Personnel Psychology Since 1940," *Psychological Bulletin*, 66 (1966): 134–149.
47. Kipnis, D. "A Non-cognitive Correlate of Performance among Lower Aptitude Men," *Journal of Applied Psychology*, 46 (1962): 76–80.
48. Kirchner, W. K. "Real Life" Faking and the Edwards Personal Preference Schedule by Sales Applicants," *Journal of Applied Psychology*, 46 (1962): 128–130.
49. Latham, G. P., K. N. Wexley, and E. D. Pursell. "Training Managers to Minimize Rating Errors in the Observation of Behavior," *Journal of Applied Psychology*, 60 (1975): 550–555.
50. Layton, W. L. "Interest Measurement. Theory and Research on the Strong Vocational Interest Blank: A Conference Report," *Journal of Consulting Psychology*, 2 (1955): 10–12.
51. Levine, E. L., and S. M. Rudolph. *Reference Checking for Personnel Selection: The State of the Art*. American Society for Personnel Administration, 1977.
52. Levine, P. R., and R. Wallen. "Adolescent Vocational Interests and Later Occupation," *Journal of Applied Psychology*, 38 (1954): 428–431.
53. Levine, R., and H. T. Reis. "Fear of Failure in Males: A More Salient Factor than Fear of Success in Females?" *Sex Roles*, 2, no. 4 (1976): 389–398.
54. Lopez, F. M., Jr. *Evaluating Executive Decision Making*. American Management Association Research Study 75. New York: American Management Association, 1966.
55. Matarazzo, J. D., H. F. Hess, and G. Saslow. "Frequency and Duration Characteristics of Speech and Silence Behavior during Interviews," *Journal of Clinical Psychology*, 18 (1962): 416–426.
56. Matarazzo, J. D., M. Weitman, G. Saslow, and A. N. Wiens. "Interviewer Influence on Duration of Interviewee Speech," *Journal of Verbal Learning and Verbal Behavior* 1 (1963): 451–458.

57. Mausner, B. Situational Effects on a Projective Test," *Journal of Applied Psychology,* 45 (1961): 186–192.
58. Mayfield, E. C. "The Selection Interview: A Re-evaluation of Published Research," *Personnel Psychology,* 17 (1964): 239–260.
59. McClelland, D. *The Achieving Society.* Princeton, N. J.: D. Van Nostrand, 1961.
60. McClelland, D. C. "N Achievement and Entrepreneurship: A Longitudinal Study," *American Psychologist,* 20 (1965): 321–333.
61. McClelland, D. C., and D. G. Winter. *Motivating Economic Achievement.* New York: Free Press, 1969.
62. McMurray, R. N. "Validating the Patterned Interview," *Personnel,* 23, no. 4 (1947): 263–272.
63. Meyer, H. D. "An Exploratory Study of the Executive Position Description Questionnaire in the Jewel Tea Company, Inc." In *Describing Managerial Work: The Conference on the Executive Study.* Princeton: Educational Testing Service, 1961.
64. Meyer, H. H., W. B. Walker, and G. G. Litwin. "Motive Patterns and Risk Preferences Associated with Entrepreneurship," *Journal of Abnormal and Social Psychology,* 63 (1961): 570–574.
65. Miner, J. B. "The Concurrent Validity of the PAT in the Selection of Tabulating Machine Operators," *Journal of Projective Techniques,* 24 (1960): 409–418.
66. Miner, J. B. "The Validity of the PAT in the Selection of Tabulating Machine Operation: An Analysis of Predictive Power," *Journal of Projective Techniques,* 25 (1961): 330–333.
67. Miner, J. B. 'Personality and Ability Factors in Sales Performance," *Journal of Applied Psychology,* 46 (1962): 6–13.
68. Miner, J. B. "Motivational Potential for Upgrading among Minority and Female Managers," *Journal of Applied Psychology,* 62 (1977), 691–697.
69. Miner, J. B. "Implications of Managerial Talent Projections for Management Education," *Academy of Management Review,* 2 (1977): 412–420.
70. Miner, J. B. *Sentence Completion Scale: Multiple Choice Version.* Atlanta, Georgia: Organizational Measurement Systems Press, 1977.
71. Miner, J. B., and J. K. Anderson. "The Postwar Occupational Adjustment of Emotionally Disturbed Soldiers," *Journal of Applied Psychology,* 42 (1958): 317–322.
72. Minor, F. J. "The Prediction of Turnover of Clerical Employees," *Personnel Psychology,* 11 (1958): 393–402.
73. Morrison, R. F., and M. L. Sebald. "Personal Characteristics Differentiating Female Executive from Female Nonexecutive Personnel," *Journal of Applied Psychology,* 59 (1974): 656–659.
74. Mosel, J. N., and H. W. Goheen. "The Validity of the Employment Recommendation Questionnaire in Personal Selection: I. Skilled Trades," *Personnel Psychologist,* 11 (1958): 481–490.
75. Mosel, J. N., and H. W. Goheen. "The Employee Recommendation Questionnaire: III. Validity of Different Types of References," *Personnel Psychology,* 12 (1959): 469–477.
76. Otis, J. L., H. H. Campbell, and E. P. Prien. "Assessment of Higher-Level

Personnel: VII. The Nature of Assessment," *Personnel Psychology*, 15 (1962): 441–446.

77. Owens, W. A. "Background Data." In M. D. Dunnette (ed.), *Handbook of Industrial and Organizational Psychology*. Chicago: Rand McNally, 1976.

78. Owens, W. A., and E. R. Henry. *Biographical Data in Industrial Psychology: A Review and Evaluation*. Creativity Research Institute, Richardson Foundation, 1966.

79. Pace, L. A., and L. F. Schoenfeldt. "Legal Concerns in the Use of Weighted Applications," *Personnel Psychology*, 30 (1977): 159–166.

80. Peres, S. H., and J. R. Garcia. "Validity and Dimensions of Descriptive Adjectives Used in Reference Letters for Engineering Applicants," *Personnel Psychology*, 15 (1962): 279–286.

81. Petty, M. M. "A Multivariate Analysis of the Effects of Experience and Training upon Performance in a Leaderless Group Discussion," *Personnel Psychology*, 27 (1974): 271–282.

82. Powers, M. K. "Permanence of Measured Vocational Interests of Adult Males," *Journal of Applied Psychology*, 40 (1956): 69–72.

83. Ray, M. L., and E. J. Webb. "Speech Duration Effects in the Kennedy News Conferences," *Science*, 153 (1966): 899–901.

84. Reeves, E. T. "Utilization of the Isolate in Industry." Unpublished manuscript. Louisiana State University, 1959.

85. Rundquist, E. A. "Development of an Interview for Selection Purposes." In G. A. Kelly (ed.), *New Methods in Applied Psychology*, 85–95. College Park, Maryland: University of Maryland, 1947.

86. Schrader, A. D., and H. G. Osburn. "Biodata Faking: Effects of Induced Subtlety and Position Specificity," *Personnel Psychology*, 30 (1977): 395–403.

87. Schwab, D. P., and H. G. Heneman. "Relationship between Interview Structure and Interviewer Reliability in an Employment Situation," *Journal of Applied Psychology*, 53 (1969): 214–217.

88. Scollary, R. W. "Personal History Data as a Predictor of Success," *Personnel Psychology*, 10 (1957): 23–26.

89. Skinner, H. A., and D. N. Jackson. "The Missing Person in Personnel Classification: A Tale of Two Models," *Canadian Journal of Behavioral Science*, 9 (1977): 147–159.

90. Smith, W. J., L. E. Albright, J. R. Glennon, and W. A. Owens. "The Prediction of Research Competence and Creativity from Personal History," *Journal of Applied Psychology*, 45 (1961): 59–62.

91. Springbett, B. M. "Factors Affecting the Final Decision in the Employment Interview," *Canadian Journal of Psychology*, 12 (1958): 13–22.

92. Stockford, L. D., and K. R. Kunze. "Psychology and the Paycheck," *Personnel*, 27, no. 1 (1950): 129–143.

93. Strong, E. K., Jr. *Vocational Interests 18 Years after College*. Minneapolis: University of Minnesota Press, 1955.

94. Super, D. E., and J. O. Crites. *Appraising Vocational Fitness*. New York: Harper, 1962.

95. Sydiaha, D. "Bales' Interaction Process Analysis of Personnel Selection Interviews," *Journal of Applied Psychology*, 46 (1962): 344–349.

96. Terborg, J. R. "Women in Management: A Research Review," *Journal of Applied Psychology,* 62 (1977): 647–664.
97. Thomas, D. S., and G. D. Mayo. "A Procedure of Applying Knowledge Results to the Predictions of Vocational Counselors," *Educational and Psychological Measurement,* 17 (1957): 416–422.
98. Tiffin, J., B. T. Parker, and R. W. Habersat. "The Analysis of Personnel Data in Relation to Turnover on a Factory Job," *Journal of Applied Psychology,* 31 (1947): 615–616.
99. Trankell, A. "The Psychologist as an Instrument of Prediction," *Journal of Applied Psychology,* 43 (1959): 170–175.
100. Tullar, W. L., and G. V. Barrett. "The Future Autobiography as a Predictor of Sales Success," *Journal of Applied Psychology,* 61 (1976): 371–373.
101. Tversky, A., and D. Kahneman. "Judgment under Uncertainty: Heuristics and Biases," *JSAS Catalog of Selected Documents in Psychology,* 5 (1975): 182.
102. Ulrich, L., and D. Trumbo. "The Selection Interview since 1949," *Psychological Bulletin,* 63 (1965): 100–116.
103. Wagner, R. "The Employment Interview: A Critical Summary," *Personnel Psychology,* 2 (1949): 17–46.
104. Wainer, H. A., and I. M. Rubin. "Motivation of Research and Development Entrepreneurs," *Journal of Applied Psychology,* 53 (1969): 178–184.
105. Watterson, D. G., J. M. Schuerger, and G. I. Melnyk, "The Addition of Personality Measures to Ability Measures for Predicting and Understanding School Achievement," *Multivariate Experimental Clinical Research,* 2 (1976): 113–122.
106. Webster, E. C. *Decision Making in the Employment Interview.* Montreal: McGill University, 1964.
107. Weiss, D. J., and R. V. Dawis. "Objective Validation of Factual Interviewer Data," *Journal of Applied Psychology,* 44 (1960): 381–385.
108. Wernimont, P. F. "Re-evaluation of a Weighted Application Blank for Office Personnel," *Journal of Applied Psychology,* 46 (1962): 417–419.
109. Wesley, S. M., D. Q. Corey, and B. M. Stewart. "The Intra-individual Relationship between Interest and Ability," *Journal of Applied Psychology,* 34 (1950): 193–197.
110. West, E. D. "The Significance of Interpersonal Relations in Job Performance," *Occupations,* 29 (1951): 438–440.
111. Wiens, A. N., R. H. Jackson, T. S. Manaugh, and J. D. Matarazzo. "Communication Length as an Index of Communicator Attitude: A Replication," *Journal of Applied Psychology,* 53 (1969): 264–266.
112. Wood, M. M., and S. T. Greenfeld. "Women Managers and Fear of Success: A Study in the Field," *Sex Roles,* 2 no. 4 (1976): 375–387.
113. Yonge, K. A. "The Value of the Interview: An Orientation and a Pilot Study," *Journal of Applied Psychology,* 40 (1956): 25–31.

12 INTEGRATING INFORMATION FOR PERSONNEL SELECTION AND PLACEMENT

IN BRIEF An integrated view of the selection-placement process is presented, building upon what has been covered in the preceding chapters on personnel psychology. Stressed is the interdependence of sequential decision phases from job analysis to placement. At each phase, consideration must be given to the nature of information required to make decisions to reject or to pass candidates to subsequent phases. The utility of proposed information sources is seen as a function of *costs* of information gathering, the *validity* of information sources available, *selection ratios,* and other factors. A useful tool in aiding the decision maker in the estimation of gains to be expected from implementing a proposed selection technique is provided by the *Taylor-Russell tables.*

The initial phases in the decision process — job analysis, recruiting, and initial screening — are followed by *selection* (decisions, typically based on test information, to accept or reject a candidate for organization membership), and *placement* (the process of allocating already selected organization members to appropriate jobs).

In the selection phase, a wide variety of information sources may be combined in various ways into *test batteries* to forecast success in different task areas. The nature of test data, other psychometric information, and interviewers' judgments, as well as *moderator* variables affect the utility of selection programs.

Management and engineering have received particular attention from personnel specialists. Some success has been achieved with various assessment programs in matching job requirements in these areas with candidates' abilities, interests, and needs.

The fundamental purpose of the preceding chapters on personnel psychology has been to present and analyze findings from the behavioral sciences that can enhance the effectiveness of work force utilization from the perspective of both the organization and its individual members. The underlying theme in the work of the personnel psychologist is *optimal matching* of an organization's work requirements— systematically understood through the process of job analysis and equitably balanced through job evaluation procedures (Chapter 7) — with the abilities, needs, values, interests, and personality characteristics of prospective members, assessed through procedures described in Chapters 9, 10, and 11.

We are now prepared to draw together the various themes of the past chapters into an integrated view of the process of matching people and jobs.

SELECTION AND PLACEMENT: SEQUENTIAL DECISION MAKING

The selection-placement process can usefully be considered as an interrelated series of decisions on the part of both organizations and their prospective members.[26] Figure 12–1 presents a simplified overview of the main phases involved in the process, along with indications of the types of decisions and information required in each phase.

The Initial Phases

JOB ANALYSIS AND EVALUATION   The process of matching individuals with organizations typically begins with the organization's definition of its needs, in the form of job descriptions and job requirements. A personnel requisition, based on some form of job analysis and job evaluation process, normally specifies requirements regarding education level, experience, and skills, as well as information about job location, travel requirements, salary, and other necessary data.

Clearly, the job requirements developed in this first phase are fundamental determinants of the nature and scope of the selection-placement process which follows. If, at one extreme, job requirements are sufficiently undemanding that 99 per cent of the population could perform adequately with little training or prior experience, it is obvious that only a very

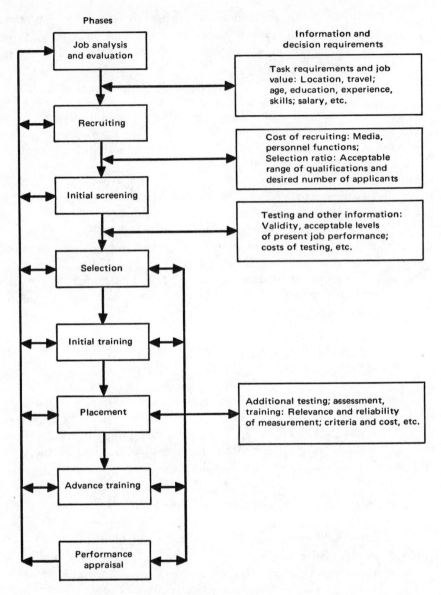

Figure 12–1. An overview of phases and decisions in the selection-placement process.

simple selection process need be involved. At the other extreme — for example, the selection of astronauts for future space missions — the combination of abilities required for successful performance may be so unique in the general population as to demand a highly elaborate, expensive, and thoroughly tested formal selection procedure.

RECRUITING   Given task requirements, the second phase in the process involves *recruiting,* usually by one or more personnel specialists. As we shall see, each of the phases in the process may require "backing up" to modify decisions made in previous phases (see Figure 12–1). For example, NASA's original request for astronauts may have specified the following requirements: Ph. D. in astrophysics, 2,000 hours of jet flight logged, ten years' military experience at officer rank, age less than thirty-two years, and excellent physical condition (including detailed physiological minimum demands). Either before any recruiting attempts (based on knowledge of available manpower) or, more likely, after fruitless initial recruiting efforts, the recruiter will demand a reanalysis of job requirements that leads to relaxations in some or all of the specifications.

The two basic decisions required at the recruiting phase concern the related questions of *cost of recruiting* and *selection ratio.* In our astronaut example, very high skill requirements imply a very small number of potentially qualified applicants in relation to the number of positions to fill; i.e., the *selection ratio,* or number to be hired from the total number of qualified applicants, will be large or *unfavorable.* Ideally, the most favorable situation, from the organization's point of view, is a large number of qualified applicants relative to the number of openings. Given stiff skill requirements, the selection ratio can only be improved by increasing the *cost of recruiting,* i.e., by widening the search. With very high requirement hurdles and unfavorable selection ratios, exorbitant recruiting costs may lead to the selection of "ready-made" astronauts, with little further effort required in testing, training, or performance appraisal.

A more typical outcome of the tradeoff between selection ratio and recruiting costs is relaxation of the skill requirements. This has obvious implications for the burdens this decision places on the remaining steps in the process. By lowering astronaut requirements to Bachelor's degrees in science or engineering, five years of relevant experience, pilot's licenses, age to thirty-eight years, and good physical condition, we would have to expect to have a much greater number of "qualified" applicants, but the remaining phases in the process would now require much greater efforts. In effect, we shift the burden of optimal matching of man and job to later phases in the process.

SCREENING   With recruiting costs acceptable and selection ratios relatively favorable, the resulting applications are then typically subject to an *initial screening* process. Based an knowledge of the validity and reliability of application blanks and other biographical information (see Chapter 11), and considering the relatively great expense involved in passing applicants to the next phase of the process, we would expect that a relatively intensive initial screening of applications, including perhaps reference checks, multiple-rater or panel reviews, and other rating procedures

(Chapter 8), might be undertaken in cases where high levels of qualifications are required. In the case of the Gemini/Apollo program, for example, 350 astronaut candidates were medically evaluated before 9 were selected.[42]

DECISION ERRORS   Before turning to the central phase of the selection process, we need to explore the nature of "allowable" errors in the decision process. Beginning with the initial screening phase, decision makers are confronted with choices to accept (i.e., to pass along to the next phase) or to reject the applicant. With each such decision, no matter which alternative is chosen, there is associated some likelihood of errors. Throughout the selection-placement process, the decision maker is forced to weigh carefully the potential costs of false positives and false negatives.

An *erroneous rejection* is a candidate who is rejected at any phase, according to the screening or selection standards used at that phase, but who would have succeeded on the job if passed through. In most cases, erroneous rejections are never recognized, and are not typically regarded as "costly" to the rejecting organization. Well-known examples exist, however, to underline the fact that erroneous rejections do represent potential costs that organizations should strive to minimize: In the field of sports, the player rejected on a team's initial draft choice goes on to become a competitor's "superstar." In business, the bypassed middle manager quits and becomes the effective president of the organization's largest competitor.

The costs of an *erroneous acceptance* are much more evident. An erroneous acceptance is an individual who is passed through and fails to meet standards on the job — the incompetent and often disastrously expensive failure.

Clearly, organizations would like to minimize both erroneous rejections and erroneous acceptances. The problem is that although tighter screening or selection criteria may decrease the erroneous acceptances, they will simultaneously tend to increase the erroneous rejections. Two approaches based on the evaluation of risks are commonly observed in organizations' attempts to decide between the costs of erroneous rejections and the costs of erroneous acceptances.

In the first approach, organizations opt for the avoidance of erroneous acceptances because the costs of ineffective performance are judged to be excessive. For our astronauts, the tremendous costs involved in potential failure of an individual, even at early training stages, imply rigidly high screening and selection standards, even at the probable cost of excluding candidates who might have been as good or better. A more familiar example is provided by selection policies in many first-rate universities. Organizations choosing this approach apply high initial screening and selection criteria, tend to experience relatively low levels of turnover or failure, and tend to allocate productive resources more evenly among selected members (e.g., "rookie" astronauts, professional football players, and freshmen have about the same access to training facilities and faculty time as "veterans" or seniors).

The second approach risks erroneous acceptances in order to minimize erroneous rejections. The philosophy here is that the development of competence is a long-term process requiring the provision of maximum exposure to learning opportunities where the initial costs of failure can be kept relatively small. Many top-rated universities (especially the public or land-grant schools) follow this approach, and other organizations in recent years have successfully adopted it with regard to hiring or admitting members of minority groups (see Chapter 18). In this approach, screening-selection, placement-performance, evaluation-promotion, and so on, represent a continuous, sequential process. Turnover and failure tend to be relatively high at lower levels, but there is no reason to believe that the ultimate qualifications of those who achieve high positions in such organizations are less than those of equivalent levels in organizations with the opposite approach.

Most modern firms combine their approaches, while tending to emphasize the second, sequential process. Thus, the Big Eight public accounting firms do a great deal of recruiting and screening. Nevertheless, a large number of those college graduates they hire do not remain more than a few years with the public company. Much of the lower level staff work is accomplished by these new hires who in turn receive considerable training and necessary experience. Many transfer to private client firms so that a link remains with the public firm for future business. Others transfer to public regulatory agencies. Again, a useful link is forged. But the most meritorious are promoted to partnership levels. The process of promotion and transfer based on merit represents, in effect, a constant series of decisions to select and place personnel, which tends to assure the development of effective organization members at all levels. Three extended examples of such approaches to management selection, placement, and development are provided later in this chapter.

The Selection Phase

At the selection stage decision makers are concerned with gathering information on which they can make rational choices to reject or to pass applicants through to the subsequent phases. They are guided in their choice of information sources by considerations of *utility* and *cost*.

Clearly, it would be ideal if the decision makers could administer a wide range of valid test batteries, situational tests, focused interviews, and other observation and information-gathering techniques to every applicant. Unfortunately, information gathering entails *costs* for both the organization and the individual involved. For many jobs in most organizations, high costs of testing and observation cannot be justified. Decision makers are forced to limit their information-gathering efforts to only those procedures for which the utility of additional information clearly exceeds the costs of information gathering. These considerations imply, of course, risks of erroneous acceptances, but the decision is typically made to shift the burden of weeding out erroneous acceptances to subsequent phases in the process.

The *utility* of any proposed information-gathering procedure depends on several factors, of which the most important are the *validity* of the procedure (see Chapter 9), the *selection ratio* (see below), and the *percentage of employees who are considered to be performing at satisfactory levels* on the job in question (if such information is available).

VALIDITY   As discussed in Chapter 9, the use of an information source that does not predict future criterion behavior beyond chance levels is very unlikely to add anything to the selection process, beyond satisfying some needs for establishing contacts or maintaining good public relations (as is the case in many job interview situations). Also, there may be some utility in having a testing program even without validity coefficients greater than chance, because there is some evidence that the existence of a testing program per se tends to draw better applicants.[89] Of course, the test results could not and should not be used for selection for legal and ethical reasons.

SELECTION RATIO   If all applicants who are tested are actually placed on the job (i.e., a selection ratio of 1.00), it is obvious that the testing procedure is not being used to select and reject. With valid tests for measuring the required abilities, as the selection ratio is reduced (i.e., the number of potentially qualified applicants becomes greater than the number of slots to be filled), the average ability level of the applicants actually hired will be increased. It also follows that low selection ratios can make up for low test validities to some extent. That is, high selection ratios require testing procedures with high validity coefficients in order to assure that testing is of any utility to the organization; with a low selection ratio, the testing procedure need only be moderately able to distinguish between likely successes and likely failures to be useful. In estimating the utility of testing, we see here systematic tradeoffs among selection ratios, cost of recruiting, cost of selection errors, cost of testing, and the test procedure's validity. Thus, we can improve the selection ratio by increased recruiting of applicants who will try to pass the test hurdle. Yet there are drawbacks and hidden as well as open costs for the increased recruiting efforts.

Suppose that the education requirement is set at the tenth grade level to attract more applicants for positions as social workers, instead of the usual requirement of two years or more of college, and that a content-valid examination is used to screen applicants. With the usual minimum college requirement, 100 individuals may apply for 20 positions, giving a selection ratio of 0.2, or the selection of 1 in 5. With the tenth grade minimum requirement, 100 additional applicants may apply, but none of them may have the knowledge or skills required to pass the content-valid test. While the selection ratio, with 200 applicants for 20 positions, will be 0.1, or the selection of 1 in 10, this has no practical value. In addition to the increased costs of recruiting and testing, expectations have been raised among the additional 100 applicants that cannot be met, causing a public relations or possibly even a legal problem for the agency. More applicants *are not always better* for an organization.

PERCENTAGE CONSIDERED SATISFACTORY   In the selection of new employees for jobs already being performed in the organization, where presently employed workers were selected without testing or with other testing procedures, the decision to add new tests or to revise the entire testing procedure will do little to increase job performance levels if they are already considered to be high. No matter how valid the tests or how favorable the selection ratio, if a very high proportion of present employees are appraised as good performers, adding new tests is not likely to increase average performance levels to any significant extent. On the other hand, if present performance levels are low, the addition of valid tests is likely to have utility in increasing average performance levels. As we will see, how much current employees actually vary from each other in performance is a key to test utility.

ESTIMATING THE UTILITY OF A PROPOSED SELECTION SYSTEM   The *Taylor-Russell tables* were devised to integrate the factors of *validity, selection ratios,* and *percentage considered successful* to permit organizations to estimate the utility of a proposed set of predictors.[92] Based on several statistical assumptions, including that of a linear relationship between criteria and predictors,[84] the tables allow predictions concerning the amount by which the selection process will be improved by using a given testing procedure, given different combinations of the three factors discussed.

The information from the Taylor-Russell tables can be displayed graphically in *expectancy charts.* As an illustration, Figure 12–2 shows hypothetical data for astronauts with varying test scores. This is an individual expectancy chart. An organizational expectancy chart could be constructed to show the proportion of satisfactory astronauts as a function of the selection ratio.[55]

As we have already noted, the utility of a test depends on a number of factors, including its validity. Application of a test with a predictive

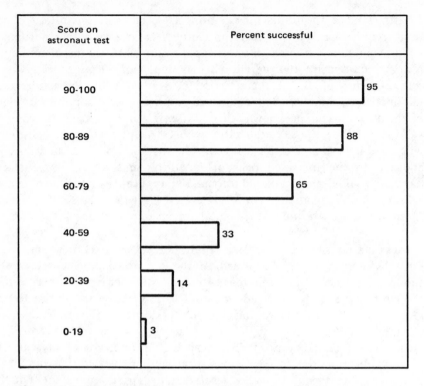

Figure 12–2. Hypothetical expectancy chart for astronauts.

validity coefficient of 0.40, in comparison to a test with a validity of 1, results in a 40 per cent gain on the criterion.[15] This is so despite the fact that only $(0.40)^2 \times 100$ per cent, or 16 per cent, of the variance in criterion performance is accounted for by the variance in test scores.

One way to define a test's utility is to determine how much of a per cent gain on the criterion of job performance occurs if we use a test to select applicants rather than hiring all applicants. This is the *efficiency* of the test.

$$\text{Efficiency} = \frac{\substack{\text{Criterion} \\ \text{mean selected} \\ \text{sample}} - \substack{\text{Criterion} \\ \text{mean unselected} \\ \text{sample}}}{\substack{\text{Criterion} \\ \text{mean} \\ \text{unselected} \\ \text{sample}}} \times 100 \text{ per cent}$$

This efficiency is a product of the validity coefficient, the criterion variance, and the selection ratio, as shown below:

$$\text{Efficiency} = \frac{\text{Validity}}{\text{coefficient}} \times \frac{\text{Criterion variance}}{\text{Criterion mean}} \times \frac{\text{Height of the normal probability curve at the point of selection}}{\text{Selection ratio}}$$

This equation is a matter of simple algebra[48] and makes no additional assumptions other than that the relations are linear. We see that the efficiency, as just noted, increases directly with increases in the validity coefficient. But it is also greater the more workers vary in the criterion of job performance (relative to their mean criterion performance). Thus, no test will be of any use if everyone is the same in criterion performance. This can occur, for example, where everyone's job performance depends on the pace of an assembly line. And finally, as we have noted before, the utility of a test is inversely related to the selection ratio. The smaller the ratio, the greater is the utility of the test.

Cost accounting procedures can be applied to estimate savings from introducing a selection procedure with specified test validities, selection ratios, variances in job performance, and costs of accounting and testing. For instance, a savings of over $150,000.00 was estimated if a biographical information blank with a validity of 0.46 were to be used to select nurses' aides.[80] In a similar analysis, a savings of $250,000 was estimated over a 25-month period for clerical employees.[56]

COMBINING PREDICTIVE INFORMATION

We will assume that the preconditions have been met — that relevant criteria, valid predictors, favorable selection ratios, and evidence of a need for performance improvement because of low performance levels of present employees have all been found — so as to establish the usefulness of adopting a proposed set of tests, or other information-gathering procedures. How should these various techniques be combined into a test battery, and how should their results be used?

Trial test batteries, larger than a final battery, are chosen to represent the range of characteristics thought to be appropriate. Even if the validity of each individual test in the battery is known, the validity of the combination will depend not only on the individual validities but also on the correlations among the tests. The predictive power of any given battery must be assessed for each battery as a package. In practice, the predictive power of a test battery does not continue to increase substantially as more and more tests are included.[68] Because pure factor tests are seldom available in practice, it is typically found that after roughly four to six tests are given, the intercorrelations among the tests are so high that redundancy begins to outweigh the added predictive power of another test, although larger valid batteries on occasion may be found.[40]

Typically, the test developer is confronted with two practical problems: Highly valid, independent pure factor tests are ideals seldom realized. Second, validities (as we noted in Chapter 9) change as a function of the characteristics of the sample chosen. As a result, when measures are combined to maximize the accuracy of prediction, sometimes that accuracy is enhanced by measures that by themselves are not related to the criterion to be predicted. One condition that provides techniques for dealing with the practical problems noted above is the use of measures as moderators.

Moderator Variables

As we saw in Chapter 9, the validity of a test (or combination of tests) is not an inherent characteristic of the test (or tests). Rather, it is a complex function of purposes, situations, and the attributes of the particular sample to whom the test is given. Because test results are thus *moderated* by sample characteristics, it is often useful to include a *moderate variable* in a test battery. This action allows the overall sample to be divided into subgroups based on the attribute in question. Moderator variables do not act to increase the predictive validity of the overall test battery, but rather permit the user to identify those special groups for which the battery is most valid.

For example, it has been found in various nontest circumstances that women are less influenced than men by extraneous environmental distractions when taking a test. This might result in a particular situation in a test validity of 0.50 for women and perhaps 0.30 for men. Subsequently, if we knew the sex of applicants and their test scores, we could make more discriminating predictions about them. Sex would be a moderator variable. Sex is, in fact, a moderator variable in predicting college grades. According to a review of research on the matter, college grades of women are more predictable than college grades of men.[84] It is important to note that this moderator variable is itself unrelated to the criterion: women's grades are neither better nor worse than those earned by men, just more predictable.

Intelligence was found to be such a variable in trying to forecast academic grades when the task orientation scores of students were known. Task orientation forecasts success of students, but only among those with IQs over 110.[33] Only capable students who were task-oriented earned better grades. For less capable students, task orientation was irrelevant.

Another likely moderator is age. For example, for applicants over forty, a test of accuracy might be expected to discriminate more accurately among those who will perform better or worse subsequently on the job.

For applicants under forty, a test of speed might be more valid. The reason that this might occur is that older persons are handicapped by speed tests, so that a particular test of speed might severely depress the scores of all older applicants, reducing or eliminating their validity for predicting job performance.[34,36,49]

USES Several methods have been developed to exploit the use of moderators. Ghiselli[34,35] constructed "moderator tests." First, he calculated for each of a group of examinees the discrepancy between their criterion success predicted from their test scores and their actual success. A distribution of the group was thus obtained according to these discrepancy scores. Now test items were keyed to discriminate among those with high and low discrepancy scores. The key was cross-validated so that what emerged was a scoring key for a moderator test, a test to determine whose performance can or cannot be accurately forecast.

A second method divides examinees into those with high and low criterion scores or high and low predictor scores to see whether prediction is better for those with high values than for those with low values.

Of particular social significance has been the question of how much race or membership in a disadvantaged group moderates the accuracy of prediction from test scores.[21] This important issue will be discussed in Chapter 18 on public policy. Unfortunately, moderator approaches have severe technical and conceptual problems that make them difficult to use in operating selection programs.

We can now proceed to examine some ways of combining the information from test and nontest sources available about an applicant to maximize the accuracy of forecasts of his/her success on a particular job.

Alternative Approaches

Eight possible modes of collecting and combining predictive information have been identified by Sawyer.[79] The data can be gathered from objective tests and measures by *mechanical* means requiring no human judgment, or they can be gathered as *judgmental* impressions from an interview, letters of recommendation, and application forms, or some combination of both methods can be employed. Similarly, the data, however collected, can be combined through interviewer *judgment* at one extreme or through purely *mechanical* processes at the other. Again, some combination of both approaches can be used.

The eight modes are charted in Table 12–1: (1) pure judgment; (2) trait ratings; (3) profile interpretation; (4) pure statistical; (5) judgmental composite; (6) mechanical composite; (7) judgmental synthesis; and (8) mechanical synthesis.

Table 12–1. Classification of prediction methods.

Mode of data collection	Mode of data combinaiton	
	Judgmental	Mechanical
Interview	1. Pure judgment	2. Trait ratings
Mechanical	3. Profile interpretation	4. Pure statistical
Both	5. Judgmental composite	6. Mechanical composite
Either or both	7. Judgmental synthesis	8. Mechanical synthesis

Adapted from Sawyer, "Measurement and Prediction, Clinical and Statistical," *Psychological Bulletin*, 66 (1966):178–200.

1. Pure judgment: Judgmental data combined by judgment No objective test data are collected. Information is gathered by the interviewers into a judgment of the likely success of the applicants. The interviewers usually have in mind some traits and standards that they think are important to consider in judging whether applicants will be successful on the job, if hired. But the interviewers do not necessarily make them explicit. This approach has been used to forecast the success of C. A. A. pilot trainees.[30] Compared with other more systematic approaches, the pure judgments of interviewers were *least predictive* of ratings of pilot potential after training.

2. Trait ratings: Judgmental data mechanically combined Here the interviewers make a formal series of ratings about the applicant based on what they have seen and heard from the applicant. But instead of having the interviewers make a final prediction about the likely success of the applicant, the various judgmental ratings made by the interviewers to describe the applicant are mechanically combined by some statistical method (to be described below). This mechanical combining of judgments has been contrasted with various other approaches and found to be *equal or less accurate* in forecasting rated performance in officer candidate school of 1,000 officer candidates.[71]

3. Profile interpretation: Mechanically collected data, combined by judgment Here an employment officer reviews all the test scores and measures obtained for an applicant and then, without seeing the applicant personally, makes a prediction about the applicant's likely success. This is a common practice when applicants live in one city and apply for jobs in another.

This method also has *not been very effective*. For example, 3 to 7 clinical psychologists were given a description of the requirements to be a successful military pilot. Then they were given in batches of 20 the personality test protocols of aviation cadets, half of whom subsequent to testing had succeeded in flight training and half of whom had been eliminated because of overt personality stress. The clinicians did little better than chance in judging from the personality test profiles which cadets had succeeded and which ones had failed. [5]

4. Pure statistical   This is a method of gathering and combining information requiring no human judgment once the rules for gathering and combining the test scores and measurements have been decided. It is a favorite approach of personnel psychologists. In its simplest form, applicants' scores on each of the tests and measures found valid for predicting success on the job are converted to some type of standard scores, so that each score (Z) is now in a form relative to a normal distribution of all applicants under consideration. The means and standard deviations are the same for the set of scores on each test, so that with K tests and measures the K scores can be added across tests and measures and each will have *equal weight* in the composite:

$$\text{Composite score} = Z_1 + Z_2 + Z_3 \cdots + Z_k.$$

A second method assigns different weights to the scores. For example, job analysis suggests that verbal skill is twice as important as mathematical skill on a job; therefore, twice as much weight is assigned to a verbal test as is assigned to a math test. The same rational approach could be employed with a number of tests giving each unequal weight in the composite:

$$\text{Composite score} = aZ_1 + bZ_2 + cZ_3 \cdots + kZ_i$$

where $a, b, c,$ through k are the different assigned weights.

Better yet, some plan for maximizing the accuracy with which the composite score predicts the criterion of job success may be employed. That is, multiple regression analysis can establish what the weights $a, b, c,$ and k should be so that the sum of the errors (squared) is minimized between the composite score for every examinee and the criterion measure of job success. Usually, a given test will achieve a greater weight if it is a more valid predictor than other tests in the battery, i.e., if its correlation with the criterion is relatively high compared with the other tests. It will also achieve a greater weight if it is independent or uncorrelated with the other tests.

From the standpoint of multiple regression, the ideal battery of tests is one in which each test is highly reliable, homogeneous, or internally consistent, measuring validly just one factor when the factor is uncorrelated with any of the other factors assessed by other similarly reliable tests of the battery.[38] It has been shown that a collection of relatively short tests like this when combined for multiple prediction purposes can serve as well as much longer ones.[16]

Nevertheless, even with as few as five tests, unweighted composites often yield results as accurate as various more mathematically elegant weightings of combinations of test scores. For example, Trattner[96] gave thirteen aptitude tests to civil service journeymen in each of twelve blue collar trades. Included were tests of name-matching, dexterity, word meaning, spelling, abstract reasoning, following oral directions, arithmetic computation, and so on. Each trade group was divided into two samples. For one of the samples he then applied three weighting procedures to obtain composite scores for each trainee and correlated the composite scores against relevant criteria of job performance. Finally, he cross-validated the composite scores with the second sample for each of the 12 trades. The three methods used for combining scores were (1) multiple regression (a statistically optimal number of differentially weighted tests); (2) rational (tests selected according to their validity for measuring abilities rated as important for a particular job); and, (3) equal weighting (the five tests with the highest validities are given equal weight).

Table 12–2 shows the cross validities found for each of the 12 trades using each of the mechanical combining methods. It can be seen that the particular trade makes more difference in the accuracy of predictions than does the method of combining test scores. Cross-validities are higher for welders, mechanics, and carpenters than for sheet metal and power unit assemblers, regardless of the method used.

While multiple regression is supposed to yield that equation for combining predictors containing a minimum of error, its frequent failure to provide much more accuracy than equal weighting can be attributed to a number of limitations. First, multiple regression assumes that the underlying assessments in question can be added together for the best possible prediction rather than combined in other more complicated ways. Second, it assumes that all the relevant relations among the predictors and between the predictors and the criteria of job success are linear — changes on the predictors are associated in a constant way with changes on the criteria. Third, with small sample sizes regression weights have considerable error. Therefore simple weighting procedures are superior.[32]

The pure statistical or *compensatory methods* assume that a deficiency in one attribute of individuals can be compensated for by above-average scores on other attributes. In contrast, the *multiple-cutoff method* assumes that some attributes of an individual are so critical for job performance that deficiencies cannot be compensated for by other attributes. Most individual judgments of applicants are probably based on some sort of implicit multiple-cutoff concept. The multiple-cutoff method can also be made very explicit by specifying minimum scores for each test in a battery, as the United States Employment Service does.[39]

5. Judgmental composite: Judgmental and mechanical data combined by judgment The judgmental composite is probably the most common

Table 12–2. Cross-validation coefficients of test batteries assembled by three methods.

	Job series			
Test battery selection method	Radio-radar equipment installer N = 63	Aircraft welder N = 60	Aircraft sheet metal worker N = 125	Aircraft sheet metal manufacturer N = 100
Multiple regression	.31	.41	.23	.19
Rational	.31	.43	.24	.16
Equal weighting	.35	.39	.29	.26

	Job series			
Test battery selection method	Plumber steamfitter N = 72	Carpenter N = 65	Warehouseman N = 99	Aircraft power unit assembler N = 95
Multiple regression	.32	.37	.35	.15
Rational	.33	.45	.29	.20
Equal weighting	.30	.35	.28	.25

	Job series			
Test battery selection method	Aircraft mechanic N = 100	Aircraft disassembler N = 60	Airframe assembler N = 74	Aircraft hydraulic systems mechanic N = 100
Multiple regression	.42	.35	.23	.26
Rational	.48	.46	.30	.32
Equal weighting	.46	.40	.34	.35

Correlations equal to or above 0.20 are significant at the 0.05 level or beyond.
After Trattner "Comparison of Three Methods for Assembling Aptitude Test Batteries,"
Personnel Psychology 16 (1963):230.

method used. An interviewer pools together all the test and interview information about an applicant, and then makes a final judgment about whether or not to hire the applicant based on what is judged to be the applicant's chances of success on the job. For example, researchers asked a team of consultants to integrate their biographical information, intelligence, aptitude, and personality test scores.[2] The consultants then pooled this information to rank the 31 managers on sales forecasting, sales performance, and interpersonal competence. These predictions were correlated with corresponding ratings of the managers by their superiors and peers. The consultants' judgments correlated 0.49, 0.58, and 0.43 with respective criterion ratings of the managers by their superiors and peers.

In the same way, psychological test data were combined by judgment for 780 applicants for positions as S. A. S. pilots. Correlations of 0.75 and 0.51 were obtained between final judgments by psychologists and subsequent criteria of retention on the job.[95]

Often, boards of judges are assembled to discuss and then to subjectively combine available data on applicants. For example, South African Civil Service Examining Boards made final predictions based on objective test data, biographical data, several individual interviews, and a leaderless group discussion among applicants.[98] Such boards are likely to add reliability to the judgments in the same way that multiplying the length of a test would increase its reliability. Validity may be enhanced as well. Thus, in a comparable study, tests alone correlated 0.32 with criterion ratings of U. S. Air Force officer effectiveness, but assessment board judgments based on the tests plus three days of observation of the examinees correlated 0.47 with criterion ratings.[60] However, the danger here is that the most vocal and prestigious of the judges will exert undue influence over the final judgments.

Various profile methods have been tried that do not require adding together predictors. They involve looking at the scattering of an individual's test scores around a grand mean of those scores. Predictions are developed from mechanical indices based on the shape of the individual's profile (on which tests scores are high rather than low), on the grand mean score on all tests, and on the extent of variation or scattering among the different scores.[103] One study contrasted three profile methods with multiple regression but found none to yield predictive validities as high as multiple regression.[9] Computers do allow applied psychologists to refine their statistical methods; nevertheless, the evidence indicates that many of their refinements are often more precise than the data warrant.[54]

6. Mechanical composite: Judgmental and mechanical data combined mechanically Test information, application blank scores, and recommenders' and interviewers' ratings are combined statistically to yield a prediction of the likely success of the applicant. This seldom-used method nevertheless may yield the greatest accuracy of predictions, since it extracts both from judgmental data and from test data only those portions that are valid, eliminates overlapping, and takes account of the predictive error contained in the various kinds of information available on the applicant — both judgmental and mechanical. A study designed to forecast the grades of college freshmen mechanically combined self-estimates and aptitude test information to make the predictions.[28] The method yielded more accurate results than a judgmental composite of the same data.

7. Judgmental synthesis All available information is first mechanically combined into a prediction. Then this prediction is evaluated subjectively in the light of other judgmental information. For example, all test data about an applicant are added together in a multiple regression equation to yield a forecast of the likelihood of job success by the applicant. This forecast is then taken into account in conjunction with the evaluations of the applicant by a number of interviewers. A final judgment is then made as to whether or not to hire the applicant. Managers and professors tend to like this approach because they can continue to feel in control of the final decision to accept or reject the applicant.

One investigator employed this approach to forecast freshman grades of University of Minnesota entrants from high school grades, interviews, and test data, and found it equal in validity to more mechanical ways of combining the data.[64]

8. Mechanical synthesis All information is reviewed to make a judgment or prediction of success. This prediction is then mechanically combined with other available data or predictions. For instance, employment officers might review the reference letters, past work history, and interview impressions they obtained about an applicant. From the review they would make a prediction about the applicant's likely job success. This prediction could be combined mechanically with test data available on the applicant to formulate the decision as to whether or not to hire the applicant. This method was used to forecast the final class standing of 1,900 Coast Guard officer candidates from aptitude test data and psychiatric ratings.[11] It was equal to but not better than purely statistical approaches to forecasting success.

COMPARISON OF METHODS Sawyer uncovered 75 comparisons in 45 studies of the relative efficiency of two or more of the eight methods of combining assessments.[79] As can be seen in Table 12–3, the pure judgmental method was never better than other methods with which it was compared, while *statistical, mechanical composite, and mechanical synthesis were always equal or superior to other methods.*

To sum up, one seems better off depending on some statistical combining of data than on combining by judgment. The efficiency of prediction is improved further by using judgment but treating the judgments as bits of data to be combined mechanically or synthesized mechanically with available test scores for an applicant. In all 20 studies of predicting success in flying, college, and so on, the predictions made mechanically were equal or superior to those made by judgment.[62,63] One qualification should be made. Most of the studies were not cross-validated, an omission that may result in a bias for the statistical approaches that optimize on chance results.[65]

Despite this qualification, there are several possible reasons why some mechanical combination is likely to yield better results. First, the accuracy of prediction may depend on proper weighting of the predictors. Such weighting is likely to be almost impossible to judge with any degree

Table 12–3. Comparisons among methods of combining assessments.

Number of comparisons with other methods	Method	Percentage of comparisons where method was —		
		Superior	Equal	Inferior
10	Pure judgmental	0%	40%	60%
14	Trait ratings	7	72	21
13	Profile interpretation	0	77	23
41	Pure statistical	27	73	0
34	Judgmental composite	0	53	47
12	Mechanical composite	50	50	0
6	Judgmental synthesis	0	100	0
20	Mechanical synthesis	50	50	0

Adapted from Sawyer, "Measurement and Prediction, Clinical and Statistical," *Psychological Bulletin,* 66 (1966):191.

of accuracy. Second, as information about new applicants is added to what is already available, statistical-mechanical methods can continually be improved by the additional information. On the other hand, interviewers depending on pure judgment are likely to reach a plateau beyond which they will be unable to continue to make modifications in their judgmental tendencies as evidence on new applicants is accumulated. Third, judges can only hope to match or do less well than statistical routines. If they become completely systematic and objective with a file of information, they can only do as well as the appropriate statistical equation—but not any better.[77] Fourth, interviewers are likely to add considerable error if we depend on them to combine or synthesize their trait ratings and test data about applicants. They are likely to be victimized by their own private assumptions, which may or may not be valid. These assumptions will depend on their own past experience, their relations with authority, their rigidity, and the theories about personality to which they happen to subscribe. They must guard against letting their own sets, needs, and wishes interfere with the accuracy of their subjective combination of the information they have about the applicant. Such errors may appear when an interviewer is called upon to make trait ratings about an interviewee, but if the ratings are subsequently combined or synthesized mechanically, allowance will be made for such error. Thus, if there is invalid bias in how the interviewer rates the applicant's drive, this will show up when an effort is made to add the drive rating to a mechanical composite of other ratings and test scores. The drive rating will simply disappear from the final statistical equation that emerges.

Systematically different methods were compared in an assessment of 107

superiors from 31 companies.[47] Predictions of job criteria were based on
(1) a collection of interview ratings alone; (2) projective tests alone; (3)
paper-and-pencil tests alone; (4) complete test and interview information;
and (5) a judgmental report prepared by a psychologist using all available
information. All predictions and criteria were intercorrelated and factor-
analyzed. A general validity factor emerged, signifying some amount of
agreement among all methods of assessment and judgment. But unique
halo or set factors appeared for each of the methods. For example, much
of the common variance of the interview was unique to the interview,
and the same was true for the tests and for the criteria. Other factors involving motivation and intellectual ability also were revealed. What this
means is that each method to some extent assesses applicants on irrelevancies. It is these irrelevancies that need to be removed by statistical
or mechanical means. If the final decision to hire or not depends on
subjective judgment, or on whatever other information a subjective
judgment is based, it is likely to contain much irrelevant error.

THE PLACEMENT PHASE

If applicants could be selected for specific jobs, with well-defined, relevant,
and reliable criteria, and if valid tests could assure high levels of intelligence, skills, aptitudes, interests, and personality factors to meet the
criterion requirements, problems of motivation, training, performance appraisal, and placement would largely disappear. Ideal matching of job
and employee would occur.

Unfortunately, few such ideal matches are ever realized. Criteria are
seldom, if ever, completely relevant or reliably measurable; no testing
procedure has been found that is anywhere near perfectly valid; people
are less than perfectly reliable; and, above all, situational and interpersonal
factors may be equally or more important in determining on-the-job behavior than any of the individual factors measured in testing programs
(see, for example, Chapter 6). As a result, failure to view selection as only
one phase in a complex process of matching job and employee may lead
management to devote insufficient attention, effort, and financial support
to questions of job analysis and task design, performance appraisal techniques, training, or other available approaches to increasing the effectiveness of the job-employee match.

In practice, applicants are often selected not only for their abilities to
perform on initial "entry level" jobs, but also in the hope that they may
be able to handle ever-increasing levels of responsibility. They may be
selected with the expectation that they will demonstrate abilities to perform new and different tasks as organizational requirements change. It
has been estimated that a given level of accuracy in matching employees

and jobs could be achieved with about half the amount of testing. What is needed is equivalent emphasis on other phases of the sequential decision-making process. Placement is one such phase of particular importance.[26]

Placement involves assigning new hirees to the different jobs available. To optimize the utilization of new hirees requires a process of estimating job success for all new hirees with respect to all possible assignments. A prime example of the complexities of the placement problem is provided by the armed forces. In the framework of the sequential decision-making process, relatively little emphasis is given to problems of recruiting for specific jobs (the range of job requirements to be filled is extremely great), initial screening, or testing and selection; selection ratios are typically quite unfavorable (a large proportion of "candidates" are actually "hired"); and initial testing costs are to be minimized. As a consequence, greater emphasis is placed on subsequent phases — especially placement and training — than would be the case if screening and selection were more narrowly job-related.

The predicted success of each individual must be established for each assignment. Figure 12–3 presents a simple illustration of the problem. Assume that four astronauts are to be assigned to four different positions. The figures in the cells indicate the predicted criterion performance of each astronaut for each task. The problem is to optimize the total performance of the organization by placing each astronaut in a position so that the four in combination will yield the highest level of performance. Mathematically optimal techniques are available for solving this assignment problem,[78] as well as simpler nonoptimal solutions.[81]

While the military has pioneered in the development of optimum placement, other large organizations as they mature are increasingly facing

Figure 12–3. Efficiency of four astronauts in each of four positions.

Position	Astronaut 1	Astronaut 2	Astronaut 3	Astronaut 4
Pilot A	10	32	14	11
Copilot B	15	29	8	20
Navigator C	27	17	14	13
Ground Control D	13	21	19	12

the problem. For example, firms dealing in advanced technology products found themselves in the 1970s faced with considering the pool of engineering talent they had employed in aerospace manufacturing and research and development as candidates for transfer to new kinds of jobs in energy and environmental technology.

Placement, compared to selection, offers some important advantages. The same tests may have different validities for different jobs, so that only one test battery can be used in dealing with many different job criteria. Only the weights would need to differ as we considered different possible employee-job matches. Second, if we have 10 different types of jobs to fill with 10 employees each, and we test just 100 applicants we still have a very favorable selection ratio for any one of the jobs (one in ten). The cost of recruiting applicants is less. Better relations are maintained with the pool of applicants, most of whom are more likely to be placed than if they were being tested for possible employment in 1 type of job rather than 10. Schoenfeldt [83] developed such an assessment-classification system that successfully matched individuals with jobs so that both individual job satisfaction and success were maximized. [66]

OTHER PHASES

Following selection and placement at entry level positions, the organization's efforts to improve the match between employee and job center primarily on *training* techniques (to be discussed in detail in Chapter 13) and on the appropriate use of information provided by *performance appraisal* (as reviewed in Chapter 8). As with every phase in the sequential process, the effectiveness of those techniques is a function of the relevance and reliability of criteria and information sources, as well as cost considerations.

FORECASTING SUCCESS AS A MANAGER

We have looked at the ways in which we can assess specific individual attributes, such as verbal aptitude or need for achievement. Then we have examined ways of combining such measures to optimize predictions. Now let us illustrate what combinations of information sources have been found likely to forecast success for selected important occupational groups, such as managers and engineers.

While these groups of occupations have some common patterns of screening, selection, placement, training, and performance review procedures, within each group there are also wide divergencies associated with specific differences in job demands.

INTELLIGENCE   As we have noted in Chapter 6, many different factors are involved in what managers may do, such as planning, supervising, and maintaining business controls. Nevertheless, success as an executive, administrator, administrative trainee, or manager has been repeatedly forecast by a battery of assessments. The battery included a difficult test of intelligence capable of discriminating readily among candidates for the managerial positions. For instance, Ghiselli[37] noted that middle and upper managers are likely to be in the top 4 per cent of the general population in intelligence, while first-line supervisors are at about the same level as skilled workers. He also noted that those executives above average in intelligence were more successful than those of lower intelligence. Modern managers must have the learning ability to keep up with new technological and economic developments. They have to learn to live with the computer. They also have to be able to solve problems effectively.

ACADEMIC ACHIEVEMENT   Critics argue that grades do not predict subsequent success in life — in particular, managerial performance.[57] Yet the facts are that academic performance does predict managerial performance. As early as the 1920s, rank in college graduating class was shown to be a valid predictor of success in American Telephone and Telegraph. These results were replicated in the 1950s.[14]

In more recent studies of master's graduate students in business administration at Carnegie-Mellon and Stanford Universities, grade point average predicted managerial compensation as long as 10 years after graduation.[41,100] And we might parenthetically add that both college grades and the Graduate Record Examination predict the future performance of scientists, as to both income and the number of times that their publications are cited.[25]

INTERPERSONAL COMPETENCE   Interpersonal competence does not necessarily imply the need for close relations with others. On the contrary, the typical manager is likely to avoid what the interaction-oriented are seeking — gratification from close relations with other persons. Managers usually have to be socially mobile, able to make and break friendships easily as they move from one position to another or one geographic location to another.[1] What interpersonal competence does imply is consideration for others, motivating others through concern for their needs. The Ohio State Leadership Opinion Questionnaire (previously discussed in Chapter 6) taps the extent to which managers emphasize such consideration in their interpersonal relations and has been found valid as a forecaster of supervisory success.[7,8] On the other hand, a widely used, more complex questionnaire and test of information about supervision ("How Supervise"), requiring endorsement or rejections of various supervisory practices and company policies, has failed to have much predictive validity.[76] Similarly, multiple choice information tests about supervisory practices[17] have generally not proved valid either, although a correlation of 0.65 was obtained between post office supervisors, tested human relations knowledge, and the volume of mail processed by their subordinates for one year.[20] Interpersonal competence seems to be assessed consistently with more validity for forecasting leadership potential by buddy or peer ratings.[44,101]

Managerial Assessment Programs

When a vacancy occurs, if an employee's tested potential is on file, management can quickly respond with a replacement. There may be a vacancy with two contenders for the position. Both may have been equally successful in their present position (as indicated by their appraisals), but one individual's test scores may show a greater potential than the other's. In this case, the management group may decide to promote the person with the greater potential, with the expectation that he or she will gain valuable experience in the position and continue to rise in the organization. Other reasons (such as special technical job demands) may, however, require choosing the individual with lesser promotion potential.[51]

Many firms and agencies have spent a great deal of time and effort in developing batteries of tests and other assessment procedures to predict executive performance. Positive results have usually been obtained. We will describe three well-known programs developed separately by American Telephone and Telegraph, Sears, and Exxon. Each has taken a slightly different approach to the identification of management potential.

AMERICAN TELEPHONE AND TELEGRAPH'S ASSESSMENT PROGRAM The management progress study in the Bell Telephone System began in 1956. The purpose of the study was to try to understand what characteristics were important in the growth of employees as they moved into middle and upper management levels. Over 400 participants were included in this investigation. The assessment program required the managers to spend three and one-half days at an Assessment Center in groups of 12. During this time, the individual's abilities, aptitudes, and motivational and personality characteristics were assessed by tests and ratings by the assessment staff.

A total of 25 attributes were defined and measured at the Assessment Center. The attributes included general mental ability, oral and written communication skill, human relations skill, creativity, need for approval by superiors, innerwork standards, need for advancement, need for security, primacy of work, Bell System value orientation, realistic expectations, energy, and decision making. The assessed variables did not all predict management advancement. For example, the Bell System value orientation was not predictive of success in the organization. (This finding should dispel some notions expressed that, to be successful in an organization, one must completely adopt the values of the organization.) In contrast, attributes such as human relation skills, need for advancement, oral communication skills, resistance to stress, energy, range of interests, and tolerance of uncertainty were all related to future advancement in the organization.

The twenty-five assessment variables have been grouped into seven categories, as follows:

1. Administrative skills — a good manager has the ability to organize work effectively and make high-quality decisions;
2. Interpersonal skills — the forceful personality makes a favorable impression on others with good oral skills;
3. Intellectual ability — a good manager learns quickly and has a wide range of interests;
4. Stability of performance — good managers are consistent in their performance, even under stressful conditions or in an uncertain environment;
5. Work motivation — good managers will find positive satisfaction from their jobs and believe that work is more important than other areas of their lives; they are concerned with doing a good job for its own sake;
6. Career orientation — a good manager wants to advance in the organization very quickly, but is not as concerned about a secure job; the manager does not want to delay rewards for too long a period of time;
7. Dependence upon others — good managers are not as concerned about getting approval from either superiors or peers and are unwilling to change their life goals.

Administrative skills were best assessed by the manager's performance on the in-basket test. The evaluation of the interpersonal skills was obtained from the staff's judgment of the manager's performance in group exercises. A measure of intellectual ability was reliably obtained from standardized general ability tests. The stability of performance measure was obtained from the individual's performance in the simulations. The work motivation measure was obtained from projective tests and the interview, with some contribution from the simulations. Career orientation was seen both in interviews and projective tests and to some extent from the personality questionnaires. The measure of dependency was gained mostly from the projective tests.

Following the assessments, data were collected annually on the managers' progress. In addition, each manager was periodically interviewed and given various questionnaires to complete. One objective of the study was to develop ways to predict managerial success. Another objective was to study how each manager developed and how the personnel policies and practices of the company aided or hindered this progress.

ASSESSMENT CENTERS   One result of the program was the widespread use of the assessment center in the Bell System. By 1968, there were some 52 assessment centers throughout the system, and over 16,000 individuals had gone through them.[13] Subsequently, over 1,000 such assessment centers were started in the United States and elsewhere.

The assessment staffs were made up of management personnel who were two levels above that of the candidates being assessed. While the assessors were nonprofessionals in one sense, they underwent a 3-week training period, which in the final week included a dry run with 12 subjects.

At the end of the assessment period, the assessment staff rated each candidate on 20 qualities. Staff members were not given detailed instructions on how to weight the various assessment devices they used. They were told to use their own experience in making the final judgments of the candidates.

PREDICTIVE VALIDITY   In the original study, the assessment center staff judged the potential of lower-level management participants to reach middle management. These judgments were kept confidential. Eight years later, of those predicted to reach middle management, 64 per cent had done so; of those predicted not to, only 32 per cent had succeeded in reaching middle management. This demonstrated that the assessment center significantly improved upon the ordinary college recruiting and screening process for selecting manager trainees.

About half the candidates at the assessment center were described by the staff in the original study as lacking in potential for promotion. This was a surprising finding because the only individuals sent to the assessment center were those who, by an earlier management judgment, possessed the potential for early advancement. The assessment staff rated 10 per cent of the 400 college graduates as exceptionally able to become high-level managers. During the eight years that followed, none of them were discharged, although of the whole 400, 19 per cent were discharged.

The two most significant factors in predicting success were leadership skills as assessed in a face-to-face situation and administrative ability. The other four important factors were intellectual ability, stability of performance when faced with stress and uncertainty, work motivation, and active career orientation. Administrative skill was correlated with intellectual ability and leadership skills with stability of performance, so the dimensions are not completely independent of each other.

The measure of intellectual ability is the factor most readily and cheaply assessed by paper-and-pencil tests before an individual enters the organization. It was found that unless an individual is of at least average mental ability, the other characteristics important for success are much less likely to be helpful. Potential for both work motivation and career orientation could be assessed by an interview. It should be stressed that the interviews

Table 12–4. Assessment predictions and attainment of middle management eight years later.

	N	Number reaching middle management	Percentage reaching middle management
Predicted to reach middle management	61	39	64
Predicted to fail to reach middle management	62	20	32
Total	123	59	48%

From D. W. Bray, R. J. Campbell, and D. C. Grant. *Formative Years in Business.* New York: John Wiley & Sons, 1974, p. 69.

were conducted by well-trained professionals, who spent at least an hour and a half with each candidate before dictating a long report, which was then carefully scored in a standardized manner for all candidates.

OPERATIONAL VALIDITY   To illustrate what results are now possible, see Table 12–4. It shows over an eight-year period those assessed candidates for management positions who reached middle management in the telephone system and those who failed to do so. It can be seen that 64 per cent of the 123 candidates who were expected to reach middle management did so but only 32 per cent who were expected by assessors to fail reached middle management levels in the following eight years.[14]

Subsequent Changes in Assessees

The importance of a dynamic approach to test-criterion is to be seen in the eight-year follow-up of 400 assessed Bell System candidates by Bray, Campbell and Grant.[14] The results showed the relationship of the candidates' assessments and changes in life themes to continued success in the organization. The candidates who proved to be more successful were more involved with their jobs initially. Their concern for their work continued to rise throughout the eight years of the study. In contrast, those who failed to attain middle management started at a lower level of concern for their work and continued to decline in this respect over the years.

"ENLARGERS" VERSUS "ENFOLDERS"   Two contrasting life styles were identified: "enlargers" and "enfolders." The enlarging life style is one that emphasizes innovation, change, self-development, and movement away from traditional ways of thinking and doing things. In contrast, the enfolding life style is oriented more toward tradition, toward maintaining close family and friendship ties, and toward recreational and social activities. Typically, enfolders are less likely to leave their hometown area and are much less apt to engage in any self-improvement activities. Those who attained middle management levels were enlargers; those less likely to do so were enfolders.

SKILL CHANGES The assessment procedure was repeated for the sample of managers after the eight-year period, providing an opportunity to examine changes in ability levels. Although it is generally believed that cognitive ability shows little change over time among young adults, decided gains during this period were found in intellectual ability, critical thinking, and knowledge of contemporary affairs. The last gain was particularly striking: eight years later individuals were much more aware of the events occurring around them than they had been as recent college graduates.

Surprisingly, there was no difference between the assessment and the reassessments for administrative skills; for interpersonal skills, there was an actual drop upon reassessment. Eight years in management roles thus had unexpected impacts. Cognitive skills improved, administrative skills were unchanged, and interpersonal skills declined. In addition, the managers became less dependent upon others, had more regard for their own achievement, had more interest in influencing others, were more aggressive, and were less interested in affiliation and deferring to others.

DIFFERENTIAL CHANGES The changes in the assessments of the successful and the unsuccessful managers were compared. Consistent with earlier findings that "enlargers" were more successful than "enfolders," concern for their work continued to increase among the more successful and decrease among the less successful managers. Likableness was associated with success in the first assessment, but not in the assessment eight years later. Lack of tact was associated with failure among the management recruits, but it was no longer an issue eight years later.

WHICH IS CAUSE, WHICH IS EFFECT? It is often hard to determine what is cause and what is effect in this type of study. As employees become more successful in the organization, they may have less time for their usual family ties, and they gain increasingly more satisfaction from their job as they are rewarded both financially and in other ways for their success. In contrast, those who are less successful in the job may derive less satisfaction from it, in both a psychological and material sense and therefore have more time for involvement in family and recreational activities. However, the evidence that most successful people were higher to start with in concern for work-related themes suggests that individuals bring to their job at least some rudiments of a life style that contributes to their success in the organization. These results are consistent with what we know from studies of management success, need for achievement, task orientation, and management motivation discussed in Chapter 11 and earlier.

UTILITY   A practical question often asked concerning assessment centers is "Why not just use the immediate supervisors' ratings of potential for management success, instead of going through the expense of an assessment center?" * Or why not just use supervisors' ratings of present on-the-job performance as a basis for promoting individuals into management positions?

First of all, the reliability of assessment center ratings of potential was higher than could be obtained from pairs of supervisors rating potential from job performance. According to Bray, Campbell and Grant, supervisors were more lenient in their on-the-job ratings of Bell System personnel. Also they used more restricted ranges of scale values. It thus appeared that ratings of potential from assessment centers were of higher quality than from supervisors.

Second, assessment centers yield better predictors of subsequent rise to managerial positions than do the predictions of the first-line supervisors of operating personnel. This is not too surprising when one considers that the first-line supervisors of operating personnel are at the lowest managerial level in the organization themselves in contrast to the staff psychologists and upper-level managers who make the judgments at assessment centers. The first-line supervisors are unlikely to be as fully conversant with the demands and qualities required for effective performance at higher levels of the organization.[14]

Third, there is evidence that the assessment center is fair to both minority and nonminority group members. Over 4,000 women have been assessed by the Bell System. The assessment centers have predicted success in management for women as well as for men.[67] There has been one study indicating that white males may receive higher ratings when the group being assessed contains a larger number of white males.[82] The effects found have only marginal practical significance. Still, if that effect is reliable, the composition of the group or another measure will have to change to eliminate any sex or race bias.

The assessment center does, of course, eliminate any possibility of immediate supervisor bias although supervisors may be involved in recommending who should go to an assessment center.[46] Whereas the assessment center is a standardized situation, job conditions may be somewhat different for each employee. For example, some jobs may be more or less demanding than others so that judgments based on the job performance may be invalid.[93]

* Estimated in 1979 in the Bell System to be $1500 per candidate assessed.

In the mid-1970s, it was estimated that in the United States alone over 1,000 assessment centers were in operation. Yet validation has depended on using managerial advancement, salary growth, or superior's ratings of potential as criteria for managerial success. Only a few validation studies have used actual managerial job performance, the satisfaction of subordinates, or departmental productivity as criteria. When actual managerial performance has been used, a decided drop has occurred in the correlation with assessment center predictions. It may be that the usual correlation obtained between assessment center predictions and managerial advancement holds true because assessment staff members anticipate how other managers (who are their colleagues) will judge candidates in making promotion decisions.[50]

Recent research indicates that the order of presentation of the exercise does not affect performance [23] and that assessment ratings are not completely influenced by test scores.[81]

The assessment center may actually provide too much information for the most accurate judgments — a condition of information overload. There is evidence from other areas of psychology that too much information can lower predictive efficiency.[16] For example, the first large-scale assessment program in the United States was set up during World War II by the Office of Strategic Services to select spies for overseas assignments. The one-day assessment used therein proved to be more predictive than the three-day assessment.[103] More information, then, may not mean more accurate prediction. Given the possibilities of information overload on the decision to promote as well as the cost per candidate for an assessment it becomes useful to predict in advance by inexpensive means who will do well and who will do poorly in an assessment center. Just as was found by Vernon that a one hour leaderless group discussion assessment correlated 0.75 with three days of assessment, so unpublished research now indicates that pre-screening of sociability and ascendancy correlate 0.60 with three day assessment results. Considerable savings can be effected by screening out in advance those highly likely to receive poor assessment ratings.[98]

Fears of a "crown prince" or "kiss of death" effect due to performance in the assessment center have not been found in companies like IBM. A high rating does not guarantee promotion, nor does a low rating eliminate promotion possibilities.[52] Generally, assessments also form the basis of counseling with the candidates on career plans and ways to improve performance on the job.

Sears Program to Predict Executive Behavior

The Sears program for executive personnel testing extends over a period of 25 years and illustrates a second type, one that rests heavily on standardized and custom-made tests and inventories. A battery of tests has evolved tapping intellectual ability, personality, values, and interests, which in combination are able to predict the promotability of executives. An interesting aspect of the Sears results is the ability of the executive test battery scores to predict subordinate morale. As can be seen in Table 12–5,

Table 12–5. Multiple correlations between mean employee morale scores and executive battery test scores for executives responsible for supervising the employees.

	Multiple correlations	
Morale areas	48 Store managers	42 Higher-level supervisors
I. Operating efficiency		
a. Effectiveness of administration	.77	.51
b. Technical competence of supervision	.74	.43
c. Adequacy of communication	.59	.61
II. Personal relations		
a. Friendliness of fellow employees	.37 (zero-order) †	.57
b. Supervisor-employee relations	.68	.54
c. Confidence in management	.59	.52
III. Individual satisfactions		
a. Job security	.40	.30 (zero-order)
b. Status and recognition	.69	.62
c. Identification with the company	.51	.52
d. Opportunity for growth and advancement	.37 (zero order)	.67
IV. Financial rewards		
a. Employee benefits	.54	.57
b. Pay	−.30 (zero-order)	.48
V. Job and conditions of work		
a. Working conditions	.36	.40
b. Job demands	.00	.00 (zero order)
c. Overall morale score	.47	.54

All correlations significant at 5% level of confidence or beyond.
† Zero order correlations refer to those between a *single* test variable and a morale category.
From V. J. Bentz "The Sears Experience in the Investigation, Description and Prediction of Executive Behavior." In J. A. Myers, Jr. (ed.), *Predicting Managerial Success*. Ann Arbor: Foundation for Research on Human Behavior, 1968, p. 71.

there are positive relationships between employee morale and the psychological characteristics of the executives. It would appear that the psychological characteristics measured by the Sears test battery play an important role in influencing employee attitudes in the organization.[10] It is imperative that an organization consider not only its present needs but also its future needs. That is, the personnel — specifically, the executives — who perform well in the organization at the present time may not perform so well in the future, if conditions change.

When the program began, Sears saw itself as a rapidly expanding company requiring certain unique qualities both now and in the future. Its analysis indicated four areas of needed change in the executive manpower pool. First, it saw a need for individuals who were several notches higher in mental ability than those presently occupying executive posts. Second, it foresaw the need for psychological qualities that would allow for innovation and change in the organization. Third, the analysis revealed a need for even greater administrative skill and decision-making abilities, especially under conditions where the information was quite complex. Fourth, Sears saw a need to continue to have people who both were emotionally stable and also had personal aggressiveness and the desire to contribute in a meaningful way to the organization.

The Sears executive battery of psychological tests was then modified and changed to include measures to tap flexible intellectual functioning, such as the Sears adaptation of the California F-Scale. To measure creative ingenuity and ability to initiate change, a number of tests were constructed, including tests for preference of complexity, a biographical history form, an adjective checklist, a verbal fluency test, and a self-rating of role definition, all designed to tap some aspect of the creative executive role.

To tap the area of administrative skill and decision making, a special Sears in-basket test was devised, along with two leaderless group problem-solving situations, one of which is described in Figure 12–4. In addition, three problem-solving simulations were designed. To measure emotional stability and competitive drive, the Guilford-Martin inventory was modified especially for this purpose.

The multiple correlation of the combination of predictor measures with various criteria such as supervisory ratings ranged from 0.49 to above 0.80. Both the specially designed Sears in-basket test and the specially designed group problem-solving simulations demonstrated good predictive power.

Exxon's "Early Identification of Managerial Potential" Program

More similar to the Sears than to the Bell Telephone approach, an extensive program was designed to measure and differentiate Exxon managers. In 1955, eight hours of tests and measurements were administered to over

---

(1) *Situation One*

The group was asked to reconsider the in-basket they had already solved but within a different role structure.

It will be recalled that the in-basket was a situation in which the ex-manager had died and the subject was to deal with the materials that were left in the in-basket. This, each of the subjects was to have done. In the group situation, the men were confronted with the in-basket materials in a somewhat different framework. The instructions are as follows:

"You and the men at your table are members of a staff group that reports to Frank Hastings, Zone Manager of the Mid-Central Zone.

"Last Saturday the Exville store manager died of a heart attack. Sunday Mr. Hastings drove to Exville to take a look at the store. He reported the store wasn't in as good a shape as he thought it might be. Mr. Hastings had given each of you a copy of the material found in the manager's in-basket and asked that you come together as a staff group for the purpose of making an analysis of the store and its problems, and then decide upon a series of recommendations that the new manager might follow in rebuilding the Exville store. Together, the analysis and recommendations should form a kind of managerial strategy that could effectively rebuild Exville."

The group then proceeds to discuss for 45 minutes. Two observers are present for rating purposes. At the conclusion of the exercise the men do peer ratings on quality and quantity of ideas contributed and make a first and second choice nomination for manager of the store.

Figure 12-4. Group problem-solving simulation. (From V. J. Bentz, "The Sears Experience in the Investigation, Description and Prediction of Executive Behavior." In J. A. Myers, Jr. (Ed.), *Predicting Managerial Success.* AnnArbor: Foundation for Research on Human Behavior, 1968, p. 98.)

400 managers. At that time, their salaries ranged from $14,000 to $225,000. The assessments included measures of intellectual functioning and personality, biographical information, and an interview. The prediction problem was especially difficult because the managers were divided into two groups according to three criteria. The criteria were organizational level attained, salary grade achieved, and rated managerial effectiveness. There were really no unsuccessful managers, since they were all operating in the organization, but some managers were identified as being more successful for their age than others. The difficult task was to develop a method to differentiate between individuals who have been just successful enough to reach a managerial position from those who have done very well in the organization.

IMPORTANCE   The testing program at Exxon was seen as important because ratings by superiors of the potential of managers and prospective managers had previously been insufficiently reliable; i.e., they did not agree well from year to year. Potential was usually rated as being either below average or average. There was also little relationship between what prospective managers were observed doing on their present jobs and what would be expected of them when they became managers. Moreover, it was suspected that the immediate supervisors of newer employees, although in the best position to rate the performance of such employees on their current jobs, were unlikely to assess managerial potential accurately. The reason, again, is that these immediate supervisors were not themselves high-level managers [53] and were thus relatively unfamiliar with the requirements for success at higher levels.

VALIDATION   After the tests were administered and criterion data collected, correlations were computed. Based on them, the Exxon tests were combined into a battery to maximize discrimination between the more successful and less successful managers. The results are shown in Figure 12–5. All the tested managers are grouped into 10 per cent intervals, going from high to low on the basis of their total weighted test scores. On the far right, it can be seen that for those with the highest test scores, 95 per cent were highly successful managers, while 5 per cent were in the middle in success; no one who had a top test score was found to be low in success as a manager. Conversely, a look at the bottom 10 per cent of test scores shows that none of the lowest-scoring examinees were highly successful managers, while 21 per cent were found to be in the middle range and 79 per cent were low in success.

APPLICATION   It is interesting to look at how the program was put into operation in the various subsidiaries of the corporation. One Exxon subsidiary — Humble Oil — began operations by first carefully explaining the program to its management. First, all currently employed managers were tested. Newcomers were usually tested within six months after entering the company, i.e., after the selection and initial placement phases.

New examinees were told that the test scores were to be used in their career development as one piece of information, along with their actual performance on the job. Employees did not receive feedback about their test results.

The test results for each examinee are presented to a management group along with current performance appraisals. This presentation allows the management group to discuss each individual, and particularly to explore in more depth any situations where the data might be in conflict. If the employee shows a high potential score and is also appraised quite highly, then the decision can be quickly made to give the individual more opportunity for growth, which will usually take the form of increased responsibility and advancement in the organization. Of greater concern and requiring more investigation is the case where the test data and current performance appraisal are in conflict. Suggestions may be raised either to change the individual's field of work or possibly to change the individual's supervisor.

FURTHER IMPROVEMENT IN PREDICTION USING LIFESPACE * VARIABLES   Vicino and Bass obtained data on 400 Humble examinees six years after Exxon testing.[99] Four "lifespace" measures were generated for each examinee:

1. How much task challenge had been perceived on the entry job into Humble Oil,
2. How much life stress (off and on the job) had been experienced in the preceding several years,
3. How well did the examinees match their first supervisor's personality test scores, and
4. How meritorious was their first supervisor.

These lifespace variables were related to success beyond what could be predicted from the Exxon test scores shown in Figure 12–5. For example, managerial success was greater than would be predicted from test scores if more task challenge had been perceived by the examinee, if less stress had been experienced, if the first supervisor was more meritorious (and thus more influential "upstairs"), and if the examinees and their supervisor *differed* in personality traits. Perhaps the old adage "opposites attract" has some value. As with the Bell System research, a challenging initial task assignment in one's Exxon career experience resulted in overachievement. If the supervisor was successful this also resulted in overachievement.[99] This research illustrates the importance of integrating personnel and organizational psychology.

FORECASTING SUCCESS IN RESEARCH AND ENGINEERING

With the importance of industrial and national investment in research and development in advanced industrial countries has come a considerable increase in studies of engineering and research personnel. Tests of spatial, mechanical, and numerical aptitude, of abstract reasoning, and of general intelligence all tend to be positively related to success in these fields. But evaluating success is a challenging problem and, we shall see, requires considerable attention to motivation and personality.

Productivity in Research and Engineering

What criteria of performance are we trying to predict? What constitutes successful and effective effort in research and engineering? Objective counts

---

* By "lifespace" variables, we mean to cover experiential moderators both on and off the job which intervene in their effects between initial selection testing and final criterion collection.

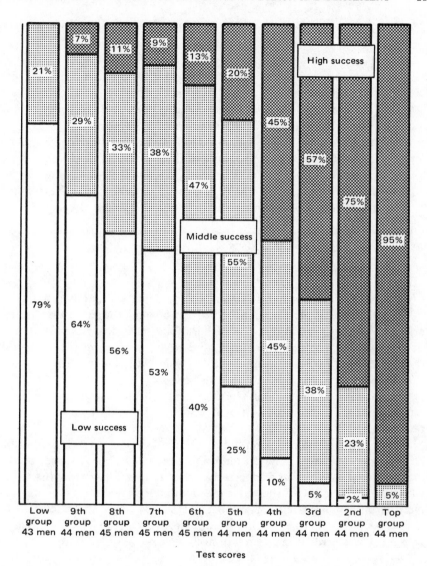

Figure 12–5. Test performance of high, middle, and low success managers. (From H. Laurent, "Research on the Identification of Management Potential." In J. A. Myers, Jr. (ed.), *Predicting Managerial Success.* Ann Arbor: Foundation for Research on Human Behavior, 1968, p. 15.)

of the number of research papers produced or number of patents earned [99] may occasionally be useful, but more psychologically meaningful differentiations depend on subjective evaluations of on-the-job performance. Buel was able to cluster examples of independent sets of items on which chemists, geologists, physicists, and engineers could be scaled in effectiveness,[18] as follows:

A. Conversant with the latest technical developments in their field; use the latest techniques to solve problems assigned to them.

B. Have not overlooked significant implications of their work; have not neglected significant facts arising from their work.

C. Can transform theory into practical application; present convincing technical arguments in support of their point of view.

D. Are technical perfectionists; carry out exhaustive literature searches.

E. Are not disorganized when their work is interrupted; have not expressed a desire to work on only one problem at a time.

Assessing Creativity in Architecture, Research and Engineering

Creative behavior in general is seen as: (1) novel and containing statistically infrequent ideas; (2) adaptive to reality; and (3) based on sustained original insights, evaluations, and elaborations.[59] But what exactly is meant by creativity in engineering? An analysis of why actual engineering solutions to test problems are seen as creative suggested four elements: novelty, worth, independence, and comprehensiveness.[86]

What is meant by originality? Often included are uncommon responses, remote, unusual, or unconventional associations, and rated cleverness of responses.[104]

Strong drive, sustained effort, and clear-cut interest are important for achieving eminence in physical and biological research.[75] A survey analysis differentiated creative and uncreative chemists and psychologists. Those who were more creative showed more dominance and initiative, and were more strongly motivated for intellectual success than their less creative colleagues.[22] Similarly, maturation and interest are particularly important to the achievement of eminence in architecture.

Highly creative architects, according to nominations by other architects, were compared at the Institute for Personality Assessment Research in tested personality, ability, and background with architects with less eminent reputations. What was found most generally characteristic of the most creative architect was

. . . a high level of effective intelligence, . . . openness to experience, . . . freedom from petty restraints and impoverishing inhibitions, . . . aesthetic sensitivity, . . . high level of energy, . . . unquestioning commitment to creative endeavor and . . . unceasing striving for creative solutions to the evermore difficult architectural problems. . . .[58]

Highly creative architects are likely to describe themselves as inventive, determined, independent, individualistic, enthusiastic, and industrious rather than responsible, secure, reliable, dependable, clear-thinking, tolerant, and disciplined. During college days, in comparison to the average student, future eminent architects were likely to earn As in courses that caught their interest and do little work in others. Like creative mathematicians, scientists, and writers, creative architects had parents who respected them, who allocated responsibilities to them, but were not emotionally close to them. Like other creative people, they now tend to be introverted; more interested in art, music, poetry, drama, and literature; high in interest in theoretical and aesthetic matters; and likely to prefer the asymmetrical and the complex.[59] Observers of the sample of creative architects sorted 100 statements of personal functioning into categories most and least descriptive. Table 12–6 shows items correlating with the tendency of architects to be judged more creative.

SCIENTISTS VERSUS ARTISTS   While the creative scientists and engineers at one extreme share much in common with the creative artists and writers, they differ also in that the technical specialists are more concerned about orderliness, control, and careful planning, while the artists and writers tend to remain more open and receptive to new experience.[59] Scientists and

Table 12–6. Item correlates (0.40 or higher) of the rated creativeness of architects.

r	Item
+.53	Is an interesting, arresting person.
+.46	Able to see the heart of important problems.
+.45	Is productive; gets things done.
+.45	Thinks and associates to ideas in an unusual way; has unconventional thought processes.
+.43	Has hostility toward others.
+.40	Has social poise and presence; appears socially at ease.
	• • •
−.41	Is vulnerable to real or fancied threat, generally fearful.
−.42	Favors conservative values in a variety of areas.
−.45	Feels cheated and victimized by life; self-pitying.
−.49	Is uncomfortable with uncertainties and complexities.
−.51	Is self-defeating.
−.52	Reluctant to commit self to any definite course of action; tends to delay or avoid action.

D. W. MacKinnon, "Assessing Creative Persons." Reprinted from the *Journal of Creative Behavior,* 2 (1967): 298. Published by the Creative Education Foundation, Buffalo, New York.

engineers generally score high in spatial, numerical, and mechanical aptitude.

This same lack of conformity to social demands and greater ego strength are characteristic of eminent artists and writers.[29] Productivity as a scientist is seen to depend mainly on dislike of regimentation, individualism, and technical competence.[97] Similarly, others have argued that engineers are handicapped when placed in administrative or supervisory roles because of their hostility toward authority, their emphasis on technical exactness and perfection, and their avoidance of close interpersonal relations.[72]

In contrast to 100 nonengineers, 100 mechanical engineers were reported to be more motivated about their work, more concerned about detail, more self-sufficient, yet more casual about interpersonal matters.

Research and Engineering Productivity

Supervisors and subordinates of engineers rated engineers with whom they had worked as most and least productive.[87,88] Supervisors' responses clustered in five factors that differentiated the productivity:

1. *General Productive Behavior:* good overall work performance, analytical thinking, work-oriented organizing behavior, independent action and good technical report writing.
2. *Affability:* agreeable, pleasant, nonaggressive, good group members (note this does not necessarily imply close interpersonal relations).
3. *Motivation:* industrious, interested in job, extra effort, not patient or calm.
4. *Ability to Communicate Effectively.*
5. *Creativity:* imagination, versatility, ingenuity.

Subordinates believed that productive and unproductive engineers differ in their interest in their work, independence, initiative, and acceptance of responsibility.

In contrast to those who produce fewer inventions and publications (holding age constant), scientific and technical personnel who are productive describe themselves as more original, imaginative, curious, enthusiastic, impulsive, and self-confident and less contented, conventional, inhibited, and formal.[97] Owens was able to predict the creativity of over 900 mechanical engineers nine years after they left college.[70] The best predictors indicated that the more creative engineers were cognitively complex (able to integrate a lot of information to arrive at a solution).

BIOGRAPHICAL DATA   What makes for successful scientists or engineers? Answers have been sought in many studies of the biographical information differentiating more from less creative technical personnel. A biographical inventory was an excellent predictor of productivity and creativity among physical scientists at Air Force research centers and scientists at NASA research centers.[91] The creative scientists had several distinguishing characteristics. They were very confident they could perform at a high level, very independent (a common finding), intellectually oriented, very hard-working and dedicated to work, and set high levels of aspiration for themselves.

The biographical inventory used by Taylor and Ellison [90] in predicting the success in science of over 2,000 scientists consists of 300 questions arranged in four parts: developmental history (up to age twenty-one), parents and family life, academic background, and adult activities. The criteria usually consisted of the number of patents and publications, official NASA records, and special rating forms completed by the supervisor. A cross-validation obtained a correlation of 0.67 with the criterion corrected for unreliability. This indicated that almost half of the variation in creativity of the scientists was accounted for by the biographical inventory score.

Similarly, correlations have been obtained of 0.22 to 0.43 between specially scored BIB keys and creativity ratings by supervisors and peers, patent disclosures, and performance ratings of engineering personnel.[61] A cross-validated analysis of 132 pharmaceutical research and technical personnel found the following positive biographical indicators of creativity: wide interests, positive self-image, a need for independence socially and at work, permissive parents, overinvolvement in job-related activities, positive reactions to challenge, interest in contemplative activities, and interest in unstructured work situations.[19]

SUMMARY OF FORECASTING   Summing up what we know about forecasting success in research and engineering, we see that biographical information forms have been very effective in predicting scientists' and engineers' productivity and creativity. Productivity and creativity have been found to be closely related. In order to be creative, an individual must produce a minimum amount. In fact, those judged most creative are also producing a great deal.

Studies have also shown some consistent personality and work patterns for creative individuals. They are extremely task-oriented and devoted to their work, putting in exceptionally long hours. They are invariably confident about their ability to do good work and are extremely independent. Intelligence is important for creative engineers and scientists. They must have an intelligence level equal to or higher than that of the average college graduate. Beyond that point, creativity seems to be determined more by motivational and personality characteristics that are often developed early in life.[59,5] The climates of both school and organizations [43] have an influence on expression of creativity, as was discussed in Chapter 5.

SUMMARY

Aptitude tests, tests of interests, values, and personality, and other sources of information about potential jobholders represent some of the most useful tools available to organizations interested in effective utilization of manpower resources. Despite imperfect measurements and legitimate objections to testing programs that incompetently or unwisely fail to measure fairly and with relevance, virtually everyone interested in either effective job performance or increased job satisfaction would agree on the need to avoid the costly human and economic waste that results from selection and placement errors. It is our conviction that it is ethically wrong — as well as economically inefficient — to do less than the best job possible in matching work requirements with the aptitudes, values, interests, and personality characteristics of individual job applicants. (We will reserve further discussion of social and ethical issues in testing for detailed investigation in Chapter 18.)

We began our discussion of the process of effective employee utilization by examining, in Chapter 7, the techniques used to define job activities and requirements. In Chapter 8, we reviewed problems associated with measuring performance on the job, with the aim of providing tools that both permit job performers to be appropriately rewarded and allow decision makers to identify those who could be effectively promoted, transferred, or trained. In Chapters 9, 10, 11, and 12, we saw that tests and other information sources can, with proper attention to reliability and validity, be used to aid decision makers in the sequential process of matching job requirements with individual characteristics.

Our emphasis has been on the interdependent nature of phases in the personnel matching process, stressing the need to balance organizational efforts, avoiding the costs both to the organizations and to individual candidates that arise from considering these phases in isolation from each other.

Once we have some confidence in having selected and placed employees by the best available methods, we are likely to improve the effectiveness of our work force even further by employing a broad range of training and development techniques. Chapters 13 and 14 focus on these applications of behavioral science.

REFERENCES

1. Abegglen, J. C. "Personality Factors in Social Mobility: A Study of Occupationally Mobile Businessmen," *Genetic Psychology Monograph,* 58 (1958): 101–159.
2. Albrecht, P. A., E. M. Glasser, and J. Marks. "Validation of a Multiple-Assessment Procedure for Managerial Personnel," *Journal of Applied Psychology,* 48 (1964): 351–360.

3. Alf, E. F., and J. H. Wolfe. "Comparison of Classification Strategies by Computer Simulation Methods," *U.S. Naval Personnel Research Activity Technical Bulletin*, St B 68–11, June 1968.

4. Arbous, A. G. "The Validation of Test Procedures for the Selection and Classification of Administrative Personnel: Summary of Report," *Bulletin of the National Institute of Personnel Research* (Johannesburg), 3, no. 1 (1951): 27–33.

5. Barron, F. *Creativity and Psychological Health*. Princeton, N. J.: Van Nostrand, 1963.

6. Bartlett, C. J., and C. G. Green. "Clinical Prediction: Does One Sometimes Know Too Much?" *Journal of Counseling Psychology*, 13 (1966): 267–270.

7. Bass, B. M. "Leadership Opinions as Forecasts of Supervisory Success," *Journal of Applied Psychology*, 40 (1956): 345–346.

8. Bass, B. M. "Leadership Opinions as Forecasts of Supervisory Process: A Replication," *Personnel Psychology*, 11 (1958): 515–518.

9. Bell, R. Q. "A Comparison of Profile Prediction Methods and Multiple Correlation." Unpublished Ph.D. dissertation, Stanford University, 1951.

10. Bentz, V. J. "The Sears Experience in the Investigation, Description and Prediction of Executive Behavior." In J. A. Myers (ed.), *Predicting Managerial Success*, 59–152. Ann Arbor: Foundation for Research on Human Behavior, 1968.

11. Bobbitt, J. M., and S. H. Newman. "Psychological Activities at the United States Coast Guard Academy," *Psychological Bulletin*, 41 (1944): 568–579.

12. Bowers, D. G. "Self-Esteem and the Diffusion of Leadership Style," *Journal of Applied Psychology*, 47 (1963): 135–140.

13. Bray, D. W. "Choosing Good Managers." In J. A. Myers (ed.), *Predicting Managerial Success*, 153–166. Ann Arbor: Foundation for Research on Human Behavior, 1968.

14. Bray, D. W., R. J. Campbell, and D. C. Grant. *Formative Years in Business: A Long-Term AT & T Study of Managerial Lives*. New York: John Wiley & Sons, 1974.

15. Brogden, H. E. "On the Interpretation of the Correlation Coefficient as a Measure of Predictive Efficiency," *Journal of Educational Psychology*, 37 (1946): 64–76.

16. Brokaw, L. D. *The Comparative Composite Validities of Batteries of "Short" versus "Long" Tests*. Res. Bull., 1950, 50–51. San Antonio, Texas: Lackland Air Force Base Air Training Command, Human Resources Research Center, 1950.

17. Bruce, M. M., and D. B. Learner. "A Supervisory Practices Test," *Personnel Psychology*, 11 (1958): 216–217.

18. Buel, W. E. "The Validity of Behavioral Rating Scale Items for the Assessment of Individual Creativity," *Journal of Applied Psychology*, 44 (1960): 407–412.

19. Buel, W. E. "Biographical Data and the Identification of Creative Research Personnel," *Journal of Applied Psychology*, 49 (1965): 318–321.

20. Carp, F. M., B. M. Vitola, and F. L. McLanathan. "Human Relations Knowledge and Social Distance Set in Supervisors," *Journal of Applied Psychology*, 47 (1963): 78–80.

21. Cascio, W. F. *Applied Psychology in Personnel Management*. Reston, Va.: Reston Publishing Company, Inc., 1978.
22. Chambers, J. A. "Relating Personality and Biographical Factors to Scientific Creativity," *Psychological Monographs: General and Applied*, 78 (1964), Whole No. 584.
23. Cohen, S. L., and L. Sands. "The Effects of Order of Exercise Presentation on Assessment Center Performance: One Standardization Concern," *Personnel Psychology*, 31 (1978): 35–46.
24. Comrey, A. L., W. S. High, and R. C. Wilson. "Factors Influencing Organizational Effectiveness: VII. A Survey of Aircraft Supervisors," *Personnel Psychology*, 8 (1955): 245–257.
25. Creager, J. A., and L. R. Harmon. *On-the-job Validation of Selection Variables*. Tech. Rep. No. 26. Washington, D. C.: Office of Scientific Personnel, National Academy of Sciences—National Research Council, April 15, 1966.
26. Cronbach, L. J., and G. C. Gleser. *Psychological Tests and Personnel Decisions*. Urbana, Ill.: University of Illinois Press, 1965.
27. Cropley, A. J., and T. W. Field. "Achievement in Science and Intellectual Style," *Journal of Applied Psychology*, 53 (1969): 132–135.
28. Doleys, F. J., and G. A. Renzaglic. "Accuracy of Student Predictor of College Grades," *Personnel Guidance Journal*, 41 (1963): 528–530.
29. Drevdahl, J. E., and R. B. Cattell. "Personality and Creativity in Artists and Writers," *Journal of Clinical Psychology*, 14 (1958): 107–111.
30. Dunlap, J. W., and M. J. Wantman. *An Investigation of the Interview as a Technique for Selecting Aircraft Pilots*. Report No. 33. Washington, D. C.: Civil Aeronautics Administration, 1944.
31. Dunnette, M. D. *Personnel Selection and Placement*. Belmont, Calif.: Wadsworth, 1966.
32. Einhorn, H. J., and R. M. Hogarth. "Unit Weighting Schemes for Decision Making," *Organizational Behavior and Human Performance*, 13 (1975): 171–192.
33. Frye, R. L. "The Effect of Feedback of Success and Effectiveness on Self-, Task-, and Interaction-Oriented Group Members." Unpublished Ph.D. dissertation, Louisiana State University, 1961.
34. Ghiselli, E. E. "Differentiation of Individuals in Terms of Their Predictability," *Journal of Applied Psychology*, 40 (1956): 374–377.
35. Ghiselli, E. E. "Differentiation of Tests in Terms of the Accuracy with Which They Predict for a Given Individual," *Educational and Psychological Measurement*, 20 (1960): 675–684.
36. Ghiselli, E. E. "The Prediction of Predictability," *Educational and Psychological Measurement*, 20 (1960): 3–8.
37. Ghiselli, E. E. "Managerial Talent," *American Psychologist*, 18 (1963): 631–642.
38. Guilford, J. P. *Fundamental Statistics in Psychology and Education*. New York: McGraw-Hill, 1955.
39. Guion, R. M. *Personnel Testing*. New York: McGraw-Hill, 1965.
40. Gulliksen, H. *Theory of Mental Tests*. New York: Wiley, 1950.
41. Harrell, M. S., T. W. Harrell, S. H. McIntyre, and C. B. Weinberg. "Predict-

ing Compensation among MBA Graduates Five and Ten Years after Graduation," *Journal of Applied Psychology,* 62 (1977): 636–640.

42. Hartman, B. O., and R. C. McNee. *Psychometric Characteristics of Astronauts.* Aeromedical Review no. 1–77. Brooks Air Force Base, Texas: USAF School of Aerospace Medicine, Aerospace Medical Division, March 1977.

43. Hasan, P., and H. J. Butcher. "Creativity and Intelligence: A Partial Replication with Scottish Children of Getzel's and Jackson's Study." *British Journal of Psychology,* 57 (1966): 129–135.

44. Hollander, E. P. "Buddy Ratings: Military Research and Industrial Implications," *Personnel Psychology,* 7 (1954): 385–393.

45. Holtzman, W. H., and S. B. Sells. "Prediction of Flying Success by Clinical Analyses of Test Protocols," *Journal of Abnormal and Social Psychology,* 49 (1954): 485–490.

46. Huck, J. R., and D. W. Bray. "Management Assessment Center Evaluations and Subsequent Job Performance of White and Black Females," *Personnel Psychology,* 29 (1976): 13–30.

47. Huse, E. F. "Assessments of Higher Level Personnel: IV. The Validity of Assessment Techniques Based on Systematically Varied Information," *Personnel Psychology,* 15 (1962): 195–205.

48. Jarrett, R. F. "Percent Increase in Output of Selected Personnel as an Index of Test Efficiency," *Journal of Applied Psychology,* 32 (1948): 135–145.

49. Kahnemann, D., and E. E. Ghiselli. "Validity and Non-linear Heteroscedastic Models," *Personnel Psychology,* 15 (1962): 1–11.

50. Klimoski, R. J., and W. J. Strickland. "Assessment Centers—Valid or Merely Prescient?" *Personnel Psychology,* 30 (1977): 353–361.

51. Kolb, H. D. "The Adminstrative Use of Data for Early Identification of Management Potential?" In J. A. Myers (ed.), *Predicting Managerial Success,* 35–58. Ann Arbor: Foundation for Research on Human Behavior, 1968.

52. Kraut, A. I., and G. J. Scott. "Validity of an Operational Management Assessment Program," *Journal of Applied Psychology,* 56 (1972): 124–129.

53. Laurent, H. "Research on the Identification of Management Potential." In J. A. Myers (ed.), *Predicting Managerial Success,* 1–34. Ann Arbor: Foundation for Research on Human Behavior, 1968.

54. Lawshe, C. H. "Statistical Theory and Practice in Applied Psychology," *Personnel Psychology,* 22 (1969): 117–124.

55. Lawshe, C. H., and R. A. Bolda. "Expectancy Charts: I. Their Use and Empirical Development," *Personnel Psychology,* 11 (1958): 353–365.

56. Lee, R., and J. M. Booth. "A Utility Analysis of a Weighted Application Blank Designed to Predict Turnover for Clerical Employees," *Journal of Applied Psychology,* 59 (1974): 516–518.

57. Livingston, J. S. "Myth of the Well-Educated Manager," *Harvard Business Review* 49, no. 1 (1971): 79–89.

58. MacKinnon, D. W. "The Personality Correlates of Creativity: A Study of American Architects," *Proceedings, XIVth International Congress of Applied Psychology,* Amsterdam 1961.

59. MacKinnon, D. W. "The Nature and Nurture of Creative Talent," *American Psychologist,* 17 (1962): 484–496.

424   PERSONNEL PSYCHOLOGY

60. MacKinnon, D. W., et al. *An Assessment Study of Air Force Officers.* Institute for Personality Assessment and Research, Berkeley, Calif.: University of California Press, 1958.
61. McDermick, C. D. "Some Correlates of Creativity in Engineering Personnel," *Journal of Applied Psychology,* 49 (1965): 14–19.
62. Meehl, P. E. *Clinical vs. Statistical Prediction.* Minneapolis: University of Minnesota Press, 1954.
63. Meehl, P. E. "Seer over Sign: The First Good Example," *Journal of Experimental Research in Personality,* 1 (1965): 27–32.
64. Melton, R. S. "A Comparison of Clinical and Actuarial Methods of Prediction with an Assessment of the Relative Accuracy of Different Clinicians." Unpublished Ph.D. dissertation, University of Minnesota, 1952.
65. Mitchel, J. O. "Assessment Center Validity: A Longitudinal Study," *Journal of Applied Psychology,* 60 (1975): 573–579.
66. Morrison, R. F. "A Multivariate Model for the Occupational Placement Decision," *Journal of Applied Psychology,* 62 (1977): 271–277.
67. Moses, J. L., and V. R. Boehm. "Relationship of Assessment-Center Performance to Management Progress of Women," *Journal of Applied Psychology,* 60 (1975): 527–529.
68. Myers, M. S. "Every Employee a Manager," *California Management Review,* 3 (1968): 9–20.
69. Nunnally, J. C. *Psychometric Theory.* New York: McGraw-Hill, 1978.
70. Owens, W. A. "Cognitive, Noncognitive, and Environmental Correlates of Mechanical Ingenuity," *Journal of Applied Psychology,* 53 (1969): 199–208.
71. Parrish, J. A., W. A. Klieger, and A. J. Drucker. *A Self-Description Blank for Officer Candidate School Applicants.* USA Personnel Research Branch Report, 1954, Washington, D. C. no. 1091.
72. Pearse, R. F., E. I. Worthington, and J. J. Flaherty. *A Program for Developing Tool Engineers into Manufacturing Executives.* ASTE Tool Engineering Conference Paper, 22T5. Detroit, 1954.
73. Randle, C. W. "How to Identify Promotable Executives," *Harvard Business Review,* 34, no. 3 (1956): 122–134.
74. Rimland, B., E. F. Alf, and L. Swanson. *Studies in the Computerization of Enlisted Classification. U. S. Naval Personnel Research Activity Research Memorandum* SRM 67–10. San Diego, November 1966.
75. Roe, A. "A Study of Imagery in Research Scientists," *Journal of Personality,* 19 (1951): 459–470.
76. Rosen, N. A. "How Supervise?—1943–1960," *Personnel Psychology,* 14 (1961): 87–100.
77. Sarbin, R. R., R. Taft, and D. E. Bailey. *Clinical Inference and Cognitive Theory.* New York: Holt, Rinehart & Winston, 1960.
78. Sasieni, M., A. Yaspan, and L. Friedman. *Operations Research: Methods and Problems.* New York: Wiley, 1959.
79. Sawyer, J. "Measurement and Prediction, Clinical and Statistical," *Psychological Bulletin,* 66 (1966): 178–200.
80. Schmidt, F. L., and B. Hoffman. "An Empirical Comparison of Three Methods of Assessing the Utility of a Selection Device," *Journal of Industrial and Organizational Psychology,* 1 (1973): 1–11.

81. Schmitt, N. "Interrater Agreement in Dimensionality and Combination of Assessment Center Judgments," *Journal of Applied Psychology*, 62 (1977): 171–176.

82. Schmitt, N., and T. E. Hill. "Sex and Race Composition of Assessment Center Groups as a Determinant of Peer and Assessor Ratings," *Journal of Applied Psychology*, 62 (1977): 261–264.

83. Schoenfeldt, L. F. "Utilization of Manpower: Development and Evaluation of an Assessment-Classification Model for Matching Individuals with Jobs," *Journal of Applied Psychology*, 59 (1974): 583–595.

84. Seashore, H. W. "Women are More Predictable than Men." Paper presented at American Psychological Association Meeting, New York, 1961.

85. Smith, M. "Cautions Concerning the Use of the Taylor-Russell Tables in Employee Selection," *Journal of Applied Psychology*, 32 (1948): 595–600.

86. Sprecher, T. B. "A Study of Engineers' Criteria for Creativity," *Journal of Applied Psychology*, 43 (1959): 141–148.

87. Stolz, R. E. "Factors in Supervisors' Perceptions of Physical Science Research Personnel," *Journal of Applied Psychology*, 43 (1959): 256–258.

88. Stolz, R. E. "Subordinates' Perception of the Productive Engineer," *Journal of Applied Psychology*, 43 (1959): 306–310.

89. Stromberg, E. L. "Testing Programs Draw Better Applicants," *Personnel Psychology*, 1 (1948): 21–30.

90. Taylor, C. W., and R. L. Ellison. "Biographical Predictors of Scientific Performance," *Science*, 155 (1967): 1075–1080.

91. Taylor, C. W., W. R. Smith, B. Ghiselin, and R. Ellison. *Exploration in the Measurement and Prediction of Contributions of One Sample of Scientists*. Report No. ASD–RR–61–69. Lackland Air Force Base, Texas: Personnel Laboratory, 1961.

92. Taylor, H. C., and J. T. Russell. "The Relationship of Validity Coefficients to the Practical Effectiveness of Tests in Selection, Discussion and Tables," *Journal of Applied Psychology*, 23 (1939): 565–578.

93. Thomson, H. A. "Comparison of Predictor and Criterion Judgments of Managerial Performance Using the Multitrait-Multimethod Approach," *Journal of Applied Psychology*, 54 (1970): 496–502.

94. Thorpe, R. P., and R. P. Conner. *A Computerized Model of the Fleet Personnel Distribution System*. U. S. Naval Personnel Research Activity Report USNPRA-SSR 66–13, San Diego, 1966.

95. Trankell, A. "The Psychologist as an Instrument of Prediction," *Journal of Applied Psychology*, 43 (1959): 170–175.

96. Trattner, M. H. "Comparison of Three Methods for Assembling Aptitude Test Batteries," *Personnel Psychology*, 16 (1963): 221–232.

97. Van Zelst, R. H., and W. A. Kerr. "Personality Self-Assessment of Scientific and Technical Personnel," *Journal of Applied Psychology*, 38 (1954): 145–147.

98. Vernon, P. E. "The Validation of Civil Service Selection Board Procedures," *Occupational Psychology*, 24 (1950): 75–95.

99. Vicino, F. L., and B. M. Bass. "Lifespace Variables and Managerial Success," *Journal of Applied Psychology*, 63 (1978): 81–88.

100. Weinstein, A. G., and V. Srinivasan. "Predicting Managerial Success of Master

of Business Administration (MBA) Graduates," *Journal of Applied Psychology*, 59 (1974): 207–212.

101. Weitz, J. "Selecting Supervisors with Peer Ratings," *Personnel Psychology*, 11 (1958): 25–35.

102. Whitehead, R. F., R. N. Suiter, and R. P. Thorpe. *The Development of a Computer-Assisted Distribution and Assignment (CADA) System for Navy Enlisted Personnel*. U. S. Naval Personnel Research Activity Report, NPRA–SRM 70–1, August 1969.

103. Wiggins, J. S. *Personality and Prediction: Principles of Personality Assessment*. Reading, Mass.: Addison-Wesley, 1973.

104. Wilson, R. C., J. P. Guilford, and P. R. Christensen. "The Measurement of Individual Differences in Originality," *Psychological Bulletin*, 50 (1953): 362–370.

13 TRAINING IN INDUSTRY

IN BRIEF   Training is an important, if not the most important, way to achieve improved individual productivity, job satisfaction, and overall organizational performance. However, training objectives and techniques need to be chosen that accurately match individual and organizational needs. Training requirements are determined by analyzing the work to be done, the personnel resources available, and the present and future environmental demands on the organization.

A broad range of training techniques is available, including both on-site approaches such as on-the-job training, apprentice training, and job rotation and off-the-job programs such as lectures, films, programmed instruction, conferences, case discussions, role playing, and simulations.

Evaluations are a necessity. However, there is no evaluation strategy that can be completely free of validity threats. The optimum strategy is determined from a cost-benefits analysis. There seem to be clear upper limits to how much we can do to increase productivity and satisfaction through appropriate recruiting, selection, and placement of employees. Training usually adds considerably to the effort to increase such productivity and satisfaction.

As much as 10 per cent of payrolls are spent on personnel training and development. That can total one hundred billion dollars! Gilbert has arrived at that estimate for the total amount spent in the United States each year on training for adult work.[28] One German chemical firm, Hoescht, spends 60,000,000 marks (about $25,000,000) annually just on its apprenticeship training. (In Germany, private industry accounts for one-third of all expenditures for education and training.)

Another evidence of the importance of training is the number of professionals involved in the activity. The American Society for Training and Development has about 10,000 members. The figures are comparable in most other industrialized as well as developing countries.

Training opportunities are the rule rather than the exception in most firms and agencies of any size engaged in the production of goods or services. Smaller organizations also take advantage of the many public short courses and programs that are available. In the United States, an important function of community colleges is providing one- and two-year training for technicians and paraprofessionals in conjunction with local industries and service institutions. Numerous reasons lie behind these managements' expenditures:

1. Seniority rules Seniority arrangements as well as pension plans are making lifetime employment with a single firm quite common. Often, union shop rules require the firm to provide employees with a permanent position 90 days after they have been hired. At this point, employees must join the union; then they are protected by the union from loss of their jobs. They are also put in a position to apply for more important jobs, providing they can qualify or be trained for them.

2. Affirmative action There is increasing pressure to hire women, blacks, Spanish-surnamed persons and Orientals, some of whom may not have the usual minimum qualifications. This means much more emphasis must be placed on training. Furthermore, when selection tests are used, they must be more specifically linked to behavioral objectives and valid training efforts.

3. Technological advances The average firm is likely to be mechanizing or automating many of its processes. Unskilled jobs are disappearing. For workers to remain employed with the firm, even at entry jobs, requires that they engage in training programs of various kinds to upgrade themselves. The introduction of new processes calls for specialized training programs to familiarize workers with the new processes and production techniques.

The proportion of technical, supervisory, and professional employees to blue-collar workers is gradually increasing as industry as a whole becomes more technologically oriented. Each of these higher-level employees is seen as an important investment to the firm. The firm, as a consequence, is willing to spend considerable funds in their training and education. As new management and technical developments appear, these higher-level employees in particular need to be refreshed. The professionals among them need to keep up with the current developments in their own fields of specialization. The average firm is usually continuously concerned with its management practices and sees in training a way of increasing the proficiency of its supervision.

4. Importance of management   One of the most important bases on which modern companies are evaluated is the quality of its management. It is assumed that good management is essential for the health of the firm. The training and education of a company's management is seen as a continuing process in development of critical importance to the firm.

At the management level of training, many benefits are expected of it. Training can produce better technical performance by trainees, who may be kept informed of scientific and technical progress in their respective fields through special training programs. A successful supervisory training program should bring about both increases in departmental productivity and increases in employee satisfaction. One may expect increased understanding from a training program, and increased interest in the organization. Management training programs may focus on developing more self-understanding. Training programs increase the attractiveness of a firm to outsiders, making possible the promotion of management from within the firm. The organization becomes more flexible as a consequence of the "reserves" of management talent created. In all, successful management development programs promote long-term survival of the company through an orderly succession process. Thus, over half of the top one thousand executives of General Motors were promoted during one five-year period and 20 per cent had received two promotions during this period.[81]

5. Increased efficiency of training   As a consequence of the attention paid to training, techniques are improving. The introduction of programmed textbooks, for instance, may result in considerable increase in the efficiency of training, at a reduced cost coupled with the increased flexibility with which such a program can be administered. There is greater willingness to invest in training as its greater payoff to the firm is seen.

6. Training benefits the individual and the organization   Training can benefit the person who receives the training. Thus, 50,000 individuals who participated in U.S. government personnel training programs in 1964 were contrasted with 70,000 who had not. Using Social Security's Continuous Work History Sample, Jacobson demonstrated that training increased subsequent annual earnings by about 5 per cent over what would have been expected without training.[41]

Training ordinarily is intended, of course, to benefit the organization that invests in the training effort. Often the investment is mandatory. In many jobs, employees cannot begin to function effectively for the organization without specific training. In many countries training expenditures can be shared with the government in many different ways. For example, in Brazil all personnel training costs can be counted double for income-tax purposes until the amount equals 10 per cent of the company net profit. The costs can include building construction, equipment, machinery, salaries of administrative and technical personnel involved in training, salaries of technicians contracted to conduct classes, and the costs of instructional materials.

The gains to the organization from training programs, when evaluated, may be quite dramatic, reinforcing the belief that training programs pay off. For instance, the amount of life insurance sold by a salesperson tends to decline after the first year. After four years, 52 per cent of 243 Canadian agents were selling 10 per cent less than in their first year, while only 29 per cent of this sample were selling 10 per cent more. Another group comprising 230 salespersons were given three four-week training periods of classes at Purdue University, following which they carried out training assignments on the job for the remainder of the year. For each trainee, a control salesperson was matched in terms of aptitude, sales volume, marital status, and age. Table 13–1 shows the production per month of trainees before, during, and after training in comparison to the agents who did not receive training. Although the agents without training decreased in production per month by 10 per cent, the trainees increased in the volume of insurance they sold by 23 per cent during the period of investigation.[97]

Caveat

Although this was one of the most carefully controlled efforts to evaluate the effects of training, it still was not a foolproof demonstration. Later,

Table 13–1. Comparison in sales of 230 life insurance agents trained at the life insurance marketing institute and 230 matched untrained agents.

	Median sales volume per month	
	Trained	Untrained
Before training	$13,900	$13,900
During training	13,200	12,000
After training	17,100	12,500

Data adapted from Wallace and Twitchell, "An Evaluation of a Training Course for Life Insurance Agents," *Personnel Psychology*, 6(1953):25–43.

we will consider an evaluation design to eliminate many other plausible explanations for the results.

DESIGNING THE TRAINING EFFORT

Sometimes training programs are introduced into a company as fads. The ABC Company introduces a "basic economics" program for its supervisors because the president's son attended a conference at which an executive from another organization spoke on their program in basic economics, and how this program was now being introduced in many different firms. So the ABC personnel, whether or not they need it, like it, or want it, are given a special program in basic economics. This is hardly an efficient way to decide on introducing a training program. Instead, three kinds of analyses should be completed. First, one ought to have available an *analysis of the work to be done,* such as can be obtained from an appropriate job analysis. Second, one should have available *an analysis of the available personnel* to do the work, their current weaknesses and capabilities for training. Third, one must have some *awareness of the organizational environment* in which the personnel are to do the work, how much support exists for the training program, and how much the organization will reinforce what is learned in training when the employee goes back to his or her job.

The Systematic Approach versus Unsystematic On-the-Job Training

The training program is designed to meet the needs revealed in the analyses of work, of personnel, and of organization. A pilot test usually follows. Then the training program is made operational. Subsequent evaluation may lead to modifications and improvements in the training effort. This is the systematic approach — analysis of needs, selection and/or design of training to meet the needs, administration, evaluation, and redesign, if necessary. The systematic approach can be contrasted with unsystematic on-the-job training of a new worker without a specific program by an experienced employee. The experienced employee simultaneously continues to perform regular duties while also training the new worker. At Johns-Manville, 20 plastic-extruder-machine operators who were individually given the benefit of a systematic training program were compared with 20 operators who were given the usual unsystematic on-the-job training. Job competency was achieved on the average in 4.55 hours by the systematically trained employees, while it took an average of 16.3 hours by those given unsystematic on-the-job training. Average production waste was 5.29 pounds for the systematically trained and 22.03 pounds for the on-the-job trainees. Systematically trained employees also solved 2.3 times more readily production problems that arose than those without systematic training did. Now that the systematic training program is in place, as new employees are hired, Johns-Manville continues to benefit from the original investment in designing the training program.[15]

Where productivity strongly depends on skill level attained rather than, say, quality of materials or engineering, even more dramatic payoffs can be demonstrated from training. The percentage of costly wheels broken by untrained disc-cutters was 12 per cent after two months of experience; 9 per cent after five months; and above 5 per cent after nine months. With training, the 12 per cent rate was reached in two weeks; the 9 per cent rate in four weeks, and breakage was close to zero with 12 weeks of training in the coordination of hands and feet that was required for doing the job well. This level of competence could never have been reached on the job without such training.[63]

Ordinarily, investment in development of training programs and the use of them to train personnel is likely to pay for itself many times over, both to the trainee as well as to the sponsor. This is particularly true if the training is part of a demonstrably needed experience sponsored by a local organization in which the training graduate will find employment. At the same time, if personnel and organizational needs are neglected, vast sums can be misspent training people for whom no jobs will be available. Such a thing happened in an effort to train the hard-core unemployed for work in supermarkets without the involvement of the prospective employers.[54]

Analysis of the Work to be Done

Special attention can be devoted to training needs during the completion of job analyses (Chapter 7). Abstraction of the results of these analyses provides the basis for outlining what should be included in a training program for employees to be placed on these jobs and families of jobs. In collecting job information for the purposes of formulating training programs, particular attention must be focused on the standards of performance to be required of the employees, the tasks in which they will be engaged, the methods that will be used on the job, and, most important, how these methods and performances are learned.[72]

Especially in developing programs for training workers to operate or to maintain complex equipment, analyses must consider the component tasks involved in the operations, the learning of which is necessary to complete the final performance. For example, police patrol officers prevent crime. They investigate, detect, and follow up on criminal activity. They use force appropriately. They handle domestic disputes. They maintain and control traffic. They give first aid. They work as team members. They have administrative duties, including report writing. They are responsible for maintaining good public relations. Each of these job responsibilities translates into a training activity.

Analyses aimed at establishing requirements are based on the same kinds of information sources used to provide job descriptions: observation, interviews with employees and their supervisors, and comparative studies by tests, surveys, and available records on good versus poor employees. External sources, such as the *Dictionary of Occupational Titles (DOT)*, may be especially useful. Useful in job analysis and evaluation, there is a supplement to the *DOT* that gives estimates of physical demands, working conditions, and training time for approximately 14,000 listed occupations.[22]

SELF-REPORTS   Employees themselves can be a good resource to identifying training needs. A 291-item questionnaire administered to 2,054 first-line production supervisors at General Motors provided much information for cataloguing their training and development needs. The ten greatest difficulties on the first supervisory job were seen as follows: (1) handling employees who presented special problems; (2) maintaining a neat and orderly workplace; (3) dealing with crises or unexpected problems; (4) controlling costs; (5) meeting quality requirements; (6) learning how much authority one had; (7) handling complaints, grievances, or labor relations problems; (8) motivating employees; (9) meeting work deadlines or production requirements; and (10) writing reports and handling paper work.

SETTING STANDARDS   The job requirements derived from these varied sources of information are typically set without respect to the abilities or personal attributes of present jobholders or any other specific persons; they represent standards to be met by any potential or actual employee.

Training needs are translated into behavioral objectives. For example, suppose we have established that as one of their tasks filling-station attendents must collect cash and make change rapidly and accurately without requiring paper-and-pencil computations. Three behavioral objectives may be specified such as: (1) always provide correct change for a single purchase such as gasoline up to the total cost of $20; (2) always provide correct change up to $100; and (3) complete 20 trials accurately and rapidly by providing the correct change.

Such objectives tell trainer, trainee, and program designer what's expected of the training effort. They indicate the conditions under which training is to be transferred into performance on the job and they indicate the criteria for evaluating the trainee's progress.[30]

Analysis of Available Personnel

Given job requirements, the determination of training needs depends on analyses of available personnel, including both present employees and potential job applicants. Personnel analyses result in the establishment of manpower inventories, which include records of individual workers' test results and performance evaluation, as well as notations regarding special skills and interests and judgments concerning promotability or qualifications for transfers. In addition to manpower inventories on current personnel, it is often useful to conduct *surveys of local labor markets* to determine the probable characteristics of potential job applicants. The availability of such inventories and survey results helps greatly to avoid frequently made training errors — the wasteful provision of unneeded, unwanted, inappropriate, or "faddish" training.

If observations, performance appraisals, test results, or other sources of information indicate gaps between job requirements and available personnel, training may be needed to close those gaps. The prescription of training, however, requires that other, possibly more effective, alternatives have been investigated. If, for example, the presently available work force already possesses the required range of skills and attributes, but these are less than optimally assigned, substandard performance may be more effectively improved by transferring or replacing employees than by instituting a training program. Similarly, engineering modifications in the job may bring employee performance up to standard, or new equipment or processes may be better solutions than training to the problem of inadequate performance. Above all, the prescription of training requires knowledge of the specific areas in which employees require training, and in which areas they do not, to minimize the cost and amount of training time required.

Often, improved performance can result from a combination of non-training techniques (such as improved selection and classification procedures, compensation programs, and job design) with training. For instance, inspector errors proved a problem to a large aerospace company. Chaney and Teel convincingly demonstrated that inspector performance could be improved by using both training and visual aids during inspection tasks.[10] They found that training the inspectors in a program consisting of four one-hour sessions resulted in a 32 per cent increase in defects detected, while the use only of improved visual aids during inspection resulted in a 42 per cent increase in efficiency. But the best gain was accomplished by using both the visual performance aid and the training, with a 71 per cent detection-rate increase. These gains were not artifactual, since a control group matched by their performance before the program began did not change. The savings to an organization from this type of program are not trivial; in this case a $50,000 research effort yielded a return of over $200,000 per year in documented savings to the organization.

At the management level, diagnosis of training needs takes the form of evaluation mainly by superiors and staff personnel. For example, at RCA Victor Division (Camden, N. J.), appraisals by a management committee of each individual executive result in a statement of specific development needs covering such areas as major strengths and weaknesses in current performance and unresolved problems at work. Developmental actions needed are mutually agreed upon by superior and subordinate following a goal-setting session together.

Analysis of the Organizational Environment

How well employee development takes place depends strongly on the prevailing organizational climate and attitudes toward employee development. For instance, in the case of management development, it is suggested that training is primarily a line responsibility. A manager's supervisor does most of the teaching of the manager. The staff expert can only help and advise. Yet often operational demands leave line management little time to do a good job of training their subordinates. Moreover, the subordinates may be better in every respect to the supervisors who are supposed to be helping them. The superiors may be insecure and afraid to develop their subordinates. Furthermore, few managers are in a position to observe their subordinates as they actually perform their jobs; consequently, they rarely are in an advantageous position to coach their subordinates effectively.[94]

Insufficient attention has been paid to the *climate* in which the learning is to take place. A study of the learning climate at the Graduate School of Business at the University of Pittsburgh emerged with five factors that M. B. A. students say make a difference in the effectiveness with which learning takes place there: (1) the grading process; (2) task relationships with the faculty (for example, faculty don't value student experience, interests, and willingness to learn); (3) physical environment; (4) social relationships with faculty; and (5) course material presentation.

MANAGEMENT SUPPORT Numerous studies disclose that lack of management support for the objectives of a particular training program reduces or eliminates the potential gains from the training program. Management development is likely to be given short shrift if the board of directors of the firm is more interested in maintaining current dividends than in the position of the firm in the industry twenty years hence. In the same way, formal training is likely to be ineffective if what is to be learned is counter to management ideology. For example, supervisors from two divisions of one large company were given supervisory training. In the first division, employees became more satisfied with their supervisors after training. In this division, three supervisors in turn said they had received considerable encouragement from their bosses. In the second division, employees were more dissatisfied with their supervisors following training, and here, supervisors reported that their new methods had not been encouraged by their bosses.[35] At International Harvester, supervisors who received two weeks' training aimed at increasing their tendency to be considerate of their subordinates all showed such improvements in attitudes immediately following the training program. However, six months later, only those supervisors who returned to bosses who wanted their supervisors to be considerate maintained this new attitude of consideration toward subordinates.[23]

Only supervisors who returned to climates approving of considerate supervision were likely to be seen by their subordinates as having increased in consideration as a consequence of the training program. Conversely, a deterioration in human relations was seen as a consequence of an attempt at supervisory training where the program was in conflict with unionism, where recruitment for the program was poor, and where the program itself became a matter of indoctrinating a captive audience.[70] Ideally, the attitudes and actions of higher-level management need to be consistent with the course content of the supervisory training program. Top management needs to be exposed to the program and its objectives, and to support actively the training as well as to reinforce what is learned in the training program.[49] One of the most common suggestions arising at the end of the typical supervisory training program is "I sure wish my boss could take this program; he needs it more than I did."

RELATED ACTIONS   Often training must be supported by other organizational actions to bring about the changes aimed at by training. For instance, a supervisory training program directed at reducing employee absenteeism had an effect on lowering absenteeism when quantitative data about the absences of their own subordinate personnel were fed back to the supervisors following training.[70]

Still another organizational consideration of considerable importance, particularly in management development, is the necessity of projecting the major trends in what will be needed during the careers of the current management force. Current training programs and plans for subsequent management development programs need to consider the changes taking place in business management. Increased attention must be paid to the applications of the physical and social sciences to business administration, to the nonmarket responsibilities of management, to the increased focus on long-range planning for successful administration of technically advanced industries, to different types of careers likely for management trainees in the same firm, and so on.[51]

INTEREST AND ABILITY TO LEARN   When we consider the continuously changing nature of modern business and the typical job mobility of the career manager, it may very well be that our major effort in management education ought to be focused on motivating managers to engage themselves in a lifelong learning process and teaching them how to learn or how to teach themselves. Our training programs possibly ought to concentrate on providing the essentials for subsequent learning by managers after training. It may be most important to concentrate on the fundamentals of applied mathematics, English, reading speed and comprehension, basic economics, science, and technology, along with those sociopsychological issues dealing with the managers themselves as the learners.

Study skills can be taught. Many universities now have courses on the subject. Matched students who complete such courses do tend to do a better job of learning than those without such skill training. Executives with satisfactory study skills know how to skim, read with a questioning frame of mind, alter the speed of their reading as a function of the material they are reading, keep a dictionary handy and use it, take advantage of opportunities to teach others, thereby reinforcing their own knowledge of particular material, comprehend charts and graphs with ease, for example.

Designing the Training Program

Generally, training programs are designed as a consequence of the experience and the attitudes of the training staff. After reviewing the needs analyses, they set the program's objectives and design it, assuming that the techniques they prescribe will move the trainee toward the stated objectives. Some techniques work better than others; some don't work at all.

"The analysis of job tasks and performance requirements, and the matching of these behaviors to those produced by the training environment, is . . . as much an art as a technology" (p. 22).[30] The total task to be learned must be organized into a set of distinct components that contribute to final task performance. These components should be in the training program. There should be an effective transfer of learning from training to on-the-job performance.[26] Thus, in our needs analyses, we must identify the components that contribute to final task performance. We must place these components into the training activity and arrange them in the best possible sequence for learning.[7]

To illustrate, Vallance, Glickman, and Vasilas uncovered 1,072 critical incidents in the performance of new Navy officers on destroyers.[96] These were then checked against the subject matter of Navy Officer Candidate School.[29] Folley completed a similar critical-incidents analysis for retail sales personnel according to customers' narratives and observations.[24] Effective salespersons tended to volunteer information on such matters as the care and use of items, while ineffective salespersons gave little or inaccurate information about the items. Effective salespersons were speedy with service; ineffective ones were slow. Effective ones were courteous; ineffective ones weren't. Effective salespersons gave exclusive attention to a customer; ineffective ones did not. Training designs were constructed accordingly. But how?

Gagné, however, did not find as much help from accepted principles of learning in designing particular task-learning experiences as might have been expected after a century of research to develop understanding of learning.[26] Nevertheless, generally a training technique to meet a training need is likely to work better if it can be designed to conform to the better substantiated principles of learning. These can be grouped into three areas: (1) the nature of the stimulating situation; (2) the required responses; and (3) the feedback of the consequences of the responses to the stimulating situations.

STIMULUS   Stimuli in training must correspond to stimuli on-the-job that impact on the task to be learned. They must be identified for the trainee so that he or she can discriminate which responses are appropriate for which stimuli.

RESPONSE AND REINFORCEMENT   Appropriate responding must be demonstrated and/or guided; there must be sufficient opportunity for trainee practice accompanied by suitable reinforcement — feedback or knowledge of results of the adequacy of the trainee's responses to particular stimuli. Ordinarily, generalized learning of responses is sought to a variety of similar stimuli as well as learning about differences among classes of stimuli calling for different responses. Sequences of responses are sought so that a chain is formed in which the reinforcer of one response becomes the stimulus for the next response.

Our design may or may not pay attention to individual differences.[30] We may design one fixed program for all trainees. Or we may design a variety of training programs, each suitable for trainees with differing goals. (While college-bound students take calculus, terminal high-school graduates take business arithmetic.) Or programs can be designed based on diagnoses of current errorful performance. Or programs can be designed to make use of different methods for different trainees.

Behavior modification   Behavior modification is a technology built to apply these principles with particular emphasis on providing discriminating cues to the learner and on arranging the reinforcements for responses that will be contingent on the appropriateness of the responses. Reinforcements are scheduled so that they become intermittent as the trainee improves his or her performance.[86] Other, more specific, principles based on human and animal experimental studies of learning include (1) avoiding the use of punishment as a primary means of obtaining desired behavior; (2) positive reinforcement of desired behavior and, where feasible, the ignoring of undesirable behavior; (3) minimizing the time lag between desired response and reinforcement, or bridging the gap with verbal mediation (using words to link the response with its consequence); (4) the relatively frequent application of positive reinforcement, preferably on a variable ratio schedule (reinforcement is erratic); (5) ascertaining the response level of each individual and using a *shaping* procedure to obtain a final complex response; (6) ascertaining reinforcers by examining the relationship between outcomes and increases or decreases in target behaviors; and (7) specifying the desired behavior in operational terms.[40]

Numerous illustrations are now available of the successful application of behavior modification to industrial training.

1. A performance audit at Emery Air Freight disclosed that although employees felt that 90 per cent of the time they were responding to customers' inquiries within 90 minutes, they actually were meeting the 90-minute target only 30 per cent of the time. A similar discrepancy was found between how much the employees believed they were combining small packages into large containers. Behavior modification was instituted. Timely feedback was provided. Employees kept records of their own progress and improvement. Several million dollars were estimated to have been saved as the employees' behavior was modified over the following three years.[20] (Note that employee involvement and acceptance of the effort was of critical importance.)

2. Positive reinforcement improved the speed and efficiency of training at Northern Systems. In their programmed learning activity, the Northern Systems Company structured the feedback system in such a way that trainees received positive feedback only when they demonstrated accurate performance at the tool station. The absence of feedback was experienced by the trainees when they failed to perform correctly. Through positive reinforcement, the trainees learned that correct behavior obtained for them the satisfaction of their needs, and that incorrect behavior did not.[33]

3. Morasky developed a "self-shaping" training process for sales interviewing.[74] He designed a model interviewing procedure, which was given to the trainees to increase their retention of information they obtained in interviews. Morasky's program specified behavioral objectives to be used by the trainees as a standard against which to compare their own behavior. They redirected their behavior to closer and closer approximations of the model, thus engaging in a self-shaping process.

4. Hard-core unemployed persons were trained by means of behavior-modification procedures. Tasks to be learned were broken into small behavioral components. Appropriate behavior was reinforced by points that were convertible into money, as well as by verbal reinforcement. The reinforcement was dispensed only part of the time to sustain the behavior over long periods without it. Back on the job, verbal praise was used to reinforce behavior that had been learned in training, once pay schedules returned to the company's "noncontingent" format — hourly pay.[6]

TRANSFER   Of particular importance is to build transfer onto the job into the match of training and training needs. The transfer of the training to the job must be fostered. To illustrate, a management training program featured, during training, an increase of considerate behavior by trainees.

As a self-feedback mechanism for promoting transfer of training to the job for six weeks following training, trainees filled out a daily behavioral checklist to keep a record of their own managerial behaviors on the job.

On the daily checklist a trainee noted whether that day he or she had done such things as:

> (a) praised subordinates and commented to them on a job well done; (b) thanked subordinates for a suggestion, wrote it down, and told them that I would get back to them within a day or two; (c) remembered to go back within a day or two to subordinates who had given me an idea or suggestion; (d) called my subordinates together and told them I wanted them to help each other with the work; (e) helped the subordinates with the work to be done by actually working with them on their jobs; (f) gave subordinates an immediate answer to a question that they had asked; (g) assigned a job and let subordinates perform it without interfering by checking on their progress; and (h) asked subordinates to explain why they had broken a rule before deciding to take any disciplinary action against him (p. 447).[99]

Further transfer was promoted by the trainer:

> Once after the 1st week and once after the 3rd week, the trainer met with trainees on their job to review the behaviors checked and to provide consultation on any particular problems the trainees might be having in applying the behaviors learned in the workshop to their job. The trainer used the first on-the-job interview to assign the trainees specific performance goals for their subsequent meeting the 3rd week. This involved encouraging trainees to emit these behaviors not previously checked and to continue to display those behaviors emitted in the past (p. 447).[99]

Sixty days after training, subordinates reported significant and sizably greater amounts of considerate behavior without any difference in their initiation or production emphasis by their trained managers than corresponding reports received about an untrained group of managers.[99]

Evaluation of Training

Although of the greatest importance, evaluations often are avoided because negative results may threaten the existence of the training program. The evaluations may be seen as an invasion of privacy, as costing more than they are worth or as superfluous as trainees and trainers are satisfied with the status quo. Nevertheless, effective evaluations help justify the continued expense of training, they diagnose parts of the training program needing improvement, they provide information to the trainer where his efforts need to be concentrated, and they give trainees a measure of progress. Hesseling has prepared a five-by-five classification of the purposes served by evaluations according to who makes the assessment and for whom it is done.[38] Figure 13–1 displays his 25 possibilities. For example, evaluations by trainees for trainers provide direct feedback about the instructional process; evaluations by scientists for the policy makers or sponsors of the training provide preparation for decision-making.

PSEUDOEVALUATION   What often constitutes an evaluation is a survey of student opinions at the end of a course. (These are Hesseling's Types 2, 4 or 5 in Figure 13–1.) Although these may help on occasion to pinpoint problems with the course, they are fraught with error connected with the popularity and likability of the instructor. A total of 293 students in undergraduate calculus were divided into 12 recitation sections. They attended common lectures on other days and used a common syllabus on 40 paradigm problems. Their final-exam performance was the number of such problems successively passed. They also rated the effectiveness of the teaching performance of their recitation section instructor. The correlation of the average subjective evaluation received by each instructor and the mean increase in calculus performance from beginning to end of course was -0.75, which means that the best-liked instructor was least effective.[83] Consistent with these results are findings with hoax arrangements in which trained actors doubletalk a lecture in front of students and receive strong positive evaluations. In the same way, controlled postsession comparisons show that students learn more from videotaped lectures without humor than from the same lectures laced with relevant or irrelevant jokes, but, of course, the funny lecturers receive higher student evaluations.[77]

Often the conclusion that training improved the trainees is invalidated by many of the threats first enumerated in Chapter 2.[44] For example, changes in trainees from before to after training can be due to parallel events or changes taking place during the same period. Thus, events other than training can occur between pre- and post-tests of training that affect the test changes. A new supervisor may be appointed or production quotas revised in between pre-test and post-test.

The trainees grow older between pre-test and post-test. They may gain more job experience parallel to their training effort, raising their post-test performance beyond what was due to training.

The test used to measure change from before to after training may be unreliable. The post-test scores will then be random changes from the pre-test scores. They may reflect a regression toward the mean test score. Taking the pre-test provides practice; therefore improvement on the post-test may be due mainly to test practice rather than the training effort. The measure

Assessment for Whom

Assessment by whom	Trainees	Trainers	Supervisors	Policy makers	Scientists
Trainees	1 gradual clarification of learning process; looking glass for each other's behavior	2 feedback from learner-teacher relation; process control	3 reporting personal impressions	4 reporting personal impressions (usually via superiors)	5 data for further analysis; direct observation, interviews, tests
Trainers	6 feedback from teacher-learner relation; steering evaluation	7 exchange of experiences: e.g., trainers' conferences	8 formal reporting on activities	9 reporting suggestions for follow-up (usually via supervisors)	10 data for further analysis; first step evaluation
Supervisors	11 formal appraisal based upon job performance and training appraisal	12 depending on position of trainer; appraisal or indication for support	13 exchange of experience; preparation for policy	14 major indication for success or failure, suggestions for policy	15 data for further analysis; organizational variables
Policy makers	16 sometimes formal introduction or conclusion of training program	17 depending on position; determination of training objectives and general standards of performance	18 formal appraisal of training activities	19 general appraisal of training objectives and means; long-term policy	20 organizational variables and starting point for evaluation research
Scientists	21 in adapted form material for reading and lecturing	22 guidelines for improved training; standards of training	23 support for appraisal; standards of performance	24 preparation for decision making; practical prognoses	25 understanding dynamics of change; methodology and theory of change

Figure 13–1. Evaluation research methods. (From Hesseling, *Strategy of Evaluation Research.* Assen, Netherlands: Van Gorcum, 1966.)

after training may be different from the measure before training. For example, different raters may be used, so that the higher scores after training than before may owe more to the change of raters than to training.

The better performance of trained compared to untrained employees may be due to a variety of other differences than the training between the two groups. The "Hawthorne effect" may have stimulated the effort of trainees singled out for special training to do better than the untrained employees. The trainees may see themselves in a "win-lose" competition with untrained employees. They may exert extra effort, which as a consequence will be reflected in better test scores after training than those of untrained employees. The trainees may be a select group compared to the untrained control group. They may be volunteers, and their subsequent better scores compared to controls may be caused by this rather than the training. For instance, take another look at the evaluation of the 230 trained versus untrained Canadian life insurance agents reported earlier in Table 13–1. There were other plausible explanations for the results. Thus, the agents selected for training by their superiors were only those seen to possess greater potential. Also, those who volunteered for training or paid their own way were likely to be more committed to the field than those who did not enter training.

Various experimental designs help to reduce or eliminate these threats to conclusions about the effects of training.

Those designs are as follows:

1. Classic experiment Two groups are drawn randomly from the same population; both are pretested. One group is trained; the other is not. Both are retested.

Experimental group	Test	Train	Retest
Control group	Test		Retest

The matched-group design is an important variant. Here, for each member of the experimental group, we match a person for the control group, alike in as many respects as possible, but not to be given training. Extraneous random differences are controlled by the matching process.

2. Post-test only This is the same as the classic experiment. The two groups are drawn randomly, except that there is no pretesting, so there can be no practice effect of the pre-test on the post-test.

Experimental group	Train	Test
Control group		Test

Again, having matched groups is an important variant.

The volunteer effect, or the threat if experimental subjects see themselves differently from control subjects, can be eliminated by organizing the post-test experiment in a "holdout" variant. All subjects are trained. One portion still is assigned to the experimental group that receives training first. The other portion is assigned to the control group which receives training second. But all trainees are evaluated at the same time, which happens to occur *after* the experimental group has completed training but before the control group has begun training. The "holdout" design is as follows:

Experimental group	Train	Test	
Control group		Test	Train

The "holdout" design gives all participants, experimental and control, the opportunity for the training. Assuming that training is beneficial, the approach is a more socially responsible one than one in which controls are diagnosed into being tested but receive no training benefits.

3. Four-group design [88]   Two additional control groups are added to the classic experiment, and various comparisons are possible to reduce selected validity threats. For instance, control group 2, when compared to the experimental group, can show whether the pretesting sensitized the experimental group to the training.

Experimental group	Test	Train	Retest
Control group 1	Test		Retest
Control group 2		Train	Test
Control group 3			Test

More often than not in industry, we cannot employ these true experiments. Much more often, we make use of *quasiexperimental* designs. Here are some examples.[44]

The extremely common *nonequivalent control group* design is like the classic experiment except that we use naturally available groups. Thus, department A receives the training; department B does not. This is a quasiexperimental design. In *the interrupted-time series* there is no control group. Repeated periodic measurements are made before and after training. Thus, we pick up measures monthly on the frequency with which the library is used for nine months preceding and following a library training program. (With no control group, this design is particularly susceptible to the rival hypothesis that events other than training have led to the observed changes from before to after the training.) In the *multiple-time series design,* such a control group is added which receives no training. The library use for the eighteen months by persons who received no training can serve as the control.

The *discontinuity design* requires that we determine in advance the tested aptitude for training of the whole sample, but to be practical, we administer training only to those above a certain cutoff score in tested aptitude. (Remember who gets sent to expensive training programs and who does not.) Then, instead of a smoothly increasing cumulative frequency curve of performance, if training has an effect, we would find a sudden discontinuity in the curve at the cutoff point, as shown in Figure 13–2. All those above the cutoff would show as an accumulated group performance elevated above what would have been expected if they had not been trained. (See Figure 13–2.)

A variety of other designs is available in which we predict post-training test scores from pre-training test scores, then see how much higher the post-training scores were than predicted from the pre-training test scores. (Table 13–2 later on will be an illustration.)

For us, it is most important to note that even more complex or sophisticated ones, making use of multiple time series of measurements before and after training, the 4-group design of three different control groups to control for measurement and environmental effects, or correlational analyses to yield contrasts with predicted outcomes, never completely rid themselves of several of the validity threats. The completely controlled evaluation is an impossibility.

No amount of resources or resourcefulness in designing an evaluation of training can eliminate all possible threats to the validity of the conclusions of the evaluation. At some point, we must fall back on judgment about the relative plausibility of the various threats to invalidate the conclusion about training effect. Moreover, realistic considerations make many of the sophisticated designs impossible. For instance, while it is one thing for us to propose that all those life insurance agents be sent through training so we can reduce the validity threats in our evaluation, it is another to ask management to pay the costs for the training and the time for training of the agents who the management believes are likely to quit soon after the completion of training.

Kane proposes therefore that we step back and ask ourselves to consider selecting the best possible training evaluation for the circumstances.[44] To make the decision, he offers a series of questions:

1. Can participants in the evaluation study be selected from the target population in the manner required by this design?
2. Can participants be assigned to training and control/comparison groups in the manner required by this design?
3. Are there any naturally existing groups that could serve as comparison groups?
4. Is the progression (simultaneous or sequential) of people through the training that is required by this design feasible?

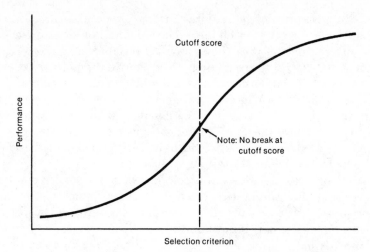

Illustration of the continuity expected between the curves for persons
above and below the selection cutoff if no training was given.

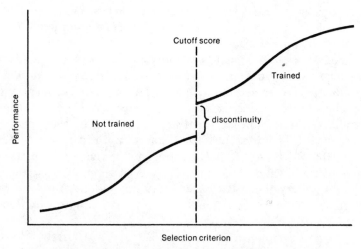

Illustration of the discontinuity expected between the curves for persons
above and below the selection cutoff if the former persons received effective training.

Figure 13–2. The regression discontinuity design. (Adapted from
J. Kane, "The Evaluation of Organizational Training Programmes," *Journal of European Training*, 5, no. 16 [1976]:
289–338.)

5. Will it be feasible to administer the criterion measure the necessary
    number of times prior to training?
6. Will it be feasible to obtain the necessary number of post-training
    criterion measures for each participant?

7. Can the necessary degree of synchronization between training administrations and between criterion measurements be achieved?
8. Can sufficient numbers of participants be obtained to serve in the
   training and/or control groups to permit the statistics required by
   the design to be computed?

Answers to these questions indicate which design it would be feasible
to employ. Kane next proposes that all the possible threats to validity
controlled by one or more of the feasible designs be identified that are
considered plausible and of concern to the evaluator or the sponsorship.
The monetary and nonmonetary costs of each feasible design would then
need to be estimated. Kane then provides a method for weighing the costs
of control of each feasible design against the benefits of controlling its
validity threats. The best possible design is selected to achieve the greatest
amount of control that can be afforded over the threats to validity.

We now turn to the available techniques for training, first looking at
those conducted on-site, then those administered off-site.

ON-SITE TRAINING TECHNIQUES

Clearly, on-the-job training is still the most common way, particularly in
smaller firms, for orienting new employees and teaching them the skills
required for the job for which they have just been hired. An older employee
or the supervisor briefs the new employees, individually, as they start to
work on the job and follows up their performance with additional briefings
until the employees seem to understand what they must do.

On and near-site training includes on-the-job training, near-the-job training, apprentice training, coaching, and job rotation. Characteristically, on-
site or near-site training involves the whole job and the whole employee,
whereas off-site education often deals with only parts of the job or some
skills relevant to the job.

On-the-Job Training

Because it requires no special space and equipment, on-the-job training
is probably the most common way in which employees receive instruction
in industry. Moreover, employees earn while they learn and produce while
they learn. They practice at what they eventually must do at the place
where they will work and with the equipment they will be using after
training is complete. Transfer is maximized.

However, there are many disadvantages. Training may be casual, unsystematic, and poorly planned. Training will be given less emphasis than pro-

duction. There is a fair chance that the trainer is a poor one compared to a professional instructor. Expensive equipment and materials are tied up for training. Waste may be high. The trainee has to learn while under the pressures of the job demands, at a pace set for already-trained workers. The trainee's progress will be appraised according to his productive output, which is likely to reveal little to him about the reasons for his mistakes and failures.[72] These disadvantages are illustrated by the already-mentioned Johns-Manville comparison of machine operators with systematic training with those operators limited to on-the-job training.[15]

Near-the-Job Training

In order to give more attention to trainee needs and to employee instructors who are specialists, a "vestibule school" may be set up in an area off the production line. Similar equipment and materials are used, but the school may be more costly than on-the-job training if only a few workers are in training at any one time. Such training areas are only feasible for teaching semiskilled jobs like machine operating, inspection, or packing.[72]

The effects of vestibule training were studied for 208 female sewing machine operators engaged in manufacturing women's lingerie. They received either one, two, or three days of vestibule training. The longer they were in vestibule training, the much lower was their subsequent turnover rate during their first 40 working days but slightly lower also was their average productivity! The best arrangement was achieved, however, with a fourth group, who were in vestibule training the first day, on the factory floor the second day, and back in vestibule training on the third day before going full-time into the factory. This integrated group produced as much or more than the other groups and also was relatively low in quitting rate. Lefkowitz, the investigator, felt that the integration of vestibule and on-the-job training worked best because it afforded an opportunity for trainees to ventilate early anxieties when they reassembled on the third day in the vestibule after the second day on the factory floor. (The trainer had been encouraged to promote conversation among the trainees and between them and herself.)

It would appear that the opportunity provided for job-oriented discussion on the day following first exposure to factory production is extremely beneficial. Reports from the trainer indicated that discussions were mainly among the women themselves, rather than their questioning her. The content of the discussions focused on topics which were areas of pragmatic difficulties ("How do you set up your schedule at home to coincide with work?") or sources of job-related tension ("The operation is really hard") . . . and the discussions appeared to provide an opportunity for group problem solving and tension reduction.

In addition, the author received informal reports that first-line supervisors paid greater attention to these trainees during their first day in the factory because they knew that [other] trainees . . . would be returning the next day to the training room and could "report" back to the trainer. This extra concern may account for the initially high rate of productivity of this group (p. 86).[59]

Apprentice Training

In formal apprenticeship programs for learning the various skilled trades, the trainees are placed under a supervisor for a specified number of years, at the end of which time they are examined or automatically promoted. If it is done well, the program offers the opportunity to move back and forth from classroom instruction to practice on the job under supervision. But too often apprentice programs are not systematically planned. The length of time in training may be unnecessarily long. Different trainees are likely to be able to learn at considerably different rates, but the fixed length of most programs and the time spent in various phases ignore this.

Apprentice programs may represent a particularly important investment in personnel development for a company or agency. As mentioned above, the German multinational chemical firm, Hoechst, conducts 3-year apprenticeship programs in 50 vocations. For 3 days a week, for 3 years, 4,500 of its employees, approximately 16 to 19 years of age, attend company schools or engage in near-job or on-the-job learning experiences. For two days, they continue to attend public schools. Apprentices can continue after graduation to pursue an engineering education.

In much of post-industrial society, the salaries of blue-collar craftspersons have long since passed those of white-collar sales and clerical personnel of equivalent education and experience and often are comparable to management salaries. As a consequence, we should be seeing an upsurge of interest in apprenticeship training in preparation for careers in the skilled blue-collar trades.

Coaching

At management levels, coaching of immediate subordinates by their managers is common. In surveys of American corporations, coaching was heavily emphasized as a management-training technique.

Coaching is likely not to be as effective as less directive approaches, such as nondirective counseling or sensitivity training, if the trainee's shortcomings are emotional or personal.[37] Coaching will be ineffective if relations between trainee and coach are ambiguous, in that the trainee cannot trust the coach; for example, the trainee might wonder, "Is the coach telling me why I am not entitled to a raise in pay or giving me helpful feedback so that I can improve myself?"

Coaching will be less effective if the coach sees the trainees as rivals, if the dependent needs of the trainee are rejected out-of-hand, if the coach is intolerant of mistakes or does not allow sufficient time for coaching. Some coaches will withhold information as a means of maintaining power in their own hands or because of antagonism toward their trainees. They may feel that certain information is of no interest to their subordinates-in-training, or they are apprehensive about the way the information might be used. They feel more secure if they hold back.[93] On the other hand, coaching will work well if the trainee can identify with the coach, and if the coach provides a good model for the trainee, if they can be open with each other, if the coach accepts responsibilities fully, and if the trainee subordinates are provided with suitable rewards and recognition for their improvement.[62]

Coaches are likely to be more effective also if they set clear standards, if they are in tune with their subordinates' capabilities, interests, and expressed needs for improvement; if they practice delegation frequently coupled with suitable followup; if they encourage completion of assignments; and if they allow their subordinates to substitute for them at times.[31] To be effective, coaches have to be good in observation, questioning, listening, and demonstrating.

Coaching thrives in a "climate of confidence," a climate in which subordinates respect the integrity and capability of their superiors.[66] And coaching can take greatest advantage of the possibilities of individualized instruction concentrating on those specific stimulus situations subordinates find hardest to deal with, those specific performances subordinates find hardest to improve, and the kind and quality of feedback which can have great impact on subordinates.

Job Rotation

With a clear understanding of its management structure and the objectives and practices of the various positions within it, and with a good way of reviewing its personnel periodically to determine their developmental needs and aspirations, managements maintain job rotation to "grow a good executive crop." Trainees may be rotated in observational assignments to acquaint them with the work of various department heads. They may fill various successive training assignments. They may rotate as "assistants" to department heads. Or they may transfer and/or spiral upward in the organization across departmental leaderships that offer opportunities to continue to "learn by doing" in different sectors of the organization.[100]

Systematic job rotation plans transfer trainees so that they gradually can move to positions of increasing responsibility. Trainees benefit to the extent to which skills learned on one job can be transferred. They gain different perspectives as they spend months or years in different company locations and absorb through experience the different problems and approaches in the marketing, production, finance, and engineering divisions. They become familiar with personnel in many different parts of the firm. The different departments are constantly stimulated with fresh viewpoints as trainees rotate into them. At the same time, job rotation offers to the trainees a prospective series of new, stimulating challenges.

Rotation fosters organizational flexibility. In case of sudden need for an executive replacement, former rotatees are likely to be available with experience to take over the situation. Rotation, which provides diagonal upward promotions, avoids the problems that may arise where a newly promoted executive must supervise his former peers. Finally, managers, particularly those at lower and middle levels, prefer to rotate rather than staying put. Rotation may offer new challenges, recognition for past performance, and a sense of progress with the firm. A survey of 1,958 managers disclosed that those at lower and middle management levels tend to be more satisfied with their jobs if they remain on them for relatively shorter periods of time. They are more satisfied, in particular, with their opportunities for self-actualization if they are moved more frequently.[55]

Job rotation also affords the trainee opportunity to see the interactions between divisions. One oil executive commented on his chagrin at finding that he had been transferred to heading an operating unit that was involved in trying unsuccessfully to execute a plan that (he discovered after his transfer) he had himself developed while heading the planning department six months earlier!

Job rotation may serve to tie executives to the firm as a whole, at the expense of their loyalty to the department to which they are assigned for only a period of time. Executives who expect to rotate cannot afford to develop strong socioemotional attachments to any group of subordinates. Their families, as well, may have to be mobile, ready to break camp and move from one city to another. Again, this may serve to tie both executives and their families to the firm or agency at the expense of loyalty to community or region.

The social and emotional costs to the family are neglected — one drawback among many of the dependence on job rotation. Executives can be rotated too fast, so they fail to gain any sense of accomplishment. If they expect only brief tenure in a particular position, they may be encouraged to become "short-term maximizers," pushing hard for immediate production and profits at the expense of long-term departmental development and morale. Two management classes may be established — those who rotate and those who don't. Those who remain fixed with a department as rotators come and go may develop a variety of ways of working against the best interests of the rotators and the organization as a whole to protect what they see are the best interests of their department and themselves. Customers and clients may experience dissatisfaction in dealing with a department whose head changes frequently.

Rotation may waste time and talent. A chemical engineer who spends one year as director of personnel may not have the readiness for really learning much during the year, and could possibly have learned more about what he particularly needed to know by a briefer course of carefully planned instruction and reading.[1]

OFF-SITE TRAINING

Off-site education and training ranges from lectures to computer-assisted instruction and, as said before, often deals with one or at most only several parts of the job at one time.

Lectures and Reading

The formal lecture has a place. It can economically transmit information to large numbers of trainees. And, sometimes, it can work well. Miner successfully used a lecture method to increase the favorableness of attitudes of 72 research and development supervisors toward accepting responsibility for their leadership role above and beyond their professional roles.[73] Nevertheless, when compared with the other available methods ranging from case discussions to programmed texts, lectures are the least popular with training directors.[9] Although a rousing instructor may stimulate employees, the lecture is unlikely to change attitudes as well as might small-group discussions about the same issues.[61]

The lecture is primarily one-way communication. There is little opportunity to clarify meanings, to check on whether trainees really understand what is being transmitted, and to handle the wide diversity of ability, attitude, and interest that may prevail among the trainees.[5] Often suitable reading matter for the better-educated readers might better serve the same aims as the lecture, for the readers can stop when necessary, make notes more easily, check back on earlier portions to clarify meanings, consult other books as they learn the material, ask other trainees about what they are reading, and so on. Company and departmental libraries are becoming important management aids.

It is commonplace to distribute reading lists to executives and professionals. Journals are circulated among employees. A certain portion of every day, on the job, may be spent by executives in keeping up with their areas of specialization, reading appropriate journals and books. Particularly sensitive to this need to keep up are the technically educated. Electrical engineers will find themselves obsolete ten years after graduation if they do not keep up with their rapidly changing fields of concentration. Obsolescence can be avoided by continued reading in the field and attending professional meetings.

Films, Filmstrips, Videotape Cassettes, and Slides

A great deal of effort and expense can go into planning a film, filmstrip, videotape cassette, or slide presentation. Editing can increase the extent to which they conform to good learning principles. Once they are "canned," they are available repeatedly thereafter. The subject matter can be organized optimally and presented by the most skillful lecturer available. Animation can be employed to make dynamic diagrams that a lecturer could show only in static forms. The cause-effect relationships to be learned can be dramatically illustrated.

The advantages of these pictorial approaches over nonpictorial ones were demonstrated in a series of thirteen experiments on the training of employees to complete various tasks such as electric wiring and soldering of joints as well as quite different assembly operations such as salad making, breading of food, and placement of plates, rolls, and coffee at a banquet. Comparisons were made of the effects of verbal instruction, typed lists of instructions, picture (slide) instructions, and combinations of these such as words plus pictures of performance.

Pictures were found best. Error rates were reduced from one-third to one-tenth and the time was usually cut in half using them alone or in combination with other training directions.[53]

Films have obvious advantages when competent instructors are not available or travel costs are prohibitive. The terminal performance expected in a complex motor sequence, particularly where highly standardized requirements are demanded, can best be recorded and displayed on film. Where slowing up or speeding up time is useful, film serves as an ideal medium of display. It can also bring into the classroom dramatic events in all their detail for close examination by instructor and students.[30] Films are more effective as media for learning if students are directed in advance what to look for and attend to in the film. In the same way, films maintain such effectiveness if they are followed by carefully led classroom discussion.

Live Television

Whether a lecture or demonstration is presented locally or by live TV does not seem to affect learning or retention. A review of 114 experimental studies of college and military investigations comparing TV and classroom instruction noted that nine yielded results favoring TV, 17 yielded results favoring classroom instruction, and 88 found no significant differences.[85] Videotape feedback permits interaction between trainee and trainer, but TV, as such, does not. Nevertheless, like films, it can make use of the most skillful instructor and the most efficiently organized subject matter. It can provide closeups of apparatus and demonstrations despite large class sizes. Evidently these advantages balance out the disadvantage of no interaction with the instructor (as is true in the large lecture hall, anyway). In some large groups, television closeups may be used in conjunction with face-to-face lectures.

As with any media, TV can be made more effective for learning. Simplicity, good organization, stimulation of interest, response opportunities with feedback, rest pauses, and cues that direct attention on what is most important to learn all make for more effective TV instructional programs.[11] The mass efficiency of TV is illustrated by the TV secretarial course "From Nine to Five," sponsored by the federal government, whose secretarial employees number in the hundreds of thousands. According to supervisory ratings, viewing the TV course led to a 59 per cent reduction in need for other training.[71]

A particularly useful video training application has emerged—the videotape cassette showing a skilled operator doing the job. Trainees play the tape as often as needed to model their behavior on that shown on the cassette. No trainer is needed.

Videotape Recording (VTR) Feedback

By the late 1970s, as a consequence of reduced costs for equipment, this medium had become an important adjunct for training of a wide variety of skills from skiing to selling, from investigating to interviewing. It appears to provide trainees with the maximum possible feedback concerning the adequacy of their actual performance. Not only do they have the consequences of their performance, but they can play and replay the performance to study specifically what they did well and what they did poorly. The next decades ought to see the development of ways to insure that we make the most out of this technological innovation.

An early evaluation of the use of VTR was made with American overseas advisors. They were able to view a videotape of their interactions with an actor trained to play the role representative of a particular foreign culture. A trainer criticized the advisor's performance as he watched the tape. Trainees learned more effectively and retained more with this approach than did a control group who only read the training manual covering the same points.[48]

Programmed Instruction (PI)

Training can remain highly structured as before, yet increase opportunities for the trainee to be an active participant in the learning process, through the use of programmed instruction. By 1970, over 2,300 such programs had appeared, dealing with topics ranging from blueprint reading to analyses of income tax returns.[95]

Teaching machines and self-instructional textbooks promote several learning conditions: (1) trainees are active, participate, and set their own pace of learning; (2) the trainees have to deal only with discrete bits of material facing them; at any one time they receive immediate knowledge of the results of their response to the material; and (3) the action occurs in an efficient sequence of such discrete steps. The organization of the material that precedes and follows the particular problem currently faced is carefully planned and tested to see that the sequence enhances learning rather than interfering with it. Each stimulus is checked to see how well it indicates what response is required. As much as possible, all irrelevant material is discarded.

The most common approach to PI has these characteristics:

1. A single item of information is revealed in each step, called a frame. The first frame requires completing blanks without aid; the second gives a choice among alternatives. All the frames together — as many as are required to complete mastery of the material under study — are called a program.

2. Frames appear in correct subject-matter sequence. Each frame uses knowledge gained from the frame or frames preceding it. The first frames are easy. Succeeding frames gradually grow more difficult.

3. At each step, the trainees must provide an answer. They remain active and attentive throughout the learning process.

4. The trainees see the correct answer immediately after giving their own answers. They can then compare the correct answer with theirs. The answer is covered during study but can be seen when the trainees advance the program. In one major variant of programming, if the trainees select a wrong alternative they are directed to a branch of instruction that informs them why they are in error. Corrective steps follow. But this bypath is avoided if the trainees respond correctly initially.[14]

5. Each program is tested to insure that almost all trainees for whom the program is being prepared will get about 95 per cent of the answers right, depending on the nature of the material.

6. Trainees work individually, at their own pace.

7. A program may be presented in book form with the answers to each frame covered by a simple mask — a ruler or sheet of paper. Or the program may be presented by a teaching machine. The trainees turn a knob or press a button to bring each frame before a window in the face of the

machine. They present their answers, turn the knob a little farther (or press another button) to uncover the correct answer, then compare answers before proceeding.[27]

Programmed instructional materials profit greatly from the fact that the programmers must first methodically break down into its minute details the complex job information about which they are to write an instructional program. Moreover, the program of separate steps they write can be tested, step-by-step, to see the extent to which certain steps are too big for too many trainees, or wrong ideas are generated by the questions and answers at that step. The main advantages of programmed instruction lie here in the precise, orderly analysis of what is to be taught by the program, and in the opportunity to test in advance of routine application the adequacy of each step in the program. In addition, programmed instruction contributes to the efficiency of the learning situation. The trainees are less likely to be distracted during the course of learning. All appropriate questions are likely to be faced and answered; no such guarantee can be made for traditional classroom procedures. If properly prepared, the program leaves no gaps in the presentation of information. The trainees are active rather than passive learners, engaged in responding in a continuous exchange of information between themselves and the program.

Motivation to learn is enhanced. Generally, the trainees' experiences are mainly successful as they proceed from easier to more difficult material in short stages. When they make mistakes, it is nonpersonal, nonthreatening; each is the only person involved. They receive no reproof for their errors. Moreover, they correct their own mistakes by retrial of the problem. Bright trainees can proceed quickly and do not suffer frustrating delays waiting for others to catch up. Less capable trainees are not pushed; they move ahead as fast as they can. Relatively dull, detailed, rote material can be programmed, freeing the classroom instruction for broader discussion rather than repetitious drill.[27]

UTILITY   Programmed instruction in the industrial setting seems to be as effective as, if not more than, normal teaching methods, perhaps because industrial training usually has very specific goals and objectives and can be fitted easily into a step-by-step training procedure.[60]

The Life Insurance Agency Management Association evaluated the effectiveness for over 1,500 employees in seven companies of a 625-frame, self-instructional text on life insurance fundamentals. As in many previous studies, the programmed learning was found to be as effective as conventional teaching procedures, but with considerable saving of the trainer's time.[98]

IBM converted into five programmed textbooks what had been presented in 15 hours of conventional classroom work on the parts, names, functions, and data-processing procedures of the IBM 7070, a large high-speed com-

Table 13–2. Comparison of achievement test scores and experimental groups (scores adjusted for pretraining differences in aptitude among trainees).

Group	Observed Means		
	Pretraining aptitude	*Achievement test scores following training*	*Posttraining * achievement test scores adjusted for pretraining aptitude*
Control	51.2	86.2	86.9
Experimental	58.2	95.1	94.7

* This adjustment is made by an analysis of covariance to determine what the differences between experimental and control trainees in posttraining achievement scores would have been if they were due only to the pretraining aptitude of the trainees, then subtracting these predicted differences from the posttraining differences actually observed. The residual of these adjusted differences cannot then be attributed to the pretraining differences of the two groups of trainees.

Adapted from Hughes and McNamara, "A Comparative Study of Programmed and Conventional Instruction in Industry," *Journal of Applied Psychology,* 45(1961): 228.

puter. While 42 trainees, serving as controls, took the conventional 15-hour course, 70 other trainees spent approximately 11 hours or less during a three-day period with the programmed texts. They could take the texts home with them, but actually 60 per cent of the trainees taught by program did less home study than the classroom-trained subjects. Table 13–2 compares the achievement test scores of the trainees taught in the classroom and those taught by programmed texts. Since the trainees taught by program were initially somewhat higher in tested aptitude, the posttraining differences were adjusted by statistical analysis to remove the effects of these differences. Even so, the trainees taught by programmed text were clearly more knowledgeable about the IBM 7070 after training than those given classroom instruction. Training time with PI was 11 hours compared to 15 hours for the control group. Ninety per cent mastery was achieved by 89 per cent of the experimental group and only 45 per cent of the control group. The results could not be attributed to a Hawthorne effect, in which the experimental trainees taught by program did better because they knew they were part of an experiment, for neither the experimental trainees nor the controls knew an experiment was being conducted. Instruction to both groups was treated as routine training operations.

Sixty-nine of the trainees taught by program mentioned afterward liking particularly such aspects as the gradual and logical sequence of presentation, the repetition of important points, the ability to set one's own pace, and the ease with which one could maintain attention and concentration

Table 13–3. Comparisons of programmed instructions versus conventional methods for each criterion in studies that include two or more criteria.

N		Conventional method superior	No significant difference between methods	Programmed instruction superior
32	Training time	1	2	29
32	Immediate learning	3	20	9
26	Retention	5	16	5

From Nash, Muczyk, and Vettori, "The Relative Practical Effectiveness of Programmed Instruction," *Personnel Psychology*, 11(1971): 57–59.

on the program. Forty of these same trainees felt that some items were repeated too frequently. Some were annoyed by the constant need to turn pages and to write all answers; others missed the classroom and the human instructor; still others missed adequate summaries and outlines of the subject. But on the whole, 87 percent of the trainees liked PI more than conventional instruction and 83 per cent would prefer using it in future courses.

A review of 128 comparisons between the effects of programmed instruction and more conventional methods summarized in Table 13–3 clearly identifies that training time generally tends to be shorter with programmed instruction with no loss in immediate learning or in subsequent retention.[75]

The savings multiply themselves many times over in industry once the initial investment has been made in a programmed text or activity, since once the time-saving program is available for nurses or technical service representatives or switchboard operators, it becomes available at relatively little cost everywhere.

DISADVANTAGES   Programmed instruction has serious limitations. If a company training program is bad to start with, programming will not make it much better. Programming can only facilitate learning. If what is to be taught is highly disorganized, the programmer's main contribution may be to initiate action to encourage the training department's careful analysis and reorganization of what must be taught.

As educational "engineers," the programmers may be forced to abandon much of what was presented in the classroom or in manuals, because their analyses show that the material does not contribute to the desired performance objectives.

Initially, programming is expensive and time-consuming. Careful planning of objectives is required. Programming requires painstaking, creative, step-by-step development. Finally, much testing and tinkering is necessary before a program can be made operational. Investment in programs thus must be limited to activities involving large numbers of prospective trainees over a substantial period of time, in order to justify the costs of programming. Activities likely to become obsolete quickly may not be worth programming.

Certain kinds of material seem less suitable than others for programming. For instance, although some effort has been made to program human-relations material, it is more difficult to write an effective program where what is to be taught involves shadings of opinion, sensitivity to fuzzy socio-emotional issues, and an unclear notion as to order of steps in which learning takes place. Thus, at the management level, programs may teach executives applied mathematics or managerial economics, but it is harder to write programs to facilitate learning to increase one's effectiveness in interpersonal relations with subordinates. For these purposes, conference procedures, discussions, case study, role-playing, gaming, and sensitivity training are likely to continue to be more commonly used. However, in this area, Fiedler successfully developed the "cultural assimilator." [21] This is programmed learning to teach sensitivity to foreign societies.

Computer-Assisted Instruction (CAI)

A logical extension of programmed instruction is computer-aided instruction, with the same step-by-step progressions, branching, and immediate feedback of results. Considerable success has been obtained in the development of such programs in subjects ranging from elementary mathematics to Russian. Learning has been found as effective as or more so than that obtained from conventional classroom procedures.[92,13] IBM used computer-assisted instruction to provide course material for such things as a basic introduction to data processing systems. Over a fairly wide range of material, computer-assisted instruction was as effective as programmed instruction and in several cases resulted in a savings in training time.[65]

CAI lends itself to adapting learning task difficulty to how well the trainee currently performs.[45] It is what the skilled teacher or instructor does when an individual or trainee is learning a task. With computers, though, the task of increasing the difficulty of the problem can be done automatically and far better than an individual instructor could do it, especially when dealing with large groups of students at one time. This *adaptive training* technique is often applied to the learning of complex skills such as that of piloting a helicopter.[8] The technique has also been applied to perceptual decision-making tasks such as simulations of the airport traffic-control problem.

TASKTEACH   Illustrative of CAI and what it can do is TASKTEACH.[82] It provides trainees with variable amounts of learning support, as they request it, to help them organize the material and the processes that lead to mastery. During each learning session, TASKTEACH continuously updates the record of the trainee's progress and the state of the equipment or task that it is simulating. The logic for the satisfactory operation of particular equipment or tasks is contained in computerized lists that describe elements and relationships among them in sufficient detail for the simulation. These lists replace the conventional, frame-by-frame description of the typical CAI instructional sequence.[19]

TASKTEACH can be used to learn to troubleshoot electronic devices. The program can simulate a failure in a particular circuit of the equipment. The computer displays front-panel indicator symptoms that the malfunction produces. The trainee proceeds to collect symptoms from indicators by manipulating the front-panel controls in patterns that will (1) make particular kinds of information visible on each indicator when the equipment is functioning normally, and (2) uncover all possible symptoms of abnormal functioning. TASKTEACH provides detailed knowledge of results that allow the trainee to test hypotheses about the malfunction. The trainee learns about the effectiveness of each test. Knowledge of possible causes of symptoms is increased. This improves troubleshooting strategy.[19]

In addition to the troubleshooting program, TASKTEACH includes a program to help trainees learn other types of tasks. Radio operators, for example, can learn how to tune transmitters. Similarly, a mechanic can learn how to disassemble, repair, and reassemble a mechanical device such as a carburetor. Programs are made specific to a particular task by computerized lists that describe goals, subgoals, actions, and constraints that specify the ways these elements are organized sequentially. Since almost all human work can be described in terms of goal-action hierarchies, this part of TASKTEACH is potentially widely applicable.[82]

PLATO-TUTOR With the PLATO system and an instructional programming language, TUTOR, Hauser and Spencer have applied CAI to interpersonal skill training in feedback communication, goal setting, problem solving, decision-making, effective rewards and punishments, and the use of power and authority.[36] Trainees were company commanders responsible for Navy recruit training. Compared to controls who received the same pre- and post-test assessments and were involved in the same regular duties, considerable skill learning (appropriate response to hypothetical cases) was obtained.

JOINING CAI AND TELECOMMUNICATIONS CAI can be coupled with telecommunication facilities to make available standardized instruction at many different locations. United Air Lines has been able to train thousands of its agents in 116 cities quickly, uniformly, and inexpensively in this way. United Air Lines linked a computerized reservations system to 900 desk consoles in a nationwide network connected to a computer in Denver. The training material is fed into the system but remains separate from data for issuing flight and passenger information. The training material has a separate, simple numerical code which makes it possible for the reservation agent to use his or her regular desk console as a teaching aid.

The employee simply places a small cardboard mask over the keyboard of his or her desk, automatically keying it for the learning/testing operation. The trainee reads the question from the sheet, selects one of the multiple-choice answers, and presses a button corresponding to that answer's code. The responses are recorded on a punched card placed in the ticket slot of the agent's console, thus providing the trainee with an immediate progress record.

The effectiveness of CAI as a training device was assessed by testing 3,000 agents. They took an average of 46 minutes to show proficiency and retention of information as opposed to 75 minutes for a control group of 175 agents receiving the standard lecture-demonstration in classroom instruction. CAI trainees averaged 92 per cent in retention while classroom pupils attained only 88 per cent.

With CAI in place, agents can study during slack periods without loss of time on the job. Information can be distributed on the basis of need. Finally, the training staff automatically is provided a monitoring system.[18]

CAI AND CABLE TV   Two-way cable TV technology is now available to bring CAI activity into the home. In Ottawa, Canada, for instance, in 1977, a homeowner with cable TV and touch telephone can call up a program on his or her TV screen and respond on the telephone.

UTILITY OF CAI   There is a big gap between the availability of the CAI technology and the economic and social viability of its use. Koerner lists these problems among many more keeping open the gap: (1) the hardware often is of low reliability and high cost of maintenance; (2) hardware quickly becomes obsolete; (3) the programming or "software" has lagged behind the hardware development; (4) developing software is still an art, and in a rudimentary state; and (5) the new technology may be thrust on instructors to whom it may represent a downgrading inconvenience.[52]

Nevertheless, CAI can individualize instruction most efficiently. It is infinitely patient when repetitive drill is required for effective learning. It does not have preconceived ideas about a trainee. Mistakes produce red lights or objective program statements, not sarcastic comments.[30]

Conference or Discussion

Lectures can arouse audiences and stimulate thinking. But numerous comparisons of lecture versus discussion approaches to helping employees to change their ways of behaving suggest that discussion of the material in small groups is likely to be more effective, particularly if attitudes must be changed before the new ways will be put into operation by the trainees.

Discussion is favored over lecture when the material to be presented is likely to need much clarification and amplification. For instance, learning from a large lecture can be facilitated, if, following a period of lecture, small "buzz groups" are formed to share opinions about the lecture, raise questions, and consider alternatives. Each buzz group can summarize its deliberations for the entire lecture room or engage in question-and-answer interchange with the lecturer. Individuals who would hesitate to question the lecturer will do so through the medium of their group spokesperson; many questions can be resolved within the group; others can be posed for the lecturer.

The promotion of two-way communication through discussion between instructor and groups of trainees increases motivation of trainees and enables them to check to see whether they are in error about certain ideas as well as to note whether others have accepted certain formulations that have been generated by the discussion. Supervisors trained in human relations, compared with those without such training, were found to lead groups into more effective and creative solution of a problem in changing work methods.[68]

Discussion leaders hope to promote learning and retention by fostering the discovery process. Rather than answering the questions they pose, they create conditions enabling trainees to discover answers for themselves and to evaluate such answers. In a way, effective discussion technique parallels programmed learning but with much less system.

The effectiveness of the discussion in reducing resistance to change, promoting learning of new behaviors, as well as in bringing about modifications in attitudes, depends a great deal on the discussion leader's skill, education, and personality. Untrained leaders can turn a discussion into a lecture or a promotion of their own prejudices. Or the discussion can degenerate into a pooling of ignorance when the leaders have no notion about the course they expect learning to take.

Participation can be shared more fully by employing a number of strategies. Members can be regrouped in successive meetings so that new groups containing only the less talkative of earlier sessions are formed. In such groups, primarily silent trainees will be "forced" into taking leadership roles in dealing with discussions about behavior relations. They will have much more opportunity to practice than if they remain mixed with more normally talkative individuals. A sample of 20 supervisors, so treated, was found six months later to earn more meritorious ratings as supervisors than a control sample in which members were not shuffled.

In the same way, asking each trainee to submit in writing an idea, a problem, or a suggestion, then pooling the written materials, will greatly increase the extent to which all trainees will involve themselves in discussions that follow.[43]

CASE DISCUSSION   A case for study and discussion can range from a paragraph statement of a specific problem to a 50-page description of the history and current status of a business firm, with a delineation of the problems facing it. At the one extreme, it can be presented for discussion without any structuring of what the student should attend to in the case. At the other extreme, a series of choices can be offered that have been pretested and scaled to assess the ability of the trainee to detect and employ the important cues in the situation.[56]

It is suggested that case discussion allows executives to exercise thought procedures to promote self-discoveries. Learning may occur to the extent that one's own conclusions and the ways one arrived at answers are adequately evaluated by one's colleagues. The method sets participants to thinking in terms of multiple causes and effects, reducing the tendency to be satisfied with simple answers. This is one reason why case discussion is a favorite method for teaching business policy, a subject matter involving integration of marketing, production, research and development, finance, and personnel. General principles and issues can be illustrated or highlighted by case discussion. Participants may feel themselves experiencing what is happening to the protagonists in the case. They learn what are the important elements to attend to in making a business decision and how to proceed systematically to make such decisions. The case leads them to focus on business objectives, environmental conditions, analyses of available resources, and alternative solutions.

The parables of the New Testament or the anecdotes of Lincoln were similar pedagogical devices, which illuminated a single issue by humanizing and personalizing a theoretical position or point of view. But even more personally involving is role-playing.

Role-Playing

Instead of just talking about a case, once the situation has been described and the trainees brought up to date on what has taken place so far, trainees are assigned to play the parts of the various characters in the case, as if they were the people with the problem. Instead of talking about solving the problems at hand, the trainees try to play out solutions to the problems spontaneously as they see them, according to their impressions of the views of the persons whose roles they are playing.

Role-playing takes advantage of the interest trainees have in acting. Pertinent situations can be dramatized. Experiments show that when persons are forced to verbalize a set of opinions as they play a role, they shift their own private opinions in the direction of the role they are playing more than if they remain passive. They are also more confident about their shifted attitudes than if they had remained passive.[42]

Further experiments show that if persons are required to defend a viewpoint, they are more likely to end up convincing themselves of its validity. It is not whether or not they are satisfied with their performance as such that matters, but the fact that they have been forced to improvise a defense.[49] As a consequence, an effective technique for developing appreciation of the "other point of view" is *role reversal*. Real-life foremen are asked to play the part of shop stewards, and vice versa. All players will shift from their own extreme position toward sharing the opposing point of view as they are forced to defend this reversal of their own original feelings.[89]

Whenever a strong difference of opinion appears between two persons, a trainer may ask each person to exchange roles with the other and continue the scene. Two executives can be asked to exchange roles, but not jobs, for the purposes of mutual training. A critique follows their playing out a problem.[90] Not only are opposing opinions ameliorated, but each player may develop more insight and understanding of what the opposition feels and wants.

APPLICATIONS TO HUMAN RELATIONS TRAINING   Role-playing appears to add to the ability to develop successful solutions to human-relations problems. For instance, small teams drawn from 440 supervisors met in either 22 case discussion groups or 23 role-playing exercises. They discussed or role-played one of two problems, one concerning the assignment of a new truck to a crew of utility repairmen and the other how to change a work procedure. In role-playing, each participant took the part of one of the repairmen and the crew foreman. In the case discussion, they simply talked about solutions to the problem. Conditions were similar with a change-of-work-procedure problem. Forty-six per cent of the role-playing teams developed integrated, new solutions to the problems. For instance, instead of assigning a new truck to the man with the oldest truck, they replaced the oldest truck but enabled each person in the crew to switch to a newer truck. On the other hand, only 15 per cent of the case discussions came up with such integrated solutions.[87]

In *multiple role-playing,* a large audience divides itself into small teams, each member of which receives instructions to play a particular role. Following the role-plays within each team, the whole audience reassembles and shares experiences.[69] The different teams can (without having been told) be given systematically different instructions, so the effects of these differences on what occurs during the interactions among the players is dramatically revealed during the critique.

SPECIFIC PURPOSES   Roles can be engineered to bring about specific attitude changes. In the self-guided exercise PROSPER, after a brief description of a case of an insubordinate black engineer and some preliminary in-basket decisions, each player receives a role as one of five different managers in a firm, gathered to discuss the case. Each of the five roles is built around a different attitudinal factor involved in the upgrading of black employees: for example, black employees can be competent, or black employees need to feel they belong. All participants verbalize favorable positions on at least one of the factors while they hear favorable information about all the rest. Analyses for 2,293 managers indicate that their attitudes on the five issues are more favorable immediately after the experience than their responses to attitude scales were before they began. After three to five months, some of the effects still remain. A comparable self-guided program of multiple role-playing, PROFAIR, deals with the corresponding issues involved in the upgrading of women employees.[4]

DISADVANTAGES   Role-playing has its disadvantages. It may be seen as immature, illegitimate, and irrelevant.[67] Players are likely to overdramatize and overact, putting more emphasis on acting than problem-solving.[64] The management trainee playing the role of the union steward is likely to fight too much and too hard; the sales trainee playing the customer unrealistically "needles" the trainee who is playing the salesperson. Players need to be instructed in the subtleties of the roles they are being asked to play. A useful procedure with multiple role-playing is to bring together first all those who are going to play the same role. They can discuss the role to develop better understanding of it and reinforce each other on how to focus on its important aspects. How much is learned depends on the context in which the role-playing takes place. For instance, whether or not role-playing by supervisor-trainees increased their measured sensitivity to employee feelings and understanding of the employees' point of view depended on whether the role-playing was part of the analysis of case material and whether adequate discussions were held after the role-play.[57]

UTILITY   Why use role-playing? A superficial argument can be advanced that role-playing, particularly reverse role-playing, is a manipulative means, which cannot be justified by its ends. It is "beyond freedom and dignity" in that it forces participants to play roles and as a consequence of their role efforts brings about changes in their attitudes through manipulation. But it is our contention that the means are justified by the ends *if the participants fully understand the game, the reasons for playing it,* and the intent, which is to cover a variety of issues in interesting and challenging ways in less time than would be required with more didactic approaches. Further, more people can be reached readily than in the typical "question-

and-answer" framework that passes for audience participation, where only the more outspoken in the audience have much opportunity to participate. Finally, many participants are reached who would be closed to challenge and change.

A role-play or a simulation, if well constructed, is no different and no more manipulative from the structuring by a curator of a presentation of works of art in a gallery. The curator selects only a few for display from among these; only a subset is highlighted. In the same way, the simulation is carefully designed and tested to evoke selected values, attitudes, and behavior. Its creation has some analogy to a work of art, which is structured to evoke a pattern of responses.

Simulation

Suppose instead of talking about a case or playing the role of individuals who were in the case, we recreate the major elements in the case and ask trainees to take on the assignments and challenges of those who were originally involved. In short, we simulate the original real-life problem, engaging trainees in the experience from which we hope we have abstracted the important conditions that were true in real life. For instance, we wish to teach managers the need to balance their objectives, to avoid allocating too much of their resources to any one need, permitting some but not too much concentration of effort in reaction to changing markets. Instead of discussing cases that exemplify the problems, or role-playing an executive faced with allocation decisions, we may design a game in which, periodically, the trainees must commit their available resources. If they err in overcommitments in some areas, they receive feedback that their competitors, other trainees, are capitalizing on their failure to cover other areas. Conversely, they may learn that they have risked too much for too little in still other expenditures.

For training, the ideal simulation experience would have the same characteristics as programmed instruction. But instead of presenting single frames of material, the simulation would present a set of increasingly complex, contrived experiences, each calling for a response or set of responses, followed by feedback to the trainees of the consequences of their actions.

One simulation that has the potential for achieving these attributes is the in-basket test,[25] which we have already mentioned in Chapter 10 as an assessment technique. Suitably modified for training executives, the in-basket can be used to stimulate and evaluate complex decisions.

BUSINESS GAMES   The business game is a living case. Trainees must make decisions and then live with them. There is intrinsic motivation to energize and direct behavior; it is not acting, as in role-playing. Feedback of results is rapid.[16] It was estimated that over 30,000 executives [91] had participated in one or more of the hundred or so business games that appeared in the first five years following the introduction in 1956 by the American Management Association of its Top Management Decision Simulation.[80] The prototypical game and most of its successors present a set of budgetary decisions to the players, requiring them to decide at each successive play how much to invest in raw materials, plant, equipment, advertising, research, labor, and so forth. They also may have to set competitive prices, buy market information, borrow money, locate plants, and so on. Specialized games are available for a wide assortment of executive activities, ranging from warehousing to stock market portfolio management.[58] The consequences of each play are revealed in a profit-and-loss statement, often calculated by computer. Players may compete individually or in teams against each other or against computer models of the environment.

In the more complex games, which literally might be played for a year or more, such as the Carnegie Tech management game, students can apply linear programming solutions, carry out extensive statistical analysis, deal with workmen's strikes, work out computer programs to assist the decision-making process, and engage in complex auditing procedures. More experienced executives may serve as the "board of directors" to advise the team of players.[12]

Human relations problems requiring solution may be generated by a game in which player-managers must literally obtain the cooperation of player-workers to produce for a "market" paper products made by cutting, assembling, and stapling. Players can be hired and fired, and tangible products and raw materials processed, bought, and sold.[2]

Despite its high initial development cost, the business game has numerous advantages over on-the-job training for executives, and contrasts favorably with specialized study or other participative techniques. Time is compressed, so that the trainees can make and experience the effects of many more decisions than they could on the job. Indeed, in the game, the players usually receive feedback about decisions. In real life, they might receive such feedback seldom, if at all. At the same time, involvement in the game is likely to be much higher than in a case discussion.

Raia has shown that a business game, simple or complex, can add more to performance and final exams about case problems than discussions and readings about the cases.[79]

The game can cue the key factors to be discerned by the trainees in order for them to understand the business they are to manage. It may illustrate which factors are important, which are not, and the approximate quantities involved. Players are given the opportunity to see the effects of executive decisions in particular areas. At the same time, they are forced to establish policies, long-range plans, and strategies. The game affords the trainees practice in using a variety of executive tools such as break-even charts, linear programs, and statistical inventory controls. The game may illustrate for the trainees the value of mathematical models to optimize decisions.[32]

Games can be designed to teach students how to interpret and use data about complex reporting and control systems, how to coordinate the various parts that make up the system, and how to deal rationally with risk.[17] Games may be designed to teach facts about the business, the importance of imaginative and creative behavior, and the credibility of various kinds of results of decisions.[12]

Nevertheless, games have shortcomings as learning situations. They may be overly expensive and lengthy experiences if their main purpose is to teach a few institutional facts, for example, which could be taught more quickly and easily in a manual or lecture. In many games designed so far, *some* trainees can discover, after a few plays, that if they follow a particular mathematical function, they can thereafter always show a comfortable profit. The game becomes a matter of making successive calculations with nothing else to be learned.[5] Games also may fail to work because they do not allow players to distinguish between good and bad strategies.[76] The mass of data provided by a game may not be considered informative. More reasonable information systems are needed, with concentration on the stimulation and evaluation of the participants' performance as executives in confronting the problems generated by the game.[34]

Electromechanical simulators have been used to train individuals to operate everything from diesel locomotives to the most sophisticated aircraft. One of the earliest simulators was the Link Trainer, used during World War II to acquaint prospective aviators with some of the procedural tasks involved in flying, but the Trainer had relatively low fidelity. The fidelity of simulation refers to how closely the operational task is represented by the training device. The fidelity of simulation can be thought of as having three different components: (1) equipment fidelity, (2) environment fidelity, and (3) psychological fidelity.[50]

Equipment fidelity refers to how closely the simulator duplicates the operational equipment such as the displays and controls of an aircraft. Environmental fidelity refers to the approximation of the simulator to the stimulation that an individual would receive in a real situation. This would include the visual scene and motion. A third element, psychological fidelity, is the trainee's perception of the simulator. This simulation depends on the sensory-perceptual capabilities of the individual involved. For example, a simulator of high-speed aircraft may not feed back all the motion cues to the trainee, but, since the trainee is not sensitive to the cues, the fidelity may seem almost perfect. In Chapter 2 we discussed the effects of lack of motion cues on drivers in an automobile simulation. As our technology increases and the level demanded by individuals on jobs increases, we will expect to see more computer-based complex simulation systems such as those presently used by the aerospace industry.

Simulation can be particularly useful in confronting trainees with particular job hazards while allowing them to act safely or unsafely (at no real risk to themselves). Thus, a source of possible injury inherent in the use of an offhand grinder is the explosion of the grinding wheel. To avoid injury in the event of an exploding wheel, it is necessary only that the operator stand to the side of the machine, out of the plane of rotation of the grinding wheel during the startup phase of the grinding operation.

Accident simulation was used as a training procedure and compared with training using written instructions and demonstrations. A bench grinder was modified to allow the simulation of an accident when an unsafe operation was performed. Subjects trained by accident simulation methods performed significantly fewer unsafe acts and retained their superior habit pattern for at least six months. Further, it was found that the training effect was transferable to a pedestal grinder.[84]

SIMULATION OF WHOLE SYSTEMS Teams and staffs that must remain highly coordinated can be trained together in simulations of the whole system they are learning to operate. An illustration would be the air control systems of persons and equipment that must control all incoming and outgoing flights from airports and maintain cognizance of airplanes while en route.[47] A more specialized function is maintained by those who run the air defense network of the United States. These networks are complex systems in which up to 40 monitors of radar scopes direct interceptors to suspected targets. This involves a team function both for the staff of the individual defense site and for their interaction with other defense sectors. It is necessary for all defense sectors to work together when they are attempting to identify or intercept an unknown aircraft traveling at a high rate of speed.

System simulation has proved to be highly effective. One study showed that trained crews could perform up to four times what was considered to be a heavy workload before the training program began.[78]

Commercially Available Standardized Training Programs

Programmed instruction is only one type of standardized, "off-the-shelf," ready-to-use training materials that provide the training stimulation, the opportunities for response and feedback. There are many more of such ready-to-use materials available. Didactic Systems lists 300 such packaged training programs (many of which are self-guided) in its annual catalogue. PROFAIR and PROSPER, mentioned earlier, dealing with affirmative action, illustrate such programs, with pre- and post-measures of progress, case discussion, and multiple role-playing.[4] All required materials are contained within a booklet, which each participant receives.

Just as physicians no longer must prepare their own prescriptions for their patients but can rely on a highly developed pharmaceutical industry heavily engaged in doing research and development, so each time trainers identify a *need* for training or development, they do not have to custom-make the educational effort to meet the need. They do not have to reinvent the wheel. There are many good instrumented programs and standardized training and development exercises on the market ready to try out for use. These are likely to do as good or better a job at lower cost than they could develop themselves unless they have comparable time and resources available for the R & D task required to plan, design, test and improve an effective training program (p. 519).[3]

Yet before they can decide whether or not to try out such packaged material training directors must be able to obtain answers to the following questions: What is the training material really about? Is this what fits what has been determined as needed for the trainees? How does the design of the material contain the three elements required for learning: effective cues, elicited behavior within the repertoire of the trainee, and reinforcements? How well are learning and progress measured? What antecedent conditions and ancillary outcomes are associated with progress? How permanent are the observed changes? For what population of trainers and trainees is the material effective? [3]

SUMMARY

Beginning with orientation of new recruits and ending with programs on how to plan for retirement, training is present everywhere, particularly in larger organizations. Training should be evaluated on how well its design meets the needs of the trainee. Accurate training-needs analysis is critical. Effective training designs call for performance models that are clear to the trainees (VTR tape cassettes are ideal for this purpose). Required responses by the trainees must be within their repertoire and followed by appropriate feedback. Then, for transfer of learning to the job to take place, transfer must be taught.

Error-free evaluation is not feasible. The only threats to the validity of the evaluation that we can afford to control are the ones we think more plausible explanations than the training itself for improved trainee performance.

Training techniques vary from "sink or swim" simplicity on-site training to computer-assisted instruction and simulations of whole systems. To some extent, the effectiveness of such training depends on organizational effectiveness, the subject of the next chapter.

REFERENCES

1. Bass, B. M. "The Management Training Laboratory—A way to Improve Organizational Effectiveness," *Advanced Management*, 25, no. 7 (1960): 11–15.

2. Bass, B. M. "Business Gaming for Organizational Research," *Management Science,* 10 (1964): 545–556.
3. Bass, B. M. "Quality Standard for 'Ready-to-Use' Training and Development Programs," *Journal of Applied Behavioral Science,* 13 (1977): 518–532.
4. Bass, B. M., W. F. Cascio, J. W. McPherson, and H. J. Tragash. "Prosper— Training and Research for Increasing Management Awareness about Affirmative Action in Race Relations," *Academy of Management Journal,* 19 (1976): 353–369.
5. Bass, B. M., and J. A. Vaughan. *Training in Industry: The Management of Learning.* Belmont, Calif.: Wadsworth, 1966.
6. Beatty, R. W., and C. E. Schneier. "Training the Hard-Core Unemployed Through Positive Reinforcement," *Human Resource Management,* 11, no. 4 (1972): 11–17.
7. Campbell, J. P. "Personnel Training and Development," *Annual Review of Psychology,* 22 (1971): 265–602.
8. Caro, P. W., Jr. "Adaptive Training—An Application to Flight Simulation," *Human Factors,* 11 (1969): 569–576.
9. Carroll, S. J., Jr., F. T. Paine, and J. J. Ivancevich. "The Relative Effectiveness of Training Methods—Expert Opinion and Research," *Personnel Psychology,* 25 (1972): 495–510.
10. Chaney, F. B., and K. S. Teel. "Improving Inspector Performance through Training and Visual Aids," *Journal of Applied Psychology,* 51 (1967): 311–315.
11. Chu, G. C., and W. Schramm. *Learning from Television: What the Research Says.* Washington, D.C.: National Association of Educational Broadcasters, 1967.
12. Cohen, K. J., and E. Rhenman. "The Role of Management Games in Education and Research," *Management Science,* 7 (1961): 131–166.
13. Cooley, W. W., and R. Glaser. "The Computer and Individualized Instruction," *Science,* 166 (1969): 574–582.
14. Crowder, N. A. "Automatic Tutoring by Means of Intrinsic Programming." In E. Galanter (ed.), *Automatic Teaching: The State of the Art.* New York: Wiley, 1959.
15. Cullen, J. G., S. Sawzin, G. R. Sisson, and R. A. Swanson. "Training, What's It Worth?" *Training and Development Journal,* 30, no. 8 (1976): 12–20.
16. Cyert, R. M. "Integration of the Game into the Curriculum." In W. R. Dill, J. R. Jackson, and J. W. Sweeney (eds.), *Proceedings of the Conference on Business Games.* Baton Rouge: Louisiana State University, 1961.
17. Dill, W. R., J. R. Jackson, and J. W. Sweeney. *Proceedings of the Conference on Business Games.* Baton Rouge: Louisiana State University, 1961.
18. *Employee Relations Bulletin,* National Foremen's Institute, Waterford, Conn., 1964.
19. Farr, M. "Computer-Assisted Instruction." *Naval Research Reviews,* 25, no. 9 (1972): 8–16.
20. Feeney, E. J. "Performance Audit, Feedback, and Positive Reinforcement." *Training and Development Journal,* 26, no. 11 (1972): 8–13.
21. Fiedler, F. E. "The Effect of Culture Training on Leadership, Organizational Performance, and Adjustment," *Naval Research Reviews* (July 1968): 7–13.
22. Fine, S. A. "The Use of the *Dictionary of Occupational Titles* as a Source of

Estimates of Educational and Training Requirements," *Journal of Human Resources,* 3 (1968): 363–375.

23. Fleishman, E. A. "The Measurement of Leadership Attitudes in Industry," *Journal of Applied Psychology,* 37 (1953): 153–158.

24. Folley, J. D., Jr. "Determining Training Needs of Department Store Sales Personnel," *Training and Development Journal,* 23 (1969): 24–27.

25. Frederiksen, N. "In-Basket Tests and Factors in Administrative Performance." In H. Guetzkow (ed.), *Simulation in Social Science: Readings.* Englewood Cliffs, N. J.: Prentice-Hall, 1962.

26. Gagné, R. M. "Military Training and Principles of Learning," *American Psychologist,* 17 (1962): 83–91.

27. General Programmed Teaching Corporation. *Guide to Programmed Teaching.* Albuquerque, N. M., 1963.

28. Gilbert, T. F. "The High Cost of Knowledge," *Personnel,* 53, no. 2 (1976): 11–23.

29. Glickman, A. S., and T. R. Vallance. "Curriculum Assessment with Critical Incident," *Journal of Applied Psychology,* 42 (1958): 329–335.

30. Goldstein, I. L. *Training: Program Development and Evaluation.* Belmont, Calif.: Wadsworth, 1974.

31. Goodacre, D. "Stimulating Improved Management," *Personnel Psychology,* 16 (1963): 133–143.

32. Greene, J. R., and R. L. Sisson. *Dynamic Management Decision Games.* New York: Wiley, 1959.

33. Hamner, W. C., and E. P. Hamner. "Behavior Modification on the Bottom Line," *Organizational Dynamics,* 4 (1976): 3–21.

34. Hand, H. H., and H. P. Sims. "Statistical Evaluation of Complex Gaming Performance," *Management Science,* 21, no. 6 (1975): 708–717.

35. Hariton, T. "Conditions Influencing the Effect of Training Foremen in Human Relations Principles." Unpublished Ph.D. dissertation, University of Michigan, 1951.

36. Hauser, D., and G. Spencer. *Application of Computer-Assisted Instruction to Interpersonal Skill Training.* MAVTRAEQUIPCEN 74C–0110, Final Report. Ann Arbor, Mich.: Institute for Social Research, 1975.

37. Hayden, S. J. "Getting Better Results from Post-Appraisal Interviews," *Personnel,* 31 (1955): 541–550.

38. Hesseling, P. *Strategy of Evaluation Research.* Assen, Netherlands: Van Gorcum, 1966.

39. Hughes, J. L., and W. J. McNamara. "A Comparative Study of Programmed and Conventional Instruction in Industry," *Journal of Applied Psychology,* 45 (1961): 225–231.

40. Jablonsky, S. F., and D. L. DeVries. "Operant Conditioning Principles Extrapolated to the Theory of Management," *Organizational Behavior and Human Performance,* 7 (1972): 340–358.

41. Jacobson, L. S. "The Use of Longitudinal Data to Assess the Impact of Manpower Training on Earnings," Labor Department contract L–72–86, Public Research Institute, Arlington, Va., 1973.

42. Janis, I. L., and B. T. King. "The Influences of Role Playing on Opinion Change," *Journal of Abnormal and Social Psychology,* 49 (1954): 211–218.

43. Jennings, E. E. "Dynamics of Forced Leadership," *Journal of Personnel and Administrative Industrial Relations,* 1 (1954): 110–118.

44. Kane, J. S. "The Evaluation of Organizational Training Programmes," *Journal of European Training,* 5, no. 6 (1976): 289–338.

45. Kelley, C. R. "What Is Adaptive Training?" *Human Factors,* 11 (1969): 547–556.

46. Kelman, H. C. "Attitude Change as a Function of Response Restriction," *Human Relations,* 6 (1953): 185–214.

47. Kidd, J. S. "A Comparison of Two Methods of Training in a Complex Task by Means of Task Simulation," *Journal of Applied Psychology,* 45 (1961): 165–169.

48. King, P. H. *A Summary of Research in Training for Advisory Roles in Other Cultures by the Behavioral Sciences Laboratory.* (AMRL–TR–66–131) Wright Patterson Air Force Base, Ohio: Aerospace Medical Research Laboratories, 1966.

49. King, B. T., and I. L. Janis. "Comparsion of the Effectiveness of Improvised versus Non-Improvised Role-Playing in Producing Opinion Changes," *Human Relations,* 9 (1956): 177–186.

50. Kinkade, R. G., and G. R. Wheaton. "Training Devices and Training Systems," *Experimental Publication System,* 1969, no. 2, Ms. no. 078B.

51. Kirkpatrick, F. H. "Collegiate Business Education in the Next Quarter Century," *West Virginia University Business Economic Study,* 5, no. 4 (1958).

52. Koerner, J. "Educational Technology: Does It Have a Future in the Classroom?" *Saturday Review Supplement,* 1, May 1973, 42–46.

53. Konz, S. A., and G. L. Dickey. "Manufacturing Assembly Instructions: A Summary," *Ergonomics,* 12 (1969): 369–382.

54. Kozoll, C. E. "The Air Left the 'bag'—A Training Program That Failed," *Training and Development Journal,* 25, no. 7 (1971): 22–25.

55. Lawler, E. E. III. "How Long Should a Manager Stay in the Same Job?" *Personnel Administration,* 27, no. 5 (1964): 6–8, 27.

56. Lawshe, C. H., R. A. Bolda, and R. L. Brune. "Studies in Management Training Evaluation: I. Scaling Responses to Human Relations Training Cases," *Journal of Applied Psychology,* 42 (1958): 396–398.

57. Lawshe, C. H., R. A. Bolda, and R. L. Brune. "Studies in Management Training Evaluation: II. The Effects of Exposures to Role Playing," *Journal of Applied Psychology,* 43 (1959): 287–292.

58. Leavitt, H. J., and B. M. Bass. "Organizational Psychology," *Annual Review of Psychology,* 15 (1964): 371–398.

59. Lefkowitz, J. "Effect of Training on the Productivity and Tenure of Sewing Machine Operators," *Journal of Applied Psychology,* 54 (1970): 81–86.

60. Leib, J. W., J. Cusack, D. Hughes, S. Pilette, J. Werther, and B. L. Kintz. "Teaching Machines and Programmed Instruction: Areas of Application," *Psychological Bulletin,* 67 (1967): 12–26.

61. Levine, J., and J. Butler. "Lecture versus Group Decision in Changing Behavior," *Journal of Applied Psychology,* 36 (1952): 29–33.

62. Levinson, H. "A Psychologist Looks at Executive Development," *Harvard Business Review,* 40, no. 5 (1962): 69–75.

63. Lindahl, L. G. "Movement Analysis as an Industrial Training Method," *Journal of Applied Psychology,* 29 (1945): 420–436.

64. Liveright, A. A. "Role Playing in Leadership Training," *Personnel Journal,* 29 (1951): 412–416.

65. Long, H. S., L. R. O'Neill, and H. A. Schwartz. "Exploratory Results from the Application of Computer Assisted Instruction to Industrial Training," *Proceedings of XVIth International Congress on Applied Psychology,* Amsterdam, 1969.

66. Mace, I. M. *The Growth and Development of Executives.* Boston: Division of Research, Graduate School of Business Administration, Harvard University, 1950.

67. MacHaver, W. V., and F. E. Fisher. "The Leaders' Role in Role Playing," *Journal of Industrial Training,* 7, no. 1 (1953): 6–16.

68. Maier, N. R. F., and L. R. Hoffman. "Organization and Creative Problem Solving," *Journal of Applied Psychology,* 45 (1961): 277–280.

69. Maier, N. R. F., and L. F. Zerfoss. "MRP: A Technique for Training Large Groups of Supervisors and Its Potential Use in Social Research," *Human Relations,* 5 (1952): 177–186.

70. Mann, F. C., and J. E. Sparling. "Changing Absence Rates," *Personnel,* 32 (1956): 392–408.

71. Mathewson, F. W. *From Nine to Five.* United States Government Memorandum, U. S. Civil Service Commission. Washington, D. C.: U. S. Government Printing Office, 1969.

72. McGehee, W., and P. W. Thayer. *Training in Business and Industry.* New York: McGraw-Hill, 1961.

73. Miner, J. B. "The Validity of the PAT in the Selection of Tabulating Machine Operation: An Analysis of Productive Power," *Journal of Projective Techniques,* 25 (1961): 330–333.

74. Morasky, R. L. "Self-Shaping Training Systems and Flexible-Model Behavior, I.E., Sales Interviewing," *Educational Technology,* 11, no. 5 (1971): 57–59.

75. Nash, A. N., J. P. Muczyk, and F. L. Vettori. "The Relative Practical Effectiveness of Programmed Instruction," *Personnel Psychology,* 24 (1971): 397–418.

76. Neuhauser, J. J. "Business Games Have Failed," *Academy of Management Review,* 1 (1976): 124–129.

77. Pascoe, G. C., and R. M. Kaplan. "Laughing More and Learning Less," *Human Behavior,* 9 (1976): 8.

78. Porter, L. W., and M. M. Henry. "Job Attitudes in Management: V. Perceptions of the Importance of Certain Personality Traits as a Function of Job Level," *Journal of Applied Psychology,* 48 (1964): 31–36.

79. Raia, A. P. "A Study of the Educational Value of Management Games," *Journal of Business,* 39 (1966): 339–352.

80. Riccardi, F. M., C. J. Craft, D. G. Malcolm, R. Bellman, C. Clark, J. M. Kibbee, and R. H. Rawdon. *Top Management Decision Simulation.* New York: American Management Association, 1957.

81. Riegel, J. W. *Executive Development. A Survey of Experience in Fifty American Corporations.* Ann Arbor, Mich.: University of Michigan Press, 1952.

82. Rigney, J. W., and D. M. Towne. *Research in Computer-Aided Performance*

Training. Final report, Department of Psychology. Los Angeles: University of Southern California, 1972.

83. Rodin, M., and B. Rodin. "Student Evaluations of Teachers," *Science,* 117 (1972): 1164–1166.

84. Rubinsky, S., and N. Smith. "Safety Training by Accident Simulation," *Journal of Applied Psychology,* 57 (1973): 68–73.

85. Schramm, W. "Mass Communication," *Annual Review of Psychology,* 13 (1962): 251–284.

86. Skinner, B. F. "The Science of Learning and the Art of Teaching," *Harvard Educational Review,* 24 (1954): 86–97.

87. Solem, A. R. "Human Relations Training: Comparison of Case Study and Role Playing," *Personnel Administration,* 23 (1960): 29–37.

88. Solomon, R. L. "An Extension of Control Group Design," *Psychological Bulletin,* 46 (1949): 137–150.

89. Speroff, B. J. "The Group's Role in Role Playing," *Journal of Industrial Training,* 7, no. 1 (1953): 3–5.

90. Speroff, B. J. "Rotational Role Playing Used to Develop Executives," *Personnel Journal,* 33, no. 2 (1954): 49–50.

91. Stewart, L. "Management Games Today." In J. M. Kibbee, C. J. Craft, and B. Nanus (eds.), *Management Games.* New York: Rinehart, 1962.

92. Suppes, P., and M. Morningstar. "Computer-Assisted Instruction," *Science,* 166 (1969): 343–350.

93. Tannenbaum, R., V. Kallejian, and I. R. Weschler. "Training Managers for Leadership," *Instructions on Industrial Relations,* No. 35. Los Angeles: University of California Press, 1954.

94. Taylor, E. K. "Review of Developing Executive Skills," *Personnel Psychology,* 11 (1958): 605–609.

95. U. S. Civil Service Commission, *Programmed Instruction: A Brief of Its Development and Current Status.* Washington, D. C.: U. S. Government Printing Office, 1970.

96. Vallance, T. R., A. S. Glickman, and J. N. Vasilas. *Critical Incidents in Junior Officer Duties aboard Destroyer-Type Vessels. USN Bureau of Naval Personnel Research Technical Bulletin,* no. 54-4, 1954.

97. Wallace, S. R., Jr., and C. M. Twichell. "An Evaluation of a Training Course for Life Insurance Agents," *Personnel Psychology,* 6 (1953): 25–43.

98. Welsh, P., J. A. Antoinetti, and P. W. Thayer. "An Industry Wide Study of Programmed Instruction," *Journal of Applied Psychology,* 49 (1965): 61–73.

99. Wexley, K. N., and W. F. Nemeroff. "Effectiveness of Positive Reinforcement and Goal Setting as Methods of Management Development," *Journal of Applied Psychology,* 60 (1975): 446–450.

100. Zeira, Y. "Job Rotation for Management Development," *Personnel,* 51, no. 4 (1974): 25–35.

14 ORGANIZATIONAL DEVELOPMENT

IN BRIEF Organizational development (OD) should begin with strategic planning. OD can be the implementation of such planning. Following an assessment of what is needed, OD aims to build trust and openness, improve decision-making and commitment to decisions reached, and increase understanding of processes that affect what happens in the organization. Analyses of resistance to change lead to a variety of alternative interventions. Most common among these are team-building, process consultation, and survey feedback by internal or external change agents. Top-management support is one of several factors required for interventions to succeed.

What Is It?

Organizational development (OD) is a process for implementing the improvement of the organization — particularly the effectiveness of relations among its members. It aims to improve the way that the organization meets its needs and the needs of its members as the members interact with each other. It aims to help members to accomplish their mutual objectives and meet the objectives of their organization.

An OD effort in the Social Security Administration (SSA) with the problems described in Chapter 1 might entail examining by interview and/or survey what is going on, then feeding back to appropriate individuals and groups in the SSA information about where it is failing to use its human resources effectively and why. OD consultants would go further and assist the SSA in finding and implementing solutions to its problems in using its human resources effectively.

OD involves the whole organization, not just a few individuals or groups. In the same way, OD involves a complete planned change: scouting, entry, diagnosis, planning, action, evaluation, and termination.

> In the scouting phase the change agent looks for the best point of entry and assesses the degree to which he thinks that he is an appropriate resource for the system. The second phase, entry, entails the development of a "contract" as to the roles, expectations, goals, and methods of the persons and groups involved in subsequent steps of the change efforts. Diagnosis, the third step, starts with the client's felt problems and moves toward clearer identification of specific goals for the improvement of the functioning of the client system. . . . Diagnosis also consists of an assessment of the resources of the client as well as the consultant available for bringing improvement in the problem. That is, the skill and readiness of both parties are important factors. . . .
>
> Planning . . . starts with the results of the diagnosis, [and] involves a careful articulation of the goals and possible resistances and action steps. . . . The action phase is the implementation of the developed plans. . . . The sixth phase, evaluation, is undertaken periodically; the success of the development activities in terms of subgoals should be monitored by the client and consultant in order to determine if termination or if replanning is necessary. The last phase, termination, can be consummated after success or failure" (pp. 5–6).[28]

Who Does It?

A review of the 1973 *OD Network Roster* indicated that by then 475 OD professionals were serving in business and industry. Ten per cent of the "Fortune 500" industrial corporations were represented. Another 115 were with management consulting firms and firms specializing in OD consultation.

In addition to its use in business and industry, OD efforts have appeared in multinational organizations, domestic political movements, government agencies, professional and religious associations, school systems, and higher education.[4] In addition, OD is becoming institutionalized in various military organizations; the U. S. Navy beginning in 1970, and the U. S. Army beginning in 1976. OD also was employed to improve the effectiveness in combat of the Israeli Army during the Yom Kippur War in 1973.[33] In the same way, it was found useful in improving the operations of county jails and a wide variety of public service agencies such as mental health centers, hospitals, and police forces.[30]

Relation to Training

We can take what we have said about the training process in Chapter 13 and apply it to the development of the organization and its membership. Again, we must focus our needs analysis on designs of special efforts (interventions) to meet the needs, and on evaluative processes that provide to the organization feedback about the extent to which its needs are being met by the interventions.

OD NEEDS ANALYSIS

Ideally, needs analyses derive from strategic planning for the organization and from internal surveys of the individuals and groups who constitute the organization. For example, as we will describe in detail later, OD efforts began at Weldon, an unprofitable garment manufacturer, when it was taken over by a new management who saw that Weldon's potential required improving its internal operations.[47] This is the ideal place to begin, but, of course, in practice one is more likely to begin with an organization that sees itself in trouble and seeks the help of an outside professional. The professional starts by searching for what is ailing the organization. Nevertheless, let's look at a better way to begin.

Strategic Planning — A Place to Begin

To plan its strategy, the top management of the firm or agency, often assisted by staff planners, ideally should begin with an examination of their organization's objectives — what they are and what they should be. These should reflect internal-attitude survey information, budget justifications, and suggestions from lower levels in the organization. Then, management needs to estimate the present and potential opportunities and threats in the organization's environment. They should examine the current and near-future economic, social, political, technological, and competitive factors likely to be of consequence to their ongoing organization's advantages — their own size, the way in which their internal resources are distributed, their strengths and weaknesses. (Note the importance here, as in Chapter 5, of an open-systems view of organizations, that what goes on inside an organization is affected by what is happening outside it.) Then they should consider alternative strategies to reach what they have perceived to be their organization's objectives. They next should identify and choose the most appropriate strategy to follow on the basis of an appraisal of their environment and of their internal resources.

This is an ideal time for an OD effort to begin. OD, beginning with

organizational needs analysis, can come to the forefront, because to implement the selected strategy requires the development of an organizational
structure and climate to fit with the strategy. It also requires short-range
policies, plans, and programs to match the task demands of the grand
strategy. Human, material, financial, and ideational resources must be
effectively matched with the task demands.[31] Figure 14–1 displays this
model for strategic planning.

Integration of Individual and Organizational Needs

Ordinarily, matching individual needs to task demands is a strategy of
change or renewal. The chosen strategy is likely to call for expanding,
contracting, or modifying the ongoing organization or components of it.
New tasks are to be attempted, old ones to be abandoned. (In the 1960s
change usually involved growth and expansion. In the 1970s, it often
concerned changing a growth-oriented organization toward one more stable
in size.) Ideally, *organizational development* involves the implementation
of strategy. It deals with efforts to change the organization and its members
and coping with resistance to such efforts. It is far more than just an
intellectual engineering task involved in rearranging equipment, materials
and people. Individual employees (as in Chapter 3) are seen as much more
than just simple, standardized pieces of machinery who can be modified,
moved around, or replaced at will. Rather, all members of the organization,
whatever their level in it, have different potential and needs. *Ideally,* if the
organization is to prosper and survive over the years, all of its members
need opportunities to actualize their individual potentials.

The Needs of the Individual

If the chosen strategy is to succeed, it must engage the commitment and
interest of the members at all levels in the organization in the changes
required to meet the new task demands. And for this to happen, whatever
their level in the hierarchy, the individuals' needs for growth must be
integrated with the needs for change of the larger group of which they
are members. In turn, their group's and organization's objectives need to
be congruent. Thus, as an ideal, organizational development aims to
integrate individuals with their group and organization.[5]

To accomplish this, the individual members have to participate in setting
objectives that are mutually acceptable to their group, to their organization,
and to themselves. Such participation in planning, as we have noted in
Chapter 5, leads to heightened commitment, understanding, productivity,
and development.

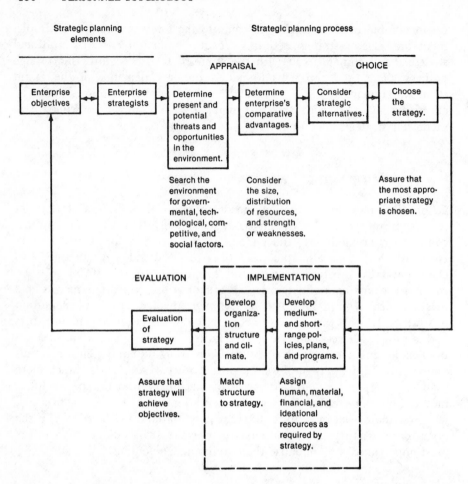

Figure 14–1. A model of strategic planning. (From *Business Policy: Strategy Forma-tion and Management Action,* by W. F. Glueck. Copyright © 1975 by McGraw-Hill Book Company. Used with the permission of McGraw-Hill Book Company.

Rational Planning and OD

While the chosen strategy of top management or its staff planners empha-sizes the rational, OD *per se* adds concern for the social, emotional, and human issues. Overall strategy, if it attempts to be completely rational, concentrates on what tasks have to be accomplished and what organiza-tional goals have to be met; OD introduces concern for the processes and dynamics of interpersonal interaction — who will do what to whom and why. Completely rational strategies more often are concerned with reliability and order; OD adds individual autonomy and flexibility. Com-pletely rational strategies usually emphasize productivity; OD often adds concern for creativity. Completely rational strategies usually suggest dependence on management controls; OD adds the use of trust.

Rational strategies tend to have lengthy time perspectives, connecting past performance with future efforts. But OD needs analysis is concerned with the existential, the here-and-now, the present. Existentialism focuses on learning from understanding and feeling the present socioemotional state of affairs within the organization.[26] If these current dynamics are inconsistent with the goals of the organization and with its various constituent parts, either the dynamics need to be changed, the resources and their uses modified, or the goals changed. Here is where the OD intervention directs attention with the aim of helping to resolve the detected conflicts.

OD, the Individual, the Work Unit, and the Organization

For individual members, at whatever their level in the organization, OD may concern itself with the processes by which they are assimilated into the organization, how they become fully "joined up." Here OD would concentrate on the discrepancies between where employees are in their career, where they want to be, and how much of their own progress is under their own control. In OD, individual development is self-development. The organization is responsible for providing realistic expectations for opportunities and challenges; the individual for developing understanding and action plans. Many firms, ranging across industries from General Electric to General Foods, see utility in giving their employees a major role in planning their own careers with the organization.

For the work unit, OD emphasizes teamwork, how the unit's objectives can become consistent with those of the larger organization, how its members can influence each other's performance, what can be done to improve their combined efforts, and how they can build on each other's efforts. In OD, with its concern for the growth of the individual and the group, consensual decision making and participative leadership are stressed.

Of basic importance between work units is the coordination of their efforts and the resolution of their conflicts. In OD, the biasing effect of intergroup competition is seen as a warp interfering with the achievement of such resolutions when, in fact, such competition can be constructive.

For the organization as a whole, OD helps the top management strategists to look at how they work together, to detect differences between their needs and their objective appraisals of alternatives, so that their aspiration levels are more realistic. Resistances are uncovered that are due to interpersonal barriers to trust within the top management group itself. Such barriers are likely to be lowered as a consequence of OD efforts. Indeed, at all levels, OD examines what can be done to lower these barriers to communication between individuals, between work units, and between different levels in the organization.

To sum up, ideally OD needs analysis takes place in the larger context of a strategy for organizational improvement. It reflects the organizational need to change with the changing demands of the organization's environment, its resources, and the felt needs of its members. The data for organizational needs analyses may be gathered from questionnaires, interviews, and participant observation. Or special problem diagnosis workshops may be employed.[7] Some of the kinds of questions asked for OD needs analysis have already been noted in Chapter 5. They may deal with how effectively communications flow, how well human resources are utilized, whether the climate is encouraging rather than discouraging, whether decisions are made at the levels of the organization at which the most information is available, and so on.[61]

OD INTERVENTIONS

Objectives and Values

Psychotherapy and traditional training and education concentrate on changing the individual. OD interventions ordinarily are directed toward changing relations between individuals, within and between groups, and within organizations. At the same time, OD interventions are based on the assumption that what motivates the individual includes both the intrinsic as well as extrinsic rewards of work. Instead of tight controls and threats, OD efforts seek to provide challenging work and responsibilities for accomplishing organizational objectives to which individuals, as members of teams, are committed.

Such commitment requires the expression of feelings that people have about each other and the direction they and their organization are taking. This requires the development of trust, openness, and willingness to risk, but this means that a wider range of choices in reaching decisions becomes available. For instance, decisions about the composition of two-person teams may give as much weight to how the two people feel about working together as to how their different skills will complement each other.

The aim is to utilize effectively the available human resources to the organization's and the individual's satisfaction. But to achieve this aim, means and ends must be set that are ones to which the individual members are truly committed in thought and feeling. For this to occur, effective decision-making is required. More often than not, this is most likely to occur where participative leadership is practiced, where the individual members of a team can participate in the search for consensus, where they can feel free to express whatever ideas and feelings they may have and to influence and be influenced by others. Yet, before this can happen, a sense of trust and openness must be developed among the members. So the route to effective utilization of human resources lies from trust-building to effective decision-making to commitment, first at the interpersonal level, then organization-wide.[29]

And so, specific objectives of typical OD programs according to Sherwood include:

1. To build trust among individuals and groups throughout the organization, and up-and-down the hierarchy.
2. To create an open, problem-solving climate throughout the organization—where problems are confronted and differences are clarified, both within groups and between groups, in contrast to "sweeping problems under the rug" or "smoothing things over."
3. To locate decision-making and problem-solving responsibilities as close to the information sources and the relevant resources as possible, rather than in a particular role or level of the hierarchy.
4. To increase the sense of "ownership" of organizational goals and objectives throughout the membership of the organization.
5. To move toward more collaboration between inderdependent persons and interdependent groups within the organization. Where relationships are clearly competitive, e.g., limited resources, then it is important that competition be open and be managed so the organization might benefit from the advantages of open competition and avoid suffering from the destructive consequences of subversive rivalry.
6. To increase awareness of group "process" and its consequences for performance—that is, to help persons become aware of what is happening between and to group members while the group is working on the task, e.g., communication, influence, feelings, leadership styles and struggles, relationships between groups, how conflict is managed, etc.[58]

SPECIFYING OBJECTIVES   These aims can be translated into specific measurable behavioral objectives.[15] For example, behavioral change in leadership from OD efforts may include changes in:

1. Support. Behavior enhancing other persons' feelings of their own worth and importance.

2. Interaction facilitation. Behavior encouraging members of the group to develop close, mutually satisfying relationships.

3. Goal emphasis. Behavior stimulating an enthusiasm for meeting the group's objective or achieving excellent performance.

4. Work facilitation. Behavior enabling attainment of the objective by such activities as scheduling, coordinating, planning, and by providing resources such as tools, materials, and technical knowledge.

CONSTRAINTS AND STIMULATIONS: FORCE FIELD ANALYSIS   A favorite approach
to questioning is for OD consultants to ask their clients to list the restraining forces in the field of forces (analogous to physics) that maintain the
problem situation, that inhibit change and improvement, that block implementation of improvements. Then, clients are asked to list the forces that
may improve the situation. These restraining forces and forces for improvement may be internal or external to the organization. For the Social
Security Administration (SSA), an example of an internal force are any
Civil Service regulations for government agencies that prevent introduction
of an effective merit system. An example of an external force on the SSA
is the Civil Service employees' union, the largest in the AFL-CIO, which
ordinarily pushes hard for cost-of-living and seniority rather than merit
increases.

Action steps can follow in terms of answering questions about how to
remove or counteract the restraining forces and about how to augment the
forces for change. For example, forces restraining improvement in the
quality of work completed may include overzealous supervisors who check
on workers excessively. This increases worker anxiety and worker tendencies to confirm the supervisors' beliefs that the workers cannot be
trusted. Forces for improvement may include clearer understanding by
workers of quality requirements, specialized training, or more immediate
feedback about the adequacy of one's performance.

Let's first look in more detail at these restraining forces, then at some
principles of intervention for dealing with them successfully.

SOURCES OF RESISTANCE TO CHANGE

Lack of Cues, Capability, and Reinforcement

In the last chapter, we suggested that we change behavior by learning to
discriminate among selected cues or stimuli. We respond in alternative
ways to those stimuli. We repeat those that are reinforced or strengthened
by their consequences. This reinforcement usually is in the form of feedback of the appropriateness of the response to the discriminated cue.
Resistance to such change in behavior, therefore, is due to one of three
sets of conditions: lack of situational clarity, lack of response capability,
or lack of appropriate reinforcement.

LACK OF SITUATIONAL CLARITY   We can't make out to what we are supposed to respond. We are receiving mixed signals from the organization.
Or we are receiving signals which are too weak. For example, two departments, Supply and Assembly, are quarreling about scheduling. Delays in
shipments from the supply department to the assembly department force
the assembly department to shut down lines. A division head in charge
of both departments won't permit the assembly department to build up an

inventory. He says it is too costly. He won't let the shipping department deliver more flexibly according to the needs of the assembly department. He claims both solutions are too costly. In fact, he doesn't even understand that he enjoys keeping his subordinate managers of supply and assembly distracted by quarreling with each other because he is concerned that he is to be given early retirement and one or the other of his subordinates is being groomed by top management to take his place.

LACK OF RESPONSE CAPABILITY   Even if what needs to be done is properly diagnosed, even if the situational requirements are clarified, the organization may not have the capability to make the necessary changes. For example, in the above circumstance, communication barriers may have been erected. The assembly manager may no longer speak to the supply manager unless she absolutely must. She mainly conveys her dissatisfactions to the division head, who keeps the two department managers apart "to avoid angry scenes."

LACK OF APPROPRIATE REINFORCEMENT   Appropriate responses to coping with the stimulating situation fail to yield consequences valued and understood by the two managers in conflict. Their needs are not met without undue costs to them. They don't receive feedback when they try to solve the problem. Or, if it is given, they don't sense it or understand it. The supply department manager may resist increasing the flexibility of his shipments because he runs a profit center. Getting a bonus depends on the profitability of the operations of his department. Nevertheless, department costs increase as he permits flexibility of shipment loads in response to the assembly manager's needs.

If the supply manager does on occasion respond to the importuning of the assembly department manager, instead of being praised by the division head, he may receive feedback from the division head in the form of questioning the variance and increased costs of the performance of the supply department. And the division head's resistance to change due to his concern about "early retirement" is reinforced by rumors floating around in the organization that a number of such retirements are being planned by top management. From his point of view, leaving things as they are and avoiding angry confrontations seems better than risking change to what might prove to be more costly to the organization as well as to himself.

Systems Failings

Using concepts from open-systems theory (Chapter 5), Alderfer has detailed what maintains resistance to change of any system.[2,3] The system's boundaries regulate the flow of matter, energy, and information in and out of the system. With completely impermeable boundaries, the system closes and eventually dies. For example, the medieval Greenland colonies, too weak to survive by themselves, disappeared when annual contacts with Norway by ship were broken. With too permeable boundaries, the system becomes indistinguishable from its environment. For instance, Jewish communities in India and China disappeared through intermarriage with their Gentile neighbors. The integration, coherence, and stability of a system depend on the relations developed. If only *internal* relationships are formed, the system closes and dies. Thus, Non-Linear Systems built high-quality products and a happy work force, but couldn't sell its products competitively. If only *external* relationships form, the system disintegrates into its environment. (It is impossible to keep an academic department healthy if all faculty members are totally concerned about their consultantships to outside organizations or their publications for their profession and unconcerned about their students, their colleagues, or campus problems.) Both internal and external relationships are required.

Further, relations that feature mutuality of exchange between individuals or units of the system are ideal for the healthy, dynamic organization. There is give-and-take among components of the system. For example, managers listen as well as talk to their subordinates. The nonmutuality of exchange is seen as detrimental to healthy growth.

Both positive and negative inputs and outputs are shared in the healthy system. Positive inputs nurture and sustain the system's boundaries, while negative inputs stimulate and challenge the system. The negative inputs signal a potential need for change and keep the system adaptable and flexible. Nevertheless, the system that receives *only* positive inputs risks becoming complacent. If it receives *only* negative inputs it is likely to become closed in order to defend itself. The negative output of waste products saves a system from being choked by its own refuse. The positive output of products useful to the system's environment makes it valuable to its environment, increasing the chances of obtaining resources required for survival and growth.[2,3]

Alderfer goes on to show how impermeable boundaries and/or lack of mutuality or balanced positive and negative inputs and outputs result in resistance to change of the individual, the group, and the organization.

INDIVIDUAL RESTRAINTS   Some specific factors that contribute to resistance to change reside with the individual members. Well-documented are the "close-minded," authoritarian personalities.[1] They blame their difficulties on forces outside their own control. They are likely to be dogmatic and rigid in diagnosing organizational problems.[54]

Other individual characteristics also affect readiness or resistance to change. Kirton and Mulligan found that the resistance of 258 British managers to adopting a new appraisal scheme was strongly associated with stated lack of self-confidence, with age, lower organizational level, and unfavorable attitudes toward change in general.[41] Emotionally stable introverts and emotionally unstable extroverts tended to support innovation, while emotionally unstable introverts and emotionally stable extroverts did not.

GROUP RESTRAINTS   In the ordinary meeting or work group, overt expression of feelings is likely to be suppressed. Members are likely to "hide behind polite facades." Trust may be absent. Willingness to risk or to lose face is absent. The group remains incapable of responding in a way that will lead to change. The group leader can dampen any efforts toward bringing out into the open how members feel about each other in order to deal adequately with such feelings, which inhibit real progress of the group in solving its problems. And groups that are less open tend to be less adept at solving problems that require rare, unusual, or original responses. Members don't dare to take the chance of being laughed at for unusual ideas that they may have. They can't build on each other's unspoken ideas. Physical isolation of groups or failure to introduce new members into groups as the groups age also result in increasing their rigidity and resistance to change.

ORGANIZATIONAL RESTRAINTS   The current boundary conditions inside and outside organizations form strong barriers to change. Prisons have obvious strong boundaries. There is the strong boundary between the prison and the outside world. Inside, there is the strong boundary between the inmates and the staff. And prisons are notoriously resistant to change. In addition to the sharp internal boundaries, there is lack of mutuality of relationships.[3] The staff sees itself as just, moral, and upright, while the inmates see them as condescending, high-handed, and mean. The staff views the inmates as secretive and untrustworthy, while the inmates themselves feel inferior, weak, and blameworthy. Each party behaves toward the other in ways that maintain these stereotypes. Each party evokes self-fulfilling reactions from the other.[32] Prison history is usually characterized by long periods of resistance to change coupled with sudden internal explosions.

SOME PRINCIPLES FOR EFFECTIVE INTERVENTION

Given what we know about resistance to change, some principles for dealing with such restraints include: appropriate entry, good timing, congruence with current conditions, optimum boundaries, unfreezing and mutualization of relations.

1. Appropriate entry   There is some optimum location in the organization, its leverage or entry point, at which to begin change efforts, where change will enjoy its greatest likelihood of success. Thus, one might elect to begin in a division of the organization led by a particularly progressive manager who is already strongly oriented toward employee development. It is easiest to make the change requirements clear at this entry point. The sympathetic division head provides power and authority to support the change effort and can serve to reinforce it as it takes place.[43]

2. Good timing   Planned change requires careful scheduling so that each change event has time to provide impact on the next. Too much attempted too soon may lead to stimulus confusion, lack of response capability, and inadequate feedback. On the other hand, stretching out change efforts too long may result in failure to exploit the impact of momentum of one change on the one that follows.

3. Congruence with current conditions   Interventions must fit with the current internal conditions and readiness of the organization.[15]

Interventions must be what the particular organization members are ready to find clear and reinforcing; they must stimulate required responses of which the members are capable. For example, suddenly appealing for mass participation in three weeks of sensitivity training for everyone belonging to an extremely hierarchical, authoritarian-led organization would be completely incongruent.

4. Optimizing boundary conditions   The nearly closed, but not yet dead system needs to be opened with new people, new ideas, new understandings, and added resources. Conversely, the "too-open" system, whose boundaries are disappearing, needs to find ways of structuring what the system is and what it is not. Members need to feel "joined up," as belonging to an organization of consequence and value.[3]

5. Unfreezing-refreezing   When data about needs are gathered and shared through feedback, the system is disturbed and complacency is reduced. Only after such unfreezing has occurred is it possible to gain acceptance of proposals for improvement. As these proposals begin to be implemented and to work, the organization is once again frozen into a new state of satisfaction with itself. Eventually, a new unfreezing will be required before further improvement can be proposed.[55]

6. Mutualization of relations   The organization is likely to improve if it increases the balance of the flow of relevant information, matter, and energy between individuals and between groups that form the system.[3] For instance, consultation and participation in decision-making are likely to increase the balanced sense of give-and-take between top management and those at lower levels in the organization. Such power redistribution is seen as a most important process for organizational improvement, along with a shared effort to change at all relevant levels in the system.[34] That is, top management cannot hope to introduce effectively considerate, participative, democratic supervision on the shop floor yet maintain a one-man autocracy in the boardroom.

SOME INTERVENTIONS AND OD PRACTICES

A better understanding of the aims, values, and principles of OD may come from looking in detail at the "laboratory method" and sensitivity training that began in the late 1940s and was the precursor of the OD movement. This, sensitivity training, making heavy use of T-groups or encounter groups, now often called team-building, is the single practice that most consultants or change agents are likely to agree is "definitely doing OD."[48]

Sensitivity Training: The Laboratory Approach

It has been suggested that firms may be in one of four stages in the progressiveness of their management or professional training. In the most primitive stage, such training involves company executives' lecturing to their subordinates about company issues. In the next stage upward, outside speakers are imported into the program to lecture, demonstrate, and provide new ideas for the firm. In the third stage, management will spend time in case discussions, role-playing, and gaming. But only in the most advanced stage will management be ready to further its education by examining itself — the laboratory approach to management development.

WHAT IS IT? For from three days to three weeks, several small groups of trainees, usually professional or managerial employees, concentrate on activities aimed at promoting their understanding of themselves and each other. They are likely to discuss a variety of topics, bring up personal cases and problems, and be directed in role-playing and simulation exercises, each demonstrating the significance of specific human relations issues. But at least half of their time will be spent in sensitivity training groups. Initially, in these T-groups (T for training), there are no agenda, no structure, no agreed-on procedures. Trainers usually are present to assist the group, but they do not direct it, except through relatively infrequent interventions.

The management training laboratory is a procedure for getting members of management to relate better to each other and to their employees. Paradoxically, it succeeds in doing this by taking the management group away from its organization, stripping away the organization from the training group and essentially forcing the members of management to get together without any organization at all. This results in the individual members fumbling and stumbling when they try to come to grips with the problem of developing a set of procedures for interacting with the other laboratory members in their group. Previously dependent on the organizational rules as the source of information for many of the decisions on how to interact with other members of management, now the trainees must rely on themselves and their colleagues for the answers (pp. 12–13).[8]

As the group develops norms, goals, and procedures, the members observe as well as participate in the development. With the aid of the training staff, they learn what to watch for and how to conceptualize the processes they observe. Members give each other feedback, indicating what they think they have noticed in themselves and others, what kinds of problem-solving have seemed effective, who has been trying to dominate the group, et cetera. Other participative activities are scheduled so as to contribute to the growth of the T-group. For instance, members may rate each other's influence in the laboratory. Then the actual rank of the members, their status outside the laboratory, will be matched against their current influence. The high correlation triggers T-group discussion dealing with status differences that suppress the attempts to contribute by those of lower rank in the company, the power of those of high status, and so on.

OBJECTIVES   The laboratory tries to demonstrate the efficacy of establishing certain norms of behavior among industrial employees. Mutual trust and openness are necessary if the organization is to bring to bear on important decisions the information and attitudes of its members. Consensual decision-making is shown to be most effective if the organization seeks to commit its members to carry out its decisions. Shared leadership is fostered, as are management by objectives, spontaneity, and informality in interaction.

Still another matter learned is that people may not be saying what they mean and what is actually going on in the group may be due to an agenda which is not an open one known to all but an agenda based on some concealed desires (which may not even be apparent to those with such desires). Such hidden agenda are likely to be detected after a while by other members of the group. Bringing these hidden agenda out into the open may be helpful . . . to persons having these hidden feelings as well as to the group as a whole for its progress (p. 15).[8]

ALTERNATIVES   Companies may decide to send one or more of their executives to a public training laboratory such as those run by the National
Training Laboratories (NTL), in the same way that they might send
these executives to a special program offered at a university. But the impact
of this training is likely to be greater if the program is held within the
plant, so that within a reasonable amount of time, all relevant personnel
have received the training. More important, the in-plant program permits
considering the various human-relations issues within the context of the
actual live organization from which all the people come. While such programs usually have composed training groups from "diagonal" slices of the
organization, so that different echelons are represented in the group but
no persons are with their own boss, "team-building" laboratories have
deliberately been made up of "family" groups of people who work directly
with each other in the plant in superior-subordinate relationships.[51] Such
a laboratory organized around the operating, organizational, and supervisory relationships of the plant brings to the training setting many of
the plant's intergroup problems that affect work.

UTILITY   T-groups do increase interpersonal sensitivity or empathy.[23]
But the effects of T-groups on the behavior of individuals in organizations
are less clear. In an extensive review of the research studies, Campbell and
Dunnette found that training does induce some behavioral changes in
participants when they go back to their home organizational setting.[18]
The problem (as we have already emphasized in Chapter 6) is that the
attitudes and behavior emphasized in training of trust, consensus, and
spontaneity may be in conflict with the organizational climate back at
the plant. A change in behavior may or may not be helpful to the organization in question. At times, behavior patterns of managers might be
changed in such a way as to make the managers counterproductive in the
organization. There is also the problem that since the sensitivity training
sessions are often emotionally charged, some participants will experience
some emotional hurts. "Some companies see more harm than good in
sensitivity training."[17]
    Nevertheless, the T-group technique is a powerful one for many indi-
viduals in the context of management development.[38]

INSTRUMENTATION   T-groups have different effects on different individuals
for a number of reasons. First, the sessions are not standard, and trainers
vary in proficiencies and techniques. Second, the very nature of the group
itself may influence the process and the learning the individuals gain
from their experience.
    As a consequence, many different standardized approaches to sensitivity
training and team-building, with instruments such as questionnaires,

guides, audio cassettes, and so on, are now available to provide somewhat more uniform experiences and outcomes. Blake and Mouton pioneered in the development of the "instrumented" laboratory.[12] No trainer is present. Instead, standard questionnaires and instructions create a quasi-T-group situation. The best known of these is the managerial GRID lab. Here, the laboratory dilemmas, encounters, and confrontations are integrated around participants' attitudes and performance. The ideal is sought on the two-way grid (Figure 14–2) of "9-9" on nine-point scales of concern for production and concern for people.[12] A more general interpersonally oriented team-building experience also is provided by PROCESS, a self-guiding set of integrated exercises for small groups. Self-scored pre- and postquestionnaires provide measures of improvement in personal and interpersonal styles of behavior. Demonstrable improvements have been obtained with PROCESS in controlled experiments.[63] Likewise, the more

Figure 14–2. The Managerial Grid. ® (From *The New Managerial Grid,* by Robert R. Blake and Jane Srygley Mouton. Houston: Gulf Publishing Company, copyright © 1978, p. 11. Reproduced by permission.)

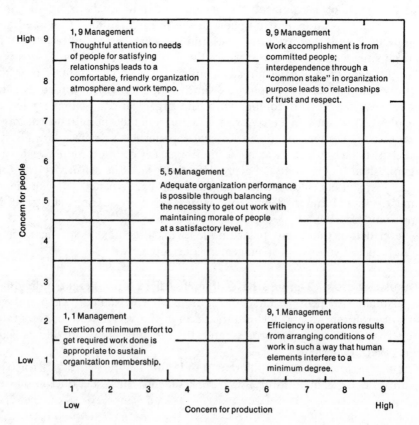

widely-used GRID has been shown in field studies to make significant contributions to the OD effort.[34]

BROADER OBJECTIVES T-group training branched in the 1960s in three directions. The objective of teaching group dynamics and leadership with which it had begun were continued as team-building experiences in larger OD efforts. But, in addition, a second branch, encounter groups, turned its focus onto personal growth, while a third branch centered attention on sensory awareness. Innumerable further variants, sensible to nonsensical, appeared from the 1960s on.[44]

TRANSFER OF TRAINING A central problem has been how to transfer what is learned in the artifically contrived T-group setting to the organization back home. The role of the T-group in the larger context of the development of the organization is determined by the ways in which transfer can be effected. In fact, there is indirect evidence of negative transfer — the T-group experience reduces subsequent performance in real life. First, Deep, Bass, and Vaughan showed that intact T-groups that subsequently went on to play as teams in a business game did much worse in the adequacy of their decisions than did T-groups that were fragmented before being reassembled in new groupings to form teams for the game.[21] Hellebrandt and Stinson went further, showing that the intact T-group also did worse in the subsequent business games than control participants did who received no T-group training.[37] Again, Bowers unearthed strong indications in organizational development efforts in 23 organizations of negative effects of the T-group on the subsequent improvement of the organization's performance, in contrast to interventions such as survey feedback (to be discussed next) without the T-group experience.[14] Why? Perhaps because how to transfer what was learned in the T-group was not taught effectively.

Using a questionnaire that measured the diagnostic approaches to interpersonal work problems of middle managers who participated in T-groups, Oshry and Harrison found that new diagnostic orientations were learned as a result of the training but that, nevertheless, participants were unable to convert these learnings into action back on the job because they saw no clear connection between the new perceptions and the job.[53]

What may be needed to obtain positive transfer from the T-group experience to performance on-the-job back home is to try some of the following procedures.

1. Build real organizational problems for examination and solution into the relations among the T-groups meeting together in a common laboratory.[51]

2. Gradually reduce time in the laboratory devoted to pure T-group activities, replacing them with exercises, problems, simulations, and dis-

cussions about organizational phenomena, finally dealing with real-live, back-home organizational problems.[51]

3. Center the T-group experience around the need to construct an attitude survey or some other organizational task for the back-home organization.[49]

4. Continue contact between the trainer and the T-groups after they return to the job to discuss problems of transfer and application. Move the OD effort from the T-group to process consultation by the trainer in the real organization.[20,25]

5. Use real-life groups to teach T-group ideas. This is process consultation.

Process Consultation

This approach to transfer OD learning to performance most directly was pioneered by Bamforth.[6] Dispensing with the T-group experience altogether, he changed from the role of a T-group trainer to that of a process consultant to functioning, formal, work-group meetings, where he helped the groups to recognize their boss-subordinate difficulties, colleague relations, role classifications, communication difficulties, resistance to the disclosure of initially unrecognized dynamics, anxieties about using or not using authority, and other sociopsychological problems.

> . . . as a group works on its own real problems, the consultant slowly and gradually introduces process analysis of what is taking place, beginning possibly with some questions on how the group feels about its progress to date. The discussions about the group's performance may eventually move the group into a general program of education about group and organizational dynamics, using the group's own current experiences as the continuing basis for discussion and analysis (p. 224).[9]

Thus, T-group trainers take their techniques for helping their group to focus on its dynamics, into the ongoing work situation. The trainers facilitate the awareness of processes and how to clarify goals. The intervention is on a continuing basis. The trainers expand the influence of T-group training into the organization's culture. They deal with individual growth as well as improving the effectiveness of the task group. The whole organization is kept in mind. Groups are helped by such process consultants to construct and maintain sociotechnical systems that support their individual members' right to be "authentic" both in relation to one another and in the performance of their tasks. Anxiety resulting from the absence of certainty is dealt with, as is the need to face current crises of responsibility and change.

INTERVENTIONS Process consultants intervene to legitimize the expression of feelings and the taking of risk to express those feelings about interpersonal relations, the need to make choices, and the task to be accomplished. The consultants encourage disclosure of here-and-now emotions. They interpret or question the here-and-now behavior of others. Their interventions point toward the ways in which people avoid or disengage from contact with one another or with work tasks. The consultants endeavor to be supportive and encouraging when others finally begin to examine their own crises and dynamics.[19]

BEGINNINGS Actually, cases in which the rudiments of such process consultation were applied appeared as early as 1945.[27] Whyte and Hamilton observed and interviewed people in five departments and top management in the "Tremont Hotel" and developed solutions to problems through group meetings of those involved.[64] The organizational changes that resulted included redefined roles, improved productivity and safety records, decreased turnover, and improved interpersonal relations.

Jaques began work in the late 1940s with the Glacier Metal Company in England.[39] The research team developed methods of offering technical assistance to groups that requested help in exploring underlying and concealed forces — psychological, cultural, structural, or technological — that were impeding their progress or otherwise reducing their efficiency. The research team observed and interviewed members at work, and offered their impressions and interpretations at group meetings to help clarify underlying issues.

Today, such a consultation is a widely practiced OD intervention.

ORGANIZATION MIRROR This is a variant of process consultation. It is described as follows:

> An organizational unit that is experiencing difficulties with units to which it is work-related, may ask key people from those other units to come to a meeting to provide feedback on how they see the host unit. The consultant often interviews the people attending the meeting, before the meeting takes place, in order to get an idea of the problems and their magnitude; to prepare the participants; and to answer any questions the participants may have.
>
> After opening remarks by the host manager, who notes . . . that there is genuine interest in hearing how the unit is perceived, the consultant feeds back to the total group information from the interviews. The outsiders "fishbowl" to discuss and explore the data presented by the consultant. [A fishbowl is a group seated in a talking configuration in which there is an inner circle of chairs for people who talk, and an outside circle of observers.] The fishbowl allows the invited participants to talk about the host unit in a natural, uninterrupted way, while the host group listens and learns. Following this, the host group members fishbowl and talk about what they have heard, ask for any clarification, and generally seek to understand the information they have heard. There may, at

this time, be a general discussion to ensure that everyone understands what is being said, but at this time the participants do not start to work on the problems that have been uncovered.

For actually working on the problems, the subgroups — composed of both host group members and invited participants — are formed. The subgroups are asked to identify the most important changes that need to be made to improve the host unit's effectiveness. After the small groups have identified the key problems, the total group convenes to make a master list to work out specific action plans for bringing about the changes deemed most important. The total group hears a summary report from each subgroup. Action plans are firmed up; people are assigned to tasks; and target dates for completion are agreed upon.

In a short period of time, an organization can get the feedback it needs to improve its relations with significant work-related groups (pp. 81–82).[62]

Action Research

While the T-group or team-building, as such, may not be used in a particular OD intervention, many of the T-group's values and objectives are likely to appear in the intervention. In the same way, most interventions make use of action research. There is extensive collaboration between an OD consultant and the organization, in which data are gathered in some way from individuals and groups. The data are analyzed and fed back to key members of the organization or groups, and collaborative planning is undertaken for the organization as a consequence.[58]

More will be said about specific action-research plans later in this chapter in discussing survey feedback.

Planned Renegotiation

In planned renegotiation, process consultation becomes an integral part of working relations between participants, who take responsibility for serving as their own consultants. The length of time from data-gathering to feedback to planning is systematically shortened until it becomes among coworkers a continuing ongoing process of sharing information, negotiating commitments, maintaining a period of stability and production, reviewing experience, and renegotiating a new contract or agreement. One doesn't wait for the annual retreat meeting to provide information calling for organizational changes. It is shared as needed. Feedback is a mutual responsibility. Givers need to be willing and able to transmit; receivers, to listen and accept. Actions don't require waiting for the end of a period of time. The process of such planned renegotiation is displayed in Figure 14–3.

Once information has been gathered and shared, expectations can be

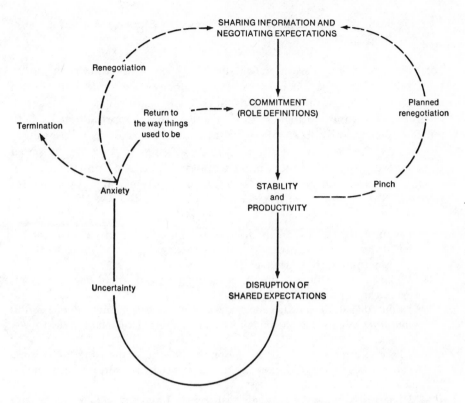

Figure 14–3. An introduction to organizational development. Sherwood and Glide-well, "Planned Renegotiation: A Norm-setting OD Intervention. In W. W. Burke (ed.), *Contemporary Organization Development.* Washington, D.C.: NTL Institute for Applied Behavioral Science, 1972, pp. 35–36. © Sherwood and Glidewell, 1971.

formed. Commitments can be made, refining each member's role. Stable, productive relations can be established.

DISRUPTIONS Sooner or later disruption occurs because of changes in the external environment that impact on the system. Or a disruption occurs because of violations of expectations by the interacting participants.

> Disruptions may be external in origin, such as a new person assigned to a work group, a loss of personnel, an assignment of a new task or higher quota, a budgetary cut and reallocation of resources, or reorganization of personnel and subsequent reassignment of duties. . . . Disruptions may also be internal in origin, such as, the sharing of information which was not made available earlier when expectations were being negotiated. Persons also change as a consequence of new experiences, training, and education. When the changed person returns

to the unchanged role, expectations may be violated leading to a disruption of the relationship.[59]

CONSEQUENCES   The disruption of shared expectations results in uncertainties and anxieties. Then there may be undesirable consequences such as complete termination of relations. Such a situation can be avoided with openness, trust, and willingness to risk, and with an appreciation by both parties of the possibilities of a planned renegotiation of relationships. What is required is that one party be able to express to the other "a signal of the possibility of an impending disruption." This is a "pinch."

Some examples of pinches in two-person or in person-group relations that raise the possibility of renegotiation are:

— "I think I am now ready to go to New York on a buying trip without you."
— "I find that I am defensive with you,.because you judge others so harshly. I don't want you judging me that way."
— "While I will continue to do all the drafting work, I would like to do some engineering work on this project."
— "I think that I somehow have to know all the answers, because no one in this group ever admits that they don't know something. I therefore bluff my way along."
— "I have to begin saying, 'no,' to you or you have to stop adding to my workload. I will be unable to meet the commitments I have already made unless something is changed."
— "I like you a lot, and I suddenly realize that I am very hesitant to disagree with you for fear that you will then dislike me" (pp. 4–5).[59]

Expressing the "pinch" can result in constructive renegotiation. Such renegotiation is planned for in advance. It starts a new cycle of sharing information, commitment, and a new stability of relations.[59]

Other OD Interventions and Practices

Some other OD interventions include:

1. *Intergroup problem solving:* groups are brought together for the purpose of reducing unhealthy competitiveness between the groups or to resolve intergroup conflicts over such things as overlapping responsibilities or confused lines of authority, and to enhance interdependence when it appropriately exists.

   Intergroup problems sometimes exist between different functional groups which must work together, e.g., sales and engineering; or between line and staff; or labor and management; or between separate organizations involved in a merger.

2. *Confrontation meeting:* is a problem solving mechanism when problems are known to exist. An action-research format is used. The entire management

group of an organization is brought together, problems and attitudes are collected and shared, priorities are established, commitments to action are made through setting targets and assigning task forces.

3. *Goal-setting and planning:* supervisor-subordinate pairs and teams throughout the organization engage in systematic performance improvement and target-setting with mutual commitment and review. Goal setting or management-by-objectives becomes a way of life for the organization. [See Chapters 3, 4, and 5.]

4. *Third party facilitation:* involves the use of a skilled third person to help in the diagnoses, understanding and resolution of difficult human problems — e.g. difficult one-to-one relationships between two persons or groups.

5. *Consulting pairs:* often managers can benefit from a close and continuing relationship with someone outside their own organization (a consultant, either internal or external to the organization), with whom they can share problems early (p. 3).[58]

One variant that combines intergroup problem-solving, confrontation, and action research is the *joining-up process.*

The *joining-up process* aims to increase the speed of assimilating new members into the organization. Failure of such "joining up" and identifying with the organization may lead to dissatisfaction and quitting. Unrealistic expectations and a sense of violating them may result in role conflicts of new members with older members. Organizational effectiveness will suffer. The "joining-up" process is an OD intervention that addresses itself to this problem in the form of a workshop among three groups representing new college trainees, promotees, or newly transferred managers with a minimum of six month's experience; experienced middle managers; and recruiters, top management, and personnel administrators.

Other kinds of team-building activity have gone on before, so that participants are aware of the differences between process and content observations and the importance of trust, feedback, and effective decision making.

A questionnaire is completed in advance, dealing with participants' expectations about what they will give to, and receive from, the firm. The focus of the workshop is on the mismatches between each group's expectations of the other two groups.

Here are some examples of mismatches that have surfaced in the joining-up process and how the conflicts in expectations have been resolved:

1. Salary policy   New members overestimated the salaries of old members. They thought that salaries and salary policies were kept secret. Resolution was achieved in an examination of what was offered to college graduates, the effects, and what progress they could expect.

2. Feedback between boss and subordinate   Most members felt they did not regularly get enough feedback from their boss. It was agreed that neither boss nor subordinate understood the basic feedback process; the boss was giving too little, and the subordinate was expecting too much.

3. College recruiting information Some new people felt that there was a sharp mismatch between both verbal and written information they had been given in college and by recruiters, about how perfect everything was in the firm. Later, they were disillusioned by the actual situation. The firm was not so perfect, not so clean, and not so well managed as they had been led to believe. They were surprised at the irresponsible attitudes of some management and employees. Resolution lay in accepting reality and changing recruiting information.

4. Career planning Some participants thought that the firm had a ready-made five-year career plan for each new member. They were surprised that they were expected to take major action in planning and developing their own careers.

Other mismatches dealt with shift assignments, management bonuses, communication, loose working hours, personnel policies, extracurricular activities, use of first names, overtime pay for management, dress codes, credibility gaps, educational opportunities, conformity of dress, time commitment, personal development, and management power.

The workshop is completed in mixed groups discussing such questions as: What can we do in the future to keep our expectations of each other clear? What can we do to plan our careers and assure promotion in the firm?[42]

Survey Feedback (or "Survey-Guided" Feedback)

Increasingly, data collection for OD needs analysis, and diagnosis is being standardized by means of survey instruments that can stand the tests of reliability and validity. That is, sufficient numbers of items are asked on the questionnaire to reach satisfactory levels of internal consistency, rate-rerate reliability, and concurrent and/or predictive validity. By far the most widely used of these instruments is the *Survey of Organizations* of the Institute of Social Research (University of Michigan).[61] With application in many large industrial organizations as well as the U. S. Navy, the *Survey* had been completed by several hundred thousand participants by 1977. It is derived from Likert's theory that organizational development implies movement of organizations away from System I, an autocracy, toward System IV characterized by trust, commitment, and self-control. The four systems are partly shown in Figure 14–4.

Typical items of the survey* completed by participants are:

* © Copyright 1969, The University of Michigan.

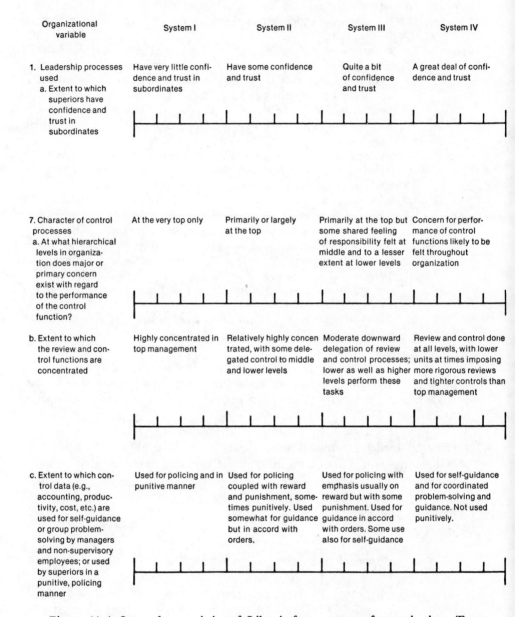

Figure 14–4. Some characteristics of Likert's four systems of organization. (From *The Human Organization* by Likert. Copyright © 1967 by McGraw-Hill Book Company. Used with permission of McGraw-Hill Book Company.)

34. How are objectives set in this organization?
    1. Objectives are announced with no opportunity to raise questions or give comments
    2. Objectives are announced and explained, and an opportunity is then given to ask questions
    3. Objectives are drawn up, but are discussed with subordinates and sometimes modified before being issued
    4. Specific alternative objectives are drawn up by supervisors, and subordinates are asked to discuss them and indicate the one they think is best
    5. Problems are presented to those persons who are involved, and the objectives felt to be best are then set by the subordinates and the supervisor jointly, by group participation and discussion
39. Which of the following best describes the *manner* in which problems between units or departments are generally resolved?
    1. Little is done about problems — they continue to exist
    2. Little is done about problems — they work themselves out with time
    3. The problems are appealed to a higher level in the organization — *but often are still not resolved*
    4. The problems are appealed to a higher level in organization — *and are usually resolved there*
    5. The problems are worked out at the level where they appear through mutual effort and understanding

The areas covered by the survey include leadership and relations with peers, technological readiness, communication flow, motivational conditions, and decision-making practices, and satisfaction with company, supervisor, job, pay, and work group.

Also included are items dealing with responsibility for company success, loyalty toward company and work group, trust and confidence in supervisor and work group. Finally, the instrument contains questions that measure respondent demographic characteristics, perceived work group effectiveness, and supervisory needs in several areas that may help in the data feedback process.

Approaches to Feedback of Survey Data

The feedback process of the survey data is of critical importance. Feedback of the results (usually computerized displays) of the survey can be given in a variety of ways. As shown in Figure 14-5 Plan A is the traditional way in which the results of attitude surveys of lower levels in the organization were fed back to the top management, who took appropriate organization actions and, in turn, then filtered down what they felt was necessary. In Plan B, feedback is to groups of subordinates and their immediate supervisor. In Plan C, feedback is to the immediate supervisor of each

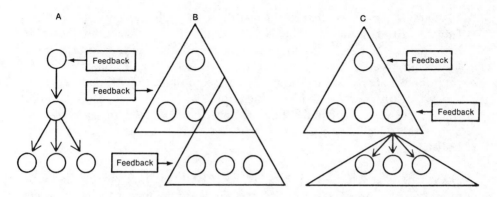

Figure 14–5. Three approaches to feedback. (Adapted from Mann, "Studying and Creating Change." In W. Bennis et al. (eds.), *The Planning of Change.* New York: Holt, Rinehart and Winston, 1961, and Frohman and Sashkin, "The Practice of Organization Development: A Selective Review." Unpublished report.)

group. Plan A is weakest. Seldom do the results fed back in Plan A filter down far enough. Even if they do, they are likely to be seriously changed as they pass on down the line. This is probably why, while 70 to 90 per cent of employees surveyed think such surveys are a good idea, only 10 to 30 per cent think any actions will be taken by management as a consequence of the survey results.

Plan B, feedback to groups, is most consistent with emphasis on sharing and participation. As a consequence of much trial and error, Mann concluded, "The process (Plan B) which finally appeared to maximize the acceptance and utilization of survey and research findings can be described structurally as an interlocking chain of conferences."[46] Managers or supervisors are the heads of one "family group" and also of another family group composed of their peers and their superiors. The organization is a pyramid of interlocking groups.[28]

PLAN B IN OPERATION   Feedback of the *Survey of Organizations* results uses Plan B. It is a "waterfall." The change agent or team of change agents starts with the group at the top of the organization. The top manager and his or her immediate subordinates are given lists of the divisions or units as a whole that report to them. Next, feedback sessions are held with groups composed of these subordinates of the top manager, each in a group with their own subordinates, who deal with the data appropriate to their units. As one proceeds downward in the organization, managers receive feedback in two groups. One is a group composed of their bosses and peers; the other is a group composed of their subordinates and themselves. As such they become *linch pins* between the two groups in dealing with the data appropriate to each of the groups. Plan B can run into some problems.

It contains some risk that the supervisors of such groups may be confronted with data they are not ready to deal with. Supervisors may be also handicapped if the consultant providing the displays of data usurps their leadership role in the group. For these reasons, Plan C fits with more traditional notions. It may be particularly appropriate with authoritarian supervisors in traditional hierarchies, for Plan C gives supervisors more time to get ready to handle the data that they are receiving, and it also avoids the possible usurpation by the consultant of their role as group leader.

PLAN C IN OPERATION   The Bass-Valenzi PROFILE is a survey feedback procedure that uses Plan C.[10] It gives feedback to managers about their group of subordinates and themselves. This feedback covers the system of inputs into the group, superior-subordinate relations, and the outputs of the group. The discrepancies and similarities in the way that the managers and their subordinates view the work situation and their relationship with each other provide a basis for locating areas for improvement. PROFILE conforms to a contingent view of the leadership process as described in Chapter 6. It is a 31-variable open systems model developed from analyses of surveys in a variety of organizational settings.[11] It is depicted below.

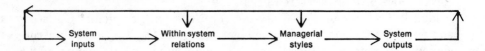

System inputs are factors of the organization, the task, the work group, and the individual's attitude with which the managers and their subordinates must work. The mix of system inputs ties with *within-system relations* between the managers and their subordinates. These are described by factors focusing on the relative amounts of power and relative amounts of information possessed by the managers and their subordinates. Besides power and information, within-system factors also include the nature of the manager's objectives — whether they be short-run or long-run — and the extent to which their relations with their subordinates are tightly or loosely structured.

The combination of *system inputs* and *within-system relations* is associated with particular *managerial styles*. The five styles are as described in Chapter 6. These are directive, negotiative, consultative, participative, and delegative. Managers can display all styles to varying degrees. For example, particular managers can be seen by their subordinates as both highly directive and highly delegative, although typically this is not likely to happen.[11]

System outputs are likely to be a consequence of the preceding factors as well as have a substantial impact on them. Concentration is on three outputs: effectiveness of the work unit, as defined by the attainment of immediate organizational goals, job satisfaction, and satisfaction with one's supervisor.

A personal computer printout displays the survey scores of a single manager and the mean and range of scores of that manager's subordinates for each factor in the survey. A sample is shown in Figure 14–6.

Let us take a closer look at a Plan C feedback session in a workshop of supervisors, who all receive their own individualized printouts for the groups they have been supervising. They are instructed to look at the data and to ask themselves which results they feel best about and which outcomes are most bothersome. They then can share these reactions with a small group of their peers. They are asked to locate the biggest discrepancies between themselves and their subordinates; between their peers in the workshop and themselves; between national norms provided by the consultant and themselves; between their ideals and themselves. They are asked to consider the major discrepancies among their subordinates as shown by the range of their subordinates' scores.

Other questions posed to the managers are: How satisfied are you with your management-styles pattern as seen by yourself and as seen by your subordinates? How do you feel about the effectiveness of your work unit as seen by your subordinates? Can you see a "message" coming through from your subordinates? Are they trying to tell you something?

After sufficient time is spent in examining the data and discussing the answers to the above questions, the workshop moves into the action phase. Questions include: If you could change some of the results by changing yourself or the situation which results would you change? Do you have control of the changes? Are they important to you? What can you do to bring about these changes? What can you do immediately? Later on?

And, finally, managers are asked to consider what feedback they are going to give to their subordinates.[10]

Requirements for Successful Feedback

Whatever the plan, A, B, or C, for data feedback to succeed, participants receiving it must overcome their skepticism and defensiveness and accept the data as a valid picture of the situation.[52] The data may corroborate the organization's views of itself and its functioning; the data may present information contrary to some beliefs; and/or the data may prompt interest and inquiry into why persons responded as they did.[50]

Participants must recognize that they had a hand in creating the conditions represented in the data and that they are, therefore, responsible for changing these conditions. They must focus on specific data and, using these as a basis for discussion, determine what implications the data have for action.[52]

YOUR MANAGEMENT PROFILE   DATE 02/17/76

MANAGER 80007   SUBORDINATES 5 MISSING 0   NAME BO BAY

->SYSTEM INPUTS->->->->->->WITHIN SYSTEM RELATIONS->->->MANAGERIAL STYLES->->->->->->SYSTEM OUTPUTS-->

MGR.SUBORDINATE MN RANGE				MGR.SUBORDINATE MN RANGE				MGR.SUBORDINATE MN RANGE				MGR.SUBORDINATE MN RANGE		

ORGANIZATIONAL

6	6	5-7	CONSTRAINTS
5	5	5-6	CLARITY
7	9	7-3	WARMTH
7	7	4-2	ORDER
4	3	1-5	EXTERNAL INFLUENCES

| 9 | 3 | 2-6 | BOSS POWER |
| 9 | 1 | 1-2 | SUB POWER |

| 6 | 6 | 5-8 | DIRECTIVE |

| 6 | 6 | 5-7 | EFFECTIVENESS |

WORK GROUP

4	3	1-5	INTRAGROUP CONFLICT
3	7	6-8	INTERDEPENDENCE
8	7	5-8	COMMITMENT TO GROUP

| 6 | 6 | 5-6 | BOSS INFO. |
| 6 | 5 | 4-7 | SUB INFO. |

| 5 | 3 | 2-4 | NEGOTIATIVE |

| 9 | 8 | 8-9 | JOB SATISFACTION |

TASK

8	7	6-9	CLEAR OBJECTIVES
7	6	4-8	ROUTINE
1	5	1-6	DISCRETIONARY OPP.
5	5	1-3	COMPLEXITY
8	6	2-7	MANAGERIAL ACTIVITY

| 4 | 6 | 4-9 | STRUCTURE |
| 3 | 6 | 5-7 | LONG TERM OBJECTIVES |

9	6	4-8	CONSULTATIVE
9	6	3-8	PARTICIPATIVE
5	6	4-8	DELEGATIVE

| 8 | 8 | 8-9 | SUPERVISORY SATISF. |

SELF-RATED ATTITUDES

7	6	5-7	FAIR
6	6	5-7	ASSERTIVE
2	2	2-3	EGALITARIAN
9	7	6-9	INEFFECTIVE

KEY

9	EXTREMELY HIGH
8	HIGH
7	HIGH
6	NEITHER HIGH NOR LOW
5	NEITHER HIGH NOR LOW
4	LOW
3	LOW
2	LOW
1	EXTREMELY LOW

Figure 14–6. Management Profile copyright 1973, Transnational Program Corp., Scottsville, New York 14546.

Numerous other conditions modify whether feedback will be effective. For instance, feedback seemed to have effects on the organization (according to follow-up interviews with 86 subordinates six months later) when the feedback data indicated the existence of serious problems that needed solution.

> Subordinates tended to report that something [of consequence to improvement] had happened in their workgroup . . . when ordinarily the organizational arrangements had not been clear . . . , activities had been unplanned and disorganized . . . , harmony between members of the workgroup was low . . . , little feedback was being provided concerning how well one was doing on the job . . . , subordinates tended to believe that people act unfairly . . . , and subordinates were relatively dissatisfied with their supervisors (p. 591).[60]

The presence in the group of highly assertive subordinates also made it more likely for actions to be taken as a consequence of the feedback to the supervisors.[60]

The Utility of Survey Feedback

Bowers was able to demonstrate dramatically the greater benefit-to-costs ratios in OD efforts using survey feedback in contrast to task consultation, process consultation, and T-grouping.[14] He was able to compare before-and-after surveys, using the Michigan *Survey of Organizations,* of 14,812 employees in 23 organizations. Improvement generally was most likely as a result of survey feedback. Next in effectiveness was process consultation. Least effective was concentration on T-grouping. And, in addition, dollar costs were far greater for providing T-group experiences than for the survey feedback.

In addition to its cost-effectiveness relative to other OD interventions, survey feedback with standardized questionnaires also, unlike the usual informal data gathering of OD change agents, contains the seeds of its own improvement as well as opportunities for cross-department, cross-function, cross-organizational, and cross-national research.

THE ROLE OF THE CHANGE AGENT OR THE CONSULTANT TO THE CLIENT ORGANIZATION

Professionals engaged in OD are either *internal* or *external* change agents. About half of those who belonged to the OD network in 1973 were internal change agents, working full-time with one firm, agency, or institution. The other half were in practice external to the organizations with which they consulted. Generally, it is the larger organizations with over 10,000 employees who maintain internal change agents.[16] Internal change agents, typically, are members of the employee relations departments of large organizations; typically they are members of consulting firms, universities, and other agencies and associations or engage in private practice.

"Internals" differ from "externals" to some extent in how they see their roles. For example, according to a survey of 46 internals and 24 externals, internals see OD as more of a self-taught art than do externals. Only 37 per cent of the internals see the use of behavioral science knowledge as important in OD, while 53 per cent of the externals do, but externals attach greater importance to responding to the client's felt need (74 per cent for externals versus 50 per cent for internals).[48] Locating decision-making close to its source of information and action (power-sharing) is subscribed to as an OD objective by only 20 per cent of the internals and 53 per cent of the externals but, conversely, internals place more emphasis on supporting the growth and development of people (39 per cent) than do externals (26 per cent).

In establishing a relationship with the client, a firm, or an agency, Scurrah, Shani, and Zipfel note that external change agents come into the situation as outside experts with certain skills to be made available to the client organization.[56] External change agents are likely to be seen as more objective and more professional. Their motives are less open to suspicion. On the other hand, internal agents may already have considerable valid knowledge about the people, technology, and problems before their consultation is sought by the client.

But the effectiveness of a change agent, whether internal or external, crucially depends on the nature of the relationship between the change agent and the members of the client organization. One important aspect of this relationship concerns the length of time the change agent devotes to the client organization, and, in particular, the time devoted to diagnosis before the program is launched and consulting with the organization is continued afterward. Friedlander has shown that the goals of increased interpersonal competence and more effective problem-solving in group meetings were more likely to be reached if the change agent had this longer relationship with the client organization.[25] In comparing three different groups with three different styles and tactics of training, it was observed that when consultants spent considerable time before the actual laboratory training session in learning about the organizational structure and the problems within the organization, then conducted their training laboratory, and afterward remained involved in the training process, there was much greater overall effectiveness in terms of the OD program's stated goals.

Depth of Involvement

Change agents differ in how deeply they become involved in the client's problems. At one extreme, the consultants work on the relatively impersonal. They review the publicly observable activities and relationships of client members. Here, organizational improvements can result from changing roles and functions, or redistributing tasks and resources, with relatively little attention devoted to the unique characteristics of the people in the client organization. Examples of work at this level include operations research, job design, or organization structure design.

At the opposite extreme is the focus on deeply personal feelings, attitudes, or perceptions that organization members have about themselves or their colleagues. Here, organizational effectiveness can be improved by broadening individual sensitivity and awareness or developing trust and openness between persons. The change agent working at this level devotes great attention to the unique personal characteristics of organization members. Examples of techniques used at this level include T-groups or counseling.[35]

The crucial problem, according to Harrison, is the choice of the appropriate depth of change-agent intervention. Frequently, clients tend to define their problems at relatively impersonal surface levels, while professional change agents tend to see problems at much deeper personal and interpersonal levels.

If the depth of involvement is determined solely by the client's definition, the OD program may be dealing only with symptoms, ignoring deeper causes, so that similar or related problems persist after the program. At the same time, interventions at relatively superficial levels have the advantage of depending on readily available, often public, information sources, and results can be easily communicated and implemented in the form of job descriptions, organization charts, new policies and procedures, and the like. Such changes are likely to be less dependent on personal factors — more controllable and predictable — and thus more lasting.

As normally understood, OD involves interventions at deeper, more personal levels. As interventions become deeper, organizations may benefit greatly from improvements in interpersonal relations and individual effectiveness, but certain risks are involved. Deeper interventions are more costly in time and effort devoted to gathering information; they depend more on the special competences of the change agent, and therefore may not be capable of effective implementation after he/she leaves the client organization. Above all, deeper, more personal interventions have less predictable and organizationally controllable results; there is greater risk of unintended consequences for both individuals and their organizations.

As a result of these considerations, Harrison recommends that change agents "intervene at a level no deeper than that required to produce enduring solutions to the problems at hand," and that such interventions go "no deeper than that at which the energy and resources of the client can be committed to problem solving and change." [35:181]

Effects of the Change Agent

Franklin was able to show how in 21 to 25 organizations the change agent influenced the success of OD efforts as measured by changes in before-and-after questionnaire surveys.[24] He concluded (see Table 14–1) that "internal change agents with the ability to assess strengths and weaknesses in organizational functioning and to prescribe on the basis of such assessments" were more likely to be successful in their OD intervention.

SOME EXAMPLES OF SUCCESSFUL INTERVENTIONS

We will conclude this chapter with several cases to illustrate how OD interventions work to bring about improvements.

Harwood-Weldon

One of the best documented cases of an OD effort that was successful and the effects of which were still apparent seven years afterward was the case of the merger of Harwood and Weldon, both in the garment industry. Harwood had been run rather participatively; Weldon was more authoritarian. But Harwood was making money in 1962; Weldon was losing it. Despite Weldon's technical, fiscal, and market strengths, it was near the point of disaster because of errors of strategy and work performance, high absenteeism, and high turnover. It was bought by Harwood. The renewal

Table 14–1. Primary responsibility for change activities.

	Successful	Unsuccessful	Total
Internal change agents	5	1	6
External change agents	1	7	8
Both ICA's and ECA's	4	3	7
	10	11	21

From Franklin, *Characteristics of Successful and Unsuccessful Organizational Development.* Ann Arbor, Michigan: Institute for Social Research, University of Michigan, 1975.

program for Weldon combined improvements in technology with an overall OD effort helped by the fact that the board chairman of Harwood, Alfred Marrow, held a Ph.D. degree in industrial psychology. The OD program for Weldon between 1962 and 1964 involved introduction of joint problem-solving, participative team efforts that included employees from the plant manager down to the production workers. Generally, job attitudes between 1962 and 1964 improved and had held up when reassessed in 1969, five years later. Actually, almost half the employees in 1969 had not even been in the company when the change effort had been carried out in 1962–1964, illustrating the obvious fact that an organization's health and potential is much more than just the satisfaction and skills of each of its current employees. Productivity had increased from 87 per cent of standard to 114 per cent by 1964 and had only slightly declined in the next five years. Financially a loser in 1962, Weldon had become profitable by 1964 and remained so through 1969, when last examined by Seashore and Bowers.[57]

The success at Weldon was attributed to its attention to Weldon's inter-personal needs at the time when new technologies were to be introduced *as part of the overall strategic plan for improvement*. Here it was seen that there were reasons for strong employee resistance to change. The company had poor labor relations. Employees were dissatisfied. There was lack of mutual trust, making employees feel they had no job security. Under these circumstances, an OD effort, before or in parallel with the effort to introduce the new technology, was most helpful in overcoming employee resistance to change to the new technologies.[47]

Other Examples

More briefly, similar kinds of success experiences were reported in a variety of organizational settings.

1. In a petrochemical refinery with 800 managers and professionals, an OD effort was built around the managerial grid and its ideology of con-cern for productivity *and* concern for people. During the year (1963) when the OD program was in effect, total production rose somewhat (with fewer employees), and profits more than doubled. Also recorded were increased frequency of meetings and improved criteria for management appraisals. Survey questionnaires also revealed perceived improvements during the year in boss-subordinate relationships and relations within de-partments and between work groups.[13]

2. Kimberly and Nielsen evaluated the effects of an OD intervention in an automobile plant consisting of 2,600 hourly and 200 salaried em-ployees. For 15 months all managers in the plant participated in skill-building, data feedback, team-building, and intergroup problem-solving. Before-and-after analyses of questionnaire data showed improvements in

organizational climate and supervisory behavior. In addition, production rates, which had been declining before the OD intervention, recovered to their predecline level. In addition, there were increases in both quality of production and overall profits earned by the plant.[40]

3. Hautaluoma and Gavin evaluated an OD effort with the employees and management of a small midwestern manufacturing company.[36] They used a research group to collect diagnostic data, to feed it back to the system, and to plan team-building for top management and supervisory-skills training for first-level management and some blue-collar employees. Before-and-after measurements indicated that managers and employees had improved in attitudes. Turnover decreased significantly from before to after the intervention, and time-series analyses of absenteeism showed a significant decrease from before to after the OD intervention.

Reasons for Successes or Failures

But Weldon and other such single cases of successful OD experiences can only be suggestive. They are single cases without comparison to control organizations which did not undergo the OD interventions.

Our conclusions here were drawn from single cases where we obtained before-and-after tests of performance. The design was as follows:

Case: Test   Interventions   Retest

Without any control, the conclusions are subject to every threat to their validity mentioned in previous chapters. Alternative plausible explanations can be readily drawn. For instance, it was suggested that one of the reasons for the Weldon success was that the intervention combined improvements in technology with improvements in interpersonal relations. In the petro-chemical refinery, success of the OD effort was attributed to such reasons as: (1) a demanding but tolerant headquarters; (2) an enthusiastic and involved top manager and senior management group; (3) an educational plan that effectively and continuously built team problem-solving and mutual support into work-related issues; and (4) an organization whose work required some interdependent effort and common values.

CASE SURVEY   One way to deal with dubious conclusions is to treat the problem as a descriptive survey of cases. Fortunately, enough such single cases are now available so that we can provide stronger evidence about some of the conditions in 25 organizations that underlay interventions that succeeded in comparison to some that failed. And the evidence is based on using the same standardized measurements before and after the inter-vention. With pre-post use of the Michigan *Survey of Organizations*, Frank-

Table 14-2. Presence of unions and success or lack of success of OD efforts.

	Successful	Unsuccessful	Total
Union	5	0	5
Non-Union	6	14	20

From Franklin, *Characteristics of Successful and Unsuccessful Organizational Development.* Ann Arbor, Michigan: Institute for Social Research, University of Michigan, 1975.

lin was able to determine what characteristics of 25 organizations made their OD effort more likely to be a success or a failure.[24] Success was measured in terms of generally positive changes of responses to the Michigan *Survey of Organizations* from before the OD intervention to one year after. As interventions, the 25 organizations employed either survey feedback, task consultation (direct assistance in improving how the work was to be done), process consultation, or T-grouping.

The organization's environment made a difference. Those in national rather than regional markets were a bit more likely to have had a successful experience. More important, those whose markets were increasing were more successful; those in steady or declining markets were less likely to have succeeded.

The work force made a difference. Those organizations paying lower wages and drawing their labor force from cities rather than from rural or suburban areas were less likely to succeed.

Industry and function made a difference. Less success was likely in the insurance industry and in office or sales work, in general, than in production activities in heavy industry.

Table 14-2 shows the effects of unionization. The absence of a union increased the likelihood of failure; although its presence didn't increase chances of success.

Particularly salient was the organization's reputation for being innovative. Innovative organizations (according to independent ratings) were much more likely to have had successful OD experiences; noninnovative were much more likely to fail (see Table 14-3).

Consistent with what we have said about the need for top management

Table 14-3. Innovative reputation and success or lack of success in OD efforts.

	Successful	Unsuccessful	Total
Innovative	8	3	11
Noninnovative	3	11	14

From Franklin, *Characteristics of Successful and Unsuccessful Organizational Development.* Ann Arbor, Michigan: Institute for Social Research, University of Michigan, 1975.

support and involvement, Franklin found that OD efforts were much more likely to succeed if the initial contact with the Michigan research staff came from some top manager such as the company president or plant manager. Successes were less frequent if the initial contact came from the personnel director or the internal change agent.

And, as we noted earlier, OD efforts were more likely to be successful if internal rather than external change agents took primary responsibility for the efforts. Again, as noted earlier, emphasis on survey feedback was characteristic of successful interventions; emphasis on T-groups, of unsuccessful ones.[24]

A NONEQUIVALENT CONTROL GROUP DESIGN   In a few cases, even more control has been possible using the nonequivalent control group design to study the effects of OD. As noted in Chapter 13, the design is as follows:

Unit A	Test	Interventions	Retest
Unit B	Test		Retest

Units A and B are selected because they are similar in many respects, but it is a practical impossibility to select two units exactly alike in all conditions likely to affect the changes in test to retest.

Doraville was one of two GM Assembly Division plants located near Atlanta. Between 1960 and 1969 it had established a reputation for operaing effectiveness with a heavy emphasis on Likert's System IV (see Figure 14–4). Lakewood, the other plant, was a disaster. Doraville's plant manager, who was a strong supporter of Likert's System IV approach to management, was transferred to take charge of Lakewood in 1969. Survey of Organization scores on a 15 per cent sample of hourly employees were obtained at both Lakewood and Doraville from before to after the intervention of the new plant manager and his two OD internal agents.

The interventions at Lakewood included special training of some of the executives and feedback of the first survey of their own subordinates' results to all managers (Plan B). Lakewood was a System II operation according to this survey — little trust, concentrated decision-making, and much management-dominated control.

Training at all levels was pushed as well as the general flow of information in the system. Supervisors were given assistants to provide help in their nonsupervisory functioning.

In the retest, a year after the first survey, Lakewood moved in its employees' perceptions much closer to Doraville. But during this same period (1969–1970) productivity dropped and production costs increased.

The reason seems to be a combination of factors: First, improvements in human organization required initially heavy dollar outlays in increased manpower and training and facility changes. Second, and more important, it simply takes time for improved management practices to be accepted and implemented, time for improved management practices to be reflected in improved employee attitudes, and still more time for these improved attitudes to be reflected in improved performance (p. 29).[22]

However, by 1971 and 1972 overall improvement, compared in plant efficiency to 1969, was substantial. The effects showed up in reduced tool breakage, lower scrap costs, improved quality, and reduced grievances as well as in other labor costs.

SUMMARY

We examined the who, what, why, where, and when of OD theory and practice and how it could be related to an organization's strategic planning. It was seen that fundamental to OD is the value and importance of integrating the individual's and the organization's needs.

The processes of OD begin with the change agent's efforts to enter the organization. Next, a contract is negotiated with the client. Diagnosis, feedback, and exploration of remedial efforts follow. The effects are evaluated, and a new cycle is started or the contract is terminated.

Understandings first learned in sensitivity training played a key role in the improvement of the OD processes. Examples of successful OD interventions, particularly when contrasting experience can be identified, provide a growing body of evidence about ways to increase the change agent's usefulness in the OD effort.

In this chapter, we have concentrated on the *social* side of sociotechnical improvements. In the next chapter, we look at the *technical* side. That is, we will now look at how we can rearrange the way work gets done in the organization to enhance personal and interpersonal reactions as well as to increase productivity and contributions to the improvement of the organization.

REFERENCES

1. Adorno, T. W., E. Frenkel-Brunswik, D. J. Levinson, and R. N. Sanford. *The Authoritarian Personality*. New York: Harper & Brothers, 1950.
2. Alderfer, C. P. "Boundary Relations and Organizational Diagnosis." In L. Meltzer and F. Wickert (eds.), *Humanizing Organizational Behavior*. Springfield, Ill.: Thomas, 1976.
3. Alderfer, C. P. "Change Processes in Organizations." In M. D. Dunnette (ed.), *Handbook of Industrial and Organizational Psychology*. Chicago: Rand-McNally, 1976.

4. Alderfer, C. P. "Organization Development," *Annual Review of Psychology* 28 (1977): 197–223.
5. Argyris, C. *Interpersonal Competence and Organizational Effectiveness.* Homewood, Ill.: Irwin-Dorsey, 1962.
6. Bamforth, K. "T-Group Methods within a Company." In G. Whitaker (ed.), *ATM Occasional Papers 2.* Oxford, England: Blackwell, 1965.
7. Bartee, E. M., and F. Cheyunski. "A Methodology for Process-Oriented Organizational Diagnosis," *Journal of Applied Behavioral Science,* 13 (1977): 653–658.
8. Bass, B. M. "The Management Training Laboratory — A Way to Improve Organizational Effectiveness," *Advanced Management,* 25, No. 7 (1960): 11–15.
9. Bass, B. M. "Social Behavior and the Orientation Inventory: A Review," *Psychological Bulletin,* 68 (1967): 260–292.
10. Bass, B. M. "A Systems Survey Research Feedback for Management and Organizational Development," *Journal of Applied Behavioral Science,* 12, No. 2 (1976): 215–229.
11. Bass, B. M., and E. Valenzi. "Contingent Aspects of Effective Management Styles" In J. G. Hunt and L. L. Larson (eds.), *Contingency Approaches to Leadership.* Carbondale: Southern Illinois University Press, 1974.
12. Blake, R. R., and J. S. Mouton. *The Managerial Grid.* Houston: Gulf Publishing, 1964.
13. Blake, R. R., J. S. Mouton, L. B. Barnes, and L. E. Greiner. "Breakthrough in Organization Development," *Harvard Business Review,* 42 No. 6 (1964): 133–135.
14. Bowers, D. G. "OD Techniques and Their Results in 23 Organizations: The Michigan ICL Study," *Journal of Applied Behavioral Science,* 9 (1973): 21–43.
15. Bowers, D. G., J. L. Franklin, and P. A. Pecorella. *A Taxonomy of Intervention: The Science of Organizational Development.* Center for Research on Utilization of Scientific Knowledge, Institute for Social Research, University of Michigan, ONR contract N00014–67–A–0181–0013, 1973.
16. Browne, P. J., and C. C. Cotton. "Who Are We? A Profile of Internal OD Practitioners," *OD Practitioner,* 5, No. 3 (1973): 7.
17. Calame, B. E. "The Truth Hurts — Some Companies See More Harm than Good in Sensitivity Training," *Wall Street Journal,* July 14, 1969, p. 191.
18. Campbell, J. P., and M. D. Dunnette. "Effectiveness of T-Group Experiences in Managerial Training and Development," *Psychological Bulletin,* 70 (1968): 73–104.
19. Clark, J. V. "Task Group Therapy: Intervention and Problems of Practise," *Human Relations,* 23 (1970): 383–403.
20. Davis, S. "An Organic Problem-Solving Method of Organizational Change," *Journal of Applied Behavioral Science,* 3 (1967): 3–21.
21. Deep, S., B. M. Bass, and J. Vaughan. "Some Effects on Business Games of Previous Quasi-T-Group Affiliation," *Journal of Applied Psychology,* 51 (1967): 426–431.
22. Dowling, W. F. "Systems 4 Build Performance and Profits," *Organizational Dynamics,* 3, No. 3 (1975): 23–38.
23. Dunnette, M. D. "People Feeling Joy, More Joy and the Slough of Despond." Paper presented at meeting of American Psychological Association. Washington, D. C., 1967.

24. Franklin, J. L. *Characteristics of Successful and Unsuccessful Organizational Development*. Ann Arbor, Michigan: Institute for Social Research, University of Michigan, 1975.

25. Friedlander, F. "A Comparative Study of Consulting Processes and Group Development," *Journal of Applied Behavioral Science*, 4 (1968): 377–399.

26. Friedlander, F. "OD Researches Adolescence: An Exploration of Its Underlying Values," *Journal of Applied Behavioral Science*, 12 (1976): 7–21.

27. Friedlander, F., and L. D. Brown. "Organization Development," *Annual Review of Psychology*, 25 (1974): 313–341.

28. Frohman, M. A., and M. Sashkin. "The Practice of Organization Development: A Selective Review." Unpublished report.

29. Gibb, J. R. "The T-Group as a Climate for Trust Formation." In L. P. Bradford, J. R. Gibb, and K. D. Benne (eds.), *T-Group Theory and Laboratory Method: Innovation in Re-Education*. New York: Wiley, 1964.

30. Gluckenstern, N. B., and R. W. Packard. "The Internal-External Change-Agent Team: Bringing Change to a 'Closed Institution,'" *Journal of Applied Behavioral Science*, 13 (1977): 41–52.

31. Glueck, W. F. *Business Policy: Strategy Formation and Management Action*. New York: McGraw-Hill, 1975.

32. Goffman, E. *Asylums*. New York: Anchor, 1961

33. Greenbaum, C. W., I. Rogovsky, and B. Shalit. "The Military Psychologist during Wartime: A Model Based on Action Research and Crisis Intervention," *Journal of Applied Behavioral Science*, 13 (1977): 7–21.

34. Greiner, L. E. "Patterns of Organization Change," *Harvard Business Review*, 45, No. 3 (1967): 119–130.

35. Harrison, R. "Choosing the Depth of Organizational Intervention," *Journal of Applied Behavioral Science*, 6 (1970): 181–202.

36. Hautaluoma, J. E., and J. F. Gavin. "Effects of Organizational Diagnosis and Intervention on Blue-Collar Blues," *Journal of Applied Behavioral Science*, 11 (1975): 475–496.

37. Hellebrandt, E. T., and J. E. Stinson. "The Effects of T-Group Training on Business Game Results," *Journal of Applied Psychology*, 77 (1971): 271–272.

38. House, R. J. "T-Group Education and Leadership Effectiveness: A Review of the Empiric Literature and a Critical Evaluation," *Personnel Psychology*, 20 (1967): 1–32.

39. Jaques, E. *The Changing Culture of a Factory*. New York: Dryden, 1952.

40. Kimberly, J. R., and W. R. Nielsen. "Organization Development and Change in Organizational Performance," *Administrative Science Quarterly*, 20 (1975): 191–206.

41. Kirton, M. J., and G. Mulligan. "Correlates of Managers' Attitudes toward Change," *Journal of Applied Psychology*, 58 (1973): 101–107.

42. Kotter, J. P. "The Psychological Contract: Managing the Joining-up Process," *California Management Review*, 15, No. 3 (1973): 91–99.

43. Leavitt, H. J. "Applied Organizational Change in Industry." In J. G. March (ed.), *Handbook of Organizations*. Chicago: Rand-McNally, 1965.

44. Leavitt, H. J. "Beyond the Analytic Manager II," *California Management Review*, 17, No. 4 (1975): 11–21.

45. Likert, R. *The Human Organization: Its Management and Value*. New York: McGraw-Hill, 1967.

46. Mann, F. "Studying and Creating Change." In W. Bennis et al. (eds.), *The Planning of Change*. New York: Holt, Rinehart and Winston, 1961.

47. Marrow, A. J., D. G. Bowers, and S. E. Seashore. *Management by Participation*. New York: Harper and Row, 1967.

48. Marsh, P. J., and W. D. Merkle. "What Is OD?—Some Issues and an Operating Definition," *OD Practitioner*, 5, No. 3 (1973): 1–3.

49. Miles, M. B. "Learning Processes and Actions in Human Relations Training." In E. H. Schein and W. G. Bennis (eds.), *Personal and Organizational Change through Group Methods*. New York: Wiley, 1965.

50. Miles, M., et al. "The Consequence of Survey Feedback, Theory and Evaluation." In W. Bennis et al. (eds.), *The Planning of Change*. New York: Holt, Rinehart and Winston, 1969.

51. Morton, R. B., and B. M. Bass. "The Organizational Training Laboratory," *Training Directors Journal*, 18, No. 10 (1964): 2–18.

52. Neff, F. "Survey Research: A Tool for Problem Diagnosis and Improvement in Organizations." In S. Miller and A. Gouldner (eds.), *Applied Sociology*. New York: Free Press, 1965.

53. Oshry, B., and R. Harrison. "Transfer from Here-and-Now to There-and-Then: Changes in Organizational Problem Diagnosis Stemming from T-Group Training," *Journal of Applied Behavioral Science*, 2 (1966): 185–198.

54. Rokeach, M. *The Open and Closed Mind*. New York: Basic Books, 1960.

55. Schein, E. H. *Process Consultation*. Reading, Mass.: Addison-Wesley, 1969.

56. Scurrah, M., M. Shani, and C. Zipfel. "Influence of Internal and External Change Agents in a Simulated Educational Organization," *Administrative Science Quarterly*, 16 (1971): 113–122.

57. Seashore, S.E., and D. G. Bowers. "Durability of Organizational Change," *American Psychologist*, 25 (1970): 227–233.

58. Sherwood, J. J. "An Introduction to Organizational Development." *Experimental Publication System*, 1971, Ms. No. 396–1.

59. Sherwood, J. J., and J. C. Glidewell. "Planned Renegotiation: A Norm-Setting OD Intervention." In W. W. Burke (Ed.), *Contemporary Organization Development*, Washington, D. C.: NTL Institute for Applied Behavioral Science, 1972.

60. Solomon, R. J. "An Examination of the Relationship between a Survey Feedback O. D. Technique and the Work Environment," *Personnel Psychology*, 29 (1976): 583–594.

61. Taylor, J. C., and D. G. Bowers. *The Survey of Organizations: A Machine-Scored Standardized Questionnaire Instrument*. Ann Arbor, Michigan: Institute for Social Research, 1972.

62. Tippin, G. L. "Organization Development Strategies/Interventions." Unpublished report.

63. Vicino, F. L., J. Krusell, B. M. Bass, E. L. Deci, and D. A. Landy. "The Impact of PROCESS: Self-Administered Exercises for Personal and Interpersonal Development," *Journal of Applied Behavioral Science*, 9 (1973): 737–756.

64. Whyte, W. F., and E. L. Hamilton. *Action Research for Management*. Homewood, Ill.: Irwin-Dorsey, 1964.

15 JOB DESIGN AND THE QUALITY OF WORKING LIFE

IN BRIEF Historically there has been continued concern about the quality of working life. Mass-production jobs have been seen as dehumanizing. Automation, both in the plant and in the office, has often failed to improve the quality of working life. Currently there is some disagreement about employees' satisfaction with work and whether or not dissatisfaction is greater than in the past. A number of different approaches to job design have evolved with various concepts. The time-and-motion approach to job design emphasizes certain universal design principles, which apply to all individuals. At the other extreme, congruency approaches to job design concentrate on employee differences. Human factors engineering, sociotechnical design, sociological approaches, motivation-hygiene theory, and organizational development have all made a contribution to understanding the design of jobs and work systems. A number of interacting factors, including management support and extrinsic rewards, can influence the success of new job-design changes in organizations.

At the beginning of the industrial era, attention was first focused upon the physical working conditions of the employee. As they improved, concern developed regarding the attitudes of workers toward their jobs. In the 1930s, a reaction against mass production and principles of scientific management began to emerge. A contrast was made between the assembly-line technology, in which people appeared to lose control of their pace and method of work, and the idealized model of crafts workers who controlled their own work and could take pride in the fruits of their own labor. Charlie Chaplin's vivid portrayal of the pathetic and harassed assembly-line worker in *Modern Times* was an artistic expression of these problems. Social critics argued that every person's work should be meaningful and give the individual a source of satisfaction. One of the first of this long line of social commentators was Marx and Engels' *Communist Manifesto* of 1847, which criticized the fractionization and routinization of industrial tasks. Since that time, industrialization has progressed, technology has changed and evolved, and concern has been expressed about mass-production jobs and automation especially.

Concern about Productivity and Quality of Working Life

Annual U. S. gains in productivity — output per worker per hour — averaged 3.2 per cent per year from 1948 to 1966, 2.1 per cent from 1966 to 1973, 1.0 per cent from 1973 to 1978 and actually declined in 1979. Yet increasing worker productivity has been the key to increasing living standards. Such productivity has depended on improving production methods and employee motivation along with technical innovation and investment in new plants and equipment. In this chapter, we will examine how production methods and employee motivation dovetail to affect productivity. Jobs can be redesigned to both increase employee productivity as well as commitment to better job performance.

At the same time, we have seen the growth of interest in the quality of working life. Work can be made a satisfying experience to the worker. As we have seen in Chapter 3, productivity and job satisfaction do not necessarily contribute to each other. Rather each are of value in its own right. In improving the design of jobs, we seek both productivity and satisfaction.

Concern about Mass-Production Jobs

Before the advent of automation, the characteristic feature of our industrial complex was the assembly line. This mass-production method is based on the standardization and interchangeability of parts, the orderly progression of the product through the manufacturing process, the mechanical delivery of the parts to and from the manufacturing process, the mechanical delivery of the parts to and from the assemblers, and a simple breakdown of each operation required of the assembler. This concept of mass production — from Eli Whitney, who standardized parts for guns, to Henry Ford, who developed the concept of the assembly line — is a grouping of characteristics common to each sequence of the total job. By the very nature of the continuous assembly line, there is a mechanical pacing of the work. Each separate operation is continually repeated, the techniques and tools employed are predetermined, and, as a result, typically only surface mental attention is required to perform the operations. Of course, there are many variations of assembly-line jobs; the characteristics noted here refer specifically to the automobile assembly line.

Walker and Guest's study of automotive workers highlighted some of the perceived problems with assembly-line jobs.[41] The investigation disclosed that the workers' interest in their work was directly related to the number of operations being performed — the more operations, the more interest in the work. As a group, the automotive workers disliked the mechanical pacing of the work, the repetitiveness of their tasks, and the minimal skill required to perform the tasks. The only aspect of their job that the majority of the workers liked was the high pay and other material benefits. (Similar results were reported subsequently in other manufacturing industries. Thus, Wyatt and Marriott found that the number of minutes spent by workers on a job's cycle was related to their satisfaction with their jobs.) [46]

Automation as a Design Problem

Automation is a technological change seen both as a specter and savior of humanity. It has been evolving since 1763, when James Watt introduced the concept of feedback to control the operation of his steam engines. A common example of the feedback principle found in the home is the interaction between a thermostat and the furnace. If the room temperature drops below a preset degree, the thermocouple in the thermostat unit makes an electrical connection, closing the circuit, which turns on the furnace. The circuit breaks when the room is heated above the preset degree, and the furnace is shut off.

Automation can take many different forms, ranging from an automated elevator to the automated refining of gasoline. In recent years, with the introduction of computers and data-processing equipment, automation has taken over many office procedures. Automation implies extensive use of automatic equipment, mechanization of the transfer of working units from process to process, and the use of closed-loop feedback systems (for processes requiring continuous control) as a means of control.

There have been a number of studies concerning the effects of automation on employees in diverse industries. These industries include power plants, steel mills, engine factories, banks, and a variety of office situations. In summarizing the studies, it is clear that automation can take many forms, and it is unwise to make broad generalizations concerning its effects upon the workers. For example, some investigations conclude that there is less teamwork, less interdependence, and more feelings of social isolation in an automated plant than in a nonautomated plant. Some have even gone so far as to suggest that an additional incentive, "loneliness pay," be given to those working in automated plants. In contrast, other studies conclude that there is greater interdependence and socialization among the workers because of the introduction of automation.[8,20,24,25,40] The substitution of computers for clerical data-processing created a large demand for both high-level jobs as programmers as well as low-level jobs as keypunch operators. Banks of clerks were replaced by programmers and keypunch operators.

Current Concerns with the Quality of Working Life

In the 1970s, the popular press and television focused upon a new national illness, the "blue-collar blues," or at times, the "Lordstown Syndrome." According to many of these sources, most of the American workers are bored, frustrated, and rebellious. Absenteeism and turnover are reported to be at all-time high rates, and productivity is perceived to be at its lowest rate. This widespread concern was reflected in the federal government by a 1973 report from the Health, Education, and Welfare Department, which reported that, although the work ethic is alive, a large number of employees at all occupational levels are very dissatisfied with their work. The report concluded that the principle sources of discontent are work specialization and diminished work autonomy. At this point, we should explain that the concept of "quality of working life" does not have any one well-accepted definition. Both employee satisfaction and more objective indices such as rate of absenteeism, mental health, and extent of drug abuse are seen by some investigators as entering into any index of the quality of working life. Other investigators infer the quality of working life from job satisfaction alone.

In a popular book entitled *Where Have All the Robots Gone? Worker Dissatisfaction in the 70s,* Sheppard and Herrick reported that dissatisfaction with the job content of the work itself was widespread among blue-collar workers.[35] In particular, the negative attitudes were most prevalent among younger workers with some college graduates, black workers, and females under thirty.

While these two representative studies reported a rather bleak picture concerning the quality of working life, other surveys have challenged the pervasive worker discontent. In what is perhaps the most comprehensive review of national surveys of American workers since 1958, a somewhat different picture is drawn.[31] In particular, this review indicated that there had been *no* widespread decline in overall job satisfaction during the prior fifteen years. Through most of that period of time, approximately 15 per cent of the workers could be classified as dissatisfied.

Despite the contradictory evidence, there is still a broadly based movement that questions the basic thesis that industrial life that provides through improved productivity a high standard of living must also result in a dehumanized working life. There appears to be a growing number of social commentators, political leaders, and concerned citizens throughout the industrialized world who will not accept alienation or the dehumanized work as consequences of a productive society.

There have evolved a number of new conceptual approaches that attempt to give a framework for redesigning jobs in order to enhance the quality of working life for all employees. We will deal with some of the older approaches such as time-and-motion study before discussing some of the newer ones.

Two broad themes differentiate approaches to job design. One holds that there are certain universal principles that apply to all workers and jobs; another says that there are moderating factors and that there is no *one* simple job design solution which would apply to all individuals. Perhaps one of the chief faults of time-and-motion study as an approach to job design is that it attempts to apply universal principles to all employees performing the same job.

APPROACHES TO JOB DESIGN

Time-and-motion study, human factors engineering, sociotechnical design, sociological methods, motivation-hygiene theory, expectancy theory, congruence approaches, and organizational development are differing approaches to job design that we will consider. Illustrative studies will be presented to highlight the features of each.

Time-and-Motion Study

Frederick Winslow Taylor has been called the father of "scientific management," but as noted in Chapter 5, most effort toward the rationalization of work preceded his popularization of the approach. As early as 1881, he presented methods and principles for developing means of reorganizing such jobs as handling pig iron and shoveling coal. His goal was to obtain more production from workers for less cost to management, enabling more money to be paid to employees. Taylor's method consisted in selecting the best man to do the job, instructing him in the most efficient method of performing the work, and giving him extra money as an incentive to produce at a higher rate. Not only did Taylor introduce new designs and shapes of shovels for each task, but he also invented the modern spoon-shaped tennis racket! Frank B. Gilbreth carried on Taylor's work and by 1920, with his wife Lillian, developed micromotion analysis. This technique made use of motion pictures to study the movements of workers on the job. Essentially, the Gilbreths attempted to find the best way of doing a job with a given machine and job setup. For the Gilbreths, the best method was the one in which the most work was done for what seemed to be the least expenditure of time and energy.

Time-and-motion study of jobs, as initially developed by Taylor and the Gilbreths, is widely used today. However, the scientific verification of the principles that need to be understood to engineer jobs has become, to some extent, the work of applied psychologists. The Taylor-Gilbreth approach to the engineering of jobs makes use of logical, common-sense principles following detailed analysis of a given job. Some of these principles fail to stand up when subjected to experimental verification; others, until now, have stood the test of time and constitute a core that has been valuable in improving the efficiency of work and methods.

Human-Factors Engineering

The human-factors approach to job design is concerned with the physical, physiological, and psychological capacities of individuals. The design process begins with an in-depth knowledge of people's capacities. Changed methods may be introduced on the basis of knowledge of how individuals process information. For example, efficiency in inspecting a complex electronic chassis was found to be 90 per cent more effective when the inspector searched for one characteristic defect at a time by scanning the whole chassis. The alternate, and less efficient method, involved looking for all types of defects at the same time.[15]

Sociotechnical Design

The sociotechnical system takes into account not only the technical aspects of the job, but also the social considerations in any organization. The practitioners of sociotechnical design argue that engineers have a great deal of knowledge about the technical aspects of a system, but they have not fully taken into account the social requirements. The sociotechnical process has evolved at least nine principles that serve as rough guidelines for the design process.[5]

PRINCIPLE 1: COMPATIBILITY   The process of design itself must be compatible with its objectives. For example, if one of the objectives of the design is to create a system that can be capable of adapting to changed circumstances by making use of the individual capabilities in the organization, then the individual should be given an opportunity to participate in the design process. As we will note below, such participation is commonly practiced in sociotechnical planning.

PRINCIPLE 2: MINIMAL CRITICAL SPECIFICATION   The design process should identify what is essential to be accomplished in a task, and no more should be specified than what is absolutely essential. For example, while the design process may be very precise about what needs to be done, it should leave maximum latitude about what method the employee can use to accomplish the task.

Time-and-motion enthusiasts argue that "there is one best way for everyone." Typically, discussion and search reveal a variety of acceptable ways a task can be completed. One way may be better for one employee, another way for another.

PRINCIPLE 3: THE SOCIOTECHNICAL CRITERIA   Any unprogrammed event in the work process is a variance. If a variance cannot be eliminated, then it should be controlled as near to the point of origin as is feasible. For example, a variance is the production of faulty parts by workers. In most organizations, this is controlled by inspectors who reject those parts that do not meet established standards. Typically, the inspection department is a separate department, removed both in location and in time from the individuals actually making the part, who are responsible for the key variance. The solution to this problem is to allow the workers producing the part the responsibility for inspecting their own products. The role of the inspector is changed from that of a "watch dog" to that of one who trains workers on how to inspect their own work accurately.

PRINCIPLE 4: THE MULTIFUNCTIONAL PRINCIPLE   For an organization to be sufficiently adaptive to meet environmental demands, it is necessary for its members to be ready, willing, and able to perform more than one function, or to perform the same function in a variety of ways to meet changing circumstances. This principle reflects the idea, discussed in Chapter 5, of equifinality, which means that there are several ways to reach the same goal.

PRINCIPLE 5: BOUNDARY LOCATION   In most organizations, the boundaries around the departments are typically based on either the technology involved, time, or territory.[26] Examples of boundaries based on *technology* are typing pools or rooms of keypunch operators. In contrast, departments may be based upon *contiguity in time*. For example, they may contain all the equipment that is necessary to convert raw materials into finished products. All the switchboard operators at a large central installation are bound together in the same *territory* because of the design of the equipment. The important consideration for boundary location is that the boundaries should be drawn so that they do not interfere with the sharing of knowledge and information that can accomplish the task. This would include, as we discussed above in Principle 3, the task of inspecting one's own product.

PRINCIPLE 6: INFORMATION FLOW   The organization should be designed so that relevant information comes to the person who should take the action. Too often, information in the organization goes to the supervisors or to upper levels of the organization, where it then must be directed downward to the others in the organization. Providing the feedback directly to those workers actually doing the job contributes a great deal to the control of the variances in their performance.

PRINCIPLE 7: SUPPORT CONGRUENCE   The total organization should be designed so that there is a reinforcement of the behaviors that the organizational structure was designed to produce. For example, if the design requires a team operation with shared responsibility for a function, payment should be based upon team productivity and not on individual performance.

PRINCIPLE 8: DESIGN OF HUMAN VALUES   The design should be compatible with human needs and should provide effective individuals with quality in their working lives. Quality of working life would include such things as an optimal variety of tasks in any one job, a pattern of tasks that has some meaning to the worker, an opportunity to learn on the job, some decision-making relevant to the job, for which the individual can feel responsible, recognition by others of the individual's role in the workplace, and some feeling that the job has some value to society.

PRINCIPLE 9: INCOMPLETENESS   Any design should be a reiterative process. It should have built into it a plan of continual review and improvement — a process of redesign.

PARTICIPATION IN THE DESIGN PROCESS   Typically, sociotechnical designing allows employees to participate in the design process. This technique has two important advantages. First, since the workers are usually the best informed about their jobs, they should have available the technical information necessary to make improvements. Second, there should be increased motivation because of participation in designing their own jobs. We previously talked quite extensively about participative techniques in Chapters 3 and 6, and about the importance of self-planning in Chapter 5.

To implement the concepts of participation in manufacturing job design, six North American Rockwell Corporation supervisors were carefully trained in the techniques of participative management. The training session included ten hours of group sessions and, what was considered to be the most important of all, individual coaching, which varied from 30 to 60 minutes for each meeting. This individual coaching, although time-consuming, was thought to be quite beneficial, giving supervisors an immediate feedback on their techniques in a group setting. An attitude questionnaire was administered to 6 groups of about 60 employees, for whom performance measures and participation ratings were available. The degree of participation actually fostered by the supervisors with their groups was judged by two psychologists, whose independent ratings agreed. Two groups were then assigned to high, medium, and low participation. The control group of 26 employees was also given the same attitude questionnaire. The results of the experiments are shown in Figure 15–1. As can be seen, there were distinct differences among the groups. Both performance and attitude were improved for those groups who participated the most in the job design.

In the most successful high-participation groups, the supervisor used a technique of goal-oriented problem-solving. The supervisor typically presented data on the past performance of the group and then stated new objectives. The group then discussed the problems and decided how to meet its new commitments. Specific suggestions for improving the design of the job included modification of hand tools used in computer assembly operations, new gauges, and special nonmagnetic tweezers.[4]

Figure 15–1. Impact of group participation on production performance and employee attitude. (From *Human Factors,* 11, 1969, p. 104. Copyright 1969 by The Human Factors Society, Inc., and reproduced by permission.)

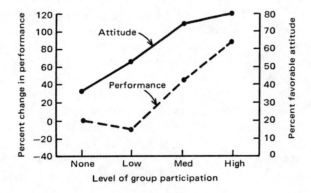

It is clear that the interaction of both technical changes and greater commitment to goals through participation was effective in greatly increasing the productivity of the groups.

Sociological Approaches to Job Design

Turner and Lawrence found that the effectiveness of a job design depended on the background of the workers assigned the job.[38] Workers from a small-town setting differed from those from urban areas. Urban workers were more willing to accept repetitive jobs. They were less interested in challenging jobs than rural workers were. In the same way, Faunce noted that automobile workers from a rural background were more dissatisfied with automated jobs than were the urban workers.[8] Again, among over 2,500 female manual workers in the British electronics industry, those from rural areas were less apt to accept paced work than those from the urban areas.[21,45] But such rural-urban differences do not emerge consistently.[33,37]

Nevertheless, we remain unclear as to whether the rural-urban differences are due to ethnic and religious effects, to growing up in a rural or urban community, or to gravitation toward rural rather than urban life as an adult.

In addition to lower taxes, land costs and congestion, one of the reasons firms choose to relocate factories in rural areas despite added distance to markets and sources of supply and labor is the belief that rural workers after training are less likely to unionize and are more committed to the work ethic. Hulin and Blood did find that the work norms of the rural or small-town employee more closely approximated the Protestant Ethic-middle-class belief in the intrinsic value of hard work, the value of striving to do well, and achievement in an occupation of one's choice. In contrast, urban workers were likely to be alienated from the usual middle-class values, including the conventional ideas about the Protestant Ethic.[3] Figure 15-2 illustrates whether or not one is satisfied with an enriched job — a job with more meaning to the occupant, more challenge, more responsibility, and more variety — depends on whether the occupant subscribes to middle-class values. Hulin and Blood suggest that an enriched job fails to result in increased job satisfaction for those who are alienated from middle-class norms. From the evidence they present, they believe that the case for job enrichment has been drastically overstated. They contend that there must be a congruence between the task performed and the values of the workers. There is some indication that the Hulin and Blood findings have more validity when the employee's present community location, rather than where the employee lived as a child, is used as

Concern for
middle-class values

Alienated	Endorses
Yes	No

Will job enrichment increase job satisfaction?

Figure 15–2. Interaction of alienation and job enrichment resulting in differing levels of job satisfaction.

a possible sign of alienation. Recent and current socializing processes seem more important than early history of the employees.

Motivation-Hygiene Job-Design Approach

Herzberg's two-factor theory of work motivation (Chapter 3) led him to formulate an approach to job design. As we noted in Chapter 3, according to Herzberg, job *content* factors such as achievement, recognition, the work itself, and responsibility are both determinants of job satisfaction and the factors that motivate workers on the job. While the presence of such job content factors will lead to increased satisfaction, their absence will not lead to dissatisfaction. It is job *context* variables such as pay, company policy, working conditions, and supervision that lead to job dissatisfaction. Improving the so-called hygiene factors — the context variables — may eliminate dissatisfaction for the employees, but will not motivate them.

Herzberg has distinguished between *job enrichment* and *job enlargement* as well as horizontal and vertical job-loading.[16] Horizontal job-loading is equated with job enlargement. It typically consists of adding more tasks to a short-cycle, repetitive job. It is Herzberg's contention that this approach should be avoided. He advocates job-enrichment approaches that involve vertical job-loading in order to increase the motivational properties of a job. Vertical job-loading involves (1) removing some controls of the employee while retaining accountability, (2) increasing individuals' accountability for their own work, (3) giving an employee a complete natural unit of work, (4) granting additional authority to an employee, (5) making periodic reports directly to the employee, rather than to the employee's supervisor, (6) introducing new and more complex tasks not previously undertaken by the employee, and (7) assigning employees specific and specialized tasks.

Herzberg's ideas have been introduced in a variety of organizations, including American Telephone and Telegraph. His approach to job redesign involves training key individuals in motivation-hygiene theory and internal consultants working with supervisors to generate job design changes. Such proposed job changes are then submitted to a committee of middle managers for approval. The approved changes are then reviewed in general with top management before being put into operation. Documented evidence of the massive benefits to AT&T were summarized by Ford.[9]

An important point to note is that participation of the worker is neither sought nor considered important by Herzberg. This is in contrast to the sociotechnical approach, in which participation by the job-holder is an integral part of the job design change. Nor, are the sociological — rural versus urban — issues of consequence to Herzberg. Many other firms have adopted the Herzberg approach with striking reports of benefits. For example, in one job-enrichment program involving complex avionics equipment, annual savings of over $350,000 were reported.[17]

In job enrichment, we have a case in which a controversial theory, whether it is valid or not, results in an effective application of behavioral science to improving performance and satisfaction. The history of technology is filled with such examples. The first successful steam engine was designed according to the theory that heat was a material substance called phlogiston.

Expectancy Theory of Job Design

Figure 15-3 graphically illustrates Hackman and Oldham's expectancy theory of job design.[13] The theory is based upon the interaction of three distinct sets of variables. First, they postulate that there is a core set of job dimensions: skill variety, task identity, task significance, autonomy, and feedback. This core set determines the employee's *critical psychological states*. These critical psychological states are the meaningfulness of the work, responsibility for the outcome of the work, and knowledge of the results of the work experienced by the employee. (Workers can see what's due to their efforts.) The third part of the model focuses upon differences among employees in *strength of growth needs* — the desire to develop one's competencies. If an individual is high in such growth needs, the result will be positive personal and work outcomes. Work will be of high quality and satisfying to do when the core dimensions of skill variety, task identity, task significance, antonomy and feedback are present in necessary amounts in the job.

In a study of over 200 telephone company employees, Hackman and Lawler presented evidence that individuals whose jobs were high on the

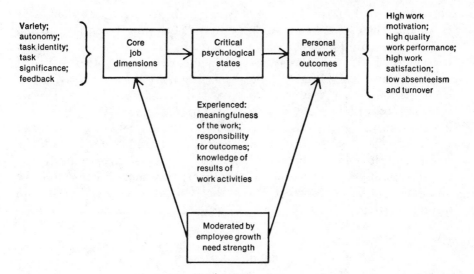

Figure 15-3. Expectancy theory of job design. (Adapted from Hackman and Oldham, "Motivation through the Design of Work: Test of a Theory," *Organizational Behavior and Human Performance,* 16 [1976]: 250–279.)

core dimensions and who also desired growth in competency tended to have higher self-rated motivation, higher self-rated job satisfaction, and better attendance records, and were rated by their supervisors as doing higher-quality work.[12] As predicted, these relationships were not found for employees with little interest in growth.

The strategy developed for enriching jobs following the expectancy theory of job design begins with a diagnostic phase. Workers are administered the Job Diagnostic Survey to measure their job satisfaction, the motivating potential of the job in terms of the core set of dimensions, and the strength of needs for growth. The second step involves determining the actual job changes required to improve the core set of job dimensions. In order to raise values on the core dimensions, consideration is given to combining tasks, forming natural work units, establishing client relationships, vertical loading (giving more responsibility to the employee), and opening feedback channels.[14]

CONTEXT FACTORS   Hackman and Oldham extended their theory of job design to include contextual factors in the organization such as satisfaction with pay, security, social conditions, and supervision.[13] Individuals achieved the highest performance and were most satisfied with an enriched job when they desired personal growth and were satisfied with factors such as pay. Further, they found that if persons in an organization are uninterested in growth and are dissatisfied with context factors in their work, their performance is adversely affected. As an illustration, they noted that there was a correlation between motivating potential and job performance only for individuals with strong needs for growth, who also were satisfied with social aspects of their organization. In other words, if employees see their job motivating them, their performance will be better if, at the same time, they want to grow and are satisfied with the social relationships within their organization. On the other hand, other employees who rate their jobs just as highly motivating will fail to perform well if they lack interest in their own growth and are dissatisfied with the social conditions in the organization. This points out the complexity of the relationships to be found in an organization and demonstrates the importance of a congruence between the individual, the task itself, and the organizational context.[29]

A Congruence Model of Job Design

The main features of the congruence model of job design are illustrated in Figure 15–4. This model suggests that an optimum match of an employee's abilities, preferred job attributes, and expectancies on the one hand and job characteristics on the other, will result in the greatest individual job performance and satisfaction.

Unlike the Hackman and Oldham expectancy theory of job design, the congruence model gives a more central role to the employees' abilities as directly influencing their job performance and, at times, work satisfaction. The congruence model assumes that our preference for work that involves learning new skills, variety, responsibility, and feedback depends on our abilities and value orientations. For instance, brighter people prefer jobs on which they can continue learning. Individuals with greater numerical, verbal, spatial, and mechanical abilities prefer jobs on which they can learn new skills. Preferences for jobs with complexity, variety, and learning new skills have been consistently related to specific and general ability measures. Preferences for other job content such as responsibility are not related to ability levels but to intrinsic work orientations. Preferences for jobs with responsibility and independence, while unrelated to individual ability levels, are instead consistently related to certain value orientations such as *intrinsic* work orientation — interest in the work itself, rather than the *extrinsic* rewards associated with the work.

One other important consideration concerning abilities must be emphasized. For certain positions, the individual with the most ability, and subsequently the highest rated performance, may be least satisfied with the work itself. This has been found in both field and laboratory studies of monitoring tasks.[2] So for monitoring tasks such as are found in many inspection jobs, if the organization hires as an inspector the individual

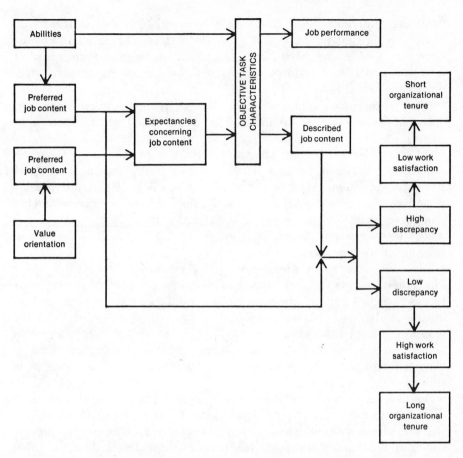

Figure 15–4. An overview of the congruence model. (Adapted from Barrett, "Task Design, Individual Attributes, Work Satisfaction, and Productivity." In A. Negandhi and B. Wilpert (eds.), *Work Organization Research: European and American Perspectives.* Kent, Ohio: Kent State University Press, 1978.)

with the most ability, it also may be hiring the individual who will be least satisfied performing the job and most likely to quit.

EXPECTATIONS   As part of the model, it can be seen that expectations concerning job content affect how employees describe their jobs and thereby influence how satisfied they are with the jobs. In order to examine this phenomenon, a series of studies involving a maintenance problem-solving task was designed in which the physical task was identical for two groups, but variation was introduced into the expected job content. In a "negative" condition, participants were given a task described as low in responsibility, feedback, task identity, and learning new skills. In a "positive" treatment, individuals were told that a substantial number of these attributes were present in the task they would perform. These manipulations were presented as part of the written task instructions and were periodically reinforced by a training session and the written instructions given during the actual task.

After performing the physical task, subjects in the "negative" condition did describe the task as significantly lower in the attributes such as responsibility than did subjects from the "positive" condition. They also rated themselves as feeling they were working on a job with greater intrinsic worth when working in the psychologically manipulated "positive" job condition. Assuming that the set could be maintained over a period of time in real-world operations, the evidence appears that even though we may be performing identical tasks, the way the task is presented to us or our expectations concerning this task will influence our subsequent feelings about the task and its worth to us.

King conducted a year-long study of a clothing manufacturer which illustrates the importance of expectations in the evaluation of any organizational change.[22] Four plants with similar production levels were utilized in the study. Two plants completed a job-enlargement program; two plants, a job-rotation plan. Managers from one of the job-enlargement plants and from one of the job-rotation plants were informed that the change program would result in greater productivity. The managers of the other job-enlargement and job-rotation plants were told the change would only improve relations with employees. There was no significant difference in production levels as a result of job enlargement alone, but the two plants with positive expectations (one job enlargement, one job rotation) did have significantly higher production levels than the other two plants.

Attitude surveys indicated that the expectations were transmitted through the managers to the employees. In this case, management expectations of improved performance became a self-fullfilling prophecy. The expectations were more important than the substantive changes in job design!

THE UTILITY OF CONGRUENCE   The congruence between what content one prefers in a job before performing it and how one describes the job after performing it has been found to be highly related to work satisfaction as well as to supervisor-rated job performance.

Figure 15–5 illustrates how both individual performance and satisfaction for a task were near-optimized. Individuals with high ability were selected for a monitoring task, whose preferred and described job content were congruent. They usually were less concerned about job variety. These individuals exhibited relatively good performance (87 per cent), accuracy, and the highest satisfaction (30.1) of any of the four groups.

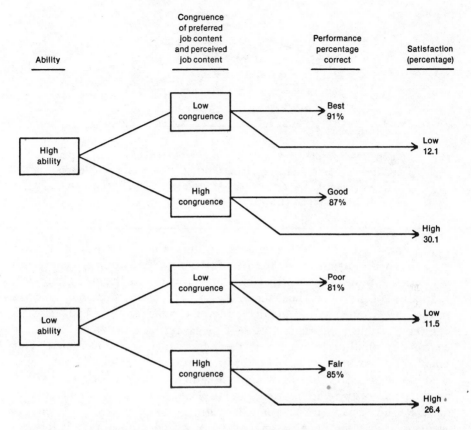

Figure 15–5. Congruence of ability and job structural attributes for monitoring tasks. (Adapted from Barrett, "Task Design, Individual Attributes, Work Satisfaction, and Productivity." In A. Negandhi and B. Wilpert [eds.], *Work Organization Research: European and American Perspectives.* Kent, Ohio: Kent State University Press, 1977.)

CONGRUENCE BETWEEN PERSONALITY PREDISPOSITIONS, JOB DESIGN CHARACTERISTICS, AND ORGANIZATIONAL VARIABLES   Morse and Wagner have presented a model integrating the major variables of the task, the personality of the individual, and the organization.[28] As shown in Figure 15–6, a proper congruence among these three aspects results in increased productivity and high quality of working life. As before, job content includes such factors as the variety individuals find in their jobs, feedback from the jobs and from others, task significance of the jobs, and the autonomy the employees have in their jobs. Another important consideration is the information rate that is inherent in the task itself. The personality predispositions include factors such as the employee's attitude toward individualism, tolerance for ambiguity, and attitude toward authority.

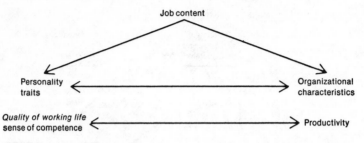

Figure 15–6. Congruence among job characteristics, employee personality, and organizational characteristics. (From Morse, "Person-Job Congruence and Individual Adjustment and Development," *Human Relations,* 28 [1975]: 841–861.)

The organizational characteristics include the influence of control patterns in the organization, the coordination of the work behavior, and the leadership and supervision which are provided in the organization.

In a test of his congruence model, Morse asked supervisors and managers to rate the routineness and predictability of various jobs in a bank, including those of teller and clerk-typist.[27] This gave a measure of job certainty. Personality predisposition traits of the job occupants were measured. This enabled the investigator to place into relatively *certain* jobs 39 employees who revealed a low tolerance for ambiguity, were comfortable in controlling authority relations, preferred working on simple problems, and were low in seeking to be aroused. Thus, personality and job demands were congruent for these 39 employees. A second group of 34 employees with opposite personalities were placed on more *uncertain* jobs, which were less routine and less predictable. An additional 42 employees were placed in jobs with no attempt to match their personality predispositions and the nature of the jobs.

The results of this field study showed that in comparison to the control group, employees placed with congruence between their personalities and jobs revealed a higher sense of competence in performing their jobs. There was no such change in the sense of competence of the individuals in the control group, for whom no personality–job content matching had been attempted.

There were no differences between the congruent groups working on certain or uncertain jobs. This means that both the sense of competence and the increase in sense of competence after being assigned to a more congruent job did not significantly differ between the two groups — one working on more routine, one on less routine tasks. This is a strong statement. It contradicts the universal theory, (a truth applicable to everyone) which derides routine, predictable jobs as dysfunctional and as dissatisfying for all individuals. In other words, those individuals working on routine, predictable jobs can be just as satisfied with such work as those who work on more uncertain, complex jobs. The important factor is the congruence between the individual's personality and the nature of the job itself.

The importance of a personality-job fit was seen in a study involving over 300 individuals working in technical jobs.[30] Figure 15–7 shows that for those individuals with challenging jobs and intrinsic work orientation, both performance and satisfaction were higher than for those people

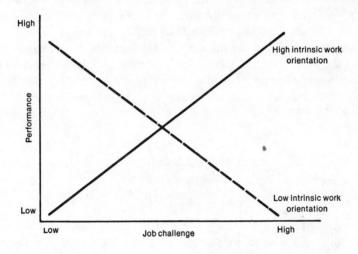

Figure 15–7. Congruence of personality and job challenge. (Adapted from O'Reilly, "Personality-Job Fit: Implications for Individual Attitudes and Performance," *Organizational Behavior and Human Performance*, 18 [1977]: 36–46.)

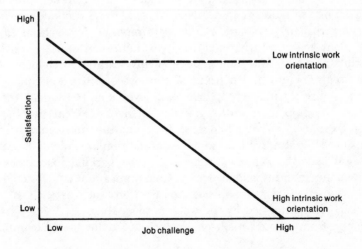

with less intrinsic interest in the work. Conversely, for those personnel
with jobs lacking in challenge, performance and satisfaction were higher
for those who were extrinsically oriented than for those with an intrinsic
work orientation.

Need for Congruence of Routinization and Information-Handling Responsibilities

We have continually emphasized in this book that as the field of indus-
trial/organizational psychology has developed, there has been a movement
away from universal theories of job behavior that take the point of view
that one simple theory can allow us to predict behavior for all individuals
and for all situations. More recent theories have stressed the moderating
effect of different variables upon our prior simpler models. For example,
the industrial engineering approach to job design has as a basic premise
that one job design will be optimal for all individuals — there is one best
way. In the same manner, Herzberg's motivation-hygiene theory as applied
to job design assumes that one prescription can apply to everybody.
Congruence theories point to different job designs for different personalities.

SOME CASES OF REDESIGN OF WORK

Organizational Development and Job Design: Pet Food Plant

Redesigning jobs is often part of an OD effort. As such, it has been argued
that there is no simple, standard procedure that can be applied to all
organizations to redesign jobs.[18] Nevertheless, some general principles can
be discerned. Fairly dramatic results were reported for such an effort in a
large plant manufacturing pet food.[42] Traditional work roles were re-
structured. Since it was a new plant, many innovative changes could be
introduced. These included teams of employees to perform functions with
their pay directly related to their skill level. Employees had the opportunity to develop their skill levels to the highest extent possible. There
was a great deal of interchange of jobs and functions among the team
members. All status symbols were removed from the plant. For instance,
the plant manager was not assigned a special parking space, as is almost
always done in firms and agencies. Communication was fostered among
all those in the firm, and specialized functions such as those of a safety
engineer were performed by the workers themselves.

Benefits from the new plant design included reduction in manufacturing costs, higher quality, decreased employee absenteeism, and a reported annual saving of $600,000 per year.

However, critics argue that the benefits could have been due mainly to the fact that the organization was selective in hiring only "good" prospective employees. Actually, an extensive screening and selection process was conducted for the initial group in an effort to see that each worker's personality was congruent with the OD-inspired design of enriched tasks and roles for the new plant.

Along with the benefits have come unforeseen costs and problems. In reviewing the seven-year history of the dog food plant, Walton found some definite cycles in the satisfaction of the employees with the new system.[44] While job satisfaction at most times has been extremely high, various factors have seen some erosion in the quality of work life. Team evaluation of members for pay increases has been a continuing problem. Cliques developed within teams which made suspect team evaluations of the qualifications of some team members. Other factors had a depressing effect on the new work system; they included the feeling that the larger organization, General Foods, did not fully support the innovations. Perhaps most important was the failure to develop a process for dealing with plant-wide issues that cut across the work teams. In the future, new mechanisms may be implemented to maintain commitment to the work system.

Success and Failures of a Job Enrichment Program: A Federal Agency Effort

While a majority of the many reports about the successes of job enrichment programs focus on their success in improving both productivity and satisfaction, a study conducted in a Federal agency illustrates some of the problems in job enrichment programs.[23] The study involved clerical workers performing relatively routine tasks, such as sorting mail and filing folders. A diagnostic attitude survey conducted before the actual experiment indicated little enthusiasm for and satisfaction with the job itself. Work units were matched in terms of type of activity and were designated as either experimental or control groups. In the experimental group, the innovations included dividing some members into teams and allowing rotation of jobs. In addition, members could decide among themselves how to divide up the various operations. An attempt was made to give employees more responsibility, autonomy, some feedback concerning their performance, and to provide more variety to all members of the units. An extensive training program was conducted for both first-line supervisors and one or two employees from each group. Participation was actively sought in redesigning and enriching the jobs. The control group was left "as was."

Table 15-1. Comparison of enriched and control units.

	Enriched units (percentage of change)	Control units (percentage of change)
Productivity	+23	+ 2
Absenteeism	− 5	+ 7
Turnover	− 6	+20
Attitudes	No Change	No Change

Adapted from Locke, Sirota, and Wolfson, "An Experimental Case Study of the Successes and Failures of Job Enrichment in a Government Agency," *Journal of Applied Psychology,* 61(1976): 701–711.

The results are summarized in Table 15-1. Productivity increased significantly in the enriched working units, and absenteeism and turnover declined in comparison to the control units without the job-enrichment changes. However, the experimental job-enrichment program produced no change in enthusiasm and satisfaction with the job, as such.

This was surprising. If the findings were valid, then the changes in productivity have to be accounted for by some mechanism other than simply improved attitudes toward the work in the organization. As is true in almost all job-enrichment projects, there were changes in work methods, procedures, and the use of personnel, which in and of themselves could result in the increased productivity of the workers. These, of course, are elements in any good industrial engineering approach to increasing worker productivity.

The failure to find any attitude change could first be explained by the fact that the enrichment project, while it did help the work to move in a smoother fashion, did not go far enough in providing increased intrinsic rewards that would have been desired. Second, and perhaps even more important, is the fact that there was no increase in extrinsic rewards for the employees' efforts; pay, raises, and promotions remained as before. In effect, employees now had acquired new skills and responsibilities, but there were no compensating increases in extrinsic rewards for them. This explanation came from interviews conducted after the experiment. Employees viewed their jobs instrumentally; that is, as a means to some desired end. They were extrinsically oriented. Their main concern was with promotions and higher pay. This is not to imply that these employees did not care about more satisfying content in their work, but it was less important to them than the pay and other benefits the job could give them. As was discussed in Chapter 3, this type of attitude concerning a job is quite common among many blue-collar employees and others relatively low on the occupational hierarchy. These results contradict Herzberg's assertion that extrinsic rewards are *not* necessary when designing job-enrichment programs.

Despite the improved productivity resulting from job enrichment, the idea of job enrichment did not spread to other areas of the agency and, in fact, most of the enriched units reverted back to their old style of work, resulting in some bitterness from the employees involved.

INTERACTING EFFECTS

Wage Rates

The Federal agency results are similar to those reported by Sheppard in examining the interaction of wage rates paid to blue-collar employees and the variety, autonomy, and skill challenge of their jobs.[34] The greatest satisfaction was found for those employees who had both high earnings *and* enriched job content. High wages *and* an enriched job combined to provide job satisfaction. But the enriched jobs had no influence upon workers' perceptions of the adequacy of their take-home pay. This finding should alleviate some fears of union leaders who believe that job enrichment may be an endeavor to make employees more satisfied with low wages. Similar results have been obtained with professional white-collar employees. For example, accountants were not willing to give up a raise to enrich the content of their job by "having the opportunity to demonstrate their own ideas". They were willing to give up a raise for a two-hour reduction in their work week.[36]

Specified Goals

In a controlled field experiment by Umstot, Bell, and Mitchell, part-time employees were hired by a firm especially created for the study.[39] The task the "employees" performed was fairly complex; it involved determining the proper zoning code for land plots by comparing two maps. In the enriched condition, skill variety was induced by having the employees choose whatever work strategies they thought were appropriate; in the unenriched condition, they were told what method to use. To promote employee identification with the task, the employees were allowed to select the community where they wanted to work and to write their names on a large wall chart, indicating their responsibility for a given area. In the unenriched condition, the employees were simply given appropriate maps. To make the task meaningful, the enriched groups were given a briefing explaining the importance of their job. Autonomy was manipulated by allowing the enriched groups to choose their own break times and the amount of time they could spend on these breaks. They were also allowed to obtain their own supplies and materials as required. In contrast, the unenriched employee groups remained at their work stations

542 PERSONNEL PSYCHOLOGY

until they were given announced breaks. In addition, the enriched groups were told that they would be responsible for their own work; the unenriched employees were told that their work would be checked. Moreover, with the unenriched groups, the supervisors remained in the employees' workroom, but they were in another room for the enriched groups. To obtain feedback from the job, the enriched groups received computer cards indicating completion of a task that was left in front of them for a full day; but for the unenriched employees, the completed tasks were collected at least once every hour and never mentioned again. The experiment was terminated shortly.

The results of this study were in line with expectations about satisfaction but not productivity. The work satisfaction of the employees in the enriched condition was significantly higher than in the unenriched condition. This was particularly true when no goals were set for the employees. If goals were set, then there was no difference between enriched and unenriched groups that could be attributed to enrichment alone.

In terms of performance, the control group without enrichment actually produced significantly more than the enriched group. If goals were assigned to the groups, then no difference was found between enriched and unenriched groups. This result points out the possibility that when task goals are not set, the enrichment may actually decrease the quantity of production of employees. On the other hand, in view of what has been seen, for instance, in the Lakewood OD program, where in comparison to Doraville, productivity first slumped and began climbing only after a year or more after the introduction of the innovations, it may be that this experiment with part-time employees was too short-lived to yield productivity effects although it did produce the expected results on job satisfaction.

PROBLEMS AND POTENTIALS

There are many pitfalls in job redesign that need to be guarded against. Insufficient attention is paid to what happens to other individuals in surrounding work systems whose jobs are not changed. There is too often little systematic diagnosis of the jobs to be changed. The redesign processes are not systematically evaluated. The consulting staff, line managers, and union officials are not fully informed concerning the projects. The redesign projects are often managed by traditional bureaucratic standards and practices that may be dysfunctional. In order to overcome these problems, Hackman proposes five basic ingredients in successful job redesign projects: (1) key individuals need to be identified, and these individuals must attack the difficult problems from the beginning of the project; (2) diagnosis of the change should be based on a theory of job design before the implementation is begun; (3) specific job design changes are to be explicitly discussed and based on the prior diagnosis with the employees; (4) contingency plans need to be prepared before the project begins to deal with problems and opportunities that may arise as a result of the job redesign; (5) the project is to be continuously evaluated in order to make any changes.[10,11]

Finally, we must note the problems in diffusion of results within firms and agencies. Walton reviewed the comprehensive work redesign projects of eight major organizations of the United States and Europe, including Corning Glass, General Foods, and Volvo.[43] Generally, he found that the success of the redesign projects was well publicized, but the diffusion of the innovation of the projects was often small or nonexistent. Only at Volvo did they find that the innovations had spread throughout the company.

SUMMARY

We have examined a number of different job design concepts along with some available evidence for each approach. It is probably obvious to the student that although there is a fair degree of overlap among the approaches, there are also some significant differences. For example, the motivation-hygiene theory would emphasize change without employee participation and no need to increase salary for added responsibility, while other approaches would take the opposite point of view.

At the present time, a wide array of case studies involving job redesign are available. Unfortunately, few permit us to generalize results since most are not controlled experiments but rather simultaneously change work methods, supervision, pay, actual task, co-workers, and rest pauses.

Our best guess is that job enrichment works well with employees who want to grow, who subscribe to the work ethic, and who will earn more in pay and promotions from enriched jobs.

Despite apparent problems, there have been enough positive results to be confident that new forms of job design will evolve. Management has become aware of alternatives to the traditional work system. As will be seen in the next chapter, the work place can be designed to further improve the system of worker, equipment, and work to be done.

REFERENCES

1. Barrett, G. V., F. Dambrot, and G. Smith. "The Relationship between Individual Attributes and Job Design: Review and Annotated Bibliography," *JSAS Catalog of Selected Documents in Psychology,* 7 (1977): 118 Ms. No. 1608.

2. Barrett, G. V. "Task Design, Individual Attributes, Work Satisfaction, and Productivity." In A. Negandhi and B. Wilpert (eds.), *Work Organization Research: European and American Perspectives,* Kent, Ohio: Kent State University Press, 1978.

3. Blood, M. R., and C. L. Hulin. "Alienation, Environmental Characteristics, and Worker Responses," *Journal of Applied Psychology,* 51 (1967): 284–290.

4. Chaney, F. B. "Employee Participation in Manufacturing Job Design," *Human Factors,* 11 (1969): 101–106.

5. Cherns, A. "The Principles of Sociotechnical Design," *Human Relations,* 29 (1976): 783–792.

6. Davis, L. E., A. B. Cherns, and associates (eds.). *The Quality of Working Life,* Vol. 1. *Problems, Prospects and the State of the Art.* New York: Free Press, 1975.

7. Davis, L. E., A. B. Cherns, and associates (eds.). *The Quality of Working Life,* Vol. II. *Cases and Commentary.* New York: Free Press, 1975.

8. Faunce, W. A. "Automation and the Automobile Worker," *Social Problems,* 6 (1958): 68–78.

9. Ford, R. N. *Motivation through the Work Itself.* New York: American Management Association, 1969.

10. Hackman, J. R. *On the Coming Demise of Job Enrichment* (Technical Report no. 9). New Haven: Yale University, 1974. Contract NONR N00014–67–A–0097–0026, NR 170–744, Office of Naval Research.

11. Hackman, J. R. "Is Job Enrichment Just a Fad?" *Harvard Business Review,* 53, No. 5 (1975): 129–138.

12. Hackman, J. R., and E. E. Lawler. "Employee Reactions to Job Characteristics," *Journal of Applied Psychology,* 55 (1971): 259–286.

13. Hackman, J. R., and G. R. Oldham. "Motivation through the Design of Work: Test of a Theory," *Organizational Behavior and Human Performance,* 16 (1976): 250–279.

14. Hackman, J. R., G. R. Oldham, R. Janson, and K. Purdy. "A New Strategy for Job Enrichment," *California Management Review,* 17, No. 4 (1975): 57–71.

15. Harris, D. H., and F. B. Chaney. *Human Factors in Quality Assurance.* New York: Wiley, 1969.

16. Herzberg, F. "One More Time: How Do You Motivate Employees?" *Harvard Business Review,* 12, No. 1 (1968): 53–62.

17. Herzberg, F. I., and E. A. Rafalko. "Efficiency in the Military: Cutting Costs with Orthodox Job Enrichment," *Personnel,* 52, No. 6 (1975): 38–48.

18. Hulin, C. L. "Worker Background and Job Satisfaction: A Reply," *Industrial and Labor Relations Review,* 26 (1973): 853–855.

19. Huse, E. F., and M. Beer. "Eclectic Approach to Organizational Development," *Harvard Business Review,* 49, No. 5 (1971): 103–112.

20. Jacobson, E., D. Trumbo, G. Cheek, and J. Nangle. "Employee Attitudes toward Technological Change in a Medium Sized Insurance Company," *Journal of Applied Psychology,* 43 (1959): 349–354.

21. Kempner, T., and R. W. Wild. "Job Design Research," *Journal of Management Studies,* 10 (1973): 62–81.

22. King, A. S. "Expectation Effects in Organizational Change," *Administrative Science Quarterly,* 19 (1974): 221–230.

23. Locke, E. A., D. Sirota, and A. D. Wolfson. "An Experimental Case Study of the Successes and Failures of Job Enrichment in a Government Agency," *Journal of Applied Psychology*, 61 (1976): 701–711.

24. Mann, F. C., and L. R. Hoffman. *Automation and the Worker: A Study of Social Changes in Power Plants*. New York: Henry Holt, 1960.

25. Mann, F. C., and L. K. Williams. "Some Effects of the Changing Work Environment in the Office," *Journal of Social Issues*, 18 (1962): 90–101.

26. Miller, E. J. "Technology Territory and Time: The Internal Differentiation of Complex Production Systems," *Human Relations*, 12 (1959): 243–272.

27. Morse, J. J. "Person-Job Congruence and Individual Adjustment and Development," *Human Relations*, 28 (1975): 841–861.

28. Morse, J. J., and F. R. Wagner. "The Congruence of Employee Personality Characteristics, Job Design, and Work System Variables: Implications for Worker Productivity and Experienced Quality of Life at Work." In A. Negandhi and B. Wilpert (eds.), *Work Organization Research: European and American Perspectives*, Kent, Ohio: Kent State University Press, 1978.

29. Oldham, G. R., J. R. Hackman, and J. L. Pearce. "Conditions under Which Employees Respond Positively to Enriched Work," *Journal of Applied Psychology*, 61 (1976): 395–403.

30. O'Reilly, C. A., III. "Personality-Job Fit: Implications for Individual Attitudes and Performance," *Organizational Behavior and Human Performance*, 18 (1977): 36–46.

31. Quinn, R. P., G. L. Staines, and M. R. McCullough. *Job Satisfaction: Is There a Trend?* Manpower Research Monograph 30 (1974).

32. Schrank, R. "On Ending Worker Alienation: The Gaines Pet Food Plant." In R. P. Fairfield (ed.), *Humanizing the Workplace*. Buffalo, N. Y.: Prometheus Books, 1974.

33. Shepard, J. "Worker Background and Job Satisfaction: Reply," *Industrial and Labor Relations Review*, 26 (1973): 856–859.

34. Sheppard, H. L. "Task Enrichment and Wage Levels as Elements in Worker Attitudes," *Journal of Management Studies*, 13 (1976): 49–61.

35. Sheppard, H. L., and N. Q. Herrick. *Where Have All the Robots Gone? Worker Dissatisfaction in the 70's*. New York: Free Press, 1972.

36. Stern, D. "Willingness to Pay for More Agreeable Work," *Industrial Relations*, 17, No. 1 (1978): 85–90.

37. Susman, G. I. "Job Enlargement: Effects of Culture on Worker Responses," *Industrial Relations*, 12 (1973): 1–15.

38. Turner, A. N., and P. R. Lawrence. *Industrial Jobs and the Worker: An Investigation of Response to Task Attributes*. Cambridge: Harvard University Press, 1965.

39. Umstot, D. D., C. H. Bell, Jr., and T. R. Mitchell. "Effects of Job Enrichment and Task Goals on Satisfaction and Productivity: Implications for Job Design," *Journal of Applied Psychology*, 61 (1976): 379–394.

40. Walker, C. R. "Life in the Automatic Factory," *Harvard Business Review*, 36, No. 1 (1958): 111–119.

41. Walker, C. R., and R. H. Guest. *The Man on the Assembly Line*. Cambridge: Harvard University Press, 1952.

42. Walton, R. E. "How to Counter Alienation in the Plant," *Harvard Business Review*, 50, No. 6 (1972): 70–81.

43. Walton, R. E. "The Diffusion of New Work Structures: Explaining Why Success Didn't Take," *Organizational Dynamics*, 3 (Winter 1975): 3–22.

44. Walton, R. E. "The Topeka Story: Teaching an Old Dog Food New Tricks," *The Wharton Magazine*, 2, No. 2 (1977): 38–46.

45. Wild, R. W., and T. Kempner. "Influence of Community and Plant Characteristics on Job Attitudes of Manual Workers," *Journal of Applied Psychology*, 56 (1972): 106–113.

46. Wyatt, S., and R. Marriott. "A study of attitudes to factory work." In P. R. Lawrence et al. (eds.), *Organizational Behavior and Administration*. Homewood, Ill.: Richard D. Irwin, 1961.

16 THE COSTS OF WORK

IN BRIEF In the search for improved systems performance and human satisfaction at work, psychologists concern themselves with the design of jobs, equipment, workplaces, job performance aids, information systems, and aspects of the work environment. They concentrate on the role of human factors, or the personnel subsystem, in the complex man-machine-environment systems that constitute working organizations.

Since World War II, psychologists have devoted special attention to the problems of workers as monitors in complex systems. Vigilance and inspection tasks make special demands on workers, whose roles are increasingly those of overseers or standby controllers of more or less automatic machine systems or information display equipment.

Simulation of man-machine-environment complexes has become increasingly sophisticated, and is now employed in a wide range of problem areas, including selection, training, proficiency measurement, and systems research and development. The use of simulation is expected to contribute greatly to our understanding of complicated systems ranging from automobile driving to space travel.

Selection and classification try to match employees with appropriate jobs; then training prepares them better for their work. Psychologists also deal

547

with the design of appropriate jobs, equipment, workplace, and environment so that the performance of employees selected and trained for the job will be fast, accurate, of high quality, and satisfying to the job occupant. Economic considerations will also govern the design of work, as do the human costs of accidents, fatigue, boredom, training time, and the energy expenditure required. These human costs will be a main concern of this chapter. However, before discussing them, we need to consider employees at work with tools, equipment, and machines, and how we study such work.

Prescientific Beginnings

People have been toolmakers for over a million years. Probably the first events in tool development occurred when our ancestors discovered that they could extract edible roots from the earth more easily with a stick than with their hands and could crush a nut more readily with a stone. An important step occurred in the evolutionary process of tool design some 35,000 years ago when they learned routinely to make and use tools, thus enabling them to perform their tasks more efficiently.

An efficient tool or implement has to fulfill several requirements. First, the tool must perform effectively the function for which it was intended. An axe, for example, must separate wood fibers cleanly and be withdrawn easily. Second, tools have to be proportioned to the body dimensions of the operator. Third, they should be suitably adjusted to the strength and work capacity of the user. Fourth, they should not cause unnecessary fatigue while being used. Fifth, they must be adapted to our senses. Sixth, the initial and maintenance costs of the tool must be economical. By application of the techniques of applied biomechanics it is possible, using the above standards, to study the various implements used by our ancestors, such as the axe, rake, and scythe. It is interesting that the folk norms concerning the optimum dimensions of tools, such as the axe, correspond very closely to what biomechanical analysis shows to be optimal.[21]

While the evolution of the optimal tool design was an exceedingly long process, there were times when tools evolved much more quickly through the efforts of one or two people. The pace of tool design is often increased by the exigencies of war. Shaka, the famous Zulu leader and warrior, made a dramatic change when he redesigned the traditional fighting spear. In Zulu tribes an extremely long throwing spear was used by the combatants. The warring tribes would stand some distance apart and throw the long spears at each other while protected by shields. Shaka introduced a shorter, thicker spear. The warrior could then rush forward, use the spear to catch the enemy's shield to turn it aside, and then plunge the spear into the adversary.

Post-1940

The evolutionary approach or the genius of one person proved effective with simple tools; however, this approach has not been particularly effective in the development of more complex systems of personnel and machines. Although there were scattered applications of human-factor principles during World War I, a concentrated attack on the problems of operator-machine interaction was brought about by the demands of World War II.

Before that time, machines generally were designed by engineers for their mechanical efficiency. But during World War II, machines became more complex and were so critical that an integration of skills was needed to design optimal operator-machine systems. Some of the early problems concerned the design of radarscopes, antiaircraft systems, and aircraft cockpits. It was during this period that psychologists were especially concerned with the layout of workplaces and the design of controls and displays. This is sometimes called the "knobs and dials" era, since certain basic principles related to such hardware were developed and applied. As the field has evolved, emphasis has shifted from first, the *retrofit* (changing the original design) of machines, to second, the design of elements of a machine (the knobs and dials), to third, the fitting of machines to their human operators. The fourth and present phase of the evolution is taking the systems approach to the combination of machine and operator, beginning at the conceptual level well before any equipment is built.[12]

Systems Analysis

There is little doubt that the systems approach to problem-solving has had a great deal of impact upon psychology. Systems analysis for operators with machines, materials and equipment has been described as organized common sense or logical problem-solving. Of course, systems analysis involves more than this; it includes a set of techniques for management decision-making, planning, and design of both complex equipment and more intangible programs. Fundamentally, the systems analyst attempts to look at a complex process as a whole with the idea that the best results are obtained when a system is seen in total perspective. The components of any system can then be broken into parts suitable for analysis.

The process of systems analysis implies a sequence of activities that includes a definition and a detailed description of the system, usually in terms of its overall requirements. (A system can be considered to be any combination of operator and machine components interacting for some purpose.) * A functional description is then given in terms of the com-

* Examples of such complex operator-machine systems are an automobile assembly line, a roadside hamburger stand, a typist and a typewriter, and a first-aid station.

ponent subsystems and how they interact with each other. Then overall objectives and criteria of system performance must be stated as explicitly as possible. In Chapter 7 we discussed in detail the criterion problem; the difficulties encountered there are also found in system analysis projects. Once the criteria for optimal system performance are determined, it is possible to consider different configurations of the system in order to approach optimum performance. Often it is feasible to simulate the alternate systems by mathematical models. By use of an appropriate model and computer techniques it is possible to compare all possible systems on a multitude of selected variables. One system may be found to satisfy one set of criteria, while another system meets another set. For example, in the design of urban transportation, a bus system might be cheaper but slower, while a subway system would be faster but more expensive. This is a typical case of a trade-off—by gaining one advantage you lose another. Often the trade-off is between improved performance with higher cost, or poorer performance with lower cost.

There are various techniques of system analysis, including the following:

System pictogram, where an overall picture of the system is given, listing and depicting all the operator-machine components and the conditions under which they operate.

Functional analysis, where each requirement of the system is stated in detail and the drawing of a diagram shows the various functions to be performed and the relationships among these functions.

Decision analysis, where a chart is prepared showing what decision the operator must make, what information is required for the decision, and what action the operator has to take to execute the decision.

Activity analysis, where data are collected on each of the operator's tasks during the day and presented in chart form, showing the percentage of time spent on each activity.

Flow analysis, where the events in a system are depicted sequentially, perhaps with a time scale.[57]

Since the systems analysis approach has been successful in bringing into operational use many multimillion-dollar complex military systems, it is understandable that political leaders see this as a promising new tool for attacking other problems such as water pollution, air pollution, health problems, and urban blight.[51] The application of systems analysis is particularly interesting to applied psychologists, since the problems of any complex system invariably involve people as a component. By taking a comprehensive view of a problem, systems analysis requires the coordinated efforts of engineers, psychologists, mathematicians, physiologists, and political scientists. More generally, the systems analysis approach to management and decision-making is becoming more widespread because of its broad usefulness.

Personnel Subsystem

The introduction of the personnel subsystem into the Air Force management philosophy in 1960 was, in effect, the application of the systems approach to industrial and organizational psychology. This was an important achievement because all major systems now had to take into account the important aspects of personnel in the system, not after the equipment had been built, but in the very early planning and conceptual stages.[36]

The personnel subsystem concept involves systematically answering a number of questions such as:

1. Should personnel be in the system?
2. If personnel should be in the system, what functions should they perform?
3. What type of personnel should be selected to perform the functions?
4. How should the task and equipment be designed so that personnel can perform most effectively?
5. How should personnel be trained in the most effective manner?

To answer these questions, systematic study is made of the qualitative and quantitative personnel requirements. These concern how many persons will be required to operate and maintain the contemplated system and what their qualifications will need to be. Once these questions are answered, it is possible to design the equipment and associated tasks required of the personnel in the system. After the type and number of people are determined and an idea of the equipment they will use and the tasks they will perform are decided, the personnel subsystem specialists can evolve a complete training program. This will include the training concepts and plan, and a determination of the equipment, such as simulators, that will be used in training.

This personnel planning is needed before any equipment is ever built because people are a functional part of the total system. The design must integrate them comfortably into the system once the equipment for it has been built. This is the principle of *concurrency*, meaning that all aspects of the system should become operational, or usable, at the same time. If we were to wait until the equipment is built to select and train personnel, there would naturally be a considerable lag time between the completion of the system and its ultimate use.

The final phase of the personnel subsystem program is the testing and evaluation of the system. This is to verify that the system can perform its functions.

The Bell Telephone Company has successfully used the personnel subsystem concept in developing a number of systems. For example, the directory assistance operator's position involves more than 44,000 people at an annual cost of $300 million. For over fifteen years, studies were conducted by psychologists to develop a computer and cathode-ray-tube system that would be optimal for the task demands. The human factors were considered before large sums of money were committed to the new computer-based system. It was introduced only after determining that the new computer system could save sufficient operator time to make it cost-effective.[44]

SIMULATION

In the study of operator-machine systems, the process of simulation has become of prime importance. Munsterberg used an early form of a simulator to represent a street intersection and traffic situation.[59] Since his 1913 report, five ways have been developed for using simulators. First, a simulator can be used to *select* individuals. Viteles' simulation of the motor operator's job is illustrative,[88] as are leaderless group discussions used in assessment centers to simulate managerial and social situations.

Second, simulation is used in *training*. A simulator can be effectively used to train individuals such as future astronauts or pilots in a safe environment, allowing them to perform and perfect maneuvers that would be either impossible or uneconomical by any other method. Such simulators result in significant fuel savings. This becomes increasingly important when fuel is in short supply. During the 1970s, the federal government spent over $5,000,000 per year for the development of simulators for flight training.

Third, a simulator can be used for *proficiency measurement*. It may be important to know if a pilot still retains certain skills on critical maneuvers. For example, emergency situations can be simulated that would not be safe in a real situation, and the reaction of the pilot can be tested.

A fourth use of simulation is as a *performance aid* to managers. The flow of materials in a refinery may be simulated. Managers can manipulate the complex variables in the simulation to see potential effects of their decisions to make changes in the system.

A fifth use is for *systems research and development*. The supersonic transport (SST) was to be a very complex aircraft with a control task often requiring five operators at a time. An SST simulator was tied to the Federal Aviation Agency's National Aviation Facility Experimental Center. By using this simulator, operators could perform real time flight in a simulated 400-by-400-nautical-mile air traffic control area around New York City, interacting with 100 other aircraft. In this manner, they could determine the effects of the air traffic control system on the supersonic transport design and also determine what effects the supersonic transport would have on the air traffic control system. So, before an extremely expensive and complex aircraft becomes operational, simulation will actually help to design the aircraft itself, and in the same manner help to determine what new equipment and requirements will be imposed on the air traffic control system by this large, extremely fast aircraft. And it can also help in the decision on whether to go ahead with a total system such as the SST or to abandon it as too costly.

The Automobile Driving Simulator — An Example

Let's look in detail at how a psychologist uses the automobile driving simulator as a research tool. The advantages of using a simulator for studying automobile driving behavior are manifold and vary with the specific research question.

1. COMPLETE CONTROL OF VEHICLE VARIABLES   In a sophisticated simulator, the computer which controls the characteristics of the simulated vehicle can be programmed to reflect the variables of any vehicle now on the road or of those planned for the future (much as the supersonic transport simulator previously mentioned is used). Vehicle acceleration and deceleration, and a standard steering ratio can readily be modified to meet the needs of the research design. The vehicle variables will remain constant until changed.

2. CONTROL OF HIGHWAY VARIABLES   In the real-world research situation, investigators wanting to study driving behavior in a controlled situation must do it in an artficial testing area. Or they can go onto the real-world highways, but they run a concurrent risk of knowing that they cannot control the behavior of the other vehicles on the road. In contrast, in a simulator, the highway can be designed to fit the needs of the research investigation. Important variables such as types of lanes, buildings, curbs, and traffic controlling devices can be varied according to the purpose of the study. This control, of course, is usually impossible in the real world.

3. CONTROL OVER ENVIRONMENTAL CONDITIONS   When the investigators want to study varied behavior out in the real world, they know that much time will be lost and conditions will change radically for their sample of drivers, since at different times it may rain, snow, or be hazy. In contrast, the simulator gives the examiners both control over and flexibility in their

choice of environmental conditions. Varying light conditions can be precisely controlled, including illumination at dusk and night. Extreme environmental conditions such as heavy rain can be introduced. Road or tire coefficients of friction can be changed, allowing simulation of wet or icy road conditions. This allows research design to reflect important variables that are extremely difficult to repeat in the real world.

4. SAFETY OF PARTICIPANTS AND RESEARCH PROGRAMS   The researchers who study driving behavior in the real world must always be conscious of the fact that there is a certain degree of risk or hazard involved in their investigation. Since they have control neither of the other vehicles nor of the driving behavior of their subject, a degree of uncertainty is involved. Obviously, there are large and broad numbers of important studies that cannot be attempted by investigators in the real world. Emergency situations cannot be presented to the driver in the real world because of the hazards involved.

One of the chief advantages of a simulator is that the participants in the research program are perfectly safe. This fact allows researchers to contrive situations where, for example, a driver could approach an unmarked intersection at 40 miles per hour while other intersecting cars pass through the intersection at the same speed or higher speeds. A situation such as this could not be duplicated in the real world because of risk of injury to the driver and the vehicle.

5. EFFECTIVE UTILIZATION OF SUBJECTS   The laboratory simulator allows researchers, utilizing the appropriate research design, to study the same subjects under a variety of conditions. Subjects can be tested under one condition and then can be immediately retested with variables such as vehicle, highway, or environmental conditions changed. The subjects can also be placed in a stressful situation or be administered alcohol or drugs without hazard. No elaboration of this point is needed. This type of research is just not feasible for researchers in the real world.

6. MEASUREMENT OF INDEPENDENT AND DEPENDENT VARIABLES   Much of the preceeding discussion directly relates to this main point: in general, researchers in the real world have little control over relevant variables. Researchers with a simulator, on the other hand, measure all relevant variables in the research design. Both own vehicle's and other vehicle's position as a function of time can be measured adequately. This sort of measurement is usually impossible in the real world. Also, researchers have greater control over experiments, since irrelevant variables such as change in light levels can be eliminated from the situation. In essence, this means that any number of subjects can be studied under exactly identical conditions.

7. GENERATION OF HYPOTHESES FOR VERIFICATION IN THE REAL WORLD   The final advantage that the simulator enjoys over investigations in the real world is largely a function of the above considerations. Since the simulator allows experimenters to control their variables precisely, there is less error variance introduced into the research design. This means that if there is a relationship between the variables, the simulated situation should reveal it. Because of the number of uncontrolled variables in real-world driving research, such as differential exposure and differing environmental conditions, test effects may be obscured. Research results from a simulated situation can, however, be cast as hypotheses to be tested in the real world. In this way, the prominent variables revealed by simulation research can be investigated rather than the myriads of variables that initially face researchers.

The preceding discussion, while specifically related to an automobile simulator, can of course be applied to simulations of space, undersea, and avionic equipment, as well as industrial processes and equipment requiring skilled human operators. Often the most compelling reason for using simulation is that the processes can be studied in no other way. This has been most obvious for the space situation, but even in the more mundane driving task this can be shown to be the case.

Problems in Simulation

AMOUNT REQUIRED   One of the most critical questions in simulation technology is: How much fidelity is required to reach a particular desired objective? Often simple simulators are adequate for procedural training but more sophisticated devices are essential for certain research problems.[14] Increasing the fidelity of a simulation to approximate the real world more closely usually increases its cost. Examples can be cited to illustrate the effects of both inadequate and excessive fidelity. Thus, in evaluating the performance of two types of aircraft displays to follow terrain, a simulation that lacked fidelity in the processing of terrain data uncovered only a negligible difference between the two differing displays. Nevertheless, when the comparison was made with a simulation of greater fidelity, decided differences were obtained between the two displays.[71] These differences were later substantiated during actual flight tests. In the same manner, there have been cases of excessive expenditures for fidelity.

VARIABLES TO BE SIMULATED   Sometimes a simulated variable, previously considered surplus and irrelevant, has drastically changed the results of an investigation.[55] A comparison was made between an "inside-out" display (view of terrain from inside aircraft) and an "outside-in" display (view of terrain and aircraft from outside) of aircraft. In a stationary vibrationless simulator, the outside-in display was clearly superior; with motion, there was little or no difference between displays. The results support the contention that motion is an extremely relevant variable in the evaluation of displays that are to be used under conditions of motion.

AN EXAMPLE: LUNAR GRAVITY SIMULATION AND HUMAN PERFORMANCE   The trade-off between fidelity and cost is an extremely complex consideration, but as yet there are no clear rules specifying the degree of fidelity required for any specific problem. Illustrative of alternatives is how we can simulate gravity on the moon. Since the moon has one-sixth the earth's gravity, lunar gravity can be simulated (1) in an aircraft in a parabolic trajectory; (2) in a swimming pool to provide comparable buoyancies; (3) by attaching counterweights-in-balance to yield lift (Figure 16–1); (4) by placing subjects on inclined planes; and (5) by attaching motor-driven springs. Each has its advantages and disadvantages. For example, the flight trajectory can last a maximum of one minute only, there are special monotony problems with water immersion, and so on.[76]

RESULTS OF LUNAR GRAVITY SIMULATION   The lunar gravity simulations have been of value both for training of astronauts and for design improvements. In an investigation of maintenance tasks, it was determined that lunar gravity and a pressurized suit imposed a 150 per cent decrement in performance compared with the usual shirt-sleeve performance.[77] This

Figure 16–1. Counterbalance techniques for lunar gravity simulation. (From *Human Factors, 10,* 1968, p. 396. Copyright 1968 by The Human Factors Society, Inc., and reproduced by permission.)

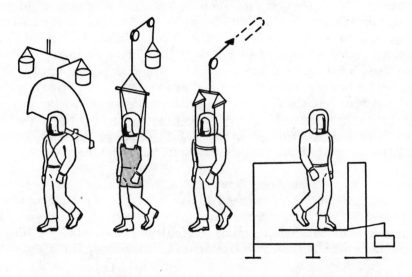

finding led to specific recommendations on how to perform specific tasks and specific design recommendations.

Simulation is a major approach to studying accident behavior—the bodily cost of work—along with the more traditional methods of case studies, analyses of personnel records of severity and frequency, and controlled experiments on the speed and accuracy of operating equipment and using tools.

ACCIDENTS

For psychology, the study of accidents is of central importance, because accidents loom large as a cost of work. The cost is personal and social as well as economic. Accidents pose a confusing but extremely important problem, since they result in significant loss to our nation both in life and in economic costs. Unfortunately, few topics are so shrouded in mythology and on few topics are so many people willing to voice their uninformed opinion, no matter how naive it might be.

Scope of the Problem

The probability of death from motor vehicles and commercial aviation alone (per hour of exposure) is equivalent to the probability of death from disease for the entire U.S. population.[81] And we don't even consider accidents at work, at home or in recreational activities.

The magnitude of the accident problem can be illustrated by a few simple figures. In the United States the accident-death toll has been above 100,000 per year since 1963. This is despite increasing attention to safer cars, speed limits of 55 miles per hour and industrial safety legislation. In addition, disabling injuries are over 10 million per year (disabling injuries are those which result in an employee being off the job at least one day or longer) and about 400,000 people per year are permanently disabled. In terms of financial loss, the cost of accidents has been estimated at over $21 billion per year, including medical expenses and loss of wages. For young adults in the United States, up to the age of thirty-five, automobile accidents are the major cause of death. Newer information from the World Health Organization shows that this social tragedy is now taking place in the younger developing countries of Africa and South America. For example, in the Latin American countries of Chile, Costa Rica, and Venezuela, the leading cause of death in young adults is now traffic accidents.

Approximately a quarter of a million people are killed throughout the world in traffic accidents every year. More than seven million are injured.

The United States still has the highest number of people killed each year in traffic accidents, but it also has one of the lowest rates of fatalities per motor vehicle mile. For example, there are usually approximately 6 fatalities per 100,000,000 passenger miles, while in some developing countries in Africa, there will be 60 fatalities per 100,000,000 passenger miles. In India the rate is 10 to 15 times higher than in the United States.

The World Health Organization believes that this epidemic of traffic accidents, which seems to be a continually growing phenomenon, can be conquered by using the same methods that conquered smallpox and that control malaria.

This contention is extremely doubtful. Unlike such diseases, traffic accidents have mutiple causes and there is no possibility of making every individual an effective driver by some simple procedure. Additionally, concentration on the problem is hampered by the fatalistic attitude toward accidents. They are considered by many as "acts of God" or chance phenomena, and therefore outside the realm of scientific inquiry.[38] This is illustrated by a newspaper headline, "FAA [Federal Aviation Agency] Boss Writes Off Disaster as 'Fate.' "

We have tended to concentrate on motor vehicle accidents, since for most industrial employees and the readers of this text the possibility of injury or death while traveling to work far exceeds the risk of an accident on the job! In addition, a large number of employees in many organizations are required to drive vehicles as a major or minor part of their jobs, resulting in approximately one-third of all work-related injury deaths.[37] An exception is in certain high-risk occupations such as mining. However, even for Air Force pilots, automobile driving is a greater hazard than flying an airplane. The automobile statistics are also related to the fact that over the past twenty-five years the frequency of job-incurred injuries has been reduced by 40 per cent.[67]

The Causes

Until the mid-1960s, it was axiomatic that human negligence was the prime cause of death of over 50,000 people on American highways each year. Ralph Nader's controversial book *Unsafe at Any Speed* was the first popular, yet thoughtful, analysis of the driver-accident problem.[60] Looking at the driver-vehicle-highway system, Nader emphasized that often the vehicle or highway, rather than the driver, was to blame for an accident.

An illustration was what happened to W. Haddon, the first federal Traffic Safety Administrator. His accelerator pedal stuck under the carpet while he was driving a new automobile on an expressway. In this particular automobile, the carpet was so positioned that the accelerator pedal stuck when pressed down to the full throttle position. Although a mishap was avoided by Haddon, if a fatal accident had occurred, the cause of death would undoubtedly have been labeled by the investigating officer "driver error—driving at an excessive speed." This small incident illustrates an important point: often the direct or contributing cause of an accident may not be the fault of the person driving the vehicle but the poor design or assembly of the vehicle; nevertheless the accident may be reported as due to a human failure.

Dealing with Infrequent Events

But paradoxically, while accidents take an enormous toll on life and property, they are infrequent events. The average motorist must drive 60,000 miles to be involved in a traffic accident. It is impossible to observe drivers passively until they are involved in an accident. Therefore, we turn to alternatives to learn indirectly about accidents. We create simulated emergencies to study driver reactions. Or, we survey near-accidents, more frequent events, where accidents could have happened but were avoided. We can study simulated emergencies and near-accidents to learn more about the accident problem. Simulators become of central importance in the study of responses to emergencies and near accidents.

SIMULATED EMERGENCIES   Simulators have been constructed to study how individuals actually do react in emergency situations that could potentially lead to accidents. In an unprogrammed simulator, the driver has complete control over all aspects of the driving task. The driver sits in a typical automobile. The screen in front displays a highway and surrounding terrain. When the key is turned, the start of the motor is heard, and when the driver shifts into first gear and lets out the clutch, there is movement on the screen and the driver experiences the illusion of driving. The driver is free to go as fast as possible, make any turns, and stop at any time.

The illusion of driving is provided by the various elements in the terrain model of both rural and urban highways, with trees, billboards, and houses, which the driver sees only on the TV projection on the front screen. A TV camera rides on a transport system above the terrain model. The driver controls the movement of the TV camera over the terrain model as the simulated auto is "driven." What is seen on the screen in front depends on the driving. Exact measurements of driver performance can be recorded, such as reaction time, rate of brake depression, speed, longitudinal and latitudinal distance on the terrain model, and steering wheel turns.

Under the above simulation conditions, reaction to emergencies was studied as follows. Each driver was familiarized first with the terrain and the simulated auto by "driving" around the terrain model several times.

Each driver was instructed to attempt to obtain certain selected speeds with the speedometer covered on a straight highway. On the return trip, a small shed was passed, located beside the road. The driver drove past this shed at a constant speed a number of times before a pedestrian dummy emerged onto the highway at a controlled rate when the driver was a specified distance away. The speed of the simulated automobile was controlled by instructing the driver to press or let up on the accelerator pedal before the shed was approached. Effectiveness (reaction time, braking, timing, et cetera) in responding to the emergency was found to relate to perceptual style. Field-independent people could respond more effectively than field-dependent ones (see below).

It is interesting to note that these effects would have been missed had we merely been measuring simple reaction time of the drivers to stop-and-go signals, for what one experiences when driving down the usual highway is a myriad of impinging stimuli. The scene in front of the driver is perceptually very complex, with a constantly shifting panorama of cars, people, and scenery. From this perceptually complex world, the driver has to extract and react to specific significant aspects of the environment and ignore other parts of it. For example, on considering the pedestrian emerging from the shed, the driver is looking down a supposedly deserted highway when unexpectedly a figure emerges into the field of vision. First, the driver has to extract this figure from the complex background. Once extracted, the figure must be identified and responded to appropriately. If what is extracted and identified is a human, the driver must immediately attempt to stop the car. If a flying piece of newspaper had been extracted, it might have been ignored. Thus, using reaction time to a simple red light to measure driver proficiency is much too simple an analog to the complex driving situation.

PERCEPTIONS AND SIMULATED EMERGENCIES Considered to be much more appropriate was the type of test that would require extracting a figure from a more complex background. Witkin and others, in a long series of studies, have identified those people who are most capable of extracting a simple figure from a more complex one as being *field-independent,* and those less proficient as being *field-dependent.*[98] In addition to using the type of test illustrated, Witkin has also measured this ability by a *rod and frame* test. Both tests were used to determine individual driver perceptual styles.

Field independence correlated 0.67 with simple reaction time, 0.74 with deceleration rate, and 0.50 with whether or not the driver hit the pedestrian.[5] The smallest relationship was found with tendency to hit or miss the pedestrian—which, just as in the real world, is the biggest problem. Near-misses are more predictable than actual accidents.

The results of the simulation have been confirmed in the real world. A group of 60 commercial drivers was tested on both field-dependence and selective attention, another measure of information-processing ability. Using a postdictive design (Chapter 9) and accident records for the previous five years, investigators found that both tests correlated with accident involvement. It is interesting to note that the selective-attention test, which previously predicted both pilot and bus driver performance, is a task involving competition between auditory messages. There is no visual component in the selective-attention test. This supports the view that the driver effectiveness is based on the efficiency of central information processing ability.[56]

In sum, these research results support the hypothesis that field-independent drivers with effective information-processing ability are more competent in responding to emergency situations. Commercial drivers can be tested for field-independence quite easily. This would contribute to reducing the accident rate. But unfortunately, such a screening program before granting a license to all drivers would be politically difficult to introduce. Yet it would be quite possible to provide extra training for these individuals who are field-dependent and lack information-processing ability, so that they could overcome their perceptual deficits to become more effective drivers. Such a training program, designed to improve these information-processing abilities, was conducted for older drivers, using a Solomon 4-group design (Chapter 13). Results were positive, as had been hypothesized.[83] A "costs versus benefits" analysis suggested that identifying drivers with deficient information-processing ability and increasing those processing attributes would in five years produce savings (from reduced accidents) matching the cost of screening and training.[4]

NEAR-ACCIDENTS Along with research on driver errors and performance in simulated emergencies, an approach used to offset the infrequency of occurrence of accidents is to concentrate on near-accidents.

Actual accidents occur much less often than unsafe behavior. We are all too aware of drivers who are reckless in their operation of the automobile but manage to avoid many accidents—although one expects that their time will come eventually. For example, a worker may remove a safety guard on the press in order to speed up production. The worker's hand may slip into the unguarded area but he or she may be fortunate and escape injury because the press was fully depressed when the unsafe act was performed. Other workers may be equally reckless but their hands may slip into the dangerous area before the presses are fully extended, resulting in crushed hands. At times, most of us have engaged in unsafe behavior and then wondered if things had been slightly different, how badly we might have injured ourselves or have injured others because of our actions. Because unsafe behavior does occur more frequently than actual accidents and since the less frequent actual accidents, when they do occur, involve some degree of chance (the same unsafe behavior may at one time cause an accident and may not another time), researchers have found it useful to study near-accidents. Whitlock, Clouse, and Spencer developed a critical-incidents checklist of unsafe behaviors which has proved to be quite reliable (0.74 to 0.93).[94] They also found that the unsafe measures of behavior are about as predictive during subsequent years of actual injuries on the job as were data on injuries themselves predictive of subsequent accidents. The checklist focused on personal safety, alertness, an interest in safety of fellow employees, housekeeping, and safety in operating machines and equipment. These factors are illustrated in Figure 16–2 with some examples of unsafe behavior found in one plant.

The Accident-Prone Individual

The accident-prone individual is seen as someone who runs into an unusually large share of errors, mishaps, and accidents either at home, at work, or while driving. Empirically, some people do have more accidents than others. Nevertheless, some or all of this may be due to the fact that some individuals are exposed to more hazards than others and therefore have a greater probability of having some sort of accident.[15] As an illustration, we know that the accident frequency of miners is three times that of individuals working in manufacturing firms, and that this accident frequency is undoubtedly higher than that of librarians. One would hesitate to call miners more accident-prone than librarians simply because miners have more accidents on their jobs. So, obviously, we must take into account the degree of risk in each occupation and job. This same reasoning, of course, applies to drivers on the road. Some drivers will drive two or three times as many miles in a year as other drivers. Therefore, they will have a much greater exposure than those who drive less.

It is evident that we must refine our original statement of accident-proneness and take into account the risk of accidents. We need to define accident prone to those individuals who have more accidents than others exposed to the same risks. Yet even this statement needs qualification. If we compute the frequency of accidents of 100 employees working in the same kind of job in a plant, suppose we find that 10 of the 100 have been injured in each of two successive years. Suppose the same person is injured twice. Is the person accident-prone? To be labeled as accident-prone, a person must be the victim of accidents more frequently than expected by

---

FACTOR I—Personal Safety

Ran up steps instead of walking. Ran down steps. Ran through work area instead of walking. Walked under or worked under suspended lead on crane. Failed to wear safety glasses in work areas. Failed to wear face shields and neoprene gloves when taking generator levels or adding electrolyte to F_2 generators. Failed to wear face shields and neoprene gloves when entering day tank room. Failed to wear face shields and neoprene gloves when taking UF_4 samples from reactor. Failed to wear respirators when working in the vacuum cleaner room. Failed to observe "no smoking" rules in operating area. Carried open cigarette packs in contaminated areas.

FACTOR II—Alertness to and Interest in Safety of Fellow Employees

Failed to actuate crane bell before moving the crane. Failed to actuate bell at intervals while the crane bridge is in motion. Participated in horseplay. Failed to clear up oil spills (floor). Failed to sweep up sweeping compound from floor. Failed to clean up water spills (floor). Failed to close tower pit hatch door. Failed to adequately purge system before system is opened.

FACTOR III—Housekeeping (Work Area)

Blocked safety showers or walkways or exits with drums, equipment, supplies, or debris. Failed to immediately clean up powder spills. Failed to store UF_6 cylinder lifting device in its proper location. Failed to store drum carts, equipment handling chokes in their proper location. Failed to report system leaks or breaks to the foreman-in-charge. Failed to put paper or container on floor to contain power or UF_6 spillage. Failed to pick up contaminated tools, vacuum cleaner hose, and other such equipment at the end of a job. Failed to report to the foreman or to pick up bolts, nuts, pipe, or other obstacles that constitute a tripping or stumbling hazard. Failed to keep equipment or material storage areas orderly so that material and equipment can be safely moved into and out of the storage area.

FACTOR IV—Operation of Machines and Equipment

Left Modine trap valving manifold when Modine trap was draining. Failed to check valves downstream of rupture disc before heating cold traps. Failed to leak test system before valving on stream. Failed to personally check system valving. Failed to valve system properly. Failed to install safety wire on Chicago couplings. Failed to report improperly guarded pulleys or gears to foreman-in-charge. Failed to report faulty drive belts to foreman-in-charge. Failed to keep equipment sufficiently clean so that equipment failures can be detected at the beginning. Left valving station when transferring HF from storage to "Dry Tank." Failed to report the existence or use of improvised or make-shift equipment or accessories to the foreman-in-charge.

Figure 16–2. List of unsafe incidents. (Adapted from Whitlock, personal communication, 1964.)

chance on a job and above and beyond the accident rate expected from the hazards of the job. No, the person is not necessarily accident-prone, because by chance alone we would expect some individuals to have more accidents than others, while in the same period the majority would have no accidents at all.

Despite these qualifications, there is some evidence that women who have kitchen accidents are also more apt to have automobile accidents. Guilford observed over two hundred women in a kitchen laboratory.[35] Their near-accidents, personal injury, and property damage were recorded while they prepared two meals over a two-hour period. The near-accidents were related to actual accidents in the kitchen. The fact that women who had the most kitchen accidents under controlled conditions also had the most automobile accidents gives support to the "accident-proneness" concept.

Experience and Age as Related to Accidents

In one of the most extensive and well-controlled investigations of the relationship between accidents and age, accident records of over 2,500 employees in a copper plant were studied.[87] An examination of the employees from a large department indicated that accidents were more frequent for newer employees. Accidents reached a plateau after five months of employment. This plateau was maintained for a period of over 5 years. But those who terminated their employment after 30 months on the job revealed a consistently higher accident frequency than those who remained on the job. This is consistent with the often-stated hypothesis that a natural selection process does occur. Those who are most suited for the work experience fewer accidents and also remain on the job, while those less suited have more accidents and tend to leave. Accidents and quitting are both forms of withdrawal from the job (Chapter 3).

After a formal training program was initiated, the especially frequent accident rate experienced by new employees was reduced and a plateau was reached at the end of 3 months instead of 5 months.

As a direct test of accident rates of the older and younger worker, two groups of workers were matched in terms of job experience, but with approximately a 12-year mean difference in age. The younger group were in their twenties and the older group in their forties. The younger group exhibited higher accident rates than did their older work companions—a result similar to that seen in driving.[31]

Transient States and Accident Behavior

We all feel at times that we are having "a bad day." People exhibit emotional swings in mood from one day to the next. Some fluctuate more than others. Evidence indicates that when people are in an emotionally depressed state they are more likely to have accidents.[46] Similarly, individuals who are continually faced with either physical or emotional stress, according to several investigations, tend to have more accidents than those who are not.[42,75]

Stress research suggests that when faced with stress, individuals on a new job that requires new modes of responding are apt to show a change in the quality of their work. We would therefore suspect that those individuals who are under stress while performing new jobs or tasks would be more apt to make errors, some of which may produce accidents.

A "popular magazine" theory of *biorhythm* proposes that there are basic cyclical rhythms that occur from birth. These cycles alternate between positive and negative periods for a physical cycle, emotional cycle, and intellectual cycle. The change from a positive to a negative cycle results in critical days. On critical days it has been postulated that more accidents occur as a consequence of one's biorhythms. (These should not be confused with *circadian* rhythm, the daily cycle we experience, to be discussed later.)

Data were obtained from pilot crashes, traffic accident, and on-the-job accidents along with the individual's birthdate. Analysis showed no significant difference as a whole in accidents on the critical days beyond that expected by chance.[11,48,52,100] Moreover, the theory behind it makes little sense, since it depends on consistency and uniformity of cycles that are known to vary considerably.

Socioemotional Well-Being and Accident Behavior

British coal miners suffering from changing economic conditions and new technological requirements experienced substantially increased accident rates.[65] As we previously mentioned, mining, in general, is a most hazardous occupation with severe accident rates. An effort was made to reduce the accident rate by building cohesiveness and team spirit by means of small group meetings, planned social activities, and the painting of a special yellow band around mine support posts as a symbol of the group or team spirit. The yellow lines placed around the supports also represented an important design improvement in the job. With the horizontal lines around the supporting posts, the miners could more easily set them vertically in the mine shaft. Since the collapse of these posts due to improper placement was an important cause of accidents, the yellow symbol also had properties that were more than symbolic. Miners working some distance away who did not have this attention paid to them served as a control group. We can see that there were a number of confounding influences, including the well-known Hawthorne effect, but the results were quite positive. There was a 54 per cent decrease in the accident rate. Although this field experiment lacked full scientific rigor, it illustrates the practical value of engineering several changes that in combination yield considerable benefits to the miners involved.

The Factory Environment as a Contributor to Accidents

Improper design of the working environment contributes to industrial and other types of accidents. For example, failure to provide proper lighting, ventilation, or labeling of dangerous substances has led to serious injury. Many features can be incorporated in the design of plant and equipment to reduce hazards or the severity of accidents. For instance, showers can be provided in areas where there is danger of chemicals being spilled on a worker. Or special meters registering exposure to radiation can be provided personnel working near an atomic reactor.

A large-scale five-year study of environmental elements in the factory contributing to accidents was conducted in a tractor plant employing over 7,000 employees. Eight knowledgeable judges in the company rated 44 shop departments in the plant on variables such as pressure to get things done, comfortable shop environment, degree of crew work, manual effort, degree of obvious danger, and job prestige. Uncomfortable shop environment induced by noise, heat, dirt, et cetera, correlated 0.70 with frequency of accidents. Partial correlations showed that uncomfortable conditions were not confounded with others such as manual effort. Over half of the variance among departments in accidents was accounted for by the lack of comfort of the departments independent of the specific tasks performed in them.[47]

Similarly, a study of 147 plants employing over a quarter of a million workers found accident frequency related to such things as seasonal layoffs, poor attitudes toward the high producers, and generally poor working conditions.[78]

A surprising finding was that the accidents in a department were not correlated so much with the *obvious* hazards as with some unrelated activity such as stapling tags or opening envelopes. Possibly, obvious dangers engage the attention of the workers so much that they become less attentive to other, nonobvious hazards.

The degree of crew work of departments correlated 0.33 with accident rates. Thus, where the typical job required the interaction of more people, there was a higher rate of accidents. Many of these activities required coordination and varying responsibility among the workers in the crew. Any lapse of attention could cause an injury to someone in the group.

Accident severity in terms of days lost due to accidents has been related to factors such as extreme work temperatures and nonegalitarian eating facilities. Thus, as has been noted in our discussion in Chapter 3, while frequency of accidents seems to be a form of withdrawal from dissatisfying working conditions, severity seems more a consequence of extreme discomfort and annoyances.

Forces for Safety

At least five forces pressure management and government administrators into spending to reduce environmental hazards. First, insurance rates depend on accident experience. A poor record means high rates or even cancellation of policies. Second, legislation or union demands force safety measures. The Occupational Safety and Health Act of 1970 provided for the establishment within industry of safety standards along with periodic inspections. Third, enlightened management voluntarily opts for safer conditions for moral reasons, better worker morale, better public image, and so on. Fourth, employees demand extra pay to continue to work in hazardous conditions. And fifth, if hazards are too great, very few people will be found willing to accept the jobs in question.

What are the factors that account for differences in accident rates of manufacturing plants? Surveys and comparison of matched pairs of low- and high-accident factories coincide in implicating several important factors. First, management commitment and involvement appears to be essential. Second, management was generally more efficient in varying all aspects of their business, resulting in greater financial stability. Third, a more humanistic approach was characteristic of low-accident plants where worker-supervisor interaction was encouraged. Fourth, the low-accident plant had better housekeeping and was concerned with keeping the plant clean. Fourth, experienced fellow employees rather than supervisors were used to train new workers in the low-accident plants. Fifth, better selection procedures were followed by low-accident plants.[80]

Another set of investigators completed a similar study, for high- and low-accident coal mines. There was a commonality of findings between the manufacturing plants and the mines. As was true in the factories, it was found that management involvement in making safety an organizational goal was an important factor in the low-accident mines but not in the high-accident mines. The behavior of management in the low-accident mines emphasized the importance of safety. Of particular importance was the stress management placed upon maintenance and safety of health equipment, with the higher-accident mines failing to make this an organizational priority.

It also appeared that the organization of work was not as well structured in the high-accident mines. Miners in the high-accident mines often reported that they had to do a lot of things at the same time and often had to work without clearcut duties, as compared to those in low-accident mines.

Training was an important consideration, since most of the accidents in mines were due to human error, which might have been prevented if proper training had been initiated. Miners in low-accident mines indicated that their training in how the electrical power system worked and how to deal with hazards such as gas were better than reported training from miners in the high-accident mines. One training technique is by example. Supervisors in the high-accident mines were reported to wear respirators less often in dusty conditions than foremen did in low-accident mines. There was evidence that the management concern should have been translated through all levels, with the supervisors setting an appropriate example for the workers.

In low-accident mines there was an increased effort to keep the work area clean, as was reported in low-accident manufacturing plants. The results of the studies in both manufacturing plants and coal mines indicate that psychological factors are important and can affect the safety and health of industrial employees.[69]

In hazardous occupations such as underground coal mining, it is anticipated that management will eventually apply even more sophisticated techniques of analyzing the risks and thereby stimulating remedial action.[19]

There is considerable evidence that injuries can be reduced, given sufficient concern about safety. For example, a Du Pont chemical plant had no disabling injuries during 67,000,000 people hours of operation. Even hazardous industries such as the explosives industry can maintain a low injury rate.[37]

PSYCHOLOGICAL AND PHYSIOLOGICAL COSTS OF WORK

Work demands inputs of energy from workers. These inputs are costs to them. If the demands become excessive, they are stressed. Their performance may suffer as a consequence. The stress or excess costs of labor to workers have changed radically in the past generation. Until well into the twentieth century, over half the population was employed in agricultural work, and a substantial portion of the remainder was engaged in some form of manufacturing operation. Both endeavors required heavy physical exertion under both hot and cold environmental conditions. Today the picture has changed. Most of the population is now engaged in more sedentary tasks in the office, in light manufacturing or as service workers. This means that the extreme environmental stress imposed by muscular exertion, heat, and often intense noise has been moderated so that now a large proportion of the population works under conditions where there is almost no environmental stress. Although this generalization is true, there are still jobs in industry that require heavy energy expenditure.

Some have labeled our civilization the Age of Anxiety. There is an implication that the hard-driving corporation employee now is under stress of a different nature. While once it may have been backbreaking labor, it is now mind-rending stress. In the next section, we will look not only at the more usual environmental factors that may stress industrial workers, but also at the psychological costs to them of doing their jobs. Specifically, we will look at such sources of decrement in performance as heat, noise, fatigue, monotony, and boredom. We will also examine the newer forms of stress which are important in our present-day world of work. Among the most important of these are the physiological and psychological costs to the employee on shift work.

Shift Work

As equipment becomes more complex and expensive, it becomes more important for industrial organizations to utilize fully their equipment around the clock. Service organizations such as hospitals, police forces, fire departments, railroads, and electric power plants have had to maintain staffs throughout a twenty-four-hour period. Shift work has been commonplace for blue-collar workers in manufacturing industries, but now it has also become common for white-collar workers in companies with large computer facilities which must be operated sixteen to twenty-four hours a day to justify their cost. Also, as process industries such as petroleum and chemicals become automated, with added expensive capital investments, there is increasing economic pressure to keep the processing plants running continuously. Both white- and blue-collar workers are involved here.

An analysis of over 1,700 major collective bargaining agreements showed that over 90 per cent in manufacturing industries had provisions in the contract for afternoon or night work. The analysis also showed that about two-thirds of the contracts in nonmanufacturing segments of concerns had similar provisions. One survey by the Department of Labor indicated that there is considerable variation from city to city in the number of people working second or third (graveyard) shifts. For example, in Detroit almost 32 per cent of the manufacturing employees worked on late shift, while in New York only 13 per cent were so engaged.[58]

Shift work is a sensitive issue for industrial firms. Efforts to study the subject have met with considerable resistance from the firms. Industrial management's reluctance to permit research about shift work lies in the fear of stirring up the often strong, negative, crystallized opinions of workers. But these negative feelings about shift work serve to make us aware of the importance of our natural circadian rhythm and what happens when work demands that we interfere with it.

CIRCADIAN RHYTHM The term "circadian rhythm" has come into general use to denote biological rhythms that have a duration of about one day.[86]

For example, body temperature follows a cycle with its highest value in the evening and a low point early in the morning. (Circadian rhythm is a scientific concept with extensive empirical support, while biorhythm is a popular concept with no empirical support. The two ideas are not related.)

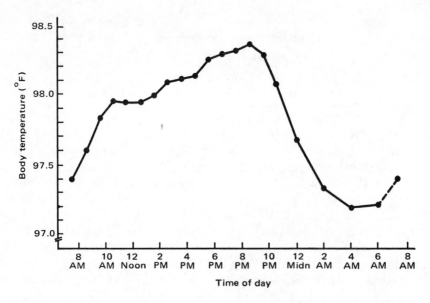

Figure 16–3. Two-point rolling mean body temperature of 59 subjects at 20 times of day (average of two trials). (From Colquhoun, Blake, and Edwards, "Experimental Studies of Shift-Work. 1: A Comparison of Rotating and Stabilized 4 Hour Shift Systems, *Ergonomics,* 11 [1968]: 451.)

This rhythm of temperature is shown in Figure 16–3. Body temperature increases from 8:00 in the morning until approximately 8:00 at night, when it drops sharply until it reaches a low point sometime around 4:00 in the morning. Human performance during a day is closely related to this rhythm of body temperature. A close relationship exists between performance on a vigilance task and body temperature—a result that has been found for many other tasks as well.[13]

When diurnal (day-night) norms of body temperature are changed (for example, for travelers crossing many time zones in a day), body temperature rather than time of day becomes the significant factor associated with effective performance. Thus, body temperature seems to reflect the underlying state of arousal of the organism (discussed previously in Chapter 3 on motivation). It would follow that the optimum time for individuals to work would be when the body temperature was high, which of course ordinarily corresponds with the usual day shift working arrangements. There seems to be no organ or function in the human body that does not exhibit similar daily rhythms. These rhythms can be thought of as an expression of a "physiological clock." [3] The circadian rhythm is influenced by periodic environmental factors. The day-night light cycle is the most important.

The evidence seems clear that a disruption of the usual sleep-wakefulness cycles usually results in poorer job performance, which is independent of the total hours slept.[84]

Our recent concern with circadian rhythm rests on the increased numbers of people engaging in shift work and those who fly from one time zone to another, both as passengers and crew, whose established diurnal cycles and performances are disturbed. It is now possible to fly from New York to Tokyo in half a day. There is a time difference of 14 hours. One is ready for noon lunch at 2:00 A.M. Tokyo time. More dramatic is the case of those few individuals in space or deep within the ocean who have to adjust to the establishment of a new work-rest cycle.

TYPES OF SHIFT PATTERNS   Most often, the twenty-four-hour day is divided into three shifts: day, afternoon, and night (graveyard). In a *rotating shift,* the three shifts are often manned by four separate crews so that after working a number of days on one shift, the crew can have one or two days off and then work a different shift. These rotating shift patterns can take many different forms. For example, workers may spend anywhere from one day to a month on one shift before they move to another shift. The common pattern is seven days on each shift. Less common is a *split shift,* where workers have a break in their working hours. This pattern is used in the military, especially for watches in the navy. Usually, each shift is eight hours, but it is not uncommon for the night shift to work fewer hours for the same pay. For example, switchboard operators in some telephone companies working the night shift are paid for eight hours but only work a six-hour shift. Obviously, everything in a shift pattern can be varied, such as the starting time of each shift and the rotation of the shift. Unfortunately, the shift patterns are usually more a function of habit and custom than of established evidence concerning the most efficient pattern for either the worker's well-being or organizational productivity.

A new pattern of four six-hour shifts is developing in some countries (e.g., the Netherlands). Shifts begin at 6 A. M., noon, 6. P. M., and midnight, with no midspell breaks. Workers can rotate these shifts every third day or so.

In the United States a recent trend is a four-day work week, ten hours each day with three consecutive days off. The potential inefficiencies of having too long a workday may be offset by the increased satisfaction of workers with the arrangement and the ability to recruit and retain employees in jobs that might have otherwise been less attractive to them. More will be said about this later.

Much less complex than a rotating shift is the *fixed shift* pattern, where the employee works only one of the three shifts. At first glance, it might seem that the rotating shift is more equitable, since all the workers have to work on the supposedly more undesirable night shift. Nevertheless, it may be the most harmful to the worker and to the organization, as will be seen.

SHIFT WORK PREFERENCES When workers are allowed to choose either working on a permanent day shift, a permanent rotating shift, or on permanent nights, according to numerous surveys, habit is the most important factor in determining the worker's choice.[18] Thus, in one study, employees tended to choose the shift on which they were working. Approximately 27 per cent chose a permanent night shift and 61 per cent chose a permanent day shift, while the remainder chose a rotating shift. The statement "I'm used to it" was the most frequent response concerning the reason for picking and staying with a shift.

ADVANTAGES AND DISADVANTAGES OF THE DIFFERENT SHIFTS
Steady day shift The steady day shift, the one worked by most people, presents the least difficulty for most workers. The day schedule fits in well with the activities of the family and society in general. One strong reason a day-shift person will give for disliking the night shift is a spouse's dislike of being left alone at night. Another reason day workers give for their dislike of the night shift is the alleged bad effect they feel it would have on their health.

While the evidence is somewhat controversial, there is no indication that night-shift workers necessarily suffer poorer health than day-shift employees. The evidence is complicated because when a symptom such as ulcers is studied, it is difficult to tell when the illness first occurred. More objective evidence of the medical records of workers on night and day shifts has not shown any differences among them.

Steady afternoon shift A worker on the afternoon shift usually leaves for work at 3:00 or 4:00 in the afternoon and does not come home again until 11:00 at night. This means that if the employee is a father or mother with young children of school age, they will never see that parent except on days off. While this may be considered an advantage by some parents, it is considered an inconvenience by most. Few mothers could work a steady afternoon shift. Also, all social activities with friends are curtailed unless the workers socialize with those working on the same shift. However, there is little conflict with the circadian rhythms of employees on this shift, since they can sleep during the normal hours at night and sleep late in the morning if they wish.

Steady night shift Many people believe that the night shift causes a great deal of inconvenience to workers; nevertheless, this shift seems to interfere less than either the afternoon or rotating shift with family and social obligations of the employee.

One of the main reasons stressed by those preferring night work is the amount of "useful free time" available to them. An objective analysis of the work records indicates that a more accurate statement might be that employees on the night shift do not work fewer hours but are better paid for the hours they do work. Workers on the night shift often wish to work overtime. It would appear that working the night shift allows them to earn more money and live a little better than their counterparts on the day shift. Also, night employees may not be required to work as hard, as is revealed by the fact that, according to one report, they produced between 57 per cent and 81 per cent of what the day workers produced. There seems to be less demand for production on the night shift than on the day shift.[18] Other reports have found less difference in performance, more on the order of 3 per cent less production.[54]

Contrary to expectations, antisocial aspects of night work have not been found. Night workers on permanent shifts appear to have no more difficulties in adjustment than those on day work. Also, since these employees are on permanent night work, there is an opportunity for the circadian rhythm to make the adjustment and adapt to the changed life cycle.[66]

Surveys have shown that at least one-quarter of the working population actually prefers night work and actually has more favorable attitudes about social life and home life than workers on other shifts.[18]

One of the main difficulties of the night shift is the reported difficulty in sleeping. This is undoubtedly due to the night shift employee's need to sleep during the day when there is a lot of family and other activity going on. But only a small proportion of the night-shift workers had any real difficulty in adjusting their circadian rhythms to the night cycle.

Rotating shift As we previously mentioned, there are many pattterns of the rotating shift; the most common is one where employees spend a week on each of the three shifts. Since the individuals are on all of the three shifts, they experience advantages and disadvantages of each when they are working that shift. Perhaps the most critical one is the fact that the circadian rhythm does not have time to make the adjustment required, since the employees are usually on one shift for only seven days, and by the time physiological adjustment is made, it is time to start a new working cycle. Evidently, for this reason, many people report various physical complaints on this shift pattern. Perhaps one of the worst features of this plan is the fact that while one survey showed that three out of four workers at one plant wanted to change from a rotating shift, there was no alternative. A rotating shift is usually plantwide. Even the alternation between day and night shift has been found to have negative consequences.[1]

A second type of rotating shift, rapidly rotating, may cause more difficulties for employees even if they are not aware of the problem. In reviewing the absence records of over 700 ship workers who changed to a rapidly rotating schedule with changes of shift every two or three days, the number of certified absences because of sickness rose 36 per cent. The employees liked the rapidly rotating shift better than the common weekly rotation and appeared to be unaware of the negative consequences of rapid rotation.[70]

RESOLVING THE PROBLEM OF SHIFT WORK   From all of the evidence presented, it would appear that the rotating shift has the most disadvantages of any of the working arrangements and few of the advantages. One then wonders why this sort of shift is the most popular one in the process industry. The primary reason seems to be that studies done by management indicate that this type of rotating shift system is less expensive to operate than a fixed shift system. The savings are due to the use of fewer employees for the same jobs. This, of course, is only one factor and does not take into account the discomfort and cost to the workers who have to work this type of shift. Another reason that the rotating shift is maintained is the fact that in all organizations and plants, workers tend to be satisfied at least in a nominal way with what they have adjusted to. For example, in Chapter 3, we saw that the employee was most satisfied with whatever compensation plan he worked under. Similarly, workers under a rotating shift tend to become satisfied with it despite its shortcomings. Habit is the overriding consideration. The difficulty is that the workers have not had experiences with other modes of shift work that might be more suited to their needs.

Frequent vacations   The rotating shift can be improved for workers by giving them more free time between work periods. For example, one company arranged rotating shifts so that the worker received four ten-day vacation periods throughout the year. Another possibility is to increase the time spent on each shift. If it were possible for the employee to work one month on a shift before being changed to a new shift, this would permit the individual's circadian rhythm cycle to adjust.

Consider preferences   A definite portion of the working force (perhaps as many as 25 per cent) does prefer an evening shift, while about half would avoid working nights. Night work makes it possible to hold two jobs (moonlighting). These preferences should be taken into account whenever possible. It is also true that some workers do have difficulty in adjusting their circadian rhythms to rotating shifts and they should be allowed to transfer to shifts that best meet their needs. It has been suggested that only a very small premium should be paid for the afternoon and night shifts, since these shifts do meet the needs of many workers, for example, those who have marital difficulties or circadian rhythms that best match working in the afternoon or night. If night work pays little more than day work, many young employees with families would not be tempted to work night shifts, which may place a strain on both the family and the social relationships of the employee.[58]

Change community functioning One of the problems of shift work is that the social and community activities are not geared to the shift worker. Dunham found that in a community oriented toward shift workers, there was no difference in satisfaction between day and night workers.[22] Conversely, in a plant with similar jobs, but in a community that was not oriented to shift work, the night worker had the lowest satisfaction. The greater the frequency of shift work in a community, the more likely it is that shift-related problems will be minimized.

Evidently there are many options and ways the situation could be handled. Unfortunately, it would appear that management has often taken the easiest course, dictated either by purely economic criteria, without consideration of possible costs to the employee, or by past practices.

SHORTER WORK WEEK We have mentioned earlier working ten hours a day for four days instead of the normal five-day week, then having a three-day weekend. Despite the interest aroused by the idea, actually more employees in the late 1970s were working a seven-day week (1.9 per cent of the labor force) than a four-day week (1.2 per cent of the labor force).[89]

A one-year study in a pharmaceutical company showed overall positive feelings toward the change to a four-day work week. Specifically, female workers saw more positive influence on home life than males did.[62] There is even some evidence that employee performance is higher while working a four-day week.[45]

Acceptance of the four-day work week was more often endorsed by those hospital employees who believed the change resulted in a job with more status and responsibility.[26] This was an unanticipated result of changing to a four-day week and may be an important factor in other organizations where an extended workday means that the employee performs job duties usually performed by others.

One negative note has been sounded from supervisors who fear supervision will be less adequate if they continue to work the regular eight hours a day five days a week, while different sets of their employees work the extended days.[41] When supervisors are themselves on a four-day work week, personal dissatisfaction has been expressed because only a small number reported that they could regularly take their day off.[34]

From what we know about fatigue and boredom, to be discussed below, the ten-hour day is more likely to be as productive as the eight-hour day if (1) the work is not too heavy, (2) sufficient rest pauses are permitted, and (3) various devices to mitigate boredom, such as job rotation, are practiced.

Fatigue

The concept of fatigue is a broad one; there are many definitions of the term. We will consider fatigue first as a physiological cost to the employee resulting from muscular exertion or environmental stress and second as a subjective feeling usually expressed as boredom or tiredness. Both tend to result in observed decrement and variability in performance.[27]

PHYSIOLOGICAL COST OF WORK   As the nature of the industrial process has changed, so has the energy expenditure required of industrial employees. Nowadays, the physiological cost to the typical worker on the job averages about two calories per minute, which is less than the physiological cost of off-the-job activities.[25] Physiological measurements of heart rate, blood pressure, cardiac output, pulmonary ventilation, oxygen consumption, chemical composition of the blood and urine, and body temperature have been used to assess the physiological costs of work imposed on the worker.

Severe conditions   Under conditions of severe rationing of food, the calorie intake of a worker is an accurate prediction of production. For example, in the Ruhr district of Germany, between 1939 and 1944, a miner required about 1,200 calories for each ton of coal mined. Fatigue served as a homeostasis (adjustment) mechanism. When cigarettes were given to 20 railroad workers as an additional incentive to produce more, the relationship between available calories and output was lost, resulting in the workers' losing weight as they worked harder for the additional reward.[20,49]

Milder conditions   The evidence is clear that measurements such as heart rate are not an indication of fatigue for most workers in the modern industrial situation because the physiological costs to individuals in most occupations are so low that the measurements do not register much effect. This is not to say that there are not industries that do impose a physiological cost on the individual. One of the few remaining occupations entailing such costs, and one of the most strenuous, is that of lumberjack, where individuals may use from 6 to 11 calories per minute.[64,25] A more moderate expenditure of energy of 3 to 5 calories per minute is typical of the steel worker's job. In the usual factory jobs, the cost to the worker usually is below these levels.

For white-collar workers, who are now a majority in American society, such as those in clerical and service occupations, the energy cost to workers is much below that which they will expend on the bowling team. Leisure-time activities such as dancing, golf, tennis, skiing, and swimming take from 5 to 11 calories per minute, while a clerk's job takes from 1.5 to 2.4 calories per minute.[25]

There is some evidence that pupillography (measurement of pupil diameter) is a good objective measure of fatigue for white-collar jobs such as telephone directory assistance.[29] Pupil diameter reliably decreases as a result of fatigue. But even in modern factories, there are still certain jobs requiring heavy energy expenditure. One example is loading boxcars. While workers loading a boxcar may never lift over 100 pounds at one time, still in a four-hour period, working at a normal pace, they will handle over 40,000 pounds apiece.[17]

Controlling energy expenditures   At Kodak, the physiological cost of doing work on specific jobs is measured and then recommendations are made to reduce the cost if it is excessive. Actual measurement of physiological cost of a job often shows unexpected results. For example, it was a company policy to take older workers off the production line and transfer them to the supposedly easier cleaning tasks. Surprisingly, more effort was required in the cleaning task than on the production line. This caused a reversal in company policy. Now, younger employees work first in the cleaning jobs, and then, as they grow older, are transferred to the production line.

Individual differences   Complicating matters is the extreme variation among individuals doing the same work in what energy they need to expend. Personality characteristics of the employee may be more significant than the actual energy requirements of the job. For example, one surgeon may perform a very difficult two-hour operation with only a slight increase in his/her cardiac mobilization. In contrast, another surgeon performing an equally difficult operation for the same length of time may show greatly increased cardiac mobilization and physiological cost. At this point, investigators have not been extremely successful in relating the personality needs to physiological costs of the job, but they have shown extreme variation among individuals performing objectively the same job.

It has been found that there is less physiological cost for managers who are in good physical condition and are nonsmokers. The normal stresses of the workday appear to have significantly less effect on those who maintain themselves in good physical condition.[39]

Physiological cost and skill level   There is evidence from more highly skilled occupations such as piloting a plane and for workers in other situations performing both mental and physical labor that physiological cost is lower for those who are more skilled. Experienced scuba divers will consume less than half the tank air than novices will. This makes good sense, as the inexperienced worker has not learned a stable pattern of response to the job situation.

Physiological cost of mental work   There is a rise in energy cost when people perform operations such as reading, writing, and arithmetic. For example, a 6 per cent rise in the cardiac level was recorded for subjects performing mental arithmetic.[24] Similar 1 to 11 per cent increases were reported in energy or metabolism when mental work is performed and the muscular activity is kept to a minimum. The metabolic cost seemed to be highest when subjects first began the task, but as they learned how to perform the activity, the metabolic cost dropped several per cent, and tension as measured by muscle potentials dropped markedly.[82] This finding is consistent with the proposition that skilled workers are less affected by stress conditions since the cost of performing the activity becomes less with practice.

Fatigue and the quality of work   As the work period proceeds, there is a decrement in performance in all tasks including light sedentary ones, but the decline will be negligible in the speed of work on light sedentary tasks unless the individual works faster than his/her preferred speed.[53] Thus, 234 typists made progressively more errors as the work period progressed from 1 to 30 minutes. Less skilled typists showed an increase in errors during the 30-minute trial, but skilled typists showed less of a change in accuracy. Speed remained about the same for both.[92]

FLEXITIME   The Germans pioneered "flexitime," which allows employees to choose the times they will come to work. The early riser may start at 7:00 A.M and quit at 3:00 P.M., while the later riser may come to work at 11:00 A.M. and quit at 7:00 P.M. Over 17 per cent of the German labor force is on flexitime, and a number of United States firms are trying the plan.[79] The important element is that employees who need to coordinate their work overlap their hours sufficiently to do so. Usually a "core time" is established when all employees are expected to be at work.

Individualized work schedules and self-control of working time has been found to result in greater personal satisfaction.[32,33] A field experiment involving approximately 250 clerical employees found that flexible working hours resulted in no adverse effects on measured productivity. For some clerical groups there was an indication that flexible time resulted in increased productivity.[74]

There is some union opposition to the concept of flexitime because the intensity of the work may increase and the employer may forgo some overtime payments. For unionized organizations, there are a number of

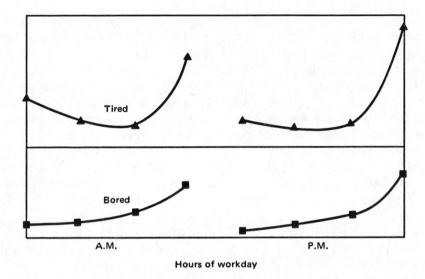

Figure 16–4. Smoothed curves of employee response. (From Nelson and Bartley, "The Pattern of Personal Response Arising during the Office Work Day," *Occupational Psychology,* 42 [1968]: 82.)

issues such as this to be resolved before flexitime will receive widespread union support.[63]

BOREDOM AND TIREDNESS   Research with a variety of occupations has shown consistently that both feelings of boredom and of being tired depend on the time of day. Figure 16–4 shows this relationship for office workers, one very similar to that obtained for manual and supervisory workers as well.[61] As shown, the individual worker comes into the office in the morning not particularly bored but somewhat tired. Boredom increases during the morning and reaches a peak right before the noon hour. The feeling of tiredness is actually reduced in the middle of the morning but then it rises to a peak as the boredom curve does. Before the employee starts work again in the afternoon, the feelings both of boredom and of being tired are at a fairly low point but rise sharply to a peak for the whole day during the last hour of work. The data presented are very stable and hold over large groups of people in various occupations, but we do not know how results are influenced by job attitude.

RESERVE CAPACITY   One of the theoretical and practical problems in measuring the effects of extreme environmental demands on individuals is the fact that an individual who is well motivated can often overcome such factors as extreme heat, cold, or psychological pressure. The individual may overcome these by exerting more effort with more skill to perform a task in a satisfactory manner. But the increased effort may not be great enough to show as an added physiological cost. Only by observing performance on a *secondary task* carried on simultaneously can we estimate the cost of performing the primary task.

Let us suppose, as an example, that we are testing alternate control systems for driving a 30-ton truck. The most straightforward way to test the two control systems would be to have matched groups of individuals operate the vehicle with identical simulated loads. Then tracking performance and fuel consumed could be obtained as measures. What one might find is that the two control mechanisms, A and B, give identical performance scores over the test track, but they might put quite different demands on the driver. The reserve capacity of the drivers operating the control systems could be tested by giving them a second task to be performed while driving the vehicle, such as listening to a string of digits being spoken and saying "now" whenever two odd numbers were heard. Performance on the second task would measure the reserve capacity left to the driver. Under these experimental conditions, one might find that with control system A, the driver, as before, could negotiate the test course and the secondary task quite well. The drivers might do as well with the control system B but make more errors on the secondary task. This would indicate that control system A left the driver a great deal more reserve capacity than control system B. This might be important if during real operations the driver might be faced with unusual stresses such as a rapid rise in ice on the road or a distracting emergency.[9]

Noise

There are three important aspects of noise that we will consider here: (1) what noise levels will lead to physiological damage to the industrial worker; (2) what the effect of noise is on the performance of employees in an organizational setting; and (3) what the subjective reaction to noise is.

NOISE AND HEARING LOSS   Those exposed to certain noise intensities for a continuous period of time will suffer a hearing loss. Risk levels for damage have been set for given intensities (perceived as loudness of sound) and given frequencies (perceived as pitch of sound). But it is difficult to state damage levels specifically for all combinations of frequency and intensity. It is even more difficult to evaluate the effect of intermittent noise, since the experimenter cannot risk hearing loss of test subjects to determine when loss occurs.

In weaving mills and similar high-intensity situations, suitable protection against noise is required. This is usually done by having the employee wear ear plugs. You can see them being worn by employees who must work around jet aircraft engines at airports. The greatest difficulty exists in persuading employees that they should wear ear plugs because the damage is not usually noticeable, but is accumulative and may occur a number of years after the employee has been exposed to the noise hazard. We can expect considerable damage of this type to be occurring to the musicians and frequent visitors to the discotheques where electronic amplifications have raised intensities and frequencies to unhealthy levels. Environmental noise pollution is being seen as a world-wide health problem.

EFFECTS ON PERFORMANCE   In regard to performance under noise conditions, the evidence indicates that noise per se has little effect on the efficiency of the employee unless the noise interferes with communication that is necessary to the job. These results have been found even in environments where prolonged exposure to the noise would produce permanent hearing loss.[50] While evidence indicates that noise does not affect efficiency, there is evidence that it does have a bearing on the amount of effort required by employees to maintain their performance. This physiological cost of noise is seldom taken into account.

Laboratory studies utilizing either the concept of reserve capacity or the differential effects of noise on selected tasks have found quite different results. Reaction time, persistence, intellectual performance, and memory have all shown decrements under noise conditions.[7,23,90,91,99,85] The nature of the decrement is dependent upon both the type of noise and the specific task.

The annoyance aspect of noise is probably of most concern to many people who work in environments where noise, as such, is not usually a significant factor. In evaluating the extent to which noise is annoying, one should keep two factors in mind. First, the loudness of a sound as established by physical measurements does not directly correspond with the loudness and noisiness as judged subjectively.[50] Second, there is a difference between loudness and noisiness. It has been established that noisiness increases at a greater rate than loudness does as (a) the pitch of sound is raised, (b) the complexity of the spectrum is increased, and (c) the duration is increased beyond 200 milliseconds.[50]

There is a cost to individuals when they have to adapt to aversive noise. A laboratory study showed that it is not only the physical intensity but also the psychological conditions that moderate the effect of noise. When the noise was unpredictable, there was lowered tolerance and a drop in subsequent performance on a task, compared with those for predictable noise. In a similar fashion, after exposure to unpredictable noise that the subjects perceived they could terminate if they desired, there was a substantial reduction in the postnoise performance levels compared with the performance of those subjects who believed they could not control the noise.[30]

It seems to be a nearly universal characteristic of individuals to want to have control over their environment and behavior. If noise in the environment is predictable and the employees believe they can terminate the annoyance, there is much less effect on behavior.

Stress and Occupation

Although our modern industrial society does not usually impose physical stress on individuals, it is often stated that in this age of anxiety there are other costs in certain occupations. For example, business executives are often singled out as overly ambitious who pay the price of their success in terms of early heart attacks. They drive themselves hard and have early success, but an early grave is the reward for their striving. But in our discussion earlier, we gave some indication that the real physiological cost was more a function of the individual than of the occupation. As we shall see, generalizing about ambitious executives and heart attacks is another instance of an erroneous idea. In actual fact, executives as a class may be among the most physically healthy in our society.

EXECUTIVE STRESS   The tension and stress that are equated with success in business are reported to be not only psychological but also physical. Bitter jokes are often made about one-, two-, and three-ulcer jobs. The most dreaded physical effect is that of a heart attack. It is widely assumed that when executives reach a top level in their organization, they are more prone to physical ailments such as heart attacks than their subordinates. Actually, the opposite was shown for the Bell Telephone System, where a study of the onset of disabling coronary heart disease revealed that executives as a group were less susceptible to heart attacks than other persons in the company.[43] In fact, the heart disease rate of both the workers and the first-level supervisors was over double that of the executive group!

What about those who rise rapidly and achieve success early? Data again disconfirmed the expectation that they would be more subject to heart attacks. Executives who were promoted most rapidly had rates no higher than others of the same age and length of service.

Another frequently cited cause of stress in the United States is the mobility and frequent transfer of employees from one location to another. Again, the results contradict the stereotype that those who are transferred often and moved around from location to location have a greater incidence of heart disease. These results have been replicated by studies in the oil and chemical industries.[68]

Other evidence indicates that the risk of coronary heart disease is more a function of early childhood or adolescent experience than of organizational mobility and executive achievement. And, equally important, better-educated executives take better care of themselves than blue-collar workers do. They are more likely to engage in active sports, watch their weight, avoid smoking, and be under better medical care. It is no wonder that it is the blue-collar workers who are much less likely to say they are in good health.[46]

There is also the factor of subjective stress. As previously mentioned, it would appear that *the increased physiological cost of occupations resides more in the individual than in the job itself. The same appears to apply to subjective stress.* For persons in the same type of work, some suffer much tension; others do not. For example, one survey of over 6,000 executives showed that the workday of average tension-sufferers was no longer than that of their more relaxed colleagues, *but their behavior was quite different from that of the more relaxed executive.* This is illustrated in Table 16–1, where it can be seen that their lives seem much more strenuous than those of their relaxed executive colleagues.

PSYCHOLOGICAL STRESS   In most job situations, employees are not placed where they are forced to perform under a great deal of stress. There are a few occupations, though, where the employee's job is structured so that at certain times he or she must perform on a very high level while subjected to some form of outside stress. Examples of this would be occupations such as those of fire fighter, police officer, pilot, military man or woman, doctor, nurse, and even the motion picture projectionist when a projector breaks down during a movie.

THE USE OF SIMULATION TO STUDY STRESS   Army trainees and experienced soldiers were systematically subjected to stressful simulated emergencies under carefully controlled conditions. While we do know that performance does decline under psychological stress, there is very little quantitative evidence concerning the degree of decrement. Laboratory studies have attempted to approach the problem, but the subjects usually realize that it is an artificial situation. The series of studies devised by researchers working with an army population depended on realistic simulations of stressful events that might conceivably happen to a soldier while on duty.[6] Unfortunately, in order for the simulations to work, they had to be conducted without the voluntary approval and awareness of the participants of what they were getting themselves into.

In one situation designed to induce psychological stress, each soldier was told that he was going to participate in a large-scale military exercise. The soldier was taken to an isolated outpost and given a two-way radio. He was told his job was to report any aircraft flying overhead. He was

Table 16–1. Executive stress.

A study of more than 6000 executives by New York's Life Extension Foundation showed that the average workday of the tension-sufferers was no longer than that of their more relaxed colleagues. Nevertheless, they led far more strenuous lives. Of the tense group:

67% more eat breakfast on the fly (under 5 minutes)

86% more gulp down their lunch (under 15 minutes)

21% more hurry through their dinner (under 30 minutes) and

1 out of 3 on diets are nursing gastric disorders.

47% fewer get some form of regular exercise

20% fewer have extracurricular interests (church, civic, etc.)

18% more have no hobby at all and

1 out of 5 get no recreation whatsoever.

46% more average 6 or fewer hours of sleep at night

139% more rarely have weekends free for family and self and their vacation time is 20% less than the overall average.

50% more are heavy cigarette smokers

32% more have cocktails for lunch (155% more drink more than 2)

9% more have cocktails before dinner (39% drink more than 2).

150% more use sleep-inducing sedatives and

165% more quiet their lives with tranquilizers.

335% more report boredom

174% more report job insecurity

60% more report greater desire to retire by age 55

206.8% more have a suspicion they are not receiving fair credit for efforts and

633% more have a fear of self-expression.

Adaped from Feinberg, "The Truth about Executive Stress." Reprinted by special permission from *Dun's Review,* August, 1964. Copyright © 1964, Dun & Bradstreet Publications Corporation.

also required to monitor the radio. After about one-half hour of routine messages, the soldier heard the voice of the command post become excited and say that artillery rounds were bursting outside the designated impact area. At about the same time he received this message, a five-pound charge of TNT, which was buried about 150 yards from the subject, was detonated. This was done to simulate the burst of incoming artillery fire. A few minutes later, he was addressed by the command post and told to report his position because it had not heard from him in quite some time. A few more minutes passed and then he was told to convert to emergency transmission. Twenty more minutes passed and he was then told it was urgent that he repair his radio so that he could be located because his position had been lost by the command post. He was told that it was imperative that he be located since there was no other way to find him and remove him from the impact area. At various times, six more shells were simulated, with the bursts coming increasingly closer to the supposedly trapped soldier.

Unknown to the subject, he was always in real contact with the command post and when he was instructed to convert to emergency transmission, he in effect began a standardized performance test. Again, there was significant decrement from the control group, which was not subjected to psychological stress. The stressed group's performance was 33 per cent lower than that of the control group. It should be noted that contributing to the lower scores was the fact that one-third of the 24 soldiers in the experimental stress condition deserted their posts even though they had been specifically told to remain and repair the radio sets so they could be rescued.

In the previous simulation, the soldier himself was subjected to stress by having his life threatened. In the last simulation of the series, the soldiers were subjected to stress by being made to believe that they were responsible for the life of someone else. Each soldier was taken to an area where there was an isolated bunker. He was instructed to connect certain colored wires onto terminals as part of preparation for the installation of a remote-control switch box for explosives. The explosives were to be detonated in a nearby canyon. He was then told that the rest of the personnel in the party were going down into the canyon while he completed the wiring job. He had two communication devices: an army field telephone switchboard in the bunker and a conventional intercom, which was supposedly connected to the canyon. It took the soldier about five minutes to finish the connections and throw a switch as he was instructed. The throwing of the switch set off a five-pound charge of TNT in the canyon. This explosion rocked the bunker and sometimes knocked items off the shelves. Immediately after this, a voice came over the intercom telling the soldier that there had been an explosion down in the canyon and someone was hurt. He was further instructed to stay where he was and not touch anything. He was also asked if he had completed the wiring correctly, with the implication that his wiring had set off the explosion. A few minutes later, he heard another message asking him to telephone the hospital because medical assistance was needed for a man who was injured. The soldier then discovered that the phone did not work, and he was told to follow the instructions posted on it for restoring it to service. During the next 45 minutes, as he worked on the phone, he was continually given messages concerning the difficulty of keeping the injured man alive and his possible fault in the accident.

The field telephone was again a performance test, which measured in a quantitative fashion how effectively the subject performed the task. The stress group performed 18 per cent below the level of a comparable control group.

The simulations seemed to produce genuine stress, for performance declined, a measure of subjective feeling showed the subjects to be genuinely concerned, and there were also physiological changes.

A comparison was made between raw recruits and experienced soldiers. In each case, the experienced troops performed better in a stressful condition than the raw recruits, but not as well as the raw recruits in the control conditions. In other words, when the experience and maturity of the experienced troops could be brought into play, they were more effective, but, in the situations that did not produce stress, they tended to see the exercises as "play" and made less effort to perform at their highest level.

Soldiers were also investigated in terms of their personal qualities. In general, those individuals who were poor performers also scored higher on a test of anxiety (Taylor Manifest Anxiety Scale).

While much may have been learned from these studies, this series raises an ethical issue of the investigator's obligation and responsibility in placing subjects in such stressful situations without their consent. Alternative approaches could have been designed to yield similar findings which did not raise ethical considerations.

INTERACTION OF STRESSES   One of the more complicated problems is the interaction among stresses. While we have fairly good information on any one stress acting by itself, we have relatively little information concerning interaction of two or more stresses on the performance of employees. For example, we do know that beyond 81°F, heat seems to play a fairly significant role in decreasing performance of employees. What we do not know is whether or not certain stresses, when in combination, add to or possibly cancel out each other in terms of the employee's performance.[8]

Some of the stresses have been connected to general arousal of the person. Loss of sleep, for example, can be viewed as reducing the level of arousal, while noise has been viewed as increasing arousal levels. When performance does break down, it has been found that the people who have lost sleep perform poorly because they do too little, whereas in high-noise-level situations persons perform poorly by doing the wrong thing.[8]

There will be a decided drop in performance on a task that lasts over a half-hour when the subject has experienced loss of sleep.[96]

Stresses may interact to decrease or actually improve performance. For example, with a low blood alcohol level and sleep deprivation, performance was superior to the condition of low alcohol and normal sleep. Performance on a reaction time task was the poorest under conditions of high alcohol blood level and sleep deprivation.[97]

It is clear that different stresses may interact in ways that cannot be predicted from their single effects. Both noise and sleep deprivation have been found to impair performance. But when noise and sleep deprivation act together, they oppose each other's effect, and performance is better than under normal conditions.[95]

ROLE OVERLOAD: ORGANIZATIONAL ROLE AS A STRESS FACTOR Role overload occurs when employees are faced with a set of obligations that, when taken as a whole, require them to do more than they are able to in the time available.[72] Overload may be objective or subjective, and the two may be unrelated. Observers may see other workers as being asked to accomplish the impossible but they may not see it as being true of themselves. Or, where they are asked to do what all of their associates do, they alone feel overloaded.

The findings are clear that when employees are subjected to *objective* overload, there are biochemical changes. Tax accountants show fairly low serum cholesterol levels during the early part of the year, but experience a sharp increase six weeks before the April 15 tax deadline.[28]

The results with *subjective* overload are not as clear, since there is some indication that individuals who are objectively overloaded with work, but who enjoy what they are doing and feel a sense of accomplishment in doing it, actually have a reduction in the biochemical effect on them.[72] While the evidence is still weak, it would appear that those individuals working on unsatisfying jobs would tend to have adverse biochemical reactions. This, of course, does not mean that these individuals will automatically have a higher rate of coronary disease. As was previously shown, managers who advance very fast in an organization were not necessarily those who had a higher rate of coronary disease. In fact, they had a lower rate.

Sales and House correlated occupational morale with observed rates of death from coronary disease.[73] For both blue- and white-collar occupations, they found that those expressing the most job dissatisfaction had the highest death rates.

The type A personality (hard-driving, involved in work) has been found to be most susceptible to coronary heart disease. Type B persons are the opposite, with a lower risk of coronary disease. Under objective work stress conditions, a strong relationship has been found between work load and anxiety for Type A individuals. Anxiety is also significantly related to pulse rate for Type A persons.[10]

Another factor of importance in coping with objective stress is the individual's locus of control. "Internals" are individuals who attribute success or failure in work to themselves; "externals" tend to attribute job performance to environmental factors such as luck rather than their own personal abilities. Investigators measured the locus of control (Rotter's I-E Scale) of ninety owner-managers after an extensive and damaging flood. After two and a half years, the entrepreneurs with the internal orientation had the more successful businesses (credit bureau ratings), and in general displayed more task-centered coping with stress.[2]

SUMMARY

The personnel subsystem is an effective technique for systematically taking into account the human in any system. Simulation has a variety of applications in studying complex problems dealing with human performance. Simulation can be an effective research approach when dealing with infrequent events such as accidents. Although the causes of accidents are many, an understanding of the factors in both vehicle and factory injuries is gradually emerging. The physiological costs of work have a direct bearing on determining the best form of shift work.

Fatigue has both a physiological and psychological component. Techniques are available for measuring both types of costs. Stress in an organization can take many forms, with wide individual reaction to objectively the same stressful situation.

Newer forms of working arrangements such as the European concept of flexitime are designed to make working more pleasant and less stressful. With multinational corporations becoming commonplace, we can expect a continuing flow of ideas between countries. In the next chapter, we will specifically discuss the influence of cross-cultural issues on organizations.

REFERENCES

1. Akerstedt, T., P. Patkai, and K. Dahlgren. "Field Studies of Shiftwork: II. Temporal Patterns in Psychophysiological Activation in Workers Alternating between Night and Day Work," *Ergonomics*, 20 (1977): 621–631.
2. Anderson, C. R. "Locus of Control, Coping Behaviors, and Performance in a Stress Setting: A Longitudinal Study," *Journal of Applied Psychology*, 62 (1977): 446–451.
3. Aschoff, J. "Circadian Rhythms in Man," *Science*, 148 (1965): 1427–1432.
4. Barrett, G. V., R. A. Alexander, and J. B. Forbes. "Analysis of Performance Measurement and Training Requirements for Driving Decision Making in Emergency Situations," JSAS *Catalog of Selected Documents in Psychology*, 7 (1977): 126 (Ms. No. 1623).
5. Barrett, G. V., and C. L. Thornton. "The Relationship between Perceptual Style and Driver Reaction to an Emergency Situation," *Journal of Applied Psychology*, 52 (1968): 169–176.
6. Berkum, M. M. "Performance Decrement under Psychological Stress," *Human Factors*, 6 (1964): 21–30.
7. Boggs, D. H., and J. R. Simon. "Differential Effect of Noise on Tasks of Varying Complexity," *Journal of Applied Psychology*, 52 (1968): 148–153.

8. Broadbent, D. E. "Differences and Interactions between Stresses," *Quarterly Journal of Experimental Psychology*, 15 (1963): 205–211.

9. Brown, I. D. "A Comparison of Two Subsidiary Tasks Used to Measure Fatigue in Car Drivers," *Ergonomics*, 8 (1965): 467–474.

10. Caplan, R. D., and K. W. Jones. "Effects of Work Load, Role Ambiguity, and Type A Personality on Anxiety, Depression, and Heart Rate," *Journal of Applied Psychology*, 60 (1975): 713–719.

11. Carvey, D. W., and R. G. Nibler. "Biorhythmic Cycles and the Incidence of Industrial Accidents," *Personnel Psychology*, 30 (1977): 447–454.

12. Christensen, J. M. "The Evolution of the Systems Approach in Human Factors Engineering," *Human Factors*, 4 (1962): 7–16.

13. Colquhoun, N. P., M. J. F. Blake, and R. S. Edwards. "Experimental Studies of Shift-Work: I. A Comparison of Rotating and Stabilized 4-Hour Shift Systems," *Ergonomics*, 11 (1968): 437–455.

14. Crawford, M. P. "Dimensions of Simulation," *American Psychologist*, 21 (1966): 788–796.

15. Crawford, P. L. "Hazard Exposure Differentiating Necessary for the Identification of the Accident-Prone Employee," *Journal of Applied Psychology*, 44 (1960): 192–194.

16. Davis, H. L., T. W. Faulkner, and C. I. Miller. "Work Physiology," *Human Factors*, 11 (1969): 157–166.

17. Davis, H. L., and C. I. Miller. "The Use of Work Physiology in Job Design." Paper presented at AIIE National Conference, Atlantic City, May 1962.

18. De La Mare, G., and J. Walker. "Factors Influencing the Choice of Shift Rotation," *Occupational Psychology*, 42 (1968): 1–22.

19. Denny, V. E., K. J. Gilbert, R. C. Erdmann, and E. T. Rumble. "Risk Assessment Methodologies: An Application to Underground Mine Systems," *Journal of Safety Research*, 10, No. 1 (1978): 24–34.

20. Dill, D. "The Nature of Fatigue," *Geriatrics*, 10 (1955): 474–478.

21. Drillis, R. J. "Folk Norms and Biomechanics," *Human Factors*, 5 (1963): 427–442.

22. Dunham, R. B. "Shift Work: A Review and Theoretical Analysis," *Academy of Management Review*, 2, No. 4 (1977): 624–634.

23. Finkelman, J. M., and D. C. Glass. "Reappraisal of the Relationship between Noise and Human Performance by Means of a Subsidiary Task Measure," *Journal of Applied Psychology*, 54 (1970): 211–213.

24. Ford, A. "Bioelectrical Potentials and Mental Effort," *Journal of Comparative and Physiological Psychology*, 46 (1953): 347–351.

25. Ford, A., and H. Hellerstein. "Work and Heart Diseases," *Circulation*, 18 (1958): 823–832.

26. Fottler, M. D. "Employee Acceptance of a Four-Day Workweek," *Academy of Management Journal*, 20 (1977): 656–668.

27. Fraser, D. C. "Recent Experimental Work in the Study of Fatigue," *Occupational Psychology*, 32 (1958): 258–266.

28. Friedman, M., R. H. Rosenman, and V. Carroll, "Changes in the Serum Cholesterol and Blood-Clotting Time of Men Subject to Cyclic Variation of Occupational Stress," *Circulation*, 17 (1957): 852–861.

29. Geacintov, T., and W. S. Peavler. "Pupillography in Industrial Fatigue Assessment," *Journal of Applied Psychology*, 59 (1974): 213–216.

30. Glass, D. C., J. E. Singer, and L. N. Friedman. "Psychic Cost of Adaptation to an Environmental Stressor," *Journal of Personality and Social Psychology*, 12 (1969): 200–210.

31. Goldstein, L. G. "Human Variables in Traffic Accidents: A Digest of Research and Selected Bibliography." National Academy of Sciences, National Research Council, Washington, D. C., 1962.

32. Golembiewski, R. T., R. Hilles, and M. S. Kagno. "Longitudinal Study of Flexitime Effects: Some Consequences of an OD Structural Interaction," *Journal of Applied Behavioral Science*, 4 (1974): 503–532.

33. Golembiewski, R. T., S. Yeager, and R. Hilles. "Factor Analysis of Some Flexitime Effects: Attitudinal and Behavioral Consequences of a Structural Intervention," *Academy of Management Journal*, 18 (1975): 500–509.

34. Goodale, J. G., and A. K. Aagaard. "Factors Relating to Varying Reactions to the 4-Day Workweek," *Journal of Applied Psychology*, 60 (1975): 33–38.

35. Guilford, J. S. "Prediction of Accidents in a Standardized Home Environment," *Journal of Applied Psychology*, 57 (1973): 306–317.

36. Gustafson, C. E., and M. R. Rockway. "The Air Force Personnel Subsystem Concept." Paper presented at meeting of Southwestern Psychological Association, Fort Worth, 1962.

37. Haddon, W., Jr., and S. P. Baker. *Injury Control*. Washington, D. C.: Insurance Institute for Highway Safety, 1978.

38. Haddon, W., E. A. Suchman, and D. Klein. *Accident Research*. New York: Harper & Row, 1964.

39. Hennigan, J. K., and A. W. Wortham. "Analysis of Workday Stresses on Industrial Managers Using Heart Rate as a Criterion," *Ergonomics*, 18 (1975): 675–681.

40. Hersey, R. "Some Neglected Aspects of Accident Prevention," *Personnel*, 27 (1950): 231–236.

41. Hilgert, R. L., and J. R. Hundley III. "Supervision: The Weak Link in Flexible Work Scheduling," *The Personnel Administrator* (January 1975): 24–26.

42. Hinkle, L. E., and N. Plummer. "Life Stress and Industrial Absenteeism," *Industrial Medicine*, 21 (1952): 363–375.

43. Hinkle, L. E., L. H. Whitney, E. W. Lehman, J. Dunn, B. Benjamin, R. King, A. Plakun, and B. Fleshinger. "Occupation, Education and Coronary Heart Disease, *Science* 161 (1968): 238–246.

44. Holt H. O., and F. L. Stevenson. "Human Performance Considerations in Complex Systems," *Science*, 195 (1977): 1205–1209.

45. Ivancevich, J. M. "Effects of the Shorter Workweek on Selected Satisfaction and Performance Measures," *Journal of Applied Psychology*, 59 (1974): 717–721.

46. Kahn, R., D. M. Wolfe, R. P. Quinn, J. D. Snock, and R. A. Rosenthal. *Organizational Stress: Studies in Role Conflict and Ambiguity*. New York: Wiley, 1964.

47. Keenan, V., W. Kerr, and W. Sherman. "Psychological Climate and Accidents in an Automobile Plant," *Journal of Applied Psychology*, 35 (1951): 108–111.

48. Khalil, T. M., and C. N. Kurucz. "The Influence of 'Biorhythm' on Accident Occurrence and Performance," *Ergonomics*, 20, No. 4 (1977): 389–398.

49. Kraut, H., and E. Muller. "Calorie Intake and Industrial Output," *Science*, 104 (1946): 495–497.

50. Kryter, K. D. "Psychological Reactions to Aircraft Noise," *Science,* 151 (1966): 1346–1355.

51. Large, A. J. "Are Computers Better than Politicians?" *Wall Street Journal,* April 1967.

52. Latman, N. "Human Sensitivity, Intelligence and Physical Cycles and Motor Vehicle Accidents," *Accident Analysis and Prevention,* 9 (1977): 109–112.

53. Lundervold, A. "Electromyographic Investigations during Typewriting," *Ergonomics,* 1 (1958): 11–19.

54. Malaviga, P., and K. Ganesh. "Shift Work and Individual Differences in the Productivity of Weavers in an Indian Textile Mill," *Journal of Applied Psychology,* 61 (1976): 774–776.

55. Mathney, W. G., D. J. Dougherty, and J. M. Willis. "Relative Motion of Elements in Instrument Displays," *Aerospace Medicine,* 34 (1963): 1041–1046.

56. Mihal, W. L., and G. V. Barrett. "Individual Differences in Perceptual Information Processing and Their Relation to Automobile Accident Involvement," *Journal of Applied Psychology,* 61 (1976): 229–233.

57. Morgan, C. T., J. S. Cook, A. Chapanis, and M. W. Lund. *Human Engineering Guide to Equipment Design.* New York: McGraw-Hill, 1963.

58. Mott, P. E., F. C. Mann, Q. McLoughlin, and D. P. Warwick. *Shift-Work.* Ann Arbor, Michigan: University of Michigan Press, 1965.

59. Munsterberg, H. *Psychology and Industrial Efficiency.* Boston: Houghton Mifflin, 1913.

60. Nader, R. *Unsafe at Any Speed.* New York: Grossman, 1965.

61. Nelson, T. M., and S. H. Bartley. "The Pattern of Personal Response Arising during the Office Work Day," *Occupational Psychology,* 42 (1968): 77–83.

62. Nord, W. R., and R. Costigan. "Worker Adjustment to the Four-Day Week: A Longitudinal Study," *Journal of Applied Psychology,* 58 (1973): 60–66.

63. Owen, J. D. "Flexitime: Some Problems and Solutions," *Industrial and Labor Relations Review,* 30, No. 2 (1977): 139–160.

64. Passmore, R., and J. Durnin. "Human Energy Expenditure," *Physiological Review,* 35 (1955): 801–840.

65. Paterson, T. T., and F. J. Willet. "An Anthropological Experiment in a British Colliery," *Human Organization,* 10 (1951): 19–25.

66. Patkai, P., T. Akerstedt, and K. Pettersson. "Field Studies of Shiftwork: I. Temporal Patterns in Psychophysiological Activation in Permanent Night Workers," *Ergonomics,* 20 (1977): 611–619.

67. Pearson, M. W. "Pareto's Law and Modern Injury Control," *Journal of Safety Research,* 1 (1969): 55–57.

68. Pell, S., and C. A. D'Alonzo. "Three Year Study of Myocardial Infarction in a Large Employed Population," *Journal of the American Medical Association,* 175 (1961): 463–470.

69. Pfiefer, C. M., Jr., J. L. Stefanski, and C. B. Grether. *Psychological, Behavioral, and Organizational Factors Affecting Coal Miner Safety and Health.* (Technical Report No. BSC–5). National Institute for Occupational Safety and Health, Contract No. HSM–99–72–151, July 1976.

70. Pocock, S. J., R. Sergean, and P. J. Taylor. "Absence of Continuous Three-Shift Workers: A Comparison of Traditional and Rapidly Rotating Systems," *Occupational Psychology,* 46 (1972): 7–13.

71. Ruby, W. J., E. H. Jocoy, and F. M. Pelton. "Simulation for Experimenta-

tion: A Position Paper." For Aerospace Flight Conference, Columbus, Ohio, August 26–28, 1963.

72. Sales, S. M. "Organizational Role as a Risk Factor in Coronary Disease," *Administrative Science Quarterly,* 14 (1969): 325–336.

73. Sales, S. M., and J. House. "Job Dissatisfaction as a Possible Contributor to Risk of Death from Coronary Disease." Unpublished manuscript, 1970.

74. Schein, V. E., E. H. Maurer, and J. F. Novak. "Impact of Flexible Working Hours on Productivity," *Journal of Applied Psychology,* 62 (1977): 463–465.

75. Schulzinger, M. S. *The Accident Syndrome: The Genesis of Accidental Injury.* Springfield, Ill.: Charles C. Thomas, 1956.

76. Shavelson, R. J. "Lunar Gravity Simulation and Its Effect on Human Performance," *Human Factors,* 10 (1968): 393–402.

77. Shavelson, R. J., and J. L. Seminara. "The Effect of Lunar Gravity on Man's Performance of Basic Maintenance Tasks," *Journal of Applied Psychology,* 52 (1968): 177–183.

78. Slivnick, P., W. Kerr, and W. Kosinar. "A Study of Accidents in 147 Factories," *Personnel Psychology,* 10 (1957): 43–51.

79. Smith, L. "Flexitime: A New Work Style Catches On," *Dunn's Review* (March 1977): 61–63.

80. Smith, M. J., H. H. Cohen, A. Cohen, and R. J. Cleveland. "Characteristics of Successful Safety Programs," *Journal of Safety Research,* 10, No. 1 (1978): 5–15.

81. Starr, C. "Social Benefit versus Technological Risk," *Science,* 165 (1969): 1232–1238.

82. Stauffacher, J. "The Effect of Induced Muscular Tension upon Various Phases of the Learning Process," *Journal of Experimental Psychology,* 21 (1957): 26–37.

83. Sterns, H. L., G. V. Barrett, R. A. Alexander, J. P. Greenawalt, T. Gianetta, and P. E. Panek. "Improving Skills of the Older Adult Critical for Effective Driving Performance." Paper presented at Symposium, Gerontological Society, Louisville, Kentucky, October 1975.

84. Taub, J. M., and R. J. Berger. "The Effects of Changing the Phase and Duration of Sleep," *Journal of Experimental Psychology: Human Perception and Performance,* 2 (1976): 30–41.

85. Theologus, G. C., G. R. Wheaton, and E. A. Fleishman. "Effects of Intermittent, Moderate Intensity Noise Stress on Human Performance," *Journal of Applied Psychology,* 59 (1974): 539–547.

86. Trumbull, R. "Diurnal Cycles and Work-Rest Scheduling in Unusual Environments," *Human Factors,* 8 (1966): 385–398.

87. Van Zelst, R. H. "The Effect of Age and Experience upon Accident Rate," *Journal of Applied Psychology,* 38 (1954): 313–317.

88. Viteles, M. S. *Industrial Psychology.* New York: W. W. Norton, 1932.

89. *Wall Street Journal.* "Seven-Day Work Weeks Exceed Those with Four," March 7, 1977.

90. Weinstein, N. D. "Effect of Noise on Intellectual Performance," *Journal of Applied Psychology,* 59 (1974): 548–554.

91. Weinstein, N. D. "Noise and Intellectual Performance: A Confirmation and Extension," *Journal of Applied Psychology,* 62 (1977): 104–107.

92. West, L. J. "Fatigue and Performance Variability among Typists," *Journal of Applied Psychology*, 53 (1969): 80–86.

93. Whitlock, G. H. Personal communication, 1964.

94. Whitlock, G. H., R. J. Clouse, and W. F. Spencer. "Predicting Accident Proneness," *Personnel Psychology*, 16 (1963): 35–44.

95. Wilkinson, R. T. "Interaction of Noise with Knowledge of Results and Sleep Deprivation," *Journal of Experimental Psychology*, 66 (1963): 332–337.

96. Wilkinson, R. T. "Some Factors Influencing the Effect of Environmental Stressors upon Performance," *Psychological Bulletin*, 72 (1969): 260–272.

97. Wilkinson, R. T., and W. P. Colquhoun. "Interaction of Alcohol with Incentive and Sleep Deprivation," *Journal of Experimental Psychology*, 76 (1968): 623–629.

98. Witkin, H. A., R. B. Dyk, H. F. Faterson, D. R. Goodenough, and S. A. Karp. *Psychological Differentiation: Studies of Development*. New York: Wiley, 1962.

99. Wohlwill, J. F., J. L. Nasar, D. M. DeJoy, and H. H. Foruzani. "Behavioral Effects of a Noisy Environment: Task Involvement versus Passive Exposure," *Journal of Applied Psychology*, 61 (1976): 67–74.

100. Wolcott, J. H., R. R. McMeekin, R. E. Burgin, and R. E. Yanowitch. "Correlation of General Aviation Accidents with the Biorhythm Theory," *Human Factors*, 19, No. 3 (1977), 283–293.

17 CROSS-CULTURAL ISSUES IN INDUSTRIAL AND ORGANIZATIONAL PSYCHOLOGY

IN BRIEF   The rapid emergence of organizations whose activities go far beyond national boundaries raises important questions about the applicability of principles and techniques across cultures, societies, and economic and political systems. Principles and practices of selection, training, organization, performance evaluation, compensation, and supervision found to be effective in the United States may not be acceptable elsewhere.

While commonalities exist across cultures, there is also strong evidence of differences in values, attitudes, goals, and preferences among cultures. These differences may require the design and implementation of testing procedures, leadership styles, compensation patterns, and other practices quite different from those described in previous chapters. Furthermore, special training techniques may be required to permit multinational managers to operate effectively in different cultures.

Dealing with cross-cultural problems at the workplace is an old problem for industrial psychologists. Sixty years ago much of industry in the United States was multinational in that a large proportion of its workers were recent immigrants from many nations. At that time industrial psychologists were concerned about the proper technique for assimilating into one organization individuals from many nations having differing attitudes, values, and behavior.[19] With the passing of that phase, the wheel has turned. Our concern again shifts to whether what is true about work, workers, and the workplace in one country is applicable in other countries. We have become particularly sensitive to this question because of the many multinational corporations.

The Multinational Corporation

In the past, international business was mainly a matter of arranging for the trading of goods between supply in one country and demand in another. But increasingly, multinational firms are emerging that take a world outlook in all their activities, not only trading, but also financing, manufacturing, and developing products. They use their combined resources in many countries. One of the best multinational examples is IBM. Two of its ten models of the 360 computer were developed in Europe.[25] It now markets in over 100 countries. While some multinational organizations like Exxon had their origins in the last century, the past 30 years have witnessed the transformation of many major domestic corporations into multinational firms. Such firms not only manufacture and market their products in many countries, but they also tend to integrate their efforts across countries. The carburetor of an engine may be designed in Britain on the basis of research done in Belgium. It may be manufactured in Germany for assembly in an automobile in Brazil.

By the late 1970s hundreds of billions had been invested by United States firms in foreign affiliates. Investment is not a one-way street, since many multinational firms originating abroad also invest in the United States. For example, Shell, Unilever, Sony, Volkswagen and Nestlé are well-known companies whose parent firms come from outside the United States but which have extensive investments in the United States — an estimated $38 billion by 1972 for manufacturing alone.[2] The rate of foreign investment in banking, and real estate, along with manufacturing, accelerated dramatically in the 1970s. It climbed 78 per cent in just one year — 1977–1978.

THE MULTINATIONAL CORPORATION AND INTERNATIONAL RELATIONS By 1980, the overseas subsidiaries of American firms were generating and repatriating enough revenue to help substantially to offset the 50 billion dollar outflow for foreign aid. Yet more than this, the multinational corporations, both U. S. and foreign in origin, are likely to do much to integrate the peoples of the world.[32]

The specter is often raised that European business is being dominated by American companies. In fact Servan-Schreiber lists the "United States in Europe" as one of the world's largest economies.[40] But economic control does not necessarily mean management or labor dominance. For instance, in Europe, IBM employed some 65,000 people as of 1969, but only 200 of these were Americans. The president of IBM World Trade in the early seventies was French.[25]

The true multinational firm is beginning to become international at its highest levels. The board of directors of Exxon, heretofore exclusively American, by the 1970s was coopting Venezuelans, Canadians, and nationals of other countries.

DEVELOPMENT OF THE MULTINATIONAL ORGANIZATION   There are three approaches to how a multinational firm organizes itself to adapt to its environment, according to Perlmutter.[33]

1. Ethnocentric   The home country is superior to the foreign organization in all respects, and all decisions and methods will be controlled by the home country.

2. Polycentric   The organization is host-country-oriented since foreign cultures are different and local people are able to make the best decisions about the firm's progress.

3. Geocentric   The organization is world-oriented and a balanced view is taken of the local national interests and the objectives of the multinational firm. Managerial positions are filled by people having the most talent regardless of national background.

As a multinational organization matures, it moves from ethnocentric to geocentric organizational patterns.

Although many American managers in a typical multinational firm will never leave the United States nor work with nationals from other countries, it is probable that they will become involved in marketing, manufacturing, financial, or personnel decisions that involve foreign cultures, people, and conditions. There is a need to understand how the European, Asian, African, and Latin American worlds of industry differ in many significant ways from the American scene.

We devote a chapter to this in the belief that many of the principles of selection, training, and organization we have advanced in earlier chapters have to be qualified if they are to be applied across national boundaries. Evidence continues to accumulate that often what was regarded as the best way to deal with a particular personnel problem turns out to be merely the American way. We are also discovering that on many dimensions such as those of competitiveness, emphasis on participation and leadership, Americans tend to be relatively atypical in comparison to personnel from most other countries.[3]

PROBLEMS OF MULTINATIONAL FIRMS   In its efforts to become integrated, the multinational firm experiences many problems. These range from union disputes over tea breaks in England to dealing with the Spanish siesta with its long midday break from 2:00 until 5:00 P.M. Some companies (e.g., Raytheon, General Electric, and Chrysler) have been forced to close down certain operations or drastically modify their mode of operation because of problems like these. And many of the organizational problems of the domestic firm are compounded in the multinational company. They must operate in a variety of cultures with different values, beliefs, supervisory practices, compensation plans, and motivational schemes. As an illustration of a typical problem, consider what happens if Greeks and Americans have to cooperate in a business activity.

According to a survey of Greek and American stereotypes, Greeks tend to look on Americans as "well-organized work horses," but, in other respects see them as being loud, rigid, and aloof. On the other hand, Americans cannot understand how Greeks accept decisions based purely on friendship or political grounds, rather than on logic. In Greece, public or industrial organizations may administer a number of tests to applicants for a position. But the applicant with the lowest score on the test is selected by the top executive because the applicant is the cousin of another person from whom a favor is needed. This gives the Americans an extremely poor impression of the Greeks.[45]

It is interesting to note that in some countries, at least, multinational firms may attract potentially more productive and accommodating types of host-country managers into their ranks than comparable domestic firms do. For example, one survey showed that highly task-oriented Flemish business school graduates prefer to work for American or German companies rather than for their own native-managed organizations.[46]

PARENT, HOST, AND THIRD-COUNTRY NATIONALS

Within the multinational firm, different national origins of the current employees are an important fact of life, adding to organizational complexity. Likewise, it makes a difference whether the firm itself originated in the United States, in Britain, or Japan. A comparison of managers in a British-Dutch firm from those countries and from other nations in Europe, the Caribbean, Venezuela, Nigeria, Singapore, Malaysia, and Asia offers convincing evidence of the wide diversity of attitudes possible in the same multinational firm. A questionnare survey concluded that the non-Europeans were much more dissatisfied with the company's image than were Europeans. Moreover, as might be expected, the British and Dutch were relatively most satisfied with the company as a place to work and with opportunities to obtain responsibility and authority.[34]

In a survey of parent-country nationals (e.g., Britons managing a Mexican subsidiary of a British-owned multinational corporation), host-country nationals (e.g., Mexicans managing the Mexican subsidiary of the British firm), and third-country nationals (e.g., Germans managing the Mexican subsidiary of the British firm) found different perceptions of managerial behavior.[52]

The survey results suggested that parent-country nationals and third-country nationals tended to impose headquarters' managerial patterns on their host-country peers and subordinates. For example, the British or German managers of the British subsidiary in Mexico tended to impose British managerial patterns and procedures when they were running the British subsidiary in Mexico. According to the headquarters' personnel directors, this multinational uniformity facilitated comparisons of the achievements of individual managers in subsidiaries in different countries. These managers could then continue their advancement to top positions on returning to the multinational headquarters. Uniformity was also thought to keep up the firm's reputation in different countries and make it easier to introduce policy changes.

But host-country nationals (e.g., the Mexicans managing in the British subsidiary in Mexico) disagreed. Of the 248 questioned by Zeira, 186 felt that the parent-country or third-country nationals maintained such uniformity of policies and practices for their own self-interests, not to further the interests of the corporation.

The host-country nationals felt that the parent-country and third-country nationals at top management levels (e.g., the British or German managers of the British firm in Mexico) were not motivated to try to make improvements locally and to adapt to local needs. They were seen to be insensitive to the discrepancies between their own behavior and the expectations of their local subordinates.

The host-country nationals saw many other conflicts brought about by top managers from other countries. Because the expatriates were representatives of their multinational corporations, they could achieve entry into the upper-class social life of the local communities. They could enter social circles that they could never reach in their previous positions at headquaters. They obtained special fringe benefits as part of their compensation abroad, such as company car, travel expenses, special insurance, rent subsidies, and education expenses, which made it possible for them to enjoy a standard of living considerably higher than that of their local peers and higher than what they could expect upon their return to headquarters.

Host-country managers were particularly critical of the tendency of multinational corporations to centralize decisions. With headquarters demanding uniformity, and the expatriate managers enforcing the demands, it was impossible to adapt to the needs of the local marketplace. Furthermore, host-country managers tended to mistrust expatriate top managers. Also, they felt that their promotion to higher level was blocked by their not being nationals of the parent country.

On the other hand, the rotation of third-country nationals (e.g., a German to a supervisory job in a British subsidiary in Mexico) into lower-level positions in the host country was seen as a favorable solution by host-country nationals.

On the basis of his surveys and interviews, Zeira recommends that multinational firms need to equip parent-country nationals and third-country nationals with adequate knowledge of the complex human problems of international enterprises and with sufficient self-confidence to adapt their managerial behavior to the needs of the subsidiary.[52] They need to be given opportunities and rewards for administering more flexible, localized policies. At the same time, multinationals must include host-country national experts in the composition of their central personnel departments to increase the empathy of these departments with morale problems abroad.

SOME CURRENT PSYCHOLOGICAL ISSUES

Does what we know about selection, training, motivation, leadership and organization in one country or culture have validity in others? As we move from one country or culture to another, how must we modify our expectations and understandings as well as our policies, plans, and ways of relating to others?

Answers to these questions are sought by cross-national study in industrial/organizational psychology and are of particular importance to multinational enterprises.[4]

Selection in Different Cultures

UTILITY IN DEVELOPING COUNTRIES   One area of high payoff for selection and testing is in the developing nations. Developing nations have a shared problem in identifying and developing manpower. This means that it is quite important that people with the most aptitude are placed in the limited number of training programs.

An extensive program was undertaken in Nigeria by the American Institute for research to develop a testing program.[39] In this program, provision was made for teaching examinees every response they were expected to make through the use of visual aids, supplemented by active demonstration and oral instructions.

Changes required were not in a test itself, but in how to explain the test to people from non-Western cultures. The research program demonstrated that it is quite feasible to design and modify aptitude tests that have been devised in the Western culture. The tests were administered to over 2,000 Nigerians of various backgrounds and were able to discriminate validly between those who performed well and not so well in training programs. It was estimated that when these tests became fully operational, the average quality of the Nigerian trainee would be on the level of the current outstanding trainee before selection by tests. Tests developed in Nigeria were also suitable for Kenya and elsewhere in Anglophone black Africa.

TRANSFERABILITY OF VALIDITY STUDIES   In Chapter 12 we discussed Exxon's Early Identification of Management Potential (EIMP) program, which involved extensive use of tests. Exxon is a multinational energy corporation with executives in many countries of the world. To determine if the original EIMP study in the United States could be validated cross-nationally, 800 managers from Norway, Denmark, and the Netherlands were studied. The criterion was an index based on salary adjusted for age and organization salary structure.[26]

As shown in Table 17–1, there was a remarkable degree of correspondence between the efficiency of the tests in the United States and in the other three European countries. This study presents fairly convincing evidence that the same traits and ability levels that are predictive of success of a United States manager are also predictive of success of managers in other countries *working in the same multinational corporation*. Similar results appear in Latin America as well. Several reasons may be involved. First, it may be that there are universal traits of leadership. Second, Exxon may recruit and attract into its ranks "Americanized" Europeans and Latin Americans, and the organizational climate may impose uniformities in requirements which transcend cultures. Third, some common test constructs may lie across cultures.

VALUES AS PREDICTIVE OF MANAGERIAL SUCCESS   There is a limited amount of information that relates managerial values to success in an organization. Managers from all countries do have distinct values that can be charac-

Table 17–1. Forecasting accuracy of a battery of tests and measurements for the early identification of Exxon managers in four different countries.

Test	U.S.	Norway	Denmark	Netherlands
Part A	.44	.59	.61	.55
Part B	.64	.65	.57	.62
Part C	.33	.29	.34	.27
Part D	.52	.43	.34	.45

Adapted from Laurent, "Cross-Cultural Cross-Validation of Empirically Validated Tests," *Journal of Applied Psychology*, 54 (1970): 421.

terized as pragmatic. Using the personal values questionnaire developed by England, it was found that managerial values are related to success in the organization.[17] The cross-national study showed a similar degree of relationship between managerial values and managerial success in India, Australia, and the United States, but not in Japan.[49]

PERSONNEL SELECTION DECISIONS Culture or nationality introduce biases into the personnel selection process. Triandis asked 100 Illinois students, 100 Greek students, 32 Illinois personnel directors, and 20 Greek personnel directors to complete a questionnaire about 32 job candidates for various jobs in accounting and finance.[45] The hypothetical candidates were systematically different in competence, age, sex, race, religion, sociability, and wealth. Respondents were asked to rate each candidate on a 7-point scale ranging from "I strongly oppose" to "I strongly recommend."

Candidates were described in different combinations of five characteristics each as either highly competent or barely competent; fifty-five or thirty years of age; female or male; Christian or Jewish; black or white; sociable or unsociable; and rich or poor. Not all combinations were used. A complex analysis of variance showed the effect of changing any one of the characteristics. For example, for the 32 Illinois personnel directors, 54 per cent of the variance in their ratings of the candidates was accounted for by whether candidates were described as highly competent or barely competent. But such competence accounted for only 24 per cent of the ratings of the Greek personnel directors. Table 17–2 shows the dis-

Table 17–2. Percentage of variance accounting for support or opposition to recommending candidates for comptroller or manager of accounting and finance division by Americans and Greeks.

	Americans		Greeks	
	Personnel directors	Students	Personnel directors	Students
Competence	54.0	70.0	24.0	46.0
Race	8.2	3.0	6.1	1.2
Age	0.0	1.8	46.0	2.1
Sex	8.0	0.4	2.1	4.2
Religion	0.7	1.5	0.0	5.0
Sociability	10.2	11.2	1.0	30.6
Wealth	0.0	0.2	0.2	2.8
Interactions	18.9	12.1	18.7	7.8

Adapted from Triandis, "Factors Affecting Employee Selection in Two Cultures," *Journal of Applied Psychology,* 47 (1963): 93.

tribution of the percentages of variance accounted for by the characteristics for the four samples. It can be seen that competence was more important (although they may not have been conscious about the importance) to the Americans than to the Greeks, more so to the students than to the personnel directors. Race was more important than religion, particularly to the American personnel directors. Age was particularly important to the Greek personnel directors, accounting for 46 per cent of the variance in their ratings. (They were unanimous in not hiring the fifty-five-year olds. But this emphasis on age was not due to culture but to Greek law. It had no relevance for the Greek students, who probably were unacquainted with the Greek law involved. Provisions of Greek law require relatively large compensation at the time of retirement or termination so Greek personnel directors reject older candidates, who will only be able to work for a relatively short period of time.) Sociability was particularly important to the Greek students.

It is clear that while the validities of tests of competence may generalize across countries, we cannot completely generalize what is likely to influence the more subjective employment interviewers' decisions across countries or cultures. These are likely to be affected by national and cultural biases and constraints that we will need to take into account.

Training and Personnel Development

Two issues stand out here. First, there is concern for specialized training to prepare employees for work in other countries. Second, there is training that is particularly relevant for some countries, such as training to speed a country's national development.

CROSS-CULTURAL TRAINING As more managers from various countries work in multinational organizations, the training they receive will increase in importance. While it is evident that training in the customs and history of the country and becoming proficient in the language of the host country are helpful, there are other areas of training that can be initiated for the multinational manager. In Chapters 13 and 14 we discussed a number of training and OD techniques, including sensitivity training and the use of programmed experiences. These techniques can also be used for cross-cultural training. The common model for the sensitivity training group is to have individuals from various countries involved in the same session. Other techniques include role-playing, where the participant is asked to play parts in various common situations which might arise in a country. A modified form of role-playing has been called "contrast culture." [42] In this technique the modal values of the culture are identified. Then various situations and roles are created that will demonstrate the extreme contrast between various roles individuals from different cultures can play.

Another technique is the use of cultural assimilators. They involve critical episodes with individuals from different countries and possible ways of dealing with the situation or issue given. The trainee chooses one of the four alternatives and then the correctness of the response is explained.[19] Other methods use similar techniques, and these include critical incidents from different cultures, which can be studied.

The authors are involved with many others in a cross-national training and research program using simulations of organizational issues. From the data of 20 or more countries, norms can be drawn that allow managers from diverse nations and organizations to compare their attitudes, values, and behavior with others. We will look at some of this comparative data later in this chapter.

Cross-cultural training aims to prepare trainees for their cross-cultural encounter. People who have never been out of their own culture are liable to *culture shock*. At home, they have learned to behave in ways that are readily understood by their family, friends, colleagues, and others; they in turn understand the behavior of others and participate in a give-and-take of psychological and emotional gratification. Yet they carry on at home without awareness of this process, since they acquire these skills during early socialization and take such gratification for granted. When the same people are suddenly transplanted to an alien cultural environment, they find themselves at a loss in understanding the behavior patterns of the host-country nationals. Often they misinterpret the motives and responses of their hosts and become critical of the hosts' behavior. The many unfamiliar situations and sundry cues that confront them call for responses that are not available in their familiar repertoire of responses that once were adequate and gratifying.

In his first lecture in Madras, India, the first author was extremely frustrated by his audience. They continually shook their heads from side to side, a gesture that he interpreted as disagreement and negative feedback. What he did not know at that time was that in South India people move their heads sideways to show appreciation and say "yes," and move their heads vertically to indicate "no."

Preparation for the cross-cultural encounter involves learning about one's own culture as well as the new culture into which one is moving.

THE DEVELOPMENT OF NEED FOR ACHIEVEMENT   In earlier chapters we talked about need for achievement. McClelland and his associates have designed an achievement stimulation course for developing countries. The argument is that national development depends on achievement motivation. This can be increased by enrolling entrepreneurs of a developing country in a course to stimulate their need for achievement. Participants learn to detect and create achievement imagery. They learn what such imagery is associated with. Cases of persons high and low in need for achievement are presented. These are then related to the participants' own lifestyles and plans.

Seventy-six achievement-trained subjects (in India) were compared with seventy-three who did not participate in such a program. In comparison to the control group, trainees significantly increased in new business activities, capital investment, and gross income from before to two years after the course.[29]

Motivation

ORGANIZATIONAL OBJECTIVES   In Chapter 1, we saw how corporate objectives influence what role industrial psychology plays in a country. But such objectives vary from one country to another. As we stated in Chapter 1, Exercise Objectives, a training experience, was designed to assess managers' rankings of corporate objectives.[11] Following group discussion, managers rate the importance of six goals that they may have had in mind as they made their personal decisions. Comparisons of between-country samples have shown a significant difference between managers from various countries both in their problem-solving decisions and their listing of corporate objectives. But instead of cultural variables being most important, the economic dimension comes to the fore. For example, managers from developing countries attribute less importance to meeting competition than do managers from the United States, Britain, and the Netherlands. The developed countries put greater stress on the objectives of growth and competition. Conversely, maintaining satisfactory organizational operations appears to be more important to those from the developing countries.[6]

Table 17–3 shows the extent to which 5,122 managers in 12 national groupings were willing to budget money for each of five organizational needs: safety, strike settlement, morale, product quality, and pollution control. For these data, collected between 1968 and 1972, it can be seen that there were wide variations among managers from country to country in their willingness to budget the necessary expenditures. National variation was widest in dealing with pollution control. European and Japanese managers seemed much less willing to spend money on pollution controls than those from elsewhere. Compared with those from everywhere else, the Japanese were least likely to spend for morale improvement. In the same way, the French were the most willing to continue advertising a shoddy product rather than to spend to improve the product's quality.

But there were unusual elements operating also. In all twelve national groupings, managers who had a higher rate of career advancement (were younger at higher levels in larger organizations) were less willing to budget

Table 17–3. Willingness to budget for five organizational needs by 5,122 managers in 12 national groupings (percentages).

Number and Nation		Safety	Settle strike	*Need* Morale	Product quality	Pollution control
Anglo-American						
344	United States	67	64	70	84	65
1,348	Britain	60	68	62	75	35
Low Countries						
592	Netherlands	76	57	70	86	46
642	Belgium	73	52	73	80	45
Nordic						
292	Germany/Austria	67	74	72	77	48
336	Scandinavia	73	62	75	76	44
Latin						
370	France	65	63	78	60	38
599	Italy	74	54	77	72	50
153	Iberia	67	66	84	74	51
256	Latin America	66	66	83	79	71
Asiatic						
133	India	66	56	72	83	65
57	Japan	59	60	47	83	46
Rate of Advancement						
2,413	Higher	67	60	77	77	45
2,709	Lower	69	64	78	76	47
5,122	Both	68	62	71	77	46

Adapted from Bass et al., *Assessment of Managers: An International Comparison* (New York: Free Press, 1979), p. 102.

money for any of the five organizational needs than were managers with lower rates of career advancement. From 13 to 21 per cent of the variance in decision to spend or not spend was due to nationality. But, of course, much more than cultural differences were involved, for the nations differed in legal requirements, wealth, market competition, inflation rates, and so on. Nevertheless, for whatever reasons, national differences exist and must be taken into account in personnel policies, training, and motivational programs in the different countries.[12]

VALUES AND MOTIVES OF DIFFERENT CULTURAL GROUPS We discussed in Chapter 3 some of the diverse motives of individuals in organizations — and these differ in different countries. For instance, cultures differ in how central work and organization are to the individual employee's life. Thus, Table 17–4 compares United States and Japanese workers in terms

Table 17–4. Meaning of company to United States and Japanese employees.

	United States (Percentage)	Japan (Percentage)
I think of my company as:		
1. The central concern in my life and of greater importance than my personal life	1	9
2. A part of my life at least equal in importance to my personal life	23	56
3. A place for me to work with management, during work hours, to accomplish mutual goals	54	26
4. Strictly a place to work and entirely separate from my personal life	23	6

Adapted from Whitehill, "Cultural Values and Employee Attitudes: United States and Japan," *Journal of Applied Psychology,* 48 (1964): 71.

of how central to their life is their company.[48] As can be seen, 56 per cent of the Japanese workers perceived the company to be at least equal in importance to their personal life, while only 23 per cent of the Americans felt the same way.

The value system of a culture plays an important role in individual expectations of organizational rewards.[18] In the United States workers see themselves receiving wages in exchange for services, but the model is quite different in Asia. In the Orient, compensation is an obligation of the employer, who is responsible for employee welfare; compensation is often not directly related to the services performed but is more directly related to the individual's needs. The whole concept of performance appraisal is often rejected in the Orient.[21]

The attitudes and values that a culture holds can have definite influences on the functioning of an organization and thereby the economic development of a country. This has been illustrated in studies of South American board meetings. Heller found that few of these boards either precirculated agenda or maintained and circulated minutes of the previous meeting.[23] This meant that there was a great deal of inefficiency. Since past board decisions were not recorded, over half the meeting time was spent in talking about decisions that had been previously made. In contrast, for those few organizations that did maintain minutes of the meetings, less than one-quarter of the time was spent going over and discussing past decisions. Further study determined that only a small percentage of the decisions made in the board meetings without recorded minutes were actually implemented.

These findings illustrate one of the primary conflicts with which a multinational company must deal. There are in a culture certain attitudes and beliefs that may be counterproductive for organizational efficiency. In order to be an effective organization in terms of the economic marketplace, it may be necessary for the organization to eliminate practices that are counterproductive. But doing this may in turn alienate members of the organization for whom the practices have special significance.

Work attitudes and values, effective management of resources, investment decisions, and national policies affect a nation's productivity. All of these were involved in the decline of Great Britain from first to tenth among the Western European industrial democracies in rate of growth of its gross national product per capita between the 1950s and 1980. Similarly, the rise of Japan and West Germany as industrial superpowers reflects all of these forces in combination, as well as the effects of being able to replace, en masse, old, bombed-out factories with new facilities.[16]

MANAGERIAL ROLE CONFLICT The importance of differences in values and culture within a country is seen in a Canadian investigation by Auclair, who studied over 3000 French- and English-Canadian managers.[3] On most dimensions, the conflict between family and business roles was less for the English-Canadian managers than for their French-speaking counterparts. French-Canadian managers placed a high value on their family role and, because of this, experienced conflict with business role demands.

GOALS OF MANAGERS FROM DIFFERENT COUNTRIES Some of the differences between countries can be explained by what managers in each country considered to be important to their lives. As shown in Table 17–5, there are distinct differences among managers from twelve national groupings.[12] Table 17–5 shows the percentage of managers in each national grouping who ranked each of eleven life goals as first, second, or third in importance. Thus, 58 per cent of U.S. managers ranked self-realization as first, second, or third, as did similar high percentages from everywhere else. The Japanese were highest in percentage (74 per cent), and the Indians were lowest (42 per cent) in this regard. Leadership was most important to Germans and Austrians (51 per cent) and least so for the Dutch (20 per cent) for whom expertise (50 per cent) was more important. But expertise was lowest for the Italians (22 per cent) relative to the other eleven groups. Note that despite outsiders' stereotypes, it is the British who had the highest percentage of managers emphasizing pleasure (29 per cent), while the Spaniards (9 per cent) and Latin Americans (10 per cent) were relatively low in this regard.

Relatively speaking, wealth is more important to the Indian and American manager and least important to the Japanese. Independence is most important to the Germans and Austrians and least important to the Indians.

Table 17–5. Percentage placing life goal in top three in importance in each of twelve national groups.

National grouping	N	Self-realization	Leadership	Expertness	Wealth	Independence	Prestige	Duty	Service	Affection	Security	Pleasure
Anglo-American												
United States	227	58	48	32	14	37	14	14	18	27	21	18
Britain	426	56	34	29	9	33	9	9	21	36	34	29
Low countries												
Netherlands	119	64	20	50	4	50	12	25	18	20	21	20
Belgium	202	55	33	40	8	40	11	29	22	29	20	10
Nordic countries												
Germany/Austria	142	68	51	34	8	54	17	7	13	20	22	4
Scandinavia	160	59	24	32	5	40	3	9	31	36	36	26
Latin countries												
France	102	63	24	47	7	32	3	20	30	45	16	15
Italy	234	65	30	22	5	51	10	13	10	44	32	18
Iberia	128	69	31	45	6	25	11	22	29	24	28	9
Latin America	119	57	33	39	9	30	33	13	26	24	21	10
Asiatic countries												
India	84	42	34	44	17	29	20	34	27	26	21	6
Japan	43	74	46	39	2	49	2	46	2	19	16	2

Adapted from Bass et al., *Assessment of Managers: An International Comparison* (New York: Free Press, 1979), p. 65.

Prestige is most important to the Latin Americans and least important to the Japanese, for whom duty is most important. Service is relatively most important to the Scandinavians. Affection for family and friends is most important to the Italians and French, and security to the Scandinavians and British.

These clusterings of Anglo-American, Nordic, Latin, and so on, derive from a survey completed by Haire, Ghiselli, and Porter involving 3,600 managers from 14 different countries.[22] Their analysis showed that when the survey responses from each country were compared with one another, certain clusters of countries emerged. Within each cluster the common link was similiarity in cultural background. The clusters that emerged were as follows: Nordic-European (Denmark, Germany, Norway, and Sweden), Latin-European (Belgium, France, Italy, and Spain), Anglo-American (England and United States), and Japan. Exceptions to these cultural clusters were the three developing countries in the sample — Argentina, Chile, and India — which formed a tight cluster by themselves, even though India is culturally quite distinct from Argentina and Chile. Except for the three developing countries, the other clusters include countries that are quite heterogeneous in their level of industrialization and economic development. Thus, when managerial attitudes are considered, cultural background of the managers seems to be a major influence.

PERCEIVED EQUITY IN WORK REWARDS   While everyone is agreed that there should be a systematic appraisal of equity, there is almost no information on national differences in what is equitable.

The training activity, Exercise Compensation, was designed to obtain data concerning managers' perceptions of equitable merit increases based on different performance and extenuating job conditions.[9] Each manager has to make decisions regarding the recommended salary increase (as a percentage of present wage) to be offered to each of ten hypothetical engineers. Three of the engineers differed in merit, one being at the ninetieth percentile in performance, one at the fiftieth percentile, and the last at the tenth percentile. In addition, the remaining seven engineers were average performers (fiftieth percentile) but had some extenuating job condition. These job conditions were: no security; no opportunity for advancement; bad working conditions; low prestige; unfriendly co-workers; boring job; and competitive offer.

Ryterband and Thiagarajan compared managers from two highly industrialized areas (the United States and Scandinavia) and two less industrialized countries (India and Colombia) on Exercise Compensation.[37] All managers rewarded the best engineer equally: the ratio was about one-half again as much as the average performer. The real difference between countries was revealed, however, in the merit increases awarded the least productive engineer. Managers from developed countries consistently gave the poor performer less than the average engineer (about 32 per cent less), while managers from the developing countries gave the poor performer almost the same salary increase as that of the average performer. The managers from the developed countries awarded the best performer approximately 2.4 times the increase awarded the poorest performer. The corresponding salary increase given by managers from the developing countries was approximately 1.5 times the increase given the poorest performing engineer.

The managers from the developing countries also differed in their treatment of the seven engineers who were average performers but who had extenuating job circumstances. The managers from the developing countries made wide distinctions among the various job conditions, while managers from the developed countries tended not to do this.

It was clear that managers from the developed countries value merit more than do those from the developing countries. It appeared that in the developing countries pay is not perceived to be as closely linked to performance as it is in developed countries. Sociologists concerned with the modernization of man assert that the belief that rewards and punishments should be according to contribution is true only of modern man.[24]

Styles of compensation do change. In Russia traditionally scientists and technical workers have been paid according to their academic degree. More recently incentive payments as high as 30 per cent above the base salary and "reverse incentive" wage units have been introduced into Russian research organizations.[1] With modernization, pay associated with merit is becoming more commonplace in developing countries.

Superior-Subordinate Relationships

Survey evidence on supervisory-subordinate relations in different countries comes from several different sources: grid seminars, surveys of IBM personnel, questionnaire surveys of managers in training centers, and responses of managers to simulated supervisory-subordinate situations. Likert contended that the participative form of management has universal application throughout the world.[27] The same argument was advanced by Mouton and Blake.[31] More specifically, Rus [35] in Yugoslavian organizations confirmed the findings of Tannenbaum [43] in the United States for managers' and workers' perceptions of the distribution of influence in an organization. Rus found that despite the fact that the Yugoslav organization has workers' councils, which theoretically should bring about maximum participation and influence by the workers in their organization, both managers and workers saw influence concentrated in top management.[35] But consistent with U. S. findings, in Yugoslavia as well, both managers and workers in the more efficient organizations reported that they had greater influence than their counterparts in inefficient organizations. In other words, the more total influence everyone felt they had in the system, the greater was the total system efficiency both in the United States and in Yugoslavia. But, as we will see, there is undeniable evidence to refute these arguments that participation is a universal panacea.

GRID SEMINARS Self-reports of almost 2,500 middle and upper managers from eight countries during grid seminars show a great deal of similarity. For the particular comparative analysis they reported, the general question asked of the participants was "What is the best way for a company to operate?" Twenty questions, each presenting a variety of alternatives about organizational performance, were discussed in a group and a consensus was reached. For each question the participants could choose one of five alternatives, ranging from "most sound" to "least sound." There was agreement in all eight countries that the 9, 9 management style is the ideal for the corporation. The 9, 9 style is maximally concerned with both production and people.[31]

The main difficulty with these findings is that all the results are based on data obtained during and after the participants' indoctrination in a management development course. The results could be merely a reflection of the completeness of the indoctrination.

These uniform results are in contrast to the way the managers viewed their own self-reported conduct at the end of the seminar. The managers in the United States rated themselves as being maximally concerned with both people and production. The opposite trend was found for managers from Japan and South America, who were more concerned with production than with people. The Middle East stood out as an area that was maximally concerned with neither production or people, as evidenced by the 55 per cent who endorsed their style as being 5, 5.

IBM SURVEY   The attitudes of 23,000 IBM employees toward their supervisors were surveyed in 45 countries.[41] One of the questions dealt with the preferred and perceived leadership styles of their manager as originally proposed by Tannenbaum and Schmidt.[44] They paralleled four of the five styles we discussed in Chapter 6:

Directive   Managers usually make their decisions promptly and communicate them to subordinates clearly and firmly. They expect them to carry out decisions loyally and without raising difficulty.

Negotiative   Managers usually make decisions promptly, but, before going ahead, try to explain them fully to subordinates. They give them the reasons for decisions and answer whatever questions subordinates may have.

Consultative   Managers usually consult with their subordinates before they reach their decision. They listen to their advice, consider it, and then announce their decision. They then expect all to work loyally to implement it, whether or not it is in accordance with the advice they gave.

Participative   Managers usually call a meeting of their subordinates when there is an important decision to be made. They put the problem before the group and invite discussion. They accept the majority viewpoint as the decision.

Table 17-6 shows results from four selected countries.

It is clear that the management style preferred by the majority of IBM employees is consultative, but we also note that there are some distinct differences among countries. In Brazil, for example, an additional 29 per cent of the employees opted for participative leadership. Consultation is considerably higher in preference in Australia and the U.K. than in Brazil or Japan. Note how little participative leadership is perceived anywhere. These results are consistent with data gathered using the Management Styles Survey in the United States, Spain, Sweden, Finland, and

Table 17-6. Preferred and perceived managerial style of IBM employees, given as percentages.

Manager	Australia	Britain	Brazil	Japan
Preferred				
Directive	1	5	8	1
Persuasive	25	25	21	42
Consultative	65	61	42	44
Participative	9	9	29	13
Perceived				
Directive	22	14	23	19
Persuasive	32	30	24	26
Consultative	30	34	17	26
Participative	5	8	12	10
None of these	11	14	24	19

Adapted from Sadler and Hofstede, *Leadership Styles, Preferences and Perceptions of Employees of an International Company in Different Countries.* International Studies of Management and Organization, 1976, 6, 3, 87–113, p. 106.

India.[14] Consultation is preferred over participation everywhere and is more frequently seen everywhere. In all the countries in the IBM survey and in those just mentioned, directive supervision is favored less by the vast majority of subordinates and their supervisors. Nevertheless, in some other countries, such as India and Greece, we find considerable preference for such authoritarian or directive supervision.[4,7]

EXERCISE SUPERVISE   In this training exercise for managers, half played the role of supervisor; the other half played subordinates. Most managers completed the exercise in their native language, but some did so in international training programs so that unequal numbers of supervisors and subordinates were in the samples from different countries. Also, nonmanagers who were in the exercise were removed from the analysis.

"Subordinates" met with three different kinds of "supervisors" to complete three sets of decisions: authoritarian-directive, persuasive-negotiative, and participative. The "supervisors" met with three kinds of "subordinates": highly involved, moderately involved, or passive-uninvolved in the decision. Afterward, "subordinates" noted which "supervisor" they met was most satisfactory to work with. Supervisors did the same.

On a chance basis, 33 per cent of all subordinates should report being most satisfied with participative supervisors. Likewise, on a chance basis, 33 per cent of all supervisors should be most satisfied with uninvolved, passive subordinates.

Data from 669 managers in Table 17-7 shows the reported satisfaction

Table 17–7. Reported satisfaction of "subordinates" following decision-making with participative, persuasive, and directive "supervisors" on exercise supervise.

N	National Grouping	Percentage of "subordinates" who were most satisfied in decision-making with "participative" supervisors
66	Dutch-Flemish	64.7
50	Nordic (Germany, Austria, Switzerland, Scandinavia)	56.4
97	Anglo-American (U.S., U.K., Eire, Australia)	53.0
78	Latin (Brazil, Colombia, France, Italy, Spain, French Switzerland, Walloon Belgium)	52.6
37	Japanese	50.0
17	Indian	29.4
18	Greek	22.2

Adapted from Cascio, "Functional Specialization, Culture, and Preference for Participative Management," *Personnel Psychology,* 27 (1974): 599, and Bass, *A Preliminary Report on Manifest Preferences in Six Cultures for Participative Management* (Technical Report No. 21). Rochester: University of Rochester, 1968), p. 13.

of those who played "subordinates." It can be seen that while almost 65 per cent of Dutch or Flemish subordinates preferred working with a participative supervisor and at least 50 per cent of European, American, and Japanese managers did so, only 25 per cent Indian and 22 per cent of Greek subordinates did so.

Table 17–8 shows the percentage of "supervisors" who favored returning to work with uninvolved, passive subordinates: "yesmen." It can be seen that the Japanese, Europeans, and Americans were much less appreciative of such subordinates than were the Greek or Indian managers.[12]

Again, the results are not just cultural. Indians and Greeks do live in a more authoritarian world, in which subordinates and supervisors find it more difficult to trust each other as easily as is possible elsewhere. But, economic, educational, legal, political, and historical differences support the preferences for authoritarian relationships and the discomfort with participative approaches. For example, with underemployment endemic as in India, managers are much more security-conscious and find it more comfortable to remain passive with superiors, avoiding the possibilities of conflict and job loss.[15]

Peru is another place where preference for more directive supervision has been found. Peruvian white-collar workers preferred supervisors who were directive, but there were exceptions. While participative and consultative management has found acceptance, particularly in the United States, it is clear that managers in some cultures actually prefer a more autocratic

Table 17–8. Reported satisfaction of "superiors" following decision-making with vitally involved, moderately involved, and uninvolved "subordinates."

N	Culture of managers	Percentage of "supervisors" who were most satisfied in decision-making with uninvolved "subordinates"
16	Japanese	18.1
34	Dutch-Flemish	21.4
62	Nordic	28.0
93	Latin	28.2
98	Anglo-American	29.8
12	Greek	41.7
17	Indians	75.0

Adapted from Cascio, "Functional Specialization, Culture, and Preference for Participative Management," *Personnel Psychology*, 27 (1974): 600, and Bass, *A Preliminary Report on Manifest Preferences in Six Cultures for Participative Management* (Technical Report No. 21). Rochester: University of Rochester, Management Research Center, 1968, p. 14.

form of supervision and more passive subordinates. Whyte had shown that the Peruvians as a whole tended to have a low level of faith in people.[50] Using a faith-in-people scale, Peruvian workers were sorted into high-, medium-, and low-trust groups. They found that those workers high in interpersonal trust favored participative or consultative supervision. In contrast, those low in interpersonal trust were more satisfied with supervision which was more authoritarian.[51]

EXERCISE COMMUNICATION   Results from a training activity, Exercise Communication,[8] were analyzed for more than 2,329 managers from 20 countries.[5] This exercise is concerned with the communication of geometric patterns. Two geometric patterns are sent. The first pattern is sent via one-way communication. The receivers do not watch and cannot talk to the sender. The second pattern is communicated via the two-way technique, which allows the receiver to ask questions of the sender.

Variation from country to country in preference as a receiver for one-way communication correlated 0.82 with the Haire, Ghiselli, and Porter measure of propensity to avoid sharing information and objectives.[22] Also, variation from country to country in preference for one-way communication as a receiver correlated 0.89 with subordinates' preference for authoritarian supervision as previously measured in Exercise Supervise.[37]

Thus, as already noted in both the supervisory and the communication exercises, managers from such countries as India tended to favor directive, authoritarian supervision as well as one-way communication, while in other locations such as the United States or Great Britain more consultation, participation, and two-way communication are favored. Consistent with this is an experimental replication of the classic Lippitt and White [28] study of leadership in India by Meade,[30] which demonstrated that both morale and productivity were higher under authoritarian rather than under democratic leadership in India. This was a reversal of the Lippitt and White results in the United States.

We interpret all the above studies on superior-subordinate relationships to indicate that there are differences among countries in preferred styles of leadership. These differences in leadership styles appear to be largely culturally based, and at this point in time it would be naive to advocate one model of leadership style as being optimal for all cultural groups. The widely advocated American model of participative or consultative management may not be optimal for all cultures and in fact may be dysfunctional in some.

SUMMARY

The United States' international trade has turned into large multinational organizational efforts during the past century. And, as well, in the 1970s we have seen the burgeoning of direct investment by foreign-led multinationals in the United States. Managers of these firms increasingly are from the host country, although parent-country and third-country nationals still play important roles, particularly at higher levels.

We are faced with the overriding question of how much we can transfer the techniques of selection, training, motivation, and supervision across countries, particularly from the developed to the developing countries. Needless to say, we cannot automatically make transfers without adequate testing of results in the local situation. Local history, culture, institutions, educational systems, and so on affect whether or not a particular personnel practice, found effective in the United States, for example, will be effective in Belgium, Japan, or Nigeria.

Industrial/organizational psychology also has relevance for the human resources management issues of countries, as countries; that is, for national policies. This forms the substance of our next chapter.

REFERENCES

1. Anonymous. "Russia Sets Program of Wage Incentives in Scientific Work," *Wall Street Journal*, June 1, 1970, p. 12.
2. Arpan, J. S., and D. A. Ricks. *Directory of Foreign Manufacturers in the United States.* Atlanta: Georgia State University, 1975.
3. Auclair, G. "Managerial Role Conflict: A Cross-Cultural Comparison." Paper

presented at 76th Annual Convention, American Psychological Association, San Francisco, September 1968.

4. Barrett, G. V., and B. M. Bass. "Cross-Cultural Issues in Industrial and Organizational Psychology." In M. D. Dunnette (ed.), *Handbook of Industrial and Organizational Psychology*. New York: Rand-McNally, 1976.

5. Barrett, G. V., and R. H. Franke. "Communication Preference and Performance: A Cross-Cultural Comparison," *Proceedings, 77th Annual Convention, American Psychological Association*, 1969, pp. 597–598.

6. Barrett, G. V., and E. C. Ryterband. "Cross-Cultural Comparisons of Corporate Objectives on *Exercise Objectives.*" Paper presented at 76th Annual Convention, American Psychological Association, San Francisco, August 31, 1968.

7. Bass, B. M. A Preliminary Report on Manifest Preferences in Six Cultures for Participative Management (Technical Report No. 21). Rochester: University of Rochester, Management Research Center, 1968.

8. Bass, B. M. *Exercise Communication.* Scottsville, N. Y.: Transnational Programs Corporation, 1975.

9. Bass, B. M. *Exercise Compensation.* Scottsville, N. Y.: Transnational Programs Corporation, 1975.

10. Bass, B. M. *Exercise Life Goals.* Scottsville, N. Y.: Transnational Program Corporation, 1975.

11. Bass, B. M. *Exercise Organizational Objectives.* Scottsville, N. Y.: Transnational Program Corporation, 1975.

12. Bass, B. M., P. Burger, R. Doktor, and G. V. Barrett. *Managerial Career Advancement: An International Comparison.* New York: Free Press, 1979.

13. Bass, B. M., and K. M. Thiagarajan. "Differential Preferences for Long- vs. Short-Term Payoffs in India and the United States," *Proceedings of the XVIth International Congress of Applied Psychology*. Amsterdam: Swets & Zeitlinger, 1969, pp. 423–428.

14. Bass, B. M., E. R. Valenzi, D. L. Farrow, and R. J. Solomon. "Management Styles Associated with Organizational, Task, Personal, and Interpersonal Contingencies," *Journal of Applied Psychology*, 60 (1975): 720–729.

15. Cascio, W. F. "Functional Specialization, Culture, and Preference for Participative Management," *Personnel Psychology*, 27 (1974): 593–603.

16. Denison, E. F. *Why Growth Rates Differ: Postwar Experience in Nine Western Countries.* Washington, D. C.: The Brookings Institute, 1967.

17. England, G. W. "Personal Value Systems of American Managers," *Academy of Management Journal*, 10 (1967): 53–68.

18. England, G. W., and R. Koike. "Personal Value Systems of Japanese Managers," *Journal of Cross-Cultural Psychology*, 1 (1970): 21–40.

19. Fiedler, F. E., T. Mitchell, and H. C. Triandis. "The Culture Assimilator: An Approach to Cross-Cultural Training," *Journal of Applied Psychology*, 55 (1971): 95–102.

20. Frost, E. "What Industry Wants and Does Not Want from the Psychologist," *Journal of Applied Psychology*, 4 (1920): 18–24.

21. Gellerman, S. W. "Passivity, Paranoia, and 'Pakikisama,'" *Columbia Journal of World Business* (1967): 59–66.

22. Haire, M., E. E. Ghiselli, and L. W. Porter. *Managerial Thinking: An International Study.* New York: Wiley, 1966.

23. Heller, F. A. "The Role of Business Management in Relation to Economic Development." Based on a paper presented to the American Psychological Association's 74th Meeting, New York, September 1966.

24. Inkeles, A. "The Modernization of Man." In M. Weiner (ed.), *Modernization*. New York: Basic Books, 1966.

25. Larsen, R. "The Challenge of Multinational Business," *Fortune*, 80, No. 2 (1969): 73–74.

26. Laurent, H. "Cross-Cultural Cross-Validation of Empirically Validated Tests," *Journal of Applied Psychology*, 54 (1970): 417–423.

27. Likert, R. "Trends toward a World-Wide Theory of Management," *Proceedings, CIOS XIII. International Management Congress*, 2 (1963): 110–114.

28. Lippitt, R., and R. K. White. "An Experimental Study of Leadership and Group Life." In E. E. Maccoby, T. M. Newcomb, and E. E. Hartley (eds.), *Readings in Social Psychology* (3rd ed.). New York: Holt, 1958.

29. McClelland, D. E., and D. G. Winter. *Motivating Economic Achievement*. New York: Free Press, 1969.

30. Meade, R. D. "An Experimental Study of Leadership in India," *Journal of Social Psychology*, 72 (1967): 35–43.

31. Mouton, J. S., and R. S. Blake. "Issues in Transnational Organization Development." In B. M. Bass, R. Cooper, and J. A. Haas (eds.), *Managing for Accomplishment*. Lexington, Mass.: D. C. Heath, 1970.

32. Multinational Corporation, The. Papers presented at Department of State Conference, Office of External Research, March 1969.

33. Perlmutter, H. V. "The Tortuous Evolution of the Multinational Corporation," *Columbia Journal of World Business*, 4 (1969): 9–18.

34. Peter, H. "Cross-Cultural Survey of Managers in Ten Countries." Paper presented at the 77th Annual Convention, American Psychological Association, Washington, D. C., 1969.

35. Rus, V. "Influence Structure in Yugoslav Enterprise," *Industrial Relations*, 9 (1970): 148–160.

36. Ryterband, E. C., and G. V. Barrett. "Managers' Values and Their Relationship to the Management of Tasks: A Cross-Cultural Comparison." In B. M. Bass, R. C. Cooper, and J. A. Haas (eds.), *Managing for Accomplishment*. Lexington, Mass.: D. C. Heath, 1970.

37. Ryterband, E. C., and K. M. Thiagarajan. *Managerial Attitudes toward Salaries as a Function of Social and Economic Development*. (Technical Report No. 24.) Rochester: University of Rochester, Management Research Center. Contract No. NONR N00014-67(A), 1968.

38. Sadler, P. J., and G. H. Hofstede. *Leadership Styles, Preferences and Perceptions of Employees of an International Company in Different Countries*. IBM Europe Personnel Research Study, No. 5, October 1969.

39. Schwartz, P. A. *Aptitude Tests for Use in the Developing Nations*. Pittsburgh: American Institute for Research, 1961.

40. Servan-Schreiber, J. J. *The American Challenge*. New York: Atheneum, 1969.

41. Sirota, D. "International Survey of Job Goals and Beliefs." Paper presented at 16th International Congress of Applied Psychology, Amsterdam, Netherlands, 1968.

42. Stewart, E. C., and J. Priel. "A Participant Technique in Area Training."

Paper presented at American Psychological Association Symposium, New York, September, 1966.

43. Tannenbaum, A. *Control in Organizations.* New York: McGraw-Hill, 1968.

44. Tannenbaum, R., and W. H. Schmidt. "How to Choose a Leadership Pattern," *Harvard Business Review,* 36, No. 2 (1958): 95–101.

45. Triandis, H. C. "Interpersonal Relations in International Organizations," *Organizational Behavior and Human Performance,* 51 (1967): 1–24.

46. Triandis, H. C. "Factors Affecting Employee Selection in Two Cultures," *Journal of Applied Psychology,* 47 (1963): 89–96.

47. Vansina, L. S., and T. C. Taillieu. "Comparative Study of the Characteristics of Flemish Graduates Planning Their Careers in National or International Organizations." In B. M. Bass, R. C. Cooper, and J. A. Haas (eds.), *Managing for Accomplishment.* Lexington, Mass.: D. C. Heath, 1970.

48. Whitehill, A. M., Jr. "Cultural Values and Employee Attitudes: United States and Japan," *Journal of Applied Psychology,* 48 (1964): 69–72.

49. Whitely, W., and G. W. England. "Managerial Values as a Reflection of Culture and the Process of Industrialization," *Academy of Management Journal,* 20 (1977): 439–453.

50. Whyte, W. F. "Culture, Industrial Relations and Economic Development: The Case of Peru," *Industrial and Labor Relations Review,* 16 (1963): 583–593.

51. Williams, L. K., W. F. Whyte, and C. S. Green. "Do Cultural Differences Affect Workers' Attitudes?" *Industrial Relations,* 5 (1966): 105–117.

52. Zeira, Y. "Overlooked Personnel Problems of Multinational Corporations," *Columbia Journal of World Business,* 10, No. 2 (1975): 96–103.

18 INDUSTRIAL/ORGANIZATIONAL PSYCHOLOGY AND PUBLIC POLICY

IN BRIEF There is increasing concern that industrial/organizational psychology make a relevant contribution to the betterment of humanity. At times industrial/organizational psychology has been perceived to be deleterious to human welfare, as in the case of testing of job applicants. Such testing has been criticized as being unfair to minority groups, yet it can be the most valid and fairest selection technique, if implemented correctly.

Recent advances have been made in programs to train those who have been unemployed for long periods of time.

Public policy should take into account the behavioral science knowledge in areas such as noise pollution, accident prevention, and water pollution.

One of the main problems industrial/organizational psychology has in influencing public policy is the limited knowledge most people have of the field. This makes it difficult for psychological findings to become a basic part of public policy. "Pop" psychology is given credence while scientific research is ignored.

Behavioral Science and Public Policy

Expenditures of federal and state funds for research in the behavioral and social sciences run into the hundreds of millions of dollars annually.

While this may seem like large sums, the amounts are small compared with those spent on the other sciences. The total impact must be spread over many different disciplines and areas. A report on the behavioral and social sciences recommends the establishment of graduate schools of applied behavioral science where training would be multidisciplinary and problems would be attacked on a much broader conceptual and methodological level than is now the case.[74]

American aid fostered the establishment in many countries in Europe and elsewhere of National Productivity Centers, which play a key role in integrating behavioral science studies and applications to the world of work. In the United States such a National Productivity Commission was recommended in 1970, and by 1980, various public and semi-private agencies concerned with productivity and quality of working life were formed.

Along with public support has come criticism of the ways in which behavioral science techniques and knowledge are used. This is similar to criticism in all fields of science, for it is evident that atomic energy can be used either to generate power or to make bombs. In much the same way, as we have already noted earlier in the book, knowledge in the field of industrial psychology can be used either to promote human welfare or, inadvertently, to downgrade the quality of life.

Here we will review some of these uses of behavioral science and criticisms about them. We will conclude with how we think the behavioral sciences, and industrial psychology in particular, can help to shape public policies in the interests of human betterment.

CONGRESSIONAL ACTION AND BEHAVIORAL SCIENCE One of the problems the behavioral sciences will have to face, and one that has been faced by science in general, is that most of our political representatives in Congress and in state legislatures are not attuned to behavioral concepts nor to science in general. In an age where so much depends on knowledge of science and, increasingly, of behavioral science, influential members of Congress have been quoted as saying they do not even understand the metric system. In Congress there are very few individuals who have been trained in either engineering, science, or medicine. The predominant professional background of Congressmen and of most state legislators is in the field of law. This simply means that most lawmakers are not equipped to deal with the natural, physical, or behavioral sciences. Congressional leaders consider as jargon terms used in the sciences that have for scientists very precise connotations.

As we have noted in Chapter 2, scientific research is not the same as policy research. For scientists to advocate positions requires making their findings meaningful to legislators and arguing the merits of their conclusions.

The public official and the public at large have a great many built-in biases that must be overcome; in fact, the individual has to be reeducated. The problem is more difficult than in the physical and life sciences because there the administrators and the public at large have no choice but to accept the statements of the scientists working in the area, because they have little or no knowledge of the fields. The situation is quite different in the behavioral sciences, because public officials and the public at large do often have rather strong opinions about solutions to problems that have a behavioral science content. One of the most common, of course, is the frequently heard statement that the only solution to the traffic safety problem is to get rid of the "nut behind the wheel." Therefore, (1) the advancement of the public support of science must proceed through scientific lobbyists; (2) nonscientific arguments become common justifications for support or abandoment (i.e., titles of papers or controversial topics); (3) failure to understand long-term needs for basic work results in emphasis on short-range programs.

EXAMPLE OF WASTE   Government agencies such as the Office of Naval Research, the National Science Foundation, and the Department of Health, Education, and Welfare have given a major thrust to basic behavioral science research. Nevertheless, regrettably, large sums of money are often wasted on programs that have no demonstrated worth. Money is granted because a problem is recognized and a possible but untested solution to the problem is offered — a prospective solution that may have little chance of success because it lacks any foundation in earlier scientific studies of the problem. An example was given in Chapter 3 of the Zero Defects motivational programs, which are widespread both in government and in private organizations, and which are initiated and supported by the Department of Defense. Despite the fact that millions have been spent on these programs, virtually nothing has been spent on evaluation. An assumption is made that a program's existence proves its success. We have tried to show that this is not a criterion for the success of any program, and that such money could well have been spent in other ways. The failure of industrial and organizational psychologists to be more fully involved with programs of this type is not lack of desire on the part of the profession, but a combination of factors that often makes acceptance of behavioral sciences slow. First, it appears that "ignorance is bliss." Many government administrators have had so little exposure to modern behavioral science that they have no concept of what it can and cannot do for an organization. There is resistance from many administrators to apply scientific knowledge and methods to the area of human behavior. Second, there is often an unspoken fear of those in administrative positions that a newcomer with specialized knowledge will jeopardize their power and position in the organization. Third, there is also an assumption by many people in positions of authority that they "know people," and therefore nothing of consequence is to be gained from behavioral sciences. In Chapter 2, we discussed the "Barnum effect," and showed the ineffectiveness of common sense in certain situations.

Another very expensive program was an extensively publicized campaign to reduce automobile accidents. While $40 million worth of television and radio time was spent to promote the theme, the promotional campaign did not have a theoretical basis nor was there any way to determine if, indeed, the campaign had an effect on the viewers.[34] Both of these programs illustrate two important problems. First, the programs lacked theoretical or scientific bases for their designs. Second, there was no plan to evaluate the actual effectiveness of the program in terms of any scientific criteria. Despite expenditures of millions of dollars, little of practical significance was achieved, and nothing was learned that will add to our knowledge for future programs. This is, of course, a safe way for initiators to administer a program, because there is never any independent judgment of the program's worth.

EXAMPLE OF CONGRESSIONAL ACTION   The problems and needs of the older workers are now gaining more attention both from the scientific community and as the result of legislation. Perhaps the most dramatic change has been legislation passed in 1978, which extended mandatory retirement to the age of seventy. The effect of this change upon the American worker is not completely known at this time, but preliminary analysis indicates that many more people will plan to retire at seventy. Although forecasting future events is always a hazard, it would appear that at least 30 to 40 per cent of the work force will eventually choose to work past the age of sixty-five, either full- or part-time. The rate of inflation appears to have a dramatic effect upon the decision to retire at sixty-five or to continue.. For example, at Sears Roebuck, 45 per cent decided to stay on past the age of sixty-five.[64]

There will undoubtedly be a dramatic impact on job opportunities for younger employees. In the case of Sears it has been estimated that the new law will eliminate 20,000 opportunities for people to get new jobs over a five-year period.

There are a number of other consequences of early retirement, one of which is the importance of a good performance appraisal system, as discussed in Chapter 8. In order to fire or replace an older individual who is not performing his or her job, more evidence will have to be presented to justify that decision. There has been a steady increase in lawsuits charging age discrimination. The Department of Labor receives over 5,000 complaints a year.[64]

Another probable effect of this law is the slowing down of efforts to increase the proportion of minority group members and females in higher levels of the organization. With fewer people retiring, there will be fewer available slots.

One interesting question is the change in abilities of the older segment of the work force. The research is remarkably clear in showing that there are decided differences in abilities between the older and younger employees, particularly after the age of sixty-five. The ability to process information certainly does change over time. Perhaps one of the best documented is the decline in abilities required for effective accident avoidance while driving.[56] On the other hand, intellectual functions among professionals and managers seem to maintain themselves into very old age and until senility sets in. Continuing to work at problem-solving can keep one mentally younger.

Other changes may aid the performance and satisfaction gained from a job. There is evidence to indicate that the older workers' personality is more compatible with the assembly-line work than younger workers'. Older workers were more efficient and actually enjoyed paced work as much as unpaced work. In contrast, the younger workers were most satisfied in working at their own freely chosen pace.[72]

It will be a number of years before the full social and economic consequences of the legislated move to a later retirement age will be understood. Clearly, there will be ramifications in a number of areas, including testing of the older employee, for people age at different rates. Some 50 year olds have declined to the average 70 year old. Some 70 year olds are like the average 50 year old. Chronological age is not a good indicator of a particular individual's abilities.

PERSONNEL PSYCHOLOGY AND PUBLIC POLICY

Testing and Public Policy

Singled out for special attack on several counts in the last decade has been the use and misuse of tests in industry. News headlines such as "Psychological Tests Assailed" and "Personnel Tests Win Widening Business — Critics Fume" give the flavor of the controversy. There are at least four main criticisms leveled at testing. First, even a thoroughly disguised personality test can be faked by applicants if they simply respond to it by imitating what they believe to be the kind of response that will get them the job, please the boss, or match another person whom they know. (They may be wrong, but much error may be introduced, since people are likely to differ in their tendencies and directions in attempting to fake responses.)

Second, validities tend to be low or absent between some personality assessments and criteria of success. Worse yet, the tests are often employed with a pre-1915 rationale that assumes they are valid without evidence to support the contention.

Third, many of the personality items, constructed originally for use with neurotic and psychotic patients and dealing with such issues as attitudes toward sex and religion, may be regarded as obnoxious invasions of privacy.

Fourth, at times, even when the validation technology is adequate, it can be argued that tests in general and personality assessments in particular discriminate against minority groups. Further, they may serve to maintain the status-quo divisions in society. For example, suppose a positive response to the item "I believe in a definite Heaven and Hell" correlates moderately with failure as an engineer. Almost any fundamentalist Protestant will be penalized for this response to this question when being screened for a job as an engineer. The screening item may be valid to some degree, but it is also even more indicative of religiosity. And even if religiosity per se correlates with job success or failure (which does not necessarily follow in this instance), it is against public policy as well as federal and state legislation to use such religiosity as the basis of deciding to hire or promote employees.

Controversy now rages in the United States on whether it is fair to use an intelligence test to screen out prospective job trainees if performance on the test is specifically influenced by culturally deprived backgrounds, even if the test forecasts success in training to some degree. It is an important problem in many countries and handled in a variety of arbitrary ways. In 1936 the Soviet Union outlawed aptitude testing as promoting class difference (although in recent years they have begun to have second thoughts about aptitude testing). In Great Britain, France, and Germany, standardized tests of adolescents are still used to determine whether they will be permitted to pursue an academic or a vocational career.

As an alternative to the standard intelligence test, the Black Intelligence Test of Cultural Homogeneity (BITCH) was developed. It was designed to be "culture specific" and therefore fairer to blacks.[48] In testing both black and white police applicants, blacks did do better than whites. Nevertheless, the BITCH scores were unrelated to a standard intelligence test. This means that the test does not appear to measure general intelligence. In addition, the BITCH did not differentiate among the black candidates: most had fairly high scores; therefore the test has little practical value. For the BITCH to prove useful in practical situations, there will have to be a future demonstration that it predicts job-relevant behavior, at least for blacks.

IS TESTING UNFAIR?   In a survey of corporations in a major metropolitan city, 73 per cent of the respondents said that they used tests in the corporation for selection.[68] Of those companies who use tests, 90 per cent use aptitude tests, 83 per cent use intelligence tests, and 51 per cent use personality measures.

Further, companies of different sizes differ considerably in their use of tests. Ninety per cent of those companies with over 5,000 employees use tests, but only 50 per cent of the companies with fewer than 100 employees do so. Tests are used for both selection and promotion. Seventy-one per cent of the companies surveyed use tests for selection, while 97 per cent of the companies use tests for either selection or promotion. Most such tests are given to salaried employees, but 70 per cent of the companies also give them to employees paid by the hour.

Personality tests were seen as being the least accurate, with 26 per cent of the companies reporting them to be inaccurate. For tests in general, 95 per cent of the companies saw tests being used in the future. These percentages given are consistent with older reports, which show about 75 per cent of companies in the United States using some form of testing procedure.

In the sixties and seventies, some predicted that all testing would be abandoned to promote fair employment practices, but it appears that the tests are here to stay. The problem is to see that they are used efficiently and fairly.

The Motorola Case was the first well-known one concerning discrimination in hiring. It was ruled that a five-minute ability test could not be used by the company for selection because it allegedly discriminated against a black applicant. While this ruling was later reversed by the Illinois Supreme Court, the Civil Rights Act of 1964, which assured equal employment opportunity without regard to considerations such as race and sex, has raised many important questions concerning the effectiveness, appropriateness, and fairness of testing procedures. One effect has been to force many companies to put some effort into trying to validate the tests they use when previously they used the tests without concerning themselves about validation.

The Civil Rights Act of 1964 was legislation designed to end discrimination based on race, religion, sex, or national origin in all phases of the employment process. One of the important features of the Title VII was the establishment of the Equal Employment Opportunity Commission (EEOC). This administrative agency was established to supervise Title VII. The EEOC, in cooperation with other federal agencies, has published standards for personnel selection, including the proper use and validation of tests.[73] In essence, the standards for test validation follow the procedures that have been outlined in the previous chapters. Many organizations have felt that the guidelines issued by the EEOC are a burden and hard to comply with. Their alternative has been to do away with testing for selection purposes. One fact that the organizations who eliminate testing are forgetting is that *any selection procedure* has to be proven to be valid and job-oriented if there is any evidence of adverse impact. Adverse impact is defined as a difference in the proportion of people hired from that of the applicants for the position. To depend on application forms and interviews without testing could make matters worse rather than better.

To clarify this point, organizations are required to maintain records by sex of the following racial and ethnic groups: Blacks (Negroes), American Indians, Asians, Hispanics, Whites (Caucasians). As a simple example, let's assume 50 per cent of the applicants for a position are female and 50 per cent male. If 70 per cent of the individuals hired are male, then this would constitute adverse impact. Adverse impact *does not* necessarily mean that there is discrimination or that an unfair selection procedure is being used. It does mean that the organization must demonstrate that it has a valid selection program. Therefore, doing away with testing may not solve the problem and could indeed result in hiring fewer qualified individuals. It could be more difficult for a firm or agency to demonstrate that its interview was valid in comparison to the tests it eliminated from its selection process. The Equal Employment Opportunity Act of 1972 gave the EEOC the authority to initiate court suits. In 1973 alone, EEOC received over 15,000 charges against state and local governments. At one point over 77,000 cases were in existence that had not been resolved.[35]

Tests have become a highly emotional issue. They are seen as culprits that discriminate unfairly against minority groups. Like many issues in behavioral science, this conjecture deserves close scrutiny. One can become very moralistic on an issue like this and flatly declare that if the average score on a given test is lower for a minority group, then by definition the test is discriminatory. Using this reasoning, if a group of male college students were weighed on a scale and on the average were found to be heavier than a group of female students, then the scale could be called discriminatory.

In a series of court cases, the Supreme Court has ruled that tests can be fair, but they must be job-related to be so. This requires, it declared, adequate job analysis; relevant, reliable, and unbiased criterion measurement; and differential validation for the different populations involved (e.g. showing the test is valid for women, if it is they who are to be screened by the test).

There are literally thousands of state and federal court decisions dealing with testing issues. We will only review the major decisions which help to clarify the interface between public policy, the law, and personnel testing.

The first important case decided by the Supreme Court was *Griggs v. Duke Power Company* (1971). The power company had instituted both testing and a high school graduation requirement for common laborers. This resulted in considerably fewer black applicants being hired than white applicants. The court made clear that the selection procedures had to be job-related. The company did not have any evidence that either high school graduation or the tests were related to job performance of a common laborer. In fact, many employees without these qualifications continued to perform the job satisfactorily. While the high-school graduation requirement and the tests appeared to be neutral, the Supreme Court said that these selection procedures were not job relevant and therefore could not be used since they caused a disproportionate number of blacks to be rejected for the position. Thus, in *Griggs v. Duke Power,* the Court required that the validity had to be demonstrated of a test for forecasting performance on jobs for which hiring was being done. The tests had to be professionally developed, meeting the standards we have spelled out in Chapters 7, 8, 9 and 10.

The importance of job-relatedness, job analysis and obtaining good performance appraisal information on employees for a validation study was emphasized by the Supreme Court in *Albermale Paper Co. v. Moody* (1975).

In short, wnat we see is that legislation and the courts have created standards that demand high quality of personnel practice. Testing is not inherently unfair; however, its abuse and misuse is. Employers are more likely to be judged for an unfair practice if they eliminate standardized testing and depend instead on unstandardized, unreliable, indefensible interviews and other selection processes that cannot be justified as fair to applicants.

The most recent federal guidelines, Uniform Guidelines on Employee Selection Procedures (1978), have been adopted by the Equal Employment Opportunity Commission, Civil Service Commission, Department of Labor and Department of Justice. They will continue to be a standard for court decisions, which are necessary due to complexities in the testing and selection processes. Probably the best professional statement concerning unfair discrimination was made by Guion: "Unfair discrimination exists when people with equal probability of success on the job have unequal probabilities of being hired for the job." [32] There are other definitions of test bias that involve both ethical and statistical issues. It is doubtful that any one definition will be acceptable to all people. [39]

There are some real problems involved in implementing the policy that those with equal probability of success on the job have equal probability of being hired. Often the problem revolves around the administration of the testing program and not the test per se. The common response from organizations is "We feel that our tests are very good." Tests need some face validity or applicants feel they are being dealt with unfairly, complain to Congress, et cetera, particularly in civil service. The more critical question is: What are the facts about the testing program and, in particular, what is the validity of the tests in predicting subsequent job performance? Only recently have the courts begun to ask the same questions.[70]

This problem is illustrated by Rusmore, who surveyed 28 companies in California.[65] He found that at the policy level of the company there was a good knowledge of tests and testing programs. But only 13 per cent of the companies required any sort of training for those who gave the tests to prospective employees. In examining the validity of the testing programs, only 15 per cent of the companies had evidence that a better job of selection was accomplished with tests. An even smaller number, 5 per cent, had any evidence at all on the validity of their employment interviewing procedures. In making an overall evaluation of the testing program of the companies involved, the professional psychologists found that only 9 per cent of the organizations could be considered to have a good program, while 30 per cent were judged to be poor. None of the organizations was judged excellent or superior in terms of the administration of its testing program. What the survey showed was that *while the policy of the company was fair-minded, the technical implementation of the fair employment policy was very primitive.* Good intentions are of little value if time, thought, and effort are not given to the technical aspects of testing.

THE CONCEPT OF DIFFERENTIAL VALIDITY   The consistent finding that certain minority group members did not score as well on certain tests as majority group members led to the conclusion by some psychologists, social commentators, and the Supreme Court that tests were not equally valid for minority group members. Though employment tests might be valid for the whites in our culture, they would not correlate with job performance for blacks. This belief that tests may correlate differently with job performance for different subgroups in our population led to the concept of differential validity. In order to establish the existence of differential validity it is necessary to examine a large number of studies that compare validities for minority groups and whites. It would be expected that in some studies by chance alone there would be some differences in validity of tests for minority groups and whites. A review of these studies has led to the conclusion that differential validity is more of an illusion than a reality in the real world.[17,66]

Test validity is often higher for blacks than for the whites. This means that tests are more accurate in predicting job performance for blacks than for the whites. For example, if a test score of 100 predicts job performance of 100 for a white group, an equivalent test score of 100 for a black group should predict equivalent job performance. The assumption of social commentators is that a test score of 100 for a black group would not result in a job performance score of 100 but job performance of, say, 110. In other words, the tests would underpredict the actual job performance of a black employee. In fact, in many studies test scores have actually predicted job performance somewhat higher than actually obtained by minority group members. The concept of differential validity was given support because of a relatively small number of studies, with very small sample sizes, which found difference in validity between minority and white groups. This can be called a classic instance of the law of small numbers operating to give misleading generalizations.

We tend to underestimate the size of a sample required to reach reliable conclusions about differential effects. In this case, the concept of differential validity was inferred from a very small sample of blacks and whites. Social critics also believed that the tests were biased against blacks, since tests were supposedly based upon a white culture.

Humphreys takes the point of view that although there may be some superficial differences between whites and blacks, there is a high degree of biological and cultural similarity.[38] There is no a priori reason to believe that a test that predicts job performance of a white would not also predict job performance of a black.

Studies in other cultures have also studied the issue of differential validity. For example, from a sample of 7,000 males in Israel, differential validity was found for three different ethnic subgroups only when education was not controlled. When the ethnic subgroups were compared in terms of the same educational background, the effect of differential validity was almost entirely eliminated.[58]

INTERVIEW BIAS   The most difficult factor to assess is possible conscious or unconscious bias in the employment interview situation. It is quite likely that some emploment interviewers often are biased against certain minority group members because they hold certain naive stereotypes about them. This type of bias is extremely difficult to detect except in the case of large companies, where a tally could be kept of the number of minority group members interviewed by each interviewer and the percentage employed. But this would be possible only for large firms with a large number of applicants. Indeed, this type of technical deficiency in the validation procedure may be more harmful to minority groups and also to all potential applicants than so-called discrimination of some tests would be. Consciously or unconsciously, some interviewers are strongly influenced by facial features (weak chin, strong neck, or square jaw), attributes of an individual that still are likely to be associated with personality by many novelists for literary effect.

CRITERION BIAS   Another problem is that of the criterion. All validation procedures are based on the correlation between the test and a specific criterion of job performance. The criterion of job performance is often a rating by the supervisor. If this criterion rating is in some way contaminated by the bias of the supervisor doing the rating, then the true validity of the testing procedure will be impossible to determine. This is certainly likely to happen, since we know that some first-line supervisors are biased against the employment of minority group members. Nevertheless, overall, white male supervisors do not appear to be biased in rating black or women subordinates. But black and female supervisors have some tendency to favor black or women subordinates. Furthermore, there is evidence of restriction in range of performance on some criteria of employee performance. For example, we know that in some companies there is a restriction in the salaries of black as compared with white employees.[76] And some women may be underpaid compared to men doing the same work. Criterion bias (discussed in Chapter 7) is one of the more serious problems that evaluations of testing programs have to face.

UNIQUE PROBLEMS OF PERSONNEL TESTING   One matter of concern to the psychologist who uses tests is whether or not to feed results back to those who have participated in the testing sessions. At one extreme, it appears only fair that the testees have feedback and knowledge of their capabilities for better self-knowledge. At the other extreme, it is possible that those who receive lower scores on a test than they anticipated would devalue the test scores, after a period of time forgetting the results. Thus, a correlation of 0.70 was found between the favorableness of individuals' scores on a personality test and their estimates of how valid they believed the test to be. This was expected, since those who did well only confirmed their beliefs in their own self-worth. Conversely, those who did poorly could maintain their self-esteem by devaluing the test results.[69] This appears to be an almost certain problem in testing, since half the people are going to do better than average and half below average on any one test. Therefore, if you feed test results back, you run the risk of alienating a large part of the tested population. But, if you do not give back test results, a possible gain for individuals in self-knowledge is denied. Care is needed for feeding test information back so that it will be perceived not as threatening but as positive and helpful.

Bias by Sex and Ethnic Identity: What Is Adverse Impact?

If accepting applicants is influenced by their sex or ethnic identity, there should be some statistical association between the kind of applicants screened and the kind actually accepted. Bias here means a distinct pattern between a selection decision and sex or ethnic identity of an applicant. Unfair discrimination refers to a selection decision that is influenced by the sex or ethnic identity of the applicant, though this identity is not material to the selection decision.

Some of the complexities of the topic can be understood from an example. The University of California at Berkeley studied the number of applicants for graduate school and the percent actually admitted. In one year 44 per cent of the men and 35 per cent of the women applying were admitted to graduate school. Can we infer from these data that graduate admissions are biased and discriminate against women, since a smaller proportion of women are admitted than men? If we can assume that the male and female applicants are the same on important dimensions that influence selection such as grades and test scores, one might quickly jump to the conclusion that overall, discriminations exists. But a finer analysis of the data indicated that such discrimination occurred in some departments, but was reversed in others. Each department within the university was examined for potential sex bias (that is, where more men were accepted than equally qualified women, or vice versa.) Four departments were biased against women *and six biased against men.* The data indicated that men and women did not apply at random to all 85 departments in the university. A larger proportion of women applicants applied for departments that were hard to get into, while a smaller proportion applied for departments that were easy to get into. For example, two-thirds of the applicants to the Department of English were female, while only 2 per cent of the applicants to the graduate program in mechanical engineering were female. At the same time, the percentage of applicants admitted to English, male or female, was lower than to mechanical engineering. When the appropriate calculations were made by taking each department separately and analyzing for potential bias and then aggregating statistics, no evidence was found for a campus-wide bias in favor of men. In fact, the evidence was in favor of some slight bias for women. Although the example that we have used is from the academic world, the same reasoning can apply to any large organization that has various specialty areas and functions.[16] For example, if a business firm employs a large number of engineers, who might be in short supply, then almost all the engineers who applied might gain employment. There would undoubtedly be very few females among the group. Conversely, for the clerical positions, there may be a great deal of competition, with a large proportion of the applicants being female. If we aggregate the data for the whole firm, it might appear that the organization is biased against women, when in fact if separate job functions are considered no such bias would appear.

There are large differences in the number of males and females who graduate with Ph.D.s in the sciences. In psychology, nearly 25 per cent of the graduates are female, but in physics, engineering, and geosciences fewer than 3 per cent of the Ph.D.s are female. Conversely, over half the Ph.D.s in French are female. Varying proportions of minority group members in each discipline must be taken into account in determining whether or not there is bias in the organizational practices. Gross statistics often do not tell the actual story.

The problem becomes more complicated when we consider the fact that there are strong and consistent differences in religious affiliation and occupational preference. For example, certain religious groups are highly represented among doctorate degree holders in science, the humanities, and the professions. One cannot assume that preference for these occupations is distributed equally across different groups. Indeed, four times as many doctorates are produced at some religious denominational colleges compared to others.[33] While these differences probably reflect certain value orientations, such as the extent to which learning is valued, the important point is that aggregating individuals by religious denomination and proportion in various occupations may show differentiation but not discrimination.

The issue of adverse impact is a very complex topic. Before the EEOC can begin a case or file a lawsuit, there must be a showing of adverse impact. Adverse impact could be shown when there is a smaller percentage of a minority group hired than applied. Without a showing of adverse impact, there is usually no basis for an administrative or court decision. Once there is a showing of adverse impact, the question remains whether or not there has been intentional discrimination. It must be noted at this point that the U. S. Supreme Court has ruled in *Davis v. Washington* that a valid test can be used for selection even if there is an adverse impact. In the *Davis v. Washington* case a test was found to relate to training criteria. A smaller proportion of black applicants than white applicants was selected by a test. Since the test was valid, there was no finding of unfair discrimination. In the same manner, the courts have held that employment requirements such as a high school education may be appropriate despite the fact that they may have an adverse impact upon certain minority groups (i.e., a smaller proportion of minority groups than the majority group may hold high school diplomas). There are many statistical ways in which the question of adverse impact and potential discrimination can be considered, and we will make no attempt to detail these complex procedures at this point in time.[3] In the same manner, various professional qualifying exams, such as a bar examination, have been found to be legal despite the fact that a smaller proportion of minority group members than majority group members might pass the exam.

In the past, many lower courts had ruled that Title VII applied only to protected minorities. In *McDonald v. Santa Fe Transportation Company* (1976) the Supreme Court ruled that the law applied to whites as well as minorities. In this case it was found that both white and black employees were stealing from the company. The whites were fired but not the black employees. The Supreme Court decided that under Title VII the whites had to be treated in the same manner as the blacks.

In *McDonnel Douglas v. Green* (1973) the Supreme Court ruled that a company had the right not to hire an employee who committed illegal acts against it. The only qualification was that the same standards should be applied to both black and white applicants. This reemphasizes the importance of consistency in personnel practices.

The Supreme Court has also held in *NEA v. South Carolina* (1978) that a content-valid test can be defended which may have an extremely adverse impact on minority group members. South Carolina instituted an achievement test on the knowledge required of teachers to perform their teaching functions. The Supreme Court upheld the right of the state to do this despite the fact that proportionately fewer black teachers than white passed the test.

Some areas of the law seem to have been clarified. In particular, sex discrimination has been routinely outlawed as a selection procedure unless it is job-relevant. Ironically enough, many of the state laws in the past mandated that females could not be hired into positions which involved night work, lifting of heavy loads, and other job duties thought to be harmful to females. Laws enacted to protect females have been routinely found to be discriminatory by the federal courts.

The ethical and legal rights of psychologists to keep their tests confidential to ensure the validity of a selection program has been approved by the Supreme Court in *NLRB v. Detroit Edison* (1979). This decision upheld the company psychologist's refusal to reveal actual test questions or to link test scores to individual employees.

Reverse Discrimination

Affirmative action to give the disadvantaged minority group members, blacks, women, Spanish-surnamed persons, and native Americans increased access to jobs and promotion, sometimes at the expense of white male members of the majority, is a hotly debated issue at this point in our history. Some social scientists oppose a public policy that advocates affirmative-action remedies for racial discrimination. They contend that it is unconstitutional to promote hiring goals that in effect establish quotas for selection based on race or sex. Other critics take the opposite point of view. They contend it is constitutional and appropriate for the courts to give preferential treatment to minority groups that have been discriminated against in the past. There are no easy answers. Suppose in a city that is now 30 per cent black, the police force had been all-white until 1965. Normal attrition and hiring without considering race might add small percentages of blacks to the force over a twenty-year period. An affirmative-action goal might be to have a force that was 30 per cent black by 1975. This would necessitate giving blacks preference in hiring between 1965 and 1975. What about seniority rights? Suppose layoffs are necessitated. Because of discrimination against blacks before 1965, the force would face layoffs of whites unless affirmative action overrode considerations of past discrimination. Note that if to redress past discrimination against blacks, we now *favor* blacks as a group, we *discriminate against* whites as a group. Clearly we have a controversy here that is difficult to resolve, and we will make no attempt ourselves to give a definitive answer. Only the courts and new legislation will be able to resolve this issue.

THE BAKKE CASE   In 1979, the Supreme Court was faced in the *Bakke* case with a dilemma: Which was more important — to sustain through affirmative action the rights of a deprived minority, or to protect the rights of an individual member of the majority discriminated against by a quota system? The minority group position was that because of past discrimination minority group members have been denied admission to a variety of occupations and professional schools. For that reason, in order to have equal opportunity it is argued that it is necessary for minority groups to have a quota or set number of spaces reserved for admission to medical and law schools. Here equal opportunity is explicitly defined as equal opportunity for both groups to have equal representation in the professional schools. In contrast, the counterargument is that individual rights should be of predominant importance in admission to professional schools. Admission should be based solely upon individual qualifications and should not be based upon sex, race, or any other group characteristic. Mr. Bakke claimed that he was denied admission to medical school because of his white skin. He asserted that he was being treated unfairly because his grades and test scores were higher than those of minority group members who were admitted. The decision of the Supreme Court in this case was a compromise. In a close vote, it renounced the use of racial quotas, as such, in mandated affirmative action programs, but it endorsed affirmative action. It declared that the race of an applicant could be considered in any overall evaluation of that applicant. Quotas were rejected, but an evaluator could give additional credit to a minority applicant who had attained a satisfactory level of competence despite a handicapped educational background. But *Bakke* only applied to selection decisions in public education where affirmative action was mandated. Subsequently, in the private sector, in *Weber v. Kaiser Aluminum*, the Supreme Court decided that under certain conditions, employers without proven histories of discrimination may adopt racial quotas to overcome "conspicuous" and "manifest" imbalances in training and development programs when these imbalances were due to traditional segregation practices. The Court held that the spirit of the 1964 Civil Rights Act supported quotas if they were a voluntary, temporary expedient, and if they still left plenty of room for white applicants. As at Kaiser Aluminum, if seniority determined who was selected for advanced training and if blacks had been excluded by tradition from required craft union membership, then it was deemed consistent with the intent of the Civil Rights Act to favor blacks with less seniority than whites in selection for craft training.

The Kaiser Aluminum affirmative action program has resulted in company training opportunities for both unskilled whites and unskilled blacks. Previously, craftsmen (white only) were hired from outside. Now all unskilled employees, black and white, have better promotion possibilities, although blacks are favored.

Most organizations in the United States subscribe to the merit principle. Salary increases and promotions are based upon performance of the employee. In the past, failure of their performance appraisal system to identify directly their meritorious employees may have resulted in lowered morale and high turnover. Now the situation is even more serious, since failure to have a valid performance appraisal system can result in legal repercussions. For non-union salaried personnel the problem is often especially acute. For lower-level employees, usually on hourly wages or incentive pay, union contracts often specify pay and promotions based upon seniority with little attention to merit. In salaried positions, such as for management, promotions to higher levels and pay are supposedly based primarily on merit rather than seniority.

Both the Title VII and the Equal Pay Act of 1963 state that it is an unlawful practice for an employer to discriminate in the wages they pay employees based upon irrelevant factors such as sex of the employee or minority-group status. Perhaps the best known case is *Rowe v. General Motors*, where a black employee successfully challenged the company's procedure for promoting from hourly wage to salaried positions based on the supervisor's recommendation. The court found that only a small proportion of blacks was promoted by that policy. The promotion procedure had defects. These included the fact that the first-level supervisors making the decisions had no written instructions, standards for promotion were vague, and hourly employees were not notified of the promotion opportunities. The important point to be learned from litigation is that organizations will have to be extremely careful in their performance evaluation systems when they are used for promotions and pay raises. The considerations that we discussed in Chapter 8 will have to be rigidly followed by employers, or they may find themselves involved in expensive litigation, often resulting in class action suits and back payment to affected workers.[8] A case may be made that better personnel practices *for everyone* will emerge ultimately as a result of civil rights legislation and litigation.

Invasion of Privacy

There has been continuing concern that the degree to which the usual selection procedures of an organization is used may invade the personal privacy of an individual. Despite the controversy concerning the topic, the amount of empirical evidence on what constitutes invasion of privacy is quite meager. Recent legislation has mandated that certain information be open to individuals while other information remains restricted.

THE 1974 FAMILY EDUCATION RIGHTS AND PRIVACY ACT The so-called Buckley Amendment to the Privacy Act allowed a student to choose either an open or confidential placement file. In an open file, letters of recommendation could be read by the student. There has been concern that students who choose an open file will be hurt in the employment situation. A prospective employer may prefer students who choose a confidential file in the belief that the letters of recommendation will be more candid. To test this idea, biographical sketches were prepared of hypothetical applicants along with letters of recommendation indicating either high or low competence. Half the judges were told that the placement file was open and the other half were told that files were confidential. The judges did favor the individuals who selected a confidential placement file.[67]

FAMILY AFFAIRS In surveying the attitudes of over 1300 job applicants toward the privacy issue, it was found that people objected the most to being asked information about their family background and how family finances were handled. Particular items such as frequency of church attendance were perceived by many to be an invasion of privacy, as were questions concerning how the family income was budgeted. But information concerning school degrees, duties of past jobs, and names of companies who were previous employers were not considered an invasion of privacy.[62]

RELEVANCE The invasion of privacy issue is very complex. While people do not object to questions concerning areas of life that are perceived to be job-relevant, unfortunately people perceive different things as being job-relevant. Also, information relevant for one job may not be relevant for another. For example, previous criminal record has been held by the courts to be a relevant factor when an individual is applying for the position of police patrol officer — and most people would agree. For the job of assembly-line worker, past criminal record may be less relevant, and if asked might be considered by many as an invasion of privacy.

THE USE OF THE POLYGRAPH IN EMPLOYMENT SITUATIONS The polygraph is used by approximately 25 per cent of the nation's businesses, with the figure rising to 50 per cent in the categories of retailers and commercial banks. The typical polygraph relies upon physiological measures of heart rate, skin conductance, and respiration. The newest measure, the Psychological Stress Evaluator, claims to measure deception from stress in the voice.[57] The polygraph is usually used for three separate purposes. First, it is used to verify the application information provided by a prospective employee. Second, it is used to survey present employees periodically for honesty and compliance with company policies. Third, it is occasionally used when a specific theft is being investigated.

The use of the lie detector is a very controversial issue, with both the American Civil Liberties Union and the AFL-CIO taking an active stance against it.[15]

These opponents see the lie detector as an invasion of an individual's privacy. They also believe that the results from a lie detector are not nearly reliable or valid enough to be used in the employment context. Advocates of using the lie detector claim accuracy of 99 per cent.[59] Some polygraphers have claimed that they have given 20,000 polygraph interrogations and never once been proven to make a mistake.[46] Claims of this sort are, of course, naive and do not conform with better-controlled studies. The basic problem concerns the number of innocent subjects who are erroneously classified as guilty. As many as 50 per cent of innocent subjects may be classified as liars when in fact they are telling the truth.[37]

This relates to a discussion of the utility of a test in Chapter 12. In this case, an erroneous rejection of employees results in their being branded as liars when they are innocent. Any selection system may be extremely accurate in identifying those people who are liars by labeling a very large number as potentially deceptive. You may claim to detect all of the liars, but you may also brand innocent people as being deceptive who are in fact innocent. This is unacceptable ethically and poor public relations. In the same way, it has been estimated that as many as 40 per cent of prospective employees may fail the polygraph test, a large proportion of whom are false negatives.[44]

The polygraph is a selection device and therefore falls under the federal regulations requiring the demonstration of validity if there is any adverse impact. To the best of our knowledge, there has never been a study reported in the literature that shows the polygraph to be valid according to the usual procedures we have outlined in Chapter 9.

At the present time the statutes that control polygraph administration vary from state to state. Some states prohibit polygraph examination entirely, while others put a variety of controls upon the process. At this point in time, there is no national or federal regulation that specifically covers polygraph use. Over the last ten years bills have been repeatedly introduced to prohibit totally the use of polygraph tests, but they have routinely failed to be enacted into law by Congress.[44]

CONFIDENTIALITY AND PRIVACY There were about 90 million employees by 1980 in the United States, and for most of these employees there are personnel records in some form. These files contain data not only on present employees but past employees and even applicants for jobs. Recent federal and state legislation has increased both the scope and complexity of personnel records. Is is not widely recognized, but the employer-employee relationship is not one that is considered confidential by the courts. Until legislation is passed or new rulings are made by the courts, information contained in an organization's personnel files can be obtained by others such as the government, unions, or law-enforcement agencies. But there are widely different organizational policies concerning release of information on present or past employees. It also must be recognized that the data can be subpoenaed by courts, and access is mandated by certain government agencies. In particular, the Occupational Safety and Health Act (OSHA) of 1970 and the Civil Rights Act of 1964 both provide for investigation of employers' files in order to carry out their functions. At this point, all that can be emphasized is that there is no legal basis to provide protection for the employee when it comes to personnel files being held by a company. In the future, new legislation may be passed to extend the confidential relationship so that personnel files are as confidential as those in a number of professions, including law, medicine, and psychology in many states.[50]

Some organizations are formulating well-thought-out guidelines to employee privacy. IBM is in the forefront in developing principles to protect the employee's privacy. When an individual applies for a job with IBM, only job-related information is requested. Verification of the applicant's information is accomplished internally by the personnel department with the consent and knowledge of the applicant. IBM does use employment tests, but does not use the polygraph at any time. An employee is allowed to see any job-related information contained in the personnel files. This includes performance appraisals. It is a policy of IBM to retain performance appraisals for a period of three years.

With regard to off-the-job behavior, the guideline is that the management of IBM will be concerned only with off-the-job behavior that impairs the employee's job performance or reflects upon the reputation of IBM in a major way.[20]

Changing Attitudes

In the early 1950s segregation of education and employment opportunities was still legally sanctioned in much of the United States. The *Brown v. Board of Education* decision of the Supreme Court in 1954, relying heavily on arguments of social psychology, was the end of legal support for segregation and discrimination and the beginning of legal support for integration in education and employment opportunities. Subsequent legislation and court and administrative decisions moved us into legally supported "affirmative action." Not only is it illegal to discriminate against blacks, women, and other designated minorities, but also, to redress the past discrimination against these groups, employers are required to take positive steps to correct the imbalances. Up to the early 1950s, it was legal to ask for photos of job applicants so that their race or sex could be identified to discriminate unfairly against them. Then for the next decade it was illegal to identify the race or sex of applicants. This was to avoid the possibility of discriminating against applicants. But with the introduction of affirmative action in the late 1960s, again sex and race were identified. Now firms are enjoined to record their progress in meeting plans to hire and promote minority group members to bring up their proportions in the firm's work force to achieve full integration.[54]

In addition to increasing efforts to recruit, select, train and promote blacks, women, Spanish-surnamed persons, and other minorities, affirmative action may involve fostering awareness and understanding among the rest of the employees of a firm. For example, Xerox put over 5,000 of its managers and professionals through a one-day workshop. The morning was spent in an exercise called PROSPER. First, workshop participants completed a twenty-item questionnaire describing their attitudes toward five factors: I. The system is biased; II. Implementation of affirmative action is limited; III. Black employees are competent; IV. Black employees need to be included; and V. Black employees need to build self-esteem.

Next, participants completed an in-basket set of decisions about the case of a black engineer who is insubordinate because of a feeling of having been given a "dead-end" assignment. Then, the participants mass-role-played a group discussion about the decisions. Each participant was assigned a different role relevant to one of the five factors so that all either verbalized or heard arguments in favor of affirmative action for the engineer. Finally, the participants retested themselves, scored and shared the results.

Much of the afternoon was spent dealing with ways of improving the implementation of the Xerox affirmative action program based on discussions of the five factors.

Table 18–1 shows the immediate changes in attitudes as a consequence of PROSPER. It can be seen that in comparison to two small control groups who merely were tested twice without the PROSPER activity between tests, the PROSPER participants showed statistically significant gains on all five factors.

Table 18–2 shows the attitudes of 157 Xerox managers before attending the workshop and another sample of 298 managers three to five months afterward.

As can be seen in Table 18–2, the effects were still present three to five months after the workshop, although diminished in amount.[12]

Table 18–1. Mean attitude changes of PROSPER workshop participants from immediately before to after the exercise.

Factor	2293 workshop participants	44 control subjects
I. System biased	+1.16	−0.26
II. Policy implementation limited	+0.54	+0.51
III. Blacks competent	+0.53	−0.05
IV. Blacks need inclusion	+1.02	+0.54
V. Blacks need self-esteem	+1.11	−0.56

Adapted from Bass, Cascio, McPherson, and Tragash, "PROSPER Training and Research for Increasing Management Awareness about Affirmative Action in Race Relations," *Academy of Management Journal,* 19 (1976): 353–369.

THE HARD-CORE UNEMPLOYED

A central problem our society faces is the elimination of lifetime unemployment — bringing more of those individuals who have had little educational and social opportunity into organizations as productive employees. Three important issues exist for the industrial psychologist. First, what tests, if

Table 18–2. Responses to the factored questionnaire of a sample prior to attending the one-day workshop and another sample three to five months after the workshop.

Awareness factor	Pre-workshop (N = 157) (percentage)	3–5 months Afterward (N = 298) (percentage)	Difference (percentage)	t	*
1. System biased	4.4	5.5	+1.1	3.7	<.0005
2. Policy implementation limited	9.4	9.9	+ .5	1.7	<.05
3. Blacks competent	10.8	12.4	+1.6	6.9	<.0005
4. Need inclusion	9.9	10.2	+ .3	1.2	<.10
5. Need self-esteem	8.9	10.0	+1.1	4.8	<.0005
Response rate	52.3	54.2	+1.9		

* For one-tailed test.
Adapted from Bass, Cascio, McPherson, and Tragash, "PROSPER Training and Research for Increasing Management Awareness about Affirmative Action in Race Relations," *Academy of Management Journal,* 19 (1976): 353–369.

any, are optimal for differentially placing individuals who have a disadvantaged background into meaningful occupations? Second, how can we
train and increase the skill levels of those who have had limited educational opportunity in the past? The third area of concern regards the
optimal techniques of supervision and organization structure for those
who are not used to the ways of middle-class organizations.

Organizational Hiring of the
Hard-Core Unemployed

The problem is emphasized for the large industrial organizations by growing national consensus that private sectors of the economy have to play
a larger role in hiring those who have been thought traditionally to be
unemployable. Recent polls show that there has been a shift in opinion
by the general public in its attitudes toward corporate involvement in
hiring the unemployed.[27] There has been a corresponding decline in
prejudice among white employees toward working with minority group
members. For example, in 1944 only 41 per cent of white employees
thought it would be all right to put a black at work next to them. In 1956
the figure had changed to 63 per cent. In 1944, only 32 per cent of employees thought integrated departments in a factory were acceptable.
In 1956, this had changed to 62 per cent believing integrated departments
in a factory were acceptable.[27] The Civil Rights legislation of the mid-
1960s undoubtedly reflected an even greater majority accepting integration.
However, by the 1970s we were seeing some backlash.

There is also a growing consensus among managers of companies that
a special effort should be made to hire and train minority group members for skilled jobs. In a 1968 confidential study conducted among 300
managers in a major corporation, 51 per cent of the first-line supervisors
(foremen) felt the company's responsibility in this area. The number of
managers who saw this as being a responsibility steadily increased up the
corporate ranks, until at the fourth and fifth levels of management (executives) 100 per cent of those queried believed the company should make a
special effort to hire and train black workers.

The response pattern was similar, though dampened, when these same
managers were asked if the company should lower the employment qualifications in order to hire more people from disadvantaged groups. Only 16
per cent of the first-line management thought this the proper thing to do
and, while the percentage steadily increased, at the fourth and fifth levels,
78 per cent thought this was the proper policy.[27] These results provide
evidence of managerial consensus, particularly within the executive group,
that more must be done in the area of hiring the disadvantaged. It is
obvious that a real problem exists within the corporate hierarchy, since

the most prejudiced segments of the corporation are probably the rank-and-file employees and the first-line supervisors, particularly if they are white and the disadvantaged are black. The closer the black worker is competitively to a white worker, the more prone the latter to oppose black employment. Where white workers still subscribe to a "lump of labor" theory — there is only a fixed number of jobs available — the white sees the black as a direct competitor for the same job who may be willing to lower wage standards to be hired. The white sees the black as of lower status. If blacks can achieve as much as whites, the whites see themselves as losing status. White supervisors know they must get out production, and that if they have to spend time in training or give special consideration to certain employees this will hurt their performance ratings. While the top levels of management are committed to a more liberal policy in terms of hiring the disadvantaged, the supervisor on the shop floor is *least committed* to this plan, but is the person who will be *most important* in implementing a program of this sort.

There is initial resentment by many employees if the hard-core unemployed are hired without meeting the usual employment standards. One investigation of the attitude change in a utility company found that before the start of a program aimed to provide jobs for hard-core people the program was viewed positively by people in the organization. But 12 weeks after the program had been in operation, the organization as a whole was neutral. This counteracts the often naive assumption that experience of this type will give everyone a good feeling about the objectives of the program. The shift in attitude was especially notable among the rank-and-file employees. There are costs in a program of this type, and it is well for the organization to be aware of these in order to make the programs more effective.[52]

Basic Skills Training to Upgrade the Disadvantaged

In the past decade, business and industry have taken on more and more responsibility for providing promotion possibilities for individuals who, because of educational disadvantages, may not have the basic skills in reading, arithmetic, and office procedures that are required to perform many of the advanced jobs in an organization effectively. Three types of training programs carried out in Procter and Gamble were designed to develop basic skills required for production jobs, secretarial work, and technician positions in laboratories.[51] In all three training programs there was a significant increase in the average score from the beginning to the end of the training period, but perhaps more significant was the fact that according to the skill being taught, between 73 and 100 per cent of the trainees showed real gains in basic skills.

The evidence showed that individuals who come from disadvantaged backgrounds and who may lack formal schooling can improve their basic skills even when the age of the participants may be well into their thirties.

Training the Hard-Core Unemployed

One of the most difficult jobs faced by industrial organizations in the United States is the training of the disadvantaged who have seldom if ever held gainful employment. Lockheed instituted a successful program in training the hard-core employee.[36] The program had a number of features that contributed to its success. First, the training was directed toward specific jobs that the trainees knew they would have, once they had completed their training program. Second, the trainees were actually "overtrained" in that they were given a little more skill than was necessary to accomplish the stated job. This was done to give the trainees a degree of self-confidence. There were also a number of costs in this sort of program, since a great deal of time was required to train the individuals. Trainees were given much personal help by the instructors and of this help, often half the time was spent on such personal problems as bailing trainees out of jail or working on debts the trainees had incurred. A great deal of demonstration and individual instruction was required, and the student-teacher ratio was about six to one. This, of course, makes the program very expensive for an organization to administer. But since the program was successful, the benefits to the individuals were substantial. Besides the obvious benefits to the trainees, there was a benefit to society as a whole, since it was calculated in one training program having a little over a hundred trainees, that if the trainees had remained unemployed and on the public payroll as they had before, the welfare payments would have totaled over $100,000.

It was obvious that this saving could benefit society in general, and having people gainfully employed and feeling a degree of satisfaction about themselves and the work they could accomplish adds immeasurably to human welfare. One problem that does exist with hard-core programs is the fact that there are so many variables that can influence the success of the program. One investigation found 50 variables that were important for programs of this sort.[31]

Less effective are programs that focus on personal or society-related problems rather than job problems. A public utility developed a company-view orientation program stressing job-related topics, especially the benefits to be gained and penalties to be avoided with responsible and effective performance. In contrast, a quasi-therapeutic orientation program administered by a university staff based upon group discussion tended to brush aside job problems and focus on personal adjustment of the black and the problems of the black working in a white establishment. In terms of both absenteeism and turnover the company orientation was superior.[61]

THE ENVIRONMENT AND INDUSTRIAL/ORGANIZATIONAL PSYCHOLOGY

Industrial psychology has been directly involved since its inception in examining systematically how people at work are affected by temperature, noise, ventilation, and so on. However, the range of concern has broadened for the environment, for ecology, and policies that deal with pollution control as well as conservation of energy and resources. For instance, industrial/organizational psychology can contribute to environmental policies by assisting in taking into account the human elements in the development of ecological inventories.

> Resource inventories that identify potential areas for reservoirs, future parks, and utility and transportation corridors will be required along with inventories to protect features such as park areas, landscapes, and even certain types of urban areas. Coupled with such inventories, a rehabilitation index needs to be developed to cover such potential conversions as dumps to parks and slums to open space. We need an antipollution index itemizing requirements for rehabilitating water, air, and soil, as well as areas that have been adversely affected by loud noises and offensive unusual effects. There should . . . be behavioral inputs into these efforts.[9]

Ecology is the complement of psychology. Both study the interaction of people and their environment. Psychology concentrates on how people adapt and respond to their environment. Ecology deals with how their environment is modified by people.[9] Behavioral science and industrial psychology have vital roles to play in indicating and ameliorating the costs of technological advances: for example, the noise pollution generated by the supersonic transport.

Noise Pollution

There is a "band of annoyance," which varies depending on the past experience of the person. Even now, many of us are annoyed by the excessive noise in the cities and in the countryside adjacent to major highways, but of even more concern is the sonic boom generated by supersonic transports. By carefully analyzing the sonic boom intensity to be expected and the annoyance levels of individuals, Kryter showed that between 35 and 65 million Americans would experience 10 to 20 booms per day if supersonic transports (SST's) flew directly overland coast to coast, depending on the route the planes traveled.[40] Of this number, we can estimate that at least 30 per cent would feel they could not live with the boom and 70 per cent would dislike or be neutral concerning the noise. These would be the social and psychological consequences of a technological advance, unless the sonic boom were eliminated. This evidence contributed to governmental policy making about SSTs. It is clear that if we had permitted supersonic transports to fly over the continental United States, without eliminating the sonic booms, it would have been at a psychological cost to the whole American population for the benefit of only a few. Millions of people would have been subjected to annoyance by the booms so that 250 people could reduce by a few hours their travel time going from New York to Los Angeles. These psychological costs were considered in evaluating what seemed to be technological progress. For this and other reasons, Congress in 1971 voted against supporting continued development of the Boeing SST, although since 1978 Concordes from London and Paris have been permitted to land in New York, Washington, and Dallas, but only if they fly at lower, subsonic speeds over the continental United States.

Driving Accidents and Public Policy

Often public officials advocate policies such as cracking down on speeding, and claim results that contradict good experimental design.

One of the critical problems in attempting to implement positive programs of accident prevention is distortion in reporting of the effects of such programs. Campbell illustrates how distortions occur when care is not taken in the research design to avoid such errors.[19] The State of Connecticut instituted severe penalties for speeding in an effort to cut the vehicle accident death toll. At the end of a year of enforcement (1956), traffic deaths had declined from 324 to 284. The 12 per cent reduction in fatalities was ascribed to consistent enforcement by the police of the laws against speeding and the severity of the penalties. This is shown graphically in Figure 18–1, seemingly dramatic proof that the death toll could be cut by effective law enforcement. But two points in an extended time series do not tell the whole story. More complete data for the preceding years are given in Figure 18–2. Here it can be seen that there was a great deal of variability in the prior years in the accident rate and that the 1955 accident death toll was actually a large jump from previous years and could have been due to a number of factors such as unusual weather conditions which made the roads more hazardous. More sophisticated statistical techniques over a longer time period did indicate that there was a slight effect from the crackdown on speeding in reducing the death toll,

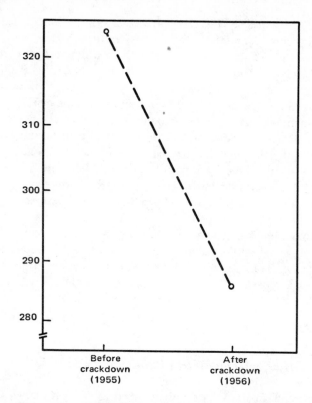

Figure 18–1. Connecticut traffic fatalities. (From Campbell, "Reforms as Experiments," *American Psychologist,* 24 [1969]: 412.)

but simply showing the decrease from 1955 to 1956 did not in itself show the efficacy of the program.[19]

A different type of legal reform in Britain showed more favorable results.[62] The British crackdown was not on speed but on the drunken driver. The British had a much better rationale than the Connecticut approach. The British approach used a breath analyzer to detect alcohol in drivers either stopped by a policeman or involved in an accident. If alcohol concentration beyond a certain level was detected, there was severe mandatory punishment, including license suspension and a fine of over $200.

The results indicated a dramatic and sustained drop in the accident rate. In comparison to the Connecticut crackdown on the speeder, the British crackdown on the drinker was more effective.

Behavioral science and industrial psychology have a great deal to offer public officials for the solution of one of our most important problems

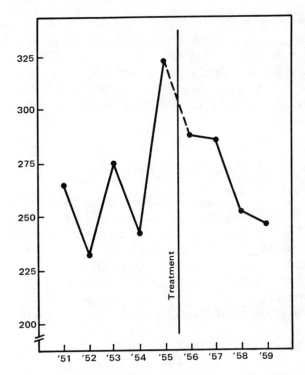

Figure 18–2. Connecticut traffic fatalities. (Same data as in Figure 18–1, presented as part of an extended time series.) (From Campbell, "Reforms as Experiments," *American Psychologist,* 24 [1969]: 413.)

— death on our highways. The problem seems to the same in this area as in many areas: that the public as a whole and officials in particular have their own ideas about what causes fatal accidents, since they consider themselves to be experienced drivers and therefore able to make informed judgments about the situation. However, public officials have neither time, training, nor inclination to review the thousands of studies in many journals that have been done in such an area, in order to formulate consistent public policy. This means that the behavioral scientists must summarize research so that the public and officials can benefit from the work that has been done; probably more important, such reviews must suggest specific policies and ways they can be implemented.

One such approach to the automobile accident problem has been suggested by Barrett, Alexander, and Forbes.[6] Their report summarizes the research on psychological factors that appear to be related to automobile accidents. They then recommended looking at the problem in much the same way as the decision theory model that was discussed in Chapter 12.[22]

By including estimates of the cost of accidents, cost of training, improvement in driving ability resulting from training, and the selection of driver applicants to be trained, they show that a substantial decrease in traffic accidents might be obtained by driver training based on present research knowledge. They have also shown that the cost of such training would be likely to pay for itself during the first four years of driving, just in reduced accident costs.

Other Environmental Policy Issues

AIR POLLUTION   Air pollution is a behavioral problem. We have increased the carbon monoxide in our blood through cigarette smoking, automobile exhaust, industrial smoke, and home heating and cooking.[28] The Northeast United States and the Midwest, with a less favorable *physical climate,* are losing industry and jobs to the sunbelt states. Part of the movement in the 1950s and 1960s was accounted for by the decision of whites to seek employment in sunny, warm, dry, snow-free weather, while blacks migrated out of the South to better their economic condition.[8]

NUCLEAR ENERGY   The public is polarized around the issue of nuclear energy plant construction. Environmentalists damn any further building; businessmen are neutral or in favor of extending the production and use of nuclear power.[11] The NUCLEAR SITE NEGOTIATION exercise[10] illustrates how interested citizens can be moved to less extreme positions and more understanding of the nuclear debate.[60]

ORGANIZATIONAL PSYCHOLOGY AND PUBLIC POLICY

Organizational psychology has probably had its main impact on public policy through the writings of its popularizers, men like Peter Drucker, Douglas McGregor, and Chris Argyris; magazines like the *Harvard Business Review, Psychology Today,* and *Fortune;* and institutions like the American Management Association, the National Training Laboratories, and graduate business schools here and abroad. Recognition has been made at the highest levels that a nation's standard of living depends on its productivity per capita and that this productivity depends on motivation to work as well as capital investment and good management practices. The psychological rewards of work are seen by policy-makers who must contend with welfare clients who refuse to accept menial jobs, with men who will volunteer for military service only under the coercion of draft eligibility, and with women's liberation forces who argue successfully and lightly that women's lack of career interest was a function of artificial, unfair barriers to advancement. The quality of working life has become the subject of national legislation enacted in the 1960s and 1970s in western Europe and under consideration in the United States at the time of this writing.

In the years to come we will expect increasing involvement of industrial/organizational psychology with public policy as the boundaries diminish between work and leisure and we move further into an administered economy.

Changing Society

Organizational policies must be ready to accommodate to the manifold changes occurring outside them. For instance, women career employees, with strong economic interests to work, are becoming increasingly commonplace in advanced industrial society. Industrial/organizational psychologists contribute to policies involved in moving into what used to be all-male jobs, in arranging for women to supervise men, in dealing with the special problems of pregnancy leaves, and in testing alternatives to the standard 8-hour day, 5-day week, and so on.

The democratization of the workplace in the advanced industrial world has been dramatic.

Industrial Democracy

In previous chapters, we have discussed, at length, workers' participation at the workplace in decisions of consequence to them. This generally has been a U. S.-centered thrust. But in many industrialized western European countries, Yugoslavia, Israel, and elsewhere, participation of workers or their representatives at different levels in the organization, including its board of directors, has been mandated by legislation. Thus, the West German codetermination law became operative in 800 large German corporations in 1976. It requires worker representation at the highest management levels.[75]

Legally constituted and supported worker councils elect their managements in Yugoslavia and involve themselves in decisions about investments as well as about production. Generally, despite legislation, the important decision-making often is left to those with power, such as the local bankers, the technocrats, and members of the Communist Party.[55]

Industrial democracy is still mainly a consequence of voluntary arrangements in such countries as Sweden and the Netherlands. In 1946, in Sweden, employer and employee organizations in firms with more than 50 employees had formed work councils, with representatives from both sides, to meet regularly to solve problems and exchange information. The Dutch *werkoverleg* is a formally constituted consultative work group that carries no particular legal support.

Drucker sees the United States moving toward industrial democracy as a consequence of empoyee stock ownership plans.[24] He argues that ESOPs will result in employee pension funds holding the controlling shares in corporations. Eventually the employee fund's directors, representing the employees' interests, will be in a position to control the firm's management.

Bass and Rosenstein suggest that industrial democracy and participative management each has its place in different aspects of employee-employer relationships.[14] The future of industrial/organizational psychology is likely to involve determination of the kinds of decisions in which each is relevant and useful. For instance, both may be important to career development or job security policies; neither may be particularly relevant for marketing or capital investment policies.

Industrial/organizational psychology has been seen as a tool of management to offset organized labor.[29] Nevertheless, progressive management has broadened its objectives from single-minded profit maximization to concern for the interests of its various constituents, including its employees. For such managements, it is easy for industrial/organizational psychologists to contribute impartially to policy on questions affecting the health of the firm that do not jeopardize the welfare of its employees. But unions may still be hurt in the process. For instance, if an industrial/organizational psychologist helps to improve an organization's climate, it reduces the need for the employees to have available a union to bargain collectively for them. The felt need for collective bargaining, according to a study of 64 professionals by Bass and Mitchell, directly depended on the extent to which the professionals had authoritarian supervisors who did not consult with them.[13] The professionals felt the need for collective bargaining also if they lacked a sense of job security, and did not trust their organization.

Quality of Working Life

The growth of industrial democracy and participative management is interlinked with the growth of concern for the quality of working life. Job design, organizational development, motivation to work and many of the other issues we have discussed in earlier chapters are now matters of public policy and subjects of legislation and public discussion.[23] The state and federal governments of developed nations such as West Germany support hundreds of experiments to try out new team approaches to the workplace such as we have described in earlier chapters. Developing nations such as Singapore now control what kinds of industries they will encourage on the basis of whether the new industries will provide jobs demanding skills and education fitting with concern for citizen and community development rather than merely jobs for unskilled, cheap labor.

Futher, public policies and discussion develop as a consequence of union interest in the quality of working life. The collective bargaining contracts, particularly with craft and professional unions, now are likely to concern making the work less onerous, easing the pace of work, and safeguarding health and safety.[4]

As we look ahead to the twenty-first century, the quality of jobs and the quality of working life may become key political issues in the United States. Between 1950 and 1980 managers and professionals have increased fourfold; unskilled workers have dropped from one in eight to one in twenty.[45] This trend is likely to level off but the comparable rise in the level of education of the population is likely to increase the oversupply of "knowledge workers" for the self-actualizing opportunities available. There may be trouble ahead in this regard.

On the one hand, if trends for those in higher-level jobs continue, we will find managers and professionals still working hard with long work weeks in complex and challenging jobs. Given the growing concern for the quality of working life, we should see increasing opportunities for creativity in such jobs and greater gratification from them. The boundaries between work and play for the creative elite will be less distinct than they are today. Future productivity will gain broadening affluence and education will provide more freedom of choice. Instead of working to produce the necessities for survival, opportunities will be increasingly available to work in pursuit of whatever goals society wishes to accomplish.[45]

On the other hand, there may be a serious oversupply in many fields of "knowledge workers" capable of handling such jobs. They will have to be content with less rewarding work, shorter hours, and more opportunities for leisure and play with income security. Some people, as well, will consciously choose to "drop out." Polarization is likely to occur between those dedicated to work, science, art, and business and those who are forced to accept uninteresting work for lack of job opportunities or who do choose to drop out. The political lines and public policies of the twenty-first century may be drawn between those whose life goals center around work and those whose life goals center around inner experiences, play, leisure, and social relations.

INDUSTRIAL/ORGANIZATIONAL PSYCHOLOGY REACTION TO CLAIMS CONCERNING BEHAVIORAL SCIENCE "INNOVATIONS"

Throughout this book we have mentioned a number of so-called innovations that their proponents have claimed will result in dramatic changes in either individual or organizational performance. Typically, these innovations are backed more by the assertions of their proponents than by any empirical facts. For example, in Chapter 3 we mentioned the widespread Zero Defects programs designed to motivate employees to higher levels of performance. Other examples include handwriting analysis for selection, assertiveness training for women, transcendental meditation for creativity, music to increase productivity, color schemes to increase performance, office landscaping to increase communication and productivity, and human relations approaches that dramatically increase quality and quantity of individual performance. Quite often these programs are financially successful and make a great deal of money for the innovators. Unfortunately, their claims of successes are often illusionary. In this section we will discuss a few of these innovations and examine some of the empirical evidence.

A major question for industrial/organizational psychologists is the amount of effort they should put forth in establishing the credibility of these so-called behavioral science innovations. Too often organizations' resources are spent in ways that are not productive or that are in fact even counterproductive for the employees in the organization. Organizations seem quite prone to fads, to grasping at a new concept or idea in hopes that it will be a panacea for the problems in the organization. We, of course, do not want to discredit all innovations, but the problem is separating the wheat from the chaff. This is often a long and painful process involving a number of empirical studies over some span of time. It is quite easy for innovators to claim that their training program will make the employee happier and more productive, but much more difficult to conduct the detailed research to refute or support that contention.[5]

COLOR AND JOB PERFORMANCE   One popular proposition is that the color of the working area can influence job performance. Quite a few studies have been consistent in showing that as a group, individuals do have preferences for colors in the green/blue region and prefer least the color yellow. But despite considerable evaluative efforts, there is literally no documented evidence from experimental studies to support the contention that color can influence job performance or performance on psychomotor tasks.[30]

GRAPHANALYSIS AS A SELECTION TECHNIQUE Handwriting analysis is a popular technique in much of Europe for analyzing personality and selecting individuals for various positions in organizations. But available validation research is not encouraging. There are few empirical investigations, and those that have been conducted fail to support the idea that job success can be predicted by analyzing handwriting samples. Despite this, graphologists analyze people's handwriting to make statements about an individual's personality, character, and likelihood of success in particular activities, and are being employed by companies for hiring purposes.[26]

Techniques like graphology and astrology rely to a large extent upon making general statements about individuals; the validity is then tested by asking individuals whose handwriting samples or horoscopes were read if the statement concerning their personalities was accurate. Invariably, the individual replies that this appears to be an accurate statement concerning his or her personality. Of course, this is the "Barnum effect," which we previously mentioned in Chapter 2. This sort of evidence, of course, cannot replace scientific empirical investigations.

TRANSCENDENTAL MEDITATION There are over a half million individuals who have been trained in the United States in transcendental meditation. One of the claims of transcendental meditation is increased creativity. No empirical evidence has been advanced by transcendental meditation advocates to support this claim. One study compared a group in transcendental meditation with several other groups, one of which was involved in a psychology course studying creativity. After a six-month period there was no change in the creativity of the transcendental meditation group, but there was a positive change in the psychology class on four of the five measures used to test for creativity.[24]

OFFICE LANDSCAPING A trend in the design of offices is open office landscaping. Conventional walls are eliminated. Screened-off work areas are substituted, using partitions, plants, and furniture. There have been conflicting reports concerning the consequences of this type of office design. The fundamental issue appears to revolve around the office workers' perception of the control they have over two-way transactions with other office workers as a result of this design change.

The negative aspect includes complaints about too much noise in the work area, too many distractions, difficulty of sustained effort on a project, and lack of clear boundary for one's own office space. The positive comments indicate that the landscaping format allows more job satisfaction, productivity, and better contact with the office workers.[49] But more pleasing esthetics may be the main justification for office landscaping rather than the claimed benefits for the costs involved.

THE EFFECTS OF MUSIC ON BEHAVIOR Certain commercial companies promote the idea that music will increase the satisfaction and performance of
employees. The actual empirical studies on the effects of music have been
quite variable in terms of their results. Some studies show no effects on
productivity and quality of performance, while others do show some increases in quality and quantity of performance with music on the job.
But quite consistently, most employees say they prefer music while they
work. A small minority of employees are against it.

In a typical study in a skateboard factory, four different types of music
were played — dance, show, folk, and popular — in order to ascertain
the effect on quality and quantity of production. No change was found
in either quantity or quality while music was being played, but the
employees were very favorable toward having music while they worked.[53]

It has also been suggested that music could have an effect upon shoppers.
In comparing soft and loud music in two large supermarkets, it was found
that there was no significant difference in sales or customer satisfaction,
but less time was spent by the customers in the store when the music
was loud.[71]

ASSERTIVENESS TRAINING FOR WOMEN Many of the training programs state
that they can "facilitate the personal growth of women." As with most
training programs, this sort of proposition is seldom put to the empirical
test. A Solomon four-group design (see Chapter 13) was used to assess an
assertiveness training program for women, which included viewing a
movie and participating in a discussion session. All of the data were
collected six weeks after the training session by having a male confederate
phone women and request that they "join an organization that would aid
in stopping inflation by asking employed American women to give their
jobs to unemployed American men." Ratings of the assertiveness and related behavior of the women showed that there were no significant differences between the experimental and control groups.

The basic issue of whether or not assertiveness training can change
women's behavior has not been substantiated, despite the widespread
publicity given to these programs.[41]

The Popular Press Reports of Events versus
Reality: The Case of Non-Linear Systems

One of the most widely publicized organizational experiments involved
Non-Linear Systems' changeover to the human relations approach. This
experiment in participative management rested upon the philosophical
basis of behavioral scientists such as Drucker, McGregor, and Maslow.
The changeover in the early 1960s was initiated by the company president,

who held all the stock of this successful maker of digital electrical measuring instruments. One of the first changes was to eliminate hourly wages and put every employee on a straight salary that involved also a 25 per cent raise in pay. Time clocks were eliminated and the employees received their pay even if they were late, left work early, or took other breaks from the work during the day. No records at all were kept on any individual employee.

The second major shift was in the organization of the plant. Before the changeover, Non-Linear Systems operated with a typical organizational structure including a board of directors, president, and managers for various areas. For the change, three "zones" were established. The first was called a trustee management and in essence consisted of the board of directors. The second zone consisted of general management and was composed of an eight-member executive council. The third zone consisted of department managers. An important change was that the executive council was to operate as a group in an advisory capacity and all decisions were to be made by mutual consent at regular meetings.

The production setup was also modified. The assembly line was discontinued. Instead, departmental units of three to twelve people were established. The manager of the group was no longer a supervisor in a traditional sense. Instead, he became a consultant to the group. This manager reported to the executive council as a whole and was not responsible to any single superior. One of the specific aspects of the study was that all record-keeping was eliminated. This followed McGregor's idea that keeping performance records would tend to kill autonomy.

The press gave many positive accounts to this experiment, uniformly stating that it was successful. For example, it was reported that "the man-hours devoted to building instruments have been cut in half" and "productivity is now averaging 50% more." There were also statements that the quality of the products had improved dramatically. The press reported that "the number of complaints from customers had dropped 70%." The facts of the situation were quite different. Indeed, as we have already mentioned, no records were kept of individual productivity, and looking at the plant as a whole, the best that could be said was that there was no change in productivity. The time required to assemble each instrument remained constant despite the 25 per cent increase in pay. Although it was true that the output of the factory rose 30 per cent, the number of employees rose 32 per cent!

Although there was no formal attitude survey conducted, the increase in salary, benefits, and more freedom in the production process would indicate that it was a good place for the shopworkers. The absenteeism rate and turnover appeared to be consistent with those of the other plants in the geographical area. The situation was quite different with regard to the lower management level, the skilled engineers and technicians, and the executive committee. They experienced a great deal of dissatisfaction, and many of them quit. Over a third of the department managers left over a three-year period after the study began.

Within five years, partly due to its failure to remain alert to its markets the company was close to bankruptcy, and then the experiment was ended. Non-Linear Systems was reorganized, going back to traditional management practices. Since there was no accurate documentation of the total process, we have to rely upon fragmentary data and a few limited generalizations one could make during the experiment. First, the concept of removing the high-level executives from the traditional job duties of planning, directing, and controlling the operations of the plant was not successful. The same finding applied to lower levels of management where job satisfaction and performance appeared to drop as a result of the experiment. On the shop floor, job satisfaction did increase, but there appeared to be no increased creativity, let alone productivity or improved quality of the product. Although the popular press was quick to note a supposedly successful reorganization by human relations principles, they were very slow to note its failure.

Most of the statements one reads in the popular press concerning innovations in organizations must be taken with a grain of salt. Typically, the statements made are based only on a reporter's impressions and may have little basis in fact. Indeed, most of the statements made by the press during the period when Non-Linear Systems was making the changes had no basis in fact since the records were not kept to support the statements.[47]

This is not to say that all of what we presented in earlier chapters on innovations in job and organization design is without foundation. Rather, here was one of many cases where the publicity ran far ahead of reality.

Popular Writers as a Source of Research Ideas

At times, popular writers can have insight into psychological problems concerning organizational behavior that will be found to have considerable validity. For example, Parkinson has formulated a number of laws of behavior. One of the most popular of Parkinson's laws is that work expands to fill the time available. This time effect has been demonstrated by allowing subjects either five or fifteen minutes to complete a task that could be completed in five minutes. Those subjects who were allowed the additional time spent significantly more time performing a second task.[1,2] This excess time effect appears to have a great deal of generality, since it can be illustrated under a variety of experimental conditions.[42]

Parkinson's generalization has been expanded to a state that "work pace is adjusted to the perceived difficulty of the task undertaken." This proposition has been supported in a laboratory and more recently in a field setting.[18] It was found that logging crews had a higher rate of production when less time was given them to meet and make deliveries of wood to the mill. When there was no pressure upon the logging crews, the output was lower.[43]

Writers, philosophers, and statesmen offer us many potentially valid propositions about people at work. But, unfortunately, we can sort out the sense from the nonsense only with considerable effort using the methods and standards we have tried to present in this book.

SUMMARY

We have discussed a wide variety of topics in the chapter. Government regulation has had an important impact on the practice of industrial/organizational psychology. Where psychology once had only professional guidelines, it now in addition must observe federal regulations and court decisions, as is the case with personnel selection. But industrial/organizational psychology's research contributes to the setting of government policy and regulation.

Congressional action to increase the retirement age will probably bring additional regulations and litigation dealing with performance evaluation of the older employee. Organizational policies may have to be modified to motivate the younger employee, whose progress may be slowed as a result of older employees remaining on the job for a longer period of time.

Formal industrial democracy is now legislated in much of noncommunist Europe while informal democratic practices are followed in the United States.

We need to sort out "pop innovations" from those that can stand the test of controlled evaluation. Many of these "pop innovations" may seem exciting, but usually greatly overstate their value to both individuals and organizations.

We believe that new congressional action, court decisions, innovations, and continued scientific progress will continue to make the field of industrial/organizational psychology relevant and stimulating.

REFERENCES

1. Aronson, E., and E. Gerard. "Beyond Parkinson's Law: The Effect of Excess Time on Subsequent Performance," *Journal of Personality and Social Psychology*, 3 (1966): 336–339.
2. Aronson, E., and E. Landy. "Further Steps beyond Parkinson's Law: A Replication and Extension of the Excess Time Effect," *Journal of Experimental Social Psychology*, 3 (1967): 274–285.

3. Baldus, D. E., and J. W. L. Cole. "Quantitative Proof of Intentional Discrimination," *Evaluation Quarterly*, 1, No. 1 (1977): 53–86.

4. Barbash, J. "Unions Advance Quality of Work through Collective Bargaining," *World of Work Report*, 2, No. 3 (1977): 31.

5. Barrett, G. V. "Symposium: Research Models of the Future for Industrial and Organizational Psychology," *Personnel Psychology*, 25 (1972): 1–17.

6. Barrett, G. V., R. A. Alexander, and J. B. Forbes. "Analysis of Performance Measurement and Training Requirements for Driving Decision Making in Emergency Situations," *JSAS Catalog of Selected Documents in Psychology*, 7 (1977): 126. (Ms. No. 1623.)

7. Basnight, T. A., and B. W. Wilkinson. "Evaluating Managerial Performance: Is Your Appraisal System Legal?" *Employee Relations Law Journal*, 3, No. 2 (1977): 240–254.

8. Bass, B. M., and R. A. Alexander. "Climate, Economy, and the Differential Migration of White and Nonwhite Workers," *Journal of Applied Psychology*, 56 (1972): 518–521.

9. Bass, B. M., and R. Bass. "Concern for the Environment: Implications for Industrial and Organizational Psychology," *American Psychologist*, 31 (1976): 158–176.

10. Bass, B. M., R. Bass, and Z. Shapira. *Nuclear Site Negotiation*. Scottsville, N.Y.: Transnational Programs Corporation, 1975.

11. Bass, B. M., R. Bass, and Z. Shapira. "Environmentalists' and Business Executives' Attitudes and Information about the Nuclear Power Controversy," *International Journal of Environmental Studies*, 10 (1977): 79–83.

12. Bass, B. M., W. F. Cascio, J. W. McPherson, and H. J. Tragash. "PROSPER—Training and Research for Increasing Management Awareness about Affirmative Action in Race Relations," *Academy of Management Journal*, 19 (1976): 353–369.

13. Bass, B. M., and C. W. Mitchell. "Influences on the Felt Need for Collective Bargaining by Business and Science Professionals," *Journal of Applied Psychology*, 61 (1976): 770–773.

14. Bass, B. M., and E. Rosenstein. "Integration of Industrial Democracy and Participative Management: U. S. and European Perspectives." In B. T. King, S. S. Streufert, and F. E. Fiedler (eds.), *Managerial Control and Organizational Democracy*. Washington, D. C.: Victor Winston & Sons, 1977.

15. Belt, J. A., and P. B. Holden. "Polygraph Usage among Major U. S. Corporations," *Personnel Journal*, 57 (1978): 80–86.

16. Bickel, P. J., E. A. Hammel, J. W. O'Connell. "Sex Bias in Graduate Admissions: Data from Berkeley," *Science*, 187 (1975): 398–404.

17. Boehm, V. R. "Differential Prediction? A Methodological Artifact," *Journal of Applied Psychology*, 62 (1977): 146–154.

18. Bryan, J. F., and E. A. Locke. "Parkinson's Law as a Goal-Setting Phenomenon," *Organizational Behavior and Human Performance*, 2 (1967): 258–275.

19. Campbell, D. T. "Reforms as Experiments," *American Psychologist*, 24 (1969): 409–420.

20. Cary, F. T. "IBM's Guidelines to Employee Privacy," *Harvard Business Review*, 54 (1976): 82–90.

21. Cascio, W. F. *Applied Psychology in Personnel Management*. Reston, Va.: Reston, 1978.

22. Cronbach, L. J., and G. C. Gleser. *Psychological Tests and Personnel Decisions.* Urbana, Ill.: University of Illinois Press, 1965.
23. Davis, L. E., A. B. Cherns, and associates (eds.). *The Quality of Working Life:* Vol. I: *Problems, Prospects and the State of the Art.* New York: Free Press, 1975.
24. Domino, G. "Transcendental Meditation and Creativity: An Empirical Investigation," *Journal of Applied Psychology,* 62 (1977): 358–362.
25. Drucker, P. *The Unseen Revolution: How Pension Fund Socialism Came to America.* New York: Harper & Row, 1976.
26. Gardner, J. "Handwriting Analysis Finds Growing Favor in Personnel Offices," *Wall Street Journal,* September 11, 1967.
27. Goeke, J. R., and C. S. Weymar. "Barriers to Hiring the Blacks," *Harvard Business Review,* 47 (1969): 144–152.
28. Goldsmith, J. R., and S. A. Landaw. "Carbon Monoxide and Human Health," *Science,* 162 (1968): 1352–1359.
29. Gomberg, W. "The Use of Psychology in Industry: A Trade Union Point of View," *Management Science,* 3 (1957): 348–370.
30. Goodfellow, R. A. H., and P. C. Smith. "Effects of Environmental Color on Two Psychomotor Tasks," *Perceptual and Motor Skills,* 37 (1973): 296–298.
31. Goodman, P. S. "Hiring, Training, and Retraining the Hard-Core," *Industrial Relations,* 9 (1969): 54–66.
32. Guion, R. M. "Employment Tests and Discriminatory Hiring," *Industrial Relations,* 5 (1966): 20–37.
33. Hardy, K. R. "Social Origins of American Scientists and Scholars," *Science,* 185 (1974): 497–506.
34. Haskins, J. B. "Effects of Safety Communication Campaigns: A Review of the Research Evidence," *Journal of Safety Research,* 1 (1969): 58–66.
35. Hill, H. "The Equal Employment Opportunity Acts of 1964 and 1972: A Critical Analysis of the Legislative History and Administration of the Law," *Industrial Relations Law Journal,* 2 (1977): 1–96.
36. Hodgson, J. D., and M. H. Brenner. "Successful Experience: Training Hard-Core Unemployed," *Harvard Business Review,* 46, No. 5 (1968): 148–156.
37. Horvath, F. "The Effect of Selected Variables on Interpretation of Polygraph Records," *Journal of Applied Psychology,* 62 (1977): 127–136.
38. Humphreys, L. G. "Statistical Definitions of Test Validity for Minority Groups," *Journal of Applied Psychology,* 58 (1973): 1–4.
39. Hunter, E. J., and F. L. Schmidt. "Critical Analysis of the Statistical and Ethical Implications of Various Definitions of Test Bias," *Psychological Bulletin,* 83 (1976): 1053–1071.
40. Kryter, K. D. "Psychological Reactions to Aircraft Noise," *Science,* 151 (1966): 1346–1355.
41. Kwiterovich, D. K., and J. J. Horan. "Solomon Evaluation of a Commercial Assertiveness Program for Women," *Behavior Therapy,* 8 (1977): 501–502.
42. Landy, D., K. McCue, and E. Aronson. "Beyond Parkinson's Law: III. The Effect of Protractive and Contractive Distractions on the Wasting of Time on Subsequent Tasks," *Journal of Applied Psychology,* 53 (1969): 236–239.
43. Latham, G. P., and E. A. Locke. "Increasing Productivity with Decreasing Time Limits: A Field Replication of Parkinson's Law," *Journal of Applied Psychology,* 60 (1975): 524–526.

44. Lee, B. "The Polygraph and Pre-Employment Screening," *Houston Law Review*, 13, No. 3 (1976): 551–570.

45. Levitan, S. A., and W. B. Johnston. *Work Is Here to Stay, Alas*. New York: Olympus, 1974.

46. Lykken, D. T. "Psychology and the Lie Detector Industry," *American Psychologist*, 29 (1974): 725–739.

47. Malone, E. L. "The Non-Linear Systems Experiment in Participative Management," *Journal of Business*, 48 (1975): 52–64.

48. Matarazzo, J. D., and A. N. Wiens. "Black Intelligence Test of Cultural Homogeneity and Wechsler Adult Intelligence Scale Scores of Black and White Police Applicants," *Journal of Applied Psychology*, 62 (1977): 57–63.

49. McCarrey, M. W., L. Peterson, S. Edwards, and P. von Kulmiz. "Landscape Office Attitudes: Reflections of Perceived Degree of Control over Transactions with the Environment," *Journal of Applied Psychology*, 59 (1974): 401–403.

50. Mironi, M. "The Confidentiality of Personnel Records: A Legal and Ethical View," *Labor Law Journal*, 25 (1974): 270–293.

51. Mollenkopf, W. G. "Some Results of Three Basic Skills Training Programs in an Industrial Setting," *Journal of Applied Psychology*, 53 (1969): 343–347.

52. Morgan, B. S., M. R. Blonsky, and H. Rosen. "Employee Attitudes Toward a Hard-Core Hiring Program," *Experimental Publication System*, 2 (1969): Ms. 074A.

53. Newman, R. I., Jr., D. L. Hunt, and F. Rhodes. "Effects of Music on Employee Attitude and Productivity in a Skateboard Factory," *Journal of Applied Psychology*, 50 (1966): 493–496.

54. Novick, M. R., and D. D. Ellis, Jr. "Equal Opportunity in Educational and Employment Selection," *American Psychologist*, 32 (1977): 306–320.

55. Obradović, J. "Workers' Participation: Who Participates?" *Industrial Relations*, 14 (1975): 32–44.

56. Panek, P. E., G. V. Barrett, H. L. Sterns, and R. A. Alexander. "A Review of Age Changes in Perceptual Information Process Abilities with Regard to Driving," *Experimental Aging Research*, 3 (1977): 387–449.

57. Podlesny, J. A., and D. C. Raskin. "Physiological Measures and the Detection of Deception," *Psychological Bulletin*, 84 (1977): 782–799.

58. Reeb, B. "Differential Test Validity for Ethnic Groups in the Israel Army and the Effects of Educational Level," *Journal of Applied Psychology*, 61 (1976): 253–261.

59. Reid, J. E., and F. E. Inbau. *Truth and Deception: The Polygraph ("Lie-Detector") Technique* (2nd ed.). Baltimore, Md.: Williams & Wilkins, 1977.

60. Reis, H. T., and B. M. Bass. "Modifying Attitudes and Knowledge about Nuclear Energy." *International Journal of Environmental Studies*, in press.

61. Rosen, H., and J. Turner. "Effectiveness of Two Orientation Approaches in Hard-Core Unemployed Turnover and Absenteeism," *Experimental Publication System*, 6 (1970), Ms. No. 218A.

62. Rosenbaum, B. L. "Attitude toward Invasion of Privacy in the Personnel Selection Process and Job Applicant Demographic and Personality Correlates," *Journal of Applied Psychology*, 58 (1973): 333–338.

63. Ross, H. L., D. T. Campbell, and G. V. Glass. "Determining the Social Effects of a Legal Reform: The British 'Breathalyser Crackdown' of 1967," *American Behavioral Scientist*, 13 (1970): 495–510.

64. Ross, I. "Retirement at Seventy: A New Trauma for Management." *Fortune,* 97 (May 1978), 106–112.

65. Rusmore, J. T. "Tests, Interviews and Fair Employment," *Personnel Administration* (March–April 1968): 50–55.

66. Schmidt, F. L., J. G. Berner, and J. E. Hunter. "Racial Differences in Validity of Employment Tests: Reality or Illusion?" *Journal of Applied Psychology,* 58 (1973): 5–9.

67. Shaffer, D. R., P. V. Mays, and K. Etheridge. "Who Shall Be Hired: A Biasing Effect of the Buckley Amendment on Employment Practices?" *Journal of Applied Psychology,* 61 (1976): 571–575.

68. Siegal, J. P. "The Use of Psychological Testing in Industry: Some Data on Local Company Practices," *Pittsburgh Business Review,* 38, No. 10 (1968): 1–3.

69. Siegal, J. P. "The Subject Evaluates the Test: Knowledge of Results and the Self-Concept," *Proceedings, 77th Annual Convention, American Psychological Association,* 1969.

70. Smith, K. U. "Human Factors and System Analysis of Psychological and Educational Testing," *Experimental Publication System* (1970), Ms. No. 132C.

71. Smith, P. C., and R. Curnow. " 'Arousal Hypothesis' and the Effects of Music on Purchasing Behavior," *Journal of Applied Psychology,* 50 (1966): 255–256.

72. Stagner, R. "Boredom on the Assembly Line: Age and Personality Variables," *Industrial Gerontology,* 2 (1975): 23–44.

73. "Uniform Guidelines on Employee Selection Procedures," *Federal Register,* 42, No. 251 (1978).

74. Walsh, J. "Behavioral and Social Sciences: NAS Report Stresses Applications," *Science,* 66 (1969): 585–586.

75. Wilpert, B. "Research on Industrial Democracy: The German Case," *Industrial Relations Journal,* 6 (1975): 53–64.

76. Wollowich, H. B., J. M. Greenwood, and W. J. McNamara. "Psychological Testing with a Minority Group Population," *Proceedings, 77th Annual Convention, American Psychological Association,* 1969, pp. 609–610.

77. Zdep, S. M., and H. B. Weaver. "The Graphoanalytic Approach to Selecting Life Insurance Salesmen." *Journal of Applied Psychology,* 51 (1967): 295–299.

AUTHOR INDEX

SUBJECT INDEX